D0527885

To the Hebrides

Samuel Johnson, a bookseller's son from Lichfield, achieved fame as a poet and moral essayist before completing his most famous work, *The Dictionary of the English Language*. James Boswell had known him for exactly ten years when they set out together for the Hebrides in 1773. Son of a Scottish judge and himself a lawyer, Boswell is celebrated as much for the disarming honesty of his diaries as for his great biography of Johnson.

Formerly a lecturer in Celtic in the universities of Glasgow and Edinburgh, **Ronald Black** is Gaelic Editor of *The Scotsman*. As well as various anthologies and studies of eighteenth- and twentieth-century Gaelic verse, he has published *The Gaelic Otherworld*, a new edition of the folklore collections of the Rev. John Gregorson Campbell of Tiree.

To the Hebrides

SAMUEL JOHNSON'S
JOURNEY TO THE WESTERN ISLANDS OF SCOTLAND

and

JAMES BOSWELL'S
JOURNAL OF A TOUR TO THE HEBRIDES

EDITED BY
RONALD BLACK

BIRLINN

First published in 2007 by
Birlinn Limited
West Newington House
10 Newington Road
Edinburgh
EH9 1QS

www.birlinn.co.uk

Second edition 2011
Notes and maps copyright © Ronald Black 2007, 2011

All rights reserved. No part of this publication may be reproduced, stored
or transmitted in any form without the express written permission of the
publisher.

ISBN: 978 1 78027 031 9

British Library Cataloguing-in-Publication Data
A catalogue record for this book is available from the British Library

Typeset by Edderston Book Design, Peebles
Printed and bound by CPI

Contents

Maps

Preface

Samuel Johnson and James Boswell toured Scotland in 1773. Their books about the trip, first published in 1775 and 1785 respectively, are monuments of English literature and of travel writing, but they also stand in line with Kirk, Martin, Burt, Pococke, Pennant, Ramsay and John Lane Buchanan as classics of Highland ethnography, the fountainhead of writings in English about the lives, traditions and beliefs of the Gaelic-speaking people of Scotland. Johnson's book, like Martin's and others, has an 'ethnographic core' (pp. 178–210 below) in which travelogue is laid aside in favour of general observations on the people's way of life.

Johnson was an Englishman who lived from 1709 to 1784. Boswell was a Lowland Scot who lived from 1740 to 1795. Beyond that there is no need to introduce our two travellers. At pp. 20–22 and 39 Boswell does it for us, and he was so satisfied with his description of Johnson that he used it again in his *Life of Samuel Johnson, LL.D.* (1791), which is rightly regarded as the best biography in the English language.

To the Hebrides looks different from any previous edition of the *Journey* or the *Tour*. But that is what it is – a new edition of these two classics. It is all here, but organised in three new ways.

Firstly, Johnson's subtitles, like 'Fall of Fiers' and 'Lough Ness', have been dispensed with; they were unhelpful anyway. Other than this, his text is as published in 1775.

Secondly, instead of presenting the whole of Johnson followed by the whole of Boswell, we have divided the material into thirteen chapters and a conclusion, thus bringing together what the two men have to say about each of the thirteen legs of the journey and highlighting their differing perspectives. This throws up intriguing differences on matters of detail – the circumstances of their arrival in Ulva, for example. Our travellers were of an age to be grandfather and grandson, and it shows.

Thirdly, thanks to the discovery of Boswell's original journal at Malahide in 1930, Frederick Pottle and Charles Bennett were able to publish *Boswell's Journal of a Tour to the Hebrides* (1936), which contained an enormous amount of previously unknown material of all kinds. This book (here referred to as the *Journal* as opposed to the *Tour*) was so successful that Pottle produced an expanded edition in 1963 containing corrections and additions to the text and a splendid 'Topographical Supplement' – the intelligent tourist's dream. Until now, the *Journal* has never been printed between the same covers as Johnson's *Journey*.

In refocusing Johnson's and Boswell's books on the Hebrides, Hugh Andrew of Birlinn felt that a composite text of the *Tour* and the *Journal* was required. Gordon Turnbull of Yale University (the owners of the manuscript) readily agreed, pointing out that this very idea had been prefigured by Pottle, who wrote in 1963 of the respective merits of the *Tour* and the *Journal*:

> Careful students of Boswell have found unique values in each version, and would probably prefer to either a text made by selecting at will from manuscript journal and printed book. Those who on the whole prefer the book would certainly like to restore from the manuscript a good many passages that Boswell in printing struck out merely because they transgressed his own very liberal standards of prudence and decorum.

The bedrock for our Boswell text is the journal as edited by Pottle and Bennett, including Pottle's corrections and additions. That is what I mean in my notes where I refer to 'the journal'. Where the *Tour* adds anything of substance, it too is incorporated. This was done by Pottle and Bennett in any case wherever the manuscript was deficient. I have modernised the orthography of these additions in line with the conventions established by Pottle and Bennett. I have also paragraphed Boswell's text afresh to aid readability. Where the *Tour* contains information which adds something to our knowledge or understanding but which would disturb the flow of the text, it is given in the endnotes.

Johnson, striving for forthrightness, wrote no footnotes, but Boswell added many to the *Tour*. These will be found here in the endnotes, clearly marked, as will translations of the Latin texts which have kindly been made for us by Mr Norman MacLeod.

In the course of 230 years the *Journey* and *Tour* have reappeared frequently in two different formats. I would call them 'landmark' and 'essay' editions. By an 'essay edition' I mean a redaction of one or both of the texts prefaced by an introductory essay; all such editions are of great value as the response of an individual to a classic work. The landmark editions have added materially to our knowledge in points of detail, and to them my debt is enormous. I have already mentioned Pottle and Bennett's; a century earlier there appeared Croker's 1831 edition of the *Life*, which included the *Tour*, annotated by Sir Walter Scott. It went through so many mutations that I have felt it best to refer to it in the endnotes by day rather than page. Then there was Robert Carruthers's edition of the *Tour* (1852). Though not a Gaelic speaker, Carruthers was editor of *The Inverness Courier*, and this provided him with a rich store of Highland insight and anecdote. In 1887 Croker's combined edition of the *Life* and *Tour* was succeeded by George Birkbeck Hill's; this was revised and further enlarged by L. F. Powell in 1934 and 1964. The result is an indispensible work in six volumes, one of which – the fifth – consists of Boswell's *Tour* and Johnson's journal of a visit to Wales in 1774. Finally there is Fleeman's 1985 edition of the *Journey*, which contains a valuable 'Chronology and Topography' section that expands and updates Pottle's topographical supplement.

The principal aim of *To the Hebrides* is to summarise existing information on the two texts as clearly as possible. However, the Gaelic and Highland perspective inevitably brings fresh insights. There is also serendipity. Earlier this year my old friend Nicholas Maclean-Bristol of Breacachadh Castle in Coll rang me up in delighted mood to tell me that he had just acquired a good many of the documents described by Boswell at pp. 326–32. They had been lost since 1897 but turned up last year in South Africa. Clearly this is a footnote to *The Treasure of Auchinleck*, and the story was duly reported in the *West Highland Free Press* (27 April 2007) under the headline 'The Treasure of Port Elizabeth'.

To the Hebrides has been planned as the first of two publications from Birlinn on Johnson and Boswell. Hugh Andrew has also asked me to prepare *To the Western Islands*, in which the Highland response to Johnson will be examined, mainly through the Rev. Donald MacNicol's *Remarks on Dr Samuel Johnson's Journey to the Hebrides* (1779), a much maligned book that is ripe for reappraisal.

My grateful thanks are due to Gordon Turnbull and the Editorial Committee of the Yale Editions of the Private Papers of James Boswell; to Norman MacLeod, Walkerburn; to the staffs of the National Library of Scotland, Edinburgh University Library and the Edinburgh Central Library; to Richard Cox, Roger Hutchinson, Jean Jones, Sheila Kidd, Anne Loughran, Mairi MacArthur, Dr John MacInnes, Rebecca MacKay, Catrìona Mackie, Nicholas Maclean-Bristol, Colm Ó Baoill and Lorna Pike; and, last but never least, to my wife Máire for the pains she has taken with design, typesetting and maps. I hope our text is free of the gremlins that have beset previous editions, such as the one in which Boswell speaks of the loo that he and Johnson 'fought for in vain' at Raasay House. See note 364 . . .

Ronald Black, Peebles, 2 May 2007

Introduction

"The sea was smooth." So begins a paragraph of Dr Johnson's at p. 176 below. Then, just four pages later, another begins: "When their grain is arrived at the state which they must consider as ripeness, they do not cut, but pull the barley: to the oats they apply the sickle."

This, to me, sums up the fascination of the present work, although I could have chosen countless other examples from Johnson's writing, Boswell's, or both. It could be described as the juxtaposition of specific experience (the sea on a given day) and of general reflection (Highland agriculture). Or, conversely, as the juxtaposition of the universal (smooth seas are timeless and within most people's personal experience) and of the specific (Highland agricultural methods in the 1770s). Or, of course, as the juxtaposition of that which was experienced and that which was merely observed – the subjective and the objective.

However the trick is analysed, it is good travel writing. A smooth sea is experienced on a particular day; the pulling up of barley by the roots is placed on record. The reader learns much about everyday life in the eighteenth-century Highlands, and the method is the pleasant one of being allowed to feel that he has joined the great writer on his journey of discovery.

Of course some one actually *did* join the great writer on his journey of discovery. Not only did Boswell accompany Johnson, he was the glue that held the 'jaunt' together, arranging, chivvying, buttering-up, filling in awkward gaps in the conversation, taking notes, apologising, and sometimes, yes, finding it all a little too much, and becoming what a journalist is never supposed to become. The story.

Boswell was a good travel-writer in all the little ways that Johnson was not. He was a 'sea was smooth' man rather than a 'barley was pulled up by the roots' man: not an objective ethnologist but a lively, subjective and percipient recorder of the immediate and transient facts of the trip. Boswell is the honestest and most celebrated diarist of the eighteenth century. The function he performs for Johnson is that performed by a camera crew on a modern expedition. For those of us whose primary interest is in what Johnson was actually seeking to tell us, and in how closely his observations approximate to the truth, Boswell provides verification, back-up, documentary evidence, names, dates, places. Had those other giants of Highland ethnography whom I listed four years ago at p. vii (Robert Kirk, Martin Martin, Edmund Burt, Richard Pococke, Thomas Pennant, John Ramsay, John Lane Buchanan) had their Boswell, our data and our understanding would be infinitely the richer, because our biographical knowledge of some of these men is rudimentary in the extreme.

If asked to name the highlights of Johnson's and Boswell's work, most commentators would probably point to Johnson's 'ethnographic core' of general information in Chapter 5 – which includes, incidentally, his perceptive disquisition on the crucial role played in Highland society by the tacksmen – and to the two men's complementary accounts of the house on Loch Ness-side in Chapter 2. Boswell's account of New Year customs in Chapter 6 (pp. 318–19) also deserves honourable mention, not least because it has only now been restored from his journal (by which I mean Pottle and Bennett's 1963 edition of the journal, as is made clear at p. viii).

That is Highland ethnography as narrowly defined, comprising writings about 'the lives, traditions and beliefs of the Gaelic-speaking people of Scotland' (p. vii). Around its outer edges, ethnography expands to embrace aspects of history, archaeology and the description of living individuals. One of the reasons why Boswell's contribution to Chapter 5 is even larger than Johnson's is that he includes in it as much as he could glean of the wanderings of Prince Charles in Skye and Raasay in 1746, and other Jacobite matters (pp. 216–29). His account of Coll's charter-chest, or rather cabinet, at pp. 326–32 is of great historical interest; it is, for example, virtually our only source of information about the Coll company of the Argyll Militia in 1745–46.

Everywhere they went, the two men took note of whatever antiquities were to be found and of their associated folklore. There are some startling differences, and some startling similarities, between what was to be found in 1773 and what attracts visitors today. No modern guide to Skye, for example, would devote as much space as Boswell does to the *annaid* or early Christian settlement at Bay (pp. 241–42); but then, he was misled into believing that it was a temple of the goddess Anaitis, and therefore of global significance. Together, Boswell and Johnson add much to our knowledge of the state of Iona's buildings in 1773, but their descriptions are not as scientific as those of Pennant, who had visited the island the year before, and our heroes' combined contribution to archaeology may ultimately lie in Johnson's remark (p. 381): "That man is little to be envied, whose patriotism would not gain force upon the plain of *Marathon*, or whose piety would not grow warmer among the ruins of *Iona!*"

The individuals portrayed by Johnson and Boswell leap off the pages with as much vividness as they possessed in 1773. Sir Alexander Macdonald (Chapter 3) fails spectacularly to live up to the model of a Highland chief. This is hardly surprising, given that for generations the Macdonalds have been following the old Campbell example of finding wives for their sons amongst the Lowland aristocracy. Sir Alexander shows the process brought one step further, for he was educated at Eton. The Rev. Donald MacQueen (Chapter 5) is highly regarded by Johnson for the opposite reason. Johnson has no tolerance of Presbyterianism but knows the history of Scotland in the seventeenth century, and expected Gaelic-speaking Presbyterian ministers to be idle placemen or raving shamans. In MacQueen he is bemused to find a measure of general learning, an interest in the classics, and a total disbelief in second sight which leaves the Englishman looking distinctly more superstitious than the Highlander. Flora MacDonald (also Chapter 5), the Jacobite heroine of heroines, now aged fifty-one, is described by Boswell as 'a little woman, of a mild and genteel appearance, mighty soft and well-bred'. Another of Prince Charles's guides in 1746, Malcolm MacLeod of Brae (Chapter 4), 'went to London to be hanged, and returned in a post-chaise with Miss Flora Macdonald'. He enjoys defying the laws against the Highland dress, and dances a reel with Boswell on the top of Dun Caan. Mrs MacKinnon of Coirechatachan, a mother of nine who remains young in spirit, welcomes our travellers twice (Chapters 3 and 5), speaks freely of her dreams, and gets on so famously with Johnson that she declares at table: "I'm in love with him. What is it to live and not love?" The laird of Coll's son (Chapter 6), aged twenty-three, seems simultaneously devoid of pretension, learning, superstition and traditional knowledge, and comes across not merely as a post-Culloden islander but as an almost twenty-first-century one: he has an amiable disposition, loves boats and horses, treats all men equally, understands psychology and is keen to find new ways of making the land yield a profit.

Also worthy of mention, by way of painting further contrasts in character, are the MacLean chiefs of Duart (Chapter 9) and of Lochbuie (Chapter 11). Duart's ancestors lost their castles and lands to the Campbells a hundred years before; now, having seen service in the army in America, he is living quietly with his daughters and servants in a couple of thatched houses on an islet which should have been his, but which he has rented from the duke of Argyll (whom we meet in the flesh in Chapter 12). Duart (or rather Sir Allan) is patiently awaiting the result of court proceedings against the duke, and Boswell is one of his counsel. Boswell treats us to some delightfully unlawyerly sentiments. He is 'agreeably disappointed' in Sir Allan, he says, because he turns out to be a religious man, and although he swears like a soldier he does not drink like one. When Boswell goes to Iona (Chapter 10) he kneels on holy ground and swears 'that I will stand by Sir Allan Maclean and his family'. Finally, John Maclaine of Lochbuie (Chapter 11) is a rascally chief of the old school who indulges freely in litigation, not because he has lost his lands but because he enjoys it as others enjoy drink, cards or women. He is known to have put men in a dungeon, and he barks, or rather bawls, at Johnson: "Are you of the Johnstons of Glencoe or of Ardnamurchan?"

Samuel Johnson was neither of Glencoe nor of Ardnamurchan. He was born at Lichfield on 18 September 1709, the son of a local bookseller, and was brought to London at the age of three to be touched for scrofula (the king's evil) by Queen Anne. The disease appears to have left him permanently blind in one eye. He remarks at Dunvegan (p. 238): "I inherited a vile melancholy from my father, which has made me mad all my life, at least not sober." When Lady MacLeod expresses surprise that he should admit it, Boswell says: "Madam, he knows that with that madness he is superior to other men."

Johnson was educated at Lichfield Grammar School and Pembroke College, Oxford, where he spent fourteen months in 1728–29 without taking a degree. Here he learned the art of disputation, and discovered that the best weapon he possessed was his brain. Boswell speaks (p. 20) of his habit of 'talking for victory', and gives (p. 56) a good example of his disputatious nature: in dicussion with Lord Monboddo on the relative merits of the savage and the London shopkeeper, Johnson naturally championed the latter, but confessed afterwards to Boswell that 'he did not know but he might have taken the side of the savage equally, had anybody else taken the side of the shopkeeper'. There is another very revealing anecdote at p. 371. Dr Johnson once called on the historian Dr John Campbell (who, incidentally, was a grandson of the perpetrator of the Massacre of Glencoe, Robert Campbell of Glenlyon, but who had lived in England since the age of five). Campbell made some remark about Tull's *Husbandry*, Johnson began to dispute it, and Campbell said, "Come, we do not want to get the better of one another. We want to increase each other's ideas." Boswell concludes: "Mr Johnson took it in good part, and the conversation then went on coolly and instructively. His candour in relating this anecdote does him much credit, and his conduct on that occasion proves how easily he could be persuaded to talk from a better motive than 'for victory'."

Johnson's father died in 1731, leaving his family in poverty, and he tried for a while to scrape a living by writing essays for the *Birmingham Journal*. In 1735 he married a widow twenty years older than himself, Mrs Elizabeth Porter, and started a private school near Lichfield. The school failed, and the marriage was childless. In 1737, in the company of one of his pupils, David Garrick, he went to London, which remained his home for the rest of his life. Garrick went on to achieve fame as an actor, while the printer Edward Cave gave Johnson a job on *The Gentleman's Magazine*, writing poems and verses in English and Latin, essays, biographies and political discourses. This at last was a solid platform for his career as a writer and lexicographer. *London: a Poem* appeared in 1738, the *Life of Mr. Richard Savage* in 1744, and *The Vanity of Human Wishes* in 1749, two years after he began work on his dictionary. In 1750 he launched *The Rambler*, a twice-weekly periodical consisting of essays on all subjects imaginable, written almost entirely by himself. It ceased publication in 1752, the year of his wife's death, but he continued to contribute to other journals.

The first edition of Johnson's *Dictionary of the English Language* appeared in 1755. It is, beyond all others, the work by which he is remembered today, though the *Lives of the Poets* and the *Journey to the Western Islands* run it close, and it is now impossible not to view Johnson's works through the prism of Boswell's. He did not produce the dictionary single-handed. He had a team of six assistants, five of whom were Scots, the senior being Alexander Macbean, a Gaelic speaker – in 1777 he examined the Rev. William Shaw's manuscript 'Analysis of the Galic Language' on behalf of Johnson, who referred to him as 'a very learned Highlander, Macbean'. His younger brother was also on the team, which makes two Gaelic speakers out of six (or seven, if we include Johnson). The *Dictionary* was more than an indispensable work of reference, and more than a means of stabilising the orthography of the English language, for the entrepreneurial, 'bottom-up' manner in which it had been undertaken was truly inspirational. I can cite only one example of this inspiration, but no doubt there are others. Sometime in the late 1760s seven Highland gentlemen formed a society with the object of compiling a Gaelic dictionary. They shared out the letters of the alphabet and made good progress. But when in 1775 they read the injudicious remarks which appear at pp. 207–10 below, the project collapsed into a welter of satirical Gaelic songs aimed at their erstwhile hero, and the publication that emerged in 1779 from the study of the member entrusted with the letters M, N and O, far from being a dictionary, was the Rev. Donald MacNicol's *Remarks on Dr Samuel Johnson's Journey to the Hebrides*.

At the age of forty-six, Johnson had become the Ursa Major of the intellectual firmament. His next great project after 1755 was an edition of Shakespeare, but, characteristically, he scribbled and boomed all the way to its publication ten years later – editing the *Literary Magazine* for a while, throwing off more biographies, contributing his 'Idler' essays to the *Universal Chronicle*, and publishing his only novel, *Rasselas*. In 1762 he was granted a pension of £300 a year by Lord Bute, in 1763 Boswell made his acquaintance, and in 1764 'The Club', later 'The Literary Club', was founded (see pp. 478–79). Its original members included Johnson, Reynolds, Burke and Goldsmith; to these Garrick, Fox and Boswell were soon added. All of these individuals, and countless others, are listed and characterised ('portrait-painter', 'statesman', 'poet and dramatist' or whatever) in the index below.

It was in 1764, also, that Johnson first met the Thrales, and so, gradually, laid down the more relaxed pattern of living that marked the last two decades of his existence. Henry Thrale was a wealthy brewer, the son of a wealthy brewer, who lived on a country estate at Streatham; he was married to a charming Welshwoman, Hester Salusbury, then aged only twenty-three, who had given birth to their first child ('Queeney') that same year. It was the kind of family that Johnson had never had, and he became an honorary member of it, revered, adored and tolerated in equal measure. For the next seventeen years, happily in love with Hester and Queeney, he gravitated between his London lodgings and Streatham, sometimes travelling to Oxford, Lichfield and elsewhere.

The journey to the Hebrides was Johnson's first and greatest venture further afield. It was inspired by his Jacobite inclinations and, as we are told at p. 18, by childhood memories of sitting in his father's shop reading Martin Martin's *Description of the Western Islands* (which clearly influenced his own choice of title). More immediately, however, the journey was provoked by Boswell's almost irresistible desire to tempt the great man on to his own turf. Johnson could see that at the age of sixty-four he could hardly explore the world on his own, and that in the absence of hotels and public transport, he had found the perfect travel companion: "Mr *Boswell*," he remarks (p. 84), "between his father's merit and his own, is sure of reception wherever he comes." Journeys to Wales and France followed in 1774 and 1775 respectively, but these were in the company of the Thrales, and, as John Wain has pointed out (*Samuel*

Johnson, pp. 341–42), "Travelling with the rich, while it undeniably has its points, never permits much involvement with the everyday life of the country. Johnson never entered an ordinary Welsh home, let alone an ordinary French home, in the way that in Scotland he entered the cottages of crofters and the cabins of trading vessels and the bedrooms of low-raftered inns. Undoubtedly an opportunity was missed. One would have given a good deal to know his reactions, in each country, to the people, his observation of their life, his judgement of their hopes and fears. But, insulated in comfort, surrounded by a thicket of servants, he saw these things as in a tapestry."

It is unsurprising, then, that there is no real Welsh or French equivalent of Johnson's *Journey to the Western Islands*, although some of his journals of these trips survived to be published posthumously. Aside from the *Journey* (1775), Johnson's output in the years of his 'retirement' consisted of *The Lives of the Poets* (1779–81) and a variety of poems, sermons, prayers, meditations and political pamphlets, of which last a couple, *The False Alarm* (1770) and *Taxation no Tyranny* (1775), are mentioned by Boswell below (pp. 107, 463). Johnson died in 1784 and was buried in Westminster Abbey. He had twice been awarded the degree of LLD – by Trinity College, Dublin, in 1765, and by his own university, Oxford, in 1775 (see note 70 at p. 464).

During his lifetime and ever since, not least in Scotland, Johnson has been the object of dislike, misunderstanding and ridicule; to these, during his lifetime only, we should add fear. Some of the reasons for it all are apparent in *To the Hebrides*. For one thing, his style owed not a little to the Latin language. At its best, as in the 'tacksman' disquisition at p. 185, it is simple, clear and dignified. At its worst it is as impenetrable as an obelisk which one may walk around without finding lock or key, as at p. 175: "If love of ease surmounted our desire of knowledge, the offence has not the invidiousness of singularity." Between these two extremes are good things and bad. He could be pedantic, as when he objected to Boswell's remark that a mountain was 'like a cone' (p. 112); he could write a perfect tableau, as at p. 84: "Once we saw a cornfield, in which a lady was walking with some gentlemen."

Johnson was always uncompromisingly himself. Unfortunately, in addition to being combative, himself was a heap of contradictions, with a dose of self-loathing thrown in. Boswell remarks at p. 314 that he 'regretted that Mr Johnson did not practise the art of accommodating himself to different sorts of people'. As a result, he was likely to receive a bad press wherever he went, leaving Boswell to pick up the pieces, as at p. 46 where the latter is forced to remark: "And here I must do Dr Johnson the justice to contradict a very absurd and ill-natured story as to what passed at St Andrews . . ."

Johnson was an Anglican, a Tory and a Jacobite, in that order. His political, religious, philosophical, social and literary views were strongly hierarchical. He visualised all good as coming from 'above', all evil from 'below'. He had no time for democratic institutions or for individuals such as Rousseau, Macpherson and Monboddo who promoted the ideal of the 'noble savage'. At p. 93 he declares that 'as government advances towards perfection, provincial judicature is perhaps in every empire gradually abolished', at p. 80 that 'politeness, the natural product of royal government, is diffused from the laird through the whole clan', and at p. 208 that 'there can be no polished language without books'. All of these statements are inherently contentious, or contain contentious elements. To Johnson, all the world was a debate, and he sought to occupy a particular piece of ground, to plant his standard upon it, and to hold it against all opposition. In many types of company this could appear graceless, and Boswell takes pains to broaden and soften the overall picture. At p. 102 he describes how, at Fort George, Sir Eyre Coote, who has travelled through the deserts of Arabia, praises the Arabs, 'their fidelity if they undertook to conduct you: that they'd lose their lives rather than let you be robbed'. It is a moment for listening and for admiration, but Johnson spoils it by saying that there is 'no superior virtue in this', clearly meaning that a breach of the eighth commandment should not be allowed to escalate into a breach of the sixth; Boswell glosses the remark by explaining that Johnson 'is always for maintaining the superiority of civilized men over uncivilized', which means in this case the superiority of Christian over Moslem. And at p. 113, as the pair ride down through Glen Shiel, Boswell gives us an insight into the nature of Johnson's ideal hierarchy, a benign autocracy: "Mr Johnson was much refreshed by this repast. He was pleased when I told him he would make a good chief. He said if he were one, he would dress his servants better than himself, and knock a fellow down if he looked saucy to a Macdonald in rags. But he would not treat men as brutes. He would let them know why all of his clan were to have attention paid to them. He would tell his upper servants why, and make them tell the others."

None of this entirely explains why Johnson should have been feared, but that 'fear' is the correct word is clearly demonstrated by the behaviour of the professors of Aberdeen and Glasgow (pp. 62, 432). It is explained, I think, by a letter from the Rev. Andrew Gallie to Charles Macintosh of the Highland Society of Scotland, published in Henry Mackenzie's Ossian Committee *Report* of 1805. The question at stake was why the Rev. Donald MacQueen had so dismally failed to convey to Dr Johnson some of the most basic facts about the Gaelic language, its antiquity, its manuscripts, its printed books and its literature, with particular reference to the wealth of Ossianic ballads and tales which were such an everyday feature of life in almost every house which the two travellers had passed from Nairn in the north to Luss in the south. Gallie wrote: "Dr Macqueen will be forgiven by many for his caution, because he saw – perhaps experienced – so much of Johnson that he might dread contradiction or opposition from him would be as running his head into the lion's mouth. I think I can recollect, that gentlemen very high in the literary circle, and most intimate with Johnson, often left the cause of truth and the field of contest to him, knowing the power and virulence of his sarcasms to be such, as would irritate beyond measure, and which he seldom restrained when opposed."

In fact, although not the ideal man for the job, MacQueen had done his best. Boswell notes at p. 137 that he (MacQueen) 'told Mr Johnson that there was an Erse Bible; that he had compared the new Erse Testament by Mr Stuart with the former one; that there were many Erse manuscripts – all of which circumstances we afterwards found not to be true'. It is not clear to me in what way any of these statements could be regarded as untrue. The language then generally referred to by non-Gaelic speakers as 'Erse' and by Gaelic speakers as 'the Highland language', and to almost all of us nowadays as 'Scottish Gaelic' or 'Gaelic' (*Gàidhlig*), is a few degrees removed from Irish, just as, say, Portuguese is from Spanish, or Dutch from German. The Bible, New Testament and manuscripts to which MacQueen was referring were all one, two or three degrees removed from Irish. If that meant that they were not in a language distinct from Irish, then spoken Gaelic was itself not a language distinct from Irish. A 'language' has been waggishly defined as 'a dialect with an army and a navy', though how this definition works for eighteenth-century Ireland and the Highlands is beyond me, except that I would point out that the Highlands had an army in 1745–46. If the 'third degree of removal' is defined as the establishment of a new, distinct and secure orthography, that stage had been reached by Scottish Gaelic in 1767, the date of publication of the above-mentioned 'new Erse Testament'. Extraordinarily, as is explained in note 279 on p. 491, Johnson himself had intervened at a crucial stage to make sure that this New Testament was published, because, as he says himself (p. 124), 'there were lately some who thought it reasonable to refuse them a version of the holy scriptures, that they might have no monument of their mother-tongue'.

The problem for Johnson was not the scriptures but Ossian's poems, concerning which he was locked into a bitter dispute with James Macpherson, whom he cordially loathed. General Norman MacLeod of MacLeod, who was just nineteen years old when our two travellers stayed with him and his family at Dunvegan, later recalled that Johnson's 'principal design was to find proofs of the unauthenticity of Ossian's poems and in his enquiries it became very soon evident that he wished not to find them genuine' (Grant, *The MacLeods*, p. 503). There is no doubt but that, after the inspiration of Martin Martin and the encouragement of James Boswell, the prospect of finding proof of the unauthenticity of Macpherson's 'translations' on his own turf had provided Johnson with a third good reason for coming. Unfortunately this part of the enterprise went badly wrong. The Highland people were loyal to Macpherson. They knew what a translation was – basic communication in one language rendered into basic communication in another, which most bilinguals could manage, more or less; or flowery speech in one language rendered into flowery speech in another, which most people regarded as neither feasible nor desirable. For generations it has been a truism that Gaelic songs 'cannot be translated'. I have heard this statement so often, and read it so many times in Gaelic books and magazines, even in reviews of translations of Gaelic songs, that I have almost begun to believe it myself. What it boils down to, I suppose, is that even if you have a hundred different translations of a creative work, none of them will ever be as good as the original. But it was difficult for Johnson to find anyone who understood both Gaelic and English and was willing to deny that Macpherson's work was a 'translation'.

Johnson encountered the problem in Raasay in the delectable shape of Miss Flora Macleod, and this gives me an opportunity to compare his account of the incident as published in 1775 with a letter written to Hester Thrale just a couple of weeks after the night in question. On 24 September 1773, at Talisker, Johnson reported to Mrs Thrale (Redford, *The Letters of Samuel Johnson*, vol. 2, p. 84):

> After supper a young Lady who was visiting, sung Earse songs, in which Lady Raarsa joined prettily enough, but not gracefully, the young Ladies sustained the chorus better. They are very little used to be asked questions, and not well prepared with answers. When one of the Songs was over, I asked the princess that sat next me, *what is it about?* I question, if she conceived that I did not understand it. For

the entertainment of the company, said she. But, Madam, what is the meaning of it? It is a love song. This was all the intelligence that I could obtain, nor have I ever been able to procure a translation of a line of Erse.

But at p. 143 below we read:

> After supper the ladies sung *Erse* songs, to which I listened as an *English* audience to an *Italian* opera, delighted with the sound of words which I did not understand.
> I inquired the subjects of the songs, and was told of one, that it was a love song, and of another, that it was a farewell composed by one of the Islanders that was going, in this epidemical fury of emigration, to seek his fortune in *America*. What sentiments would rise, on such an occasion, in the heart of one who had not been taught to lament by precedent, I should gladly have known; but the lady, by whom I sat, thought herself not equal to the work of translating.

Johnson wrote substantial letters to Mrs Thrale once or twice a week throughout the tour, with the exception of 30 September to 15 October, when he was stormbound in Coll. These letters are written in a style noticeably lighter than that of the *Journey*, and deserve to be published as an addendum to it, for they contain much of interest.

Johnson's desire to procure translations of 'Erse verse' was partially fulfilled at Erray in Mull when he met Christina MacLean (pp. 208, 345, 356, 358–59). On the face of it, it is a little curious that neither he nor Boswell reports any attempt to persuade any of their hosts to set up a performance of Ossianic ballads in the company of a competent translator, and MacLeod of MacLeod's suspicion that Johnson had come to Skye 'to find proofs of the unauthenticity of Ossian's poems' seems to be well founded. When a test was made, it was not at Dunvegan but at Ullinish, proposed by the host's son Rorie MacLeod and carried out by himself and MacQueen in the presence not of Johnson but of Boswell (p. 261). When the result was reported to Johnson, he immediately stated a conclusion which was entirely correct with regard to Macpherson's 'translations', but begged the question with regard to 'Ossian's poems' in the original: "He has found names, and stories, and phrases – nay passages in old songs – and with them has compounded his own compositions, and so made what he gives to the world as the translation of an ancient poem."

It speaks ill of Johnson that he admitted the existence of 'old songs' of this kind, but sought not to hear them, refused to believe in the existence of manuscripts that contained them, denied their antiquity, and comprehensively insulted the language in which they were sung. He had carried 'talking for victory' against James Macpherson down to the level of the grotesque, and if this was one of the purposes of his visit, it was a charade.

What then of James Boswell? In 1773 he was a rather reluctant thirty-two-year-old member of the Faculty of Advocates. Born in Edinburgh on 29 October 1740, eldest son of the circuit judge Lord Auchinleck, he was a difficult child, and was educated successively at Edinburgh High School, at home, and at the universities of Edinburgh and Glasgow. He was quick to discover the joys of sex, the stage and the Catholic Church, all of which were sternly disapproved of, and at the age of nineteen he ran away to London, where he naturally fell into bad company but was rescued by his father's connections (see p. 95). He had grand ideas of becoming a soldier, a writer or a politician, or, grander still, of meeting his father's approval. He therefore agreed to come back home, face the music and sit his examination in Civil Law.

In 1762 Boswell went to London once again, this time with his father's blessing, to seek a commission in the Guards. Like almost everything he ever undertook, the visit had unintended consequences: he failed in his prime purpose, but met Samuel Johnson, and finally agreed with his father (by letter) to pursue his law studies at Utrecht in Holland. The result was a grand tour of swashbuckling proportions. When he had completed his courses in the summer of 1764 he set off for Berlin in a coach and four with the Earl Marischal, who had taken part in the '15 and the '19 on the Jacobite side and was now a courtier of Frederick the Great.

In Switzerland Boswell sought out – and interviewed – both Voltaire and Rousseau. He travelled exhaustively in Italy (see note 108 on p. 469), then crossed to Corsica, which was in armed revolt against the Genoese Republic. He met and befriended the rebel leader, Pasquale Paoli (who was to end his life in exile in London), and made his cause his own. Following his return via France early in 1766 he wrote *An Account of Corsica, the Journal of a Tour to that Island, and Memoirs of Pascal Paoli*. On its publication in 1768 it earned him high acclaim and the nickname 'Corsica Boswell' (or, more curiously, 'Paoli', as at p. 100 below).

In summer 1766 Boswell 'passed advocate', and on 25 November 1769 he married his cousin Margaret Montgomerie. Business was good, domestic life was happy and regularly blessed with children, but despite all his resolutions his whoring resumed, as did his drinking, his gaming and his periodic fits of depression (an affliction also suffered by Johnson). He visited London twice between his marriage and the tour to the Islands, in the spring of 1772 and 1773, for what stimulated him most was the company of men of genius, and he had become an inveterate note-taker. Bennet Langton once declared with impatience that 'Boswell's conversation consists entirely in asking questions, and it is extremely offensive' (Robert Lynd, *Dr. Johnson & Company*, p. 36). He could certainly ask questions 'slapdash', as he puts it himself at p. 337 below, but in general he had a highly engaging manner. Where Johnson 'talked for victory', he claimed, he himself 'talked at random' (Lynd, p. 30). Had he lived 200 years later, he would have enjoyed a successful career in television. Politicians, writers, philosophers and stars of stage and screen would have queued up to appear on his show. He would have bedded the prettiest ones, as he did Rousseau's mistress and many others of her kind. He would have travelled far and wide, reporting wars, investigating famines, interviewing world leaders and exposing corruption with fearless impartiality. His chief characteristic, as later remembered, was his tendency to provoke mirth (Chambers, *Traditions of Edinburgh*, pp. 60–61): "It was impossible to look in his face without being moved by the comicality which always reigned upon it." We need seek no further than the following pages, however, for evidence of Boswell's character. At p. 53 Johnson tells him that 'Burke says that you have so much good humour naturally, it is scarce a virtue', thus likening this quality to a language acquired without conscious study. At p. 202 Johnson informs us gravely that in Skye 'Mr Boswell's frankness and gaiety made every body communicative'. At p. 214 Boswell cheerfully agrees with him, mentioning another man of genius while he is at it: "My *facility of manners*, as Adam Smith said of me, had fine play." At p. 343 Johnson tells him to his face that he is 'longer a boy than others', and at p. 394 it is confirmed: "I had a serious joy in hearing my voice," says Boswell, "resounding in the ancient cathedral of Icolmkill."

Boswell's life after the tour may be briefly summarised. He succeeded to his father's estate in 1782, saw Johnson for the last time in June 1784, read of his death six months later, made up his mind to move to London, published the *Journal of a Tour to the Hebrides* (with Edmond Malone's help) in 1785, and qualified as a barrister in 1786. From now on, instead of living with his wife and five children in Edinburgh and Auchinleck and making periodic visits to London, he lived with them in London and brought them on periodic visits to Edinburgh and Auchinleck. He did not prosper at the English bar, and spent increasing amounts of time working with Malone on his *Life* of Johnson. Margaret died in 1789, and the *Life* was published in 1791 to enormous critical acclaim, knocking rival biographies by Hester Thrale (1786) and Sir John Hawkins (1787) completely out of the water. Boswell did not include the tour in the *Life*, but described the itinerary in a few words and referred his readers to the *Journal*.

Although Boswell died in 1795, prematurely aged, I cannot resist making special mention of an incident in 1792 which shows him putting his fame to good use in a decent and altruistic way. A young woman from Cornwall called Mary Bryant, who had been sentenced to transportation for street-robbery and stealing a cloak, had escaped from Botany Bay with four men and succeeded in sailing a small boat with them all the way to Timor. They were brought back in irons to England. Boswell interested himself in their case, and set about obtaining an interview with the Home Secretary, a royal pardon for Bryant, and the release of the men from Newgate, in most of which he was successful. The story was filmed for television in 2006 as *The Incredible Journey of Mary Bryant*, starring Romola Garai. How Boswell would have loved it.

I do not apologise for the decision made by Hugh Andrew and myself to place Johnson and Boswell cheek by jowl in each of thirteen different locations. The arrangement of *To the Hebrides* provides those interested in specific islands with ready access to what they want to know. It also helps throw up fresh insights, comparable to the contrasts between Wheeler and Spon referred to by Johnson himself at p. 379. At pp. 360–61, for example, we discover that on the night of 16 October, according to Boswell, Captain McClure was absent from his ship in the Sound of Ulva, but that 'his men obligingly came with their long-boat and ferried us over', while Johnson – ever hierarchical! – has it that 'the master saw that we wanted a passage, and with great civility sent us his boat'. No doubt Boswell had it right. There are countless other examples of greater significance, of which the two men's different treatments of the MacLonichs in Chapter 6 (pp. 303–04, 326–27) is one.

Some of the contrasts between Johnson's and Boswell's accounts seem to be racial in origin (English and Scots). Others have more to do with class, Johnson feeling perpetually obliged to fight his corner, while the aristocratic Boswell takes things easy. Others again spring from issues of age and youth, or related matters of taste and governance, such as classical and romantic, hierarchical and democratic. The reader should also beware of differences which are more apparent than real. Johnson based his judgements not on emotion but on rigorous logic; at the same time, he had a tendency to fly to the opposite end of any prevailing argument, producing a see-saw effect. That is why, in two completely different settings – breakfasting in Mackenzie's inn at Inverness and sailing along in a boat from Ullinish to Fernilea – he erupted into identical 'fits of railing against the Scots' (pp. 104, 264). Put very simply, Scotland had been in a bad state before the Union, and had obtained benefits from it. "I am entertained," says Boswell on the first occasion, "with his copious exaggeration upon that subject. But I am uneasy when people are by who do not know him as well as I do and may be apt to think him narrow-minded. I diverted the subject."

Our complex of contrasts is best illustrated by scenery. Johnson's Augustan idea of a beautiful landscape was of a fertile and productive one. This can be found in Boswell, too, but only with respect to the Lowlands (p. 40). When it comes to the Highlands, Boswell's views appear to creep from the Classical towards the Romantic, foundering halfway between, for he remarks of Johnson (p. 74): "He always said that he was not come to Scotland to see fine places, of which there were enough in England, but wild objects – mountains, waterfalls, peculiar manners: in short, things which he had not seen before. I have a notion that he at no time has had much taste for rural beauties. I have very little."

In fact, Johnson makes his views on Highland landscape very clear indeed. While Boswell babbles about a scene that is 'as remote and agreeably wild as could be desired' (p. 106), Johnson speaks of rocks 'towering in horrid nakedness' (p. 81), of mountain streams 'discharging all their violence of waters by a sudden fall through the horrid chasm' (p. 84), and, most revealingly of all, of heather ('heath') on the Highland hills (p. 88): "They exhibit very little variety; being almost wholly covered with dark heath, and even that seems to be checked in its growth. What is not heath is nakedness, a little diversified by now and then a stream rushing down the steep. An eye accustomed to flowery pastures and waving harvests is astonished and repelled by this wide extent of hopeless sterility." Curiously for a journey made in late August and September, there is no mention of the beauty of purple heather.

All in all, one can see exactly what Johnson meant when, once the trip was over, he was asked how he liked the Highlands (p. 437). "How, sir," he replied, "can you ask me what obliges me to speak unfavourably of a country where I have been hospitably entertained? Who *can* like the Highlands? I like the inhabitants very well."

Ronald Black, Peebles, 7 June 2011

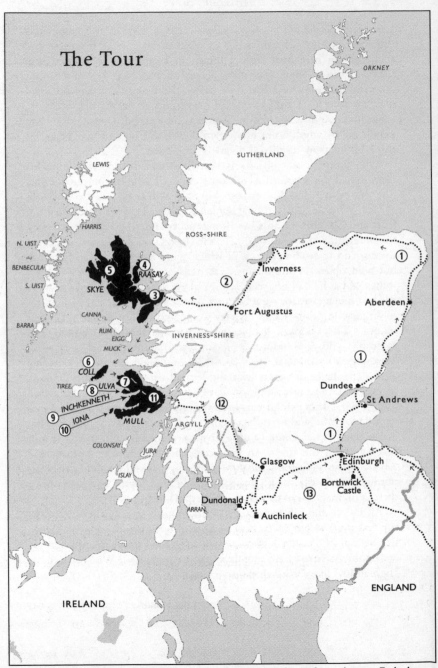

The Tour

ORKNEY

SUTHERLAND

LEWIS

HARRIS

N. UIST

BENBECULA

S. UIST

ROSS-SHIRE

⑤ ④ RAASAY

SKYE

③

Inverness

②

BARRA

CANNA

RUM

EIGG

MUCK

INVERNESS-SHIRE

Fort Augustus

Aberdeen

① ①

⑥ COLL

TIREE ⑧ ULVA ⑦

INCHKENNETH

⑨ IONA ⑪ MULL

⑩

Dundee

St Andrews

①

ARGYLL ⑫

COLONSAY

JURA

ISLAY

BUTE

Glasgow

Edinburgh

Borthwick Castle

⑬

Dundonald

Auchinleck

ARRAN

ENGLAND

IRELAND

Islands visited by Johnson and Boswell are shown in black. Numbers refer to chapters. Each chapter contains a more detailed map.

CHAPTER ONE

The Lowlands

SAMUEL JOHNSON

I had desired to visit the *Hebrides*, or Western Islands of Scotland, so long, that I scarcely remember how the wish was originally excited; and was in the Autumn of the year 1773 induced to undertake the journey, by finding in Mr Boswell a companion, whose acuteness would help my inquiry, and whose gaiety of conversation and civility of manners are sufficient to counteract the inconveniencies of travel, in countries less hospitable than we have passed.

On the eighteenth of August we left Edinburgh, a city too well known to admit description, and directed our course northward, along the eastern coast of Scotland, accompanied the first day by another gentleman, who could stay with us only long enough to shew us how much we lost at separation.[1]

As we crossed the *Frith* of *Forth*, our curiosity was attracted by *Inch Keith*, a small island, which neither of my companions had ever visited, though, lying within their view, it had all their lives solicited their notice. Here, by climbing with some difficulty over shattered crags, we made the first experiment of unfrequented coasts. Inch Keith is nothing more than a rock covered with a thin layer of earth, not wholly bare of grass, and very fertile of thistles. A small herd of cows grazes annually upon it in the summer. It seems never to have afforded to man or beast a permanent habitation.

We found only the ruins of a small fort, not so injured by time but that it might be easily restored to its former state. It seems never to have

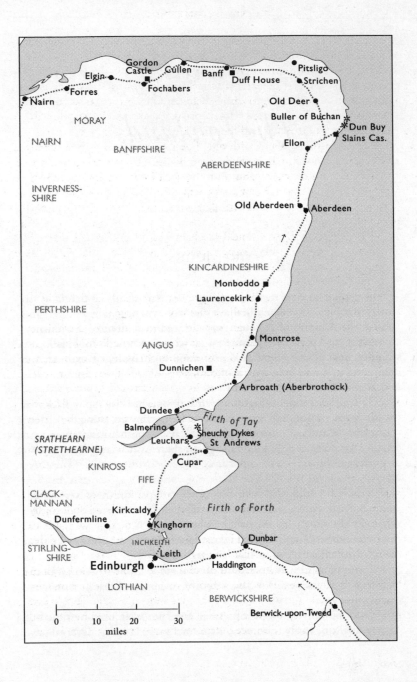

Gordon
Castle
Elgin   Cullen   Banff   Pitsligo
Forres   Fochabers   Duff House   Strichen
Nairn
                                            Old Deer
MORAY   Buller of Buchan   Dun Buy
                                                         Slains Cas.
NAIRN
            BANFFSHIRE   Ellon

INVERNESS-
SHIRE   ABERDEENSHIRE

                                    Old Aberdeen   Aberdeen

                        KINCARDINESHIRE

PERTHSHIRE   Monboddo
                            Laurencekirk

            ANGUS   Montrose

                    Dunnichen

                            Arbroath (Aberbrothock)

                    Dundee
                    Balmerino   Firth of Tay
SRATHEARN   Sheuchy Dykes
(STRETHEARNE)   Leuchars   St Andrews
        KINROSS   Cupar
                FIFE
CLACK-
MANNAN   Kirkcaldy   Firth of Forth
        Dunfermline   Kinghorn
STIRLING-   INCHKEITH   Dunbar
SHIRE   Leith
        Edinburgh   Haddington
            LOTHIAN
                        BERWICKSHIRE
                            Berwick-upon-Tweed

        0   10   20   30
                miles

been intended as a place of strength, nor was built to endure a siege, but merely to afford cover to a few soldiers, who perhaps had the charge of a battery, or were stationed to give signals of approaching danger. There is therefore no provision of water within the walls, though the spring is so near, that it might have been easily enclosed. One of the stones had this inscription: "Maria Reg. 1564." It has probably been neglected from the time that the whole island had the same king.[2]

We left this little island with our thoughts employed awhile on the different appearance that it would have made, if it had been placed at the same distance from London, with the same facility of approach; with what emulation of price a few rocky acres would have been purchased, and with what expensive industry they would have been cultivated and adorned.

When we landed, we found our chaise ready, and passed through *Kinghorn*, *Kirkaldy*, and *Cowpar*, places not unlike the small or straggling market-towns in those parts of England where commerce and manufactures have not yet produced opulence.

Though we were yet in the most populous part of Scotland, and at so small a distance from the capital, we met few passengers.

The roads are neither rough nor dirty; and it affords a southern stranger a new kind of pleasure to travel so commodiously without the interruption of toll-gates. Where the bottom is rocky, as it seems commonly to be in Scotland, a smooth way is made indeed with great labour, but it never wants repairs; and in those parts where adventitious materials are necessary, the ground once consolidated is rarely broken; for the inland commerce is not great, nor are heavy commodities often transported otherwise than by water. The carriages in common use are small carts, drawn each by one little horse; and a man seems to derive some degree of dignity and importance from the reputation of possessing a two-horse cart.

At an hour somewhat late we came to St Andrews, a city once archiepiscopal; where that university still subsists in which philosophy was formerly taught by Buchanan, whose name has as fair a claim to immortality as can be conferred by modern latinity, and perhaps a fairer than the instability of vernacular languages admits.

We found, that by the interposition of some invisible friend, lodgings had been provided for us at the house of one of the professors, whose easy civility quickly made us forget that we were strangers; and in the whole time of our stay we were gratified by every mode of kindness, and entertained with all the elegance of lettered hospitality.[3]

In the morning we rose to perambulate a city, which only history shews to have once flourished, and surveyed the ruins of ancient magnificence, of which even the ruins cannot long be visible, unless some care be taken to preserve them; and where is the pleasure of preserving such mournful memorials? They have been till very lately so much neglected, that every man carried away the stones who fancied that he wanted them.

The cathedral, of which the foundations may be still traced, and a small part of the wall is standing, appears to have been a spacious and majestick building, not unsuitable to the primacy of the kingdom. Of the architecture, the poor remains can hardly exhibit, even to an artist, a sufficient specimen. It was demolished, as is well known, in the tumult and violence of Knox's reformation.

Not far from the cathedral, on the margin of the water, stands a fragment of the castle, in which the archbishop anciently resided. It was never very large, and was built with more attention to security than pleasure. Cardinal Beatoun is said to have had workmen employed in improving its fortifications at the time when he was murdered by the ruffians of reformation, in the manner of which Knox has given what he himself calls a merry narrative.[4]

The change of religion in Scotland, eager and vehement as it was, raised an epidemical enthusiasm, compounded of sullen scrupulousness and warlike ferocity, which, in a people whom idleness resigned to their own thoughts, and who, conversing only with each other, suffered no dilution of their zeal from the gradual influx of new opinions, was long transmitted in its full strength from the old to the young, but by trade and intercourse with England, is now visibly abating, and giving way too fast to that laxity of practice and indifference of opinion, in which men, not sufficiently instructed to find the middle point, too easily shelter themselves from rigour and constraint.

The city of St Andrews, when it had lost its archiepiscopal preeminence, gradually decayed. One of its streets is now lost; and in those that remain, there is the silence and solitude of inactive indigence and gloomy depopulation.[5]

The university, within a few years, consisted of three colleges, but is now reduced to two; the college of St Leonard being lately dissolved by the sale of its buildings and the appropriation of its revenues to the professors of the two others. The chapel of the alienated college is yet standing, a fabrick not inelegant of external structure; but I was always, by some civil excuse, hindred from entering it.[6] A decent attempt, as I was since told, has been made to convert it into a kind of green-house, by planting its area with shrubs. This new method of gardening is unsuccessful; the plants do not hitherto prosper. To what use it will next be put I have no pleasure in conjecturing. It is something that its present state is at least not ostentatiously displayed. Where there is yet shame, there may in time be virtue.

The dissolution of St Leonard's college was doubtless necessary; but of that necessity there is reason to complain. It is surely not without just reproach, that a nation, of which the commerce is hourly extending, and the wealth encreasing, denies any participation of its prosperity to its literary societies;[7] and while its merchants or its nobles are raising palaces, suffers its universities to moulder into dust.

Of the two colleges yet standing, one is by the institution of its founder appropriated to Divinity. It is said to be capable of containing fifty students; but more than one must occupy a chamber. The library, which is of late erection, is not very spacious, but elegant and luminous.

The doctor, by whom it was shewn, hoped to irritate or subdue my English vanity by telling me, that we had no such repository of books in England.[8]

Saint Andrews seems to be a place eminently adapted to study and education, being situated in a populous, yet a cheap country, and exposing the minds and manners of young men neither to the levity and dissoluteness of a capital city, nor to the gross luxury of a town of commerce, places naturally unpropitious to learning; in one the desire of knowledge easily gives way to the love of pleasure, and in the other, is in danger of yielding to the love of money.

The students however are represented as at this time not exceeding a hundred. Perhaps it may be some obstruction to their increase that there is no episcopal chapel in the place. I saw no reason for imputing their paucity to the present professors; nor can the expence of an academical education be very reasonably objected. A student of the highest class may keep his annual session, or as the English call it, his term, which lasts seven months, for about fifteen pounds, and one of lower rank for less than ten; in which board, lodging, and instruction are all included.

The chief magistrate resident in the university, answering to our vice-chancellor, and to the *rector magnificus* on the continent, had commonly the title of Lord Rector; but being addressed only as *Mr Rector* in an inauguratory speech by the present chancellor,[9] he has fallen from his former dignity of style. Lordship was very liberally annexed by our ancestors to any station or character of dignity: they said, the *Lord*

General, and *Lord Ambassador*; so we still say, *my Lord*, to the judge upon the circuit, and yet retain in our Liturgy *the Lords of the Council*.

In walking among the ruins of religious buildings, we came to two vaults over which had formerly stood the house of the sub-prior. One of the vaults was inhabited by an old woman, who claimed the right of abode there, as the widow of a man whose ancestors had possessed the same gloomy mansion for no less than four generations. The right, however it began, was considered as established by legal prescription, and the old woman lives undisturbed. She thinks however that she has a claim to something more than sufferance; for as her husband's name was Bruce, she is allied to royalty, and told Mr Boswell that when there were persons of quality in the place, she was distinguished by some notice; that indeed she is now neglected, but she spins a thread, has the company of her cat, and is troublesome to nobody.[10]

Having now seen whatever this ancient city offered to our curiosity, we left it with good wishes, having reason to be highly pleased with the attention that was paid us. But whoever surveys the world must see many things that give him pain. The kindness of the professors did not contribute to abate the uneasy remembrance of an university declining, a college alienated, and a church profaned and hastening to the ground.

St Andrews indeed has formerly suffered more atrocious ravages and more extensive destruction, but recent evils affect with greater force. We were reconciled to the sight of archiepiscopal ruins. The distance of a calamity from the present time seems to preclude the mind from contact or sympathy. Events long past are barely known; they are not considered. We read with as little emotion the violence of Knox and his followers, as the irruptions of Alaric and the Goths. Had the university been destroyed two centuries ago, we should not have regretted it; but to see it pining in decay and struggling for life, fills the mind with mournful images and ineffectual wishes.

As we knew sorrow and wishes to be vain, it was now our business to mind our way. The roads of Scotland afford little diversion to the traveller, who seldom sees himself either encountered or overtaken, and who has nothing to contemplate but grounds that have no visible boundaries, or are separated by walls of loose stone. From the bank of the Tweed to St Andrews I had never seen a single tree, which I did not believe to have grown up far within the present century. Now and then about a gentleman's house stands a small plantation, which in Scotch is called a *policy*, but of these there are few, and those few all very young.

The variety of sun and shade is here utterly unknown. There is no tree for either shelter or timber. The oak and the thorn is equally a stranger, and the whole country is extended in uniform nakedness, except that in the road between *Kirkaldy* and *Cowpar*, I passed for a few yards between two hedges. A tree might be a show in Scotland as a horse in Venice. At St Andrews Mr Boswell found only one, and recommended it to my notice; I told him that it was rough and low, or looked as if I thought so. This, said he, is nothing to another a few miles off. I was still less delighted to hear that another tree was not to be seen nearer. Nay, said a gentleman that stood by, I know but of this and that tree in the county.

The Lowlands of Scotland had once undoubtedly an equal portion of woods with other countries. Forests are every where gradually diminished, as architecture and cultivation prevail by the increase of people and the introduction of arts. But I believe few regions have been denuded like this, where many centuries must have passed in waste without the least thought of future supply. Davies observes in his account of Ireland, that no Irishman had ever planted an orchard.[11] For that negligence some excuse might be drawn from an unsettled state of life, and the instability of property; but in Scotland possession has long been secure, and inheritance regular, yet it may be doubted whether before the Union any man between Edinburgh and England had ever set a tree.

Of this improvidence no other account can be given than that it probably began in times of tumult, and continued because it had begun. Established custom is not easily broken, till some great event shakes the whole system of things, and life seems to recommence upon new principles. That before the Union the Scots had little trade and little money, is no valid apology; for plantation is the least expensive of all methods of improvement. To drop a seed into the ground can cost nothing, and the trouble is not great of protecting the young plant, till it is out of danger; though it must be allowed to have some difficulty in places like these, where they have neither wood for palisades, nor thorns for hedges.

Our way was over the Firth of Tay, where, though the water was not wide, we paid four shillings for ferrying the chaise. In Scotland the necessaries of life are easily procured, but superfluities and elegancies are of the same price at least as in England, and therefore may be considered as much dearer.

We stopped a while at Dundee, where I remember nothing remarkable, and mounting our chaise again, came about the close of the day to Aberbrothick.

The monastery of Aberbrothick is of great renown in the history of

Scotland.[12] Its ruins afford ample testimony of its ancient magnificence: its extent might, I suppose, easily be found by following the walls among the grass and weeds, and its height is known by some parts yet standing. The arch of one of the gates is entire, and of another only so far dilapidated as to diversify the appearance. A square apartment of great loftiness is yet standing; its use I could not conjecture, as its elevation was very disproportionate to its area. Two corner towers particularly attracted our attention. Mr Boswell, whose inquisitiveness is seconded by great activity, scrambled in at a high window, but found the stairs within broken, and could not reach the top. Of the other tower we were told that the inhabitants sometimes climbed it, but we did not immediately discern the entrance, and as the night was gathering upon us, thought proper to desist. Men skilled in architecture might do what we did not attempt: they might probably form an exact ground-plot of this venerable edifice. They may from some parts yet standing conjecture its general form, and perhaps by comparing it with other buildings of the same kind and the same age, attain an idea very near to truth. I should scarcely have regretted my journey, had it afforded nothing more than the sight of Aberbrothick.

Leaving these fragments of magnificence, we travelled on to Montrose, which we surveyed in the morning, and found it well built, airy, and clean. The townhouse is a handsome fabrick with a portico. We then went to view the English chapel, and found a small church, clean to a degree unknown in any other part of Scotland, with commodious galleries, and what was yet less expected, with an organ.[13]

At our inn we did not find a reception such as we thought proportionate to the commercial opulence of the place; but Mr Boswell desired me to observe that the innkeeper was an Englishman, and I then defended him as well as I could.[14]

When I had proceeded thus far, I had opportunities of observing what I had never heard, that there are many beggars in Scotland. In Edinburgh the proportion is, I think, not less than in London, and in the smaller places it is far greater than in English towns of the same extent. It must, however, be allowed that they are not importunate, nor clamorous. They solicit silently, or very modestly, and therefore though their behaviour may strike with more force the heart of a stranger, they are certainly in danger of missing the attention of their countrymen. Novelty has always some power, an unaccustomed mode of begging excites an unaccustomed degree of pity. But the force of novelty is by its own nature soon at an end; the efficacy of outcry and perseverance is permanent and certain.

The road from Montrose exhibited a continuation of the same appearances. The country is still naked, the hedges are of stone, and the fields so generally plowed that it is hard to imagine where grass is found for the horses that till them. The harvest, which was almost ripe, appeared very plentiful.

Early in the afternoon Mr Boswell observed that we were at no great distance from the house of lord Monboddo. The magnetism of his conversation easily drew us out of our way, and the entertainment which we received would have been a sufficient recompence for a much greater deviation.[15]

The roads beyond Edinburgh, as they are less frequented, must be expected to grow gradually rougher; but they were hitherto by no means incommodious. We travelled on with the gentle pace of a Scotch driver, who having no rivals in expedition, neither gives himself nor his horses unnecessary trouble. We did not affect the impatience we did not feel, but were satisfied with the company of each other as well riding in the chaise, as sitting at an inn. The night and the day are equally solitary and equally safe; for where there are so few travellers, why should there be robbers?

We came somewhat late to Aberdeen, and found the inn so full, that we had some difficulty in obtaining admission, till Mr Boswell made himself known: his name overpowered all objection, and we found a very good house and civil treatment.[16]

I received the next day a very kind letter from Sir Alexander Gordon, whom I had formerly known in London, and after a cessation of all intercourse for near twenty years met here professor of physic in the King's College. Such unexpected renewals of acquaintance may be numbered among the most pleasing incidents of life.

The knowledge of one professor soon procured me the notice of the rest, and I did not want any token of regard, being conducted wherever there was any thing which I desired to see, and entertained at once with the novelty of the place, and the kindness of communication.

To write of the cities of our own island with the solemnity of geographical description, as if we had been cast upon a newly discovered coast, has the appearance of very frivolous ostentation; yet as Scotland is little known to the greater part of those who may read these observations, it is not superfluous to relate, that under the name of Aberdeen are comprised two towns standing about a mile distant from each other, but governed, I think, by the same magistrates.

Old Aberdeen is the ancient episcopal city, in which are still to be seen the remains of the cathedral. It has the appearance of a town in decay, having been situated in times when commerce was yet unstudied, with very little attention to the commodities of the harbour.

New Aberdeen has all the bustle of prosperous trade, and all the shew of increasing opulence. It is built by the waterside. The houses are large and lofty, and the streets spacious and clean. They build almost wholly with the granite used in the new pavement of the streets of London, which is well known not to want hardness, yet they shape it easily. It is beautiful and must be very lasting.

What particular parts of commerce are chiefly exercised by the merchants of Aberdeen, I have not inquired. The manufacture which forces itself upon a stranger's eye is that of knit-stockings, on which the women of the lower class are visibly employed.

In each of these towns there is a college, or in stricter language, an university; for in both there are professors of the same parts of learning, and the colleges hold their sessions and confer degrees separately, with total independence of one on the other.

In old Aberdeen stands the King's College, of which the first president was *Hector Boece*, or *Boethius*, who may be justly reverenced as one of the revivers of elegant learning.[17] When he studied at Paris, he was acquainted with *Erasmus*, who afterwards gave him a public testimony of his esteem, by inscribing to him a catalogue of his works. The stile of Boethius, though, perhaps, not always rigorously pure, is formed with great diligence upon ancient models, and wholly uninfected with monastic barbarity. His history is written with elegance and vigour, but his fabulousness and credulity are justly blamed. His fabulousness, if he was the author of the fictions, is a fault for which no apology can be made; but his credulity may be excused in an age, when all men were credulous. Learning was then rising on the world; but ages so long accustomed to darkness, were too much dazzled with its light to see any thing distinctly. The first race of scholars, in the fifteenth century, and some time after, were, for the most part, learning to speak, rather than to think, and were therefore more studious of elegance than of truth. The contemporaries of Boethius thought it sufficient to know what the ancients had delivered. The examination of tenets and of facts was reserved for another generation.

Boethius, as president of the university, enjoyed a revenue of forty Scottish marks, about two pounds four shillings and sixpence of sterling money. In the present age of trade and taxes, it is difficult even for the imagination so to raise the value of money, or so to diminish the demands of life, as to suppose four and forty shillings a year, an honourable stipend; yet it was probably equal, not only to the needs, but to the rank of Boethius. The wealth of England was undoubtedly to that of Scotland more than five to one, and it is known that Henry the eighth, among whose faults avarice was never reckoned, granted to Roger Ascham, as a reward of his learning, a pension of ten pounds a year.

The other, called the Marischal College, is in the new town. The hall is large and well lighted. One of its ornaments is the picture of Arthur Johnston, who was principal of the college, and who holds among the Latin poets of Scotland the next place to the elegant Buchanan.

In the library I was shewn some curiosities: a Hebrew manuscript of exquisite penmanship, and a Latin translation of Aristotle's Politicks by *Leonardus Aretinus*, written in the Roman character with nicety and beauty, which, as the art of printing has made them no longer necessary, are not now to be found.[18] This was one of the latest performances of the transcribers, for Aretinus died but about twenty years before typography was invented. This version has been printed, and may be found in libraries, but is little read; for the same books have been since translated both by *Victorius* and *Lambinus*, who lived in an age more cultivated, but perhaps owed in part to *Aretinus* that they were able to excel him. Much is due to those who first broke the way to knowledge, and left only to their successors the task of smoothing it.

In both these colleges the methods of instruction are nearly the same; the lectures differing only by the accidental difference of diligence, or ability in the professors. The students wear scarlet gowns and the professors black, which is, I believe, the academical dress in all the *Scottish* universities, except that of Edinburgh, where the scholars are not distinguished by any particular habit. In the King's College there is kept a public table, but the scholars of the Marischal College are boarded in the town. The expence of living is here, according to the information that I could obtain, somewhat more than at St Andrews.

The course of education is extended to four years, at the end of which those who take a degree, who are not many, become masters of arts, and whoever is a master may, if he pleases, immediately commence doctor. The title of doctor, however, was for a considerable time bestowed only on physicians. The advocates are examined and approved by their own body; the ministers were not ambitious of titles, or were afraid of being censured for ambition; and the doctorate in every faculty was commonly given or sold into other countries. The ministers are now reconciled to distinction, and as it must always happen that some will excel others, have thought graduation a proper testimony of uncommon abilities or acquisitions.

The indiscriminate collation of degrees has justly taken away that respect which they originally claimed as stamps, by which the literary value of men so distinguished was authoritatively denoted. That academical honours, or any others should be conferred with exact proportion to merit, is more than human judgment or human integrity have given reason to expect. Perhaps degrees in universities cannot be better adjusted by any general rule than by the length of time passed in the public profession of learning. An English or Irish doctorate cannot be obtained by a very young man, and it is reasonable to suppose, what is likewise by experience commonly found true, that he who is by age qualified to be a doctor, has in so much time gained learning sufficient not to disgrace the title, or wit sufficient not to desire it.

The Scotch universities hold but one term or session in the year. That of St Andrews continues eight months, that of Aberdeen only five, from the first of November to the first of April.

In Aberdeen there is an English chapel, in which the congregation was numerous and splendid. The form of public worship used by the church of England is in Scotland legally practised in licensed chapels served by clergymen of English or Irish ordination, and by tacit connivance quietly permitted in separate congregations supplied with ministers by the successors of the bishops who were deprived at the Revolution.

We came to Aberdeen on Saturday August 21. On Monday we were invited into the town-hall, where I had the freedom of the city given me by the Lord Provost. The honour conferred had all the decorations that politeness could add, and what I am afraid I should not have had to say of any city south of the Tweed, I found no petty officer bowing for a fee.

The parchment containing the record of admission is, with the seal appending, fastened to a riband and worn for one day by the new citizen in his hat.[19]

By a lady who saw us at the chapel, the Earl of Errol was informed of our arrival, and we had the honour of an invitation to his seat, called Slanes Castle, as I am told, improperly, from the castle of that name, which once stood at a place not far distant.

The road beyond Aberdeen grew more stony, and continued equally naked of all vegetable decoration. We travelled over a tract of ground near the sea, which, not long ago, suffered a very uncommon, and unexpected calamity. The sand of the shore was raised by a tempest in such quantities, and carried to such a distance, that an estate was overwhelmed and lost. Such and so hopeless was the barrenness superinduced, that the owner, when he was required to pay the usual tax, desired rather to resign the ground.[20]

We came in the afternoon to *Slanes Castle*, built upon the margin of the sea, so that the walls of one of the towers seem only a continuation of a perpendicular rock, the foot of which is beaten by the waves. To walk round the house seemed impracticable. From the windows the eye wanders over the sea that separates Scotland from Norway, and when the winds beat with violence must enjoy all the terrifick grandeur of the tempestuous ocean. I would not for my amusement wish for a storm; but as storms, whether wished or not, will sometimes happen, I may say, without violation of humanity, that I should willingly look out upon them from Slanes Castle.

When we were about to take our leave, our departure was prohibited by the countess till we should have seen two places upon the coast, which she rightly considered as worthy of curiosity, *Dun Buy*, and the *Buller of Buchan*, to which Mr Boyd very kindly conducted us.

Dun Buy, which in Erse is said to signify the *Yellow Rock*, is a double protuberance of stone, open to the main sea on one side, and parted from the land by a very narrow channel on the other.[21] It has its name and its colour from the dung of innumerable sea-fowls, which in the Spring chuse this place as convenient for incubation, and have their eggs and their young taken in great abundance. One of the birds that frequent this rock has, as we were told, its body not larger than a duck's, and yet lays eggs as large as those of a goose. This bird is by the inhabitants named a *Coot*. That which is called *Coot* in England, is here a *Cooter*.

Upon these rocks there was nothing that could long detain attention, and we soon turned our eyes to the *Buller*, or *Bouilloir* of *Buchan*, which no man can see with indifference, who has either sense of danger or delight in rarity. It is a rock perpendicularly tubulated, united on one side with a high shore, and on the other rising steep to a great height, above the main sea. The top is open, from which may be seen a dark gulf of water which flows into the cavity, through a breach made in the lower part of the inclosing rock. It has the appearance of a vast well bordered with a wall. The edge of the Buller is not wide, and to those that walk round, appears very narrow. He that ventures to look downward sees, that if his foot should slip, he must fall from his dreadful elevation upon stones on one side, or into the water on the other. We however went round, and were glad when the circuit was completed.

When we came down to the sea, we saw some boats, and rowers, and resolved to explore the Buller at the bottom. We entered the arch, which the water had made, and found ourselves in a place, which, though we could not think ourselves in danger, we could scarcely survey without some recoil of the mind. The bason in which we floated was nearly circular, perhaps thirty yards in diameter. We were inclosed by a natural wall, rising steep on every side to a height which produced the idea of insurmountable confinement. The interception of all lateral light caused a dismal gloom. Round us was a perpendicular rock, above us the distant sky, and below an unknown profundity of water. If I had any malice against a walking spirit, instead of laying him in the Red-sea, I would condemn him to reside in the Buller of Buchan.

But terrour without danger is only one of the sports of fancy, a voluntary agitation of the mind that is permitted no longer than it pleases. We were soon at leisure to examine the place with minute inspection, and found many cavities which, as the watermen told us, went backward to a depth which they had never explored. Their extent we had not time to try; they are said to serve different purposes. Ladies come hither sometimes in the summer with collations, and smugglers make them storehouses for clandestine merchandise. It is hardly to be doubted but the pirates of ancient times often used them as magazines of arms, or repositories of plunder.

To the little vessels used by the northern rowers, the Buller may have served as a shelter from storms, and perhaps as a retreat from enemies; the entrance might have been stopped, or guarded with little difficulty, and though the vessels that were stationed within would have been battered with stones showered on them from above, yet the crews would have lain safe in the caverns.

Next morning we continued our journey, pleased with our reception at Slanes Castle, of which we had now leisure to recount the grandeur and the elegance; for our way afforded us few topics of conversation. The ground was neither uncultivated nor unfruitful; but it was still all arable. Of flocks or herds there was no appearance. I had now travelled two hundred miles in Scotland, and seen only one tree not younger than myself.

We dined this day at the house of Mr Frazer of *Streichton*, who shewed us in his grounds some stones yet standing of a druidical circle, and what I began to think more worthy of notice, some forest trees of full growth.[22]

At night we came to Bamff, where I remember nothing that particularly claimed my attention. The ancient towns of Scotland have generally an appearance unusual to Englishmen. The houses, whether great or small, are for the most part built of stones. Their ends are now and then next the streets, and the entrance into them is very often by a flight of steps, which reaches up to the second story. The floor which is level with the ground being entered only by stairs descending within the house.

The art of joining squares of glass with lead is little used in Scotland, and in some places is totally forgotten. The frames of their windows are all of wood. They are more frugal of their glass than the English, and will often, in houses not otherwise mean, compose a square of two pieces, not joining like cracked glass, but with one edge laid perhaps half an inch over the other. Their windows do not move upon hinges, but are pushed up and drawn down in grooves, yet they are seldom accommodated with weights and pullies. He that would have his window open must hold it with his hand, unless what may be sometimes found among good contrivers, there be a nail which he may stick into a hole, to keep it from falling.

What cannot be done without some uncommon trouble or particular expedient, will not often be done at all. The incommodiousness of the Scotch windows keeps them very closely shut. The necessity of ventilating human habitations has not yet been found by our northern neighbours; and even in houses well built and elegantly furnished, a stranger may be sometimes forgiven, if he allows himself to wish for fresher air.[23]

These diminutive observations seem to take away something from the dignity of writing, and therefore are never communicated but with hesitation, and a little fear of abasement and contempt. But it must be remembered, that life consists not of a series of illustrious actions, or elegant enjoyments; the greater part of our time passes in compliance with necessities, in the performance of daily duties, in the removal of small inconveniencies, in the procurement of petty pleasures; and we are well or ill at ease, as the main stream of life glides on smoothly, or is ruffled by small obstacles and frequent interruption. The true state of every nation is the state of common life. The manners of a people are not to be found in the schools of learning, or the palaces of greatness, where the national character is obscured or obliterated by travel or instruction, by philosophy or vanity; nor is public happiness to be estimated by the assemblies of the gay, or the banquets of the rich. The great mass of nations is neither rich nor gay: they whose aggregate constitutes the people, are found in the streets, and the villages, in the shops and farms; and from them collectively considered, must the measure of general prosperity be taken. As they approach to delicacy a nation is refined; as their conveniencies are multiplied, a nation, at least a commercial nation, must be denominated wealthy.

Finding nothing to detain us at Bamff, we set out in the morning, and having breakfasted at Cullen, about noon came to *Elgin*, where in the inn, that we supposed the best, a dinner was set before us, which we could not eat. This was the first time, and except one, the last, that I found any reason to complain of a Scotish table; and such disappointments, I suppose, must be expected in every country, where there is no great frequency of travellers.[24]

The ruins of the cathedral of Elgin afforded us another proof of the waste of reformation. There is enough yet remaining to shew, that it was once magnificent. Its whole plot is easily traced. On the north side of the choir, the chapterhouse, which is roofed with an arch of stone, remains entire; and on the south side, another mass of building, which we could not enter, is preserved by the care of the family of Gordon; but the body of the church is a mass of fragments.[25]

A paper was here put into our hands, which deduced from sufficient authorities the history of this venerable ruin. The church of Elgin had, in the intestine tumults of the barbarous ages, been laid waste by the irruption of a Highland chief, whom the bishop had offended;[26] but it was gradually restored to the state, of which the traces may be now discerned, and was at last not destroyed by the tumultuous violence of Knox, but more shamefully suffered to dilapidate by deliberate robbery and frigid indifference. There is still extant, in the books of the council, an order, of which I cannot remember the date, but which was doubtless issued after the Reformation, directing that the lead, which covers the two cathedrals of Elgin and Aberdeen, shall be taken away, and converted into money for the support of the army.[27] A Scotch army was in those times very cheaply kept; yet the lead of two churches must have born so small a proportion to any military expence, that it is hard not to believe the reason alleged to be merely popular, and the money intended for some private purse. The order however was obeyed; the two churches were stripped, and the lead was shipped to be sold in Holland. I hope every reader will rejoice that this cargo of sacrilege was lost at sea.

Let us not however make too much haste to despise our neighbours. Our own cathedrals are mouldering by unregarded dilapidation. It seems to be part of the despicable philosophy of the time to despise monuments of sacred magnificence, and we are in danger of doing that deliberately, which the Scots did not do but in the unsettled state of an imperfect constitution.

Those who had once uncovered the cathedrals never wished to cover them again; and being thus made useless, they were first neglected, and perhaps, as the stone was wanted, afterwards demolished.

Elgin seems a place of little trade, and thinly inhabited. The episcopal cities of Scotland, I believe, generally fell with their churches, though some of them have since recovered by a situation convenient for commerce. Thus *Glasgow*, though it has no longer an archbishop, has risen beyond its original state by the opulence of its traders; and *Aberdeen*, though its ancient stock had decayed, flourishes by a new shoot in another place.

In the chief street of Elgin, the houses jut over the lowest story, like the old buildings of timber in London, but with greater prominence; so that there is sometimes a walk for a considerable length under a cloister, or portico, which is now indeed frequently broken, because the new houses have another form, but seems to have been uniformly continued in the old city.

We went forwards the same day to Fores, the town to which Macbeth was travelling, when he met the weird sisters in his way. This to an Englishman is classic ground. Our imaginations were heated, and our thoughts recalled to their old amusements.

We had now a prelude to the Highlands. We began to leave fertility and culture behind us, and saw for a great length of road nothing but heath; yet at *Fochabers*, a seat belonging to the duke of Gordon, there is an orchard, which in *Scotland* I had never seen before, with some timber trees, and a plantation of oaks.

At Fores we found good accommodation,[28] but nothing worthy of particular remark, and next morning entered upon the road, on which *Macbeth* heard the fatal prediction; but we travelled on not interrupted by promises of kingdoms, and came to *Nairn*, a royal burgh, which, if once it flourished, is now in a state of miserable decay; but I know not whether its chief annual magistrate has not still the title of Lord Provost.

James Boswell

INTRODUCTION. Dr Johnson had for many years given me hopes that we should go together and visit the Hebrides. Martin's Account of those islands had impressed us with a notion that we might there contemplate a system of life almost totally different from what we had been accustomed to see; and to find simplicity and wildness, and all the circumstances of remote time or place, so near to our native great island, was an object within the reach of reasonable curiosity.[29] Dr Johnson has said in his *Journey* that he scarcely remembered how the wish to visit the Hebrides was excited; but he told me, in summer 1763, that his father put Martin's Account into his hands when he was very young, and that he was much pleased with it. We reckoned there would be some inconveniencies and hardships, and perhaps a little danger; but these we were persuaded were magnified in the imagination of everybody. When I was at Ferney in 1764, I mentioned our design to Voltaire. He looked at me as if I had talked of going to the North Pole, and said, "You do not insist on my accompanying you?"

"No, sir."

"Then I am very willing you should go."

I was not afraid that our curious expedition would be prevented by such apprehensions, but I doubted that it would not be possible to prevail on Dr Johnson to relinquish for some time the felicity of a London life, which, to a man who can enjoy it with full intellectual relish, is apt to make existence in any narrower sphere seem insipid or irksome. I doubted that he would not be willing to come down from his elevated state of philosophical dignity; from a superiority of wisdom among the wise and of learning among the learned; and from flashing his wit upon minds bright enough to reflect it.

He had disappointed my expectations so long that I began to despair; but in spring 1773, he talked of coming to Scotland that year with so much firmness that I hoped he was at last in earnest. I knew that if he were once launched from the metropolis, he would go forward very well; and I got our common friends there to assist in setting him afloat. To Mrs Thrale in particular, whose enchantment over him seldom failed, I was much obliged. It was: "I'll give thee a wind."

"Thou art kind."[30]

To *attract* him we had invitations from the chiefs Macdonald and MacLeod, and for additional aid I wrote to Lord Elibank, Dr William Robertson, and Dr Beattie. To Dr Robertson, so far as my letter concerned the present subject, I wrote as follows:

> Our friend Mr Samuel Johnson is in great health and spirits, and, I do think, has a serious resolution to visit Scotland this year. The more attraction, however, the better; and therefore, though I know he will be happy to meet you there, it will forward the scheme if, in your answer to this, you express yourself concerning it with that power of which you are so happily possessed, and which may be so directed as to operate strongly upon him.

His answer to that part of my letter was quite as I could have wished. It was written with the address and persuasion of the historian of America:

> When I saw you last, you gave us some hopes that you might prevail with Mr Johnson to make out that excursion to Scotland with the expectation of which we have long flattered ourselves. If he could order matters so as to pass some time in Edinburgh about the close of the Summer Session, and then visit some of the Highland scenes, I am confident he would be pleased with the grand features of nature in many parts of this country; he will meet with many persons here who respect him, and some whom I am persuaded he will think not unworthy of his esteem. I wish he would make the experiment. He sometimes cracks his jokes upon us, but he will find that we can distinguish between the stabs of malevolence and *the rebukes of the righteous, which are like excellent oil,*[31] *and break not the head.* Offer my best compliments to him, and assure him that I shall be happy to have the satisfaction of seeing him under my roof.

To Dr Beattie I wrote,

> The chief intention of this letter is to inform you that I now seriously believe Mr Samuel Johnson will visit Scotland this year, but I wish that every power of attraction may be employed to secure our having so valuable an acquisition; and therefore I hope you will without delay write to me what I know you think, that I may read it to the mighty sage, with proper emphasis, before I leave London, which I must do soon. He talks of you with the same warmth that he did last year. We are to see as much of Scotland as we can in the months of August and September. We shall not be long of being at Marischal College.[32] He is particularly desirous of seeing some of the Western Islands.

Dr Beattie did better: *ipse venit.* He was, however, so polite as to waive his privilege of *nil mihi rescribas,*[33] and wrote from Edinburgh as follows:

> Your very kind and agreeable favour of the 20th of April overtook me here yesterday after having gone to Aberdeen, which place I left about a week ago. I am to set out this day for London, and hope to have the honour of paying my respects to Mr Johnson and you about a week or ten days hence. I shall then do what I can to enforce the topic you mention, but at present I cannot enter upon it, as I am in a very great hurry; for I intend to begin my journey within an hour or two.

He was as good as his word and threw some pleasing motives into the northern scale. But indeed, Mr Johnson loved all that he heard from one whom he tells us in his *Lives of the Poets* Gray found 'a poet, a philosopher, and a good man'.

My lord Elibank did not answer my letter to his lordship for some time. The reason will appear when we come to the Isle of Skye. I shall then insert my letter, with letters from his lordship both to myself and Mr Johnson.[34] I beg it may be understood that I insert my own letters, as I relate my own sayings, rather as keys to what is valuable belonging to others than for their own sake.

Luckily Mr Justice (now Sir Robert) Chambers, who was about to sail for the East Indies, was going to take leave of his relations at Newcastle, and he conducted Dr Johnson to that town. Mr Scott of University College, Oxford (now Dr Scott of the Commons), accompanied him from thence to Edinburgh.[35] With such propitious convoys did he proceed to my native city. But lest metaphor should make it be supposed he actually went by sea, I choose to mention that he travelled in post-chaises, of which the rapid motion was one of his most favourite amusements.[36]

Dr Samuel Johnson's character – religious, moral, political, and literary – nay, his figure and manner, are, I believe, more generally known than those of almost any man, yet it may not be superfluous here to attempt a sketch of him. Let my readers then remember that he was a sincere and zealous Christian, of high-Church-of-England and monarchical principles, which he would not tamely suffer to be questioned; steady and inflexible in maintaining the obligations of piety and virtue, both from a regard to the order of society and from a veneration for the Great Source of all order; correct, nay stern, in his taste; hard to please and easily offended, impetuous and irritable in his temper, but of a most humane and benevolent heart; having a mind stored with a vast and various collection of learning and knowledge, which he communicated with peculiar perspicuity and force, in rich and choice expression. He united a most logical head with a most fertile imagination, which gave him an extraordinary advantage in arguing, for he could reason close or wide as he saw best for the moment. He could, when he chose it, be the greatest sophist that ever wielded a weapon in the schools of declamation, but he indulged this only in conversation, for he owned that he sometimes talked for victory; he was too conscientious to make error permanent and pernicious by deliberately writing it.

He was conscious of his superiority. He loved praise when it was brought to him, but was too proud to seek for it. He was somewhat susceptible of flattery. His mind was so full of imagery that he might have been perpetually a poet. It has been often remarked that in his poetical pieces (which it is to be regretted are so few, because so excellent) his style is easier than in his prose. There is deception in this: it is not easier but better suited to the dignity of verse; as one may dance with grace whose motions in ordinary walking – in the common step – are awkward. He had a constitutional melancholy, the clouds of which darkened the brightness of his fancy and gave a gloomy cast to his whole course of thinking; yet, though grave and awful in his deportment when he thought it necessary or proper, he frequently indulged himself in pleasantry and sportive sallies.

He was prone to superstition but not to credulity. Though his imagination might incline him to a belief of the marvellous and the mysterious, his vigorous reason examined the evidence with jealousy. He had a loud voice and a slow deliberate utterance which no doubt gave some additional weight to the sterling metal of his conversation. Lord Pembroke said once to me at Wilton, with a happy pleasantry and some truth, that 'Dr Johnson's sayings would not appear so extraordinary were it not for his *bow-wow way*', but I admit the truth of this only on some occasions. The *Messiah* played upon the Canterbury organ is more sublime than when played upon an inferior instrument, but very slight music will seem grand when conveyed to the ear through that majestic medium. *While therefore Doctor Johnson's sayings are read, let his manner be taken along with them.* Let it, however, be observed that the sayings themselves are generally great; that, though he might be an ordinary composer at times, he was for the most part a Handel.

His person was large, robust, I may say approaching to the gigantic, and grown unwieldy from corpulency. His countenance was naturally of the cast of an ancient statue, but somewhat disfigured by the scars of that *evil* which it was formerly imagined the *royal touch* could cure. He was now in his sixty-fourth year, and was become a little dull of hearing. His sight had always been somewhat weak, yet so much does mind govern and even supply the deficiency of organs that his perceptions were uncommonly quick and accurate. His head and sometimes also his body shook with a kind of motion like the effect of a palsy; he appeared to be frequently disturbed by cramps or convulsive contractions, of the nature of that distemper called St Vitus's dance.[37]

He wore a full suit of plain brown clothes with twisted-hair buttons of the same colour, a large bushy greyish wig, a plain shirt, black worsted stockings, and silver buckles. Upon this tour, when journeying, he wore boots and a very wide brown cloth greatcoat with pockets which might have almost held the two volumes of his folio dictionary, and he carried in his hand a large English oak stick. Let me not be censured for mentioning such minute particulars. Everything relative to so great a man is worth observing. I remember Dr Adam Smith, in his rhetorical lectures at Glasgow, told us he was glad to know that Milton wore latchets in his shoes instead of buckles. When I mention the oak stick, it is but letting Hercules have his club; and by and by my readers will find this stick will bud and produce a good joke.[38]

This imperfect sketch of 'the *combination* and the *form*' of that Wonderful Man whom I venerated and loved while in this world, and after whom I gaze with humble hope now that it has pleased Almighty God to call him to a better world, will serve to introduce to the fancy of my readers the capital object of the following Journal, in the course of which I trust they will attain to a considerable degree of acquaintance with him.

His prejudice against Scotland was announced almost as soon as he began to appear in the world of letters. In his *London, a Poem*, are the following nervous lines:

> *For who would leave, unbribed, Hibernia's land?*
> *Or change the rocks of Scotland for the Strand?*
> *There none are swept by sudden fate away,*
> *But all, whom hunger spares, with age decay.*[39]

The truth is, like the ancient Greeks and Romans, he allowed himself to look upon all nations but his own as barbarians: not only Hibernia and Scotland, but Spain, Italy, and France are attacked in the same poem. If he was particularly prejudiced against the Scots, it was because they were more in his way; because he thought their success in England rather exceeded the due proportion of their real merit; and because he could not but see in them that nationality which I believe no liberal-minded Scotsman will deny. He was indeed, if I may be allowed the phrase, at bottom much of a *John Bull*, much of a *true-born Englishman*. There was a stratum of common clay under the rock of marble. He was voraciously fond of good eating, and he had a great deal of that quality called *humour*, which gives an oiliness and a gloss to every other quality.

I am, I flatter myself, completely a citizen of the world. In my travels through Holland, Germany, Switzerland, Italy, Corsica, France, I never felt myself from home; and I sincerely love 'every kindred and tongue and people and nation'.[40] I subscribe to what my late truly learned and philosophical friend Mr Crosbie said: that the English are better animals than the Scots; they are nearer the sun, their blood is richer and more mellow; but when I humour any of them in an outrageous contempt of Scotland, I fairly own I treat them as children. And thus I have, at some moments, found myself obliged to treat even Dr Johnson.

To Scotland, however, he ventured; and he returned from it in great good humour, with his prejudices much lessened, and with very grateful feelings of the hospitality with which he was treated, as is evident from that admirable work, his *Journey to the Western Islands of Scotland*, which, to my utter astonishment, has been misapprehended, even to rancour, by many of my countrymen.[41]

To have the company of Chambers and Scott, he delayed his journey so long that the Court of Session, which rises on the eleventh of August, was broke up before he got to Edinburgh.[42]

On Saturday the fourteenth of August, 1773, late in the evening, I received a note from him that he was arrived at Boyd's Inn, at the head of the Canongate.[43] I went to him directly. He embraced me cordially, and I exulted in the thought that I now had him actually in Caledonia. Mr Scott's amiable manners and attachment to our Socrates at once united me to him. He told me that before I came in the Doctor had unluckily had a bad specimen of Scottish cleanliness. He then drank no fermented liquor. He asked to have his lemonade made sweeter, upon which the waiter with his greasy fingers lifted a lump of sugar and put it into it. The Doctor in indignation threw it out of the window. Scott said he was afraid he would have knocked the waiter down. Mr Johnson told me subsequently that such another trick was played him at the house of a lady in Paris.[44]

He was to do me the honour to lodge under my roof. I regretted sincerely that I had not also a room for Mr Scott. He said, "Shall I see your lady?" BOSWELL. "Yes."

"Then I'll put on a clean shirt."

I said, "'Tis needless. Either don't see her tonight, or don't put on a clean shirt." JOHNSON. "Sir, I'll do both."[45]

Mr Johnson and I walked arm-in-arm up the High Street to my house in James's Court; it was a dusky night; I could not prevent his being assailed by the evening effluvia of Edinburgh. I heard a late baronet of some distinction in the political world in the beginning of the present reign observe that 'walking the streets of Edinburgh at night was pretty perilous and a good deal odoriferous'.[46] The peril is much abated by the care which the magistrates have taken to enforce the city laws against throwing foul water from the windows; but, from the structure of the houses in the old town, which consist of many storeys in each of which a different family lives, and there being no covered sewers, the odour still continues. A zealous Scotsman would have wished Mr Johnson to be without one of his five senses upon this occasion. As we marched slowly along, he grumbled in my ear, "I smell you in the dark!" But he acknowledged that the breadth of the street and the loftiness of the buildings on each side made a noble appearance.

My wife had tea ready for him, which it is well known he delighted to drink at all hours, particularly when sitting up late, and of which his able defence against Mr Jonas Hanway should have obtained him a magnificent reward from the East India Company.[47] He showed much complacency upon finding that the mistress of the house was so attentive to his singular habit; and as no man could be more polite when he chose to be so, his address to her was most courteous and engaging, and his conversation soon charmed her into a forgetfulness of his external appearance. BOSWELL. "I'm glad to see you under my roof." JOHNSON. "And 'tis a very noble roof."

I did not begin to keep a regular full journal till some days after we had set out from Edinburgh, but I have luckily preserved a good many fragments of his *Memorabilia* from his very first evening in Scotland. We had, a little before this, had a trial for murder, in which the judges had allowed the lapse of twenty years since its commission as a plea in bar, in conformity with the doctrine of prescription in the civil law, which Scotland and several other countries in Europe have adopted.[48] He at first disapproved of this, but then he thought there was something in it if there had been for twenty years a neglect to prosecute a crime which was *known*. He would not allow that a murder, by not being *discovered* for twenty years, should escape punishment.

We talked of the ancient trial by duel. He did not think it so absurd as is generally supposed. "For," said he, "it was only allowed when the question was *in equilibrio*, as when one affirmed and another denied; and they had a notion that Providence would interfere in favour of him who was in the right. But as it was found that in a duel he who was in the right had not a better chance than he who was in the wrong, therefore society instituted the present mode of trial and gave the advantage to him who is in the right."

We sat till near two in the morning, having chatted a good while after my wife left us. BOSWELL. "Langton is a worthy man." JOHNSON. "Sir, the earth has not a better man. But ridicule is inherent in him. There is no separating them." My wife had insisted that, to show all respect to the sage, she would give up our own bedchamber to him and take a worse. This I cannot but gratefully mention, as one of a thousand obligations which I owe her, since the great obligation of her being pleased to accept of me as her husband.[49]

SUNDAY 15 AUGUST. I had a little of a headach. He had a barber to shave him. The first rasor was bad. He was very angry. "Sir, this is digging."

Mr Scott came to breakfast, at which I introduced to Dr Johnson and him my friend Sir William Forbes, now of Pitsligo, a man of whom too much good cannot be said; who, with distinguished abilities and application in his profession of a banker, is at once a good companion and a good Christian – which I think is saying enough. Yet it is but justice to record that once when he was in a dangerous illness he was watched with the anxious apprehension of a general calamity; day and night his house was beset with affectionate inquiries, and upon his recovery *Te Deum* was the universal chorus from the hearts of his countrymen.

Mr Johnson was pleased with my daughter Veronica, then a child of about four months old. She had the appearance of listening to him. His motions seemed to her to be intended for her amusement, and when he stopped, she fluttered and made a little infantine noise and a kind of signal for him to begin again. She would be held close to him, which was a proof from simple nature that his figure was not horrid. Her fondness for him endeared her still more to me, and I declared she should have five hundred pounds of additional fortune.[50]

We talked of the practice of the Law. Sir William Forbes said he thought an honest lawyer should never undertake a cause which he was satisfied was not a just one. "Sir," said Mr Johnson, "a lawyer has no business with the justice or injustice of the cause which he undertakes, unless his client asks his opinion, and then he is bound to give it honestly. The justice or injustice of the cause is to be decided by the judge. Consider, sir; what is the purpose of courts of justice? It is that every man may have his cause fairly tried by men appointed to try causes. A lawyer is not to tell what he knows to be a lie: he is not to produce what he knows to be a false deed; but he is not to usurp the province of the jury and of the judge and determine what shall be the effect of evidence, what shall be the result of legal argument. As it rarely happens that a man is fit to plead his own cause, lawyers are a class of the community, who, by study and experience, have acquired the art and power of arranging evidence and of applying to the points at issue what the law has settled. A lawyer is to do for his client all that his client might fairly do for himself if he could. If, by a superiority of attention, of knowledge, of skill, and a better method of communication, he has the advantage of his adversary, it is an advantage to which he is entitled. There must always be some advantage on one side or other, and it is better that advantage should be had by talents than by chance. If lawyers were to undertake no causes till they were sure they were just, a man might be precluded altogether from a trial of his claim, though, were it judicially examined, it might be found a very just claim."

This was sound practical doctrine, and rationally repressed a too-refined scrupulosity of conscience.

Emigration was at this time a common topic of discourse. Dr Johnson regretted it as hurtful to human happiness. "For," said he, "it spreads mankind, which weakens the defence of a nation and lessens the comfort of living. Men, thinly scattered, make a shift, but a bad shift, without many things. A smith is ten miles off; they'll do without a nail or a staple. A tailor is far from them; they'll botch their own clothes. It is being concentrated which produces high convenience."

My wife objected to our going because Skye was a bad country. JOHNSON. "Madam, we do not go there as to a paradise. We go to see something different from what we're accustomed to see."[51]

Sir William Forbes, Mr Scott, and I accompanied Mr Johnson to the chapel founded by Lord Chief Baron Smith for the service of the Church of England.[52] The Reverend Mr Carr, the senior clergyman, preached from these words: "Because the Lord reigneth, let the earth be glad." I was sorry to think Mr Johnson did not attend to the sermon, Mr Carr's low voice not being strong enough to reach his hearing. A selection of Mr Carr's sermons has, since his death, been published by Sir William Forbes, and the world has acknowledged their uncommon merit. I am well assured Lord Mansfield has pronounced them to be excellent.

Here I obtained a promise from Lord Chief Baron Ord that he would dine at my house next day. I presented Mr Johnson to his lordship, who politely said to him, "I have not the honour of knowing you, but I hope for it and to see you at my house. I am to wait on you tomorrow."

This respectable English judge will be long remembered in Scotland, where he built an elegant house and lived in it magnificently. His own ample fortune, with the addition of his salary, enabled him to be splendidly hospitable. It may be fortunate for an individual amongst ourselves to be Lord Chief Baron, and a most worthy man now has the office;[53] but in my opinion it is better for Scotland in general that some of our public employments should be filled by gentlemen of distinction from the south side of the Tweed, as we have the benefit of promotion in England. Such an interchange would make a beneficial mixture of manners, and render our union more complete. Lord Chief Baron Ord was on good terms with us all, in a country filled with jarring interests and keen parties; and, though I well knew his opinion to be the same with my own, he kept himself aloof at a very critical period indeed, when the Douglas Cause shook the sacred security of birthright in Scotland to its foundation; a cause, which had it happened before the Union, when there was no appeal to a British House of Lords, would have left the great fortress of honours and of property in ruins.[54]

When we got home, Dr Johnson desired to see my books. He took down Ogden's *Sermons on Prayer*, on which I set a very high value, having been much edified by them, and he retired with them to his room.[55] He did not stay long, but soon joined us in the drawing-room. Mr Johnson said of himself, without any prompting at all, my drawing-room was the pleasantest room he had ever been in. I presented to him Mr Robert Arbuthnot, a relation of the celebrated Dr Arbuthnot, and a man of literature and taste. To him we were obliged for a previous recommendation which secured us a very agreeable reception at St Andrews, and which Dr Johnson in his *Journey* ascribes to 'some invisible friend'.[56] I also presented to him Mr Charles Hay, advocate, who had been at chapel.[57]

Of Dr Beattie Mr Johnson said, "Sir, he has written like a man conscious of the truth and feeling his own strength. Treating your adversary with respect is giving him an advantage to which he is not entitled. The greatest part of men cannot judge of reasoning, and are impressed by character; so that if you allow your adversary a respectable character, they will think that though you differ from him, you may be in the wrong. Sir, treating your adversary with respect is striking soft in a battle.[58] And as to Hume – a man who has so much conceit as to tell all mankind that they have been bubbled for ages and he is the wise man who sees better than they, a man who has so little scrupulosity as to venture to oppose those principles which have been thought necessary to human happiness – is he to be surprised if another man comes and laughs at him? If he is the great man he thinks himself, all this cannot hurt him; it is like throwing peas against a rock."

He added '*something much too rough*', both as to Mr Hume's head and heart: BOSWELL. "But why attack his heart?" JOHNSON. "Why, sir, because his head has corrupted it. Or perhaps it has perverted his head. I know not indeed whether he has first been a blockhead and that has made him a rogue, or first been a rogue and that has made him a blockhead."[59]

Violence is, in my opinion, not suitable to the Christian cause. Besides, I always lived on good terms with Mr Hume, though I have frankly told him I was not clear that it was right in me to keep company with him. "But," said I, "how much better are you than your books!" He was cheerful, obliging, and instructive; he was charitable to the poor; and many an agreeable hour have I passed with him. I have preserved some entertaining and interesting memoirs of him, particularly when he knew himself to be dying, which I may some time or other communicate to the world.[60] I shall not, however, extol him so very highly as Dr Adam Smith does, who says in a letter to Mr Strahan the printer (not a confidential letter to his friend, but a letter which is published with all formality), "Upon the whole, I have always considered him, both in his lifetime and since his death, as approaching as nearly to the idea of a perfectly wise and virtuous man as perhaps the nature of human frailty will permit."[61]

Let Dr Smith consider: was not Mr Hume blessed with good health, good spirits, good friends, a competent and increasing fortune? And had he not also a perpetual feast of fame? But, as a learned friend has observed to me, "What trials did he undergo to prove the perfection of his virtue? Did he ever experience any great instance of adversity?" When I read this sentence, delivered by my old Professor of Moral Philosophy, I could not help exclaiming with the Psalmist, "Surely I have now more understanding than my teachers!"[62]

While we were talking, there came a note to me from Dr William Robertson: "Sunday. DEAR SIR, I have been expecting every day to hear from you of Dr Johnson's arrival. Pray what do you know about his motions? I long to take him by the hand. I write this from the college, where I have only this scrap of paper. Ever yours, W. R." It pleased me to find Dr Robertson thus eager to meet Dr Johnson. I was glad that I could answer that he was come; and I begged Dr Robertson might be with us as soon as he could.

Sir William Forbes, Mr Scott, Mr Arbuthnot, and another gentleman dined with us.[63] "Come, Dr Johnson," said I, "it is commonly thought that our veal in Scotland is not good. But here is some which I believe you will like." There was no catching him. JOHNSON. "Why, sir, what is commonly thought I should take to be true. *Your* veal may be good, but that will only be an exception to the general opinion, not a proof against it."

Dr Robertson, according to the custom of Edinburgh at that time, dined in the interval between the forenoon and afternoon service, which was then later than now; so we had not the pleasure of his company till dinner was over, when he came and drank wine with us. And then began some animated dialogue, of which here follows a pretty full note.

We talked of Mr Burke. Dr Johnson said he had great variety of knowledge, store of imagery, copiousness of language. ROBERTSON. "He has wit too." JOHNSON. "No, sir, he never succeeds there. 'Tis low; 'tis conceit. I used to say Burke never once made a good joke.[64] What I most envy Burke for is his being constantly the same. He is never what we call humdrum; never unwilling to begin to talk, nor in haste to leave off." BOSWELL. "Yet he can listen." JOHNSON. "No, I cannot say he is good at that. So desirous is he to talk that if one is speaking at this end of the table, he'll speak to somebody at the other end. Burke, sir, is such a man that if you met him for the first time in a street where there was a shower of cannon bullets, and you and he ran up a stair to take shelter but for five minutes,[65] he'd talk to you in such a manner that when you parted you would say, 'This is an extraordinary man.' Now, you may be long enough with *me* without finding anything extraordinary."

He said he believed Burke was intended for the Law, but either had not money enough to follow it or had not diligence enough. He said he could not understand how a man could apply to one thing and not to another. Robertson said one man had more judgment, another more imagination. JOHNSON. "No, sir; it is only one man has more mind than another. He may direct it differently; he may by accident see the success of one kind of study and take a desire to excel in it. I am persuaded that had Sir Isaac Newton applied to poetry, he would have made a very fine epic poem. I could as easily apply to law as to tragic poetry." BOSWELL. "Yet, sir, you *did* apply to tragic poetry, not to law." JOHNSON. "Because, sir, I had not money to study law. Sir, the man who has vigour may walk to the east just as well as to the west, if he happens to turn his head that way." BOSWELL. "But, sir, 'tis like walking up and down a hill; one man will naturally do the one better than the other. A hare will run up a hill best, from her forelegs being short; a dog, down." JOHNSON. "Nay, sir; that is from mechanical powers. If you make mind mechanical, you may argue in that manner. One mind is a vice, and holds fast; there's a good memory. Another is a file, and he is a disputant, a controversialist. Another is a razor, and he is sarcastical."

We talked of Whitefield. He said he was at the same college with him and knew him 'before he began to be better than other people' (smiling); that he believed he sincerely meant well, but had a mixture of politics and ostentation, whereas Wesley thought of religion only.[66] Robertson said Whitefield had strong natural eloquence, which, if cultivated, would have done great things. JOHNSON. "Why, sir, I take it he was at the height of what his abilities could do, and was sensible of it. He had the ordinary advantages of education, but he chose to pursue that oratory which is for the mob." BOSWELL. "He had great effect on the passions." JOHNSON. "Why, sir, I don't think so. He could not represent a succession of pathetic images. He vociferated and made an impression. *There*, again, was a mind like a hammer."

Dr Johnson now said a certain eminent political friend of ours was wrong in his maxim of sticking to a certain set of *men* on all occasions.[67] "I can see that a man may do right to stick to a *party*," said he; "that is to say, he is a *Whig*, or he is a *Tory*, and he thinks one of those parties upon the whole the best, and that to make it prevail, it must be generally supported, though in particulars it may be wrong. He takes its faggot of principles, in which there are fewer rotten sticks than in the other, though some rotten sticks, to be sure; and they cannot well be separated. But to bind one's self to one man, or one set of men (who may be right today and wrong tomorrow), without any general preference of system, I must disapprove."[68]

He told us of Cooke who translated Hesiod and lived twenty years on a translation of Plautus for which he was always taking subscriptions; and that he presented Foote to a club in the following singular manner: "This is the nephew of the gentleman who was lately hung in chains for murdering his brother."[69]

In the evening I introduced to Mr Johnson two good friends of mine, Mr William Nairne, advocate, and Mr Hamilton of Sundrum, my neighbour in the country, both of whom supped with us. I have preserved nothing of what passed, except that Dr Johnson displayed another of his heterodox opinions: a contempt of tragic acting.[70] He said, "The action of all players in tragedy is bad. It should be a man's study to repress those signs of emotion and passion, as they are called."

He was of a directly contrary opinion to that of Fielding in his *Tom Jones*, who makes Partridge say of Garrick, "Why, I could act as well as he myself. I am sure if I had seen a ghost, I should have looked in the very same manner, and done just as he did." For when I asked him, "Would not you, sir, start as Mr Garrick does if you saw a ghost?" he answered, "I hope not. If I did, I should frighten the ghost."[71]

MONDAY 16 AUGUST. Dr William Robertson came to breakfast. We talked of Ogden on Prayer. Dr Johnson said, "The same arguments which are used against GOD's hearing prayer will serve against his rewarding good and punishing evil. He has resolved, he has declared, in the former case as in the latter."

He had last night looked into Lord Hailes's *Remarks on the History of Scotland*. Dr Robertson and I said it was a pity Lord Hailes did not write greater things. (His lordship had not then published his *Annals of*

Scotland.) JOHNSON. "I remember I was once on a visit at the house of a lady for whom I had a high respect. There was a good deal of company in the room. When they were gone, I said to this lady, 'What foolish talking have we had!' 'Yes,' said she, 'but while they talked, you said nothing.' I was struck with the reproof. How much better is the man who does anything that is innocent than he who does nothing. Besides, I love anecdotes. I fancy mankind may come in time to write all aphoristically, except in narrative; grow weary of preparation and connexion and illustration and all those arts by which a big book is made. If a man is to wait till he weaves anecdotes into a system, we may be long in getting them, and get but few in comparison of what we might get."

Dr Robertson said the notions of Eupham Macallan, a fanatic woman of whom Lord Hailes gives a sketch, were still prevalent among some of the Presbyterians; and therefore it was right in Lord Hailes, a man of known piety, to undeceive them.[72]

We walked out, that Dr Johnson might see some of the things which we have to show at Edinburgh. We went to the Parliament House, where the Parliament of Scotland sat and where the Ordinary Lords of Session hold their courts; and to the New Session House adjoining to it, where our Court of Fifteen (the fourteen Ordinaries with the Lord President at their head) sit as a court of review. Dr Johnson asked why President Duncan Forbes had a statue and no one else. He agreed, however, that if others were admitted, there was danger lest they become too common.[73] We went to the Advocates' Library, of which Dr Johnson took a cursory view, and then to what is called the *Laigh* (or under) Parliament House, where the records of Scotland (which has an universal security by register) are deposited till the great Register Office be finished.[74] I was pleased to behold Dr Samuel Johnson rolling about in this old magazine of antiquities. There was by this time a pretty numerous circle of us attending upon him. Somebody talked of happy moments for composition, and how a man can write at one time and not at another. "Nay," said Dr Johnson, "a man may write at any time if he will set himself *doggedly* to it."[75]

I here began to indulge old Scottish sentiments and to express a warm regret that by our Union with England, we were no more – our independent kingdom was lost.[76] JOHNSON. "Sir, never talk of your independency, who could let your Queen remain twenty years in captivity and then be put to death without even a pretence of justice, without your ever attempting to rescue her; and such a Queen, too! As every man of any gallantry of spirit would have sacrificed his life for." Worthy MR JAMES KER, Keeper of the

Records: "Half our nation was bribed by English money." JOHNSON. "Sir, that is no defence; that makes you worse." Good MR BROWN, Keeper of the Advocates' Library: "We had better say nothing about it." BOSWELL. "You would have been glad, however, to have had us last war, sir, to fight your battles!" JOHNSON. "We should have had you for the same price, though there had been no Union, as we might have had Swiss, or other troops. No, no, I shall agree to a separation. You have only to *go home.*"

Just as he had said this, I, to divert the subject, showed him the signed assurances of the three successive Kings of the Hanover family to maintain the Presbyterian establishment in Scotland. "We'll give you that," said he, "into the bargain."

We next went to the great church of St Giles, which has lost its original magnificence in the inside by being divided into four places of Presbyterian worship. BOSWELL. "It is made into four kirks." JOHNSON. "A Church will make many kirks. Come," said he jocularly to Principal Robertson,[77] "let me see what was once a church!"[78]

We entered that division which was formerly called the New Church and of late the High Church, so well known by the eloquence of Dr Hugh Blair.[79] It is now very elegantly fitted up, but it was then shamefully dirty. Dr Johnson said nothing at the time, but when we came to the great door of the Royal Infirmary, where, upon a board, was this inscription, "*Clean your feet!*", he turned about slyly and said, "There is no occasion for putting this at the doors of your churches!"

We then conducted him down the Post House stairs, Parliament Close, and made him look up from the Cowgate to the highest building in Edinburgh (from which he had just descended), being thirteen floors or storeys from the ground upon the back elevation, the front wall being built upon the edge of the hill and the back wall rising from the

OPPOSITE: Edinburgh *c.* 1773 (based on Edgar's map of 1742)

1. Holyrood House
2. Boyd's Inn (White Horse Inn)
3. Black Friars Wynd (Baron Smith's chapel)
4. The Town Guard House
5. The Mercat Cross
6. James's Court (Boswell's house)
7. St Giles': West or Haddo's Hole Church
8. St Giles': Tolbooth Church
9. St Giles': Old Church
10. St Giles': New (High) Church
11. Parliament House
12. Post House Stairs
13. Old Post House Close
14. Willam Forbes's Bank
15. College Wynd
16. Site of North Bridge – dotted line (built 1763–72)
17. Site of Register House
18. Edinburgh Castle
19. Mr Braidwood's College

Monday 16 August

bottom of the hill several storeys before it comes to a level with the front wall. We proceeded to the College with the Principal at our head. Dr Adam Ferguson, whose *Essay on the History of Civil Society* gives him a respectable place in the ranks of literature, was with us. As the College buildings are indeed very mean, the Principal said to Dr Johnson that he must give them the same epithet that a Jesuit did when showing a poor college abroad: "*Hae miseriae nostrae.*"[80] Dr Johnson was, however, much pleased with the library, and with the conversation of Dr James Robertson, Professor of Oriental Languages, the Librarian.[81] We talked of Kennicott's edition of the Hebrew Bible and hoped it would be quite faithful. JOHNSON. "Sir, I know not any crime so great that a man could contrive to commit as poisoning the sources of eternal truth."

I pointed out to him where there formerly stood an old wall enclosing part of the College, which I remember bulged out in a threatening manner, and of which there was a common tradition similar to that concerning Bacon's study at Oxford – that it would fall upon some very learned man. It had some time before this been taken down, that the street might be widened and a more convenient wall built. Dr Johnson, glad of an opportunity to have a pleasant hit at Scottish learning, said, "They have been afraid it never would fall."

We showed him the Royal Infirmary, for which, and for every other exertion of generous public spirit in his power, that noble-minded citizen of Edinburgh, George Drummond, will be ever held in honourable remembrance.[82] And we were too proud not to carry him to the Abbey of Holyroodhouse, that beautiful piece of architecture, but, alas! that deserted mansion of royalty, which Hamilton of Bangour in one of his elegant poems calls: "A virtuous palace, where no monarch dwells." I was much entertained while Principal Robertson fluently harangued to Dr Johnson upon the spot concerning scenes of his celebrated *History of Scotland*. We surveyed that part of the palace appropriated to the Duke of Hamilton, as Keeper, in which our beautiful Queen Mary lived, and in which David Rizzio was murdered, and also the State Rooms.

Dr Johnson was a great reciter of all sorts of things serious or comical. I overheard him repeating here in a kind of muttering tone a line of the old ballad, 'Johnny Armstrong's Last Good-Night': "And ran him through the fair body!"[83]

We returned to my house, where there met him at dinner the Duchess of Douglas, Sir Adolphus Oughton, Lord Chief Baron, Sir William Forbes, Principal Robertson, Mr Cullen, advocate. Before dinner he told us of a curious conversation between the famous George Faulkner and him. George said that England had drained Ireland of fifty thousand pounds in specie annually for fifty years. "How so, sir?" said Dr Johnson. "You must have a very great trade?"

"No trade."

"Very rich mines?"

"No mines."

"From whence, then, does all this money come?"

"Come! Why, out of the blood and bowels of the poor people of Ireland!"

He seemed to me to have an unaccountable prejudice against Swift, for I once took the liberty to ask him if Swift had personally offended him, and he told me he had not. He said today, "Swift is clear, but he is shallow. In coarse humour he is inferior to Arbuthnot; in delicate humour he is inferior to Addison. So he is inferior to his contemporaries, without putting him against the whole world. I doubt if the *Tale of a Tub* was his; it has so much more thinking, more knowledge, more power, more colour, than any of the works which are indisputably his. If it was his, I shall only say he was *impar sibi*."

We gave him as good a dinner as we could. Our Scotch moor-fowl or grouse were then abundant and quite in season; he had accused us of eating ox meat like dogs in Scotland, and so far as wisdom and wit can be aided by administering agreeable sensations to the palate, my wife took care that our great guest should not be deficient.[84]

Sir Adolphus Oughton, then our Deputy Commander-in-Chief, who was not only an excellent officer but one of the most universal scholars I ever knew, had learned the Erse language, and expressed his belief in the authenticity of Ossian's poetry. Dr Johnson took the opposite side of that perplexed question, and I was afraid the dispute would have run high between them. But Sir Adolphus, who had a very sweet temper, changed the discourse, grew playful, laughed at Lord Monboddo's notion of men having tails, and called him 'a Judge *a posteriori*', which amused Dr Johnson, and thus hostilities were prevented.[85]

At supper we had Dr Cullen, his son the advocate, Dr Adam Ferguson, and Mr Crosbie, advocate.[86] Witchcraft was introduced. Mr Crosbie said he thought it the greatest blasphemy to suppose evil spirits counteracting the Deity, and raising storms, for instance, to destroy his creatures. JOHNSON. "Why, sir, if moral evil be consistent with the government of the Deity, why may not physical evil be also consistent with it? It is not more strange that there should be evil spirits than evil men; evil unembodied spirits than evil embodied spirits. And as to storms, we know there are such things, and it is no worse that evil spirits raise them than that they rise." CROSBIE. "But it is not credible that witches should have effected what they are said in stories to have done." JOHNSON. "Sir, I am not defending their credibility. I am only saying that your arguments are not good, and will not overturn the belief of witchcraft." (Dr Ferguson said to me aside, "He is right.") "And then, sir, you have all mankind, rude and civilized, agreeing in the belief of the agency of preternatural powers. You must take evidence; you must consider that wise and great men have condemned witches to die." CROSBIE. "But an Act of Parliament put an end to witchcraft." JOHNSON. "No, sir; witchcraft had ceased, and therefore an Act of Parliament was passed to prevent persecution for what was not witchcraft. Why it ceased, we cannot tell, as we cannot tell the reason of many other things."

Dr Cullen, to keep up the gratification of mysterious disquisition, with the grave address for which he is remarkable in his companionable as in his professional hours, talked in a very entertaining manner of people walking and conversing in their sleep. I am very sorry I have no note of this. We talked of the orang-outang, and of Lord Monboddo's thinking that he might be taught to speak. Dr Johnson treated this with ridicule. Mr Crosbie said that Lord Monboddo believed the existence of everything possible; in short that all which is in *posse* might be found in *esse*. JOHNSON. "But, sir, it is as possible that the orang-outang does not speak as that he speaks. However, I shall not contest the point. I should have thought it not possible to find a Monboddo, yet *he* exists." I again mentioned the stage. JOHNSON. "The appearance of a player with whom I have drunk tea counteracts the imagination that he is the character he represents. Nay, you know, nobody imagines that he is the character he represents. They say, 'See *Garrick*! How he looks tonight! See how he'll clutch the dagger!' That is the buzz of the theatre."

TUESDAY 17 AUGUST. Sir William Forbes came to breakfast and brought with him Dr Blacklock, whom he introduced to Dr Johnson, who received him with a most humane complacency: "Dear Dr Blacklock, I am glad to see you!"

Blacklock seemed to be much surprised when Dr Johnson said it was easier to him to write poetry than to compose his *Dictionary*. His mind was less on the stretch in doing the one than the other. Besides, composing a dictionary requires books and a desk; you can make a poem walking in the fields, or lying in bed. Dr Blacklock spoke of scepticism in morals and religion with apparent uneasiness, as if he wished for more certainty.[87] Dr Johnson, who had thought it all over, and whose vigorous understanding was fortified by much experience, thus encouraged the blind Bard to apply to higher speculations what we all willingly submit to in common life; in short, he gave him more familiarly the able and fair reasoning of Butler's *Analogy*: "Why, sir, the greatest concern we have in this world, the choice of our profession, must be determined without demonstrative reasoning. Human life is not yet so well known as that we can have it. And take the case of a man who is ill. I call two physicians: they differ in opinion. I am not to lie down and die between them; I must do something."

The conversation then turned on atheism; on that horrible book, *Système de la Nature*;[88] and on the supposition of an eternal necessity, without design, without a governing mind. JOHNSON. "If it were so, why has it ceased? Why don't we see men thus produced around us now? Why, at least, does it not keep pace in some measure with the progress of time? If it stops because there is now no need of it, then it is plain there is and ever has been an all-powerful intelligence. But stay!" said he with one of his satiric laughs. "Ha! ha! ha! I shall suppose Scotchmen made necessarily, and Englishmen by choice."

At dinner this day we had Sir Alexander Dick, whose amiable character and ingenious and cultivated mind are so generally known (he was then on the verge of seventy, and is now – 1785 – eighty-one, with his faculties entire, his heart warm, and his temper gay); Sir David Dalrymple (Lord Hailes); Mr Maclaurin, advocate; Dr Gregory, who now worthily fills his father's medical chair; and my uncle, Dr Boswell.[89] This was one of Dr Johnson's best days. He was quite in his element. All was literature and taste, without any interruption. Lord Hailes, who is one of the best philologists in Great Britain, who has written papers in the *World*, and a variety of other works in prose and in verse, both Latin and English, pleased him highly. He told him he had discovered the *Life of Cheynell*, in the *Student*, to be his. JOHNSON. "No one else knows it."

Dr Johnson had before this dictated to me a law paper, upon a question purely in the law of Scotland, concerning *vicious intromission*, that is to say, intermeddling with the effects of a deceased person without a regular title, which formerly was understood to subject the intermeddler to payment of all the defunct's debts. The principle has of late been relaxed. Dr Johnson's argument was for a renewal of its strictness. The paper was printed, with additions by me, and given into the Court of Session.[90] Lord Hailes knew Dr Johnson's part not to be mine, and pointed out exactly where it began and where it ended. Dr Johnson said, "It is much, now, that his lordship can distinguish so."

In Dr Johnson's *Vanity of Human Wishes* there is the following passage:

> *The teeming mother, anxious for her race,*
> *Begs for each birth the fortune of a face;*
> *Yet Vane could tell what ills from beauty spring,*
> *And Sedley cursed the charms which pleased a king.*

Lord Hailes told him he was mistaken in the instances he had given of unfortunate fair ones, for neither Vane nor Sedley had a title to that description. His lordship has since been so obliging as to send me a note of this, for the communication of which I am sure my readers will thank me.

The lines in the tenth Satire of Juvenal, according to my alteration, should have run thus: "Yet Shore could tell . . . / And Vallière cursed . . ." The first was a penitent by compulsion, the second by sentiment; though the truth is Mademoiselle de la Vallière threw herself (but still from sentiment) in the King's way. Our friend chose Vane, who was far from being well-looked, and Sedley, who was so ugly that Charles II said his brother had her by way of penance.[91]

Mr Maclaurin's learning and talents enabled him to do his part very well in Dr Johnson's company. He produced two epitaphs upon his father, the celebrated mathematician. One was in English, of which Dr Johnson did not change one word. In the other, which was in Latin, he made several alterations. In place of the very words of Virgil, *Ubi luctus et pavor et plurima mortis imago*, he wrote *Ubi luctus regnant et pavor*. He introduced the word *prorsus* into the line *Mortalibus prorsus non absit solatium* and after *Hujus enim scripta evolve*, he added, *Mentemque tantarum rerum capacem corpori caduco superstitem crede*; which is quite applicable to Dr Johnson himself.[92]

Mr Murray, advocate, who married a niece of Lord Mansfield's, and is now one of the Judges of Scotland by the title of Lord Henderland, sat with us a part of the evening, but did not venture to say anything that I remember, though he is certainly possessed of talents which would have enabled him to have shown himself to advantage if too great anxiety had not prevented him.

At supper we had Dr Alexander Webster, who, though not learned, had such a knowledge of mankind, such a fund of information and entertainment, so clear a head and such accommodating manners, that Dr Johnson found him a very agreeable companion.[93]

When Dr Johnson and I were left by ourselves, I read to him my notes of the opinions of our judges upon the question of literary property. He did not like them, and said, "They make me think of your judges not with that respect which I should wish to do." To the argument of one of them that there can be no property in blasphemy or nonsense, he answered, "Then your rotten sheep are mine! By that rule, when a man's house falls into decay, he must lose it."[94]

I mentioned an argument of mine: that literary performances are not taxed. As Churchill says, 'No statesman yet has thought it worth his pains / To tax our labours, or excise our brains', and therefore they are not property. "Yet," said he, "we hang a man for stealing a horse, and horses are not taxed."

Mr Pitt has since put an end to that argument.[95]

WEDNESDAY 18 AUGUST. On this day we set out from Edinburgh. We should gladly have had Mr Scott to go with us, but he was obliged to return to England.[96] I have given a sketch of Dr Johnson; my readers may wish to know a little of his fellow-traveller. Think, then, of a gentleman of ancient blood, the pride of which was his predominant passion. He was then in his thirty-third year, and had been about four years happily married. His inclination was to be a soldier, but his father, a respectable judge, had pressed him into the profession of the Law. He had travelled a good deal and seen many varieties of human life. He had thought more than anybody supposed, and had a pretty good stock of general learning and knowledge. He had all Dr Johnson's principles, with some degree of relaxation. He had rather too little than too much prudence, and his imagination being lively, he often said things of which the effect was very different from the intention. He resembled sometimes 'the best good man, with the worst natured muse'. He cannot deny himself the vanity of finishing with the encomium of Dr Johnson, whose friendly partiality to the companion of his tour represents him as one 'whose acuteness would help my inquiry, and whose gaiety of conversation and civility of manners are sufficient to counteract the inconveniences of travel in countries less hospitable than we have passed'.

Dr Johnson thought it unnecessary to put himself to the additional expense of bringing with him Francis Barber, his faithful black servant, so we were attended only by my man, Joseph Ritter, a Bohemian, a fine stately fellow above six feet high, who had been over a great part of Europe, and spoke many languages. He was the best servant I ever saw. Let not my readers disdain his introduction. For Dr Johnson gave him this character: "Sir, he is a civil man, and a wise man."

From an erroneous apprehension of violence, Dr Johnson had provided a pair of pistols, some gunpowder, and a quantity of bullets; but upon being assured we should run no risk of meeting any robbers, he left his arms and ammunition in an open drawer, of which he gave my wife the charge. He also left in that drawer one volume of a pretty full and curious Diary of his Life, of which I have a few fragments, but the book has been destroyed.[97] I wish female curiosity had been strong enough to have had it all transcribed, which might easily have been done; and I should think the theft, being *pro bono publico*, might have been forgiven. But I may be wrong. My wife told me she never once looked into it. She did not seem quite easy when we left her, but away we went!

Mr Nairne, advocate, was to go with us as far as St Andrews. It gives me pleasure that by mentioning his *name* I connect his title to the just and handsome compliment paid him by Dr Johnson in his book: "A gentleman who could stay with us only long enough to make us know how much we lost by his leaving us."[98]

When we came to Leith, I talked with perhaps too boasting an air how pretty the Frith of Forth looked; as indeed, after the prospect from Constantinople, of which I have been told, and that from Naples, which I have seen, I believe the view of that Frith and its environs from the Castle Hill of Edinburgh is the finest in Europe. "Ay," said Dr Johnson, "that is the state of the world. Water is the same everywhere: *Una est injusti caerula forma maris.*"[99]

I told him the port here was the mouth of the river or water of Leith. "Not *Lethe*," said Mr Nairne.

"Why, sir," said Dr Johnson, "when a Scotchman sets out from this port for England, he forgets his native country." NAIRNE. "I hope, sir, you will forget England here." JOHNSON. "Then 'twill be still more Lethe." He observed of the pier or quay, "You have no occasion for so large a one, your trade does not require it; but you are like a shopkeeper who takes a shop, not only for what he has to put into it, but that it may be believed he has a great deal to put into it."

It is very true that there is now comparatively little trade upon the eastern coast of Scotland. The riches of Glasgow show how much there is in the west; and perhaps we shall find trade travel westward on a great scale as well as a small.

We talked of a man's drowning himself. JOHNSON. "I should never think it time to make away with myself." I put the case of Eustace Budgell, who was accused of forging a will and sunk himself in the Thames before the trial of its authenticity came on. "Suppose, sir," said

I, "that a man is absolutely sure that if he lives a few days longer, he shall be detected in a fraud, the consequence of which will be utter disgrace and expulsion from society." JOHNSON. "Then, sir, let him go abroad to a distant country; let him go to some place where he is *not* known. Don't let him go to the devil where he *is* known!"

He then said, "I see a number of people barefooted here; I suppose you all went so before the Union. Boswell, your ancestors went so when they had as much land as your family has now. Yet 'Auchinleck' is the 'Field of Stones': there would be bad going barefooted there. The Lairds, however, did it."[100]

I bought some speldings, fish (generally whitings) salted and dried in a particular manner, being dipped in the sea and dried in the sun, and eaten by the Scots by way of a relish. He had never seen them, though they are sold in London. I insisted on *scottifying* his palate, but he was very reluctant. With difficulty I prevailed with him to let a bit of one of them lie in his mouth. He did not like it.[101]

In crossing the Frith, Dr Johnson determined that we should land upon Inchkeith. On approaching it, we first observed a high rocky shore. We coasted about, and put into a little bay on the northwest. We clambered up a very steep ascent, on which was very good grass but rather a profusion of thistles. There were sixteen head of black cattle grazing upon the island. Lord Hailes observed to me that Brantôme calls it *L'Isle des Chevaux*, and that it was probably 'a *safer* stable' than many others in his time. The fort, with an inscription on it, *Maria Re.* 1564, is strongly built. Dr Johnson examined it with much attention. He stalked like a giant among the luxuriant thistles and nettles. There are three wells in the island, but we could not find one in the fort. There must probably have been one, though now filled up, as a garrison could not subsist without it. But I have dwelt too long on this little spot. Dr Johnson afterwards bade me try to write a description of our discovering Inchkeith, in the usual style of travellers, describing fully every particular, stating the grounds on which we concluded that it must have once been inhabited, and introducing many sage reflections; and we should see how a thing might be covered in words so as to induce people to come and survey it. All that was told might be true, and yet in reality there might be nothing to see. He said, "I'd have this island. I'd build a house, make a good landing-place, have a garden and vines and all sorts of trees. A rich man of a hospitable turn here would have many visitors from Edinburgh." When we had got into our boat again, he called to me, "Come now, pay a classical compliment to the island on quitting it." I happened luckily, in allusion to the beautiful Queen Mary, whose name is upon the fort, to think of what Virgil makes Aeneas say on having left the country of his charming Dido: *Invitus, regina, tuo de littore cessi.*[102] "Very well hit off!" said he.

It looked as if he and I had laid a plan to have a good ready saying. Had we been little wits, it would have been believed. We spoke of the Glengore. He said we had a law to geld lepers, and a good one, as they could do nothing but mischief. He was pleased with the sailing.

We dined at Monro's in Kinghorn, on fish with onion sauce, roast mutton, and potatoes, and then got into a post-chaise. Mr Nairne and his servant and Joseph rode by us. We stopped at Cupar and drank tea. We talked of Parliament, and I said I supposed very few of the members knew much of what was going on, as indeed very few gentlemen know much of their own private affairs. JOHNSON. "Why, sir, if a man is not of a sluggish mind, he may be his own steward. If he will look into his affairs, he will soon learn. So it is as to public affairs. There must always be a certain number of men of business in Parliament." BOSWELL. "But consider, sir, what is the House of Commons? Is not a great part of it chosen by peers? Do you think, sir, they ought to have such an influence?" JOHNSON. "Yes, sir. Influence must ever be in proportion to property, and it is right it should." BOSWELL. "But is there not reason to fear that the common people may be oppressed?" JOHNSON. "No, sir. Our great fear is from want of power in government. Such a storm of vulgar force has broke in." BOSWELL. "It has only roared." JOHNSON. "Sir, it has roared till the judges in Westminster Hall have been afraid to pronounce sentence in opposition to the popular cry. You are frightened by what is no longer dangerous, like Presbyterians by Popery." He then repeated a passage, I think in Butler's *Remains*, which ends, "and would cry 'Fire! Fire!' in Noah's flood."[103]

We had a dreary drive in a dusky night to St Andrews, where we arrived late. I *saw*, either in a dream or vision, my child, dead, then her face eaten by worms, then a skeleton of her head. Was shocked and dreary. I was sunk. Mr Johnson complained I did not hear in the chaise, and said it was half abstraction. I must try to help this.[104]

We found a good supper of *rissered* haddocks and mutton chops at Glass's Inn, and Dr Johnson revived agreeably. He said the collection called *The Muses' Welcome to King James* (first of England and sixth of Scotland), on his return to his native kingdom, showed that there was then abundance of learning in Scotland, and that the conceits in that collection, with which people find fault, were mere mode. He added, we could not now entertain a sovereign so; that Buchanan had spread the spirit of learning amongst us, but we had lost it during the civil wars. He did not allow the Latin poetry of Pitcairne so much merit as has been usually attributed to it, though he owned that one of his pieces, which he mentioned but which I am sorry is not specified in my notes, was 'very well'. It is not improbable that it was the poem which Prior has so elegantly translated.[105]

After supper we made a *procession* to St Leonard's College, the landlord walking before us with a candle and the waiter with a lantern. That college had some time before been dissolved, and Dr Watson, a professor here (the historian of Philip II), had purchased the ground and what buildings remained.[106] When we entered his court, it seemed quite academical; and we found in his house very comfortable and genteel accommodation.[107]

THURSDAY 19 AUGUST. Slept till near ten; waked well. Prayed fervently; read New Testament. Found Mr Johnson up. He shewed me his notes of yesterday's jaunt. Wonderfully minute, and exact except as to not seeing trees and hedges.

We rose much refreshed. I had with me a map of Scotland, a Bible which was given to me by Lord Mountstuart when we were together in Italy, and Ogden's *Sermons on Prayer*.[108] Mr Nairne introduced us to Dr Watson, whom we found a well-informed man of very amiable manners. Dr Johnson, after they were acquainted, said, "I take great delight in him."

His daughter, a very pleasing young lady, made breakfast. Dr Watson observed that Glasgow University had fewer home-students since trade increased, as learning was rather incompatible with it. JOHNSON. "Why, sir, as trade is now carried on by subordinate hands, men in trade have as much leisure as others, and now learning itself is a trade. A man goes to a bookseller and gets what he can. We have done with patronage. In the infancy of learning we find some great man praised for it. This diffused it among others. When it becomes general, an author leaves the great and applies to the multitude." BOSWELL. "It is a shame that authors are not now better patronized." JOHNSON. "No, sir. If learning cannot support a man, if he must sit with his hands across till somebody feeds him, it is as to him a bad thing, and it is better as it is. With patronage, what flattery! What falsehood! While a man is *in equilibrio*, he throws truth among the multitude and lets them take it as they please. In patronage, he must say what pleases his patron, and it is an equal chance whether that be truth or falsehood." WATSON. "But is not the case now that, instead of flattering one person, we flatter the age?" JOHNSON. "No, sir. The world always lets a man tell what he thinks his own way. I wonder, however, that so many people have written who might have let it alone. That people should endeavour to excel in conversation, I do not wonder, because in conversation praise is instantly reverberated."

We talked of change of manners. Dr Johnson observed that our drinking less than our ancestors was owing to the change from ale to wine. "I remember," said he, "when all the *decent* people in Lichfield got drunk every night, and were not the worse thought of. Ale was cheap, so you pressed strongly. When a man must bring a bottle of wine, he is not in such haste. Smoking has gone out. To be sure, it is a shocking thing – blowing smoke out of our mouths into other people's mouths, eyes, and noses, and having the same thing done to us. Yet I cannot account why a thing which requires so little exertion and yet preserves the mind from total vacuity, should have gone out. Every man has something by which he calms himself: beating with his feet or so.[109] I remember when people in England changed a shirt only once a week; a pandour, when he gets a shirt, greases it to make it last. Formerly, good tradesmen had no fire but in the kitchen; never in the parlour except on Sunday. My father, who was a magistrate of Lichfield, lived thus. They never began to have a fire in the parlour but on leaving off business or some great revolution of their life." Dr Watson said the hall was as a kitchen in old squires' houses. JOHNSON. "No, sir. The hall was for great occasions, and never was used for domestic refection."

We talked of the Union, and what money it had brought into Scotland. Dr Watson observed that a little money formerly went as far as a great deal now. JOHNSON. "In speculation, it seems that a smaller quantity of money, equal in value to a larger quantity, if equally divided, should produce the same effect. But it is not so in reality. Many more conveniences and elegancies are enjoyed where money is plentiful than where it is scarce. Perhaps a great familiarity with it, which arises from plenty, makes us more easily part with it."

After what Dr Johnson has said of St Andrews, which he had long wished to see as our oldest university and the seat of our Primate in the days of episcopacy, I can say little. Since the publication of Dr Johnson's book, I find that he has been censured for not seeing here the ancient chapel of St Rule, a curious piece of sacred architecture. But this was neither his fault nor mine. We were both of us abundantly desirous of surveying such sort of antiquities, but neither of us knew of this. I am afraid the censure must fall on those who did not tell us of it. In every

place where there is anything worthy of observation, there should be a
short printed directory for strangers, such as we find in all the towns
of Italy and in some of the towns in England. I was told that there is a
manuscript account of St Andrews by Martin, secretary to Archbishop
Sharp, and that one Douglas has published a small account of it.[110] I
inquired at a bookseller's, but could not get it.

Dr Johnson's veneration for the hierarchy is well known. There is no
wonder, then, that he was affected with a strong indignation while he
beheld the ruins of religious magnificence. I happened to ask where John
Knox was buried. Dr Johnson burst out, "I hope in the highway. I have
been looking at his reformations."

It was a very fine day. Dr Johnson seemed quite wrapped up in the
contemplation of the scenes which were now presented to him. He kept
his hat off while he was upon any part of the ground where the cathedral
had stood. He said well that Knox had set on a mob without knowing
where it would end; and that differing from a man in doctrine was no
reason why you should pull his house about his ears. As we walked in
the cloisters, there was a solemn echo while he talked loudly of a proper
retirement from the world. Mr Nairne said he had an inclination to retire.
I called Dr Johnson's attention to this, that I might hear his opinion if
it was right. JOHNSON. "Yes, when he has done his duty to society. In
general, as every man is obliged not only to love GOD, but his neighbour
as himself, he must bear his part in active life; yet there are exceptions.
Those who are exceedingly scrupulous (which I do not approve, for I
am no friend to scruples), and find their scrupulosity invincible, so that
they are quite in the dark and know not what they shall do; or those
who cannot resist temptations and find they make themselves worse by
being in the world, without making it better, may retire. I never read of
a hermit, but in imagination I kiss his feet; never of a monastery, but
I could fall on my knees and kiss the pavement. But I think putting
young people there, who know nothing of life, nothing of retirement,
is dangerous and wicked. It is a saying as old as Hesiod, Ἔργα νέων,
βουλαίτε μέσων, εὐχαίτε γερόντων.[111] That is a very noble line: not that
young men should not pray, or old men not give counsel, but that every
season of life has its proper duties. I have thought of retiring, and have
talked of it to a friend, but I find my vocation is rather to active life."

I said *some* young monks might be allowed, to show that it is not age
alone that can retire to pious solitude, but he thought this would only
show that they could not resist temptation.

He wanted to mount the steeples, but it could not be done. There are no good inscriptions here. Bad Roman characters he naturally mistook for half-Gothic, half-Roman. One of the steeples, which he was told was in danger, he wished not to be taken down. "For," said he, "it may fall on some of the posterity of John Knox – and no great matter!"

Dinner was mentioned. JOHNSON. "Ay, ay; amidst all these sorrowful scenes, I have no objection to dinner."

We went and looked at the castle where Cardinal Beaton was murdered, and then visited Principal Murison at his college, where is a good library-room; but the Principal was abundantly vain of it, for he seriously said to Dr Johnson, "You have not such a one in England."

The Professors entertained us with a very good dinner: salmon, mackerel, herrings, ham, chicken, roast beef, apple pie. Present: Murison, Shaw, Cook, Hill, Hadow, Watson, Flint, Brown. I observed that I wondered to see him eat so well after viewing so many sorrowful scenes of ruined religious magnificence. "Why," said he, "I am not sorry after seeing these gentlemen, for they are not sorry." Murison said all sorrow was bad, as it was murmuring against the dispensations of Providence. JOHNSON. "Sir, sorrow is inherent in humanity. As you cannot judge two and two to be either five or three, but certainly four, so, when comparing a worse present state with a better which is past, you cannot but feel sorrow. It is not cured by reason, but by the incursion of present objects, which wear out the past. You need not murmur, though you are sorry." MURISON. "But St Paul says, 'I have learnt, in whatever state I am, therewith to be content.'" JOHNSON. "Sir, that relates to riches and poverty; for we see St Paul, when he had a thorn in the flesh, prayed earnestly to have it removed, and then he could not be content."

Murison, thus refuted, tried to be smart, and drank to Dr Johnson: "Long may you lecture!"

Dr Johnson afterwards, speaking of his not drinking wine, said, "The Doctor spoke of *lecturing*" (looking to him). "I give all these lectures on water."

He defended requiring subscription in those admitted to universities thus: "As all who come into the country must obey the King, so all who come into an university must be of the Church."

And here I must do Dr Johnson the justice to contradict a very absurd and ill-natured story as to what passed at St Andrews. It has been circulated that after grace was said in English in the usual manner, he with the greatest marks of contempt, as if he had held it to be no grace in an university, would not sit down till he had said grace aloud in Latin. This would have been an insult indeed to the gentlemen who were entertaining us. But the truth was precisely thus: in the course of conversation at dinner, Dr Johnson, in very good humour, said, "I should have expected to have heard a Latin grace among so many learned men; we had always a Latin grace at Oxford. I believe I can repeat it."

Which he did, as giving the learned men in one place a specimen of what was done by the learned men in another place.

We went and saw the church in which is Archbishop Sharp's monument.[112] I was struck with the same kind of feelings with which the churches of Italy impressed me. I was much pleased to see Dr Johnson actually in St Andrews, of which we had talked so long. Professor Hadow was with us this afternoon, along with Dr Watson. We looked at St Salvator's College. The rooms for students seemed very commodious, and Dr Johnson said the chapel was the neatest place of worship he had seen. The key of the library could not be found, as Professor Hill had it. Dr Johnson told a joke he had heard of a monastery abroad where the key of the library could never be found. We saw the mace and silver arrows.[113]

It was somewhat dispiriting to see this ancient archiepiscopal city now sadly deserted. We saw in one of its streets a remarkable proof of liberal toleration: a nonjuring clergyman strutting about in his canonicals with a jolly countenance and a round belly, like a well-fed monk.[114]

We observed two occupations united in the same person, who had hung out two signposts. Upon one was, "James Hood, White-Iron Smith" (i.e. tin-plate worker). Upon another, "The Art of Fencing taught, by James Hood." Upon this last were painted some trees and two men fencing, one of whom had hit the other in the eye, to show his great dexterity; so that the art was well taught. JOHNSON. "Were I studying here, I should go and take a lesson. I remember Hope in his book on this art, says, 'The Scotch are very good fencers.'"[115]

We returned to the inn where we had been entertained at dinner, and drank tea in company with some of the professors, of whose civilities I beg leave to add my humble and very grateful acknowledgment to the honourable testimony of Dr Johnson in his *Journey*.

We talked of composition, which was a favourite topic of Dr Watson's, who first distinguished himself by lectures on rhetoric. JOHNSON. "I advised Chambers, and would advise every young man beginning to compose, to do it as fast as he can, to get a habit of having his mind to start promptly.[116] It is so much more difficult to improve in speed than in accuracy." WATSON. "I own I am for much attention to accuracy in composing, lest one should get bad habits of doing it in a slovenly manner." JOHNSON. "Why, sir, you are confounding *doing* inaccurately with the *necessity* of doing inaccurately. A man knows when his composition is inaccurate, and when he thinks fit he'll correct it. But if a man is accustomed to compose slowly and with difficulty upon all occasions, there is danger that he may not compose at all, as we do not like to do that which is not done easily; and at any rate, more time is consumed in a small matter than ought to be." WATSON. "Dr Hugh Blair has taken a week to compose a sermon." JOHNSON. "Then, sir, that is for want of the habit of composing quickly, which I am insisting one should acquire." WATSON. "Blair was not composing all the week, but only such hours as he found himself disposed for composition." JOHNSON. "Nay, sir, unless you tell me the time he took, you tell me nothing. If I say I took a week to walk a mile, and have had the gout five days and been ill otherwise another day, I have taken but one day. I myself have composed about forty sermons. I have begun a sermon after dinner and sent it off by the post that night. I wrote forty-eight of the printed octavo pages of the *Life of Savage* at a sitting, but then I sat up all night. I have also written six sheets in a day of translation from the French."[117] BOSWELL. "We have all observed how one man dresses himself slowly and another fast." JOHNSON. "Yes, sir, it is wonderful how much time some people will consume in dressing: taking up a thing and looking at it, and laying it down, and taking it up again. Every one should get the habit of doing it quickly. I would say to a young divine, 'Here is your text; let me see how soon you can make a sermon.' Then I'd say, 'Let me see how much better you can make it.' Thus I should see both his powers and his judgment."

We all went to Dr Watson's to supper. Miss Sharp, great-grandchild of Archbishop Sharp, was there, as was Mr Craig, the ingenious architect of the new town of Edinburgh and nephew of Thomson, to whom Dr Johnson has since done so much justice in his *Lives of the Poets*.[118]

We talked of memory and its various modes. JOHNSON. "Memory will play strange tricks. One sometimes loses a single word. I once lost *fugaces* in the ode '*Posthume, Posthume*.'" I mentioned to him that a worthy gentleman of my acquaintance actually forgot his own name. JOHNSON. "Sir, that was a morbid oblivion."[119]

FRIDAY 20 AUGUST. Dr Shaw, the Professor of Divinity, breakfasted with us. I took out my *Ogden on Prayer* and read some of it to the company. Dr Johnson praised him. "Abernethy," said he, "allows only of a physical effect of prayer upon the mind, which may be produced many ways as well as by prayer; for instance, by meditation. Ogden goes farther. In truth we have the consent of all nations for the efficacy of prayer, whether offered up by individuals or by assemblies; and *Revelation* has told us it will be effectual."[120]

I said Leechman seemed to incline to Abernethy's doctrine. Dr Watson observed that Leechman meant to show that, even admitting no effect to be produced by prayer respecting the Deity, it was useful to our own minds. He had given only a part of his system. Dr Johnson thought he should have given the whole.

Dr Johnson enforced the strict observance of Sunday. "It should be different," he observed, "from another day. People may walk, but not throw stones at birds. There may be relaxation, but there should be no levity."

We went and saw Colonel Nairne's garden and grotto.[121] Here was a fine old plane-tree. Unluckily the Colonel said there was but this and another large tree in the county. This assertion was an excellent cue for Dr Johnson, who laughed enormously, calling to me to hear it. He had expatiated to me on the nakedness of that part of Scotland which he had seen. His *Journey* has been violently abused for what he has said upon this subject. But let it be considered that when Dr Johnson talks of trees, he means trees of good size, such as he was accustomed to see in England, and of these there are certainly very few upon the *eastern coast* of Scotland. Besides, he said that he meant to give only a map of the road; and let any traveller observe how many trees which deserve the name he can see from the road from Berwick to Aberdeen. Had Dr Johnson said there are *no* trees upon this line, he would have said what is colloquially true, because by 'no trees' in common speech we mean 'few'. When he is particular in counting, he may be attacked.

I know not how Colonel Nairne came to say there were but *two* large trees in the county of Fife. I did not perceive that he smiled. There are certainly not a great many, but I could have shown him more than two at Balmuto, from whence my ancestors came, and which now belongs to a branch of my family.

The grotto was ingeniously constructed.[122] In the front of it were petrified stocks of fir, plane, and some other tree. Dr Johnson said, "Scotland has no right to boast of this grotto; it is owing to personal merit. I never denied personal merit to many of you."

Professor Shaw said to me as we walked, "This is a wonderful man; he is master of every subject he handles." Dr Watson allowed him a very strong understanding, but wondered at his total inattention to established manners, as he came from London. I have not preserved in my

Journal any of the conversation which passed between Dr Johnson and Professor Shaw, but I recollect Dr Johnson said to me afterwards, "I took much to Shaw."

We left St Andrews about noon, and some miles from it observing at Leuchars a church with an old tower, we stopped to look at it. The manse, as the parsonage-house is called in Scotland, was close by. I waited on the minister, mentioned our names, and begged he would tell us what he knew about it. He was a very civil old man, but could only inform us that it was supposed to have stood eight hundred years. He told us there was a colony of Danes in his parish; that they had landed at a remote period of time, and still remained a distinct people. Dr Johnson shrewdly inquired whether they had brought women with them. We were not satisfied as to this colony.[123]

We saw this day Dundee and Aberbrothock, the last of which Dr Johnson has celebrated in his *Journey*. Came to Dundee about three. Good busy town, P. Murray the landlord. Fresh chaise there. Came to Arbroath: Shaw's. Ruin very noble. I went by a window into one tower, up five steps, then twenty-two, then they broke off. We drank tea. He asked me about my being a Roman Catholic in 1759, which I resumed.[124] Upon the road we talked of the Roman Catholic faith. He mentioned (I think) Tillotson's argument against transubstantiation: "That we are as sure we see bread and wine only as that we read in the Bible the text on which that false doctrine is founded. We have only the evidence of our senses for both."

"If," he added, "GOD had never spoken figuratively, we might hold that he speaks literally when he says, 'This is my body.'" BOSWELL. "But what do you say, sir, to the ancient and continued tradition of the Church upon this point?" JOHNSON. "Tradition, sir, has no place where the Scriptures are plain; and tradition cannot persuade a man into a belief of transubstantiation. Able men, indeed, have *said* they believed it."

This is an awful subject. I did not then press Dr Johnson upon it, nor shall I now enter upon a disquisition concerning the import of those words uttered by our Saviour[125] which had such an effect upon many of his disciples that they 'went back, and walked no more with him'. The Catechism and solemn office for Communion in the Church of England maintain a mysterious belief in more than a mere commemoration of the death of Christ by partaking of the elements of bread and wine.

Dr Johnson put me in mind that at St Andrews I had defended my profession very well when the question had again been started whether a lawyer might honestly engage with the first side that offers him a fee.

"Sir," said I, "it was with your arguments against Sir William Forbes, but it was much that I could wield the arms of Goliath."

He said our judges had not gone deep in the question concerning literary property. I mentioned Lord Monboddo's opinion that if a man could get a work by heart, he might print it, as by such an act the mind is exercised. JOHNSON. "No, sir, a man's repeating it no more makes it his property than a man may sell a cow which he drives home." I said printing an abridgment of a work was allowed, which was only cutting the horns and tail off the cow. JOHNSON. "No, sir, 'tis making the cow have a calf."

About eleven at night we arrived at Montrose. We found but a sorry inn, where we dined on haddocks, pickled salmon, veal cutlets and fowl, and I myself saw another waiter put a lump of sugar with his fingers into Dr Johnson's lemonade, for which he called him: "Rascal!" It put me in great glee that our landlord was an Englishman. I rallied the Doctor upon this, and he grew quiet. Both Sir John Hawkins's and Dr Burney's *History of Music* had then been advertised. I asked if this was not unlucky: would not they hurt one another? JOHNSON. "No, sir. They will do good to one another. Some will buy the one, some the other, and compare them; and so a talk is made about a thing, and the books are sold."

He was angry at me for proposing to carry lemons with us to Skye, that he might be sure to have his lemonade. "Sir," said he, "I do not wish to be thought that feeble man who cannot do without anything. Sir, it is very bad manners to carry provisions to any man's house, as if he could not entertain you. To an inferior it is oppressive; to a superior it is insolent."

Having taken the liberty this evening to remark to Dr Johnson that he very often sat quite silent for a long time, even when in company with only a single friend, which I myself had sometimes sadly experienced, he smiled and said, "It is true, sir. Tom Tyers" (for so he familiarly called our ingenious friend, who since his death has paid a biographical tribute to his memory) "Tom Tyers described me the best. He once said to me, 'Sir, you are like a ghost: you never speak till you are spoken to.'"[126]

SATURDAY 21 AUGUST. Neither the Rev. Mr Nisbet, the established minister, nor the Rev. Mr Spooner, the Episcopal minister, were in town. Before breakfast we went and saw the town hall, where is a good dancing-room and other rooms for tea-drinking, not cleanly kept. The appearance of the town from it is very well, but many of the houses are built with their ends to the street, which looks awkward. When we came down from it, I met Mr Gleg, a merchant here. He went with us to see the English chapel. It is situated on a pretty dry spot, and there is a fine walk to it. It is really an elegant building, both within and without. The organ is adorned with green and gold. Dr Johnson gave a shilling extraordinary to the clerk, saying, "He belongs to an honest church."

I put him in mind that Episcopals were but *dissenters* here; they were only *tolerated*. "Sir," said he, "we are here as Christians in Turkey."

He afterwards went into an apothecary's shop and ordered some medicine for himself, and wrote the prescription in technical characters. The boy took him for a physician.[127]

I doubted much which road to take, whether to go by the coast or by Laurencekirk and Monboddo. I knew Lord Monboddo and Dr Johnson did not love each other, yet I was unwilling not to visit his lordship, and was also curious to see them together.[128] I mentioned my doubts to Dr Johnson, who said he would go two miles out of his way to see Lord Monboddo. I therefore sent Joseph forward with the following note:

> Montrose, 21 August. MY DEAR LORD, Thus far I am come with Mr Samuel Johnson. We must be at Aberdeen tonight. I know you do not admire him so much as I do, but I cannot be in this country without making you a bow at your old place, as I do not know if I may again have an opportunity of seeing Monboddo. Besides, Mr Johnson says he would go two miles out of his way to see Lord Monboddo. I have sent forward my servant, that we may know if your lordship be at home. I am ever, my dear lord, most sincerely yours, JAMES BOSWELL.

As we travelled onwards from Montrose, we had the Grampian Hills in our view, and some good land around us, but void of trees and hedges. Dr Johnson has said ludicrously in his *Journey* that the *hedges* were of *stone*; for instead of the verdant *thorn* to refresh the eye, we found the bare *wall* or *dike* intersecting the prospect. He observed that it was wonderful to see a country so divested, so denuded of trees.

We stopped at Laurencekirk, where our great grammarian, Ruddiman, was once schoolmaster. We respectfully remembered that excellent man and eminent scholar, by whose labours a knowledge of the Latin language will be preserved in Scotland, if it shall be preserved at all. Lord Gardenstone, one of our judges, collected money to raise a monument to him at this place, which I hope will be well executed. I know my father gave five guineas towards it. Lord Gardenstone is the proprietor of Laurencekirk, and has encouraged the building of a manufacturing village, of which he is exceedingly fond, and has written a pamphlet upon it, as if he had founded Thebes, in which, however, there are many useful precepts strongly expressed. The village seemed to be irregularly built, some of the houses being of clay, some of brick, and some of brick and stone. Dr Johnson observed they thatched well here.

I was a little acquainted with Mr Forbes, the minister of the parish. I sent to inform him that a gentleman desired to see him. He returned for answer that he would not come to a stranger. I then gave my name and he came. I remonstrated to him for not coming to a stranger, and by presenting him to Dr Johnson proved to him what a stranger might sometimes be. His Bible inculcates 'be not forgetful to entertain strangers', and mentions the same motive.[129] He defended himself by saying he had once come to a stranger who sent for him, and he found him 'a *little-worth person*'!

Dr Johnson insisted on stopping at the inn, as I told him that Lord Gardenstone had furnished it with a collection of books, that travellers might have entertainment for the mind as well as the body. He praised the design, but wished there had been more books, and those better chosen.

About a mile from Monboddo, where you turn off the road, Joseph was waiting to tell us my lord expected us to dinner. We drove over a wild moor. It rained and the scene was somewhat dreary. Dr Johnson repeated with solemn emphasis Macbeth's speech on meeting the witches. As we travelled on, he told me, "Sir, you got into our Club by doing what a man can do.[130] Several of the members wished to keep you out. Burke told me he doubted if you were fit for it, but now you are in, none of them are sorry. Burke says that you have so much good humour naturally, it is scarce a virtue." BOSWELL. "They were afraid of you, sir, as it was you who proposed me." JOHNSON. "Sir, they knew that if they refused you, they'd probably never have got in another. I'd have kept them all out. Beauclerk was very earnest for you." BOSWELL. "Beauclerk has a keenness of mind which is very uncommon." JOHNSON. "Yes, sir; and everything comes from him so easily. It appears to me that I labour when I say a good thing." BOSWELL. "You are loud, sir, but it is not an effort of mind."

Monboddo is a wretched place, wild and naked, with a poor old house; though, if I recollect right, there are two turrets which mark an old baron's residence. Lord Monboddo received us at his gate most courteously; pointed to the Douglas arms upon his house, and told us that his great-grandmother was of that family. "In such houses," said he, "our ancestors lived, who were better men than we."

"No, no, my lord," said Dr Johnson. "We are as strong as they, and a great deal wiser."

This was an assault upon one of Lord Monboddo's capital dogmas, and I was afraid there would have been a violent altercation in the very close, before we got into the house. But his lordship is distinguished not only for 'ancient metaphysics', but for ancient *politesse* – '*la vieille cour*' – and he made no reply.

His lordship was dressed in a rustic suit and wore a little round hat. He told us we now saw him as *Farmer Burnett*, and we should have his family dinner, a farmer's dinner. He said, "I should not have forgiven Mr Boswell had he not brought you here, Dr Johnson." He produced a very long stalk of corn as a specimen of his crop, and said, "You see here the *laetas segetes*."[131] He added that Virgil seemed to be as enthusiastic a farmer as he, and was certainly a practical one. JOHNSON. "It does not always follow, my lord, that a man who has written a good poem on an art has practised it. Philip Miller told me that in Philips's *Cyder, a Poem* all the precepts were just, and indeed better than in books written for the purpose of instructing, yet Philips had never made cider."

I started the subject of emigration. JOHNSON. "To a man of mere animal life, you can urge no argument against going to America but that it will be some time before he will get the earth to produce. But a man of any intellectual enjoyment will not easily go and immerse himself and his posterity for ages in barbarism."

He and my lord spoke highly of Homer. JOHNSON. "He had all the learning of his age. The shield of Achilles shows a nation in war, a nation in peace; harvest sport, nay, stealing."[132] MONBODDO. "Ay, and what we" (looking to me) "would call a Parliament-House scene: a cause pleaded." JOHNSON. "That is part of the life of a nation in peace. And there are in Homer such characters of heroes and combinations of qualities of heroes, that the united powers of mankind ever since have not produced any but what are to be found there." MONBODDO. "Yet no character is described." JOHNSON. "No, they all develop themselves. Agamemnon is always a gentleman-like character; he has always βασιλικόν τι.[133] That the ancients held so is plain from this: that Euripides in his *Hecuba* makes him the person to interpose."[134] MONBODDO. "The history of manners is the most valuable. I never set a high value on any other history." JOHNSON. "Nor I; and therefore I esteem biography, as giving us what comes near to ourselves, what we can turn to use." BOSWELL. "But in the course of general history, we find manners. In wars, we see the dispositions of people, their degrees of humanity, and other particulars." JOHNSON. "Yes;

but then you must take all the facts to get this, and it is but a little you get." MONBODDO. "And it is that little which makes history valuable." Bravo! thought I; they agree like two brothers. MONBODDO. "I am sorry, Dr Johnson, you were not longer at Edinburgh to receive the homage of our men of learning." JOHNSON. "My lord, I received great respect and great kindness." BOSWELL. "He goes back to Edinburgh after our tour."

We talked of the decrease of learning in Scotland, and of the *Muses' Welcome*. JOHNSON. "Learning is much decreased in England in my remembrance." MONBODDO. "You, sir, have lived to see its decrease in England, I its extinction in Scotland." However, I brought him to confess that the High School of Edinburgh did well.[135] JOHNSON. "Learning has decreased in England, because learning will not do so much for a man as formerly. There are other ways of getting preferment. Few bishops are now made for their learning. To be a bishop a man must be learned in a learned age, factious in a factious age, but always of eminence. Warburton is an exception, though his learning alone did not raise him. He was first an antagonist to Pope, and helped Theobald to publish his Shakespeare; but seeing Pope the rising man, when Crousaz attacked his *Essay on Man* for some faults which it has and some which it has not, Warburton defended it in the Review of that time. This brought him acquainted with Pope, and he gained his friendship. Pope introduced him to Allen, Allen married him to his niece; so by Allen's interest and his own he was made a bishop. But then his learning was the *sine qua non*. He knew how to make the most of it, but I do not find by any dishonest means." MONBODDO. "He is a great man." JOHNSON. "Yes, he has great knowledge, great power of mind. Hardly any man brings greater variety of learning to bear upon his point." MONBODDO. "He is one of the greatest lights of your church." JOHNSON. "Why, we are not so sure of his being very friendly to us. He blazes, if you will, but that is not always the steadiest light. Lowth is another bishop who has risen by his learning."

Dr Johnson examined young Arthur, Lord Monboddo's son, in Latin. He answered very well, upon which he said with complacency, "Get you gone! When King James comes back, you shall be in the *Muses' Welcome*!"[136]

My lord and Dr Johnson disputed a little whether the savage or the London shopkeeper had the best existence, his lordship, as usual, preferring the savage. My lord was extremely hospitable, and I saw both Dr Johnson and him liking each other better every hour.[137]

Mr Johnson went downstairs a little.[138] My lord spoke of his conversation as I could have wished. Mr Johnson had said, "I have done greater feats with my knife than this," though he had taken a very hearty dinner: an admirable soup, ham, peas, lamb, and moor-fowl. My lord, who affects or believes he follows an abstemious system, seemed struck with Mr Johnson's manner of living. I had a particular satisfaction in being under the roof of Monboddo, my lord being my father's old friend, and having been always very good to me. We were cordial together. He asked Mr Johnson and me to stay all night. When I said we *must* be at Aberdeen, he said, "Well, I'm like the Romans, 'happy to come, happy to depart'."

He thanked Mr Johnson for his visit. JOHNSON. "I little thought, when I had the honour to meet your lordship in London, that I should see you at Monboddo."[139]

After dinner, as the ladies were going away, Mr Johnson would stand up. He insisted that good breeding was of great consequence in society. "'Tis fictitious benevolence. It supplies the place of it among those who see each other in public, or little. Depend upon it, the want of it always produces something disagreeable to one or other. I have always applied to good breeding what Cato says of honour" (repeated the lines nobly).

> Honour's a sacred tie, the law of kings;
> The noble mind's distinguishing perfection,
> That aids and strengthens virtue when it meets her,
> And imitates her actions where she is not.

When he took up his large oak stick, he said, "My lord, that's *Homeric*."[140]

Gory, my lord's black servant, was sent as our guide, to conduct us to the high road. The circumstance of each of them having a black servant was another point of similarity between Johnson and Monboddo.[141] I observed how curious it was to see an African in the north of Scotland, with little or no difference of manners. A man is like a bottle, which you may fill with red wine or with white. He laughed to see Gory and Joseph: "Those two fellows, one from Africa, the other from Bohemia – quite at home."

He was much pleased with Lord Monboddo today. He said he would have pardoned him for a few paradoxes when he found he had so much that was good. But that from his appearance in London he was all paradox, which would not do. He observed he had talked no paradoxes today; and as to the savage and the London shopkeeper, he did not know but he might have taken the side of the savage equally, had anybody else taken the side of the shopkeeper. He had said to my lord, in opposition to the value of the savage's courage, that it was owing to his limited power of thinking; and repeated Pope's four lines in which 'Macedonia's madman' comes in, and the conclusion is 'farther than his nose'.[142] I objected to the last phrase being low. MR JOHNSON. "'Tis intended, 'tis satire. The expression is debased to debase the character."

My lord showed Mr Johnson *Hermes*, as the work of a living author for whom he had great respect. Mr Johnson said nothing. He afterwards told me that Harris was a coxcomb. Indeed, I always thought so. I used to provoke my friend Temple by laughing at the quaint affected style of his *Dialogues on Poetry, Music, Painting, and Happiness*.[143]

When Gory was going to leave us, Mr Johnson called to him, "Mr Gory, give me leave to ask you a question. Are you baptized?" Gory told him he was – and confirmed by the Bishop of Durham. He then gave him a shilling.

We had tedious driving this afternoon, and were a good deal drowsy. Last night I was afraid Mr Johnson was beginning to faint in his resolution, for he said, "If we must *ride* much, we shall not go; and there's an end on't." Today when he talked of Skye with spirit, I said, "Why, sir, you was beginning to despond yesterday. You're a delicate Londoner – you're a macaroni! You can't ride!" JOHNSON. "Sir, I shall ride better than you. I was only afraid I should not find a horse able to carry me."

I hoped then there would be no fear of fulfilling our wild Tour.

We got to Aberdeen half an hour past 11. The New Inn, we were told, was full. This was comfortless. The waiter, however, asked if one of our names was Boswell, and brought me a letter left at the inn. It was from Mr Thrale, enclosing one to Mr Johnson. Finding who I was, we were told they would contrive to lodge us by putting us for a night into a room with two beds. The waiter said to me in strong Aberdeenshire, "I thought I knew you, by your likeness to your father." My father puts up at the New Inn when on his circuit.

We had a broiled chicken, some tarts, and crabs' claws. Little was said tonight. I was to sleep in a little box-bed in Mr Johnson's room. I had it wheeled out into the dining-room, and there I lay very well.

SUNDAY 22 AUGUST. I sent a message to Professor Thomas Gordon, who came and breakfasted with us. He had secured seats for us at the English chapel. We went to it at ten. Good congregation, admirable organ, well played by Mr Tait. I was truly in a devout frame. Gordon, who officiated, had the most unhappy defects of speech. His tongue was too big. He made such efforts to articulate, 'twas like convulsions. There was no understanding him. 'Twas just the same as speaking in an unknown tongue. It was wrong to put him in orders.[144]

We walked down to the shore. Mr Johnson laughed to hear that Cromwell's soldiers taught the Aberdeen people to make shoes and stockings, and to plant cabbages. He asked if weaving the plaids was ever a domestic art in the Highlands, like spinning or knitting. He could not be informed here. But he conjectured probably that where people lived so remote from each other, it would be domestic art, as we see it was among the ancients, from Penelope.[145] I was sensible today, to a very striking degree, of Mr Johnson's excellent English pronunciation. I cannot account for it, how it struck me more now than any other day. But it was as if new to me; and I listened to every sentence which he spoke as to a musical composition. Professor Gordon gave him an account of the plan of education in his college. Mr Johnson said 'twas similar to Oxford. Waller the poet's great-grandson was studying here.[146] Mr Johnson wondered how a man sent his son so far off, as there were so many good schools in England. He said, "At a great school there is all the splendour and illumination of many minds; the radiance of all is concentrated in each, or at least reflected upon each. But we must own that neither a dull boy, nor an idle boy, will do so well at a great school as at a private one. For at a great school there are always boys enough to do well easily, who are sufficient to keep up the credit of the school; and after whipping being tried to no purpose, the dull or idle boys are left at the end of a class, having the appearance of going through the course, but learning nothing at all. Such boys may do good at a private school, where constant attention is paid to them, and they are watched. So that the question of public or private education is not properly a general one; but whether one or the other is best for *my son*."

We were told the present Mr Waller was just a plain country gentleman; and his son would be such another. I observed a family could not expect a poet but in a hundred generations. "Nay," said Mr Johnson, "not one family in a hundred can expect a poet in a hundred generations." He then repeated Dryden's celebrated lines, "Three poets," etc., and part of a Latin translation of it done at Oxford – perhaps his own. I must ask.[147]

He received a card from Sir Alexander Gordon, who had been his acquaintance twenty years ago in London, and who, 'if forgiven for not answering a line from him', would come in the afternoon. Mr Johnson rejoiced to hear of him. We sent for him to come and dine with us. I was much pleased to see the kindness with which Mr Johnson received his old friend Sir Alexander, a gentleman of good family (Lismore), but by the extravagance of his relations, to whom he left the care of his estate, had lost it. The King's College here made him Professor of Medicine, which affords him a decent subsistence. He told us Aberdeen exported stockings to the value of £100,000 in peace, and one hundred and seventy in war. Mr Johnson asked what made the difference. Here we had a proof of the different sagacity of the two professors. Sir Alexander answered, "Because there's more occasion for them in war."

Professor Thomas Gordon answered, "Because the Germans, who are our great rivals in the manufacture of stockings, are otherwise employed in time of war."

"Sir, you have given a very good solution," said Mr Johnson.

At dinner Mr Johnson eat several platefuls of Scotch broth with barley and pease in them, and was very fond of the dish. I said, "You never eat it before, sir."

"No, sir, but I don't care how soon I eat it again."

We had also skate, roasted lamb, roasted chickens, and tarts. My cousin and old flame at Inverness, Miss Dallas, was married to Mr Riddoch, one of the ministers of the English Chapel here. He was ill and confined to his room. But she sent us a kind invitation to tea, which we all accepted. I was in a kind of uneasiness from thinking that I should see a great change upon her at the distance of twelve years. But I declare I thought she looked better in every respect, except that some of her fore-teeth were spoiled. She was the same lively, sensible, cheerful woman as ever. My mind was sensibly affected at seeing her. I believe there was sincere joy on both sides. Her youngest sister was gone to Maryland with her husband, also a clergyman. I saw her other two sisters. Kate I should not have known. Anne I recollected.[148]

Mr Johnson did not talk much. He had only some jokes against Scotland: said, "You go first to Aberdeen; then to *Enbru*; then to Newcastle, to be polished by the colliers; then to York; then to London." And he laid hold of a little girl, Stuart Dallas, niece to Mrs Riddoch, and, representing himself as a giant, said he'd take her with him, telling her in a hollow voice that he lived in a cave and had a bed in the rock, and she should have a little bed cut opposite to it.

Yet he spoke well on the point as to prescription of murder. He said a jury in England would make allowance for deficiencies of evidence on account of lapse of time. But that a general rule that a crime should not be punished or tried in order to punishment after twenty years was bad. That it was cant to talk of the King's Advocate delaying prosecution from malice. How unlikely was it the King's Advocate should have malice against people who commit murder, or should even know them at all. He said if the son of the murdered man should kill the murderer who got off merely by prescription, he would help him to make his escape; though were he upon his jury, he would not acquit him. That he would not advise him to do it. On the contrary, would bid him submit to the determination of society, because a man is bound to submit to the inconveniencies of it, as he enjoys the good. But that the young man, though politically wrong, would not be morally wrong. He would have to say, "Here I am amongst barbarians who not only refuse to do justice, but encourage the greatest of all crimes. I am therefore in a state of nature. For where there is no law, it is a state of nature. I therefore upon the eternal and immutable law of justice which requires that he who sheds blood should have his blood shed, will stab the murderer of my father."

We came to our inn, and sat quietly. Mr Johnson borrowed at Mr Riddoch's a volume of Massillon, his discourses on the Psalms. But I found he read little in it. Ogden too he sometimes took up and glanced at, but threw it down again. I then entered upon religious conversation. Never did I see him in a better frame: calm, gentle, wise, holy. I said the same objection would serve against the Trinity as against transubstantiation. "Yes," said he, "if you take Three and One in the same sense. If you do so, to be sure, you cannot believe it. But they are Three in one sense and One in another. We cannot tell how, and that is the Mystery."

I spoke of the satisfaction of Christ. He said his notion was that it did not atone for the sins of the world. But by satisfying divine justice, by showing that no less than the Son of God suffered for sin, it showed to men and innumerable created beings the heinousness of sin, and therefore rendered it unnecessary for divine vengeance to be exercised against sinners, as it otherwise must have been. In this way it might operate even in favour of those who had never heard of it. As to those who did hear of it, the effect it should produce would be repentance and piety, by impressing upon the mind a just notion of sin. That original sin was the propensity to evil, which no doubt was occasioned by the Fall. He presented this great subject in a new light to me, and rendered much more rational and clear the ideas of what our Saviour has done for us, as it removed the notion of imputed righteousness in the usual sense, and the difficulty of our righteousness co-operating; whereas by his view Christ has done all already that he had to do, or is ever to do, for mankind, by making his great satisfaction, the consequences of which will affect each individual according to the particular conduct of each.[149] I would illustrate this by saying that Christ's satisfaction is like there being a sun placed to show light to men, so that it depends upon themselves whether they will walk the right way or not, which they could not have done without that sun, 'the sun of righteousness'. There is, however, more in it than merely giving light – 'a light to lighten the Gentiles'. I must think of it at leisure and with attention. Mr Johnson said, "Richard Baxter commends a treatise by Grotius, *De Satisfactione Christi*. I have never read it. But I intend to do it, and you may read it."

I said upon the principle now laid down we might explain, "They that believe shall be saved," etc. They that believe will have such an impression made upon their minds as will make them act so as that they shall be accepted by GOD.

We talked of Langton's taking ill for a length of time a hasty expression of Mr Johnson's to him, on his attempting to prosecute a subject that had a reference to religion, beyond the bounds within which the Doctor thought such topics should be confined in a mixed company. JOHNSON. "What is to come of society if a friendship of twenty years is to be broken off for such a cause? As Bacon says, 'Who then to frail mortality shall trust, / But limns in water, or but writes in dust.'"[150]

I said he should write expressly in support of Christianity, for that although a reverence for it shines through his works in several places, that is not enough. "You know," said I, "what Grotius has done, what Addison has done, you should do also."

He said, "I hope I shall."

MONDAY 23 AUGUST. Principal Campbell, Sir Alexander Gordon, Professor Gordon, and Professor Ross came to us in the morning, as did Dr Gerard, who had come in six miles from the country on purpose. We went and saw Marischal College, and at one o'clock we waited on the magistrates in the Town Hall, as they had invited us in order to present Mr Johnson with the freedom of the city, which Provost Jopp did with a very good grace.[151] Mr Johnson was pleased with this mark of attention, and received it very politely.

There was a pretty numerous company there. It was curious to hear all of them drinking "Dr Johnson, Dr Johnson" in the Town Hall of Aberdeen, and then to see him with his burgess-ticket, or diploma, in his hat, which he wore as he walked along the street, according to the usual custom. It gave me great satisfaction to observe the regard and indeed fondness, too, which everybody here had for my father.

While Sir A. Gordon conducted Mr Johnson to Old Aberdeen, Professor Gordon and I called on Mr Riddoch, whom I found to be a grave worthylike clergyman. He said that whatever might be said of Mr Johnson while he was alive, after he was dead he would be looked upon by the world with regard and astonishment on account of his Dictionary.

Mrs Riddoch, Professor Gordon, and I went and called for Mrs Dallas, whom I had not seen since I was a mere child.[152] Then he and I walked over to the Old College, which Mr Johnson had seen by this time. I stepped a little into the chapel and looked at the tomb of the Founder, Archbishop Elphinstone, of whom I shall have occasion to write in my *History of James IV*.[153]

We dined at Sir A. Gordon's. The Provost, Professor Ross, Professor Dunbar, Professor Thomas Gordon were there. After dinner came in Dr Gerard, Professor Leslie, Professor MacLeod. We had had little or no conversation in the morning. Now we were but barren. The professors seemed afraid to speak. Dr Gerard told us that Strahan the printer was very intimate with Warburton. Mr Johnson said, "He has printed some of his works, and perhaps bought property of some of 'em. The intimacy is as one of the professors here may have with one of the carpenters who is repairing the College."

"But," said Gerard, "I saw a letter from him to Strahan, in which he says that the one half of the Church of Scotland are fanatics and the other half infidels."

Mr Johnson said Warburton had accustomed himself to write letters just as he speaks, without thinking any more of what he throws out. He said when he read Warburton first and observed his force and contempt, he thought he had driven the world before him, but he found that was not the case, for Warburton by his extensive abuse made it ineffectual. He told me when we were by ourselves that he thought it very wrong in Strahan to show Warburton's letter, as it was raising him a body of enemies. He thought it foolish in Warburton to write so to Strahan, and he said the worst way of being intimate is by scribbling. He said Warburton's essay on Grace was a poor performance, and so was Wesley's answer. (He was not in spirits somehow.) Warburton had laid himself very open. In particular, he was weak enough to say that in some disorders of the imagination people had spoken with tongues – had spoken languages which they never knew before – a thing as absurd as to say that in some disorders of the imagination people had been known to fly.

Gerard said he had detected Thomas Warton in the most barefaced plagiarism in his Spenser. He copies a whole page from Abbé du Bos, and to disguise it, quotes Du Bos for a sentence in the middle of it.[154] I talked of difference of genius to try if I could engage Gerard in a disquisition with Mr Johnson. But I did not succeed. I mentioned, as a curious fact, that Locke had written verses. Mr Johnson said he knew of none but a kind of exercise prefixed to T. Sydenham's *Works*, in which he has some conceits about the dropsy, in which water and burning are united, and how Dr Sydenham removed fire by drawing off water, contrary to the usual practice, which is to extinguish fire by bringing water upon it. "I know not," said he, "if there's a word of all this, but 'tis such kind of talk."

All this, as Dr Johnson suspected at the time, was the immediate invention of his own lively imagination; for there is not one word of it in Mr Locke's complimentary performance. My readers will, I have no doubt, like to be satisfied, by comparing them; and, at any rate, it may entertain them to read verses composed by our great metaphysician, when a Bachelor in Physic.

AUCTORI, in Tractatum ejus de Febribus.

Febriles æstus, victumque ardoribus orbem
  Flevit, non tantis par Medicina malis.
Et post mille artes, medicæ tentamina curae,
  Ardet adhuc Febris; nec velit arte regi.
Præda sumus flammis; solum hoc speramus ab igne,
  Ut restet paucus, quem capit urna, cinis.
Dum quærit medicus febris caussamque, modumque,
  Flammarum et tenebras, et sine luce faces;
Quas tractat patitur flammas, et febre calescens,
  Corruit ipse suis victima rapta focis.
Qui tardos potuit morbos, artusque trementes,
  Sistere, febrili se videt igne rapi.
Sic faber exesos fulsit tibicine muros;
  Dum trahit antiquas lenta ruina domos.
Sed si flamma vorax miseras incenderit ædes,
  Unica flagrantes tunc sepelire salus.
Fit fuga, tectonicas nemo tunc invocat artes;
  Cum perit artificis non minus usta domus.
Se tandem Sydenham febrisque Scholæque furori
  Opponens, morbi quærit, et artis opem.
Non temere incusat tectæ putedinis ignes;
  Nec fictus, febres qui fovet, humor erit,
Non bilem ille movet, nulla hic pituita; Salutis
  Quæ spes, si fallax ardeat intus aqua?

Nec doctas magno rixas ostentat hiatu,
    Quis ipsis major febribus ardor inest.
Innocuas placide corpus jubet urere flammas,
    Et justo rapidos temperat igne focos.
Quid febrim exstinguat, varius quid postulat usus,
    Solari ægrotos, qua potes arte, docet.
Hactenus ipsa suum timuit Natura calorem,
    Dum sæpe incerto, quo calet, igne perit:
Dum reparat tacitos male provida sanguinis ignes,
    Prælusit busto, fit calor iste rogus.
Jam secura suas foveant præcordia flammas,
    Quem Natura negat, dat Medicina modum.
Nec solum faciles compescit sanguinis æstus,
    Dum dubia est inter spemque metumque salus;
Sed fatale malum domuit, quodque astra malignum
    Credimus, iratam vel genuisse Stygem.
Extorsit Lachesi *cultros, Pestique venenum*
    Abstulit, et tantos non sinit esse metus.
Quis tandem arte nova domitam mitescere Pestem
    Credat, et antiquas ponere posse minas?
Post tot mille neces, cumulataque funera busto,
    Victa jacet, parvo vulnere, dira Lues.
Ætheriæ quanquam spargunt contagia flammæ,
    Quicquid inest istis ignibus, ignis erit.
Delapsæ cœlo flammæ licet acrius urant,
    Has gelida exstingui non nisi morte putas?
Tu meliora paras victrix Medicina; tuusque,
    Pestis quæ superat cuncta, triumphus eris.
Vive liber, victis febrilibus ignibus; unus
    Te simul et mundum qui manet, ignis erit.

J. Lock, *A. M.* Ex Aede Christi, Oxon."[155]

We spoke of *Fingal*. He said, "If the poems were really translated, they were certainly first written down. Let Mr Macpherson deposit the MS in one of the colleges at Aberdeen where there are people who can judge, and if the professors certify the authenticity, then there will be an end of the controversy. If he does not take this obvious and easy method, he gives the best reason to doubt, considering too how much is against it *a priori*."

We sauntered after dinner in Sir Alexander's garden and saw his little grotto, which is hung with pieces of poetry written in a fair hand. It was agreeable to see the contentment and kindness of the worthy, harmless man. Professor MacLeod was brother to Talisker and brother-in-law to the Laird of Coll. He gave me a letter to young Coll.

I was weary of this day, and began to think wishfully of the post-chaise. I was uneasy to think myself too delicate, and thought Mr Johnson was quite satisfied. But he owned to me that he was fatigued and teased with Sir Alexander's doing too much. I said 'twas all kindness. "Yes, sir. But sensation is sensation."

"Yes," said I, "you feel pain equally from the surgeon's probe as from the sword of the foe."[156]

We tried two booksellers' shops and could not find Arthur Johnston's Poems. We went and sat near an hour at Mr Riddoch's. He could not tell distinctly how much education at the college here costs, which disgusted Mr Johnson. I had engaged to Mr Johnson that we should go home to the inn, and not stay supper. They pressed us, but he was resolute. I saw Mr Riddoch did not please him. He said to me, "Sir, he has no vigour in his talk." But it should have been considered that Mr Johnson was not in good humour, so that it was not so easy to talk to his satisfaction. We sat quietly at our inn. He then became merry, and observed how little we had either heard or said at Aberdeen. That the Aberdonians had not started a single *mawkin* (the Scottish word for hare) for us to pursue.

TUESDAY 24 AUGUST. We set out about eight; morning fine. Breakfasted at Ellon.[157] The landlady said to me, "Is not this the great Doctor that is going about through the country?"

I said, "Yes."

"Ay," said she, "we heard of him. I made an errand into the room on purpose to see him. There's something great in his appearance. It is a pleasure to have such a man in one's house; a man who does so much good. If I had thought, I would have shown him a child of mine who has had a lump on his throat for some time."

"But," said I, "he's not a Doctor of Physic."

"Is he an oculist?" said the landlord.

"No," said I, "he's just a very learned man."

Said the landlord: "They say he's the greatest man in England except Lord Mansfield."

Mr Johnson was highly entertained with this, and I do think he was pleased too. He said he liked the exception, for that in Scotland it must be Lord Mansfield or Sir John Pringle.[158]

He told me a good story of Dr Goldsmith. 'Telemachus' Graham was sitting one night with him and Mr Johnson, and was half drunk. He rattled away, and told Mr Johnson, "You're a clever fellow, but you can't write an essay like Addison or verses like *The Rape of the Lock*." At last he said, "Doctor, I will be happy to see you at Eton."

"I shall be glad to wait on you," answered Goldsmith.

"No," said Graham, "'tis not you I meant, Dr Minor. 'Tis Dr Major there."

Goldsmith was prodigiously hurt with this. He spoke of it himself. Said he: "Graham is a fellow to make one commit suicide."[159]

We had received a polite invitation to Slains Castle.[160] We arrived there just at three o'clock, as the bell for dinner was ringing. Though, from its being just on the Northwest Ocean, no trees will grow here, Lord Erroll has done all that can be done.[161] He has cultivated his fields so as to bear rich crops of every kind, and he has made an excellent kitchen-garden, with a hothouse. I had never seen any of the family. But there had been a card of invitation written by Mr Charles Boyd, the Earl's brother. We were conducted into the house, and at the dining-room door were met by Mr Charles Boyd, whom both of us at first took to be Lord Erroll, but he soon corrected our mistake. My lord was gone to dine in the neighbourhood at an entertainment given by Mr Irvine of Drum. Lady Erroll received us politely, and was very attentive to us in the time of dinner. There was nobody at table but she and Mr Boyd and some of the children, their governor and governess. Mr Boyd put Mr Johnson in mind of having dined with him at Cumming the Quaker's, along with a Mr Hall and Miss Williams. This was a bond of connexion between Mr Boyd and Mr Johnson. For me, my father's acquaintance was enough.[162]

After dinner my lady made her young family stand up in a row. There were eight, just steps of stairs, six girls and two boys, besides a young lady of four weeks old who did not appear. It was the prettiest sight I ever saw.

Mr Johnson proposed our setting out. Mr Boyd said he hoped we would stay all night. His brother would be at home in the evening, and would be very sorry if he missed us. Mr Boyd was called out of the room. I was very desirous to stay in so comfortable a house, and wished to see Lord Erroll. Mr Johnson was right in resolving to go if we were not asked again, as it is best to err on the safe side and be sure that one is quite welcome at a house. To my great joy when Mr Boyd returned he told Mr Johnson that it was Lady Erroll who had called him out; that she would never let Mr Johnson into the house again if he stirred that night, and that she had ordered the coach to carry us to see a great curiosity on the coast, after which we should see the house. We cheerfully agreed.

Mr Boyd was out in the year 1745–6. He escaped and lay concealed for a year in the island of Arran, the ancient territory of the Boyds. He then went to France, and was about twenty years on the Continent. He married a French lady, and now he lives very comfortably at Aberdeen, and is much at Slains Castle. He entertained us with much civility. He had a pompousness or formal plenitude in his conversation. Mr Johnson said there was too much elaboration in his talk. I liked to see him a steady branch of the family, setting forth all its advantages with much zeal. My lady had hardly said anything. But he told me she was one of the most pious and most sensible women in the island; had a good head and as good a heart. He said she did not force her children in their education. Mr Johnson said he would rather have the rod to be the general terror to all, to make them learn, than to tell children they should be more esteemed than their brothers or sisters. "The rod produces an effect which terminates in itself. A child is afraid of being whipped and gets his task, and there's an end on't; whereas by exciting emulation and comparisons of superiority, you lay the foundation of lasting mischief: you make brothers and sisters hate each other."

During Mr Boyd's stay in Arran, he had found a chest of medical books left by a surgeon there, and had read them till he acquired some skill, in consequence of which he is often consulted. There were several women here waiting for him as patients. I thought this *practice* of Mr Boyd's but a foolish amusement of vanity, and no doubt of benevolence too. We walked round the house till stopped by a gullet into which the sea comes. The house is built quite upon the shore. The windows look upon the main ocean, and the King of Denmark is Lord Erroll's nearest neighbour on the northeast.

We got into the coach and drove to Dunbuy, a rock near the shore, just an island covered with seafowl. Then to a circular basin of large extent, surrounded with tremendous rocks. On the quarter to the sea there is a high arch in the rock which the force of the tempest has driven out. This place is called Buchan's Buller, or the Bullers of Buchan, and the country people call it the Pot. Mr Boyd said it was so called from the French *bouilloire*. It may be more simply traced from *boiler* in our own language.

We walked round this monstrous cauldron. In some places the rock is very narrow, and on each side you have a sea deep enough for a man-of-war to ride in, so that it is somewhat horrid to move along. However, there is earth and grass upon the rock, and a kind of road marked out by the print of feet, so that one makes it out pretty easily. It was rather alarming to see Mr Johnson poking his way. He insisted to take a boat and sail into the Pot. We did so. He was stout and wonderfully alert. It was curious to me to observe the Buchan men all showing their teeth and speaking with that strange sharp accent which distinguishes them. Mr Johnson was not sensible of the difference of pronunciation in the north of Scotland, which I wondered at.

As the entry into the Buller is so narrow that oars cannot be used as you go in, the method taken is to row very hard when you come near it, and give the boat such a rapidity of motion that she glides in. Mr Johnson observed what an effect this scene would have had were we entering into an unknown place. There are caves of considerable depth, I think one on each side. The boatmen had never entered either far enough to know the size. Mr Boyd told us that it is customary for the company at Peterhead Well to make parties and come and dine in one of the caves here.

He told us that as Slains is at a considerable distance from Aberdeen, Lord Erroll, who has so large a family, resolved to have a surgeon of his own. So he educated one of his tenants' sons, and he is now settled in a very neat house and farm just by, which we saw from the road. By the salary which my lord allows him and the practice which he has had, he is in very easy circumstances. He had kept an exact account of all that had been laid out on his education, and he came to my lord one day, told him that he had arrived at a much higher station than ever he expected, that he was now able to repay what my lord had advanced, and begged my lord would accept of it. The Earl was pleased with the generous gratitude and genteel offer of the man, but refused it. Mr Boyd told us Cumming the Quaker first began by writing against Dr Leechman on Prayer, to prove it unnecessary, as GOD knows best what should be, and will order it without *us*.

When we returned we found coffee and tea in the drawing-room. My lady was not with us. There is a bow window in the drawing-room to the sea. Mr Johnson repeated the ode, *Jam satis terris*,[163] while Boyd was with his patients. He spoke well to Mr Boyd in favour of entails to preserve lines of men whom mankind are accustomed to reverence. He'd have as much land entailed as that they should never fall into contempt, and as much free as to give them all the advantages of property in case of any emergency. He said if the nobility were suffered to sink into indigence, they of course become corrupted; they are ready to do whatever the King chooses; therefore it is fit they should be kept from becoming poor, unless 'tis fixed that when they fall below such a standard of wealth, they shall lose their peerages. He said the House of Peers had made noble stands when the House of Commons durst not. The two last years of a session they dare not contradict the populace.

This room is ornamented with a number of fine prints. Mr Johnson said Sir Joshua Reynolds was the most invulnerable man he knew, the man with whom if you should quarrel, you would find the most difficulty how to abuse. There is a whole-length of Lord Erroll by him in this room, and portraits of my lady and Lady ———, her companion, by Miss Read. At least my lady's is by her. Mr Johnson said it wanted grace. I said the same of Lady ———'s. She has a Welsh harp before her. Her attitude is such as would as well have suited a spinning-wheel.

Mr Johnson said the prospect here was the noblest he had ever seen – better than Mount Edgcumbe, reckoned the first in England, because at Mount Edgcumbe the sea is bounded by land on the other side, and if you have a fleet, you have also the ideas of there being a dockyard, etc., which are not agreeable.[164] Slains is an excellent old house. My lord has built of brick, round or along the square in the inside, a gallery both on the first and second storey, the house being no higher, so that he has always a dry walk, and the rooms, which formerly entered through each other, have now all separate entries from the gallery, which is hung with Hogarth's works and other prints. We went and sat awhile in the library. There is a valuable and numerous collection. It was chiefly made by Mr Falconer, husband to the late Countess. This Earl has added a good many modern books.

About nine the Earl came home, and Captain Gordon of Park was with him. His lordship put Mr Johnson in mind of their dining together in London, along with Mr Beauclerk. I was excessively pleased with Lord Erroll. His stately person and agreeable countenance, with the most unaffected affability, gave me high satisfaction. From perhaps a weakness, or, as I rather hope, more fancy and warmth of feeling than is quite reasonable, my mind is ever impressed with admiration for persons of high birth.[165] I could with the most perfect honesty expatiate on Lord Erroll's good qualities as if I was bribed to do it. His agreeable look and softness of address relieved that awe which his majestic person and the idea of his being Lord High Constable of Scotland would have inspired. He talked very easily and sensibly with Mr Johnson. I observed that Mr Johnson, while he showed that respect to his lordship which he always does from principle to high rank, yet, when they came to argument, maintained that manliness which becomes the force and vigour of his understanding. To show external deference to our superiors is proper. To seem to yield to them in opinion is meanness.[166] The Earl said grace both before and after supper with much decency. He told us a story of a man who was executed at Perth some years ago for murdering a woman, who was with child to him, and a former child he had by her. His hand was cut off. He was then pulled up. But the rope broke, and he was forced to lie an hour on the ground till another rope was brought from Perth, the execution being in a wood at some distance – the place where the murders were committed. "There," said my lord, "I see the hand of Providence."

I was really happy here. I saw in my lord the best dispositions and best principles; and I saw him *in my mind's eye* to be the representative of the ancient Boyds of Kilmarnock. I was afraid he might push the bottle about, as he, I believe, used formerly to do. But he drank port and water out of a large glass himself, and let us do as we pleased. He went with us to our rooms at night, said he took the visit very kind, told me my father and he were very old acquaintance; that I now knew the way to Slains, and he hoped to see me there again.

I had a most elegant room. But there was a fire in it which blazed, and the sea, to which my windows looked, roared, and the pillows were made of some sea-fowl's feathers which had to me a disagreeable smell. So that by all these causes, I was kept awake a good time. I began to think that Lord Errol's father, Lord Kilmarnock (who was beheaded on Tower Hill in 1746), might appear to me, and I was somewhat dreary. But the thought did not last long, and I fell asleep.[167]

WEDNESDAY 25 AUGUST. We got up between seven and eight, and found Mr Boyd in the dining-room, with his greatcoat by way of nightgown, with tea and coffee before him, to give us breakfast. We were in admirable humour. Lady Erroll had given each of us a copy of an ode by Beattie on the birth of her son, Lord Hay. Mr Boyd asked Mr Johnson what he thought of it, or how he liked it. Mr Johnson, who was not very fond of it, got off very well by taking it out and reading the two second stanzas of it with much melody. This, without saying a word, pleased Mr Boyd. He observed, however, to Mr Johnson that the expression as to the family of Erroll, "*A thousand years* have seen it shine," was an anticlimax, and that it would have been better "Ages have seen, &c."[168] Mr Johnson, however, said, "So great a number as a thousand is better. *Dolus latet in universalibus.* Ages might be only two ages."

Mr Johnson talked of the advantage of keeping up the connexions of relationship, which produce much kindness. "Every man who comes into the world has need of friends. If he has to get them for himself, half his life is spent ere his merit is known. Relations are a man's friends who support him. When a man is in real distress, he flies into the arms of his relations. An old lawyer, who had much experience in making wills, told me that after people had deliberated long and thought of many for their executors, they settled at last by fixing on their relations. This shows the universality of the principle."

I regretted the decay of respect for men of family, and that a Nabob would carry an election from them. Said Mr Johnson: "The Nabob will carry it by means of his wealth in a country where money is highly valued, because nothing can be had without it; but if it comes to personal preference, the man of family will always carry it. There is a *scoundrelism* about a low man."

Mr Boyd said that was a good *ism*.

I said I believed mankind were happier in the ancient feudal state of subordination than when in the modern state of independency. Mr Johnson said, "To be sure, the *Chief* was. But we must think of the number of individuals. That *they* were less happy seems plain; for that state from which all escape as soon as they can, and to which none return after they have left it, must be less happy; and this is the case with the state of dependence on a chief or great man."

I mentioned the happiness of the French in their subordination by the reciprocal benevolence and attachment between the great and those in lower ranks. Mr Boyd gave us an excellent instance of gentility of spirit. An old Chevalier de Malthe, of ancient *noblesse* but in low circumstances, was in a coffee-house at Paris where was Julienne, the great manufacturer at the Gobelins of the fine tapestry, so much distinguished both for the figures and the *colours*. The Chevalier's carriage was very old. Says Julienne with a plebeian insolence, "I think, sir, you had better have your carriage new painted."

The Chevalier looked at him with indignant contempt, and answered, "Well, sir, you may take it home and *dye* it." All the coffee-house rejoiced at Julienne's confusion.[169]

We set out about nine. Mr Johnson was curious to see a Druid's Temple. I had a recollection of one at Strichen which I had seen fifteen years ago. So we went four miles out of our road after passing Old Deer, and went thither. Mr Fraser, the proprietor, was at home and showed it. But I had augmented it in my mind, for all that remains is the two stones set up on end with a long one laid between them, as was usual, and one stone at a little distance from them. That stone was the capital one of the circle which surrounded what now remains. Fraser was very hospitable.[170] It was Strichen Fair, and he had several of his neighbours from it at dinner. One of them, Dr Fraser, who had been in the army, remembered to have seen Mr Johnson at a lecture on experimental philosophy at Lichfield. Mr Johnson remembered being at the lecture, and he thought it curious that he should still find somebody who knew him.

Mr Fraser sent a servant along to conduct us by a short passage into the high road. I observed that I had a most disagreeable idea of the life of a country gentleman; that I left Mr Fraser just now as one leaves a prisoner in a jail. Mr Johnson said that I was right in thinking them unhappy, for that they had not enough to keep their minds in motion.

I started a thought which amused us a great part of the way. "If," said I, "our Club should go and set up in St Andrews as a college to teach all that each of us can in the several departments of learning and taste, we'd rebuild the city. We'd draw a wonderful concourse of students."

Mr Johnson entered fully into the spirit of this idea. We immediately fell to distributing the offices. I was to teach Civil and Scotch Law; Burke, Politics and Eloquence; Garrick, the Art of Public Speaking; Langton was to be our Grecian, Colman our Humanist; Nugent to teach Physic; Lord Charlemont, Modern History; Beauclerk, Natural Philosophy; Vesey, Irish Antiquities or Celtic Learning;[171] Jones, Oriental Learning; Goldsmith, Poetry and Ancient History; Chamier, Commercial Politics; Reynolds, Painting and the arts which have beauty for their object; Chambers, the Law of England. Mr Johnson at first said, "I'll trust Theology to nobody but myself." But upon due consideration that Percy is a clergyman, it was agreed that Percy should teach Practical Divinity and British Antiquities, Mr Johnson himself, Logic, Metaphysics, and Scholastic Divinity. In this manner did we amuse ourselves, each suggesting, and each varying or adding. It was really a high entertainment. Mr Johnson said we only wanted a mathematician, since Dyer died, who was a very good one. But as to everything else, we would have a very capital university. He said that we'd persuade Langton to lodge in the garret, as best for him, and if he should take a fancy of making his Will, we'd get him to leave his estate to the College.[172]

We got at night to Banff. I sent Joseph on to Duff House, but Earl Fife was not at home, which I regretted much, as we should have had a very elegant reception from his lordship. We got but an indifferent inn.[173] Here unluckily the windows had no pulleys; and Dr Johnson, who was constantly eager for fresh air, had much struggling to get one of them kept open. Thus he had a notion impressed upon him, that this wretched defect was general in Scotland; in consequence of which he has erroneously enlarged upon it in his *Journey*. I regretted that he did not allow me to read over his book before it was printed. I should have changed very little; but I should have suggested an alteration in a few places where he has laid himself open to be attacked. I hope I should have prevailed with him to omit or soften his assertion that 'a Scotsman must be a sturdy moralist, who does not prefer Scotland to truth' – for I really think it is not founded; and it is harshly said.[174]

Mr Johnson wrote a long letter to Mrs Thrale. I wondered to see him write so much so easily. He verified his doctrine that a man 'may always write when he will set doggedly to it'.

THURSDAY 26 AUGUST. We got a fresh chaise here, a very good one, and very good horses. William Bower, the owner, drove it himself, and drove briskly. Our driver from Aberdeen was rather slow. We breakfasted at Cullen. They set down dried haddocks, broiled, along with our tea, etc. I eat one. But Mr Johnson disliked their presence, so they were removed. Cullen has a snug, warm, comfortable appearance, though but a very small town and the houses mostly of a poor appearance. I observed upon one small thatched house a broad piece of freestone with an inscription bearing that this house and croft was *mortified* (left in mortmain) to the poor of the parish by one Lawter, and that the house was repaired by the present minister of the parish, who, it seems, is the founder's representative.[175]

I went and called for Mr Robertson, who has the charge of my Lord Findlater's affairs, and was formerly Lord Monboddo's clerk, was three times in France with him, and translated Condamine's Account of the Savage Girl, to which my lord wrote a Preface containing several remarks of his own. Robertson said he did not believe so much as my lord did. That it was plain to him the girl confounded what she imagined with what she remembered. That besides she perceived Condamine and Mr Burnett forming theories, and she adapted her story to them.[176]

Mr Johnson said it was a pity to see Lord Monboddo publish such notions as he has done, a man of sense and of so much elegant learning. That there would be little in a fool doing it. We would only laugh. But that when a wise man does it, we are sorry. "Other people," said he, "have strange notions, but they conceal them. If they have tails, they hide them."

I shall here put down one or two more remarks on Lord Monboddo which were not made exactly at this time, but come in well from connexion. He said Monboddo was as jealous of his tail as a squirrel. He did not approve of a judge's being '*Farmer* Burnett' and going about with a little round hat.[177] He laughed heartily at his lordship's saying he was an *enthusiastical* farmer. "For," said he, "what can he do with his *enthusiasm*?"

Here, however, I think Mr Johnson mistaken. A man may be enthusiastical, that is to say, very keen in all the occupations or diversions of life. An ordinary gentleman farmer will be satisfied with looking at his fields once or twice a day. An enthusiastical farmer will be constantly employed on them, will have his mind earnestly engaged, will talk perpetually of them. But Mr Johnson has much of the *nil admirari* in smaller concerns. That survey of life which gave birth to his *Vanity of Human Wishes* early sobered his mind. Besides, so great a mind as his cannot be moved by inferior objects. An elephant does not run and skip like lesser animals.

Mr Robertson sent a servant with us to show us through Lord Findlater's wood, by which our way was shortened, and we saw some part of his domain, which is indeed admirably laid out. Mr Johnson did not choose to walk about it. He always said that he was not come to Scotland to see fine places, of which there were enough in England, but wild objects – mountains, waterfalls, peculiar manners: in short, things which he had not seen before. I have a notion that he at no time has had much taste for rural beauties. I have very little.

Mr Johnson said there was nothing more contemptible than a country gentleman living beyond his income and every year growing poorer and poorer. He spoke strongly of the influence which a man has by being rich. "A man," said he, "who keeps his money has in reality more use from it than he can have by spending it."

I said this looked very like a paradox. But he explained it. "If," said he, "it were sure that a man is to keep his money locked up for ever, to be sure he would have no influence. But as so many want money, and he has the power of giving it, and they know not but by gaining his favour they may obtain it, the rich man will always have the greatest influence. He again who lavishes his money is laughed at as foolish, and in a great degree with justice, considering how much is spent from vanity. Even those who share of a man's hospitality have but a kindness for him in the meantime. If he has not the command of money, people know he cannot help them if he would. Whereas the rich man always can if he will, and for the chance of that will have much weight." BOSWELL. "But philosophers and satirists have all treated a miser as contemptible." JOHNSON. "He is

Thursday 26 August

so philosophically, but not in the practice of life." BOSWELL. "Let me see now. I do not know the instances of misers in England so as to examine into their influence." JOHNSON. "We have had few misers in England." BOSWELL. "There was Lowther, now." JOHNSON. "Why, sir, Lowther, by keeping his money, had the command of the county, which the family has now lost by spending it.[178] I take it he lent a great deal; and that is the way to have influence and yet preserve one's wealth. A man may lend his money upon very good security and yet have his debtor much under his power." BOSWELL. "No doubt, sir. He can always distress him for the money, as no man borrows who is able to pay on demand quite conveniently."

We dined at Elgin, and saw the noble ruins of the cathedral. Though it rained much, Mr Johnson examined them with a most patient attention. He could not here feel an abhorrence at the Scottish Reformers, for he had been told by Lord Hailes that it was destroyed before the Reformation by the Lord of Badenoch, who had a quarrel with the Bishop.[179] The Bishop's house and those of the other clergy, which are still pretty entire, do not seem to have been proportioned to the magnificence of the cathedral, which has been of great extent, and had very fine carved work. In the ———— I was pleased to see the monument of a nun remaining. The ground within the walls of the cathedral is employed as a burying-place. The family of Gordon have their vault here. But it has nothing grand. I looked through a hole in the door of it. They just bury in the earth within it.

We passed Gordon Castle this forenoon, which has a grand appearance: castle, planting, etc.[180] Fochabers is a poorlike village, many of the houses ruinous. But it is remarkable they have in general orchards well stored with apple-trees. Elgin has piazzas in many places on each side of the street. It must have been a much better place formerly. Probably it had piazzas all along, as I have seen at Bologna. I approve much of this mode. It is so convenient in wet weather. Mr Johnson disapproved of it because he said it made the under storey of a house very dark, which greatly overbalanced the conveniency, when it is considered how small a part of the year it rains; how few must then be upon the street, as many who are might as well be at home; and the small hurt supposing people to be as much wet as they commonly are in walking a street.

Baillie Leslie, at whose house we put up, gave us good fish, but beef collops and mutton chops which absolutely could not be eat. Mr Johnson said this was the first time he had got a dinner in Scotland that he could not eat.[181]

Thursday 26 August

In the afternoon, we drove over the very heath where Macbeth met the witches, according to tradition. Dr Johnson again solemnly repeated

> *How far is't called to Fores? What are these,*
> *So wither'd, and so wild in their attire?*
> *That look not like the inhabitants o' the earth,*
> *And yet are on't?*

He repeated a good deal more of Macbeth. His recitation was grand and affecting, and, as Sir Joshua Reynolds has observed to me, had no more tone than it should have: it was the better for it. He then parodied the 'All-hail' of the witches to Macbeth, addressing himself to me. I had purchased some land called Dalblair; and, as in Scotland it is customary to distinguish landed men by the name of their estates, I had thus two titles, 'Dalblair' and 'Young Auchinleck'. So my friend, in imitation of "All hail Macbeth! hail to thee, Thane of Cawdor!" condescended to amuse himself with uttering: "All hail Dalblair! hail to thee, Laird of Auchinleck!"[182]

We got to Forres at night. Found an admirable house kept by Lawson, wine-cooper from London. By the road I had, from that strange curiosity which I always have about anything dismal, stepped out of the chaise and run up close to the gallows where Kenneth Leal hangs in chains for robbing the mail.[183] As he had not hung but about two months, the body was quite entire. It was still a *man* hanging. The sight impressed me with a degree of gloom. Mr Johnson did not know of this, or, he told me afterwards, he would not have talked as he did, for he diverted himself with trying to frighten me, as if the witches would come and dance at the foot of my bed. I said he would be the most frightened of the two. But that I would rather see three witches than one of anything else. I was really a little uneasy. However, the door of my room opened into his. This gave me a security, and I soon fell asleep.

CHAPTER TWO

The Highlands

SAMUEL JOHNSON

At Nairn we may fix the verge of the Highlands; for here I first saw peat fires, and first heard the *Erse* language. We had no motive to stay longer than to breakfast, and went forward to the house of Mr *Macaulay*, the minister who published an account of St *Kilda*, and by his direction visited Calder Castle, from which *Macbeth* drew his second title.[184] It has been formerly a place of strength. The drawbridge is still to be seen, but the moat is now dry. The tower is very ancient: its walls are of great thickness, arched on the top with stone, and surrounded with battlements. The rest of the house is later, though far from modern.

We were favoured by a gentleman, who lives in the castle, with a letter to one of the officers at Fort George, which being the most regular fortification in the island, well deserves the notice of a traveller, who has never travelled before. We went thither next day, found a very kind reception, were led round the works by a gentleman, who explained the use of every part, and entertained by Sir *Eyre Coote*, the governour, with such elegance of conversation as left us no attention to the delicacies of his table.[185]

Of Fort George I shall not attempt to give any account. I cannot delineate it scientifically, and a loose and popular description is of use only when the imagination is to be amused. There was every where an appearance of the utmost neatness and regularity. But my suffrage is of little value, because this and Fort *Augustus* are the only garrisons that I ever saw.

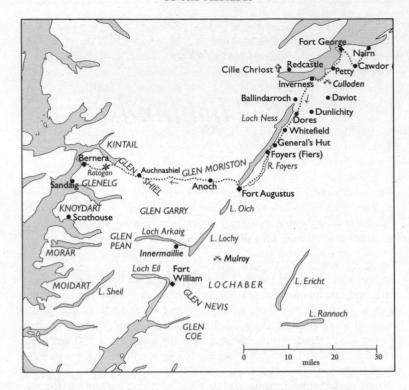

We did not regret the time spent at the fort, though in consequence of our delay we came somewhat late to *Inverness*, the town which may properly be called the capital of the Highlands. Hither the inhabitants of the inland parts come to be supplied with what they cannot make for themselves: hither the young nymphs of the mountains and valleys are sent for education, and as far as my observation has reached, are not sent in vain.[186]

Inverness was the last place which had a regular communication by high roads with the southern counties. All the ways beyond it have, I believe, been made by the soldiers in this century. At *Inverness* therefore *Cromwell*, when he subdued *Scotland*, stationed a garrison, as at the boundary of the Highlands. The soldiers seem to have incorporated afterwards with the inhabitants, and to have peopled the place with an English race; for the language of this town has been long considered as peculiarly elegant.

Here is a castle, called the castle of Macbeth, the walls of which are yet standing. It was no very capacious edifice, but stands upon a rock so high and steep, that I think it was once not accessible, but by the help of ladders, or a bridge. Over against it, on another hill, was a fort built by *Cromwell*, now totally demolished; for no faction of Scotland loved the name of *Cromwell*, or had any desire to continue his memory.[187]

Yet what the Romans did to other nations, was in a great degree done by Cromwell to the Scots; he civilized them by conquest, and introduced by useful violence the arts of peace. I was told at *Aberdeen* that the people learned from Cromwell's soldiers to make shoes and to plant kail.

How they lived without kail, it is not easy to guess: they cultivate hardly any other plant for common tables, and when they had not kail they probably had nothing. The numbers that go barefoot are still sufficient to shew that shoes may be spared: they are not yet considered as necessaries of life; for tall boys, not otherwise meanly dressed, run without them in the streets; and in the islands the sons of gentlemen pass several of their first years with naked feet.

I know not whether it be not peculiar to the Scots to have attained the liberal, without the manual arts, to have excelled in ornamental knowledge, and to have wanted not only the elegancies, but the conveniencies of common life. Literature soon after its revival found its way to *Scotland*, and from the middle of the sixteenth century, almost to the middle of the seventeenth, the politer studies were very diligently pursued. The Latin poetry of *Deliciae Poetarum Scotorum* would have done honour to any nation, at least till the publication *of May's Supplement* the English had very little to oppose.[188]

Yet men thus ingenious and inquisitive were content to live in total ignorance of the trades by which human wants are supplied, and to supply them by the grossest means. Till the Union made them acquainted with English manners, the culture of their lands was unskilful, and their domestick life unformed; their tables were coarse as the feasts of Eskimeaux, and their houses filthy as the cottages of Hottentots.

Since they have known that their condition was capable of improvement, their progress in useful knowledge has been rapid and uniform. What remains to be done they will quickly do, and then wonder, like me, why that which was so necessary and so easy was so long delayed. But they must be for ever content to owe to the English that elegance and culture, which, if they had been vigilant and active, perhaps the English might have owed to them.

Here the appearance of life began to alter. I had seen a few women with plaids at *Aberdeen*; but at *Inverness* the Highland manners are common. There is I think a kirk, in which only the Erse language is used. There is likewise an English chapel, but meanly built, where on Sunday we saw a very decent congregation.[189]

We were now to bid farewel to the luxury of travelling, and to enter a country upon which perhaps no wheel has ever rolled. We could indeed have used our post-chaise one day longer, along the military road to Fort *Augustus*, but we could have hired no horses beyond Inverness, and we were not so sparing of ourselves, as to lead them, merely that we might have one day longer the indulgence of a carriage.

At Inverness therefore we procured three horses for ourselves and a servant, and one more for our baggage, which was no very heavy load. We found in the course of our journey the convenience of having disencumbered ourselves, by laying aside whatever we could spare; for it is not to be imagined without experience, how in climbing crags, and treading bogs, and winding through narrow and obstructed passages, a little bulk will hinder, and a little weight will burthen; or how often a man that has pleased himself at home with his own resolution, will, in the hour of darkness and fatigue, be content to leave behind him every thing but himself.

We took two Highlanders to run beside us, partly to shew us the way, and partly to take back from the seaside the horses, of which they were the owners.[190] One of them was a man of great liveliness and activity, of whom his companion said, that he would tire any horse in Inverness. Both of them were civil and ready-handed. Civility seems part of the national character of Highlanders. Every chieftain is a monarch, and politeness, the natural product of royal government, is diffused from the laird through the whole clan. But they are not commonly dexterous: their narrowness of life confines them to a few operations, and they are accustomed to endure little wants more than to remove them.

We mounted our steeds on the thirtieth of August, and directed our guides to conduct us to Fort Augustus. It is built at the head of Lough Ness, of which *Inverness* stands at the outlet. The way between them has been cut by the soldiers, and the greater part of it runs along a rock, levelled with great labour and exactness, near the waterside.[191]

Most of this day's journey was very pleasant. The day, though bright, was not hot; and the appearance of the country, if I had not seen the Peak, would have been wholly new.[192] We went upon a surface so hard and level, that we had little care to hold the bridle, and were therefore at full leisure for contemplation. On the left were high and steep rocks shaded with birch, the hardy native of the North, and covered with fern or heath. On the right the limpid waters of *Lough Ness* were beating their bank, and waving their surface by a gentle agitation. Beyond them were rocks sometimes covered with verdure, and sometimes towering in horrid nakedness. Now and then we espied a little cornfield, which served to impress more strongly the general barrenness.

Lough Ness is about twenty-four miles long, and from one mile to two miles broad. It is remarkable that *Boethius*, in his description of Scotland, gives it twelve miles of breadth. When historians or geographers exhibit false accounts of places far distant, they may be forgiven, because they can tell but what they are told; and that their accounts exceed the truth may be justly supposed, because most men exaggerate to others, if not to themselves: but *Boethius* lived at no great distance; if he never saw the lake, he must have been very incurious, and if he had seen it, his veracity yielded to very slight temptations.

Lough Ness, though not twelve miles broad, is a very remarkable diffusion of water without islands. It fills a large hollow between two ridges of high rocks, being supplied partly by the torrents which fall into it on either side, and partly, as is supposed, by springs at the bottom. Its water is remarkably clear and pleasant, and is imagined by the natives to be medicinal. We were told, that it is in some places a hundred and forty fathoms deep, a profundity scarcely credible, and which probably those that relate it have never sounded.[193] Its fish are salmon, trout, and pike.

It was said at fort *Augustus*, that *Lough Ness* is open in the hardest winters, though a lake not far from it is covered with ice. In discussing these exceptions from the course of nature, the first question is, whether the fact be justly stated. That which is strange is delightful, and a pleasing error is not willingly detected. Accuracy of narration is not very common, and there are few so rigidly philosophical, as not to represent as perpetual, what is only frequent, or as constant, what is really casual. If it be true that *Lough Ness* never freezes, it is either sheltered by its high banks from the cold blasts, and exposed only to those winds which have more power to agitate than congeal; or it is kept in perpetual motion by the rush of streams from the rocks that inclose it. Its profundity though it should be such as is represented can have little part in this exemption; for though deep wells are not frozen, because their water is secluded from the external air, yet where a wide surface is exposed to the full influence of a freezing atmosphere, I know not why the depth should keep it open. Natural philosophy is now one of the favourite studies of the Scottish nation, and *Lough Ness* well deserves to be diligently examined.[194]

The road on which we travelled, and which was itself a source of entertainment, is made along the rock, in the direction of the lough, sometimes by breaking off protuberances, and sometimes by cutting the great mass of stone to a considerable depth. The fragments are piled in a loose wall on either side, with apertures left at very short spaces, to give a passage to the wintry currents. Part of it is bordered with low trees, from which our guides gathered nuts, and would have had the appearance of an English lane, except that an English lane is almost always dirty. It has been made with great labour, but has this advantage, that it cannot, without equal labour, be broken up.

Within our sight there were goats feeding or playing. The mountains have red deer, but they came not within view; and if what is said of their vigilance and subtlety be true, they have some claim to that palm of wisdom, which the eastern philosopher, whom Alexander interrogated, gave to those beasts which live furthest from men.[195]

Near the way, by the waterside, we espied a cottage. This was the first Highland Hut that I had seen; and as our business was with life and manners, we were willing to visit it. To enter a habitation without leave, seems to be not considered here as rudeness or intrusion. The old laws of hospitality still give this licence to a stranger.[196]

A hut is constructed with loose stones, ranged for the most part with some tendency to circularity. It must be placed where the wind cannot act upon it with violence, because it has no cement; and where the water will run easily away, because it has no floor but the naked ground. The wall, which is commonly about six feet high, declines from the perpendicular a little inward. Such rafters as can be procured are then raised for a roof, and covered with heath, which makes a strong and warm thatch, kept from flying off by ropes of twisted heath, of which the ends, reaching from the center of the thatch to the top of the wall, are held firm by the weight of a large stone. No light is admitted but at the entrance, and through a hole in the thatch, which gives vent to the smoke. This hole is not directly over the fire, lest the rain should extinguish it; and the smoke therefore naturally fills the place before it escapes. Such is the general structure of the houses in which one of the nations of this opulent and powerful island has been hitherto content to live. Huts however are not more uniform than palaces; and this which we were inspecting was very far from one of the meanest, for it was divided into several apartments; and its inhabitants possessed such property as a pastoral poet might exalt into riches.

When we entered, we found an old woman boiling goats-flesh in a kettle. She spoke little English, but we had interpreters at hand; and she was willing enough to display her whole system of economy. She has five children, of which none are yet gone from her. The eldest, a boy of thirteen, and her husband, who is eighty years old, were at work in the wood. Her two next sons were gone to *Inverness* to buy *meal*, by which oatmeal is always meant. Meal she considered as expensive food, and told us, that in Spring, when the goats gave milk, the children could live without it. She is mistress of sixty goats, and I saw many kids in an enclosure at the end of her house. She had also some poultry. By the lake we saw a potatoe-garden, and a small spot of ground on which stood four shucks, containing each twelve sheaves of barley. She has all this from the labour of their own hands, and for what is necessary to be bought, her kids and her chickens are sent to market.

With the true pastoral hospitality, she asked us to sit down and drink whisky. She is religious, and though the kirk is four miles off, probably eight English miles, she goes thither every Sunday. We gave her a shilling, and she begged snuff; for snuff is the luxury of a Highland cottage.

Soon afterwards we came to the *General's Hut*, so called because it was the temporary abode of Wade, while he superintended the works upon the road. It is now a house of entertainment for passengers, and we found it not ill stocked with provisions.

Towards evening we crossed, by a bridge, the river which makes the celebrated fall of Fiers. The country at the bridge strikes the imagination with all the gloom and grandeur of Siberian solitude. The way makes a flexure, and the mountains, covered with trees, rise at once on the left hand and in the front. We desired our guides to shew us the fall, and dismounting, clambered over very rugged crags, till I began to wish that our curiosity might have been gratified with less trouble and danger. We came at last to a place where we could overlook the river, and saw a channel torn, as it seems, through black piles of stone, by which the stream is obstructed and broken, till it comes to a very steep descent, of such dreadful depth, that we were naturally inclined to turn aside our eyes.

But we visited the place at an unseasonable time, and found it divested of its dignity and terror. Nature never gives every thing at once. A long continuance of dry weather, which made the rest of the way easy and delightful, deprived us of the pleasure expected from the fall of Fiers. The river having now no water but what the springs supply, showed us only a swift current, clear and shallow, fretting over the asperities of the rocky bottom, and we were left to exercise our thoughts, by endeavouring to conceive the effect of a thousand streams poured from the mountains into one channel, struggling for expansion in a narrow passage, exasperated by rocks rising in their way, and at last discharging all their violence of waters by a sudden fall through the horrid chasm.

The way now grew less easy, descending by an uneven declivity, but without either dirt or danger. We did not arrive at Fort Augustus till it was late. Mr *Boswell*, who, between his father's merit and his own, is sure of reception wherever he comes, sent a servant before to beg admission and entertainment for that night. Mr Trapaud, the governor, treated us with that courtesy which is so closely connected with the military character. He came out to meet us beyond the gates, and apologized that, at so late an hour, the rules of a garrison suffered him to give us entrance only at the postern.

In the morning we viewed the fort, which is much less than that of St *George*, and is said to be commanded by the neighbouring hills. It was not long ago taken by the Highlanders. But its situation seems well chosen for pleasure, if not for strength; it stands at the head of the lake, and, by a sloop of sixty tuns, is supplied from Inverness with great convenience.

We were now to cross the Highlands towards the western coast, and to content ourselves with such accommodations, as a way so little frequented could afford. The journey was not formidable, for it was but of two days, very unequally divided, because the only house, where we could be entertained, was not further off than a third of the way. We soon came to a high hill, which we mounted by a military road, cut in traverses, so that as we went upon a higher stage, we saw the baggage following us below in a contrary direction. To make this way, the rock has been hewn to a level with labour that might have broken the perseverance of a Roman legion.

The country is totally denuded of its wood, but the stumps both of oaks and firs, which are still found, shew that it has been once a forest of large timber. I do not remember that we saw any animals, but we were told that, in the mountains, there are stags, roebucks, goats and rabbits.

We did not perceive that this tract was possessed by human beings, except that once we saw a cornfield, in which a lady was walking with some gentlemen. Their house was certainly at no great distance, but so situated that we could not descry it.

Passing on through the dreariness of solitude, we found a party of soldiers from the fort, working on the road, under the superintendence of a serjeant. We told them how kindly we had been treated at the garrison, and as we were enjoying the benefit of their labours, begged leave to shew our gratitude by a small present.

Early in the afternoon we came to Anoch, a village in *Glenmorrison* of three huts, one of which is distinguished by a chimney. Here we were to dine and lodge, and were conducted through the first room, that had the chimney, into another lighted by a small glass window. The landlord attended us with great civility, and told us what he could give us to eat and drink. I found some books on a shelf, among which were a volume or more of Prideaux's Connection.[197]

This I mentioned as something unexpected, and perceived that I did not please him. I praised the propriety of his language, and was answered that I need not wonder, for he had learned it by grammar.

By subsequent opportunities of observation, I found that my host's diction had nothing peculiar. Those Highlanders that can speak English, commonly speak it well, with few of the words, and little of the tone by which a Scotchman is distinguished. Their language seems to have been learned in the army or the navy, or by some communication with those who could give them good examples of accent and pronunciation. By their Lowland neighbours they would not willingly be taught; for they have long considered them as a mean and degenerate race. These prejudices are wearing fast away; but so much of them still remains, that when I asked a very learned minister in the islands, which they considered as their most savage clans: "*Those*, said he, *that live next the Lowlands*."[198]

As we came hither early in the day, we had time sufficient to survey the place. The house was built like other huts of loose stones, but the part in which we dined and slept was lined with turf and wattled with twigs, which kept the earth from falling. Near it was a garden of turnips and a field of potatoes. It stands in a glen, or valley, pleasantly watered by a winding river. But this country, however it may delight the gazer or amuse the naturalist, is of no great advantage to its owners. Our landlord told us of a gentleman, who possesses lands, eighteen Scotch miles in length, and three in breadth; a space containing at least a hundred square English miles.[199] He has raised his rents, to the danger of depopulating his farms, and he fells his timber, and by exerting every art of augmentation, has obtained an yearly revenue of four hundred pounds, which for a hundred square miles is three halfpence an acre.

Some time after dinner we were surprised by the entrance of a young woman, not inelegant either in mien or dress, who asked us whether we would have tea. We found that she was the daughter of our host, and desired her to make it. Her conversation, like her appearance, was gentle and pleasing. We knew that the girls of the Highlands are all gentlewomen, and treated her with great respect, which she received as customary and due, and was neither elated by it, nor confused, but repaid my civilities without embarrassment, and told me how much I honoured her country by coming to survey it.

She had been at *Inverness* to gain the common female qualifications, and had, like her father, the English pronunciation. I presented her with a book, which I happened to have about me, and should not be pleased to think that she forgets me.[200]

In the evening the soldiers, whom we had passed on the road, came to spend at our inn the little money that we had given them. They had the true military impatience of coin in their pockets, and had marched at least six miles to find the first place where liquor could be bought. Having never been before in a place so wild and unfrequented, I was glad of their arrival, because I knew that we had made them friends, and to gain still more of their good will, we went to them, where they were carousing in the barn, and added something to our former gift. All that we gave was not much, but it detained them in the barn, either merry or quarrelling, the whole night, and in the morning they went back to their work, with great indignation at the bad qualities of whisky.

We had gained so much the favour of our host, that, when we left his house in the morning, he walked by us a great way, and entertained us with conversation both on his own condition, and that of the country. His life seemed to be merely pastoral, except that he differed from some of the ancient Nomades in having a settled dwelling. His wealth consists of one hundred sheep, as many goats, twelve milk-cows, and twenty-eight beeves ready for the drovers.

From him we first heard of the general dissatisfaction, which is now driving the Highlanders into the other hemisphere; and when I asked him whether they would stay at home, if they were well treated, he answered with indignation, that no man willingly left his native country. Of the farm, which he himself occupied, the rent had, in twenty-five years, been advanced from five to twenty pounds, which he found himself so little able to pay, that he would be glad to try his fortune in some other place. Yet he owned the reasonableness of raising the Highland rents in a certain degree, and declared himself willing to pay ten pounds for the ground which he had formerly had for five.

Our host having amused us for a time, resigned us to our guides. The journey of this day was long, not that the distance was great, but that the way was difficult. We were now in the bosom of the Highlands, with full leisure to contemplate the appearance and properties of mountainous regions, such as have been, in many countries, the last shelters of national distress, and are every where the scenes of adventures, stratagems, surprises and escapes.

Mountainous countries are not passed but with difficulty, not merely from the labour of climbing; for to climb is not always necessary: but because that which is not mountain is commonly bog, through which the way must be picked with caution. Where there are hills, there is much rain, and the torrents pouring down into the intermediate spaces, seldom find so ready an outlet, as not to stagnate, till they have broken the texture of the ground.

Of the hills, which our journey offered to the view on either side, we did not take the height, nor did we see any that astonished us with their loftiness. Towards the summit of one, there was a white spot, which I should have called a naked rock, but the guides, who had better eyes, and were acquainted with the phænomena of the country, declared it to be snow. It had already lasted to the end of August, and was likely to maintain its contest with the sun, till it should be reinforced by winter.

The height of mountains philosophically considered is properly computed from the surface of the next sea; but as it affects the eye or imagination of the passenger, as it makes either a spectacle or an obstruction, it must be reckoned from the place where the rise begins to make a considerable angle with the plain. In extensive continents the land may, by gradual elevation, attain great height, without any other appearance than that of a plane gently inclined, and if a hill placed upon such raised ground be described, as having its altitude equal to the whole space above the sea, the representation will be fallacious.

These mountains may be properly enough measured from the inland base; for it is not much above the sea. As we advanced at evening towards the western coast, I did not observe the declivity to be greater than is necessary for the discharge of the inland waters.

We passed many rivers and rivulets, which commonly ran with a clear shallow stream over a hard pebbly bottom. These channels, which seem so much wider than the water that they convey would naturally require, are formed by the violence of wintry floods, produced by the accumulation of innumerable streams that fall in rainy weather from the hills, and bursting away with resistless impetuosity, make themselves a passage proportionate to their mass.

Such capricious and temporary waters cannot be expected to produce many fish. The rapidity of the wintry deluge sweeps them away, and the scantiness of the summer stream would hardly sustain them above the ground. This is the reason why in fording the northern rivers, no fishes are seen, as in England, wandering in the water.

Of the hills many may be called with Homer's Ida *abundant in springs*, but few can deserve the epithet which he bestows upon Pelion by *waving their leaves*. They exhibit very little variety; being almost wholly covered with dark heath, and even that seems to be checked in its growth. What is not heath is nakedness, a little diversified by now and then a stream rushing down the steep. An eye accustomed to flowery pastures and waving harvests is astonished and repelled by this wide extent of hopeless sterility. The appearance is that of matter incapable of form or usefulness, dismissed by nature from her care and disinherited of her favours, left in its original elemental state, or quickened only with one sullen power of useless vegetation.

It will very readily occur, that this uniformity of barrenness can afford very little amusement to the traveller; that it is easy to sit at home and conceive rocks and heath, and waterfalls; and that these journeys are useless labours, which neither impregnate the imagination, nor enlarge the understanding. It is true that of far the greater part of things, we must content ourselves with such knowledge as description may exhibit, or analogy supply; but it is true likewise, that these ideas are always incomplete, and that at least, till we have compared them with realities, we do not know them to be just. As we see more, we become possessed of more certainties, and consequently gain more principles of reasoning, and found a wider basis of analogy.

Regions mountainous and wild, thinly inhabited, and little cultivated, make a great part of the earth, and he that has never seen them, must live unacquainted with much of the face of nature, and with one of the great scenes of human existence.

As the day advanced towards noon, we entered a narrow valley not very flowery, but sufficiently verdant. Our guides told us, that the horses could not travel all day without rest or meat, and intreated us to stop here, because no grass would be found in any other place. The request was reasonable and the argument cogent. We therefore willingly dismounted and diverted ourselves as the place gave us opportunity.

I sat down on a bank, such as a writer of Romance might have delighted to feign. I had indeed no trees to whisper over my head, but a clear rivulet streamed at my feet. The day was calm, the air soft, and all was rudeness, silence, and solitude. Before me, and on either side, were high hills, which by hindering the eye from ranging, forced the mind to find entertainment for itself. Whether I spent the hour well I know not; for here I first conceived the thought of this narration.[201]

We were in this place at ease and by choice, and had no evils to suffer or to fear; yet the imaginations excited by the view of an unknown and untravelled wilderness are not such as arise in the artificial solitude of parks and gardens, a flattering notion of self-sufficiency, a placid indulgence of voluntary delusions, a secure expansion of the fancy, or a cool concentration of the mental powers. The phantoms which haunt a desert are want, and misery, and danger; the evils of dereliction rush upon the thoughts; man is made unwillingly acquainted with his own weakness, and meditation shews him only how little he can sustain, and how little he can perform. There were no traces of inhabitants, except perhaps a rude pile of clods called a summer hut, in which a herdsman had rested in the favourable seasons. Whoever had been in the place where I then sat, unprovided with provisions and ignorant of the country, might, at least before the roads were made, have wandered among the rocks, till he had perished with hardship, before he could have found either food or shelter. Yet what are these hillocks to the ridges of Taurus, or these spots of wildness to the desarts of America?[202]

It was not long before we were invited to mount, and continued our journey along the side of a lough, kept full by many streams, which with more or less rapidity and noise, crossed the road from the hills on the other hand.[203] These currents, in their diminished state, after several dry months, afford, to one who has always lived in level countries, an unusual and delightful spectacle; but in the rainy season, such as every winter may be expected to bring, must precipitate an impetuous and tremendous flood. I suppose the way by which we went, is at that time impassable.

The lough at last ended in a river broad and shallow like the rest, but that it may be passed when it is deeper, there is a bridge over it. Beyond it is a valley called *Glensheals*, inhabited by the clan of Macrae. Here we found a village called *Auknasheals*, consisting of many huts, perhaps twenty, built all of *dry-stone*, that is, stones piled up without mortar.[204]

We had, by the direction of the officers at Fort *Augustus*, taken bread for ourselves, and tobacco for those Highlanders who might show us any kindness. We were now at a place where we could obtain milk, but must have wanted bread if we had not brought it. The people of this valley did not appear to know any English, and our guides now became doubly necessary as interpreters. A woman, whose hut was distinguished by greater spaciousness and better architecture, brought out some pails of milk. The villagers gathered about us in considerable numbers, I believe without any evil intention, but with a very savage wildness of aspect and manner. When our meal was over, Mr *Boswell* sliced the bread, and divided it amongst them, as he supposed them never to have tasted a wheaten loaf before. He then gave them little pieces of twisted tobacco, and among the children we distributed a small handful of halfpence, which they received with great eagerness. Yet I have been since told, that the people of that valley are not indigent; and when we mentioned them afterwards as needy and pitiable, a Highland lady let us know, that we might spare our commiseration; for the dame whose milk we drank had probably more than a dozen milk-cows. She seemed unwilling to take any price, but being pressed to make a demand, at last named a shilling. Honesty is not greater where elegance is less. One of the by-standers, as we were told afterwards, advised her to ask more, but she said a shilling was enough. We gave her half a crown, and I hope got some credit by our behaviour; for the company said, if our interpreters did not flatter us, that they had not seen such a day since the old laird of Macleod passed through their country.[205]

The Macraes, as we heard afterwards in the Hebrides, were originally an indigent and subordinate clan, and having no farms nor stock, were in great numbers servants to the Maclellans, who, in the war of Charles the First, took arms at the call of the heroic *Montrose*, and were, in one of his battles, almost all destroyed. The women that were left at home, being thus deprived of their husbands, like the Scythian ladies of old, married their servants, and the Macraes became a considerable race.[206]

As we continued our journey, we were at leisure to extend our speculations, and to investigate the reason of those peculiarities by which such rugged regions as these before us are generally distinguished.

Mountainous countries commonly contain the original, at least the oldest race of inhabitants, for they are not easily conquered, because they must be entered by narrow ways, exposed to every power of mischief from those that occupy the heights; and every new ridge is a new fortress, where the defendants have again the same advantages. If the assailants either force the strait, or storm the summit, they gain only so much ground; their enemies are fled to take possession of the next rock, and the pursuers stand at gaze, knowing neither where the ways of escape wind among the steeps, nor where the bog has firmness to sustain them: besides that, mountaineers have an agility in climbing and descending distinct from strength or courage, and attainable only by use.

If the war be not soon concluded, the invaders are dislodged by hunger; for in those anxious and toilsome marches, provisions cannot easily be carried, and are never to be found. The wealth of mountains is cattle, which, while the men stand in the passes, the women drive away. Such lands at last cannot repay the expence of conquest, and therefore perhaps have not been so often invaded by the mere ambition of dominion; as by resentment of robberies and insults, or the desire of enjoying in security the more fruitful provinces.

As mountains are long before they are conquered, they are likewise long before they are civilized. Men are softened by intercourse mutually profitable, and instructed by comparing their own notions with those of others. Thus Caesar found the maritime parts of Britain made less barbarous by their commerce with the Gauls. Into a barren and rough tract no stranger is brought either by the hope of gain or of pleasure. The inhabitants having neither commodities for sale, nor money for purchase, seldom visit more polished places, or if they do visit them, seldom return.

It sometimes happens that by conquest, intermixture, or gradual refinement, the cultivated parts of a country change their language. The mountaineers then become a distinct nation, cut off by dissimilitude of speech from conversation with their neighbours. Thus in Biscay, the original Cantabrian, and in Dalecarlia, the old Swedish still subsists. Thus Wales and the Highlands speak the tongue of the first inhabitants of Britain, while the other parts have received first the Saxon, and in some degree afterwards the French, and then formed a third language between them.

That the primitive manners are continued where the primitive language is spoken, no nation will desire me to suppose, for the manners of mountaineers are commonly savage, but they are rather produced by their situation than derived from their ancestors.

Such seems to be the disposition of man, that whatever makes a distinction produces rivalry. England, before other causes of enmity were found, was disturbed for some centuries by the contests of the northern and southern counties; so that at Oxford, the peace of study could for a long time be preserved only by chusing annually one of the Proctors from each side of the Trent. A tract intersected by many ridges of mountains, naturally divides its inhabitants into petty nations, which are made by a thousand causes enemies to each other. Each will exalt its own chiefs, each will boast the valour of its men, or the beauty of its women, and every claim of superiority irritates competition; injuries will sometimes be done, and be more injuriously defended; retaliation will sometimes be attempted, and the debt exacted with too much interest.

In the Highlands it was a law, that if a robber was sheltered from justice, any man of the same clan might be taken in his place. This was a kind of irregular justice, which, though necessary in savage times, could hardly fail to end in a feud, and a feud once kindled among an idle people with no variety of pursuits to divert their thoughts, burnt on for ages either sullenly glowing in secret mischief, or openly blazing into publick violence. Of the effects of this violent judicature, there are not wanting memorials. The cave is now to be seen to which one of the Campbells, who had injured the Macdonalds, retired with a body of his own clan. The Macdonalds required the offender, and being refused, made a fire at the mouth of the cave, by which he and his adherents were suffocated together.[207]

Mountaineers are warlike, because by their feuds and competitions they consider themselves as surrounded with enemies, and are always prepared to repel incursions, or to make them. Like the Greeks in their unpolished state, described by Thucydides, the Highlanders, till lately, went always armed, and carried their weapons to visits, and to church.[208]

Mountaineers are thievish, because they are poor, and having neither manufactures nor commerce, can grow richer only by robbery. They regularly plunder their neighbours, for their neighbours are commonly their enemies; and having lost that reverence for property, by which the order of civil life is preserved, soon consider all as enemies, whom they do not reckon as friends, and think themselves licensed to invade whatever they are not obliged to protect.

By a strict administration of the laws, since the laws have been introduced into the Highlands, this disposition to thievery is very much represt. Thirty years ago no herd had ever been conducted through the mountains, without paying tribute in the night, to some of the clans; but cattle are now driven, and passengers travel without danger, fear, or molestation.

Among a warlike people, the quality of highest esteem is personal courage, and with the ostentatious display of courage are closely connected promptitude of offence and quickness of resentment. The Highlanders, before they were disarmed, were so addicted to quarrels, that the boys used to follow any publick procession or ceremony, however festive, or however solemn, in expectation of the battle, which was sure to happen before the company dispersed.

Mountainous regions are sometimes so remote from the seat of government, and so difficult of access, that they are very little under the influence of the sovereign, or within the reach of national justice. Law is nothing without power; and the sentence of a distant court could not be easily executed, nor perhaps very safely promulgated, among men ignorantly proud and habitually violent, unconnected with the general system, and accustomed to reverence only their own lords. It has therefore been necessary to erect many particular jurisdictions, and commit the punishment of crimes, and the decision of right to the proprietors of the country who could enforce their own decrees. It immediately appears that such judges will be often ignorant, and often partial; but in the immaturity of political establishments no better expedient could be found. As government advances towards perfection, provincial judicature is perhaps in every empire gradually abolished.

Those who had thus the dispensation of law, were by consequence themselves lawless. Their vassals had no shelter from outrages and oppressions; but were condemned to endure, without resistance, the caprices of wantonness, and the rage of cruelty.

In the Highlands, some great lords had an hereditary jurisdiction over counties; and some chieftains over their own lands; till the final conquest of the Highlands afforded an opportunity of crushing all the local courts, and of extending the general benefits of equal law to the low and the high, in the deepest recesses and obscurest corners.[209]

While the chiefs had this resemblance of royalty, they had little inclination to appeal, on any question, to superior judicatures. A claim of lands between two powerful lairds was decided like a contest for dominion between sovereign powers. They drew their forces into the field, and right attended on the strongest. This was, in ruder times, the common practice, which the kings of Scotland could seldom control.

Even so lately as in the last years of King William, a battle was fought at *Mull Roy*, on a plain a few miles to the south of *Inverness*, between the clans of *Mackintosh* and *Macdonald* of *Keppoch*. *Col Macdonald*, the head of a small clan, refused to pay the dues demanded from him by *Mackintosh*, as his superior lord. They disdained the interposition of judges and laws, and calling each his followers to maintain the dignity of the clan, fought a formal battle, in which several considerable men fell on the side of *Mackintosh*, without a complete victory to either. This is said to have been the last open war made between the clans by their own authority.[210]

The Highland lords made treaties, and formed alliances, of which some traces may still be found, and some consequences still remain as lasting evidences of petty regality.[211] The terms of one of these confederacies were, that each should support the other in the right, or in the wrong, except against the king.

The inhabitants of mountains form distinct races, and are careful to preserve their genealogies. Men in a small district necessarily mingle blood by intermarriages, and combine at last into one family, with a common interest in the honour and disgrace of every individual. Then begins that union of affections, and cooperation of endeavours, that constitute a clan. They who consider themselves as ennobled by their family, will think highly of their progenitors, and they who through successive generations live always together in the same place, will preserve local stories and hereditary prejudices. Thus every Highlander can talk of his ancestors, and recount the outrages which they suffered from the wicked inhabitants of the next valley.

Such are the effects of habitation among mountains, and such were the qualities of the Highlanders, while their rocks secluded them from the rest of mankind, and kept them an unaltered and discriminated race. They are now losing their distinction, and hastening to mingle with the general community.

We left *Auknasheals* and the *Macraes* in the afternoon, and in the evening came to *Ratiken*, a high hill on which a road is cut, but so steep and narrow, that it is very difficult. There is now a design of making another way round the bottom.[212] Upon one of the precipices, my horse, weary with the steepness of the rise, staggered a little, and I called in haste to the Highlander to hold him. This was the only moment of my journey, in which I thought myself endangered.

Having surmounted the hill at last, we were told that at *Glenelg*, on the seaside, we should come to the house of lime and slate and glass. This image of magnificence raised our expectation. At last we came to our inn weary and peevish, and began to inquire for meat and beds.

Of the provisions the negative catalogue was very copious. Here was no meat, no milk, no bread, no eggs, no wine. We did not express much satisfaction. Here however we were to stay. Whisky we might have, and I believe at last they caught a fowl and killed it. We had some bread, and with that we prepared ourselves to be contented, when we had a very eminent proof of Highland hospitality. Along some miles of the way, in the evening, a gentleman's servant had kept us company on foot with very little notice on our part. He left us near *Glenelg*, and we thought on him no more till he came to us again, in about two hours, with a present from his master of rum and sugar. The man had mentioned his company, and the gentleman, whose name, I think, is Gordon, well knowing the penury of the place, had this attention to two men, whose names perhaps he had not heard, by whom his kindness was not likely to be ever repaid, and who could be recommended to him only by their necessities.[213]

We were now to examine our lodging. Out of one of the beds, on which we were to repose, started up, at our entrance, a man black as a Cyclops from the forge. Other circumstances of no elegant recital concurred to disgust us. We had been frighted by a lady at Edinburgh, with discouraging representations of Highland lodgings. Sleep, however, was necessary. Our Highlanders had at last found some hay, with which the inn could not supply them. I directed them to bring a bundle into the room, and slept upon it in my riding coat. Mr. Boswell being more delicate, laid himself sheets with hay over and under him, and lay in linen like a gentleman.

JAMES BOSWELL

FRIDAY 27 AUGUST. It was dark when we came to Forres last night. So we did not see what is called King Duncan's Monument.[214]

I shall now mark some gleanings of Mr Johnson's conversation. I spoke of *Leonidas*, and said there were some good passages in it. He said, "Why, you must *seek* for them." He said Paul Whitehead's *Manners* was a poor performance.[215] He said I should write down all the particulars of my first coming to London, where I eloped from the University of Glasgow, changed my name, was initiated by Derrick, the poet, afterwards Master of the Ceremonies at Bath, in the knowledge of the *town* in all its varieties of wits, players, ladies to which he could attain, and having then *surrendered* myself to the late Alexander Earl of Eglinton, was introduced by that most accomplished and friendly nobleman into the highest company both in London and at Newmarket.[216]

What Dr Johnson thought worth doing I think I shall certainly do. The account will be as like a novel as what is strictly true can be. At any rate, I am anxious to pay a grateful tribute to the memory of a noble lord to whom I was indebted for a thousand marks of kindness, who first opened my mind to the perception of the best philosophy in this state of being, the *savoir vivre*, so as to multiply pleasurable sensations as much as possible – not merely animal sensations, but those of the fine arts, of knowledge, and of reasoning. The most honourable testimony I can produce will be to arrange in good preservation all that I can collect concerning him. I have some of his conversation and several of his letters to myself. The Countess his mother presented me with all his letters to her Ladyship, and I hope to obtain some valuable communications from others. Compositions of such an elegant cast relieve the mind in intervals of laborious occupation.

He said he had a kindness for Derrick; and he had often said that if his letters had been written by one of a more established name, they would have been thought very pretty letters.[217]

This morning we got upon the origin of evil. Moral evil, he said, was occasioned by free-will, which implies choice between good and evil. "And," said he, "with all the evil that is, there is no man but would rather be a free agent than a mere machine without the evil; and what is best for each individual must be best for the whole. If," said he, "a man says he would rather be the machine, I cannot argue with him. He is a different being from me."

I said a man, as a machine, might have agreeable sensations; he might have music. "No," said he, "he could not have music, at least no power of producing music, for he who can produce music may let it alone. He who can play upon a fiddle may break it: such a man is not a machine."

The reasoning satisfied me. To be sure, there cannot be a free agent unless there is the power of being evil as well as good. We must take the inherent possibilities of things into consideration in our reasonings or conjectures concerning the works of GOD.

We came to Nairn to breakfast. It is a very poor place to be a county town and a royal burgh. Above the room where we were a girl was spinning wool on a great wheel, and singing an Erse song. "I'll warrant you," said Mr Johnson, "one of the songs of Ossian." He then repeated these lines:

> *Verse sweetens toil, however rude the sound.*
> *All at her work the village maiden sings;*
> *Nor, while she turns the giddy wheel around,*
> *Revolves the sad vicissitude of things.*

I thought I had seen these lines before. But Mr Johnson fancied I had not, as they are in a detached poem by one Gifford, a parson, of which he does not remember the name.[218]

I expected Kenneth Macaulay, the minister of Cawdor, who published the *History of St Kilda*, of which Mr Johnson is fond, would have met us here, as I had written to him from Aberdeen. But I received a letter from him telling that he could not come from home, as he was to have the sacrament next Sunday, and earnestly begging to see us at his manse. "We'll go," said Mr Johnson, which we accordingly did.

When we came to it, Mrs Macaulay received us, and told us he was in the church distributing tokens.[219] We got there between twelve and one, and it was near three before he came to us. Mr Johnson thanked him for his book, and said it was a very pretty piece of topography. Macaulay did not seem much to mind the compliment. From his conversation Mr Johnson was persuaded that he had not written the book which goes under his name. I myself always suspected so. Mr Johnson said there was a combination in it of which Macaulay was not capable, and he said to me privately, "Crassus homo est."[220]

However, he gave us a good hospitable dinner, and as we were to get a route from him for our tour among the western isles, we agreed to stay all night.

After dinner we walked to the old Castle of Cawdor, the Thane of Cawdor's residence. I was sorry that my friend, this 'prosperous gentleman', was not there.[221] The old tower must be of great antiquity. There is a drawbridge, what has been a moat, and a court. There is a hawthorn tree in one of the rooms, still undecayed, that is to say, the stock still remains. The tower has been built round it by a strange conceit. The thickness of the walls, the small slanting windows, and a great iron door at the entrance on the second storey, coming up the stairs, all indicate the rude times in which this building has been erected. There is a great deal of additional building 250 years old: some large rooms, and an excellent kitchen partly cut out of rock, with a pump-well in it. There were here some large venerable trees.

I was afraid Mr Johnson would quarrel with poor Macaulay, who talked at random of the lower English clergy not being the most respectable. Mr Johnson gave him a frowning look, and said, "This is a day of novelties: I have seen old trees in Scotland, etc., and I've heard the English clergy treated with disrespect." He did not perceive that honest Kenneth was not to be minded.

I dreaded that a whole evening at Cawdor manse would be heavy. However, Mr Grant, minister at Daviot and Dunlichity, was there, and helped us with conversation. Mr Johnson, talking of hereditary occupations in the Highlands, said there was no harm in offices being hereditary, but it was wrong to force them so, and oblige a man to be a tailor or a smith or anything else because his father had been it. This custom, however, is not peculiar to our Highlands; it is well known

Friday 27 August

that in India a similar practice prevails. Mr Grant told us a story of an apparition, which he had from the Rev. Mr Grant at Nigg, *who saw it*. I shall write to Mr Grant and have it from the fountain-head, if he will favour me with it.

Macaulay began a rhapsody against creeds and confessions. Mr Johnson showed clearly that what he called *imposition* was only a voluntary declaration of agreement in certain articles of faith, which a Church had a right to require, just as any other society can insist on certain rules being observed by its members. Nobody is compelled to be of the Church, as nobody is compelled to enter into a society. This was a very clear and very just view of the subject. But poor Macaulay could not be driven out of his track. Mr Johnson said well that he was a *bigot to laxness*.

As we had a great deal of conversation about the second sight, I mentioned to the company my uneasiness because I had seen, or had dreamed that I saw, my little daughter dead, the night that we were going from Cupar to St Andrews; and I said I should not be easy till I got a letter. I thought it best to mention it to several people, because it made a strong impression upon my mind, and in case it should unhappily prove true, I might have witnesses to attest what I said. Yet I can hardly have any pretence to the second sight, being no Highlander. However, as others have had strange supernatural communications, I knew not but it might be my case. I endeavoured to prepare my mind by pious reflections for whatever might happen. Yet I remembered Mr Johnson's doctrine among the St Andrews professors, that grief for a loss must necessarily affect the mind of man.

Mr Macaulay and I laid the map of Scotland before us, and he mentioned a route for us from Inverness by Fort Augustus to Glenelg, Skye, Mull, Icolmkill, Lorne, Inveraray, which I wrote down. As my father was to set out for the North Circuit about the 18 of September, it was necessary for us either to make our tour with great expedition, so as to get to Auchinleck before he set out, or to protract it so as not to be at Auchinleck till his return, which would be about the 10 of October. By Macaulay's calculation, we were not to land in Lorne till the 20 of September. I thought that the interruptions by bad days, or by agreeable schemes of curiosity, might make it ten days later; and I thought too that we might perhaps go to Benbecula and visit Clanranald, which would take a week of itself.

Mr Johnson went up awhile with Mr Grant to the library, which consisted of a tolerable collection, but Mr Johnson thought it rather a lady's library, with some Latin books in it by chance, than the library of a clergyman. It had only two of the Latin fathers, and one of the Greek ones in Latin.

I doubted whether Dr Johnson would be present at a Presbyterian prayer. I told Mr Macaulay so, and said that the Doctor might sit in the library while we were at family worship. Mr Macaulay said, he would omit it, rather than give Dr Johnson offence: but I would by no means agree that an excess of politeness, even to so great a man, should prevent what I esteem as one of the best pious regulations. I know nothing more beneficial, more comfortable, more agreeable, than that the little societies of each family should regularly assemble, and unite in praise and prayer to our heavenly Father, from whom we daily receive so much good, and may hope for more in a higher state of existence. I mentioned to Dr Johnson the over-delicate scrupulosity of our host. He said, he had no objection to hear the prayer. This was a pleasing surprise to me; for he refused to go and hear Principal Robertson preach. "I will hear him," said he, "if he will get up into a tree and preach; but I will not give a sanction, by my presence, to a Presbyterian assembly."[222]

Accordingly Mr Grant prayed. Mr Johnson said it was a very good prayer, but objected to his not having introduced the Lord's Prayer. He told us that Baretti said once to him, "We have in our service a prayer called the *Pater Noster* which is a very fine composition. I wonder who is the author of it." Such a strange piece of ignorance may a man of literature and general inquiry happen to have.[223]

Macaulay had a remarkably good manse. Mr Grant and I slept in the same room. Mr Johnson had a room to himself. The house was very decently furnished. Mrs Macaulay is a MacLeod of a very good family. She seemed to have a little too much value for herself on that account.

SATURDAY 28 AUGUST. Mr Johnson had brought a copy of Sallust with him in his pocket from Edinburgh. He gave it last night to Mr Macaulay's son, a smart young lad about eleven. He had a governor in the house to teach him. Mr Johnson had given an account of the education at Oxford in all its gradations. The advantages of being a servitor, to a youth of little fortune, struck Mrs Macaulay much. I observed it aloud. Mr Johnson very handsomely and kindly said that if they would send their boy to him when he was ready for the University, he would get him made a servitor, and perhaps would do more for him. He could not promise to do more, but would undertake for the servitorship. This may be a most fortunate circumstance for the lad. The father did not take it so warmly as I should have thought he would, owing to the same cause which occasioned his invincible adherence to his notions against creeds and confessions. But Mrs Macaulay was wisely and truly grateful.[224]

I should have mentioned that Mr White, a Welshman who has been many years factor on the estate of Cawdor, drank tea with us last night upon getting a note from Macaulay, and asked us to his house. We had not time to accept of his invitation.[225] He gave us a letter to Mr Fern, master of stores at Fort George. He showed it to me. It recommended 'two celebrated gentlemen: no less than Dr Johnson, *Author of his Dictionary*, and Mr Boswell, known at Edinburgh by the name of Paoli'.[226] He said he hoped I had no objection to what he had written. If I had, he would alter it. I thought it was a pity to check his effusions, and acquiesced, taking care, however, to seal the letter, that it might not appear that I had read it.

After breakfast and a conversation about saying grace to breakfast as well as dinner and supper, in which Mr Johnson observed that it is enough if we have stated seasons of prayer, no matter when, and that a man may as well pray when he mounts his horse, or a woman when she milks her cow, as at meals, and that custom is to be followed, we drove down to Fort George.[227]

When we came into the square, I sent a soldier with the letter to Fern. He came to us immediately, and along with him came Major *Brewse* of the Engineers (pronounced *Bruce*). He said he believed it was originally the same Norman name with Bruce. That he had dined at a house in London where were three Bruces, one of the Irish line, one of the Scottish, and himself of the English line. He said he was shown it in the Herald Office spelled fourteen different ways. I told him the different spellings of my name. Mr Johnson observed that there had been great disputes about the spelling of Shakespeare's name. At last it was thought it would be settled by looking at the original copy of his Will. But upon examining it, he was found to have written it no less than three different ways. This conversation passed after we had been some time together. But it comes in well here.

Mr Fern was a brisk civil man. He had been in the Fort for twenty years, but had been at different intervals in London and other places. Major Brewse was a man who seemed to be very intelligent in his profession, and spoke with uncommon deliberation and distinctness. They first carried us to wait on Sir Eyre Coote, whose Regiment (the 37) was lying here, and who commanded them. He asked us to eat a bit of mutton with him. Mr Johnson said, "That, sir, is contrary to our plan."

Saturday 28 August

"Then," said Sir Eyre, "I hope you'll alter your plan."

Mr Johnson agreed, to my great joy.

Mr Fern and Major Brewse showed us the fort very fully. The Major explained everything in fortification to us, as did Mr Fern in stores. Mr Johnson talked of the proportions of charcoal and saltpetre in making gunpowder, of granulating it, and of giving it a gloss. He made a very good figure upon these topics. He said afterwards that he had talked *ostentatiously*.

We reposed ourselves a little in Fern's house. He had everything in neat order as in England. He had a tolerable collection of books. I looked at Pennant.[228] He says little of this fort but that the barracks, etc., form several streets. This is aggrandizing. Fern observed if he had said they form a square with a row of buildings before it, he would have given a juster description. Mr Johnson observed, "How seldom descriptions correspond with realities; and the reason is that people do not write them till some time after, and then their imagination has added circumstances."

We talked of Sir Adolphus Oughton. The Major said he knew a great deal for a military man. "Sir," said Mr Johnson, "you will find few men of any profession who know more. Sir Adolphus is a very extraordinary man, a man of boundless curiosity and unwearied diligence."

I know not how the Major contrived to introduce the contest between Warburton and Lowth. Mr Johnson said, "Warburton kept his temper all along, while Lowth was in a passion. Lowth published some of Warburton's letters. Warburton drew *him* on to write some very abusive letters, and then asked his leave to publish them, which he knew Lowth could not refuse after what *he* had done. So that he contrived it so that he should publish apparently with Lowth's consent what could not but show Lowth in a disadvantageous light."

Mr Johnson said the King did him the honour to ask him what he thought of that controversy. Mr Johnson said he thought Warburton had most general learning, Lowth most scholastic learning. He did not know which of them called names best. The King said he judged of 'em very rightly. The King appeared to have read the controversy.[229]

At three the drum beat for dinner. I could for a little fancy myself a military man, and it pleased me. We went to Sir Eyre's, in the Governor's house, and found him a most gentlemanlike man. His lady was, though not a beauty, one of the most agreeable women I ever saw, with an uncommonly mild and sweet tone in her conversation. She had a young lady, a companion, with her. There was a pretty large company: Fern, the Major of Engineers, and several officers. Sir Eyre had come from the East

Indies by land, through the deserts of Arabia. He told us the Arabs could live five days without victuals, and subsist for three weeks with nothing else but the blood of their camels, who could lose so much of it as would suffice for that time, without being exhausted. He highly praised the virtue of the Arabs: their fidelity if they undertook to conduct you: that they'd lose their lives rather than let you be robbed. Mr Johnson, who is always for maintaining the superiority of civilized men over uncivilized, said there was no superior virtue in this. Colonel Pennington took up the argument with a good deal of spirit and ingenuity. Mr Johnson said, "A sergeant and twelve men who are my guard will die rather than that I shall be robbed."

"Ay," said the Colonel, "but the soldiers are compelled to do it."

"Well," said Mr Johnson, "the Arabs are compelled by the fear of infamy." COLONEL. "The soldiers have the same fear of infamy, and the fear of punishment besides; so have less virtue, because they act less voluntarily." Lady Coote observed very well that we ought to know if there is not among the Arabs some punishment for not being faithful on such occasions.

We talked of the Stage. I observed that we had not now such a company of actors as in the last age: Wilks, Booth, etc. Mr Johnson said, "You think so because there is one who excels all the rest so much. You compare them with Garrick and see the deficiency. Garrick's great distinction is his universality. He can represent all modes of life but that of an easy, fine-bred gentleman."

The Colonel said he should give over playing young parts. JOHNSON. "He does not take them now, but he does not leave off those which he has been used to play, because he does them better than any one else can do. If you had generations of actors, if they swarmed like bees, the young ones might drive off the old ones."

He said he thought Mrs Cibber got more reputation than she deserved, as she had a great sameness, though she had something very fine; though Mrs Clive was the best player he ever saw. Mrs Pritchard was a very good one, but had something affected. He imagined she had some player of the former age in her eye, which occasioned it.

Pennington said Garrick sometimes failed in emphasis, as in *Hamlet*, "I will speak *daggers* to her, but I'll use *none*," in place of "I'll *speak* daggers to her, but I'll *use* none."

Sir Eyre had something between the Duke of Queensberry and my late worthy friend Captain Cuninghame in his manner. We had a dinner of two complete courses, variety of wines, and the regimental band of music playing in the square before the windows after it. I enjoyed this day much. We were quite easy and cheerful. Mr Johnson said, "I shall always remember this fort with gratitude."

I could not help being struck with the idea of finding upon that barren sandy point such buildings, such a dinner, such company. It was like enchantment. Mr Johnson, on the other hand, said to me more rationally that it did not strike *him*, because he knew here was a large sum of money expended in building a fort. Here was a regiment. If there had been less than what he found, it would have surprised him. *He* looked coolly through all the gradations. *My* imagination jumped from the barren sand to the good dinner and fine company. Like the hero in *Love in a Hollow Tree*,[230] "Without ands or ifs, / I leapt from off the sand upon the cliffs." I had a strong impression of the power and excellence of human art.

We left the fort between six and seven. Sir Eyre, the Colonel, etc., went downstairs and saw us into our chaise. There could not be greater attention paid to any visitors. Sir Eyre spoke of the hardships which Dr Johnson had before him. Said I, "Considering what he has said of us, we must make him feel something rough in Scotland."

Said Sir Eyre to him, "You must change your name."

"Ay," said I, "to Dr Macgregor."[231]

We got safely to Inverness, and put up at Mackenzie's at the Horns. Mr Keith, the Collector of Excise here, my old acquaintance at Ayr, who had seen us at the Fort, called in the evening and engaged us to dine with him next day, and promised to breakfast with us and take us to the English Chapel; so that we were at once commodiously arranged.[232]

Mr Johnson wrote tonight both to Mrs Thrale and Mrs Williams, and I wrote to my wife. I value myself on having as constant a regard – nay, love – for her as any man ever had for a woman, and yet never troubling anybody else with it. I was somewhat uneasy that I found no letter here from her, though I could hardly expect it, as I had desired her to write to Skye. I could not help my mind from imaging it as dreary that I was to be yet for several weeks separated from her. Clouds passed over my imagination, and in these clouds I saw objects somewhat dismal. She might die or I might die; and I felt a momentary impatience to be home, but a sentence or two of the Rambler's conversation gave me firmness, and I saw that I was upon an expedition which I had wished for for years, and the recollection of which would be a treasure to me for life.

The inn was dirty and ill-furnished. The entertainment pretty good.

SUNDAY 29 AUGUST. Mr Keith breakfasted with us. Mr Johnson run out rather strongly upon the benefits derived to Scotland from the Union, and the bad state of our people before it. I am entertained with his copious exaggeration upon that subject. But I am uneasy when people are by who do not know him as well as I do and may be apt to think him narrow-minded.[233] I diverted the subject.

The chapel was but a poor one. The altar was a bare fir table, with a coarse stool for kneeling on, covered with a piece of coarse sail-cloth doubled by way of cushion. The lofts were at each end, and one before the pulpit. At the left hand of it, when you looked up to the loft, you saw just the uncovered joists. At the right hand, where the altar was, they were covered with white crown paper pasted upon them, which formed a ceiling. The congregation was small. Tait, the clergyman, read prayers very well, though with much of the Scotch accent. He preached on "Love your enemies." It was curious that when talking of the connexions amongst men, he said that some connected themselves with men of distinguished talents, and since they could not equal them, tried to deck themselves with their merit by being their companions. The sentence was to this purpose. It had an odd coincidence with what might be said of Mr Johnson and me.

After church we walked down to the quay, where I met, at Oliver's fort, Mr Alves the painter, whom I had not seen since I was at Rome in 1765. We then went to Macbeth's Castle. I had a most romantic satisfaction in seeing Mr Johnson actually in it. It answers to Shakespeare's description, which Sir Joshua Reynolds has so happily illustrated, in one of his notes on our immortal poet: "This castle hath a pleasant," etc., which I repeated. When we came out of it, a raven perched on one of the chimney-tops and croaked. Then I repeated, "The raven himself is hoarse," etc. I exulted in comparing my former hypochondriac state when at Inverness with my present soundness and vigour of mind, and I was thankful.[234]

We dined at Keith's. A Miss Duff was there. Mrs Keith was officiously attentive to Mr Johnson, asking him many questions about his drinking only water. He rebuked her by saying to me, "You may remember that not the least notice was taken of this by Lady Erroll" – showing Mrs Keith that she was not so well-bred.

Mr Johnson has the art for which I have heard my father praise the old Earl of Aberdeen: viz., that of instructing himself by making every man he meets tell him something of what he knows best. He led Keith to talk to him of the excise in Scotland. Mr Johnson told us that Mr Thrale paid £20,000 a year to the revenue; that he had four casks, each of which holds 1600 barrels – above a thousand hogsheads.

A young lady whose name I did not hear, and Mr Grant, the minister whom we had seen at Macaulay's, drank tea with us. There was little conversation that can be written down. I shall therefore here again glean what I have omitted on former days. Gerard told us that when he was in Wales he was shown a valley inhabited by Danes who still retain their own language, and are quite a distinct people. Mr Johnson said it could not be true, or all the kingdom must have heard of it. He said to me as we travelled, "These people, sir, may have somewhat of a *peregrinity* in their dialect, which is augmented to a different language."

I asked him if *peregrinity* was a word. He laughed and said, "No."

I told him this was just the second time that I had heard him make a word. When Foote broke his leg, I observed that this would fit him better for taking off George Faulkner as Peter Paragraph, poor George having a wooden leg. Mr Johnson said, "George will rejoice at the *depeditation* of Foote," and when I asked him, laughed and owned he had made the word; and that he had not made above three or four in the Dictionary.[235]

Mr Johnson told me that all the aid he had in compiling the Dictionary was having about twenty etymologies sent him by an unknown hand at the time, which he afterwards learned was Dr Pearce, Bishop of Rochester. Some of them he adopted. He never lived a great deal with Lord Chesterfield, nor was there any particular incident that produced a quarrel between them, as has been erroneously propagated. My lord had made him great professions. Yet for seven years, while Mr Johnson was engaged in his immense undertaking, the Dictionary, my lord never took the least notice of him. When the work came out, my lord fell a-scribbling in the *World* about it. Mr Johnson, with a just indignation and contempt, wrote to him a letter which was civil but showed him that he did not mind what he said or wrote, and that he had done with him. Mr Johnson kept no copy of the letter. He could repeat it, and was once persuaded to write it down from memory, but he believes he has lost the copy. I have heard Langton repeat some of it; in particular a sentence to this purpose: that Lord Chesterfield, after leaving him to struggle with the waves unassisted, stretched out his hand to welcome him on shore.

After tea Mr Keith went with us to our inn. He and I left Mr Johnson there a little and went and called for old Mr Fraser, the minister; for Redcastle's family, where I found only Miss Murdoch, whom I had never seen before; and for Mrs Anderson, formerly Miss Mackinnon, in whose mother's house I had formerly lodged along with my father at the Circuit. I am, as Mr Johnson observed, one who has all the old principles, good and bad. That of attention to relations in the remotest degree, or to worthy people in every state whom I have once known, I inherit from my father. It gave me much satisfaction to hear everybody here speak of him with uncommon regard.

Mr Keith and Mr Grant, whom we had seen at Mr Macaulay's, supped with us at the inn. We had roasted kid, which Dr Johnson had never tasted before. He relished it much.[236]

MONDAY 30 AUGUST. This day we were to begin our *equitation*, as I said, for *I* would needs make a word too.[237]

It is remarkable, that my noble, and to me most constant friend, the Earl of Pembroke (who, if there is too much ease on my part, will please to pardon what his benevolent, gay, social intercourse, and lively correspondence, have insensibly produced) has since hit upon the very same word. The title of the first edition of his lordship's very useful book was, in simple terms, *A Method of Breaking Horses and Teaching Soldiers to Ride*. The title of the second edition is, *Military Equitation*.[238]

We might have taken a chaise to Fort Augustus. But, had we not hired horses at Inverness, we should not have found them afterwards: so we resolved to begin here to ride. We should have set out at seven. But one of the horses needed shoeing; the smith had got drunk the night before at a wedding and could not rise early; so we did not get off till nine. We had three horses for Mr Johnson, myself, and Joseph, and one which carried our portmanteaus; and two Highlanders who walked with us, John Hay and Lauchlan Vass, whom Mr Johnson has remembered with credit in his *Journey*, though he has omitted their names. Mr Johnson rode very well.

A little above Inverness, I fancy about three miles, we saw just by the road a very complete Druid's temple; at least we took it to be so. There was a double circle of stones, one of very large ones and one of smaller ones.[239] Mr Johnson justly observed that to go and see one is only to see that it is nothing, for there is neither art nor power in it, and seeing one is as much as one would wish.

It was a delightful day. Loch Ness, and the road upon the side of it, between birch trees, with the hills above, pleased us much. The scene was as remote and agreeably wild as could be desired. It was full enough to occupy our minds for the time.

To see Mr Johnson in any new situation is an object of attention to me. As I saw him now for the first time ride along just like Lord Alemoor, I thought of *London, a Poem*, of the *Rambler*, of *The False Alarm*; and I cannot express the ideas which went across my imagination.[240]

A good way up the Loch, I perceived a little hut with an oldish woman at the door of it. I knew it would be a scene for Mr Johnson. So I spoke of it. "Let's go in," said he. So we dismounted, and we and our guides went in. It was a wretched little hovel, of earth only, I think; and for a window had just a hole which was stopped with a piece of turf which could be taken out to let in light. In the middle of the room (or space which we entered) was a fire of peat, the smoke going out at a hole in the roof. She had a pot upon it with goat's flesh boiling. She had at one end, under the same roof but divided with a kind of partition made of wands, a pen or fold in which we saw a good many kids.

Mr Johnson asked me where she slept. I asked one of the guides, who asked her in Erse. She spoke with a kind of high tone. He told us she was afraid we wanted to go to bed to her.[241] This coquetry, or whatever it may be called, of so wretched a like being was truly ludicrous. Mr Johnson and I afterwards made merry upon it. I said it was he who alarmed the poor woman's virtue. "No, sir," said he. "She'll say, 'There came a wicked young fellow, a wild young dog, who I believe would have ravished me had there not been with him a grave old gentleman who repressed him. But when he gets out of the sight of his tutor, I'll warrant you he'll spare no woman he meets, young or old.'"

"No," said I. "She'll say, 'There was a terrible ruffian who would have forced me, had it not been for a gentle, mild-looking youth, who, I take it, was an angel.'"

Mr Johnson would not hurt her delicacy by insisting to 'see her bedchamber', like Archer in *The Beaux' Stratagem*.[242] But I was of a more ardent curiosity, so I lighted a piece of paper and went into the place where the bed was. There was a little partition of wicker, rather more neatly done than the one for the fold, and close by the wall was a kind of bedstead of wood with heath upon it for a bed; and at the foot of it I saw some sort of blankets or covering rolled up in a heap.

The woman's name was Fraser. So was her husband's. He was a man of eighty. Mr Fraser of Balnain allows him to live in this hut and to keep sixty goats for taking care of his wood. He was then in the wood. They had five children, the oldest only thirteen. Two were gone to Inverness to buy meal. The rest were looking after the goats. She had four stacks of barley, twenty-four sheaves in each. They had a few fowls. They will live all the spring without meal upon milk and curds and whey alone. What they get for their goats, kids, and hens maintains them. I did not observe how the children lay.

She asked us to sit down and take a dram. I saw one chair. She said she was as happy as any woman in Scotland. She could hardly speak any English, just detached words. Mr Johnson was pleased at seeing for the first time such a state of human life. She asked for snuff. It is her luxury. She uses a great deal. We had none, but gave her sixpence apiece. She then brought out her whisky bottle. I tasted it, and Joseph and our guides had some. So I gave her sixpence more. She sent us away with many prayers in Erse.

We came to dinner to a public house called the General's Hut, from General Wade, who was lodged there when he commanded in the North. Near it is the meanest parish kirk I ever saw.[243] It is a shame it should be on a high road. We had mutton-chops, a broiled chicken, and bacon and eggs, and a bottle of Malaga.

After dinner we had a good deal of mountainous country. I had known Mr Trapaud, the deputy governour of Fort Augustus, twelve years ago, at a Circuit at Inverness, where my father was judge. I sent forward one of our guides and Joseph with a card to him, that he might know Mr Johnson and I were coming up, leaving it to him to invite us or not.

It was dark when we got up. The inn was wretched. Government ought to build one, or give the Governor an additional salary, as he must necessarily be put to a great expense in entertaining travellers. Joseph announced to us when we lighted that the Governor waited for us at the gate. We walked towards it. He met us, and with much civility conducted us to his house. It was comfortable to find ourselves in a well-built little square, a neat well-furnished house with prints, etc., a good supper (fricassee of moor-fowl, etc.); in short, with all the conveniencies of civilized life in the midst of rude mountains.

Mrs Trapaud and the Governor's daughter and her husband, Captain Newmarsh, were all most obliging and polite. The Governor, though near seventy, had excellent animal spirits, the conversation of a soldier and somewhat of a Frenchman, talking with importance of everything, however small. He is brother to General Cyrus Trapaud. We passed a very agreeable evening till twelve, and then went to bed.

TUESDAY 31 AUGUST. The Governor has a very neat garden. We looked at it and all the rest of the Fort, which is but small and may be commanded from a variety of hills around. We also looked at the galley or sloop belonging to the Fort, which sails upon the Loch and brings what is wanted for the garrison. Captains Ourry and D'Aripé and Lieutenant Letch breakfasted with us.[244] The two former had been in the American War, and entertained Mr Johnson much with accounts of the Indians. He said he could make a very pretty book out of them were he to stay there.

Governor Trapaud was much struck with Mr Johnson. "I like to hear him talk," said he. "It is so majestic. I should be glad to hear him speak in your Court." He wanted us to stay dinner. But I considered that we had a rude road before us, which we could easier encounter in the morning, and that it was hard to say when we might get up were we to sit down to good entertainment and good company. I therefore begged the Governor would just let us slip away. Here too I had the satisfaction of another proof how much my father is regarded. The Governor expressed the highest respect for him, and bid me tell him that if he would come that way on a Circuit to Inverness, he would do him all the honours in his power.

Between twelve and one we set out and travelled eleven wild miles till we came to a house in Glenmoriston, called Anoch, kept by one Macqueen.[245] Our landlord was a sensible fellow. He had learnt his grammar, and Mr Johnson justly observed that a man is the better for that as long as he lives. There were some books here: a treatise against drunkenness, translated from the French, a volume of the *Spectator*, a volume of Prideaux' *Connexion*, *Cyrus's Travels*.[246] Macqueen said he had more volumes, and his pride seemed to be much piqued that we were surprised at his having books.

Near to this, we had passed a party of soldiers under a sergeant at work upon the road. We gave them two shillings to drink. They came to this house and made merry in the barn. We went out, Mr Johnson saying, "Come, let's go and give 'em another shilling apiece." We did so, and he was saluted "My Lord" by all of 'em. He is really generous, loves influence, and has the way of gaining it. He said he was quite feudal. Here I agree with him. I said I regretted I was not head of a clan. I would make my tenants follow me. I could not be a *patriarchal* chief. But I'd be a *feudal* chief.

The poor soldiers got too much liquor. Some of 'em fought and left blood upon the spot, and cursed whisky next morning. The house here was built of thick turfs and thatched with thinner turfs and heath. It had three rooms in length, and a little room projected. Where we sat, the side-walls were *wainscotted*, as Mr Johnson said, with wands very well plaited. Our landlord had made all with his own hand. We had a broiled chicken, mutton collops or chops, mutton sausage, and eggs, of which Mr Johnson eat five and nothing else. I eat four, some chicken and some sausage, and drank some rum and water and sugar. Joseph had lemons for Mr Johnson, so he had lemonade. Mr Johnson said he was a fine fellow: a civil man and a wise man.

Macqueen, our landlord, sat by us awhile and talked with us. He said all Glenmoriston's people would bleed for him if they were well used. But that seventy men had gone out of the Glen to America. That he himself intended to go next year, for that his farm, which twenty-five years ago was only £5 a year, was now raised to £20. That he could pay £10 and live, but no more. Mr Johnson said he wished Macqueen Laird of Glenmoriston, and Glenmoriston to go to America. Macqueen very generously said he should be sorry for it, for Glenmoriston could not shift for himself in America as he could do.[247]

I talked of the officers whom we had left today: how much service they had seen and how little they got for it, even of fame. Mr Johnson said, "Sir, a soldier gets as little as any man can get." I observed that Goldsmith had more fame than all the officers last war who were not generals. JOHNSON. "Why, sir, you will get ten thousand to do what they did before you get one who does what Goldsmith has done. You must consider a thing is valued according to its rarity. A pebble that paves the street is in itself more useful than the diamond upon a lady's finger." I wish Goldie had heard this.

He said yesterday when I wondered how John Hay, one of our guides, who had been pressed aboard a man-of-war, did not choose to continue longer than nine months, after which time he got off: "Why, sir, no man will be a sailor who has contrivance to get himself into a jail, for being in a ship is being in a jail with the chance of being drowned."

We had tea in the afternoon, and our landlord's daughter, a modest civil girl very neatly dressed, made it to us. She told us she had been a year at Inverness and learnt reading and writing, sewing, knotting, working lace, and pastry. Mr Johnson made her a present of a book of arithmetic which he had bought at Inverness.[248]

The room had some deals laid as a kind of ceiling. There were two beds in the room. A woman's gown was hung on a rope to make a curtain of separation between them. Joseph had the sheets which we brought with us laid on them. We had much hesitation whether to undress or lie down with our clothes on. I said at last, "I'll plunge in! I shall have less room for vermin to settle about me when I strip!"

Mr Johnson said he was like one hesitating whether to go into the cold bath. At last he resolved too. I observed he might serve a campaign. Said he, "I could do all that can be done by patience. Whether I should have strength enough, I know not."

He was in excellent humour. To see the Rambler as I saw him tonight was really a curiosity. I yesterday told him I was thinking to write an Epistle to him *on his return from Scotland*, in the style of Mrs Gulliver to Captain Lemuel Gulliver, on his return to England from the country of the *Houyhnhnms*:

> *At early morn I to the market haste,*
> *Studious in ev'ry thing to please thy taste.*
> *A* curious *fowl* and *sparagrass I chose;*
> *(For I remember you were fond of those:)*
> *Three shillings cost the first, the last sev'n groats;*
> *Sullen you turn from both, and call for* oats.[249]

He laughed and asked in whose name I'd write it. I said Mrs Thrale's. He was angry and said, "Sir, if you have any sense of decency or delicacy, you won't do that."

"Then," said I, "let it be Cole, the landlord of the Mitre Tavern."

"Ay, that may do," said he.

Tonight each offered up his private devotions. After we had chatted a little from our beds, Mr Johnson said, "GOD bless us both for Jesus Christ's sake. Good night." I pronounced "Amen." Mr Johnson fell asleep immediately. I could not have that good fortune for a long time. I fancied myself bit by innumerable vermin under the clothes, and that a spider was travelling from the *wainscot* towards my mouth. At last I fell into insensibility.

WEDNESDAY 1 SEPTEMBER. I awaked very early. I began to imagine that the landlord, being about to emigrate, might murder us to get our money and lay it upon the soldiers in the barn. Such groundless fears will arise in the mind before it has resumed its vigour after sleep! Mr Johnson had had the same kind of ideas; for he told me afterwards that he considered so many soldiers, having seen us, would be witnesses should any harm be done; and the thought of that, I suppose, he considered would make us secure.[250] When I got up, I found him sound asleep in his miserable sty, I may say, with a coloured handkerchief tied round his head. With difficulty could I get him up. It put me in mind of Henry IV's fine soliloquy on sleep; for to be sure there was here an 'uneasy pallet' with a witness.[251]

Wednesday 1 September

A redcoat of the 15th regiment, whether officer or only sergeant I could not be sure, came to the house in his way to the mountains to shoot deer, which it seems Glenmoriston does not hinder anybody to do. Few indeed can do them harm. We had him to breakfast with us. We got away about eight. Macqueen walked some miles to give us a convoy. He had joined Prince Charles at Fort Augustus, and continued in the Highland army till after the battle of Culloden. As he narrated the particulars of that unlucky but brave and generous attempt, I several times burst into tears. There is a certain association of ideas in my mind upon that subject, by which I am strongly affected. The very Highland names, or the sound of a bagpipe, will stir my blood and fill me with a mixture of melancholy, and respect for courage; and pity for an unfortunate, and superstitious regard for antiquity; and inclination for war without thought; and, in short, with a crowd of sensations.[252]

We passed through Glen Shiel, with prodigious mountains on each side. We saw where the battle was in the year 1719. Mr Johnson owned he was now in a scene of as wild nature as he could see. But he corrected me sometimes in my observations. "There," said I, "is a mountain like a cone."[253]

"No, sir," said he. "It would be called so in a book; and when a man comes to look at it, he sees 'tis not so. It is indeed pointed at the top. But one side of it is much longer than the other."

Another mountain I called immense. "No," said he, "but 'tis a considerable protuberance."

We came to a rich green valley, comparatively speaking, and stopped at Auchnashiel, a kind of rural village, a number of cottages being built together, as we saw all along in the Highlands.[254] We passed many many miles today without seeing a house, but only little summer-huts or *shielings*. Ewan Campbell, servant to Mr Murchison, factor to the Laird of MacLeod in Glenelg, run along with us today. He was a fine obliging little fellow. At this Auchnashiel, we sat down on a green turf seat at the end of a house, and they brought us out two wooden dishes of milk. One of them was frothed like a sillabub. I saw a woman preparing it with such a stick as is used for chocolate, and in the same manner.[255] That dish fell to my share; but I put by the froth and took the cream with some wheat-bread which Joseph had brought for us from Fort Augustus. Mr Johnson imagined my dish was better than his, and desired to taste it. He did so, and was convinced that I had no advantage over him. We had there in a circle all about us, men, women and children, all Macraes, Lord Seaforth's people. Not one of them could speak English. I said to

Mr Johnson 'twas the same as being with a tribe of Indians. "Yes," said he, "but not so terrifying."

I gave all who chose it snuff and tobacco. Governor Trapaud had made us buy a quantity at Fort Augustus and put them up in small parcels. I also gave each person a bit of wheat-bread, which they had never tasted. I then gave a penny apiece to each child. I told Mr Johnson of this, upon which he called to Joseph and our guides, for change for a shilling, and declared that he would distribute among the children. Upon this being announced in Erse, there was a great stir: not only did some children come running down from neighbouring huts, but I observed one black-headed man, who had been among us all along, coming carrying a very young child. Mr Johnson then ordered the children to be drawn up in a row, and he distributed his copper and made them and their parents all happy. The poor Macraes, whatever may be their present state, were much thought of in the year 1715, when there was a line in a song, "And aw' the brave McCraas is coming."[256] There was great diversity in the faces of the circle around us. Some were as black and wild in their appearance as any American savages whatever. One woman was as comely as the figure of Sappho, as we see it painted. We asked the old woman, the mistress of the house where we had the milk (which, by the by, Mr Johnson told me, for I did not observe it myself, was built not of turf but of stone), what we should pay. She said, what we pleased. One of our guides asked her in Erse if a shilling was enough. She said, "Yes." But some of the men bid her ask more. This vexed me, because it showed a desire to impose upon strangers, as they knew that even a shilling was high payment. The woman, however, honestly persisted in her first price. So I gave her half-a-crown. Thus we had one good scene of life uncommon to us. The people were very much pleased, gave us many blessings, and said they had not had such a day since the old Laird of MacLeod's time.

Mr Johnson was much refreshed by this repast. He was pleased when I told him he would make a good chief. He said if he were one, he would dress his servants better than himself, and knock a fellow down if he looked saucy to a Macdonald in rags. But he would not treat men as brutes. He would let them know why all of his clan were to have attention paid to them. He would tell his upper servants why, and make them tell the others.

We rode on well till we came to the high mountain called the Rattachan, by which time both Mr Johnson and the horses were a good deal fatigued. It is a terrible steep to climb, notwithstanding the road is made slanting along. However, we made it out. On the top of it we met Captain MacLeod of Balmeanach (a Dutch officer come from Skye) riding with his sword slung about him.[257] He asked, "Is this Mr Boswell?" which was a proof that we were expected.

Going down the hill on the other side was no easy task. As Mr Johnson was a great weight, the two guides agreed that he should ride the horses alternately. Hay's were the two best, and Mr Johnson would not ride but upon one or other of them, a black or a brown. But as Hay complained much after ascending the Rattachan, Mr Johnson was prevailed with to mount one of Vass's greys. As he rode upon it downhill, it did not go well, and he grumbled. I walked on a little before, but was excessively entertained with the method taken to keep him in good humour. Hay led the horse's head, talking to Mr Johnson as much as he could; and (having heard him, in the forenoon, express a pastoral pleasure on seeing the goats browsing) just when Mr Johnson was uttering his displeasure, the fellow says, "See such pretty goats." Then *whu!* he whistled, and made them jump.

Little did he conceive what Mr Johnson was. Here was now a common ignorant horse-hirer imagining that he could divert, as one does a child, *Mr Samuel Johnson*! The ludicrousness, absurdity, and extraordinary contrast between what the fellow fancied and the reality, was as highly comic as anything that I ever witnessed. I laughed immoderately, and must laugh as often as I recollect it.

It grew dusky; and we had a very tedious ride for what was called five miles, but I am sure would measure ten. We spoke none. I was riding forward to the inn at Glenelg, that I might make some kind of preparation, or take some proper measures, before Mr Johnson got up, who was now advancing in silence, with Hay leading his horse. Vass also walked by the side of his horse, and Joseph followed behind: as therefore he was thus attended, and seemed to be in deep meditation, I thought there could be no harm in leaving him for a little while. He called me back with a tremendous shout, and was really in a passion with me for leaving him. I told him my intentions. But he was not satisfied, and said, "Do you know, I should as soon have thought of picking a pocket as doing so."

"I'm diverted with you," said I.

Said he, "I could never be diverted with incivility." He said doing such a thing made one lose confidence in him who did it, as one could not tell what he would do next. His extraordinary warmth confounded me so much, that I justified myself but lamely to him. But my intentions

Wednesday 1 September

were not improper. I wished to be forward to see if Sir A. Macdonald had sent his boat; and if not, how we were to sail, and how we were to lodge, all which I thought I could best settle myself, without his having any trouble. To apply his great mind to minute particulars is wrong. It is like taking an immense balance, such as you see on a quay for weighing cargoes of ships, to weigh a guinea. I knew I had neat little scales which would do better. That his attention to everything in his way, and his uncommon desire to be always in the right, would make him weigh if he knew of the particulars; and therefore it was right for me to weigh them and let him have them only in effect. I kept by him, since he thought I should.

As we passed the barracks at Bernera, I would fain have put up there; at least I looked at them wishfully, as soldiers have always everything in the best order. But there was only a sergeant and a few men there.

We came on to the inn at Glenelg. There was nothing to give the horses, so they were sent to grass with a man to watch them. We found that Sir Alexander had sent his boat to a point which we had passed, at Kintail, or more properly at the King's house – that it had waited several days till their provisions run short, and had returned only this day.[258] So we had nothing to say against that Knight. A lass showed us upstairs into a room raw and dirty; bare walls, a variety of bad smells, a coarse black fir greasy table, forms of the same kind, and from a wretched bed started a fellow from his sleep like Edgar in *King Lear*: "Poor Tom's a-cold."[259]

The landlord was one Munro from Fort Augustus. He pays £8 to MacLeod for the shell of the house, and has not a bit of land in lease. They had no bread, no eggs, no wine, no spirits but whisky, no sugar but brown grown black. They prepared some mutton-chops, but we would not have them. They killed two hens. I made Joseph broil me a bit of one till it was black, and I tasted it. Mr Johnson would take nothing but a bit of bread, which we had luckily remaining, and some lemonade which he made with a lemon which Joseph had for him, and he got some good sugar; for Mr Murchison, factor to MacLeod in Glenelg, sent us some, with a bottle of excellent rum, letting us know he was very sorry that his servant had not come and informed him before we passed his house; that we might have been there all night, and that if he were not obliged to set out early next day for Inverness, he would come down and wait upon us. Such extraordinary attention from this gentleman, to entire strangers, deserves the most honourable commemoration. I took some rum and water and sugar, and grew better; for after my last bad night I hoped much to be well this, and being disappointed, I was uneasy and almost fretful. Mr Johnson was calm. I said he was so from vanity. "No," said he, "'tis from philosophy."

It was a considerable satisfaction to me to see that the Rambler could practise what he nobly teaches. I resumed my riding forward, and wanted to defend it. Mr Johnson was still violent upon that subject, and said, "Sir, had you gone on, I was thinking that I should have returned with you to Edinburgh and then parted, and never spoke to you more."

I sent for fresh hay, with which we made beds to ourselves, each in a room equally miserable. As Wolfe said in his letter from Quebec, we had 'choice of difficulties'.[260] Mr Johnson made things better by comparison. At Macqueen's last night he observed that few were so well lodged in a ship. Tonight he said we were better than if we had been upon the hill. He lay down buttoned up in his greatcoat. I had my sheets spread on the hay, and having stripped, I had my clothes and greatcoat and Joseph's greatcoat laid upon me, by way of blankets. Joseph lay in the room by me, upon a bed laid on the floor.

THURSDAY 2 SEPTEMBER. I had slept ill. Mr Johnson's anger had affected me much. I considered that, without any bad intention, I might suddenly forfeit his friendship. I was impatient to see him this morning. I told him how uneasy he had made me by what he had said.[261] He owned it was said in passion; that he would not have done it; that if he had done it, he would have been ten times worse than me. That it would indeed, as I said, be 'limning in water', should such sudden breaks happen (or something to that effect);[262] and said he, "Let's think no more on't." BOSWELL. "Well then, sir, I shall be easy. Remember, I am to have fair warning in case of any quarrel. You are never to spring a mine upon me. It was absurd in me to believe you." JOHNSON. "You deserved about as much as to believe it from night to morning."

Mr MacLeod of Drynoch, to whom we had a letter from Kenneth Macaulay, breakfasted with us. A quarter before nine we got into a boat for Skye.

CHAPTER THREE

Skye

———————

SAMUEL JOHNSON

In the morning, September the second, we found ourselves on the edge of the sea. Having procured a boat, we dismissed our Highlanders, whom I would recommend to the service of any future travellers, and were ferried over to the Isle of Sky. We landed at *Armidel*, where we were met on the sands by Sir Alexander Macdonald, who was at that time there with his lady, preparing to leave the island and reside at Edinburgh.[263]

Armidel is a neat house, built where the *Macdonalds* had once a seat, which was burnt in the commotions that followed the Revolution. The walled orchard, which belonged to the former house, still remains. It is well shaded by tall ash trees, of a species, as Mr Janes the fossilist informed me, uncommonly valuable. This plantation is very properly mentioned by Dr *Campbell*, in his new account of the state of *Britain*, and deserves attention; because it proves that the present nakedness of the *Hebrides* is not wholly the fault of Nature.[264]

As we sat at Sir Alexander's table, we were entertained, according to the ancient usage of the North, with the melody of the bagpipe. Every thing in those countries has its history. As the bagpiper was playing, an elderly Gentleman informed us, that in some remote time, the *Macdonalds* of Glengary having been injured, or offended by the inhabitants of *Culloden*, and resolving to have justice or vengeance, came to *Culloden* on a Sunday, where finding their enemies at worship, they shut them up in the church, which they set on fire; and this, said he, is the tune that the piper played while they were burning.[265]

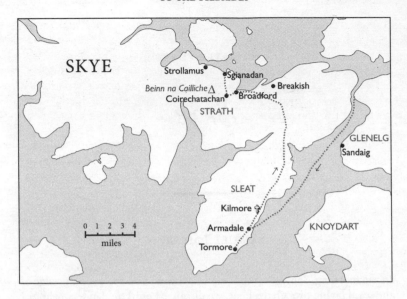

Narrations like this, however uncertain, deserve the notice of a traveller, because they are the only records of a nation that has no historians, and afford the most genuine representation of the life and character of the ancient Highlanders.

Under the denomination of *Highlander* are comprehended in Scotland all that now speak the Erse language, or retain the primitive manners, whether they live among the mountains or in the islands; and in that sense I use the name, when there is not some apparent reason for making a distinction.

In *Sky* I first observed the use of Brogues, a kind of artless shoes, stitched with thongs so loosely, that though they defend the foot from stones, they do not exclude water. Brogues were formerly made of raw hides, with the hair inwards, and such are perhaps still used in rude and remote parts; but they are said not to last above two days. Where life is somewhat improved, they are now made of leather tanned with oak bark, as in other places, or with the bark of birch, or roots of tormentil, a substance recommended in defect of bark, about forty years ago, to the Irish tanners, by one to whom the parliament of that kingdom voted a reward.[266] The leather of *Sky* is not completely penetrated by vegetable matter, and therefore cannot be very durable.

My inquiries about brogues, gave me an early specimen of Highland information. One day I was told, that to make brogues was a domestick art, which every man practised for himself, and that a pair of brogues was the work of an hour. I supposed that the husband made brogues as the wife made an apron, till next day it was told me, that a brogue-maker was a trade, and that a pair would cost half a crown. It will easily occur that these representations may both be true, and that, in some places, men may buy them, and in others, make them for themselves; but I had both the accounts in the same house within two days.

Many of my subsequent inquiries upon more interesting topicks ended in the like uncertainty. He that travels in the Highlands may easily saturate his soul with intelligence, if he will acquiesce in the first account. The Highlander gives to every question an answer so prompt and peremptory, that skepticism itself is dared into silence, and the mind sinks before the bold reporter in unresisting credulity; but, if a second question be ventured, it breaks the enchantment; for it is immediately discovered, that what was told so confidently was told at hazard, and that such fearlessness of assertion was either the sport of negligence, or the refuge of ignorance.

If individuals are thus at variance with themselves, it can be no wonder that the accounts of different men are contradictory. The traditions of an ignorant and savage people have been for ages negligently heard, and unskilfully related. Distant events must have been mingled together, and the actions of one man given to another. These, however, are deficiencies in story, for which no man is now to be censured. It were enough, if what there is yet opportunity of examining were accurately inspected, and justly represented; but such is the laxity of Highland conversation, that the inquirer is kept in continual suspense, and by a kind of intellectual retrogradation, knows less as he hears more.

In the islands the plaid is rarely worn. The law by which the Highlanders have been obliged to change the form of their dress, has, in all the places that we have visited, been universally obeyed. I have seen only one gentleman completely clothed in the ancient habit, and by him it was worn only occasionally and wantonly. The common people do not think themselves under any legal necessity of having coats; for they say that the law against plaids was made by Lord Hardwicke, and was in force only for his life: but the same poverty that made it then difficult for them to change their clothing, hinders them now from changing it again.

The fillibeg, or lower garment, is still very common, and the bonnet almost universal; but their attire is such as produces, in a sufficient degree, the effect intended by the law, of abolishing the dissimilitude of appearance between the Highlanders and the other inhabitants of Britain; and, if dress be supposed to have much influence, facilitates their coalition with their fellow-subjects.[267]

What we have long used we naturally like, and therefore the Highlanders were unwilling to lay aside their plaid, which yet to an unprejudiced spectator must appear an incommodious and cumbersome dress; for hanging loose upon the body, it must flutter in a quick motion, or require one of the hands to keep it close. The Romans always laid aside the gown when they had any thing to do. It was a dress so unsuitable to war, that the same word which signified a gown signified peace. The chief use of a plaid seems to be this, that they could commodiously wrap themselves in it, when they were obliged to sleep without a better cover.

In our passage from *Scotland* to *Sky*, we were wet for the first time with a shower. This was the beginning of the Highland winter, after which we were told that a succession of three dry days was not to be expected for many months. The winter of the *Hebrides* consists of little more than rain and wind. As they are surrounded by an ocean never frozen, the blasts that come to them over the water are too much softened to have the power of congelation. The salt loughs, or inlets of the sea, which shoot very far into the island, never have any ice upon them, and the pools of fresh water will never bear the walker. The snow that sometimes falls, is soon dissolved by the air, or the rain.

This is not the description of a cruel climate, yet the dark months are here a time of great distress; because the summer can do little more than feed itself, and winter comes with its cold and its scarcity upon families very slenderly provided.

The third or fourth day after our arrival at *Armidel*, brought us an invitation to the isle of *Raasay*, which lies east of *Sky*. It is incredible how soon the account of any event is propagated in these narrow countries by the love of talk, which much leisure produces, and the relief given to the mind in the penury of insular conversation by a new topick. The arrival of strangers at a place so rarely visited, excites rumour, and quickens curiosity. I know not whether we touched at any corner, where Fame had not already prepared us a reception.

To gain a commodious passage to *Raasay*, it was necessary to pass over a large part of *Sky*. We were furnished therefore with horses and a guide. In the islands there are no roads, nor any marks by which a stranger may find his way. The horseman has always at his side a native of the place, who, by pursuing game, or tending cattle, or being often employed in messages or conduct, has learned where the ridge of the hill has breadth sufficient to allow a horse and his rider a passage, and where the moss or bog is hard enough to bear them. The bogs are avoided as toilsome at least, if not unsafe, and therefore the journey is made generally from precipice to precipice; from which if the eye ventures to look down, it sees below a gloomy cavity, whence the rush of water is sometimes heard.

But there seems to be in all this more alarm than danger. The Highlander walks carefully before, and the horse, accustomed to the ground, follows him with little deviation. Sometimes the hill is too steep for the horseman to keep his seat, and sometimes the moss is too tremulous to bear the double weight of horse and man. The rider then dismounts, and all shift as they can.

Journies made in this manner are rather tedious than long. A very few miles require several hours. From *Armidel* we came at night to *Coriatachan*, a house very pleasantly situated between two brooks, with one of the highest hills of the island behind it. It is the residence of Mr *Mackinnon*, by whom we were treated with very liberal hospitality, among a more numerous and elegant company than it could have been supposed easy to collect.[268]

The hill behind the house we did not climb. The weather was rough, and the height and steepness discouraged us. We were told that there is a cairne upon it. A cairne is a heap of stones thrown upon the grave of one eminent for dignity of birth, or splendour of atchievements. It is said that by digging, an urn is always found under these cairnes: they must therefore have been thus piled by a people whose custom was to burn the dead. To pile stones is, I believe, a northern custom, and to burn the body was the Roman practice; nor do I know when it was that these two acts of sepulture were united.

The weather was next day too violent for the continuation of our journey; but we had no reason to complain of the interruption. We saw in every place, what we chiefly desired to know, the manners of the people. We had company, and, if we had chosen retirement, we might have had books.

I never was in any house of the Islands, where I did not find books in more languages than one, if I staid long enough to want them, except one from which the family was removed.[269] Literature is not neglected by the higher rank of the Hebridians.

It need not, I suppose, be mentioned, that in countries so little frequented as the Islands, there are no houses where travellers are entertained for money. He that wanders about these wilds, either procures recommendations to those whose habitations lie near his way, or, when night and weariness come upon him, takes the chance of general hospitality. If he finds only a cottage, he can expect little more than shelter; for the cottagers have little more for themselves: but if his good fortune brings him to the residence of a gentleman, he will be glad of a storm to prolong his stay. There is, however, one inn by the seaside at Sconsor, in Sky, where the post-office is kept.[270]

At the tables where a stranger is received, neither plenty nor delicacy is wanting. A tract of land so thinly inhabited, must have much wildfowl; and I scarcely remember to have seen a dinner without them. The moorgame is every where to be had. That the sea abounds with fish, needs not be told, for it supplies a great part of Europe. The Isle of *Sky* has stags and roebucks, but no hares. They sell very numerous droves of oxen yearly to England, and therefore cannot be supposed to want beef at home. Sheep and goats are in great numbers, and they have the common domestick fowls.

But as here is nothing to be bought, every family must kill its own meat, and roast part of it somewhat sooner than Apicius would prescribe.[271] Every kind of flesh is undoubtedly excelled by the variety and emulation of English markets; but that which is not best may be yet very far from bad, and he that shall complain of his fare in the *Hebrides*, has improved his delicacy more than his manhood.

Their fowls are not like those plumped for sale by the poulterers of London, but they are as good as other places commonly afford, except that the geese, by feeding in the sea, have universally a fishy rankness.

These geese seem to be of a middle race, between the wild and domestick kinds. They are so tame as to own a home, and so wild as sometimes to fly quite away.

Their native bread is made of oats, or barley. Of oatmeal they spread very thin cakes, coarse and hard, to which unaccustomed palates are not easily reconciled. The barley cakes are thicker and softer; I began to eat them without unwillingness; the blackness of their colour raises some dislike, but the taste is not disagreeable.[272] In most houses there is wheat flower, with which we were sure to be treated, if we staid long enough to have it kneaded and baked. As neither yeast nor leaven are used among them, their bread of every kind is unfermented. They make only cakes, and never mould a loaf.

A man of the Hebrides, for of the women's diet I can give no account, as soon as he appears in the morning, swallows a glass of whisky; yet they are not a drunken race, at least I never was present at much intemperance;

but no man is so abstemious as to refuse the morning dram, which they call a *skalk*.[273]

The word *whisky* signifies water, and is applied by way of eminence to *strong water*, or distilled liquor. The spirit drunk in the North is drawn from barley. I never tasted it, except once for experiment at the inn in *Inverary*, when I thought it preferable to any *English* malt brandy.[274] It was strong, but not pungent, and was free from the empyreumatick taste or smell. What was the process I had no opportunity of inquiring, nor do I wish to improve the art of making poison pleasant.

Not long after the dram, may be expected the breakfast, a meal in which the Scots, whether of the lowlands or mountains, must be confessed to excel us. The tea and coffee are accompanied not only with butter, but with honey, conserves, and marmalades. If an epicure could remove by a wish, in quest of sensual gratifications, wherever he had supped he would breakfast in Scotland.

In the islands however, they do what I found it not very easy to endure. They pollute the tea-table by plates piled with large slices of cheshire cheese, which mingles its less grateful odours with the fragrance of the tea.[275]

Where many questions are to be asked, some will be omitted. I forgot to inquire how they were supplied with so much exotic luxury. Perhaps the French may bring them wine for wool, and the Dutch give them tea and coffee at the fishing season, in exchange for fresh provision. Their trade is unconstrained; they pay no customs, for there is no officer to demand them; whatever therefore is made dear only by impost, is obtained here at an easy rate.

A dinner in the Western Islands differs very little from a dinner in *England*, except that in the place of tarts, there are always set different preparations of milk. This part of their diet will admit some improvement. Though they have milk, and eggs, and sugar, few of them know how to compound them in a custard. Their gardens afford them no great variety, but they have always some vegetables on the table. Potatoes at least are never wanting, which, though they have not known them long, are now one of the principal parts of their food.[276] They are not of the mealy, but the viscous kind.

Their more elaborate cookery, or made dishes, an Englishman at the first taste is not likely to approve, but the culinary compositions of every country are often such as become grateful to other nations only by degrees; though I have read a French author, who, in the elation of his heart, says, that French cookery pleases all foreigners, but foreign cookery never satisfies a Frenchman.

Their suppers are, like their dinners, various and plentiful. The table is always covered with elegant linen. Their plates for common use are often of that kind of manufacture which is called cream coloured, or queen's ware.[277] They use silver on all occasions where it is common in *England*, nor did I ever find the spoon of horn, but in one house.

The knives are not often either very bright, or very sharp. They are indeed instruments of which the Highlanders have not been long acquainted with the general use. They were not regularly laid on the table, before the prohibition of arms, and the change of dress. Thirty years ago the Highlander wore his knife as a companion to his dirk or dagger, and when the company sat down to meat, the men who had knives, cut the flesh into small pieces for the women, who with their fingers conveyed it to their mouths.[278]

There was perhaps never any change of national manners so quick, so great, and so general, as that which has operated in the Highlands, by the last conquest, and the subsequent laws. We came thither too late to see what we expected, a people of peculiar appearance, and a system of antiquated life. The clans retain little now of their original character, their ferocity of temper is softened, their military ardour is extinguished, their dignity of independence is depressed, their contempt of government subdued, and their reverence for their chiefs abated. Of what they had before the late conquest of their country, there remain only their language and their poverty. Their language is attacked on every side. Schools are erected, in which *English* only is taught, and there were lately some who thought it reasonable to refuse them a version of the holy scriptures, that they might have no monument of their mother-tongue.[279]

That their poverty is gradually abated, cannot be mentioned among the unpleasing consequences of subjection. They are now acquainted with money, and the possibility of gain will by degrees make them industrious. Such is the effect of the late regulations, that a longer journey than to the Highlands must be taken by him whose curiosity pants for savage virtues and barbarous grandeur.

At the first intermission of the stormy weather we were informed, that the boat, which was to convey us to *Raasay*, attended us on the coast. We had from this time our intelligence facilitated, and our conversation enlarged, by the company of Mr Macqueen, minister of a parish in *Sky*, whose knowledge and politeness give him a title equally to kindness and respect, and who, from this time, never forsook us till we were preparing to leave Sky, and the adjacent places.

James Boswell

It rained much when we set off, but cleared up as we advanced. One of the boatmen who spoke English said that a mile at land was two miles at sea. I then said to him that from Glenelg to Armadale in Skye, which was our sail this morning and is called twelve, was only six miles. But this he could not understand. "Well," said Mr Johnson, "never talk to me of the native good sense of the Highlanders. Here is a fellow who calls one mile two, and yet cannot comprehend that twelve such miles make but six."

It was curious to think that now at last Mr Johnson and I had left the mainland of Scotland and were sailing to the Hebrides, one of which was close in our view; and I had besides a number of youthful ideas, that is to say, ideas which I have had from my youth about the Isle of Skye. We were shown the land of Moidart where Prince Charles first landed. That stirred my mind.

We reached the shore of Armadale before one. Sir Alexander came down and received us. He was in tartan clothes. My lady stood at the top of the bank and made a kind of jumping for joy.[280] They were then in a house built by a tenant at this place, which is in the district of Sleat. There was a house here for the family, which was burnt in Sir Donald's time.[281] But there is really a good garden and a number of trees of age and size, mostly ash, and that too of a particular kind, the wood of which is very compact. There is a kind of recess here of land, as well as a kind of bay of the sea, more indeed the former. It is a pretty warm exposure. There is a little brook runs down from the hill through a tolerable bank of wood. I am a very imperfect topographer. The house is a very good tenant's house, having two storeys and garrets, but seemed very poor for a chief. Mr Johnson and I were to have had but one room. But I made the plan be altered; so one of the beds was taken out of his room and put into the next, in which I and the overseer of the farm were to lie; but happily Joseph was put in the overseer's place.

The most ancient seat of the chief of the Macdonalds in the Isle of Skye was at Duntulm, where there are the remains of a stately castle. The principal residence of the family is now at Mugstot, at which there is a considerable building. Sir Alexander and Lady Macdonald had come to

Armidale in their way to Edinburgh, where it was necessary for them to be soon after this time. Armidale is situated on a pretty bay of the narrow sea, which flows between the main land of Scotland and the Isle of Skye. In front there is a grand prospect of the rude mountains of Moidart and Knoidart. Behind are hills gently rising and covered with a finer verdure than I expected to see in this climate, and the scene is enlivened by a number of little clear brooks. Sir Alexander Macdonald having been an Eton scholar, and being a gentleman of talents, Dr Johnson had been very well pleased with him in London. But my fellow traveller and I were now full of the old Highland spirit, and were dissatisfied at hearing of racked rents and emigration; and finding a chief not surrounded by his clan. Dr Johnson said, "Sir, the Highland chiefs should not be allowed to go farther south than Aberdeen. A strong-minded man, like Sir James Macdonald, may be improved by an English education; but in general, they will be tamed into insignificance."[282]

We had at dinner a little Aberdeenshire man, one Jeans, a naturalist, with his son, a dwarf with crooked legs. Jeans said he had been at Mr Johnson's in London with Ferguson the astronomer. Mr Johnson thought it strange how he found somebody in such distant places who knew him; that he should have thought he might hide himself in Skye. We had also Rorie Macdonald in Sandaig, an old brisk Highlander of 68, a near relation of Sir Alexander's, and his wife, a sister of Raasay's; Donald MacLeod, late of Canna, a very genteel man,[283] and Donald Macdonald, son to Rorie, who was Lieutenant of Grenadiers in Montgomerie's Regiment (I took a liking to him from his first appearance), as also —— Macqueen, son to Rorie's wife by the first marriage, who was going to America, and a Captain MacLeod from Sutherland.

We had an ill-dressed dinner, Sir Alexander not having a cook of any kind from Edinburgh. I alone drank port wine. No claret appeared. We had indeed mountain and Frontignac and Scotch porter. But except what I did myself, there was no hospitable convivial intercourse, no ringing of glasses. Nay, I observed that when Captain Macdonald and Mr Macqueen came in after we were sat down to dinner, Sir Alexander let them stand round the room and stuck his fork into a liver pudding, instead of getting room made for them. I took care to act as he ought to have done. There was no wheat-loaf, but only a kind of bannock or cake, raw in the heart, as it was so thick. Sir Alexander himself drank punch without souring and with little spirits in it, which he distributed to those men who were accustomed even in their own houses to much better. He gave it with a pewter dividing-spoon which had served the broth. At tea there were few cups and no tea-tongs nor a supernumerary tea-spoon, so we used our fingers.

I was quite hurt with the meanness and unsuitable appearance of everything. I meditated setting out the very next day. At night we had only Rorie and spouse and the naturalist and his son. When Mr Johnson and I retired for rest, he said it grieved him to see the chief of a great clan in such a state; that he was just as one in a lodging-house in London. However, he resolved that we should weather it out till Monday.

FRIDAY 3 SEPTEMBER. The day was very wet. Sir Alexander's piper plays below stairs both at breakfast and dinner, which is the only circumstance of a chief to be found about him. He had two chests of books, of which Mr Johnson and I ravenously seized some of the contents. It grew fair a little before dinner, and I took a little walk with Captain Macdonald, from whom I found that Sir Alexander was quite unpopular, and that all his deficiencies were well remarked.[284] I made the Captain drink port wine today. Mrs Macdonald said that I fitted Sir Alexander in several suits better than anybody – a curious expression.[285] I asked her how the old Laird of MacLeod came to be so much in debt. She said, "You may as well read the *Spectator* as begin to tell all that"; and she said it was a pity that this young Laird should lose his *patronomic* estate when he was in no fault; meaning that he was labouring under a load of debt not contracted by himself.[286]

When Sir Alexander was out of the room, I spoke of Sir James. The Highlanders fairly cried. Neither my lady nor Mr Johnson were then present. I cried too, and we drank a bumper to his memory. It was really melancholy to see the manly, gallant, and generous attachment of clanship going to ruin.[287]

Sir Alexander composed today some Latin verses with which he presented Mr Johnson.

> *Viator, o qui nostra per æquora*
> *Visurus agros Skiaticos venis,*
> *En te salutantes tributim*
> *Undique conglomerantur oris.*
>
> *Donaldiani,—quotquot in insulis*
> *Compescit arctis limitibus mare;*
> *Alitque jamdudum, ac alendos*
> *Piscibus indigenas fovebit.*

Ciere fluctus siste, Procelliger,
Nec tu laborans perge, precor, ratis,
Ne conjugem plangat marita,
Ne doleat suboles parentem.

Nec te vicissim pæniteat virum
Luxisse;—vestro scimus ut æstuant
In corde luctantes dolores,
Cum feriant inopina corpus.

Quidni! peremptum clade tuentibus
Plus semper illo qui moritur pati
Datur, doloris dum profundos
Pervia mens aperit recessus.

Valete luctus;—hinc lacrimabiles
Arcete visus:—ibimus, ibimus
Superbienti qua theatro
Fingaliæ memorantur aulæ.

Illustris hospes! mox spatiabere
Qua mens ruinæ ducta meatibus
Gaudebit explorare cætus,
Buccina qua cecinit triumphos.

Audin? resurgens spirat anhelitu
Dux usitato, suscitat efficax
Poeta manes, ingruitque
Vi solita redivivus horror.

Ahaena quassans tela gravi manu
Sic ibat atrox Ossiani pater:
Quiescat urna, stet fidelis
Phersonius vigil ad favillam.[288]

After dinner the Knight and I met in Mr Johnson's room, where I was looking for pen and ink. I fell upon him with perhaps too great violence upon his behaviour to his people; on the meanness of his appearance here; upon my lady's neither having a maid, nor being dressed better than one. In short, I gave him a volley. He was thrown into a violent passion; said he could not bear it; called in my lady and complained to her, at the same time defending himself with considerable plausibility. Had he been a man of more mind, he and I must have had a quarrel for life. But I knew he would soon come to himself. We had moor-fowl for supper tonight, which comforted me.

Friday 3 September

We were advised by Rorie, by Donald MacLeod, and everybody to visit Raasay in our way to Dunvegan, MacLeod's house, to which we looked wishfully forward as expecting more elegance and propriety. The Rev. Mr Donald Macqueen I heard was the most intelligent man in the island. Sir Alexander should have had him here with us. I had a letter to him from Sir James Foulis.[289] I sent an express to set off early next morning with a letter to him enclosing Sir James's and begging he'd meet us at Raasay on Monday or Tuesday, as also enclosing a card to MacLeod, to inform him that we were to be at Dunvegan.

Mr Johnson was vexed that he could get no distinct information about anything from any of the people here. He wished that a good comedian saw Rorie and his wife, to take from them a Highland scene.[290]

SATURDAY 4 SEPTEMBER. Sir Alexander was in my room before I got up, with a bowl of buttermilk, of which I drank. Our quarrel was already evanished. I set Mr Johnson upon him this morning, who said that in seven years he would make this an independent island; that he'd roast oxen whole and hang out a flag as a signal to the Macdonalds to come and get beef and whisky. Poor Sir Alexander was always starting difficulties. "Nay," said Mr Johnson, "if you're born to object, I have done with you." He would have a magazine of arms. Sir Alexander said they would rust. Said Mr Johnson, "Let there be men to keep them clean. Your ancestors did not use to let their arms rust."[291]

It was in vain to try to inspirit him. Mr Johnson said, "Sir, we shall make nothing of him. He has no more ideas of a chief than an attorney who has twenty houses in a street and considers how much he can make of them. All is wrong. He has nothing to say to the people when they come about him." My beauty of a cousin, too, did not escape. Indeed, I was quite disgusted with her nothingness and insipidity. Mr Johnson said, "This woman would sink a ninety-gun ship. She is so dull – so heavy."[292]

The naturalist and son have been gone two days. Nobody dined today but Rorie and his wife. Rorie was to be dispossessed of his farm in Glenelg at Whitsunday, and was trying to get one from Sir Alexander. He and his wife only dined today. In the afternoon came Rorie's two sons, James the factor and Captain Donald;[293] Norman Macdonald, Sir James's old servant, who was in terms for a farm; and Donald MacLeod. They drank tea. The evening was heavy enough.

SUNDAY 5 SEPTEMBER. Sir Alexander and Rorie and I walked to the parish church of Sleat. It is a poor one; not a loft in it. There are no church-bells in the island. I was told there were once some. What has become of them I could not learn. The minister was from home, so there was no sermon. We went into the church and saw Sir James's monument. It is a very pretty one. The inscription is rather too verbose.[294] Mr Johnson said it should have been in Latin, as everything intended to be universal and permanent should be.

To the memory
Of Sir James Macdonald, Bart.
Who in the flower of youth,
Had attained to so eminent a degree of knowledge
in Mathematics, Philosophy, Languages,
And in every other branch of useful and polite learning,
As few have acquired in a long life
Wholly devoted to study:
Yet to this erudition he joined
What can rarely be found with it,
Great talents for business,
Great propriety of behaviour,
Great politeness of manners!
His eloquence was sweet, correct, and flowing;
His memory vast and exact;
His judgement strong and acute;
All which endowments, united
With the most amiable temper
And every private virtue,
Procured him, not only in his own country,
But also from foreign nations,
The highest marks of esteem.
In the year of our Lord
1766,
The 25th of his life,
After a long and extremely painful illness,
Which he supported with admirable patience and fortitude,
He died at Rome,
Where, notwithstanding the difference of religion,
Such extraordinary honours were paid to his memory,
As had never graced that of any other British subject,
Since the death of Sir Philip Sydney.
The fame he left behind him is the best consolation

To his afflicted family,
And to his countrymen in this isle,
For whose benefit he had planned
Many useful improvements,
Which his fruitful genius suggested,
And his active spirit promoted,
Under the sober direction
Of a clear and enlightened understanding.
Reader, bewail our loss,
And that of all Britain.
In testimony of her love,
And as the best return she can make
To her departed son,
For the constant tenderness and affection
Which, even to his last moments,
He shewed for her,
His much afflicted mother,
The LADY MARGARET MACDONALD,
Daughter to the EARL of EGLINTOUNE,
Erected this Monument,
A.D. 1768.

This extraordinary young man, whom I had the pleasure of knowing intimately, having been deeply regretted by his country, the most minute particulars concerning him must be interesting to many. I shall therefore insert his two last letters to his mother, Lady Margaret Macdonald, which her ladyship has been pleased to communicate to me.

Rome, July 9th, 1766. / MY DEAR MOTHER, / Yesterday's post brought me your answer to the first letter in which I acquainted you of my illness. Your tenderness and concern upon that account are the same I have always experienced, and to which I have often owed my life. Indeed it never was in so great danger as it has been lately; and though it would have been a very great comfort to me to have had you near me, yet perhaps I ought to rejoice, on your account, that you had not the pain of such a spectacle. I have been now a week in Rome, and wish I could continue to give you the same good accounts of my recovery as I did in my last: but I must own that, for three days past, I have been in a very weak and miserable state, which however seems to give no uneasiness to my physician. My stomach has been greatly out of order, without any visible cause; and the palpitation does not decrease. I am told that my stomach will soon recover its tone, and that the palpitation must cease in time. So I am willing to believe; and with this hope support the little remains of spirits which I can be supposed to have, on the forty-seventh day of such an illness. Do not imagine I have relapsed – I only recover slower than I expected. If my letter is shorter than usual, the cause of it is a dose of physick, which has weakened me so much to-day, that I am not able to write a long letter. I will make up for it next post, and remain always / Your most sincerely affectionate son, / J. MACDONALD.

He grew gradually worse; and on the night before his death he wrote as follows from Frescati:

MY DEAR MOTHER, / Though I did not mean to deceive you in my last letter from Rome, yet certainly you would have very little reason to conclude of the very great and constant danger I have gone through ever since that time. My life, which is still almost entirely desperate, did not at that time appear to me so, otherwise I should have represented, in its true colours, a fact which acquires very little horror by that means, and comes with redoubled force by deception. There is no circumstance of danger and pain of which I have not had the experience, for a continued series of above a fortnight; during which time I have settled my affairs, after my death, with as much distinctness as the hurry and the nature of the thing could admit of. In case of the worst, the Abbé Grant will be my executor in this part of the world, and Mr Mackenzie in Scotland, where my object has been to make you and my younger brother as independent of the eldest as possible.

It was a beautiful day. My spirits were cheered by the mere effect of climate. I had felt a return of spleen during my stay in this mean mansion, and had it not been that I had Mr Johnson to contemplate, I should have been very sickly in mind. His firmness kept me steady. I looked at him as a man whose head is turning giddy at sea looks at a rock or any fixed object. I wondered at his tranquillity. He however said, "Sir, when a man retires into an island, he is to turn his thoughts entirely on another world. He has done with this." BOSWELL. "It appears to me, sir, to be very difficult to unite a due attention to this world, and that which is to come; for, if we engage eagerly in the affairs of life, we are apt to be totally forgetful of a future state; and, on the other hand, a steady contemplation of the awful concerns of eternity renders all objects here so insignificant, as to make us indifferent and negligent about them." JOHNSON. "Sir, Dr Cheyne has laid down a rule to himself on this subject, which should be imprinted on every mind: 'To neglect nothing to secure my eternal peace, more than if I had been certified I should die within the day: nor to mind any thing that my secular obligations and duties demanded of me, less than if I had been ensured to live fifty years more.'"[295]

And although Mr Johnson was calm, yet his genius did not shine as in companies where I have listened to him with admiration. It was enough if he was not weak.[296]

I am inclined to think that it was on this day he composed the following *Ode upon the Isle of Sky*, which a few days afterwards he showed me at Raasay:[297]

> *Ponti profundis clausa recessibus,*
> *Strepens procellis, rupibus obsita,*
> *Quam grata defesso virentem*
> *Skia sinum nebulosa pandis.*
>
> *His cura, credo, sedibus exulat;*
> *His blanda certe pax habitat locis:*
> *Non ira, non mœror quietis*
> *Insidias meditatur horis.*
>
> *At non cavata rupe latescere,*
> *Menti nec ægræ montibus aviis*
> *Prodest vagari, nec frementes*
> *E scopulo numerare fluctus.*
>
> *Humana virtus non sibi sufficit,*
> *Datur nec æquum cuique animum sibi*
> *Parare posse, ut Stoicorum*
> *Secta crepet nimis alta fallax.*
>
> *Exæstuantis pectoris impetum,*
> *Rex summe, solus tu regis arbiter,*
> *Mentisque, te tollente, surgunt,*
> *Te recidunt moderante fluctus.*[298]

After dinner Sir Alexander and I walked to Tormore, the house of James Macdonald, his factor. Here we had Rorie's daughter, Miss Katie, a pretty girl enough, Captain Donald, and the rest who were with us yesterday, and drank a couple of bowls of punch. It was dark by the time we got back. I drank freely of punch by way of being social, and after supper I drank freely of port by way of keeping off a *taedium vitae*. Altogether, I had too much.

Mr Johnson told us that Isaac Hawkins Browne drank hard for thirty years, and that he wrote his poem, *De Animi Immortalitate*, in the last of these years. Sir Alexander and I had another dispute tonight upon his method of proceeding, and he was again in a passion.[299]

MONDAY 6 SEPTEMBER. I awaked a good deal uneasy from having drank too much. The morning too was very wet. So I was in bad plight. About noon it cleared, and I grew better. Sir Alexander supplied us with horses, and we set out, accompanied by Mr Donald MacLeod (late of Canna) as our guide.[300]

The day was exceedingly agreeable. We rode for some time along Sleat, near the shore. The houses in general were made just of turf, covered with grass, and the country seemed well peopled. We came into Strath, and passed along a wild moorish tract of land till we came to the shore at Broadford. There we found good verdure and whin-rocks, or collections of stones like the ruins of the foundations of old buildings. We saw, too, three cairns of considerable size. We came on a mile to Coirechatachan, a farm-house of Sir Alexander possessed by Mr Mackinnon,[301] a jolly big man who received us with a kindly welcome.

The house was of two storeys. We were carried into a low parlour, with a carpet on the floor, which we had not seen at Armadale. We had tea in good order, a *trea*, silver tea-pot, silver sugar-dish and tongs, silver tea-spoons enough.[302] Our landlord's father had found a treasure of old silver coins, and of these he had made his plate. Mr Johnson was quite well here. Mrs Mackinnon was a decent well-behaved old gentlewoman in a black silk gown. At night we had of company Coirechatachan and his wife; Mrs Mackinnon, daughter to his wife and widow of his son; Mr Macpherson, minister of Sleat, and his wife, daughter of Coirechatachan; a niece of Coirechatachan's, Miss Mackinnon; Miss Macpherson, sister to the minister; and Dr Macdonald, a physician; as also young Mr Mackinnon, son to Coirechatachan. We had for supper a large dish of minced beef collops, a large dish of fricassee of fowl, I believe a dish called fried chicken or something like it, a dish of ham or tongue, some excellent haddocks, some herrings, a large bowl of rich milk, frothed, as good a bread-pudding as I ever tasted, full of raisins and lemon or orange peel, and sillabubs made with port wine and in sillabub glasses. There was a good table-cloth with napkins; china, silver spoons, porter if we chose it, and a large bowl of very good punch. It was really an agreeable meeting;[303] and we for the first time had a specimen of the joyous social manners of the inhabitants of the Highlands. They talked in their own ancient language, with fluent vivacity, and sung many Erse songs with such spirit, that, though Dr Johnson was treated with the greatest respect and attention, there were moments in which he seemed to be forgotten. For myself, though but a Lowlander, having picked up a few words of the language, I presumed to mingle in their mirth, and joined in the choruses with as much glee as any of the company. Old Coirechatachan had hospitality in his whole behaviour, as had his wife, who was what we call a ladylike woman. Mr Pennant was two nights here. He and young Mackinnon went to the top of Ben Caillich, a very high mountain just by, on the top of which there is a cairn.[304]

Dr Johnson being fatigued with his journey, retired early to his chamber, where he composed the following Ode, addressed to Mrs Thrale:

> Permeo terras, ubi nuda rupes
> Saxeas miscet nebulis ruinas,
> Torva ubi rident steriles coloni
>   Rura labores.
>
> Pervagor gentes, hominum ferorum
> Vita ubi nullo decorata cultu
> Squallet informis, tugurique fumis
>   Fœda latescit.
>
> Inter erroris salebrosa longi,
> Inter ignotæ strepitus loquelæ,
> Quot modis mecum, quid agat, requiro,
>   Thralia dulcis?
>
> Seu viri curas pia nupta mulcet,
> Seu fovet mater sobolem benigna,
> Sive cum libris novitate pascet
>   Sedula mentem;
>
> Sit memor nostri, fideique merces,
> Stet fides constans, meritoque blandum
> Thraliæ discant resonare nomen
>   Littora Skiæ.

Scriptum in Skia, Sept. 6, 1773.[305]

How superior was our reception here to that at Sir Alexander's! Mr Johnson got a good bedroom to himself. When I went upstairs, Mrs Mackinnon received me in an opposite bedroom with three beds in it, and with an air of hearty cordiality said, "Come away and see if you can sleep among a heap of folks"; then kissed me on each side of the face, and bid me good-night. I had a good clean bed with red and white check curtains to myself. In a bed with blue worsted stuff curtains lay Donald MacLeod and Dr Macdonald; in a red one of the same kind, the minister and young Mackinnon.

Monday 6 September

TUESDAY 7 SEPTEMBER. Mr Johnson was much pleased; said we had a genteeler supper than ever we saw at Sir Alexander's. There were several good books here: Hector Boethius in Latin, Cave's *Lives of the Fathers*, Baker's *Chronicle*, Jeremy Collier's *Church History*, Mr Johnson's small Dictionary, several more books; a picture in oil colours, a mezzotinto of Mrs Brooks (by some strange chance in Skye), and a head of Prince Charles in Paris plaster.[306] Also a print of Ranald Macdonald of Clanranald, with a Latin inscription about the Culloden cruelties.[307]

It was a very wet, stormy day. So we were obliged to remain here, as it was impossible to cross the sea to Raasay. Mr Johnson called me to his bed-side this morning, and to my astonishment he *took off* Lady Macdonald leaning forward with a hand on each cheek and her mouth open – quite insipidity on a monument grinning at sense and spirit. To see a beauty represented by Mr Johnson was excessively high. I told him it was a masterpiece and that he must have studied it much. "Ay," said he.

I put off a part of the forenoon in bringing up this Journal. The rest was a little dreary from the dulness of the weather and the uncertain state in which we were in, as we could not tell but it might clear up every hour. Nothing is more uneasy to the mind than a state of suspense, especially when it depends on the weather, as to which there can be so little calculation. As Mr Johnson said of our weariness on the Monday at Aberdeen, "Sensation is sensation."

Coirechatachan, which was last night a hospitable house, was in my mind changed today into a prison. A Mr Macdonald of Breakish came at dinner. We had a good plentiful one: roast mutton, a chicken-pie, and I forget how many good dishes. After it we had several Erse songs, and a bowl of stout punch. I was plagued somewhat with the toothache. I had a slight return of that spleen or hypochondria or whatever it should be called, which formerly made me so miserable, and which operates not only as to the present, but throws a gloom upon everything, whether past or future. The blackness of the imagination blackens every object that it takes in. How much reason have I to thank GOD that I have now hardly any remains of so direful a malady! The cheerfulness and constant good sense of my valuable spouse have had the happiest influence upon my mind.

After dinner I read some of Macpherson's *Dissertations on the Ancient Caledonians*, etc. I was disgusted at the unsatisfactory conjectures as to antiquity before the days of record. I was happy when tea came. Such, I take it, is the state of those who live in the country. Meals are wished for from the cravings of vacuity of mind as well as from the desire of eating. I was hurt to find even such a temporary feebleness, and that I was so far from being that robust wise man who is sufficient for his own happiness. I felt a kind of lethargy of indolence. I did not exert myself to get Mr Johnson to talk, that I might not have the labour of writing down his conversation. Macpherson, the minister of Sleat, was a very poor companion. He teased us with pitiful scraps which he had picked up, such as, "Gay was a good poet. He made a great deal by the *Beggar's Opera*," etc. But what was worse, he told Mr Johnson that there was an Erse Bible; that he had compared the new Erse Testament by Mr Stuart with the former one; that there were many Erse manuscripts – all of which circumstances we afterwards found not to be true.[308]

Mr Johnson inquired here if there were any remains of the second sight. Macpherson said he was *resolved* not to believe it, because it was founded on no principle. "Then," said Mr Johnson, "there are many things which we are sure are true that you will not believe. What principle is there why the loadstone attracts iron? Why an egg produces a chicken by heat? Why a tree grows upwards, when the natural tendency of all things is downwards? Sir, it depends upon the degree of evidence that you have."

Young Mr Mackinnon told us of one Mackenzie who is still alive whom he had often seen faint, and when he recovered he told he had seen things. He told Mr Mackinnon that on such a place he would meet a funeral, and that such and such people would be the bearers, naming four; and three weeks after he saw just what Mackenzie had told him. The naming the very spot in a country where a funeral comes a long way, and the very people as bearers when there are so many out of whom a choice may be made, seems curious. We would have sent for Mackenzie had we not been informed that he could speak no English. Besides, the young man seemed confused in his narration.

Mrs Mackinnon, who was a daughter of old Kingsburgh, told us that her father was one day riding in Skye, and some women who were at work in a field on the side of the road told him they heard two *taiscks*, that is, two voices of persons about to die. "And what," said they, "is extraordinary, one of them is an *English taisck*, which we never heard before." When he returned, he at that very place met two funerals, and one of them was of a woman who had come from the mainland and could speak only English. This, she told us, made a great impression upon her father.[309]

Between tea and supper, Coirechatachan and I and some more of the gentlemen assembled round a good peat fire, and drank two or three bottles of porter. We had another excellent supper, and many lively Erse songs after it.

How all the people here were lodged, I know not. By putting a number of men in one room and another of women in another, thus separating men from their wives, a good deal was done. Tonight Breakish was laid with Canna. What became of Dr Macdonald, whose place was thus filled up, is more than I could guess. I observed the Highlanders were laid beside each other, and in sheets very dirty, without the least scruple. Joseph had a good bed with clean sheets made for him in the parlour. There were here two very good servants at table, a young lad bare-legged and a girl bare-headed but very decently dressed. She attended a company with uncommon alertness. I observed tonight a remarkable instance of the simplicity of manners or want of delicacy among the people in Skye. After I was in bed, the minister came up to go to his. The maid stood by and took his clothes and laid them carefully on a chair piece by piece, not excepting his breeches, before throwing off which he made water, while she was just at his back.

WEDNESDAY 8 SEPTEMBER. When I awaked, the rain was much heavier than yesterday, but the wind had abated. By breakfast, the day was better, and in a little it was calm and clear. The joy which I felt was very fine. The propriety of the expression, 'the sunshine of the breast', was evident, for the brilliant rays penetrated into my very soul. We were all in better humour than before. Mrs Mackinnon with unaffected hospitality and politeness expressed her happiness in having such company in her house, and really was capable of admiring Mr Johnson; which indeed I must say all of them did according to their capacities. When I knew she was old Kingsburgh's daughter, I did not wonder at the good appearance which she made.

She had been much in Abercairney's family. She was at Kingsburgh the night that Prince Charles was there.[310] She told me that next morning the Prince was sound asleep in a room upstairs. She went into her father's room, which was below, and waked him and suggested to him her apprehensions of a party's coming up. Her father said, "Let the poor man repose himself after his fatigues; and as for me, I care not though they take off this old grey head" (pulling off his night cap and showing it) "ten or eleven years sooner." He then pulled the clothes over his head and again fell fast asleep: "Sweet are the slumbers of the virtuous man."[311] This worthy old gentleman lived to see the family of Macdonald, of which he had taken the most faithful charge in Sir James's minority, become what it now is in the person of this wretch Sir Alexander, who neglected Kingsburgh and has quarrelled with his son.

I observed to Mr Johnson that if Sir Alexander was a fierce barbarian, there might be something grand in observing his ravages; but that so much mischief should be produced by such an insect, really vexed one. At Coirechatachan the universal voice was against him. It was one of the farms upon the estate of Mackinnon, from whom it was purchased by the family of Macdonald by a strange sale which is well known. There are five years of the lease to run. By and by Sir Alexander will be harassing the people there too. But Mrs Mackinnon talked as if their family would go to America rather than be oppressed by him. She said, "How agreeable would it be if these gentlemen should come in upon us when we're in America."

It was said Sir Alexander is very frightened at sea. Said Mr Johnson, "*He's* frightened at sea; and his tenants are frightened when he comes to land."

Coirechatachan pays but about £50 of rent. But by droving and selling meal, in the former part of his life, he has made as much money as that the interest of it will pay his rent.

We resolved to set out directly after breakfast. We had about two miles to ride to the seaside, and there we expected to get one of the boats belonging to the fleet of bounty herring-ships then on the coast, or at least a good country fishing-boat.[312] But while we were preparing to set out, there arrived a man with the following card from the Reverend Mr Donald Macqueen, to whom I had written to meet us at Raasay:

> Mr Macqueen's compliments to Mr Boswell, and begs leave to acquaint him, that fearing the want of a proper boat, as much as the rain of yesterday, might have caused a stop, he is now at Sgianadan with Macgillicallum's carriage, to convey him and Dr Johnson to Raasay, where they will meet with most hearty welcome and where MacLeod, being on a visit, now attends their motions. / Wednesday forenoon.[313]

This card was most agreeable. It was a prologue to that hospitable and truly polite reception which we were to have at Raasay. It added much to my good spirits. I was elated perhaps too youthfully. "This is right," said I. "We're now like ourselves."

In a little arrived Mr Donald Macqueen himself; a decent minister, an elderly man with his own black hair, courteous and rather slow of speech, but candid, sensible, and well-informed, nay, learned. Along with him came, as our pilot, a gentleman whom I had a great desire to see – Malcolm MacLeod, one of the Raasay family, celebrated in the year 1745 for his conducting the Prince with fidelity from Raasay to the Laird of Mackinnon's. He was now sixty-two years of age, quite the Highland gentleman; of a stout well-made person, well-proportioned; a manly countenance browned with the weather, but a ruddiness in his cheeks, a good way up which his rough beard extended; a quick lively eye, not fierce in his look, but firm and good-humoured. He had a pair of brogues, tartan hose which came up only near to his knees and left them bare, a purple camblet kilt, a black waistcoat, a short cloth green coat bound with gold cord, a yellowish bushy wig, a large blue bonnet with a gold-thread button.[314] I never saw a figure that was more perfectly a representative of a Highland gentleman. I wished much to have a picture of him just as he was. I found him frank and *polite*, in the true sense of the word.

The good family at Coirechatachan said they hoped to see us in our return. We rode down to the shore. But Malcolm walked with graceful vigour. We were accompanied on foot by young Mr Mackinnon and Breakish. We got into Raasay's *carriage*, which was a good stout open boat made in Norway.

CHAPTER FOUR

Raasay

SAMUEL JOHNSON

The boat was under the direction of Mr *Malcolm Macleod*, a gentleman of *Raasay*. The water was calm, and the rowers were vigorous; so that our passage was quick and pleasant. When we came near the island, we saw the laird's house, a neat modern fabrick, and found Mr *Macleod*, the proprietor of the Island, with many gentlemen, expecting us on the beach. We had, as at all other places, some difficulty in landing. The craggs were irregularly broken, and a false step would have been very mischievous.

It seemed that the rocks might, with no great labour, have been hewn almost into a regular flight of steps; and as there are no other landing places, I considered this rugged ascent as the consequence of a form of life inured to hardships, and therefore not studious of nice accommodations. But I know not whether, for many ages, it was not considered as a part of military policy, to keep the country not easily accessible. The rocks are natural fortifications, and an enemy climbing with difficulty, was easily destroyed by those who stood high above him.[315]

Our reception exceeded our expectations. We found nothing but civility, elegance, and plenty. After the usual refreshments, and the usual conversation, the evening came upon us. The carpet was then rolled off the floor; the musician was called, and the whole company was invited to dance, nor did ever fairies trip with greater alacrity. The general air of festivity, which predominated in this place, so far remote from all those regions which the mind has been used to contemplate as the mansions

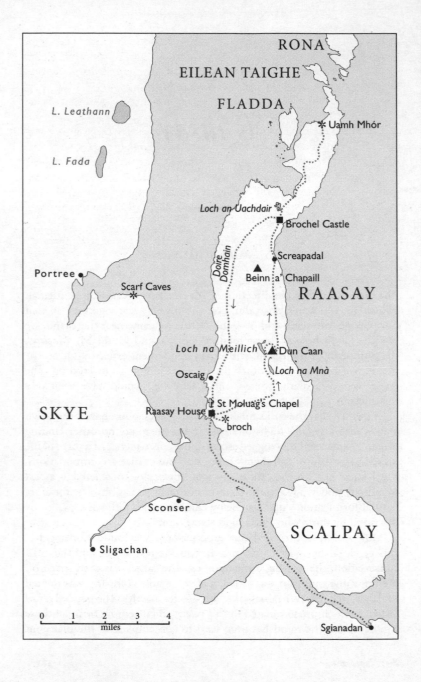

RONA

EILEAN TAIGHE

FLADDA

L. Leathann

L. Fada

✳ Uamh Mhór

Loch an Uachdair

■ Brochel Castle

● Screapadal

Portree ●

▲ Beinn a' Chapaill

Scarf Caves
✳

Doire Domhain

RAASAY

↓

↑

Loch na Meillich

⚓ ▲ Dun Caan

Oscaig ●

Loch na Mnà

↑

✝ St Moluag's Chapel

SKYE

Raasay House ■

✳ broch

↙

Sconser ●

SCALPAY

● Sligachan

↙

0   1   2   3   4
miles

Sgianadan ●

of pleasure, struck the imagination with a delightful surprise, analogous to that which is felt at an unexpected emersion from darkness into light.

When it was time to sup, the dance ceased, and six and thirty persons sat down to two tables in the same room. After supper the ladies sung *Erse* songs, to which I listened as an *English* audience to an *Italian* opera, delighted with the sound of words which I did not understand.

I inquired the subjects of the songs, and was told of one, that it was a love song, and of another, that it was a farewell composed by one of the Islanders that was going, in this epidemical fury of emigration, to seek his fortune in *America*. What sentiments would rise, on such an occasion, in the heart of one who had not been taught to lament by precedent, I should gladly have known; but the lady, by whom I sat, thought herself not equal to the work of translating.

Mr *Macleod* is the proprietor of the islands of *Raasay*, *Rona*, and *Fladda*, and possesses an extensive district in *Sky*. The estate has not, during four hundred years, gained or lost a single acre. He acknowledges *Macleod* of Dunvegan as his chief, though his ancestors have formerly disputed the preeminence.[316]

One of the old Highland alliances has continued for two hundred years, and is still subsisting between *Macleod of Raasay* and *Macdonald of Sky*, in consequence of which, the survivor always inherits the arms of the deceased; a natural memorial of military friendship. At the death of the late Sir *James Macdonald*, his sword was delivered to the present laird of *Raasay*.

The family of *Raasay* consists of the laird, the lady, three sons and ten daughters. For the sons there is a tutor in the house, and the lady is said to be very skilful and diligent in the education of her girls. More gentleness of manners, or a more pleasing appearance of domestick society, is not found in the most polished countries.

Raasay is the only inhabited island in Mr *Macleod's* possession. *Rona* and *Fladda* afford only pasture for cattle, of which one hundred and sixty winter in *Rona*, under the superintendence of a solitary herdsman.

The length of *Raasay* is, by computation, fifteen miles, and the breadth two. These countries have never been measured, and the computation by miles is negligent and arbitrary. We observed in travelling, that the nominal and real distance of places had very little relation to each other. *Raasay* probably contains near a hundred square miles. It affords not much ground, notwithstanding its extent, either for tillage, or pasture; for it is rough, rocky, and barren. The cattle often perish by falling from the precipices. It is like the other islands, I think, generally naked of shade, but it is naked by neglect; for the laird has an orchard, and very large forest trees grow about his house. Like other hilly countries it has many rivulets. One of the brooks turns a corn-mill, and at least one produces trouts.

In the streams or fresh lakes of the Islands, I have never heard of any other fish than trouts and eels. The trouts, which I have seen, are not large; the colour of their flesh is tinged as in *England*. Of their eels I can give no account, having never tasted them; for I believe they are not considered as wholesome food.

It is not very easy to fix the principles upon which mankind have agreed to eat some animals, and reject others; and as the principle is not evident, it is not uniform. That which is selected as delicate in one country, is by its neighbours abhorred as loathsome. The Neapolitans lately refused to eat potatoes in a famine. An Englishman is not easily persuaded to dine on snails with an Italian, on frogs with a Frenchman, or on horseflesh with a Tartar. The vulgar inhabitants of *Sky*, I know not whether of the other islands, have not only eels, but pork and bacon in abhorrence, and accordingly I never saw a hog in the *Hebrides*, except one at *Dunvegan*.[317]

Raasay has wildfowl in abundance, but neither deer, hares, nor rabbits. Why it has them not, might be asked, but that of such questions there is no end. Why does any nation want what it might have? Why are not spices transplanted to *America*? Why does tea continue to be brought from China? Life improves but by slow degrees, and much in every place is yet to do. Attempts have been made to raise roebucks in *Raasay*, but without effect. The young ones it is extremely difficult to rear, and the old can very seldom be taken alive.

Hares and rabbits might be more easily obtained. That they have few or none of either in *Sky*, they impute to the ravage of the foxes, and have therefore set, for some years past, a price upon their heads, which, as the number was diminished, has been gradually raised, from three shillings and sixpence to a guinea, a sum so great in this part of the world, that, in a short time, *Sky* may be as free from foxes, as *England* from wolves. The fund for these rewards is a tax of sixpence in the pound, imposed by the farmers on themselves, and said to be paid with great willingness.

The beasts of prey in the Islands are foxes, otters, and weasels. The foxes are bigger than those of *England*; but the otters exceed ours in a far greater proportion. I saw one at *Armidel*, of a size much beyond that which I supposed them ever to attain; and Mr *Maclean*, the heir of *Col*, a man of middle stature, informed me that he once shot an otter, of which the tail reached the ground, when he held up the head to a level with his own. I expected the otter to have a foot particularly formed for the act of swimming; but upon examination, I did not find it differing much from that of a spaniel. As he preys in the sea, he does little visible mischief, and is killed only for his fur. White otters are sometimes seen.

In *Raasay* they might have hares and rabbits, for they have no foxes. Some depredations, such as were never made before, have caused a suspicion that a fox has been lately landed in the Island by spite or wantonness.[318] This imaginary stranger has never yet been seen, and therefore, perhaps, the mischief was done by some other animal. It is not likely that a creature so ungentle, whose head could have been sold in *Sky* for a guinea, should be kept alive only to gratify the malice of sending him to prey upon a neighbour: and the passage from *Sky* is wider than a fox would venture to swim, unless he were chased by dogs into the sea, and perhaps than his strength would enable him to cross. How beasts of prey came into any islands is not easy to guess. In cold countries they take advantage of hard winters, and travel over the ice: but this is a very scanty solution; for they are found where they have no discoverable means of coming.

The corn of this island is but little. I saw the harvest of a small field. The women reaped the corn, and the men bound up the sheaves. The strokes of the sickle were timed by the modulation of the harvest song, in which all their voices were united. They accompany in the Highlands every action, which can be done in equal time, with an appropriated strain, which has, they say, not much meaning; but its effects are regularity and cheerfulness. The ancient proceleusmatick song, by which the rowers of gallies were animated, may be supposed to have been of this kind. There is now an *oar-song* used by the *Hebridians*.[319]

The ground of *Raasay* seems fitter for cattle than for corn, and of black cattle I suppose the number is very great. The Laird himself keeps a herd of four hundred, one hundred of which are annually sold. Of an extensive domain, which he holds in his own hands, he considers the sale of cattle as repaying him the rent, and supports the plenty of a very liberal table with the remaining product.

Raasay is supposed to have been very long inhabited. On one side of it they show caves, into which the rude nations of the first ages retreated from the weather. These dreary vaults might have had other uses. There is still a cavity near the house called the *oar-cave*, in which the seamen, after one of those piratical expeditions, which in rougher times were very frequent, used, as tradition tells, to hide their oars. This hollow was near the sea, that nothing so necessary might be far to be fetched; and it was secret, that enemies, if they landed, could find nothing. Yet it is not very evident of what use it was to hide their oars from those, who, if they were masters of the coast, could take away their boats.[320]

A proof much stronger of the distance at which the first possessors of this island lived from the present time, is afforded by the stone heads of arrows which are very frequently picked up. The people call them *Elf-bolts*, and believe that the fairies shoot them at the cattle. They nearly resemble those which Mr *Banks* has lately brought from the savage countries in the Pacifick Ocean, and must have been made by a nation to which the use of metals was unknown.[321]

The number of this little community has never been counted by its ruler, nor have I obtained any positive account, consistent with the result of political computation. Not many years ago, the late Laird led out one hundred men upon a military expedition. The sixth part of a people is supposed capable of bearing arms: *Raasay* had therefore six hundred inhabitants. But because it is not likely, that every man able to serve in the field would follow the summons, or that the chief would leave his lands totally defenceless, or take away all the hands qualified for labour, let it be supposed, that half as many might be permitted to stay at home. The whole number will then be nine hundred, or nine to a square mile; a degree of populousness greater than those tracts of desolation can often show. They are content with their country, and faithful to their chiefs, and yet uninfected with the fever of migration.

Near the house, at *Raasay*, is a chapel unroofed and ruinous, which has long been used only as a place of burial.[322] About the churches, in the Islands, are small squares inclosed with stone, which belong to particular families, as repositories for the dead. At *Raasay* there is one, I think, for the proprietor, and one for some collateral house.

It is told by *Martin*, that at the death of the Lady of the Island, it has been here the custom to erect a cross. This we found not to be true. The stones that stand about the chapel at a small distance, some of which perhaps have crosses cut upon them, are believed to have been not funeral monuments, but the ancient boundaries of the sanctuary or consecrated ground.[323]

Martin was a man not illiterate: he was an inhabitant of *Sky*, and therefore was within reach of intelligence, and with no great difficulty might have visited the places which he undertakes to describe; yet with all his opportunities, he has often suffered himself to be deceived. He lived in the last century, when the chiefs of the clans had lost little of their original influence. The mountains were yet unpenetrated, no inlet was opened to foreign novelties, and the feudal institutions operated upon life with their full force. He might therefore have displayed a series of subordination and a form of government, which, in more luminous and improved regions, have been long forgotten, and have delighted his readers with many uncouth customs that are now disused, and wild opinions that prevail no longer. But he probably had not knowledge of the world sufficient to qualify him for judging what would deserve or gain the attention of mankind. The mode of life which was familiar to himself, he did not suppose unknown to others, nor imagined that he could give pleasure by telling that of which it was, in his little country, impossible to be ignorant.

What he has neglected cannot now be performed. In nations, where there is hardly the use of letters, what is once out of sight is lost for ever. They think but little, and of their few thoughts, none are wasted on the past, in which they are neither interested by fear nor hope. Their only registers are stated observances and practical representations. For this reason an age of ignorance is an age of ceremony. Pageants, and processions, and commemorations, gradually shrink away, as better methods come into use of recording events, and preserving rights.[324]

It is not only in *Raasay* that the chapel is unroofed and useless; through the few islands which we visited, we neither saw nor heard of any house of prayer, except in *Sky*, that was not in ruins. The malignant influence of *Calvinism* has blasted ceremony and decency together; and if the remembrance of papal superstition is obliterated, the monuments of papal piety are likewise effaced.

It has been, for many years, popular to talk of the lazy devotion of the Romish clergy; over the sleepy laziness of men that erected churches, we may indulge our superiority with a new triumph, by comparing it with the fervid activity of those who suffer them to fall.

Of the destruction of churches, the decay of religion must in time be the consequence; for while the publick acts of the ministry are now performed in houses, a very small number can be present; and as the greater part of the Islanders make no use of books, all must necessarily live in total ignorance who want the opportunity of vocal instruction.

From these remains of ancient sanctity, which are every where to be found, it has been conjectured, that, for the last two centuries, the inhabitants of the Islands have decreased in number. This argument, which supposes that the churches have been suffered to fall, only because they were no longer necessary, would have some force, if the houses of worship still remaining were sufficient for the people. But since they have now no churches at all, these venerable fragments do not prove the people of former times to have been more numerous, but to have been more devout. If the inhabitants were doubled, with their present principles it appears not that any provision for publick worship would be made. Where the religion of a country enforces consecrated buildings, the number of those buildings may be supposed to afford some indication, however uncertain, of the populousness of the place; but where by a change of manners a nation is contented to live without them, their decay implies no diminution of inhabitants.

Some of these dilapidations are said to be found in islands now uninhabited; but I doubt whether we can thence infer that they were ever peopled. The religion of the middle age, is well known to have placed too much hope in lonely austerities. Voluntary solitude was the great act of propitiation, by which crimes were effaced, and conscience was appeased; it is therefore not unlikely, that oratories were often built in places where retirement was sure to have no disturbance.

Raasay has little that can detain a traveller, except the Laird and his family; but their power wants no auxiliaries. Such a seat of hospitality, amidst the winds and waters, fills the imagination with a delightful contrariety of images. Without is the rough ocean and the rocky land, the beating billows and the howling storm: within is plenty and elegance, beauty and gaiety, the song and the dance. In *Raasay*, if I could have found an Ulysses, I had fancied a *Phæacia*.[325]

JAMES BOSWELL

The wind had now risen pretty much. But we had four stout rowers, particularly a MacLeod, a fellow half naked, with a bare black head, robust and spirited, something half wild Indian, half English tar. Mr Johnson sat high on the stern like a magnificent Triton. Malcolm raised an Erse song, *Hatyin foam foam eri*, to which he gave Jacobite words of his own.[326] The tune was *O'er the moor among the heather*, Highlandized. The boatmen and Mr Macqueen chorused, and all went well. At length Malcolm himself took an oar and rowed like a hero. We sailed along the coast of Scalpay, an island belonging to Sir Alexander Macdonald, being part of the purchase from Mackinnon. It is four miles long and ———— broad.[327] Mr Johnson was for him and me buying it and having a good school and an Episcopal church (Malcolm said he would come to it) and a printing-press where we should print all the Erse that could be found.

Here again I was strongly struck with the long-projected scheme of Mr Johnson's and my visiting the Hebrides being realized. I called to him, "We are contending with seas," which I think were the words of one of his letters to me. "Not much," said he; and though the wind made the sea lash considerably upon us, he was not discomposed. After we were out of the shade of Scalpay, and in the sound between it and Raasay, which was for about a league, the wind made the sea really rough. I did not like it. Mr Johnson said, "This now is the Atlantic. If I should tell at a tea-table in London that I have crossed the Atlantic in an open boat, how they'd shudder and what a fool they'd think me to expose myself to such danger." He repeated the ode, *Otium divos rogat*.[328]

In the confusion or hurry of this rough sail, Mr Johnson's spurs, which Joseph had in his hand or on his knee, were carried overboard into the sea, and lost. This was the first misfortune that has befallen us. Mr Johnson was a little angry at first, observing that there was something wild in a pair of spurs being carried into the sea out of a boat; but then he said that, as Jeans had said upon losing his pocket-book, "It was rather an inconvenience than a loss." He said he now recollected that the night before he dreamt that he put his staff into a river and chanced to let it go, and it was carried down the stream and he lost it. "So now you see," said he, "that I have lost my spurs; and this story is better than many of those which we have as to second sight and dreams." Mr Macqueen said he did not believe the second sight; that he never met any well-attested instances; and if he did, he would impute them to chance, because all who pretend to that quality often fail in their predictions, though they take a wide range, and sometimes interpret literally, sometimes figuratively so as to suit the events. He told us that since he came to be minister of the parish where he now is, the belief of witchcraft or charms was very common, in so much that he had many prosecutions before his *session* against women, for having by these means carried off the milk from people's cows. He disregarded them; and there is not now the least vestige of that superstition. He preached against it; and in order to give a strong proof to the people that there was nothing in it, he said from the pulpit that every woman in the parish was welcome to take the milk from his cows provided she did not touch them.[329]

Mr Johnson asked him as to *Fingal*. He said he could repeat some passages in the original. That he heard his grandfather had a copy of the poem; but that he did not believe that Ossian composed that poem as it is now published. This came pretty much to what Mr Johnson has always held, though he goes farther and maintains that it is no better than such an epic poem as he could make from the song of Robin Hood; that is to say, that, except a few passages, there is nothing truly ancient but the names and some vague traditions. Mr Macqueen alleged that Homer was made up of detached fragments. Mr Johnson denied it; said that it had been one work originally, and that you could not put a book of the *Iliad* out of its place; and he believed the same might be said of the *Odyssey*.

Mr Malcolm told us that he went with the Prince from Raasay in a boat, landed near Portree, and from thence they walked all night over the mountains till they came into Strath, and the Laird of Mackinnon received him. He said the Prince went as his servant, carrying a little bundle and a bottle with a little brandy in it. When the brandy was drank out, he was for throwing away the bottle. "No," said Malcolm, "since it has served your highness, I hope to drink a cask out of it yet," and kept it. He has it still, as also a silver stock-buckle which he got from the Prince.[330] He said the Prince walked better than he did, and said he was not afraid of any party of soldiers if he was once at the distance of a musket-shot from them; but that he feared the Highlanders who were against him, as they could pursue so much better. He did not seem to be at all cast down.

I shall here put down all the particulars concerning the unfortunate Prince which I picked up at Raasay. He was two nights in a hut in that island. The present Raasay, Dr MacLeod his brother, and Malcolm were with him. There came a man near to the hut whom they did not know. They were apprehensive he might be a spy; and the Raasay gentlemen were for shooting him directly. "No," said the Prince, "God forbid. Let us not take away a man's life who may be innocent." John Mackenzie, a common Highlander who was attending them, said in Erse, "Well, well, no matter. He must be shot. You are the King. But we are the Parliament." The Prince asked what the man said; and being told it in English, he, notwithstanding the peril which he was in, laughed loud and heartily. Luckily the unknown person did not perceive that there were people in the hut; at least did not approach it, but walked on past it, unknowing of his risk. Had he come to them, they were resolved to dispatch him, for as Malcolm said to me, "We could not keep him with us, and we durst not let him go. In such a situation I would have shot my brother if I had not been sure of him."

John Mackenzie is alive. I saw him.[331] About eighteen years ago he

Wednesday 8 September

hurt one of his legs when dancing, and was obliged to have it cut off. So he was going about with a wooden leg. The story of his being a *member of Parliament* is always kept up. I took him out a little way from the house, gave him a shilling to drink Raasay's health, and talked to him of the story. With less foundation, some writers have traced the idea of Parliament and of the British Constitution in rude and early times. I was curious to know if John Mackenzie had really heard or understood anything of that subject, which, had he been a greater man, would have been strenuously maintained. "Why, John," said I, "did you think the King should be controlled by a Parliament?" He answered, "I thought, sir, there were many voices against one."

The Prince asked Dr MacLeod what kind of man Malcolm was, and Malcolm what kind of man the Doctor was, that he might know whom to trust. He told Malcolm, "Sir, I put myself into your hands. Only bring me to the Laird of Mackinnon." Malcolm proposed taking him by sea. He more wisely chose to go by land, after being in Skye. So Raasay, the Doctor, and Malcolm attended him in a boat which ferried him over. He told only Malcolm where he was to go, justly considering that it was safest to have the secret entrusted to as few as possible. He gave the Doctor a spoon and knife and fork in a shagreen case, and bid him keep them till they met again, and bid him be at Portree in a few days with some brandy and other things. Malcolm delivered him to Mackinnon, who went over with him to Morar, and delivered him to the present Morar, then a lad of seventeen.[332] Malcolm told me that in the hut the Prince would start from broken slumbers and speak to himself in different languages: French, Italian, and English (though indeed it must be considered that my worthy friend Malcolm did not probably know the difference between French and Italian), and one of his expressions in English was, "O God! Poor Scotland!" Malcolm said they had always a man keeping watch while they were in the hut, and that while they were crossing from Raasay to Skye it was somewhat rough, and the Prince asked if there was any danger; and upon being told there was none, he immediately sung an Erse song. He had learnt a good deal of Erse.

It was a most pleasing approach to Raasay. We saw before us a beautiful bay, well defended with a rocky coast; a good gentleman's house, a fine verdure about it, a considerable number of trees, and beyond it hills and mountains in gradation of wildness. Our boatmen sung with great spirit. Mr Johnson observed that naval music was very ancient. As we came to shore, the music of rowers was succeeded by that of reapers, who were busy at work, and who seemed to shout as much as to sing, while they worked with a bounding vigour. Just as we landed, I observed a cross, or rather the ruins of one, upon a rock, which had to me a pleasing vestige of religion.[333] I perceived a large company coming out from the house. We met them as we walked up. There were Raasay; his brother Dr MacLeod; his nephew the Laird of Mackinnon; the Laird of MacLeod; Colonel MacLeod of Talisker, a genteel man and a faithful branch of the family, an officer in the Dutch service; Mr MacLeod of Muiravonside, best known by the name of Sandie MacLeod, who was aide-de-camp to the Prince in 1745, and remained eighteen years in exile on that account; Mr Macqueen, a young divine, son to the Reverend Mr Donald Macqueen; Mr James MacLeod, a boy about — years of age, the future Laird of Raasay; and Mr Macqueen, a genteel young man, his tutor. We were welcomed upon the green, and conducted into the house, where we were introduced to Lady Raasay, to Miss Flora Raasay (as she is called in this part of the world for distinction), the eldest daughter or Princess, and to nine other young ladies, viz., Janet, Katherine, Margaret, Isabella, Jane, Julia, Anne, Mary, and Christian.[334] Raasay has also three sons, James, Malcolm, and John, all boys. He himself is a sensible, polite, and most hospitable gentleman. I was told that his island of Raasay, and that of Rona (from which the eldest son of the family has his title), and a considerable extent of land which he has in Skye, do not altogether yield him above £250 or at most £300 of rent; and yet he lives in the greatest plenty; and so far is he from distressing his people, that, in the present rage for emigration, not a man has left his estate.

We found here coffee and tea in genteel order upon the table, as it was past six when we arrived: diet loaf, marmalade of oranges, currant jelly; some elegantly bound books on a large table, in short, all the marks of improved life. We had a dram of excellent brandy, according to the Highland custom, filled round. They call it a *scalck*.[335] On a sideboard was served up directly, for us who had come off the sea, mutton-chops and tarts, with porter, claret, mountain, and punch. Then we took coffee and tea. In a little, a fiddler appeared, and a little ball began. Raasay himself danced with as much vigour and spirit as any man. Sandie MacLeod, who has at times an excessive flow of spirits, was, in his days of absconding, known by the name of MacCruslick, which it seems was the designation of a kind of wild man in the Highlands,[336] and so he was called here. He made much jovial noise, but was too violent for my nerves, though they are now pretty well stiffened. Mr Johnson was so delighted with this scene that he said, "I know not how we shall get away."

It entertained me to observe him sitting by while we danced, sometimes in deep meditation, sometimes smiling complacently, sometimes looking upon Hooke's *Roman History*, and sometimes talking a little, amidst the noise of the ball, to Mr Donald Macqueen, who anxiously gathered knowledge from him. He was pleased with Macqueen, and said to me, "This is a critical man, sir. There must be great vigour of mind to make him cultivate learning so much in the Isle of Skye, where he might do without it. It is wonderful how many of the new publications he has. There must be a snatch of every opportunity." Mr Macqueen told me that his brother (who is the fourth generation of the family following each other as ministers of the parish of Snizort) and he joined together and bought from time to time such books as had reputation.

Soon after we came in, a black cock and grey hen, which had been shot, were shown, with their feathers on, to Dr Johnson, who had never seen that species of bird before. We had a company of thirty at supper, and all was good humour and gaiety. Many songs were sung, one in particular to encourage the emigrants, which had a chorus ending always with *Tullishole*.[337] The glass circulated briskly, but nobody was asked to drink more than he cared to, and there was no intemperance.

I had a very good room to myself. The house has eleven fire rooms. It was built by this Raasay. His father was out in 1745, but had previously conveyed the estate to him, so there was no forfeiture; but as the Prince was known to have had an asylum in Raasay, those employed under the Government burnt every house upon the island. The family house was then just new. The tower of three storeys, which Martin mentions, stood till within a little of those latter commotions, when it was taken down and the stones of it employed in building the present house, which was consumed with the fire, all but the walls, so that 'tis partly the work of the late Raasay, partly of this. Some of the rooms have a number of beds, and so they are able to have so extensive a hospitality. We were in a new state of existence tonight.[338]

THURSDAY 9 SEPTEMBER. After a most comfortable sleep, I had goat's whey brought to my bedside. Then rose and partook of an excellent breakfast: as good chocolate as I ever tasted, tea, bread and butter, marmalade and jelly. There was no loaf-bread, but very good *scones*, or cakes of flour baked with butter. There was a plate of butter and curd mixed which they call *gruitheam*; cakes of what is called *graddaned* meal, that is, meal made of grain separated from the husks, and toasted by fire, in place of being threshed and kiln-dried.[339] This seems to be bad management, as so much fodder is consumed by it. Mr Macqueen, however, defends it by saying that it is doing the thing much quicker, as one operation serves for what is otherwise done by two. His chief reason, however, was that the servants in Skye are, according to him, a worthless, faithless pack, and steal what they can; so that much is saved by the corn passing but once through their hands, as at each time they pilfer some. It appears to me that the graddaning is a strong example of the laziness of the Highlanders, who will rather let fire do for them, at the expense of fodder, than labour themselves. There were also barley-bannocks of this year's meal, and – what I cannot help disliking to have at breakfast – cheese. It is the custom over all the Highlands to have it; and it often smells very strong, and poisons to a certain degree the elegance of an Indian breakfast.

The day was showery. However, Raasay and I took a walk and had a very solid, easy, feudal chat.[340] I conceived a more than ordinary regard for this worthy gentleman. He has had this island above four hundred years. It is the remains of the estate of MacLeod of Lewis whom he represents; and there is a question with some whether MacLeod of Harris or his family is the elder branch. However, he does not contest the chieftainship with the Laird of MacLeod.[341]

When we returned, Mr Johnson came out with us to see the old chapel. But before quitting the island in my Journal (as I am now far behind with it, for I am now writing on the 15 September), I shall put down all my observations upon it at once.[342] Mr Johnson was in fine spirits. He said, "This is truly the patriarchal life. This is what we came to find." Minute things mark civilized life. We had here variety of preserves, and two parrots in cages were set out before the door to bask in the sun.

We had a plentiful and genteel dinner, after which MacCruslick and I went out with guns to try if we could find any black cock; but we had no sport, and there came a heavy rain, by which we were a good deal wet. Malcolm had the best way of sheltering himself – under a dike with ferns upon it – that could be. We saw what is called a Danish fort. Our evening was passed as last night was. The Laird of Mackinnon was a young man of small size, delicate constitution, feebleness of voice and nearness of sight, but I was told had great knowledge, and hurt himself by too much study, particularly of infidel metaphysicians.[343] I had a small specimen of his improvement in that way when I spoke of the second sight. He immediately retailed some of the flimsy arguments of Voltaire and Hume against miracles in general. It was strangely offensive to hear infidelity from a Highland chief. It was like finding him toupé'd and essenced like a French fop. I was sorry for the young gentleman, who I

Thursday 9 September

heard was a worthy lad. I told Mr Johnson he had studied himself into infidelity. "Then," said he, "he must study himself out of it again. That is the way. Drinking largely would sober him again."

Mr Johnson showed me today two odes which he had written in Skye. One of them was to Mrs Thrale. It was very pretty. I asked it from him. He said, "I'd as soon give you my ears." But he said I might get it from her if she pleased. He said he would not swear against giving me the other. So I hope it shall enrich my Journal. I said I was entitled to have a diamond here and there in it. I would give him one if I could.[344]

I was in some doubt today whether to set out next day, in order that I might let Sir Alexander's horses get home to him the sooner, in which case I thought to return to Raasay in our way from Dunvegan to Sleat, whence we could have Sir Alexander's boat to Mull, and on return I might see the island fully. But I considered that we might perhaps get a boat from MacLeod's country, and it was better to make sure of seeing Raasay; so I resolved to have a great expedition tomorrow, and my friend Malcolm promised to call me before six.

FRIDAY 10 SEPTEMBER. Having resolved to explore the island of Raasay, which could be done only on foot, I last night obtained my fellow-traveller's permission to leave him for a day, he being unable to take so hardy a walk.[345]

Malcolm was at my bed-side between five and six. I sprung up, and he and I and Donald Canna and Mr Macqueen, the minister's son, and Joseph set out. We took a dram and a bit of bread directly. But Lady Raasay and some of her daughters were up, and a boy of the name of Stewart was sent with us as our carrier of provisions. We walked briskly along; but the country was very stony at first, and a great many risings and fallings lay in our way. We had a shot at a flock of plovers sitting. But mine was harmless. We came first to a pretty large lake, sunk down comparatively with the ground about it. Then to another; and then we mounted up to the top of Duncaan, where we sat down, eat cold mutton and bread and cheese and drank brandy and punch. Then we had a Highland song from Malcolm; then we danced a reel to which he and Donald and Macqueen sang. We then walked on over a much better country, very good pasture; saw many moor-fowl, but could never get near them; descended a hill on the east side of the island and went into a farm-house, a Maclean's.[346] It was somewhat circular in its shape. At one end sheep and goats were lodged; at the other, the family. The man and his wife had a little bedstead. The place where the servants lay was marked out upon the ground with whinstones and strewed with fern. The fire was towards the upper end of the house. The smoke went out at a hole in the roof, at some distance and not directly above it, as rain would hurt it. I found here sacks made of rushes very well plaited, so as to be strong and very compact. They really looked well and made very tolerable baskets. The art of *creeling* or working in wattles seems to be well practised among these islanders.

Let me here put down a local saying of mine against Sir Sawney. I said by driving away the gentlemen, the best people upon his estate, he would have no beams, no great timber – just a *creel clan*. He knew not well how to do about Mr Johnson and me. He did not wish us to see how much better Raasay lived than he; so he began to object, and said he heard Lady Raasay was ill. "Oh, then," said Mr Johnson, "we'll stay till we hear how she is." The animal answered, "Oh, no!" Mr Johnson was struck with his desire to get rid of us.

I saw in this hut a little house-kiln for drying corn. It was about the size of a hogshead; was made of wattles, plastered with clay very firmly both on the outside and the inside. The convenience of it was that the man could dry a little at a time, as he could afford it, and instead of having one to attend in an outhouse, it could be watched by the family sitting by their fireside. The farmer here had no children, and he and his wife spoke only Erse. Adjoining to the house was another little circular room called a *keep-house*.[347] The woman very hospitably went into it and brought us some very good milk. I went into the place. It was a kind of store-room for the few things that they had. She kept her milk in an earthen dish put within a wooden chest, which shut with a lid, so that it was very clean.

We had been met by Mr Charles MacLeod, half-brother to Raasay, a strapping young fellow. Old Raasay had most absurdly married again after the year 1746. His widow, by whom he had several children, lives in a small comfortable house which was built for him just adjoining to the old castle of the family. She has a good farm gratis, and the interest of £400 by way of jointure. Mr Charles took us to her house. She was a stout fresh-looking woman, very plainly dressed, and could not speak a word of English. She treated us with cream and barley-bread. It was not amiss to see the difference between her housekeeping and that of Raasay's. Folly on one side, and probably interested cunning on the other, had produced the second marriage. She was called only Mrs MacLeod now. I know not if ever she was called *Lady*, as her husband had previously given the estate to this gentleman.[348]

We saw the old castle, then walked over to a large cave on the north-western coast, accompanied by Mr Charles, who was to go to Raasay with us. From there we turned and made the best of our way back again, by somewhat a shorter road. I was much fatigued for a while, but recovered and did wonderfully. It was a fine fair day, with such a breeze as was refreshing. By the time we returned we had walked good four-and-twenty English miles. I got coffee and tea after I had dressed myself, and was most serene.[349]

Malcolm had told us several anecdotes today of his expedition in 1745–6. He was kept prisoner in London for a year. He was carried up in Captain John Ferguson's ship, where he said the prisoners were very ill maintained.[350] But there were some soldiers on board, who lived well, and sometimes invited him to share. At London he had the good fortune to be confined in the house of one Dick, a messenger, instead of being imprisoned. To his astonishment there could but one evidence against him be found. He said he would willingly have signed his banishment. Yet he told me he would never be so ready for dying as he was then. His spirits were kept up by thinking warmly of the good cause. Lady Primrose, who took care of Miss Flora Macdonald, sent her to Scotland in a post-chaise, and bid her have any one of her friends to accompany her. She chose Malcolm.[351] "So," said he, "I went to London to be hanged, and came down in a chaise with Miss Flora Macdonald."[352] He said when the Prince parted from him he insisted on his taking ten guineas out of his purse, though he was sure he had not above forty. But he said he would get enough on the mainland.

Malcolm and I became great friends. He offered to make me a present of the bottle, which was going a great length indeed. But I refused it, saying nobody should have it but himself. He had got a little pipe from the Prince, which he gave to a gentleman in England; and as he came down, he saw it at York in a silver case.[353]

I exerted myself in an extraordinary degree in dancing tonight, drinking porter heartily at intervals, and thinking that I was fit to lead on Highlanders.

Let me gather here some gold dust, some gleanings of Mr Johnson's conversation without regard to order of time. He said he thought very highly of Bentley; that no man now went so far in the kinds of learning that he cultivated; that the many attacks of him were owing to envy and to a desire of being known by being in competition with such a man; that it was safe to attack him because he never answered them, but let them die away. It was attacking a man who would not beat them, because his beating them would make them live the longer. And he was right not to answer, for in his hazardous method of writing he could not but be often enough wrong; so it was better to leave things to their general appearance than own himself to be wrong in particulars.[354] He said Mallet was the prettiest-dressed poppet about town, and always kept good company. That from his way of talking, he saw and always said that he had not written any of the Life of the Duke of Marlborough, though perhaps he intended to do it some time; in which case he was not culpable in taking the pension. That he imagined the Duchess was to furnish the materials and Mallet to furnish the words and the order and all that in which the art of writing consists.[355] That the Duchess was not a woman of superior parts, but a bold frontless woman who knew how to make the most of her opportunities in life. That Hooke got a great sum of money for writing her *Apology*; that he wondered how Hooke put in that saying that to tell another's secret to one's friend is no breach of confidence; though perhaps Hooke, who was a virtuous man, and whose *History* shows it, and did not wish her well though he wrote her *Apology*, might see its effect and yet put it in, since she desired it to be put in. He was acting only ministerially. I am afraid, though, that Hooke was bound to give his best advice. I speak as a lawyer. Though I have had clients that I did not wish well to, yet if I undertook their cause, I would not do anything to hurt it, even at their desire, without warning them first.

And now let me throw together what I can as to the Island of Raasay. It lies south and north, is about fifteen English miles long, and four broad. On the south quarter is the family seat, situated on a pleasing low spot. The old tower of three stories, mentioned by Martin, was taken down soon after 1746, and a modern house supplies its place. There is very good grass fields and corn lands about it, well-dressed. I observed, however, hardly any enclosing except a good garden well stocked with kitchen stuff, gooseberries, raspberries, currants, strawberries, apple-trees. There is a tolerable southern wall on which fruit-trees have been tried, but have been neglected. Dr Johnson observed to me, how quietly people will endure an evil, which they might at any time very easily remedy; and mentioned as an instance, that the present family of Raasay had possessed the island for more than four hundred years, and never made a commodious landing place, though a few men with pickaxes might have cut an ascent of stairs out of any part of the rock in a week's time.

On one of the rocks just where we landed, which are not high ones, there is rudely drawn a square with a crucifix in the middle, where it is said the Laird of Raasay in old times used to offer up his devotions.[356] I could not but kneel upon the spot and gratefully remember the death of Christ, uttering a short prayer. This I did the morning that I left Raasay, while the family accompanied us to the shore; but nobody could imagine that I was doing anything more than attentively satisfying my curiosity.

A little off the shore westward is a kind of subterraneous house. There has been a natural fissure or separation of the rock, running towards the sea. That has been roofed over with long stones, and above them turf has been laid, till the ground gradually disappears, being lost in the beach. In that place the inhabitants used to keep their oars. About a quarter of a mile or more from the house is what is called a Danish fortification. It could not be a watch tower, for on the land side it is covered by rising ground, close to it, so could not communicate intelligence by signals. It has been a pretty high circular wall built double, so as that there was a spiral passage, like that of pipes in a hothouse, to the top, roofed all along with *flag stones*, as they are called, or long pieces of freestone. In the space in the middle were the huts for the people, who were there safe, and could steal under cover to the top to explore. The middle of this was much filled up by stones having tumbled from the wall. So 'tis very imperfect.[357]

There are a tolerable number of trees near the house which grow well. Some of them are of a pretty good size. They are mostly the plane or sycamore-tree and ash. There were a few of the mountain ash or *rowan*-tree, loaded with berries and which had a rich appearance. These were between the back of the house and the garden.

A little to the west of the house is an old chapel with now no roof upon it. It has never been very curious. I at first imagined it had originally two storeys, from there being holes in the wall as if joists had been there. But Mr Johnson, who is very accurate, found that the holes were not directly opposite to each other in the two walls, and were only defects by the injury of time. In one of these holes we saw some human bones of an uncommon size. There was a heel-bone in particular which Dr MacLeod said was such that if the foot was in proportion it must have been twenty-seven inches. Mr Johnson would not look at the bones. He started back from them with a striking appearance of horror. Mr Macqueen said it was formerly much the custom in these isles to have human bones lying above ground and in the windows of churches. This chapel appears to have been a good deal filled up with earth. On the floor of it are several gravestones, but without any legible inscriptions. A little to the east of it, I suppose about twelve feet, is a ruin of a burying-place of another tribe of the MacLeods (for there were several in the island), and in the space between the two were some recent graves. On the south of the chapel is the family burying-place. Above the door on the east end of it is a small bust or image of the Virgin Mary, carved upon a stone which makes part of the wall; and to the south of the family burying-place is a smaller one said to be for another tribe. All these ruins are unroofed and full of nettles and other weeds, and look like one cluster at small distance. As they are now in a grove, they have somewhat of a venerable air; at least they affect the mind with pious awe to a certain degree.[358] There is no church upon the island, which is in the parish of Portree in Skye, and the minister comes and preaches there either in Raasay's house or some other house once in every three Sundays.[359] I could not but value the family seat more for having even this ruin of a chapel so near it. There was something comfortable in the thought of being so near a piece of consecrated ground. Mr Johnson said, "I look with reverence upon every place that has been set apart for religion," and he kept off his hat while he was within the walls of the chapel.

The eight crosses which Martin mentions as pyramids for deceased ladies stood in a semi-circular line comprehending the chapel. They have been real crosses and have marked out the boundaries of the sacred territory within which an asylum was to be had. The one which we observed upon our landing was the one which made the first point of the semi-circle. There are few of them now remaining, and they have ended at an opposite point on the west. A good way farther north there is a row of dry-stone buildings about four foot high and ———— yards around, twice what I could grasp and five hands. They run along the top of a pretty high eminence and so down to the shore on the west, in pretty much the same direction with the crosses. Raasay took them to be the marks for the asylum. But Malcolm thought them to be false sentinels, a common deception (of which instances occur in Martin) to make invaders imagine the island better guarded; and Mr Donald Macqueen, justly in my opinion, makes the crosses which form the inner circle to be the church's landmarks.[360]

The south end of the island is much covered with large stones or rocky strata. Raasay has enclosed and planted with firs one point upon the eastern quarter of that end; and he showed me part of a stone wall built and stones laid down for more, in order to enclose a considerable space, which he is also to plant.

Duncaan is a mountain three computed miles from the house. There is an ascent of the country by consecutive risings (if that expression may be used when valleys intervene), so that there is but a short rise at once;

but it is certainly very high from the sea. The palm of altitude is disputed for by the people of Raasay and those of Skye between Duncaan and the mountains in Skye over against it. I take it the latter have it; for Duncaan being not very thick, but rather like a mount framed by the landscape, it looks to be higher than it really is, whereas the mountains in Skye are vast lumps.

We went up the east side of Duncaan pretty easily. It is mostly rock all around, the points of which hem the summit of it. Sailors, to whom it is a good object as they pass along, call it Raasay's Cap. It is more like the shape of a bonnet. Within the rocky edging at the summit there is plain green ground, though here and there a piece of rock is interspersed.

Before we reached Duncaan we passed by two lakes. Of the first, Malcolm told me a strange fabulous tradition. He said there was a wild beast in it, a sea-horse which came and devoured a man's daughter. Upon which the man put on a great fire and had a sow roasted at it, the smell of which attracted the monster. The loch was in a hollow between two hills. The fire was placed on the side of the hill to the southeast, a little way down the declivity on that side away from the loch. In the fire was put a spit. The man lay concealed behind a little building of dry stones, and he had an avenue formed for the monster with two rows of large flat stones which reached from the fire over the summit of the hill, till it came on the side next to the loch. The monster came, and the man with the red-hot spit destroyed it. Malcolm showed me the little hiding-place and the rows of stones, which seemed to be artificial, though it was not certain. He did not laugh when he told this story. I recollect having seen in the *Scots Magazine* several years ago a poem upon a similar story, perhaps the same, translated from the Erse or Irish, called *Albin and the Daughter of Mey*.[361]

There is a large tract of land possessed as a common in Raasay. They have no regulations as to the number of cattle. Every man puts upon it as many as he chooses. From Duncaan northward, till you reach the other end of the island, there is a good deal of good natural pasture little hurt by stones. We passed over a spot which is appropriated for the exercising ground. In 1745, a hundred fighting men were reviewed here, as Malcolm told me, who was one of the officers that led them to the field. They returned home all but about fourte. What a princely thing is it to be able to furnish such a band! Raasay has the true spirit of a chief. He is, without exaggeration, a father to his people, so far as I could learn. Not one of them has left him.

There is plenty of limestone in the island, and a great quarry of freestone. There are some pieces of natural woods, none of any age, as they cut the trees for common country uses. There are a number of lakes with trout in them. Malcolm catched one four-and-twenty pound weight in the loch next to Duncaan, which, by the by, is certainly a Danish name, as most names of places in these islands are. Raasay put trout into that lake and into some of the others. On the western coast, not far from the old castle, there arose upon the sea a rock so like one of the ordinary huts in the island that everybody must mistake it for one.[362]

The old castle in which the family of Raasay formerly resided is situated upon a rock very near the sea. The rock is not one mass of stone, but a concretion of pebbles and earth; but so firm that it does not appear to have mouldered. I perceived no pieces of it fallen off. The entry was by a steep stair from the quarter next the sea, of which stair only three or four steps are remaining, all at the top of it. Above them the castle projects, and there is an opening in the wall from which hot water or stones could be thrown upon an invader. Upon entering the gate or door, there was what I never saw before: a sentry box or alcove in the wall on your right hand. The man placed there could only watch in case of noise. He could see nothing. The next advance was to a court or *close* as it was called, in the centre of four towers, and open above just like any other court of an old castle in the square form. Only that this seemed extraordinary, as you came to it after ascending a stair and entering a gate; but as Mr Johnson observed, it was just an ordinary court, with the difference that the rock here was as the ground in others.[363] The court here was very small. There was a fine well – just a spring in the rock – but it was now filled up with rubbish. One could distinguish tolerably that there had been four towers, but time and storms had left little but ruinous fragments: pieces of wall, pieces of stairs, a part of the battlement to the sea.

There was one small room in one of the towers quite entire. It was a little confined triangular place, vaulted as in the ancient manner. In a corner of it was a square freestone in which was cut an exact circular opening such as is in every temple of Cloacina, and from it there appears a clear communication to the bottom, that is to say anything will be carried by the outside of the rock to the bottom. They call this room the *nursery*, and say the hole was for the children. But I take it to have been the necessary-house of the castle. It was much to find such a convenience in an old tower. I did not imagine that the invention had been introduced into Scotland till in very modern days, from our connexion with England. But it seems we have forgotten something of civilized life that our ancestors knew. It is strange how rare that convenience is amongst us. Mr Johnson laughed heartily and said, "You take very good care of one end of a man, but not of the other."[364]

One should think it requires very little reflection to provide such a convenience. Raasay has none. I told him that it was a shame to see it at the old castle and not at his new house. He said it would be better. But I doubt many generations may pass before it is built.

From the castle we crossed the island, or at least cut across a part of it, to a famous cave. In our way we saw a very pretty lake with two islands upon it covered with wood. Bushes, I may say. We saw the other end of Raasay, which turns in with a crook, and is as rocky or stony as the south end; and the little Isle of Fladda, belonging to Raasay, all fine green ground; and Rona, which is of so rocky a soil that it appears to be just a pavement. I was told, however, that it has a great deal of grass in the interstices. Raasay has it all in his own hand. It keeps 160 cattle. His *bowman* or cow-keeper resides upon it with his family.[365] The cave which we went to see is in a striking situation. It is in a recess of a great cleft, a good way up from the sea. Before it the ocean roars, being dashed against monstrous broken rocks – grand and awful *propugnacula*. On the right hand, going up to it from the sea, is a longitudinal cave, very low in the roof all upon the side going in, but higher as you advance. The sea has washed it and scooped it out; I know not how it has been made more lofty as the sea went farther in. The roof of it is all covered with a kind of petrifications formed by drops which perpetually distil from it. They are like little trees. I broke off some of them. The great cave has its mouth almost built up with round pebbles. The entry is low. When you get in, it is of a good highth – no great breadth – ten paces long. It has been a place of much safety. I saw upon the floor some places for beds marked out with stones as in the cottage. I find a wretched deficiency in expressing visible objects. I must own, too, that the old castle and cave, like many other things of which one hears much, did not answer my expectations. People love to boast of the curiosities of their country, be it great or small.

This island has abundance of black cattle, sheep, and goats; a good many horses, which are used for ploughing, carrying out dung, etc. I believe the people never ride. There are indeed no roads through the island, except now and then a detached piece which use has made. Most of the houses are upon the shore, so that all the people have little boats and catch fish. There is a great plenty of potatoes here. There are blackcock in extraordinary abundance, moor-fowl, plovers, wild pigeons

– just the bluish kind which we have in pigeon-houses – in the state of nature. Raasay has no pigeon-house. There are no hares nor rabbits in the island, nor there never was known to be a fox till last year, that some malicious person landed one; which must have been the case, as a fox is a bad swimmer. He has done much mischief and they have not got him killed yet. Mr Johnson said they should set a trap for him. There is a great deal of fish caught in the sea around Raasay: rock cod, haddocks, _____[366] and in the lakes and rivers, or rather brooks, trout is taken. It is really a place where one may live in plenty, and even in luxury. There are no deer. But Raasay is to get some. Mr Johnson said, "If one had a mind to retire for study for a summer, it would be a fine place."

I said if I had my wife and little daughter with me, I would stay here long enough. The thought of my being absent from them damped my happiness. I considered that my wife is uneasy when I am away – that it is not just, and surely not kind, to leave her for such a portion of life, when she sets such a value on my company and gives up everything else for me and my interest. And weak as it may be, I could not help having that kind of tender uneasiness which a lover has when absent from his mistress. Laugh at it who will, as not to be believed or as singular, I mark it as a fact, and rejoice at it, as it is the counterpart of more than ordinary conjugal felicity.

Raasay has a barn worth remembering. The corners and a piece of wall at each door are built to the full highth of good stone and lime, to give it firmness, as a strong box is fortified in different places with brass or iron. The rest of it has a wall of the same kind about the highth of an ordinary dike, and above that is work of wattles covered on the outside with heath. It is so open that the wind gets in and the rain is kept out. And it is well thatched with heath. This is better than having slits in the walls, for the air comes more equally. In this barn he often dries his hay as well as his corn, which is a great advantage in so wet a climate, where if it stands long in the fields it may rot. They reckon nine months rain here, as it is just opposite to the western coast of Skye, where the copious clouds are broken by high mountains.[367] The hills here, and indeed all the heathy ground in general, abound with the sweet-smelling plant which the Highlanders call *gaul*, and I think with dwarf juniper in many places. There is enough of turf, which is their fuel, and it is thought there is a mine of coal.[368] I do not recollect anything more that I can put down about Raasay. I shall draw out a little account of it and get Raasay himself and his brother the doctor to revise it. They have promised to send me in writing all that they can tell of what happened in 1745.[369]

Friday 10 September

I liked to see a brother of the family a physician. He is a sensible civil man, and I am told has good skill. He was wounded at Culloden. He has had bad health of late years and has given over practice, except visiting from regard his particular friends. He has a family from Raasay upon his estate in Skye. He is married and has children. There was a son and daughter of his at Raasay. All relations are welcome there.

There has been long a league between the families of Macdonald and Raasay. Raasay has a writing concerning it, dated, as I was told, above 100 years ago, for I did not see it, as I did not hear of it till I had left the island. Whenever the head of either family dies, his sword is given to the head of the other. This Raasay has the late Sir James Macdonald's sword. But Sir Alexander, who is wrong in everything and has no generous attachment, is carrying on a lawsuit with Raasay to keep him from recovering £500 which Raasay advanced to Kingsburgh, Sir Alexander's own kinsman and tenant. Sir Alexander claims a preference as landlord. Everybody who knows the history of the families is hurt at this. I am one of Sir Alexander's lawyers in the suit. But now when I have had occasion to see worthy Raasay, been so hospitably entertained by him, and have learnt the ancient alliance, I will have nothing more to do with it.[370] The late Sir Alexander was truly friendly in 1745. "Don't be afraid, Raasay," said he. "I'll use all my interest to keep you safe; and if your estate should be taken, I'll buy it for the family." And he would have done it.

SATURDAY 11 SEPTEMBER. It was a storm of wind and rain; so we could not set out. I wrote some Journal and talked awhile with Mr Johnson in his room, and passed the day, I cannot well say how, but very easily. I was here amused to find Mr Cumberland's comedy of the *Fashionable Lover*, in which he has very well drawn a Highland character, Colin McCleod, of the same name with the family under whose roof we now were.[371]

Mr Johnson was very fond of MacLeod, who is indeed a most promising youth, and with a noble spirit is to struggle with difficulties and keep his people.[372] He has been left with £40,000 of debt and 1300 a year of annuities to pay. Mr Johnson said, "Sir, if he gets the better of all this, he'll be a hero; and I hope he shall. He's a fine fellow, MacLeod. I have not met with a young man who had more desire to learn, or who has learnt more. I've seen nobody that I wish more to do a kindness to than MacLeod."

Such was the honourable elogium, on this young chieftain, pronounced by an accurate observer, whose praise was never lightly bestowed. I do not observe exact chronology in Mr Johnson's sayings. There is no occasion.

There is neither Justice of Peace or constable in Raasay. Skye has but Ullinish, a Sheriff Depute, and no other Justice of Peace. The want of the execution of justice is much felt among the islanders. MacLeod very sensibly observed that taking away the heritable jurisdictions had not been of such service in the islands as was imagined.[373] They had not authority enough in lieu of them. What could then have been settled at once must now either take much time and trouble or be neglected. Mr Johnson said that a country was in a bad state which was governed only by laws; because a thousand things occur for which laws cannot provide and where authority ought to interpose. Now destroying the authority of the chiefs threw the people loose. It did not pretend to bring any positive good, but only to cure some evil; and he was not well enough acquainted with the country to know what degree of evil the jurisdictions occasioned. I maintained, hardly any, because the chiefs took care for their own sakes.

Mr Johnson was now wishing to move. There was not enough of intellectual entertainment for him after he had satisfied his curiosity, which he did by asking questions till he had exhausted the island. And where there was such a numerous company, mostly young people, there was such a flow of familiar talk, so much noise and so much singing and dancing, that there was not much opportunity for his majestic conversation. He seemed sensible of this; for when I told him how happy they were at having him there, he said, "Yet we have not been able to entertain them much." I was apt to be fretted with irritability of nerves on account of MacCruslick's loud rattling, romping, etc. I complained of it to Mr Johnson and said we would be better if he was gone. "No, sir," said he. "He puts something into the company, and takes nothing out of it."

Mr Johnson, however, had several opportunities of instructing the company; and they were made sensible of his powers. I can recollect nothing to put down, as he run rather into general discourse upon mechanics, agriculture, and such subjects, than into science and wit. Last night Lady Raasay showed him the operation of *wawking* cloth, that is, thickening it as is done by a mill. Here it is performed by women who kneel upon the ground. The cloth is spread upon ———, and they rub it with both their hands, with ———, singing an Erse song all the time.[374] He was asking questions in the time of it, and amidst their loud and wild howl his voice was heard even in the room above.

We had a ball again tonight. Miss Flora is really an elegant woman (tall, genteel, a pretty face), sensible, polite, and good-humoured.[375] I find it in vain to try to draw a portrait of a young lady. I cannot discriminate. She alone has been at Edinburgh. All the rest were never farther than Applecross, a gentleman's seat in Ross-shire on the opposite coast. Mr Johnson said they were the best-bred children he ever saw; that he did not believe there was such another family between this and London; that he had never seen a family where there was such airiness and gaiety. Not one of the family ever had the toothache. They dance every night all the year round. There seemed to be no jealousy, no discontent among them. I asked Miss Flora, "Why, you have no idea then of the unhappiness of life that we hear so much of?"

"No," said she. "I have reason to be thankful."

She had very good sense without any aiming at smartness more than was natural to her. The only fault Mr Johnson could find with her was that her head was too high dressed. Can there then be no misery here? What says Mr Johnson? "Yet hope not life from pain or danger free; / Or think the doom of man revers'd for thee."[376]

I must set him to inquire if evil has place in Raasay. They can never have the sufferings of savages by being in want of food, for they have plenty. And they have not the uneasiness which springs from refined life. They work in every way proper for young ladies. Miss ——— plays on the guitar. What can disturb them? I can only say that I was disturbed by thinking how poor a chance they had to get husbands. I mused on this, in the very heat of dancing. It perhaps, though, does not occur either to them or to their father.[377]

SUNDAY 12 SEPTEMBER. It was a fine day, and although we do not approve of travelling on Sunday, we resolved to set out, as we were in an island from whence we must take occasion as it serves. Besides, I had sent forward Sir Alexander's horses to Portree against his inclination. He had most inhospitably desired to have them sent back to him when we got to the shore opposite to Raasay, and thus thought to make us shift the best way we could after coming out of Raasay. He even gave me a note in my almanac how to try for horses. But since he had not proper reflection, I resolved to supply his place, upon hearing that we should hardly be able to find other horses.[378] Mr Johnson said, "Don't let us part with *them* till we get others."

I said any sensible Justice of Peace would press them for us. Mr Donald Macqueen was clear for our keeping them. It was accordingly done. But as he was to set out for Edinburgh on the 15, it was necessary to send them back to him early this week.

MacLeod and Talisker sailed in a boat of Raasay's for Sconser, to take the shortest way to Dunvegan. MacCruslick went with them to Sconser, from whence he was to go to Sleat, and so away to the mainland. We were resolved to pay a visit at Kingsburgh and see the celebrated Miss Flora Macdonald, who is married to the present Kingsburgh; so took the other road.[379]

All the family, but Lady Raasay, walked down to the shore to see us depart. I confess I felt some pain in leaving Raasay. But I thought I would come with my wife and daughter to pass an autumn there. Raasay himself went with us in a large boat with eight oars, built in his island. So did worthy Malcolm. So did Mr Donald Macqueen, Dr MacLeod, two of Raasay's sons, and their tutor. Raasay said the party under the Government in 1745 destroyed a number of the very cows and horses in Raasay. A list was taken of them. But the Act of Parliament for indemnity as to those outrages prevented redress.

CHAPTER FIVE

Skye Again

SAMUEL JOHNSON

At *Raasay*, by good fortune, *Macleod*, so the chief of the clan is called, was paying a visit, and by him we were invited to his seat at *Dunvegan*. *Raasay* has a stout boat, built in *Norway*, in which, with six oars, he conveyed us back to *Sky*. We landed at *Port Re*, so called, because *James* the Fifth of *Scotland*, who had curiosity to visit the Islands, came into it.[380] The port is made by an inlet of the sea, deep and narrow, where a ship lay waiting to dispeople *Sky*, by carrying the natives away to *America*.

In coasting *Sky*, we passed by the cavern in which it was the custom, as *Martin* relates, to catch birds in the night, by making a fire at the entrance. This practice is disused; for the birds, as is known often to happen, have changed their haunts.[381]

Here we dined at a publick house, I believe the only inn of the island, and having mounted our horses, travelled in the manner already described, till we came to *Kingsborough*, a place distinguished by that name, because the King lodged here when he landed at *Port Re*.[382] We were entertained with the usual hospitality by Mr *Macdonald* and his lady, *Flora Macdonald*, a name that will be mentioned in history, and if courage and fidelity be virtues, mentioned with honour. She is a woman of middle stature, soft features, gentle manners, and elegant presence.[383]

In the morning we sent our horses round a promontory to meet us, and spared ourselves part of the day's fatigue, by crossing an arm of the sea. We had at last some difficulty in coming to *Dunvegan*; for our way led over an extensive moor, where every step was to be taken with caution,

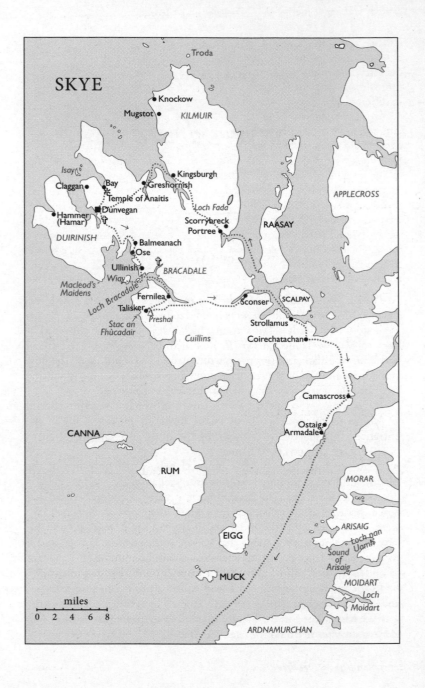

SKYE

Troda

Knockow

Mugstot

KILMUIR

Isay

Claggan

Bay

Greshornish

Kingsburgh

Temple of Anaitis

Loch Fada

APPLECROSS

Hammer
(Hamar)

Dunvegan

Scorrybreck

Portree

RAASAY

DUIRINISH

Balmeanach

Ose

BRACADALE

Ullinish

Wiay

SCALPAY

Macleod's
Maidens

Loch Bracadale

Fernilea

Sconser

Talisker

Strollamus

Preshal

Coirechatachan

Stac an
Fhùcadair

Cuillins

Camascross

Ostaig

Armadale

CANNA

RUM

MORAR

ARISAIG

Loch nan
Uamh

EIGG

Sound
of
Arisaig

MOIDART

MUCK

Loch
Moidart

miles

0   2   4   6   8

ARDNAMURCHAN

and we were often obliged to alight, because the ground could not be trusted. In travelling this watery flat, I perceived that it had a visible declivity, and might without much expence or difficulty be drained. But difficulty and expence are relative terms, which have different meanings in different places.

To *Dunvegan* we came, very willing to be at rest, and found our fatigue amply recompensed by our reception. Lady *Macleod*, who had lived many years in *England*, was newly come hither with her son and four daughters, who knew all the arts of southern elegance, and all the modes of English economy.[384] Here therefore we settled, and did not spoil the present hour with thoughts of departure.

Dunvegan is a rocky prominence, that juts out into a bay, on the west side of *Sky*. The house, which is the principal seat of *Macleod*, is partly old and partly modern; it is built upon the rock, and looks upon the water. It forms two sides of a small square: on the third side is the skeleton of a castle of unknown antiquity, supposed to have been a *Norwegian* fortress, when the Danes were masters of the Islands. It is so nearly entire, that it might have easily been made habitable, were there not an ominous tradition in the family, that the owner shall not long outlive the reparation. The grandfather of the present Laird, in defiance of prediction, began the work, but desisted in a little time, and applied his money to worse uses.[385]

As the inhabitants of the *Hebrides* lived, for many ages, in continual expectation of hostilities, the chief of every clan resided in a fortress. This house was accessible only from the water, till the last possessor opened an entrance by stairs upon the land.

They had formerly reason to be afraid, not only of declared wars and authorized invaders, or of roving pirates, which, in the northern seas, must have been very common; but of inroads and insults from rival clans, who, in the plenitude of feudal independence, asked no leave of their Sovereign to make war on one another. Sky has been ravaged by a feud between the two mighty powers of *Macdonald* and *Macleod*. *Macdonald* having married a *Macleod*, upon some discontent dismissed her, perhaps because she had brought him no children. Before the reign of *James* the Fifth, a Highland Laird made a trial of his wife for a certain time, and if she did not please him, he was then at liberty to send her away. This however must always have offended, and *Macleod* resenting the injury, whatever were its circumstances, declared, that the wedding had been solemnized without a bonfire, but that the separation should be better illuminated; and raising a little army, set fire to the territories of *Macdonald*, who returned the visit, and prevailed.[386]

Another story may show the disorderly state of insular neighbourhood. The inhabitants of the Isle of *Egg*, meeting a boat manned by *Macleods*, tied the crew hand and foot, and set them adrift. *Macleod* landed upon *Egg*, and demanded the offenders; but the inhabitants refusing to surrender them, retreated to a cavern, into which they thought their enemies unlikely to follow them. *Macleod* choked them with smoke, and left them lying dead by families as they stood.[387]

Here the violence of the weather confined us for some time, not at all to our discontent or inconvenience. We would indeed very willingly have visited the Islands, which might be seen from the house scattered in the sea, and I was particularly desirous to have viewed *Isay*; but the storms did not permit us to launch a boat, and we were condemned to listen in idleness to the wind, except when we were better engaged by listening to the ladies.

We had here more wind than waves, and suffered the severity of a tempest, without enjoying its magnificence. The sea being broken by the multitude of islands, does not roar with so much noise, nor beat the storm with such foamy violence, as I have remarked on the coast of *Sussex*. Though, while I was in the *Hebrides*, the wind was extremely turbulent, I never saw very high billows.

The country about *Dunvegan* is rough and barren. There are no trees, except in the orchard, which is a low sheltered spot surrounded with a wall.

When this house was intended to sustain a siege, a well was made in the court, by boring the rock downwards, till water was found, which though so near to the sea, I have not heard mentioned as brackish, though it has some hardness, or other qualities, which make it less fit for use; and the family is now better supplied from a stream, which runs by the rock, from two pleasing waterfalls.

Here we saw some traces of former manners, and heard some standing traditions. In the house is kept an ox's horn, hollowed so as to hold perhaps two quarts, which the heir of *Macleod* was expected to swallow at one draught, as a test of his manhood, before he was permitted to bear arms, or could claim a seat among the men. It is held that the return of the Laird to *Dunvegan*, after any considerable absence, produces a plentiful capture of herrings; and that, if any woman crosses the water to the opposite Island, the herrings will desert the coast. *Boetius* tells the same of some other place. This tradition is not uniform. Some hold that no woman may pass, and others that none may pass but a *Macleod*.[388]

Among other guests, which the hospitality of *Dunvegan* brought to the table, a visit was paid by the Laird and Lady of a small island south of *Sky*, of which the proper name is *Muack*, which signifies swine.[389] It is commonly called *Muck*, which the proprietor not liking, has endeavoured, without effect, to change to *Monk*. It is usual to call gentlemen in *Scotland* by the name of their possessions, as *Raasay, Bernera, Loch Buy*, a practice necessary in countries inhabited by clans, where all that live in the same territory have one name, and must be therefore discriminated by some addition. This gentleman, whose name, I think, is *Maclean*, should be regularly called *Muck*; but the appellation, which he thinks too coarse for his Island, he would like still less for himself, and he is therefore addressed by the title of, *Isle of Muck*.

This little Island, however it be named, is of considerable value. It is two *English* miles long, and three quarters of a mile broad, and consequently contains only nine hundred and sixty *English* acres. It is chiefly arable. Half of this little dominion the Laird retains in his own hand, and on the other half, live one hundred and sixty persons, who pay their rent by exported corn. What rent they pay, we were not told, and could not decently inquire. The proportion of the people to the land is such, as the most fertile countries do not commonly maintain.

The Laird having all his people under his immediate view, seems to be very attentive to their happiness. The devastation of the smallpox, when it visits places where it comes seldom, is well known. He has disarmed it of its terrour at *Muack*, by inoculating eighty of his people. The expence was two shillings and sixpence a head. Many trades they cannot have among them, but upon occasion, he fetches a smith from the Isle of *Egg*, and has a tailor from the main land, six times a year. This Island well deserved to be seen, but the Laird's absence left us no opportunity.

Every inhabited Island has its appendant and subordinate islets. Muck, however small, has yet others smaller about it, one of which has only ground sufficient to afford pasture for three wethers.

At *Dunvegan* I had tasted lotus, and was in danger of forgetting that I was ever to depart, till Mr Boswell sagely reproached me with my sluggishness and softness. I had no very forcible defence to make; and we agreed to pursue our journey. *Macleod* accompanied us to *Ulinish*, where we were entertained by the sheriff of the Island.[390]

Mr *Macqueen* travelled with us, and directed our attention to all that was worthy of observation. With him we went to see an ancient building, called a dun or borough. It was a circular inclosure, about forty-two feet in diameter, walled round with loose stones, perhaps to the height of nine feet. The walls are very thick, diminishing a little towards the top, and though in these countries, stone is not brought far, must have been raised with much labour. Within the great circle were several smaller rounds of wall, which formed distinct apartments. Its date, and its use are unknown. Some suppose it the original seat of the chiefs of the *Macleods*. Mr *Macqueen* thought it a *Danish* fort.[391]

The entrance is covered with flat stones, and is narrow, because it was necessary that the stones which lie over it, should reach from one wall to the other; yet, strait as the passage is, they seem heavier than could have been placed where they now lie, by the naked strength of as many men as might stand about them. They were probably raised by putting long pieces of wood under them, to which the action of a long line of lifters might be applied. Savages, in all countries, have patience proportionate to their unskilfulness, and are content to attain their end by very tedious methods.

If it was ever roofed, it might once have been a dwelling, but as there is no provision for water, it could not have been a fortress. In *Sky*, as in every other place, there is an ambition of exalting whatever has survived memory, to some important use, and referring it to very remote ages. I am inclined to suspect, that in lawless times, when the inhabitants of every mountain stole the cattle of their neighbour, these inclosures were used to secure the herds and flocks in the night. When they were driven within the wall, they might be easily watched, and defended as long as could be needful; for the robbers durst not wait till the injured clan should find them in the morning.

The interior inclosures, if the whole building were once a house, were the chambers of the chief inhabitants. If it was a place of security for cattle, they were probably the shelters of the keepers.

From the *Dun* we were conducted to another place of security, a cave carried a great way under ground, which had been discovered by digging after a fox.[392] These caves, of which many have been found, and many probably remain concealed, are formed, I believe, commonly by taking advantage of a hollow, where banks or rocks rise on either side. If no such place can be found, the ground must be cut away. The walls are made by piling stones against the earth, on either side. It is then roofed by larger stones laid across the cavern, which therefore cannot be wide. Over the roof, turfs were placed, and grass was suffered to grow; and the mouth was concealed by bushes, or some other cover.

These caves were represented to us as the cabins of the first rude inhabitants, of which, however, I am by no means persuaded. This was so low, that no man could stand upright in it. By their construction they are all so narrow, that two can never pass along them together, and being subterraneous, they must be always damp. They are not the work of an age much ruder than the present; for they are formed with as much art as the construction of a common hut requires. I imagine them to have been places only of occasional use, in which the Islander, upon a sudden alarm, hid his utensils, or his cloaths, and perhaps sometimes his wife and children.

This cave we entered, but could not proceed the whole length, and went away without knowing how far it was carried. For this omission we shall be blamed, as we perhaps have blamed other travellers; but the day was rainy, and the ground was damp. We had with us neither spades nor pickaxes, and if love of ease surmounted our desire of knowledge, the offence has not the invidiousness of singularity.

Edifices, either standing or ruined, are the chief records of an illiterate nation. In some part of this journey, at no great distance from our way, stood a shattered fortress, of which the learned minister, to whose communication we are much indebted, gave us an account.

Those, said he, are the walls of a place of refuge, built in the time of James the Sixth, by Hugh Macdonald, who was next heir to the dignity and fortune of his chief.[393] Hugh, being so near his wish, was impatient of delay; and had art and influence sufficient to engage several gentlemen in a plot against the Laird's life. Something must be stipulated on both sides; for they would not dip their hands in blood merely for Hugh's advancement. The compact was formally written, signed by the conspirators, and placed in the hands of one Macleod.

It happened that Macleod had sold some cattle to a drover, who, not having ready money, gave him a bond for payment. The debt was discharged, and the bond redemanded; which Macleod, who could not read, intending to put into his hands, gave him the conspiracy. The drover, when he had read the paper, delivered it privately to Macdonald; who, being thus informed of his danger, called his friends together, and provided for his safety. He made a publick feast, and inviting Hugh Macdonald and his confederates, placed each of them at the table between two men of known fidelity. The compact of conspiracy was then shewn, and every man confronted with his own name. Macdonald acted with great moderation. He upbraided Hugh, both with disloyalty and ingratitude; but told the rest, that he considered them as men deluded and misinformed. Hugh was sworn to fidelity, and dismissed with his companions; but he was not generous enough to be reclaimed by lenity; and finding no longer any countenance among the gentlemen, endeavoured to execute the same design by meaner hands. In this practice he was detected, taken to Macdonald's castle, and imprisoned in the dungeon. When he was hungry, they let down a plentiful meal of salted meat; and when, after his repast, he called for drink, conveyed to him a covered cup, which, when he lifted the lid, he found empty. From that time they visited him no more, but left him to perish in solitude and darkness.

We were then told of a cavern by the seaside, remarkable for the powerful reverberation of sounds. After dinner we took a boat, to explore this curious cavity. The boatmen, who seemed to be of a rank above that of common drudges, inquired who the strangers were, and being told we came one from *Scotland*, and the other from *England*, asked if the *Englishman* could recount a long genealogy. What answer was given them, the conversation being in *Erse*, I was not much inclined to examine.

They expected no good event of the voyage; for one of them declared that he heard the cry of an *English* ghost. This omen I was not told till after our return, and therefore cannot claim the dignity of despising it.

The sea was smooth. We never left the shore, and came without any disaster to the cavern, which we found rugged and misshapen, about one hundred and eighty feet long, thirty wide in the broadest part, and in the loftiest, as we guessed, about thirty high. It was now dry, but at high water the sea rises in it near six feet. Here I saw what I had never seen before, limpets and mussels in their natural state. But, as a new testimony to the veracity of common fame, here was no echo to be heard.

We then walked through a natural arch in the rock, which might have pleased us by its novelty, had the stones, which incumbered our feet, given us leisure to consider it. We were shown the gummy seed of the kelp, that fastens itself to a stone, from which it grows into a strong stalk.

In our return, we found a little boy upon the point of a rock, catching with his angle, a supper for the family. We rowed up to him, and borrowed his rod, with which Mr *Boswell* caught a cuddy.[394]

The cuddy is a fish of which I know not the philosophical name. It is not much bigger than a gudgeon, but is of great use in these Islands, as it affords the lower people both food, and oil for their lamps. Cuddies are so abundant, at some times of the year, that they are caught like whitebait in the *Thames*, only by dipping a basket and drawing it back.

If it were always practicable to fish, these Islands could never be in much danger from famine; but unhappily in the winter, when other provision fails, the seas are commonly too rough for nets, or boats.

From *Ulinish*, our next stage was to *Talisker*, the house of colonel *Macleod*, an officer in the *Dutch* service, who, in this time of universal peace, has for several years been permitted to be absent from his regiment. Having been bred to physick, he is consequently a scholar, and his lady, by accompanying him in his different places of residence, is become skilful in several languages. *Talisker* is the place beyond all that I have seen, from which the gay and the jovial seem utterly excluded; and where the hermit might expect to grow old in meditation, without possibility of disturbance or interruption.[395] It is situated very near the sea, but upon a coast where no vessel lands but when it is driven by a tempest on the rocks. Towards the land are lofty hills streaming with waterfalls. The garden is sheltered by firs or pines, which grow there so prosperously, that some, which the present inhabitant planted, are very high and thick.

At this place we very happily met Mr *Donald Maclean*, a young gentleman, the eldest son of the Laird of *Col*, heir to a very great extent of land, and so desirous of improving his inheritance, that he spent a considerable time among the farmers of *Hertfordshire* and *Hampshire*, to learn their practice. He worked with his own hands at the principal operations of agriculture, that he might not deceive himself by a false opinion of skill, which, if he should find it deficient at home, he had no means of completing. If the world has agreed to praise the travels and manual labours of the Czar *of Muscovy*, let *Col* have his share of the like applause, in the proportion of his dominions to the empire of *Russia*.[396]

This young gentleman was sporting in the mountains of *Sky*, and when he was weary with following his game, repaired for lodging to *Talisker*. At night he missed one of his dogs, and when he went to seek him in the morning, found two eagles feeding on his carcass.

Col, for he must be named by his possessions, hearing that our intention was to visit *Iona*, offered to conduct us to his chief, Sir *Allan Maclean*, who lived in the isle of *Inch Kenneth*, and would readily find us a convenient passage. From this time was formed an acquaintance, which being begun by kindness, was accidentally continued by constraint; we derived much pleasure from it, and I hope have given him no reason to repent it.

The weather was now almost one continued storm, and we were to snatch some happy intermission to be conveyed to *Mull*, the third Island of the *Hebrides*, lying about a degree south of *Sky*, whence we might easily find our way to *Inch Kenneth*, where Sir *Allan Maclean* resided, and afterward to *Iona*.

For this purpose, the most commodious station that we could take was *Armidel*, which Sir *Alexander Macdonald* had now left to a gentleman, who lived there as his factor or steward.[397]

In our way to *Armidel* was Coriatachan, where we had already been, and to which therefore we were very willing to return. We staid however so long at *Talisker*, that a great part of our journey was performed in the gloom of the evening. In travelling even thus almost without light thro' naked solitude, when there is a guide whose conduct may be trusted, a mind not naturally too much disposed to fear, may preserve some degree of cheerfulness; but what must be the solicitude of him who should be wandering, among the craggs and hollows, benighted, ignorant, and alone?

The fictions of the *Gothick* romances were not so remote from credibility as they are now thought. In the full prevalence of the feudal institution, when violence desolated the world, and every baron lived in a fortress, forests and castles were regularly succeeded by each other, and the adventurer might very suddenly pass from the gloom of woods, or the ruggedness of moors, to seats of plenty, gaiety, and magnificence. Whatever is imaged in the wildest tale, if giants, dragons, and enchantment be excepted, would be felt by him, who, wandering in the mountains without a guide, or upon the sea without a pilot, should be carried amidst his terror and uncertainty, to the hospitality and elegance of *Raasay* or *Dunvegan*.

To Coriatachan at last we came, and found ourselves welcomed as before. Here we staid two days, and made such inquiries as curiosity suggested. The house was filled with company, among whom Mr *Macpherson* and his sister distinguished themselves by their politeness and accomplishments.[398] By him we were invited to *Ostig*, a house not far from *Armidel*, where we might easily hear of a boat, when the weather would suffer us to leave the Island.

At *Ostig*, of which Mr *Macpherson* is minister, we were entertained for some days, then removed to *Armidel*, where we finished our observations on the island of Sky.

As this Island lies in the fifty-seventh degree, the air cannot be supposed to have much warmth. The long continuance of the sun above the horizon, does indeed sometimes produce great heat in northern latitudes; but this can only happen in sheltered places, where the atmosphere is to a certain degree stagnant, and the same mass of air continues to receive for many hours the rays of the sun, and the vapours of the earth. *Sky* lies open on the west and north to a vast extent of ocean, and is cooled in the summer by perpetual ventilation, but by the same blasts is kept warm in winter. Their weather is not pleasing. Half the year is deluged with rain. From the autumnal to the vernal equinox, a dry day is hardly known, except when the showers are suspended by a tempest. Under such skies can be expected no great exuberance of vegetation. Their winter overtakes their summer, and their harvest lies upon the ground drenched with rain. The autumn struggles hard to produce some of our early fruits. I gathered gooseberries in September; but they were small, and the husk was thick.

Their winter is seldom such as puts a full stop to the growth of plants, or reduces the cattle to live wholly on the surplusage of the summer. In the year Seventy-one they had a severe season, remembered by the name of the Black Spring, from which the island has not yet recovered. The snow lay long upon the ground, a calamity hardly known before. Part of their cattle died for want, part were unseasonably sold to buy sustenance for the owners; and, what I have not read or heard of before, the kine that survived were so emaciated and dispirited, that they did not require the male at the usual time. Many of the roebucks perished.[399]

The soil, as in other countries, has its diversities. In some parts there is only a thin layer of earth spread upon a rock, which bears nothing but short brown heath, and perhaps is not generally capable of any better product. There are many bogs or mosses of greater or less extent, where the soil cannot be supposed to want depth, though it is too wet for the plow. But we did not observe in these any aquatick plants. The vallies and the mountains are alike darkened with heath. Some grass, however, grows here and there, and some happier spots of earth are capable of tillage.

Their agriculture is laborious, and perhaps rather feeble than unskilful. Their chief manure is sea-weed, which, when they lay it to rot upon the field, gives them a better crop than those of the Highlands. They heap sea shells upon the dunghill, which in time moulder into a fertilising substance. When they find a vein of earth where they cannot use it, they dig it up, and add it to the mould of a more commodious place.

Their corn grounds often lie in such intricacies among the craggs, that there is no room for the action of a team and plow. The soil is then turned up by manual labour, with an instrument called a crooked spade, of a form and weight which to me appeared very incommodious, and would perhaps be soon improved in a country where workmen could be easily found and easily paid. It has a narrow blade of iron fixed to a long and heavy piece of wood, which must have, about a foot and a half above the iron, a knee or flexure with the angle downwards. When the farmer encounters a stone which is the great impediment of his operations, he drives the blade under it, and bringing the knee or angle to the ground, has in the long handle a very forcible lever.[400]

According to the different mode of tillage, farms are distinguished into *long land* and *short land*. Long land is that which affords room for a plow, and short land is turned up by the spade.[401]

The grain which they commit to the furrows thus tediously formed, is either oats or barley. They do not sow barley without very copious manure, and then they expect from it ten for one, an increase equal to that of better countries; but the culture is so operose that they content themselves commonly with oats; and who can relate without compassion, that after all their diligence they are to expect only a triple increase? It is in vain to hope for plenty, when a third part of the harvest must be reserved for seed.

When their grain is arrived at the state which they must consider as ripeness, they do not cut, but pull the barley: to the oats they apply the sickle. Wheel carriages they have none, but make a frame of timber, which is drawn by one horse with the two points behind pressing on the ground. On this they sometimes drag home their sheaves, but often convey them home in a kind of open panier, or frame of sticks upon the horse's back.[402]

Of that which is obtained with so much difficulty, nothing surely ought to be wasted; yet their method of clearing their oats from the husk is by parching them in the straw. Thus with the genuine improvidence of savages, they destroy that fodder for want of which their cattle may perish. From this practice they have two petty conveniencies. They dry the grain so that it is easily reduced to meal, and they escape the theft of the thresher. The taste contracted from the fire by the oats, as by every other scorched substance, use must long ago have made grateful. The oats that are not parched must be dried in a kiln.[403]

The barns of *Sky* I never saw. That which *Macleod of Raasay* had erected near his house was so contrived, because the harvest is seldom brought home dry, as by perpetual perflation to prevent the mow from heating.[404]

Of their gardens I can judge only from their tables. I did not observe that the common greens were wanting, and suppose, that by choosing an advantageous exposition, they can raise all the more hardy esculent plants. Of vegetable fragrance or beauty they are not yet studious. Few vows are made to Flora in the *Hebrides*.

They gather a little hay, but the grass is mown late; and is so often almost dry and again very wet, before it is housed, that it becomes a collection of withered stalks without taste or fragrance; it must be eaten by cattle that have nothing else, but by most English farmers would be thrown away.

In the Islands I have not heard that any subterraneous treasures have been discovered, though where there are mountains, there are commonly minerals. One of the rocks in *Col* has a black vein, imagined to consist of the ore of lead; but it was never yet opened or essayed. In *Sky* a black mass was accidentally picked up, and brought into the house of the owner of the land, who found himself strongly inclined to think it a coal, but unhappily it did not burn in the chimney.[405] Common ores would be here of no great value; for what requires to be separated by fire, must, if it were found, be carried away in its mineral state, here being no fewel for the smelting-house or forge. Perhaps by diligent search in this world of stone, some valuable species of marble might be discovered. But neither philosophical curiosity, nor commercial industry, have yet fixed their abode here, where the importunity of immediate want supplied but for the day, and craving on the morrow, has left little room for excursive knowledge or the pleasing fancies of distant profit.

They have lately found a manufacture considerably lucrative. Their rocks abound with kelp, a sea-plant, of which the ashes are melted into glass. They burn kelp in great quantities, and then send it away in ships, which come regularly to purchase them. This new source of riches has raised the rents of many maritime farms; but the tenants pay, like all other tenants, the additional rent with great unwillingness; because they consider the profits of the kelp as the mere product of personal labour, to which the landlord contributes nothing. However, as any man may be said to give, what he gives the power of gaining, he has certainly as much right to profit from the price of kelp as of any thing else found or raised upon his ground.

This new trade has excited a long and eager litigation between *Macdonald* and *Macleod*, for a ledge of rocks, which, till the value of kelp was known, neither of them desired the reputation of possessing.[406]

The cattle of *Sky* are not so small as is commonly believed. Since they have sent their beeves in great numbers to southern marts, they have probably taken more care of their breed. At stated times the annual growth of cattle is driven to a fair, by a general drover, and with the money, which he returns to the farmer, the rents are paid.

The price regularly expected, is from two to three pounds a head: there was once one sold for five pounds. They go from the Islands very lean, and are not offered to the butcher, till they have been long fatted in *English* pastures.

Of their black cattle, some are without horns, called by the Scots *humble* cows, as we call a bee an *humble* bee, that wants a sting.[407]

Whether this difference be specifick, or accidental, though we inquired with great diligence, we could not be informed. We are not very sure that the bull is ever without horns, though we have been told, that such bulls there are. What is produced by putting a horned and unhorned male and female together, no man has ever tried, that thought the result worthy of observation.

Their horses are, like their cows, of a moderate size. I had no difficulty to mount myself commodiously by the favour of the gentlemen. I heard of very little cows in *Barra*, and very little horses in *Rum*, where perhaps no care is taken to prevent that diminution of size, which must always happen, where the greater and the less copulate promiscuously, and the young animal is restrained from growth by penury of sustenance.

The goat is the general inhabitant of the earth, complying with every difference of climate, and of soil. The goats of the *Hebrides* are like others: nor did I hear any thing of their sheep, to be particularly remarked.[408]

In the penury of these malignant regions nothing is left that can be converted to food. The goats and the sheep are milked like the cows. A single meal of a goat is a quart, and of a sheep a pint. Such at least was the account, which I could extract from those of whom I am not sure that they ever had inquired.

The milk of goats is much thinner than that of cows, and that of sheep is much thicker. Sheeps milk is never eaten before it is boiled: as it is thick, it must be very liberal of curd, and the people of St *Kilda* form it into small cheeses.

The stags of the mountains are less than those of our parks, or forests, perhaps not bigger than our fallow deer. Their flesh has no rankness, nor is inferiour in flavour to our common venison. The roebuck I neither saw nor tasted. These are not countries for a regular chase. The deer are not driven with horns and hounds.[409] A sportsman, with his gun in his hand, watches the animal, and when he has wounded him, traces him by the blood.

They have a race of brinded greyhounds, larger and stronger than those with which we course hares, and these are the only dogs used by them for the chase.

Man is by the use of firearms made so much an overmatch for other animals, that in all countries, where they are in use, the wild part of the creation sensibly diminishes. There will probably not be long, either stags or roebucks in the Islands. All the beasts of chase would have been lost long ago in countries well inhabited, had they not been preserved by laws for the pleasure of the rich.

There are in *Sky* neither rats nor mice, but the weasel is so frequent, that he is heard in houses rattling behind chests or beds, as rats in *England*. They probably owe to his predominance that they have no other vermin; for since the great rat took possession of this part of the world, scarce a ship can touch any port, but some of his race are left behind. They have within these few years begun to infest the isle of *Col*, where being left by some trading vessel, they have increased for want of weasels to oppose them.

The inhabitants of *Sky*, and of the other Islands, which I have seen, are commonly of the middle stature, with fewer among them very tall or very short, than are seen in *England*, or perhaps, as their numbers are small, the chances of any deviation from the common measure are necessarily few. The tallest men that I saw are among those of higher rank. In regions of barrenness and scarcity, the human race is hindered in its growth by the same causes as other animals.

The ladies have as much beauty here as in other places, but bloom and softness are not to be expected among the lower classes, whose faces are exposed to the rudeness of the climate, and whose features are sometimes contracted by want, and sometimes hardened by the blasts. Supreme beauty is seldom found in cottages or work-shops, even where no real hardships are suffered. To expand the human face to its full perfection, it seems necessary that the mind should cooperate by placidness of content, or consciousness of superiority.

Their strength is proportionate to their size, but they are accustomed to run upon rough ground, and therefore can with great agility skip over the bog, or clamber the mountain. For a campaign in the wastes of *America*, soldiers better qualified could not have been found. Having little work to do, they are not willing, nor perhaps able to endure a long continuance of manual labour, and are therefore considered as habitually idle.

Having never been supplied with those accommodations, which life extensively diversified with trades affords, they supply their wants by very insufficient shifts, and endure many inconveniences, which a little attention would easily relieve. I have seen a horse carrying home the harvest on a crate. Under his tail was a stick for a crupper, held at the two ends by twists of straw. Hemp will grow in their islands, and therefore ropes may be had. If they wanted hemp, they might make better cordage of rushes, or perhaps of nettles, than of straw.[410]

Their method of life neither secures them perpetual health, nor exposes them to any particular diseases. There are physicians in the Islands, who, I believe, all practise chirurgery, and all compound their own medicines.

It is generally supposed, that life is longer in places where there are few opportunities of luxury; but I found no instance here of extraordinary longevity. A cottager grows old over his oaten cakes, like a citizen at a turtle feast.[411] He is indeed seldom incommoded by corpulence. Poverty preserves him from sinking under the burden of himself, but he escapes no other injury of time. Instances of long life are often related, which those who hear them are more willing to credit than examine. To be told that any man has attained a hundred years, gives hope and comfort to him who stands trembling on the brink of his own climacterick.

Length of life is distributed impartially to very different modes of life in very different climates; and the mountains have no greater examples of age and health than the lowlands, where I was introduced to two ladies of high quality; one of whom, in her ninety-fourth year, presided at her table with the full exercise of all her powers; and the other has attained her eighty-fourth, without any diminution of her vivacity, and with little reason to accuse time of depredations of her beauty.[412]

In the Islands, as in most other places, the inhabitants are of different rank, and one does not encroach here upon another. Where there is no commerce nor manufacture, he that is born poor can scarcely become rich; and if none are able to buy estates, he that is born to land cannot annihilate his family by selling it. This was once the state of these countries. Perhaps there is no example, till within a century and half, of any family whose estate was alienated otherwise than by violence or forfeiture. Since money has been brought amongst them, they have found, like others, the art of spending more than they receive; and I saw with grief the chief of a very ancient clan, whose Island was condemned by law to be sold for the satisfaction of his creditors.[413]

The name of highest dignity is Laird, of which there are in the extensive Isle of Sky only three, *Macdonald*, *Macleod*, and *Mackinnon*. The Laird is the original owner of the land, whose natural power must be very great, where no man lives but by agriculture; and where the produce of the land is not conveyed through the labyrinths of traffick, but passes directly from the hand that gathers it to the mouth that eats it. The Laird has all those in his power that live upon his farms. Kings can, for the most part, only exalt or degrade. The Laird at pleasure can feed or starve, can give bread, or withold it. This inherent power was yet strengthened by the kindness of consanguinity, and the reverence of patriarchal authority. The Laird was the father of the Clan, and his tenants commonly bore his name. And to these principles of original command was added, for many ages, an exclusive right of legal jurisdiction.

This multifarious, and extensive obligation operated with force scarcely credible. Every duty, moral or political, was absorbed in affection and adherence to the Chief. Not many years have passed since the clans knew no law but the Laird's will. He told them to whom they should be friends or enemies, what King they should obey, and what religion they should profess.

When the Scots first rose in arms against the succession of the house of *Hanover*, *Lovat*, the Chief of the Frasers, was in exile for a rape.[414] The Frasers were very numerous, and very zealous against the government. A pardon was sent to *Lovat*. He came to the *English* camp, and the clan immediately deserted to him.

Next in dignity to the Laird is the Tacksman; a large taker or lease-holder of land, of which he keeps part, as a domain, in his own hand, and lets part to under tenants. The Tacksman is necessarily a man capable of securing to the Laird the whole rent, and is commonly a collateral relation. These *tacks*, or subordinate possessions, were long considered as hereditary, and the occupant was distinguished by the name of the place at which he resided. He held a middle station, by which the highest and the lowest orders were connected. He paid rent and reverence to the Laird, and received them from the tenants. This tenure still subsists, with its original operation, but not with the primitive stability. Since the islanders, no longer content to live, have learned the desire of growing rich, an ancient dependent is in danger of giving way to a higher bidder, at the expence of domestick dignity and hereditary power. The stranger, whose money buys him preference, considers himself as paying for all that he has, and is indifferent about the Laird's honour or safety. The commodiousness of money is indeed great; but there are some advantages which money cannot buy, and which therefore no wise man will by the love of money be tempted to forego.

I have found in the hither parts of *Scotland*, men not defective in judgment or general experience, who consider the Tacksman as a useless burden of the ground, as a drone who lives upon the product of an estate, without the right of property, or the merit of labour, and who impoverishes at once the landlord and the tenant. The land, say they, is let to the Tacksman at sixpence an acre, and by him to the tenant at ten-pence. Let the owner be the immediate landlord to all the tenants; if he sets the ground at eight-pence, he will increase his revenue by a fourth part, and the tenant's burthen will be diminished by a fifth.

Those who pursue this train of reasoning, seem not sufficiently to inquire whither it will lead them, nor to know that it will equally shew the propriety of suppressing all wholesale trade, of shutting up the shops of every man who sells what he does not make, and of extruding all whose agency and profit intervene between the manufacturer and the consumer. They may, by stretching their understandings a little wider, comprehend, that all those who by undertaking large quantities of manufacture, and affording employment to many labourers, make themselves considered as benefactors to the publick, have only been robbing their workmen with one hand, and their customers with the other. If Crowley had sold only what he could make, and all his smiths had wrought their own iron with their own hammers, he would have lived on less, and they would have sold their work for more.[415] The salaries of superintendents and clerks would have been partly saved, and partly shared, and nails been sometimes cheaper by a farthing in a hundred. But then if the smith could not have found an immediate purchaser, he must have deserted his anvil; if there had by accident at any time been more sellers than buyers, the workmen must have reduced their profit to nothing, by underselling one another; and as no great stock could have been in any hand, no sudden demand of large quantities could have been answered, and the builder must have stood still till the nailer could supply him.

According to these schemes, universal plenty is to begin and end in universal misery. Hope and emulation will be utterly extinguished; and as all must obey the call of immediate necessity, nothing that requires extensive views, or provides for distant consequences, will ever be performed.

To the southern inhabitants of Scotland, the state of the mountains and the islands is equally unknown with that of *Borneo* or *Sumatra*. Of both they have only heard a little, and guess the rest. They are strangers to the language and the manners, to the advantages and wants of the people, whose life they would model, and whose evils they would remedy.

Nothing is less difficult than to procure one convenience by the forfeiture of another. A soldier may expedite his march by throwing away his arms. To banish the Tacksman is easy, to make a country plentiful by diminishing the people, is an expeditious mode of husbandry; but that abundance, which there is nobody to enjoy, contributes little to human happiness.

As the mind must govern the hands, so in every society the man of intelligence must direct the man of labour. If the Tacksmen be taken away, the Hebrides must in their present state be given up to grossness and ignorance; the tenant, for want of instruction, will be unskilful, and for want of admonition will be negligent. The Laird in these wide estates, which often consist of islands remote from one another, cannot extend his personal influence to all his tenants; and the steward having no dignity annexed to his character, can have little authority among men taught to pay reverence only to birth, and who regard the Tacksman as their hereditary superior; nor can the steward have equal zeal for the prosperity of an estate profitable only to the Laird, with the Tacksman, who has the Laird's income involved in his own.

The only gentlemen in the Islands are the Lairds, the Tacksmen, and the Ministers, who frequently improve their livings by becoming farmers. If the Tacksmen be banished, who will be left to impart knowledge, or impress civility? The Laird must always be at a distance from the greater part of his lands; and if he resides at all upon them, must drag his days in solitude, having no longer either a friend or a companion; he will therefore depart to some more comfortable residence, and leave the tenants to the wisdom and mercy of a factor.

Of tenants there are different orders, as they have greater or less stock. Land is sometimes leased to a small fellowship, who live in a cluster of huts, called a Tenants Town, and are bound jointly and separately for the payment of their rent. These, I believe, employ in the care of their cattle, and the labour of tillage, a kind of tenants yet lower; who having a hut, with grass for a certain number of cows and sheep, pay their rent by a stipulated quantity of labour.[416]

The condition of domestick servants, or the price of occasional labour, I do not know with certainty. I was told that the maids have sheep, and are allowed to spin for their own clothing; perhaps they have no pecuniary wages, or none but in very wealthy families. The state of life, which has hitherto been purely pastoral, begins now to be a little variegated with commerce; but novelties enter by degrees, and till one mode has fully prevailed over the other, no settled notion can be formed.

Such is the system of insular subordination, which, having little variety, cannot afford much delight in the view, nor long detain the mind in contemplation. The inhabitants were for a long time perhaps not unhappy; but their content was a muddy mixture of pride and ignorance, an indifference for pleasures which they did not know, a blind veneration for their chiefs, and a strong conviction of their own importance.

Their pride has been crushed by the heavy hand of a vindictive conqueror, whose severities have been followed by laws, which, though they cannot be called cruel, have produced much discontent, because they operate upon the surface of life, and make every eye bear witness to subjection. To be compelled to a new dress has always been found painful.[417]

Their Chiefs being now deprived of their jurisdiction, have already lost much of their influence; and as they gradually degenerate from patriarchal rulers to rapacious landlords, they will divest themselves of the little that remains.

That dignity which they derived from an opinion of their military importance, the law, which disarmed them, has abated. An old gentleman, delighting himself with the recollection of better days, related, that forty years ago, a Chieftain walked out attended by ten or twelve followers, with their arms rattling. That animating rattle has now ceased. The Chief has lost his formidable retinue; and the Highlander walks his heath unarmed and defenceless, with the peaceable submission of a French peasant or English cottager.

Their ignorance grows every day less, but their knowledge is yet of little other use than to shew them their wants. They are now in the period of education, and feel the uneasiness of discipline, without yet perceiving the benefit of instruction.

The last law, by which the Highlanders are deprived of their arms, has operated with efficacy beyond expectation. Of former statutes made with the same design, the execution had been feeble, and the effect inconsiderable. Concealment was undoubtedly practised, and perhaps often with connivance. There was tenderness, or partiality, on one side, and obstinacy on the other. But the law, which followed the victory of Culloden, found the whole nation dejected and intimidated; informations were given without danger, and without fear, and the arms were collected with such rigour, that every house was despoiled of its defence.

To disarm part of the Highlands, could give no reasonable occasion of complaint. Every government must be allowed the power of taking away the weapon that is lifted against it. But the loyal clans murmured, with some appearance of justice, that after having defended the King, they were forbidden for the future to defend themselves; and that the sword should be forfeited, which had been legally employed. Their case is undoubtedly hard, but in political regulations, good cannot be complete, it can only be predominant.[418]

Whether by disarming a people thus broken into several tribes, and thus remote from the seat of power, more good than evil has been produced, may deserve inquiry. The supreme power in every community has the right of debarring every individual, and every subordinate society from self-defence, only because the supreme power is able to defend them; and therefore where the governor cannot act, he must trust the subject to act for himself. These Islands might be wasted with fire and sword before their sovereign would know their distress. A gang of robbers, such as has been lately found confederating themselves in the Highlands, might lay a wide region under contribution.[419] The crew of a petty privateer might land on the largest and most wealthy of the Islands, and riot without control in cruelty and waste. It was observed by one of the Chiefs of Sky, that fifty armed men might, without resistance, ravage the country. Laws that place the subjects in such a state, contravene the first principles of the compact of authority: they exact obedience, and yield no protection.

It affords a generous and manly pleasure to conceive a little nation gathering its fruits and tending its herds with fearless confidence, though it lies open on every side to invasion, where, in contempt of walls and trenches, every man sleeps securely with his sword beside him; where all on the first approach of hostility come together at the call to battle, as at a summons to a festal show; and committing their cattle to the care of those whom age or nature has disabled, engage the enemy with that competition for hazard and for glory, which operates in men that fight under the eye of those, whose dislike or kindness they have always considered as the greatest evil or the greatest good.

This was, in the beginning of the present century, the state of the Highlands. Every man was a soldier, who partook of national confidence, and interested himself in national honour. To lose this spirit, is to lose what no small advantage will compensate.

It may likewise deserve to be inquired, whether a great nation ought to be totally commercial? Whether amidst the uncertainty of human affairs, too much attention to one mode of happiness may not endanger others? Whether the pride of riches must not sometimes have recourse to the protection of courage? And whether, if it be necessary to preserve in some part of the empire the military spirit, it can subsist more commodiously in any place, than in remote and unprofitable provinces, where it can commonly do little harm, and whence it may be called forth at any sudden exigence?

It must however be confessed, that a man, who places honour only in successful violence, is a very troublesome and pernicious animal in time of peace; and that the martial character cannot prevail in a whole people, but by the diminution of all other virtues. He that is accustomed to resolve all right into conquest, will have very little tenderness or equity. All the friendship in such a life can be only a confederacy of invasion, or alliance of defence. The strong must flourish by force, and the weak subsist by stratagem.

Till the Highlanders lost their ferocity, with their arms, they suffered from each other all that malignity could dictate, or precipitance could act. Every provocation was revenged with blood, and no man that ventured into a numerous company, by whatever occasion brought together, was sure of returning without a wound. If they are now exposed to foreign hostilities, they may talk of the danger, but can seldom feel it. If they are no longer martial, they are no longer quarrelsome. Misery is caused for the most part, not by a heavy crush of disaster, but by the corrosion of less visible evils, which canker enjoyment, and undermine security. The visit of an invader is necessarily rare, but domestick animosities allow no cessation.

The abolition of the local jurisdictions, which had for so many ages been exercised by the chiefs, has likewise its evil and its good. The feudal constitution naturally diffused itself into long ramifications of subordinate authority. To this general temper of the government was added the peculiar form of the country, broken by mountains into many subdivisions scarcely accessible but to the natives, and guarded by passes, or perplexed with intricacies, through which national justice could not find its way.

The power of deciding controversies, and of punishing offences, as some such power there must always be, was intrusted to the Lairds of the country, to those whom the people considered as their natural judges. It cannot be supposed that a rugged proprietor of the rocks, unprincipled and unenlightened, was a nice resolver of entangled claims, or very exact in proportioning punishment to offences. But the more he indulged his own will, the more he held his vassals in dependance. Prudence and innocence, without the favour of the Chief, conferred no security; and crimes involved no danger, when the judge was resolute to acquit.

When the chiefs were men of knowledge and virtue, the convenience of a domestick judicature was great. No long journies were necessary, nor artificial delays could be practised; the character, the alliances, and interests of the litigants were known to the court, and all false pretences were easily detected. The sentence, when it was past, could not be evaded; the power of the Laird superseded formalities, and justice could not be defeated by interest or stratagem.

I doubt not but that since the regular judges have made their circuits through the whole country, right has been every where more wisely, and more equally distributed; the complaint is, that litigation is grown troublesome, and that the magistrates are too few, and therefore often too remote for general convenience.

Many of the smaller Islands have no legal officer within them. I once asked, if a crime should be committed, by what authority the offender could be seized? And was told, that the Laird would exert his right; a right which he must now usurp, but which surely necessity must vindicate, and which is therefore yet exercised in lower degrees, by some of the proprietors, when legal processes cannot be obtained.[420]

In all greater questions, however, there is now happily an end to all fear or hope from malice or from favour. The roads are secure in those places through which, forty years ago, no traveller could pass without a convoy. All trials of right by the sword are forgotten, and the mean are in as little danger from the powerful as in other places. No scheme of policy has, in any country, yet brought the rich and poor on equal terms into courts of judicature. Perhaps experience, improving on experience, may in time effect it.

Those who have long enjoyed dignity and power, ought not to lose it without some equivalent. There was paid to the Chiefs by the publick, in exchange for their privileges, perhaps a sum greater than most of them had ever possessed, which excited a thirst for riches, of which it shewed them the use.[421] When the power of birth and station ceases, no hope remains but from the prevalence of money. Power and wealth supply the place of each other. Power confers the ability of gratifying our desire without the consent of others. Wealth enables us to obtain the consent of others to our gratification. Power, simply considered, whatever it confers on one, must take from another. Wealth enables its owner to give to others by taking only from himself. Power pleases the violent and proud: wealth delights the placid and the timorous. Youth therefore flies at power, and age grovels after riches.

The Chiefs, divested of their prerogatives, necessarily turned their thoughts to the improvement of their revenues, and expect more rent, as they have less homage. The tenant, who is far from perceiving that his condition is made better in the same proportion, as that of his landlord is made worse, does not immediately see why his industry is to be taxed more heavily than before. He refuses to pay the demand, and is ejected; the ground is then let to a stranger, who perhaps brings a larger stock, but who, taking the land at its full price, treats with the Laird upon equal terms, and considers him not as a Chief, but as a trafficker in land. Thus the estate perhaps is improved, but the clan is broken.

It seems to be the general opinion, that the rents have been raised with too much eagerness. Some regard must be paid to prejudice. Those who have hitherto paid but little, will not suddenly be persuaded to pay much, though they can afford it. As ground is gradually improved, and the value of money decreases, the rent may be raised without any diminution of the farmer's profits: yet it is necessary in these countries, where the ejection of a tenant is a greater evil, than in more populous places, to consider not merely what the land will produce, but with what ability the inhabitant can cultivate it. A certain stock can allow but a certain payment; for if the land be doubled, and the stock remains the same, the tenant becomes no richer. The proprietors of the Highlands might perhaps often increase their income, by subdividing the farms, and allotting to every occupier only so many acres as he can profitably employ, but that they want people.

There seems now, whatever be the cause, to be through a great part of the Highlands a general discontent. That adherence, which was lately professed by every man to the chief of his name, has now little prevalence; and he that cannot live as he desires at home, listens to the tale of fortunate islands, and happy regions, where every man may have land of his own, and eat the product of his labour without a superior.

Those who have obtained grants of American lands, have, as is well known, invited settlers from all quarters of the globe; and among other places, where oppression might produce a wish for new habitations, their emissaries would not fail to try their persuasions in the Isles of Scotland, where at the time when the clans were newly disunited from their Chiefs, and exasperated by unprecedented exactions, it is no wonder that they prevailed.

Whether the mischiefs of emigration were immediately perceived, may be justly questioned. They who went first, were probably such as could best be spared; but the accounts sent by the earliest adventurers, whether true or false, inclined many to follow them; and whole neighbourhoods formed parties for removal; so that departure from their native country is no longer exile. He that goes thus accompanied, carries with him all that makes life pleasant. He sits down in a better climate, surrounded by his kindred and his friends: they carry with them their language, their opinions, their popular songs, and hereditary merriment: they change nothing but the place of their abode; and of that change they perceive the benefit.

This is the real effect of emigration, if those that go away together settle on the same spot, and preserve their ancient union. But some relate that these adventurous visitants of unknown regions, after a voyage passed in dreams of plenty and felicity, are dispersed at last upon a Sylvan wilderness, where their first years must be spent in toil, to clear the ground which is afterwards to be tilled, and that the whole effect of their undertaking is only more fatigue and equal scarcity.

Both accounts may be suspected. Those who are gone will endeavour by every art to draw others after them; for as their numbers are greater, they will provide better for themselves. When *Nova Scotia* was first peopled, I remember a letter, published under the character of a New Planter, who related how much the climate put him in mind of Italy.[422] Such intelligence the *Hebridians* probably receive from their transmarine correspondents. But with equal temptations of interest, and perhaps with no greater niceness of veracity, the owners of the Islands spread stories of American hardships to keep their people content at home.

Some method to stop this epidemick desire of wandering, which spreads its contagion from valley to valley, deserves to be sought with great diligence. In more fruitful countries, the removal of one only makes room for the succession of another: but in the *Hebrides*, the loss of an inhabitant leaves a lasting vacuity; for nobody born in any other parts of the world will choose this country for his residence; and an Island once depopulated will remain a desert, as long as the present facility of travel gives every one, who is discontented and unsettled, the choice of his abode.

Let it be inquired, whether the first intention of those who are fluttering on the wing, and collecting a flock that they may take their flight, be to attain good, or to avoid evil. If they are dissatisfied with that part of the globe, which their birth has allotted them, and resolve not to live without the pleasures of happier climates; if they long for bright suns, and calm skies, and flowery fields, and fragrant gardens, I know not by what eloquence they can be persuaded, or by what offers they can be hired to stay.

But if they are driven from their native country by positive evils, and disgusted by ill-treatment, real or imaginary, it were fit to remove their grievances, and quiet their resentment; since, if they have been hitherto undutiful subjects, they will not much mend their principles by American conversation.

To allure them into the army, it was thought proper to indulge them in the continuance of their national dress. If this concession could have any effect, it might easily be made. That dissimilitude of appearance, which was supposed to keep them distinct from the rest of the nation, might disincline them from coalescing with the *Pensylvanians*, or people of *Connecticut*. If the restitution of their arms will reconcile them to their country, let them have again those weapons, which will not be more mischievous at home than in the Colonies. That they may not fly from the increase of rent, I know not whether the general good does not require that the landlords be, for a time, restrained in their demands, and kept quiet by pensions proportionate to their loss.

To hinder insurrection, by driving away the people, and to govern peaceably, by having no subjects, is an expedient that argues no great profundity of politicks. To soften the obdurate, to convince the mistaken, to mollify the resentful, are worthy of a statesman; but it affords a legislator little self-applause to consider, that where there was formerly an insurrection, there is now a wilderness.[423]

It has been a question often agitated without solution, why those northern regions are now so thinly peopled, which formerly overwhelmed with their armies the Roman empire. The question supposes what I believe is not true, that they had once more inhabitants than they could maintain, and overflowed only because they were full.

This is to estimate the manners of all countries and ages by our own. Migration, while the state of life was unsettled, and there was little communication of intelligence between distant places, was among the wilder nations of Europe, capricious and casual. An adventurous projector heard of a fertile coast unoccupied, and led out a colony; a chief of renown for bravery, called the young men together, and led them out to try what fortune would present. When Caesar was in *Gaul*, he found the Helvetians preparing to go they knew not whither, and put a stop to their motions. They settled again in their own country, where they were so far from wanting room, that they had accumulated three years provision for their march.[424]

The religion of the North was military; if they could not find enemies, it was their duty to make them: they travelled in quest of danger, and willingly took the chance of Empire or Death. If their troops were numerous, the countries from which they were collected are of vast extent, and without much exuberance of people great armies may be raised where every man is a soldier. But their true numbers were never known. Those who were conquered by them are their historians, and shame may have excited them to say, that they were overwhelmed with multitudes. To count is a modern practice, the ancient method was to guess; and when numbers are guessed they are always magnified.[425]

Thus England has for several years been filled with the atchievements of seventy thousand Highlanders employed in *America*. I have heard from an English officer, not much inclined to favour them, that their behaviour deserved a very high degree of military praise; but their number has been much exaggerated. One of the ministers told me, that seventy thousand men could not have been found in all the Highlands, and that more than twelve thousand never took the field. Those that went to the American war, went to destruction. Of the old Highland regiment, consisting of twelve hundred, only seventy-six survived to see their country again.

The Gothick swarms have at least been multiplied with equal liberality. That they bore no great proportion to the inhabitants, in whose countries they settled, is plain from the paucity of northern words now found in the provincial languages. Their country was not deserted for want of room, because it was covered with forests of vast extent; and the first effect of plenitude of inhabitants is the destruction of wood. As the Europeans spread over *America*, the lands are gradually laid naked.

I would not be understood to say, that necessity had never any part in their expeditions. A nation, whose agriculture is scanty or unskilful, may be driven out by famine. A nation of hunters may have exhausted their game. I only affirm that the northern regions were not, when their irruptions subdued the Romans, overpeopled with regard to their real extent of territory, and power of fertility. In a country fully inhabited, however afterward laid waste, evident marks will remain of its former populousness. But of *Scandinavia* and *Germany*, nothing is known but that as we trace their state upwards into antiquity, their woods were greater, and their cultivated ground was less.

That causes very different from want of room may produce a general disposition to seek another country is apparent from the present conduct of the Highlanders, who are in some places ready to threaten a total secession. The numbers which have already gone, though like other numbers they may be magnified, are very great, and such as if they had gone together and agreed upon any certain settlement, might have founded an independent government in the depths of the western continent. Nor are they only the lowest and most indigent; many men of considerable wealth have taken with them their train of labourers and dependants; and if they continue the feudal scheme of polity, may establish new clans in the other hemisphere.

That the immediate motives of their desertion must be imputed to their landlords, may be reasonably concluded, because some Lairds of more prudence and less rapacity have kept their vassals undiminished. From *Raasa* only one man had been seduced, and at *Col* there was no wish to go away.

The traveller who comes hither from more opulent countries, to speculate upon the remains of pastoral life, will not much wonder that a common Highlander has no strong adherence to his native soil; for of animal enjoyments, or of physical good, he leaves nothing that he may not find again wheresoever he may be thrown.

The habitations of men in the *Hebrides* may be distinguished into huts and houses. By a *house*, I mean a building with one story over another; by a *hut*, a dwelling with only one floor. The Laird, who formerly lived in a castle, now lives in a house; sometimes sufficiently neat, but seldom very spacious or splendid. The Tacksmen and the Ministers have commonly houses. Wherever there is a house, the stranger finds a welcome, and to the other evils of exterminating Tacksmen may be added the unavoidable cessation of hospitality, or the devolution of too heavy a burden on the Ministers.

Of the houses little can be said. They are small, and by the necessity of accumulating stores, where there are so few opportunities of purchase, the rooms are very heterogeneously filled. With want of cleanliness it were ingratitude to reproach them. The servants having been bred upon the naked earth, think every floor clean, and the quick succession of guests, perhaps not always over-elegant, does not allow much time for adjusting their apartments.

Huts are of many gradations; from murky dens, to commodious dwellings.

The wall of a common hut is always built without mortar, by a skilful adaptation of loose stones. Sometimes perhaps a double wall of stones is raised, and the intermediate space filled with earth. The air is thus completely excluded. Some walls are, I think, formed of turfs, held together by a wattle, or texture of twigs. Of the meanest huts, the first room is lighted by the entrance, and the second by the smoke-hole. The fire is usually made in the middle. But there are huts, or dwellings, of only one story, inhabited by gentlemen, which have walls cemented with mortar, glass windows, and boarded floors. Of these all have chimneys, and some chimneys have grates.

The house and the furniture are not always nicely suited. We were driven once, by missing a passage, to the hut of a gentleman, where, after a very liberal supper, when I was conducted to my chamber, I found an elegant bed of Indian cotton, spread with fine sheets. The accommodation was flattering; I undressed myself, and felt my feet in the mire. The bed stood upon the bare earth, which a long course of rain had softened to a puddle.[426]

In pastoral countries the condition of the lowest rank of people is sufficiently wretched. Among manufacturers, men that have no property may have art and industry, which make them necessary, and therefore valuable. But where flocks and corn are the only wealth, there are always more hands than work, and of that work there is little in which skill and dexterity can be much distinguished. He therefore who is born poor never can be rich. The son merely occupies the place of the father, and life knows nothing of progression or advancement.

The petty tenants, and labouring peasants, live in miserable cabins, which afford them little more than shelter from the storms. The Boor of *Norway* is said to make all his own utensils. In the *Hebrides*, whatever might be their ingenuity, the want of wood leaves them no materials. They are probably content with such accommodations as stones of different forms and sizes can afford them.

Their food is not better than their lodging. They seldom taste the flesh of land animals; for here are no markets. What each man eats is from his own stock. The great effect of money is to break property into small parts. In towns, he that has a shilling may have a piece of meat; but where there is no commerce, no man can eat mutton but by killing a sheep.

Fish in fair weather they need not want; but, I believe, man never lives long on fish, but by constraint; he will rather feed upon roots and berries.

The only fewel of the Islands is peat. Their wood is all consumed, and coal they have not yet found. Peat is dug out of the marshes, from the depth of one foot to that of six. That is accounted the best which is nearest the surface. It appears to be a mass of black earth held together by vegetable fibres. I know not whether the earth be bituminous, or whether the fibres be not the only combustible part; which, by heating the interposed earth red hot, make a burning mass. The heat is not very strong nor lasting. The ashes are yellowish, and in a large quantity. When they dig peat, they cut it into square pieces, and pile it up to dry beside the house. In some places it has an offensive smell. It is like wood charked for the smith. The common method of making peat fires, is by heaping it on the hearth; but it burns well in grates, and in the best houses is so used.

The common opinion is, that peat grows again where it has been cut; which, as it seems to be chiefly a vegetable substance, is not unlikely to be true, whether known or not to those who relate it.[427]

There are water mills in *Sky* and *Raasa*; but where they are too far distant, the housewives grind their oats with a quern, or hand-mill, which consists of two stones, about a foot and a half in diameter; the lower is a little convex, to which the concavity of the upper must be fitted. In the middle of the upper stone is a round hole, and on one side is a long handle. The grinder sheds the corn gradually into the hole with one hand, and works the handle round with the other. The corn slides down the convexity of the lower stone, and by the motion of the upper is ground in its passage. These stones are found in *Lochaber*.

The Islands afford few pleasures, except to the hardy sportsman, who can tread the moor and climb the mountain. The distance of one family from another, in a country where travelling has so much difficulty, makes frequent intercourse impracticable. Visits last several days, and are commonly paid by water; yet I never saw a boat furnished with benches, or made commodious by any addition to the first fabrick. Conveniencies are not missed where they never were enjoyed.

The solace which the bagpipe can give, they have long enjoyed; but among other changes, which the last Revolution introduced, the use of the bagpipe begins to be forgotten. Some of the chief families still entertain a piper, whose office was anciently hereditary. *Macrimmon* was piper to *Macleod*, and *Rankin* to *Maclean* of *Col*.[428]

The tunes of the bagpipe are traditional. There has been in *Sky*, beyond all time of memory, a college of pipers, under the direction of *Macrimmon*, which is not quite extinct. There was another in *Mull*, superintended by *Rankin*, which expired about sixteen years ago. To these colleges, while the pipe retained its honour, the students of musick repaired for education. I have had my dinner exhilarated by the bagpipe, at *Armidale*, at *Dunvegan*, and in *Col*.

The general conversation of the Islanders has nothing particular. I did not meet with the inquisitiveness of which I have read, and suspect the judgment to have been rashly made. A stranger of curiosity comes into a place where a stranger is seldom seen: he importunes the people with questions, of which they cannot guess the motive, and gazes with surprise on things which they, having had them always before their eyes, do not suspect of any thing wonderful. He appears to them like some being of another world, and then thinks it peculiar that they take their turn to inquire whence he comes, and whither he is going.[429]

The Islands were long unfurnished with instruction for youth, and none but the sons of gentlemen could have any literature. There are now parochial schools, to which the lord of every manor pays a certain stipend. Here the children are taught to read; but by the rule of their institution, they teach only *English*, so that the natives read a language which they may never use or understand. If a parish, which often happens, contains several Islands, the school being but in one, cannot assist the rest. This is the state of *Col*, which, however, is more enlightened than some other places; for the deficiency is supplied by a young gentleman, who, for his own improvement, travels every year on foot over the Highlands to the session at Aberdeen; and at his return, during the vacation, teaches to read and write in his native Island.[430]

In *Sky* there are two grammar schools, where boarders are taken to be regularly educated.[431] The price of board is from three pounds, to four pounds ten shillings a year, and that of instruction is half a crown a quarter. But the scholars are birds of passage, who live at school only in the summer; for in winter provisions cannot be made for any considerable number in one place. This periodical dispersion impresses strongly the scarcity of these countries.

Having heard of no boarding-school for ladies nearer than *Inverness*, I suppose their education is generally domestick. The elder daughters of the higher families are sent into the world, and may contribute by their acquisitions to the improvement of the rest.

Women must here study to be either pleasing or useful. Their deficiencies are seldom supplied by very liberal fortunes. A hundred pounds is a portion beyond the hope of any but the Laird's daughter. They do not indeed often give money with their daughters; the question is, how many cows a young lady will bring her husband. A rich maiden has from ten to forty; but two cows are a decent fortune for one who pretends to no distinction.

The religion of the Islands is that of the Kirk of *Scotland*. The gentlemen with whom I conversed are all inclined to the *English* liturgy; but they are obliged to maintain the established Minister, and the country is too poor to afford payment to another, who must live wholly on the contribution of his audience.

They therefore all attend the worship of the Kirk, as often as a visit from their Minister, or the practicability of travelling gives them opportunity; nor have they any reason to complain of insufficient pastors; for I saw not one in the Islands, whom I had reason to think either deficient in learning, or irregular in life; but found several with whom I could not converse without wishing, as my respect increased, that they had not been Presbyterians.

The ancient rigour of puritanism is now very much relaxed, though all are not yet equally enlightened. I sometimes met with prejudices sufficiently malignant, but they were prejudices of ignorance. The Ministers in the Islands had attained such knowledge as may justly be admired in men, who have no motive to study, but generous curiosity, or, what is still better, desire of usefulness; with such politeness as so narrow a circle of converse could not have supplied, but to minds naturally disposed to elegance.

Reason and truth will prevail at last. The most learned of the Scottish Doctors would now gladly admit a form of prayer, if the people would endure it. The zeal or rage of congregations has its different degrees. In some parishes the Lord's Prayer is suffered: in others it is still rejected as a form; and he that should make it part of his supplication would be suspected of heretical pravity.

The principle upon which extemporary prayer was originally introduced, is no longer admitted. The Minister formerly, in the effusion of his prayer, expected immediate, and perhaps perceptible inspiration, and therefore thought it his duty not to think before what he should say. It is now universally confessed, that men pray as they speak on other occasions, according to the general measure of their abilities and attainments. Whatever each may think of a form prescribed by another, he cannot but believe that he can himself compose by study and meditation a better prayer than will rise in his mind at a sudden call; and if he has any hope of supernatural help, why may he not as well receive it when he writes as when he speaks?

In the variety of mental powers, some must perform extemporary prayer with much imperfection; and in the eagerness and rashness of contradictory opinions, if publick liturgy be left to the private judgment of every Minister, the congregation may often be offended or misled.

There is in Scotland, as among ourselves, a restless suspicion of popish machinations, and a clamour of numerous converts to the Romish religion. The report is, I believe, in both parts of the Island equally false. The Romish religion is professed only in *Egg* and *Canna*, two small islands, into which the Reformation never made its way.[432] If any missionaries are busy in the Highlands, their zeal entitles them to respect, even from those who cannot think favourably of their doctrine.

The political tenets of the Islanders I was not curious to investigate, and they were not eager to obtrude. Their conversation is decent and inoffensive. They disdain to drink for their principles, and there is no disaffection at their tables. I never heard a health offered by a Highlander that might not have circulated with propriety within the precincts of the King's palace.

Legal government has yet something of novelty to which they cannot perfectly conform. The ancient spirit, that appealed only to the sword, is yet among them. The tenant of *Scalpa*, an island belonging to

Macdonald, took no care to bring his rent; when the landlord talked of exacting payment, he declared his resolution to keep his ground, and drive all intruders from the Island, and continued to feed his cattle as on his own land, till it became necessary for the Sheriff to dislodge him by violence.[433]

The various kinds of superstition which prevailed here, as in all other regions of ignorance, are by the diligence of the Ministers almost extirpated.

Of *Browny*, mentioned by Martin, nothing has been heard for many years. *Browny* was a sturdy Fairy; who, if he was fed, and kindly treated, would, as they said, do a great deal of work. They now pay him no wages, and are content to labour for themselves.

In *Troda*, within these three-and-thirty years, milk was put every Saturday for *Greogach*, or *the Old Man with the Long Beard*. Whether *Greogach* was courted as kind, or dreaded as terrible, whether they meant, by giving him the milk, to obtain good, or avert evil, I was not informed. The Minister is now living by whom the practice was abolished.[434]

They have still among them a great number of charms for the cure of different diseases; they are all invocations, perhaps transmitted to them from the times of popery, which increasing knowledge will bring into disuse.

They have opinions, which cannot be ranked with superstition because they regard only natural effects. They expect better crops of grain, by sowing their seed in the moon's increase. The moon has great influence in vulgar philosophy. In my memory it was a precept annually given in one of the *English* Almanacks, *to kill hogs when the moon was increasing, and the bacon would prove the better in boiling.*[435]

We should have had little claim to the praise of curiosity, if we had not endeavoured with particular attention to examine the question of the *Second Sight*. Of an opinion received for centuries by a whole nation, and supposed to be confirmed through its whole descent, by a series of successive facts, it is desirable that the truth should be established, or the fallacy detected.

The *Second Sight* is an impression made either by the mind upon the eye, or by the eye upon the mind, by which things distant or future are perceived, and seen as if they were present. A man on a journey far from home falls from his horse, another, who is perhaps at work about the house, sees him bleeding on the ground, commonly with a landscape of the place where the accident befalls him. Another seer, driving home his cattle, or wandering in idleness, or musing in the sunshine, is suddenly surprised by the appearance of a bridal ceremony, or funeral procession, and counts the mourners or attendants, of whom, if he knows them, he relates the names, if he knows them not, he can describe the dresses. Things distant are seen at the instant when they happen. Of things future I know not that there is any rule for determining the time between the Sight and the event.

This receptive faculty, for power it cannot be called, is neither voluntary nor constant. The appearances have no dependence upon choice: they cannot be summoned, detained, or recalled. The impression is sudden, and the effect often painful.

By the term *Second Sight*, seems to be meant a mode of seeing, superadded to that which Nature generally bestows. In the *Earse* it is called *Taisch*; which signifies likewise a spectre, or a vision. I know not, nor is it likely that the Highlanders ever examined, whether by *Taisch*, used for *Second Sight*, they mean the power of seeing, or the thing seen.[436]

I do not find it to be true, as it is reported, that to the *Second Sight* nothing is presented but phantoms of evil. Good seems to have the same proportion in those visionary scenes, as it obtains in real life: almost all remarkable events have evil for their basis; and are either miseries incurred, or miseries escaped. Our sense is so much stronger of what we suffer, than of what we enjoy, that the ideas of pain predominate in almost every mind. What is recollection but a revival of vexations, or history but a record of wars, treasons, and calamities? Death, which is considered as the greatest evil, happens to all. The greatest good, be it what it will, is the lot but of a part.

That they should often see death is to be expected; because death is an event frequent and important. But they see likewise more pleasing incidents. A gentleman told me, that when he had once gone far from his own Island, one of his labouring servants predicted his return, and described the livery of his attendant, which he had never worn at home; and which had been, without any previous design, occasionally given him.[437]

Our desire of information was keen, and our inquiry frequent. Mr Boswell's frankness and gaiety made every body communicative; and we heard many tales of these airy shows, with more or less evidence and distinctness.

It is the common talk of the Lowland *Scots*, that the notion of the *Second Sight* is wearing away with other superstitions; and that its reality is no longer supposed, but by the grossest people. How far its prevalence ever extended, or what ground it has lost, I know not. The Islanders of all degrees, whether of rank or understanding, universally admit it, except the Ministers, who universally deny it, and are suspected to deny it, in consequence of a system, against conviction. One of them honestly told me, that he came to *Sky* with a resolution not to believe it.[438]

Strong reasons for incredulity will readily occur. This faculty of seeing things out of sight is local, and commonly useless. It is a breach of the common order of things, without any visible reason or perceptible benefit. It is ascribed only to people very little enlightened; and among them, for the most part, to the mean and the ignorant.

To the confidence of these objections it may be replied, that by presuming to determine what is fit, and what is beneficial, they presuppose more knowledge of the universal system than man has attained; and therefore depend upon principles too complicated and extensive for our comprehension; and there can be no security in the consequence, when the premises are not understood; that the *Second Sight* is only wonderful because it is rare, for, considered in itself, it involves no more difficulty than dreams, or perhaps than the regular exercise of the cogitative faculty; that a general opinion of communicative impulses, or visionary representations, has prevailed in all ages and all nations; that particular instances have been given, with such evidence, as neither *Bacon* nor *Boyle* has been able to resist;[439] that sudden impressions, which the event has verified, have been felt by more than own or publish them; that the *Second Sight* of the *Hebrides* implies only the local frequency of a power, which is nowhere totally unknown; and that where we are unable to decide by antecedent reason, we must be content to yield to the force of testimony.

By pretension to *Second Sight*, no profit was ever sought or gained. It is an involuntary affection, in which neither hope nor fear are known to have any part. Those who profess to feel it, do not boast of it as a privilege, nor are considered by others as advantageously distinguished. They have no temptation to feign; and their hearers have no motive to encourage the imposture.

To talk with any of these seers is not easy. There is one living in *Sky*, with whom we would have gladly conversed; but he was very gross and ignorant, and knew no *English*. The proportion in these countries of the poor to the rich is such, that if we suppose the quality to be accidental, it can very rarely happen to a man of education; and yet on such men it has sometimes fallen. There is now a Second Sighted gentleman in the Highlands, who complains of the terrors to which he is exposed.[440]

The foresight of the Seers is not always prescience: they are impressed with images, of which the event only shews them the meaning. They tell what they have seen to others, who are at that time not more knowing than themselves, but may become at last very adequate witnesses, by comparing the narrative with its verification.

To collect sufficient testimonies for the satisfaction of the publick, or of ourselves, would have required more time than we could bestow. There is, against it, the seeming analogy of things confusedly seen, and little understood; and for it, the indistinct cry of national persuasion, which may be perhaps resolved at last into prejudice and tradition. I never could advance my curiosity to conviction; but came away at last only willing to believe.

As there subsists no longer in the Islands much of that peculiar and discriminative form of life, of which the idea had delighted our imagination, we were willing to listen to such accounts of past times as would be given us. But we soon found what memorials were to be expected from an illiterate people, whose whole time is a series of distress; where every morning is labouring with expedients for the evening; and where all mental pains or pleasure arose from the dread of winter, the expectation of spring, the caprices of their Chiefs, and the motions of the neighbouring clans; where there was neither shame from ignorance, nor pride in knowledge; neither curiosity to inquire, nor vanity to communicate.

The Chiefs indeed were exempt from urgent penury, and daily difficulties; and in their houses were preserved what accounts remained of past ages. But the Chiefs were sometimes ignorant and careless, and sometimes kept busy by turbulence and contention; and one generation of ignorance effaces the whole series of unwritten history. Books are faithful repositories, which may be a while neglected or forgotten; but when they are opened again, will again impart their instruction: memory, once interrupted, is not to be recalled. Written learning is a fixed luminary, which, after the cloud that had hidden it has past away, is again bright in its proper station. Tradition is but a meteor, which, if once it falls, cannot be rekindled.

It seems to be universally supposed, that much of the local history was preserved by the Bards, of whom one is said to have been retained by every great family. After these Bards were some of my first inquiries; and I received such answers as, for a while, made me please myself with my increase of knowledge; for I had not then learned how to estimate the narration of a Highlander.

They said that a great family had a *Bard* and a *Senachi*, who were the poet and historian of the house; and an old gentleman told me that he remembered one of each. Here was a dawn of intelligence. Of men that had lived within memory, some certain knowledge might be attained. Though the office had ceased, its effects might continue; the poems might be found, though there was no poet.

Another conversation indeed informed me, that the same man was both Bard and Senachi. This variation discouraged me; but as the practice might be different in different times, or at the same time in different families, there was yet no reason for supposing that I must necessarily sit down in total ignorance.

Soon after I was told by a gentleman, who is generally acknowledged the greatest master of *Hebridian* antiquities, that there had indeed once been both Bards and Senachies; and that *Senachi* signified *the man of talk*, or of conversation; but that neither Bard nor Senachi had existed for some centuries. I have no reason to suppose it exactly known at what time the custom ceased, nor did it probably cease in all houses at once. But whenever the practice of recitation was disused, the works, whether poetical or historical, perished with the authors; for in those times nothing had been written in the *Earse* language.

Whether the *Man of talk* was a historian, whose office was to tell truth, or a storyteller, like those which were in the last century, and perhaps are now among the Irish, whose trade was only to amuse, it now would be vain to inquire.[441]

Most of the domestick offices were, I believe, hereditary; and probably the laureat of a clan was always the son of the last laureat. The history of the race could no otherwise be communicated, or retained; but what genius could be expected in a poet by inheritance?

The nation was wholly illiterate. Neither bards nor Senachies could write or read; but if they were ignorant, there was no danger of detection; they were believed by those whose vanity they flattered.

The recital of genealogies, which has been considered as very efficacious to the preservation of a true series of ancestry, was anciently made, when the heir of the family came to manly age. This practice has never subsisted within time of memory, nor was much credit due to such rehearsers, who might obtrude fictitious pedigrees, either to please their masters, or to hide the deficiency of their own memories.[442]

Where the Chiefs of the Highlands have found the histories of their descent is difficult to tell; for no *Earse* genealogy was ever written. In general this only is evident, that the principal house of a clan must be very ancient, and that those must have lived long in a place, of whom it is not known when they came thither.

Thus hopeless are all attempts to find any traces of Highland learning. Nor are their primitive customs and ancient manner of life otherwise than very faintly and uncertainly remembered by the present race.

The peculiarities which strike the native of a commercial country, proceeded in a great measure from the want of money. To the servants and dependents that were not domesticks, and if an estimate be made from the capacity of any of their old houses which I have seen, their domesticks could have been but few, were appropriated certain portions of land for their support. *Macdonald* has a piece of ground yet, called the Bards or Senachies field. When a beef was killed for the house, particular parts were claimed as fees by the several officers, or workmen. What was the right of each I have not learned. The head belonged to the smith, and the udder of a cow to the piper: the weaver had likewise his particular part; and so many pieces followed these prescriptive claims, that the Laird's was at last but little.[443]

The payment of rent in kind has been so long disused in England, that it is totally forgotten. It was practised very lately in the *Hebrides*, and probably still continues, not only in St *Kilda*, where money is not yet known, but in others of the smaller and remoter Islands. It were perhaps to be desired, that no change in this particular should have been made. When the Laird could only eat the produce of his lands, he was under the necessity of residing upon them; and when the tenant could not convert his stock into more portable riches, he could never be tempted away from his farm, from the only place where he could be wealthy. Money confounds subordination, by overpowering the distinctions of rank and birth, and weakens authority by supplying power of resistance, or expedients for escape. The feudal system is formed for a nation employed in agriculture, and has never long kept its hold where gold and silver have become common.

Their arms were anciently the *Glaymore*, or great two-handed sword, and afterwards the two-edged sword and target, or buckler, which was sustained on the left arm. In the midst of the target, which was made of wood, covered with leather, and studded with nails, a slender lance, about two feet long, was sometimes fixed; it was heavy and cumberous, and accordingly has for some time past been gradually laid aside. Very few targets were at Culloden.[444] The dirk, or broad dagger, I am afraid, was of more use in private quarrels than in battles. The Lochaber-ax is only a slight alteration of the old *English* bill.

After all that has been said of the force and terrour of the Highland sword, I could not find that the art of defence was any part of common education. The gentlemen were perhaps sometimes skilful gladiators, but the common men had no other powers than those of violence and courage. Yet it is well known, that the onset of the Highlanders was very formidable. As an army cannot consist of philosophers, a panick is easily excited by any unwonted mode of annoyance. New dangers are naturally magnified; and men accustomed only to exchange bullets at a distance, and rather to hear their enemies than see them, are discouraged and amazed when they find themselves encountered hand to hand, and catch the gleam of steel flashing in their faces.

The Highland weapons gave opportunity for many exertions of personal courage, and sometimes for single combats in the field; like those which occur so frequently in fabulous wars. At Falkirk, a gentleman now living, was, I suppose after the retreat of the King's troops, engaged at a distance from the rest with an Irish dragoon. They were both skilful swordsmen, and the contest was not easily decided: the dragoon at last had the advantage, and the Highlander called for quarter; but quarter was refused him, and the fight continued till he was reduced to defend himself upon his knee. At that instant one of the Macleods came to his rescue; who, as it is said, offered quarter to the dragoon, but he thought himself obliged to reject what he had before refused, and, as battle gives little time to deliberate, was immediately killed.[445]

Funerals were formerly solemnized by calling multitudes together, and entertaining them at great expence. This emulation of useless cost has been for some time discouraged, and at last in the Isle of *Sky* is almost suppressed.

Of the Earse language, as I understand nothing, I cannot say more than I have been told. It is the rude speech of a barbarous people, who had few thoughts to express, and were content, as they conceived grossly, to be grossly understood. After what has been lately talked of Highland Bards, and Highland genius, many will startle when they are told, that the *Earse* never was a written language; that there is not in the world an Earse manuscript a hundred years old; and that the sounds of the Highlanders were never expressed by letters, till some little books of piety were translated, and a metrical version of the Psalms was made by the Synod of *Argyle*. Whoever therefore now writes in this language, spells according to his own perception of the sound, and his own idea of the power of the letters. The *Welsh* and the *Irish* are cultivated tongues. The Welsh, two hundred years ago, insulted their *English* neighbours for the instability of their Orthography; while the *Earse* merely floated in the breath of the people, and could therefore receive little improvement.[446]

When a language begins to teem with books, it is tending to refinement; as those who undertake to teach others must have undergone some labour in improving themselves, they set a proportionate value on their own thoughts, and wish to enforce them by efficacious expressions; speech becomes embodied and permanent; different modes and phrases are compared, and the best obtains an establishment. By degrees one age improves upon another. Exactness is first obtained, and afterwards elegance. But diction, merely vocal, is always in its childhood. As no man leaves his eloquence behind him, the new generations have all to learn. There may possibly be books without a polished language, but there can be no polished language without books.[447]

That the Bards could not read more than the rest of their countrymen, it is reasonable to suppose; because, if they had read, they could probably have written; and how high their compositions may reasonably be rated, an inquirer may best judge by considering what stores of imagery, what principles of ratiocination, what comprehension of knowledge, and what delicacy of elocution he has known any man attain who cannot read. The state of the Bards was yet more hopeless. He that cannot read, may now converse with those that can; but the Bard was a barbarian among barbarians, who, knowing nothing himself, lived with others that knew no more.

There has lately been in the Islands one of these illiterate poets, who hearing the Bible read at church, is said to have turned the sacred history into verse. I heard part of a dialogue, composed by him, translated by a young lady in *Mull*, and thought it had more meaning than I expected from a man totally uneducated; but he had some opportunities of knowledge; he lived among a learned people.[448] After all that has been done for the instruction of the Highlanders, the antipathy between their language and literature still continues; and no man that has learned only *Earse* is, at this time, able to read.

The *Earse* has many dialects, and the words used in some Islands are not always known in others. In literate nations, though the pronunciation, and sometimes the words of common speech may differ, as now in *England*, compared with the South of *Scotland*, yet there is a written diction, which pervades all dialects, and is understood in every province. But where the whole language is colloquial, he that has only one part, never gets the rest, as he cannot get it but by change of residence.

In an unwritten speech, nothing that is not very short is transmitted from one generation to another. Few have opportunities of hearing a long composition often enough to learn it, or have inclination to repeat it so often as is necessary to retain it; and what is once forgotten is lost for ever. I believe there cannot be recovered, in the whole *Earse* language, five hundred lines of which there is any evidence to prove them a hundred years old. Yet I hear that the father of Ossian boasts of two chests more of ancient poetry, which he suppresses, because they are too good for the *English.*[449]

He that goes into the Highlands with a mind naturally acquiescent, and a credulity eager for wonders, may come back with an opinion very different from mine; for the inhabitants knowing the ignorance of all strangers in their language and antiquities, perhaps are not very scrupulous adherents to truth; yet I do not say that they deliberately speak studied falsehood, or have a settled purpose to deceive. They have inquired and considered little, and do not always feel their own ignorance. They are not much accustomed to be interrogated by others; and seem never to have thought upon interrogating themselves; so that if they do not know what they tell to be true, they likewise do not distinctly perceive it to be false.

Mr Boswell was very diligent in his inquiries; and the result of his investigations was, that the answer to the second question was commonly such as nullified the answer to the first.

We were a while told, that they had an old translation of the scriptures; and told it till it would appear obstinacy to inquire again. Yet by continued accumulation of questions we found, that the translation meant, if any meaning there were, was nothing else than the *Irish* Bible.[450]

We heard of manuscripts that were, or that had been in the hands of somebody's father, or grandfather; but at last we had no reason to believe they were other than Irish. Martin mentions Irish, but never any Earse manuscripts, to be found in the Islands in his time.[451]

I suppose my opinion of the poems of Ossian is already discovered. I believe they never existed in any other form than that which we have seen. The editor, or author, never could shew the original; nor can it be shewn by any other; to revenge reasonable incredulity, by refusing evidence, is a degree of insolence, with which the world is not yet acquainted; and stubborn audacity is the last refuge of guilt. It would be easy to shew it if he had it; but whence could it be had? It is too long to be remembered, and the language formerly had nothing written. He has doubtless inserted names that circulate in popular stories, and may have translated some wandering ballads, if any can be found; and the names, and some of the images being recollected, make an inaccurate auditor imagine, by the help of Caledonian bigotry, that he has formerly heard the whole.[452]

I asked a very learned Minister in Sky, who had used all arts to make me believe the genuineness of the book, whether at last he believed it himself? But he would not answer. He wished me to be deceived, for the honour of his country; but would not directly and formally deceive me. Yet has this man's testimony been publickly produced, as of one that held Fingal to be the work of Ossian.[453]

It is said, that some men of integrity profess to have heard parts of it, but they all heard them when they were boys; and it was never said that any of them could recite six lines.[454] They remember names, and perhaps some proverbial sentiments; and, having no distinct ideas, coin a resemblance without an original. The persuasion of the Scots, however, is far from universal; and in a question so capable of proof, why should doubt be suffered to continue? The editor has been heard to say, that part of the poem was received by him, in the Saxon character.[455] He has then found, by some peculiar fortune, an unwritten language, written in a character which the natives probably never beheld.

I have yet supposed no imposture but in the publisher, yet I am far from certainty, that some translations have not been lately made, that may now be obtruded as parts of the original work. Credulity on one part is a strong temptation to deceit on the other, especially to deceit of which no personal injury is the consequence, and which flatters the author with his own ingenuity. The Scots have something to plead for their easy reception of an improbable fiction: they are seduced by their fondness for their supposed ancestors. A Scotchman must be a very sturdy moralist, who does not love *Scotland* better than truth: he will always love it better than inquiry; and if falsehood flatters his vanity, will not be very diligent to detect it. Neither ought the *English* to be much influenced by *Scotch* authority; for of the past and present state of the whole *Earse* nation, the Lowlanders are at least as ignorant as ourselves. To be ignorant is painful; but it is dangerous to quiet our uneasiness by the delusive opiate of hasty persuasion.

But this is the age in which those who could not read, have been supposed to write; in which the giants of antiquated romance have been exhibited as realities. If we know little of the ancient Highlanders, let us not fill the vacuity with *Ossian*. If we have not searched the *Magellanick* regions, let us however forbear to people them with *Patagons*.[456]

James Boswell

We had a most pleasant sail between Raasay and Skye; passed by a cave where Martin says fowls were caught by lighting fire in the mouth of it. Malcolm remembers this. But 'tis not now practised, as few fowls come into it.

We spoke of death. Mr Johnson gave us a short discourse worth any sermon, saying that the reflections of some men as to dying easily were idle talk, were partial views. I mentioned Hawthornden's *Cypress Grove*, where it is said that the world is just a show; and how unreasonable is it for a man to wish to continue in the show-room after he has seen it.[457] Let him go cheerfully out and give place to other spectators. "Yes," said Mr Johnson. "If he's sure he's to be well after he goes out of it. But if he is to grow blind after he goes out of the show-room, and never to see anything again; or if he does not know whither he is to go next, a man will not go cheerfully out of a show-room. No wise man will be contented to die if he thinks he is to go into a state of punishment. Nay, no wise man will be contented to die if he thinks he is to fall into annihilation. For however bad any man's existence may be, every man would rather have it than not exist at all. No, there is no rational principle by which a man can be contented, but a trust in the mercy of God, through the merits of Jesus Christ."

All this delivered with manly eloquence in a boat on the sea, upon a fine, calm Sunday morning, while every one listened with a comfortable air of satisfaction and complacency, had a most pleasing effect upon my mind. Mr Johnson observed that it seemed certain that happiness could not be found in this life, because so many had tried to find it in such a variety of ways, and had not found it.

We came into the harbour of Portree, which is a large and good one. There was lying in it a vessel to carry off the emigrants. It was called the *Nestor*. It made a short settlement of the differences between a chief and his clan: "Nestor componere lites / Inter Peleiden festinat et inter Atriden."[458] We approached her, and she hoisted her colours; at least I observed them putting them up as we came, and observed no more. Mr Johnson and Mr Macqueen remained in the boat. Raasay and I and the rest went on board of her. She was a very pretty vessel, we were told the largest in Clyde, being of ——— ton. Harrison, the Captain, showed us her. The cabin was commodious and even elegant. There was a little library, finely bound. I looked at nothing except a volume of the Rev. Mr Hervey's works lying on the table. The accommodation for the emigrants was very good. A long ward I may call it, with a row of beds on each side, every one of which was the same size every way, and fit to contain four people.

We landed at Portree, which has its name from King James V having landed at it in his tour through the Western Isles, *Ree* in Erse being 'king', as *Re* in Italian. So it is *Kingston* or *Portroyal*. We found here a very good half-finished inn, kept by James Macdonald, who is going to America.[459] On our landing I had a most agreeable letter from my dear wife, with the best accounts of her and Veronica; and Mr Johnson and I had each of us letters from Lord Elibank, sent after us from Edinburgh, which were like rich cordials to us. They are state papers in this expedition. The one to Mr Johnson was as follows:

> DEAR SIR, I was to have kissed your hands at Edinburgh the moment I heard of you, but you was gone. I hope my friend Boswell will inform me of your motions. It will be cruel to deprive me an instant of the honour of attending you. As I value you more than any king in Christendom, I will perform that duty with infinitely greater alacrity than any courtier. I can contribute but little to your entertainment, but my sincere esteem for you gives me some title to the opportunity of expressing it. I dare say you are by this time sensible that things are pretty much the same as when Buchanan complained of being born *solo et seculo inerudito*.[460] Let me hear of you, and be persuaded that none of your admirers is more sincerely devoted to you than, dear sir, your most obedient and most humble servant, ELIBANK.

Mine was also in an admirable style. But I need not engross it here, as I keep it.[461] Perhaps, too, I may be permitted to keep Mr Johnson's as his *Custos Rotulorum*, but lest I should not, I have put it down; and for the same reason I shall here put down, while it is in my head to do it, his burgess-ticket of Aberdeen.

> Diploma Abredonense pro Samuele Johnson, LL.D. Abredoniae, vigesimo tertio die mensis Augusti, Anno Domini millesimo septingentesimo septuagesimo tertio, in praesentia honorabilium virorum Jacobi Jopp, Armigeri, Praepositi; Adami Duff, Gulielmi Young, Georgii Marr, et Gulielmi Forbes, Ballivorum; Gulielmi Rainie, Decani Guildae; et Joannis Nicoll, Thesaurarii dicti Burgi. Quo die vir generosus ac doctrina clarus, Samuel Johnson, LL.D., receptus et admissus fuit in municipes et fratres Guildae praefati Burgi de Aberdeen. In deditissimi amoris et

affectus ac eximiae observantiae tesseram, quibus dicti Magistratus eum
amplectuntur. Extractum per me, ALEX^r CARNEGIE.[462]

Dr Johnson, on the following Tuesday, answered for both of us, thus:

My Lord, On the rugged shore of Skie, I had the honour of your lordship's
letter, and can with great truth declare, that no place is so gloomy but
that it would be cheered by such a testimony of regard, from a mind
so well qualified to estimate characters, and to deal out approbation in
its due proportions. If I have more than my share, it is your lordship's
fault; for I have always reverenced your judgment too much, to exalt
myself in your presence by any false pretensions. Mr Boswell and I are at
present at the disposal of the winds, and therefore cannot fix the time at
which we shall have the honour of seeing your lordship. But we should
either of us think ourselves injured by the supposition that we would miss
your lordship's conversation, when we could enjoy it; for I have often
declared that I never met you without going away a wiser man. / I am,
my Lord, / Your lordship's most obedient / And most humble servant, /
SAM. JOHNSON.[463]

At Portree, Mr Donald Macqueen went to church and officiated in
Erse, and then came to dinner. Mr Johnson and I resolved that we should
treat; so I played the landlord, having previously ordered Joseph to pay
the bill. We had a very good dinner, porter, port, and punch. We had
Mrs Macdonald, a very comely woman, James's wife, at the head of the
table, and James himself sat with us. I was quite easy with him: "Come,
Portroyal, your toast."

Sir James intended to have built a village here, which would have
done great good. A village is like a heart to a country. It produces a
perpetual circulation, and gives the country people an opportunity to
make profit of eggs and many little articles which would otherwise be in
a good measure lost. It was a dinner here *et praeterea nihil*.[464] Mr Johnson
talked none. Captain Harrison dined with us. When we came to go away,
behold Raasay had been beforehand and paid all, or at least concerted
with James Macdonald that he should pay, as it was an inn near to his
estate. This was a most uncommon degree of kindness and generosity.
I would fain have contested it with him, but seeing him resolved, I
declined it.

I parted with cordial embraces from him and worthy Malcolm,
hoping to see them again. Mr Johnson and I set out on horseback again,
accompanied by Mr Macqueen, Dr MacLeod, and Donald Canna. It was
a very rainy afternoon. We rode what they call six miles to Dr MacLeod's

Sunday 12 September

house upon Raasay's lands in Skye. On the road Mr Johnson appeared to be somewhat out of humour. When I talked of our meeting Lord Elibank, he said, "I cannot be with him much. I long to be again in civilized life, but cannot stay long." (He meant at Edinburgh.)[465] He said, "Let us go to Dunvegan tomorrow."

"Yes," said I, "if it is not a deluge."

"At any rate," said he.

This showed a kind of impatience upon his spirits, and no wonder, considering our disagreeable ride. I apprehended his giving up Mull and Icolmkill, for he said something of his fears of being detained by bad weather in going to Mull and *Iona*. However, I hoped well.

We had a comfortable dish of tea at the Doctor's, a pretty good house, where was his brother, a half-pay officer. His lady was a decent well-behaved woman.[466] Mr Johnson said he was glad to see her so. He had an esteem for physicians. The Doctor accompanied us to Kingsburgh, said to be but a mile farther, but the computation of Skye has no connexion whatever with the real distance.

It was fine to see Mr Johnson light from his horse at Kingsburgh's, who received us most courteously, and after shaking hands supported Mr Johnson into the house. He was quite the figure of a gallant Highlander – 'the graceful mien and manly looks', which our popular Scotch song has justly attributed to that character.[467] He had his tartan plaid thrown about him, a large blue bonnet with a knot of black ribbon like a cockade, a brown short coat of a kind of duffle, a tartan vest with gold buttons and gold buttonholes, a bluish filibeg, and tartan hose. He had jet-black hair tied behind and with screwed ringlets on each side, and was a large stately man, with a steady sensible countenance.

There was a comfortable parlour with a good fire, and a dram of admirable Holland's gin went round. By and by supper came, when there appeared his spouse, the celebrated Miss Flora. She was a little woman, of a mild and genteel appearance, mighty soft and well-bred. To see Mr Samuel Johnson salute Miss Flora Macdonald was a wonderful romantic scene to me. There was a Mrs Macdonald, wife to James, a brother of Kingsburgh's, and one of his sons. We had as genteel a supper as one would wish to see, in particular an excellent roasted turkey, porter to drink at table, and after supper claret and punch. But what I admired was the perfect ease with which everything went on. My *facility of manners*, as Adam Smith said of me, had fine play.

Miss Flora (for so I shall call her) told me she heard upon the mainland, as she was returning to Skye about a fortnight before this, that

Mr Boswell was coming to Skye, and one Mr Johnson, a young English buck, with him. He was highly entertained with this event, and speaking of the afternoon which we passed at Anoch, he said, "I, being a *buck*, had Miss in to make tea," or some such expression about Macqueen's daughter. He was rather quiescent tonight and went early to bed. I was in a cordial humour, and promoted a cheerful glass. The punch was superexcellent, and we drank three bowls of it. Honest Mr Macqueen said of me, "His governor's gone to bed."

My heart was sore to recollect that Kingsburgh had fallen sorely back in his affairs, was under a load of debt, and intended to go to America. However, nothing but what was good was present, and I pleased myself in thinking that so fine a fellow would be well everywhere.[468]

I slept in the same room with Mr Johnson. Each had a neat clean bed in an upper chamber.

MONDAY 13 SEPTEMBER. Last night's jovial bout disturbed me somewhat, but not long. The room where we lay was a room indeed. Each bed had tartan curtains, and Mr Johnson's was the very bed in which the Prince lay.[469] To see Mr Samuel Johnson lying in Prince Charles's bed, in the Isle of Skye, in the house of Miss Flora Macdonald, struck me with such a group of ideas as it is not easy for words to describe as the mind perceives them. He smiled, and said, "I have had no ambitious thoughts in it."[470]

The room was decorated with a great variety of maps and prints. Among others was Hogarth's print of Wilkes grinning with the cap of liberty beside him. That, too, was a curious circumstance in the scene this morning. Such a contrast was Wilkes to the above group! It was like Sir William Chambers's idea of oriental gardening, in which all odd, strange, ugly, and even terrible objects, are to be introduced for the sake of variety, and which is so well ridiculed in an *Epistle* to him.[471] I thought of the two lines in it, "Here too, O King of vengeance! in thy fane, / Tremendous Wilkes shall rattle his gold chain." Upon the table in our room I found a slip of paper in the morning, on which Mr Johnson had written with his pencil these words: "Quantum cedat virtutibus aurum."[472] What he meant by writing it I could not tell.[473] He had catched cold a day or two ago, and the rain yesterday had made it worse; so he was become very deaf. At breakfast he said he would have given a good deal rather than not have lain in the bed. I said he was the lucky man; and to be sure it had been contrived between Mrs Macdonald and him. She said, "You know young *bucks* are always favourites of the ladies."

He spoke of the Prince being here, and said to Mrs Macdonald,

"*Who* was with him? We were told in England, there was one Miss Flora Macdonald with him."

Said she, "They were very right."

She then very obligingly told him out of her own mouth, how she had agreed to carry the Prince with her out of Lewis when it was known he was there; the country was full of troops and the coast surrounded with ships.[474] He passed as her maid, an Irish girl, Betty Bourke. They set off in a small boat. The people on shore fired after them to bring them to. But they went forward. They landed in Skye. She got a horse and her maid walked beside her, which it seems is common in this part of the world, but Betty looked somewhat awkward in women's clothes. They came to Mugstot. She dined at table with Lady Margaret Macdonald, where was an officer who commanded a party watching for the Prince, at whom she often laughed in good humour afterwards as having deceived him; and her maid was – I do not remember where.[475]

Mr Johnson said all this should be written down. She said it was, and Bishop Forbes at Leith had it.[476] Mr Johnson and I were both visibly of the *old interest* (to use the Oxford expression), kindly affectioned at least, and perhaps too openly so.[477] From what she told us, and from what I was told by others personally concerned, and from a paper of information which Raasay was so good as to send me, at my desire, I have compiled the following abstract, which, as it contains some curious anecdotes, will, I imagine, not be uninteresting to my readers, and even, perhaps, be of some use to future historians.

Prince Charles Edward, after the battle of Culloden, was conveyed to what is called the Long Island, where he lay for some time concealed. But intelligence having been obtained where he was, and a number of troops having come in quest of him, it became absolutely necessary for him to quit that country without delay. Miss Flora Macdonald, then a young lady, animated by what she thought the sacred principle of loyalty, offered, with the magnanimity of a heroine, to accompany him in an open boat to Skye, though the coast they were to quit was guarded by ships. He dressed himself in women's clothes, and passed as her supposed maid, by the name of Betty Bourke, an Irish girl. They got off undiscovered, though several shots were fired to bring them to, and landed at Mugstot, the seat of Sir Alexander Macdonald. Sir Alexander was then at Fort Augustus, with the Duke of Cumberland; but his lady was at home.[478]

Prince Charles took his post upon a hill near the house. Flora Macdonald waited on Lady Margaret, and acquainted her of the enterprise in which she was engaged. Her ladyship, whose active benevolence was ever seconded by superior talents, shewed a perfect presence of mind, and readiness of invention, and at once settled that Prince Charles should be conducted to old Raasay, who was himself concealed with some select friends.

The plan was instantly communicated to Kingsburgh, who was dispatched to the hill to inform the Wanderer, and carry him refreshments. When Kingsburgh approached, he started up, and advanced, holding a large knotted stick, and in appearance ready to knock him down, till he said, "I am Macdonald of Kingsburgh, come to serve your highness."

The Wanderer answered, "It is well," and was satisfied with the plan.

Flora Macdonald dined with Lady Margaret, at whose table there sat an officer of the army, stationed here with a party of soldiers, to watch for Prince Charles in case of his flying to the isle of Sky. She afterwards often laughed in good humour with this gentleman, on her having so well deceived him. After dinner, Flora Macdonald on horseback, and her supposed maid, and Kingsburgh, with a servant carrying some linen, all on foot, proceeded towards that gentleman's house. Upon the road was a small rivulet which they were obliged to cross. The Wanderer, forgetting his assumed sex, that his clothes might not be wet, held them up a great deal too high. Kingsburgh mentioned this to him, observing, it might make a discovery. He said he would be more careful for the future. He was as good as his word; for the next brook they crossed, he did not hold up his clothes at all, but let them float upon the water.

He was very awkward in his female dress. His size was so large, and his strides so great, that some women whom they met reported that they had seen a very big woman, who looked like a man in woman's clothes, and that perhaps it was (as they expressed themselves) the *Prince*, after whom so much search was making.

At Kingsburgh he met with a most cordial reception; seemed gay at supper, and after it indulged himself in a cheerful glass with his worthy host. As he had not had his clothes off for a long time, the comfort of a good bed was highly relished by him, and he slept soundly till next day at one o'clock.[479]

On the afternoon of that day, the Wanderer, still in the same dress, set out for Portree, with Flora Macdonald and a man servant. His shoes being very bad, Kingsburgh provided him with a new pair, and taking up the old ones, said, "I will faithfully keep them till you are safely settled at St James's. I will then introduce myself by shaking them at you, to put you in mind of your night's entertainment and protection under my roof."

He smiled, and said, "Be as good as your word!"

Monday 13 September

Kingsburgh kept the shoes as long as he lived. After his death, a zealous Jacobite gentleman gave twenty guineas for them.[480] Old Mrs Macdonald, after her guest had left the house, took the sheets in which he had lain, folded them carefully, and charged her daughter that they should be kept unwashed, and that, when she died, her body should be wrapped in them as a winding sheet. Her will was religiously observed.

Upon the road to Portree, Prince Charles changed his dress, and put on man's clothes again: a tartan short coat and waistcoat, with philibeg and short hose, a plaid, and a wig and bonnet. Mr Donald Macdonald, called Donald Roy, had been sent express to the present Raasay, then the young laird, who was at that time at his sister's house, about three miles from Portree, attending his brother, Dr MacLeod, who was recovering of a wound he had received at the battle of Culloden.[481] Mr Macdonald communicated to young Raasay the plan of conveying the Wanderer to where old Raasay was; but was told that old Raasay had fled to Knoidart, a part of Glengary's estate. There was then a dilemma what should be done. Donald Roy proposed that he should conduct the Wanderer to the main land; but young Raasay thought it too dangerous at that time, and said it would be better to conceal him in the island of Raasay, till old Raasay could be informed where he was, and give his advice what was best. But the difficulty was, how to get him to Raasay. They could not trust a Portree crew, and all the Raasay boats had been destroyed, or carried off by the military, except two belonging to Malcolm MacLeod, which he had concealed somewhere.

Dr MacLeod being informed of this difficulty, said he would risk his life once more for Prince Charles; and it having occurred, that there was a little boat upon a fresh-water lake in the neighbourhood, young Raasay and Dr MacLeod, with the help of some women, brought it to the sea, by extraordinary exertion, across a Highland mile of land, one half of which was bog, and the other a steep precipice.[482] These gallant brothers, with the assistance of one little boy, rowed the small boat to Raasay, where they were to endeavour to find Captain MacLeod, as Malcolm was then called, and get one of his good boats, with which they might return to Portree, and receive the Wanderer; or, in case of not finding him, they were to make the small boat serve, though the danger was considerable. Fortunately, on their first landing, they found their cousin Malcolm, who, with the utmost alacrity, got ready one of his boats, with two strong men, John Mackenzie, and Donald MacFriar. Malcolm, being the oldest man, and most cautious, said, that as young Raasay had not hitherto appeared in the unfortunate business, he ought not to run any risk;

but that Dr MacLeod and himself, who were already publicly engaged, should go on this expedition. Young Raasay answered, with an oath, that he would go, at the risk of his life and fortune. "In GOD's name then," said Malcolm, "let us proceed."

The two boatmen, however, now stopped short, till they should be informed of their destination; and Mackenzie declared he would not move an oar till he knew where they were going. Upon which they were both sworn to secrecy; and the business being imparted to them, they were eager to put off to sea without loss of time. The boat soon landed about half a mile from the inn at Portree.

All this was negotiated before the Wanderer got forward to Portree. Malcolm MacLeod, and MacFriar, were dispatched to look for him. In a short time he appeared, and went into the public house. Here Donald Roy, whom he had seen at Mugstot, received him, and informed him of what had been concerted. He wanted silver for a guinea, but the landlord had only thirteen shillings. He was going to accept of this for his guinea; but Donald Roy very judiciously observed, that it would discover him to be some great man; so he desisted. He slipped out of the house, leaving his fair protectress, whom he never again saw; and Malcolm MacLeod was presented to him by Donald Roy, as a captain in his army.

Young Raasay and Dr MacLeod had waited, in impatient anxiety, in the boat. When he came, their names were announced to him. He would not permit the usual ceremonies of respect, but saluted them as his equals. Donald Roy staid in Skye, to be in readiness to get intelligence, and give an alarm in case the troops should discover the retreat to Raasay; and Prince Charles was then conveyed in a boat to that island in the night. He slept a little upon the passage, and they landed about day-break. There was some difficulty in accommodating him with a lodging, as almost all the houses in the island had been burnt by the soldiery. They repaired to a little hut, which some shepherds had lately built, and having prepared it as well as they could, and made a bed of heath for the stranger, they kindled a fire, and partook of some provisions which had been sent with him from Kingsburgh. It was observed, that he would not taste wheat-bread, or brandy, while oat-bread and whisky lasted: "For these," said he, "are my own country's bread and drink." This was very engaging to the Highlanders.

Young Raasay being the only person of the company that durst appear with safety, he went in quest of something fresh for them to eat; but though he was amidst his own cows, sheep, and goats, he could not venture to take any of them for fear of a discovery, but was obliged to supply himself by stealth. He therefore caught a kid, and brought it to the hut in his plaid, and it was killed and drest, and furnished them a meal which they relished much.

The distressed Wanderer, whose health was now a good deal impaired by hunger, fatigue, and watching, slept a long time, but seemed to be frequently disturbed. Malcolm told me he would start from broken slumbers, and speak to himself in different languages, French, Italian, and English. I must however acknowledge, that it is highly probable that my worthy friend Malcolm did not know precisely the difference between French and Italian. One of his expressions in English was, "O GOD! Poor Scotland!"

While they were in the hut, Mackenzie and MacFriar, the two boatmen, were placed as sentinels upon different eminences; and one day an incident happened, which must not be omitted. There was a man wandering about the island, selling tobacco. Nobody knew him, and he was suspected to be a spy. Mackenzie came running to the hut, and told that this suspected person was approaching. Upon which the three gentlemen, young Raasay, Dr MacLeod, and Malcolm, held a council of war upon him, and were unanimously of opinion that he should be instantly put to death. Prince Charles, at once assuming a grave and even severe countenance, said, "GOD forbid that we should take away a man's life, who may be innocent, while we can preserve our own."

The gentlemen however persisted in their resolution, while he as strenuously continued to take the merciful side. John Mackenzie, who sat watching at the door of the hut, and overheard the debate, said in Erse, "Well, well; he must be shot. You are the king, but we are the parliament, and will do what we choose."

Prince Charles, seeing the gentlemen smile, asked what the man had said, and being told it in English, he observed that he was a clever fellow, and, notwithstanding the perilous situation in which he was, laughed loud and heartily. Luckily the unknown person did not perceive that there were people in the hut, at least did not come to it, but walked on past it, unknowing of his risk. It was afterwards found out that he was one of the Highland army, who was himself in danger. Had he come to them, they were resolved to dispatch him; for, as Malcolm said to me, "We could not keep him with us, and we durst not let him go. In such a situation, I would have shot my brother, if I had not been sure of him."

John Mackenzie was at Raasay's house, when we were there.[483] About eighteen years before, he hurt one of his legs when dancing, and being obliged to have it cut off, he now was going about with a wooden leg.

The story of his being a *member of parliament* is not yet forgotten. I took him out a little way from the house, gave him a shilling to drink Raasay's health, and led him into a detail of the particulars which I have just related. With less foundation, some writers have traced the idea of a parliament, and of the British constitution, in rude and early times. I was curious to know if he had really heard, or understood, any thing of that subject, which, had he been a greater man, would probably have been eagerly maintained. "Why, John," said I, "did you think the king should be controuled by a parliament?"

He answered, "I thought, sir, there were many voices against one."

The conversation then turning on the times, the Wanderer said that, to be sure, the life he had led of late was a very hard one; but he would rather live in the way he now did, for ten years, than fall into the hands of his enemies. The gentlemen asked him, what he thought his enemies would do with him, should he have the misfortune to fall into their hands. He said, he did not believe they would dare to take his life publicly, but he dreaded being privately destroyed by poison or assassination.

He was very particular in his inquiries about the wound which Dr MacLeod had received at the battle of Culloden, from a ball which entered at one shoulder, and went across to the other. The doctor happened still to have on the coat which he wore on that occasion. He mentioned, that he himself had his horse shot under him at Culloden; that the ball hit the horse about two inches from his knee, and made him so unruly that he was obliged to change him for another.

He blamed one of his generals. He said perhaps it was rash in him to do it, but he thought he had good reason, for that for three days before the disastrous day that general did not obey any orders that he gave; that he was as good a colonel of a regiment as was in Europe, but was not fit for a high command. I however believe that the opinion which he had formed on this head was ill founded;[484] for I have had a good deal of conversation upon the subject with my very worthy and ingenious friend, Mr Andrew Lumisden, who was under secretary to Prince Charles, and afterwards principal secretary to his father at Rome, who, he assured me, was perfectly satisfied both of the abilities and honour of the generals who commanded the Highland army on that occasion. Mr Lumisden has written an account of the three battles in 1745-6, at once accurate and classical.[485]

Talking of the different Highland corps, the gentlemen who were present wished to have his opinion which were the best soldiers. He said, he did not like comparisons among those corps: they were all best.

He told his conductors, he did not think it advisable to remain long in any one place; and that he expected a French ship to come for him to Lochbroom, among the Mackenzies. It then was proposed to carry him in one of Malcolm's boats to Lochbroom, though the distance was fifteen leagues coastwise. But he thought this would be too dangerous, and desired that at any rate they might first endeavour to obtain intelligence. Upon which young Raasay wrote to his friend, Mr Mackenzie of Applecross, but received an answer, that there was no appearance of any French ship.

It was therefore resolved that they should return to Skye, which they did, and landed in Strath, where they reposed in a cow-house belonging to Mr Nicolson of Scorbreck. The sea was very rough, and the boat took in a good deal of water. The Wanderer asked if there was danger, as he was not used to such a vessel. Upon being told there was not, he sung an Erse song with much vivacity. He had by this time acquired a good deal of the Erse language.[486]

Young Raasay was now dispatched to where Donald Roy was, that they might get all the intelligence they could; and the Wanderer, with much earnestness, charged Dr MacLeod to have a boat ready, at a certain place about seven miles off, as he said he intended it should carry him upon a matter of great consequence; and gave the doctor a case, containing a silver spoon, knife, and fork, saying, "Keep you that till I see you," which the doctor understood to be two days from that time. But all these orders were only blinds; for he had another plan in his head, but wisely thought it safest to trust his secrets to no more persons than was absolutely necessary. Having then desired Malcolm to walk with him a little way from the house, he soon opened his mind, saying, "I deliver myself to you. Conduct me to the Laird of Mackinnon's country."

Malcolm objected that it was very dangerous, as so many parties of soldiers were in motion. He answered, "There is nothing now to be done without danger." He then said, that Malcolm must be the master, and he the servant; so he took the bag, in which his linen was put up, and carried it on his shoulder; and observing that his waistcoat, which was of scarlet tartan, with a gold twist button, was finer than Malcolm's, which was of a plain ordinary tartan, he put on Malcolm's waistcoat, and gave him his; remarking at the same time, that it did not look well that the servant should be better dressed than the master.

Malcolm, though an excellent walker, found himself excelled by Prince Charles, who told him, he should not much mind the parties that were looking for him, were he once but a musket shot from them; but that he was somewhat afraid of the Highlanders who were against him. He was well used to walking in Italy, in pursuit of game; and he was even now so keen a sportsman, that, having observed some partridges, he was going to take a shot; but Malcolm cautioned him against it, observing that the firing might be heard by the tenders who were hovering upon the coast.

As they proceeded through the mountains, taking many a circuit to avoid any houses, Malcolm, to try his resolution, asked him what they should do, should they fall in with a party of soldiers: he answered, "Fight, to be sure!" Having asked Malcolm if he should be known in his present dress, and Malcolm having replied he would, he said, "Then I'll blacken my face with powder."

"That," said Malcolm, "would discover you at once."

"Then," said he, "I must be put in the greatest dishabille possible." So he pulled off his wig, tied a handkerchief round his head, and put his nightcap over it, tore the ruffles from his shirt, took the buckles out of his shoes, and made Malcolm fasten them with strings; but still Malcolm thought he would be known. "I have so odd a face," said he, "that no man ever saw me but he would know me again."

He seemed unwilling to give credit to the horrid narrative of men being massacred in cold blood, after victory had declared for the army commanded by the Duke of Cumberland. He could not allow himself to think that a general could be so barbarous.

When they came within two miles of Mackinnon's house, Malcolm asked if he chose to see the laird. "No," said he, "by no means. I know Mackinnon to be as good and as honest a man as any in the world, but he is not fit for my purpose at present. You must conduct me to some other house; but let it be a gentleman's house."

Malcolm then determined that they should go to the house of his brother-in-law, Mr John Mackinnon, and from thence be conveyed to the main land of Scotland, and claim the assistance of Macdonald of Scothouse. The Wanderer at first objected to this, because Scothouse was cousin to a person of whom he had suspicions.[487] But he acquiesced in Malcolm's opinion.

When they were near Mr John Mackinnon's house, they met a man of the name of Ross, who had been a private soldier in the Highland army. He fixed his eyes steadily on the Wanderer in his disguise, and having at once recognized him, he clapped his hands, and exclaimed, "Alas! Is this the case?"

Finding that there was now a discovery, Malcolm asked, "What's to be done?"

"Swear him to secrecy," answered Prince Charles. Upon which Malcolm drew his dirk, and on the naked blade, made him take a solemn oath, that he would say nothing of his having seen the Wanderer, till his escape should be made public.

Malcolm's sister, whose house they reached pretty early in the morning, asked him who the person was that was along with him. He said, it was one Lewis Caw, from Crieff, who being a fugitive like himself, for the same reason, he had engaged him as his servant, but that he had fallen sick.[488] "Poor man!" said she. "I pity him. At the same time my heart warms to a man of his appearance."

Her husband was gone a little way from home; but was expected every minute to return. She set down to her brother a plentiful Highland breakfast. Prince Charles acted the servant very well, sitting at a respectful distance, with his bonnet off. Malcolm then said to him, "Mr Caw, you have as much need of this as I have; there is enough for us both: you had better draw nearer and share with me." Upon which he rose, made a profound bow, sat down at table with his supposed master, and eat very heartily.

After this there came in an old woman, who, after the mode of ancient hospitality, brought warm water, and washed Malcolm's feet. He desired her to wash the feet of the poor man who attended him. She at first seemed averse to this, from pride, as thinking him beneath her, and in the periphrastic language of the Highlanders and the Irish, said warmly, "Though I wash your father's son's feet, why should I wash his father's son's feet?" She was however persuaded to do it.

They then went to bed, and slept for some time; and when Malcolm awaked, he was told that Mr John Mackinnon, his brother-in-law, was in sight. He sprang out to talk to him before he should see Prince Charles. After saluting him, Malcolm, pointing to the sea, said, "What, John, if the prince should be prisoner on board one of those tenders?"

"GOD forbid!" replied John.

"What if we had him here?" said Malcolm.

"I wish we had, answered John; we should take care of him."

"Well, John," said Malcolm, "he is in your house."

John, in a transport of joy, wanted to run directly in, and pay his obeisance; but Malcolm stopped him, saying, "Now is your time to behave well, and do nothing that can discover him."

John composed himself, and having sent away all his servants upon different errands, he was introduced into the presence of his guest, and was then desired to go and get ready a boat lying near his house, which, though but a small leaky one, they resolved to take, rather than go to the Laird of Mackinnon. John Mackinnon, however, thought otherwise; and upon his return told them, that his chief and Lady Mackinnon were coming in the laird's boat. Prince Charles said to his trusty Malcolm, "I am sorry for this, but must make the best of it."

Mackinnon then walked up from the shore, and did homage to the Wanderer. His lady waited in a cave, to which they all repaired, and were entertained with cold meat and wine.

Mr Malcolm MacLeod being now superseded by the Laird of Mackinnon, desired leave to return, which was granted him, and Prince Charles wrote a short note, which he subscribed 'James Thompson', informing his friends that he had got away from Skye, and thanking them for their kindness; and he desired this might be speedily conveyed to young Raasay and Dr MacLeod, that they might not wait longer in expectation of seeing him again.[489] He bade a cordial adieu to Malcolm, and insisted on his accepting of a silver stock-buckle, and ten guineas from his purse, though, as Malcolm told me, it did not appear to contain above forty. Malcolm at first begged to be excused, saying, that he had a few guineas at his service; but Prince Charles answered, "You will have need of money. I shall get enough when I come upon the main land."

The Laird of Mackinnon then conveyed him to the opposite coast of Knoidart. Old Raasay, to whom intelligence had been sent, was crossing at the same time to Skye; but as they did not know of each other, and each had apprehensions, the two boats kept aloof.

These are the particulars which I have collected concerning the extraordinary concealment and escapes of Prince Charles, in the Hebrides. He was often in imminent danger. The troops traced him from the Long Island, across Skye, to Portree, but there lost him. Here I stop, having received no farther authentic information of his fatigues and perils before he escaped to France. Kings and subjects may both take a lesson of moderation from the melancholy fate of the House of Stuart; that kings may not suffer degradation and exile, and subjects may not be harrassed by the evils of a disputed succession. Let me close the scene on that unfortunate House with the elegant and pathetic reflections of Voltaire, in his *Histoire Generale*. "Que les hommes privés," says that brilliant writer, speaking of Prince Charles, "qui se croyent malheureux, jettent les yeux sur ce prince et ses ancêtres."[490] In another place he thus sums up the sad story of the family in general:

Il n'y a aucun exemple dans l'histoire d'une maison si longtems infortunée. Le premier des Rois d'Écosse, ses aïeux, qui eut le nom de *Jacques*, après avoir été dix-huit ans prisonnier en Angleterre, mourut assassiné, avec sa femme, par la main de ses sujets. *Jacques* II, son fils, fut tué à vingt-neuf ans en combattant contre les Anglois. *Jacques* III, mis en prison par son peuple, fut tué ensuite par les révoltés, dans une bataille. *Jacques* IV. périt dans un combat qu'il perdit. *Marie Stuart*, sa petite-fille, chassée de son trône, fugitive en Angleterre, ayant langui dix-huit ans en prison, se vit condamnée à mort par des juges Anglais, et eut la tête tranchée. *Charles* I, petit-fils de *Marie*, Roi d'Écosse et d'Angleterre, vendu par les Écossois, et jugé à mort par les Anglais, mourut sur un échaffaut dans la place publique. *Jacques*, son fils, septième du nom, et deuxième en Angleterre, fut chassé de ses trois royaumes; et pour comble de malheur on contesta à son fils jusqu'à sa naissance. Ce fils ne tenta de remonter sur le trône de ses pères, que pour faire périr ses amis par des bourreaux; et nous avons vu le Prince *Charles Édouard*, réunissant en vain les vertus de ses pères et le courage du Roi *Jean Sobieski*, son ayeul maternel, exécuter les exploits et essuyer les malheurs les plus incroyables. Si quelque chose justifie ceux qui croyent une fatalité à laquelle rien ne peut se soustraire, c'est cette suite continuelle de malheurs qui a persécuté la maison de *Stuart*, pendant plus de trois-cents années.[491]

The gallant Malcolm was apprehended in about ten days after they separated, put aboard a ship and carried prisoner to London. He said, the prisoners in general were very ill treated in their passage; but there were soldiers on board who lived well, and sometimes invited him to share with them: that he had the good fortune not to be thrown into jail, but was confined in the house of a messenger, of the name of Dick. To his astonishment, only one witness could be found against him, though he had been so openly engaged; and therefore, for want of sufficient evidence, he was set at liberty. He added, that he thought himself in such danger, that he would gladly have compounded for banishment. Yet, he said, he should never be so ready for death as he then was.

There is philosophical truth in this. A man will meet death much more firmly at one time than another. The enthusiasm even of a mistaken principle warms the mind, and sets it above the fear of death; which in our cooler moments, if we really think of it, cannot but be terrible, or at least very awful.[492]

Sandie MacLeod had assured us that the Prince was in London in 1759 when there was a plan in agitation for him. We could hardly believe it, and Mr Johnson said there could be no probable plan then. Dr MacLeod said with warmth that there was. The present Royal Family were all to have been seized and put aboard a ship; he was to have been in London; a number of persons of great consequence, among which was the Lord Mayor of London, were in the plot, and James III of Britain would have been proclaimed at Charing Cross; the Prince Regent would have issued writs and called a Parliament, and all would have gone well. "But," said the Doctor, "it failed from the pusillanimity of some of those who were to have acted." Mr Johnson said it could not have done, unless the King of Prussia had stopped the Army in Germany; for that the Army would have fought without orders, and the fleet would have fought without orders, for the king under whom they served.

Having related so many particulars concerning the grandson of the unfortunate King James the Second; having given due praise to fidelity and generous attachment, which, however erroneous the judgement may be, are honourable for the heart; I must do the Highlanders the justice to attest, that I found every where amongst them a high opinion of the virtues of the king now upon the throne, and an honest disposition to be faithful subjects to his majesty, whose family had possessed the sovereignty of this country so long, that a change, even for the abdicated family, would now hurt the best feelings of all his subjects.[493]

I must here explain a little Mr Johnson's political notions as well as my own. We are both *Tories*; both convinced of the utility of monarchical power, and both lovers of that reverence and affection for a sovereign which constitute loyalty, a principle which I take to be absolutely extinguished in Britain, which is one of the worst consequences of the Revolution. Mr Johnson is not properly a *Jacobite*. He does not hold the *jus divinum* of kings. He founds their right on long possession, which ought not to be disturbed upon slight grounds. He said to me once that he did not know but it was become necessary to remove the King at the time of the Revolution; and after the present family have had so long a possession, it appears to him that their right becomes the same that the Stuarts had. His difficulty is as to the right still in some measure belonging to that unfortunate family. In short, he is dubious; and he would not involve the nation in a civil war to restore the Stuarts. Nay, I have heard him say he was so dubious that if holding up his right hand would have gained the victory to the Highland army in 1745, he does not know if he would have done it. Beauclerk told me he heard him say so before he had his pension. I, again, have all that Mr Johnson has, and something more, for my high notions of male succession make me mount up to distant times; and when I find how the Stuart family's right has been formed, it appears to me as but very casual and artificial. I find not the firm feudal hold for which I wish and which my imagination figures. I might fix my eye at the point of James IV, from whom my ancestor Thomas Boswell got the estate of Auchinleck, and look no further, had I a line of males from that Prince. But Queen Mary comes in the way; and I see the sons of Lennox on the throne. Besides, I consider that even supposing Prince Charles to have the right, it may be very generous for one to support another's right at every risk, but it is not wise, and I would not do it. Mr Johnson's argument of right being formed by possession and acknowledgment of the people, settles my mind, and I have now no uneasiness. With all this, he and I have a kind of *liking* for Jacobitism, something that it is not easy to define. I should guard against it; for from what I have now put down, it is certain that my calm reasoning stops short at action, so that doing anything violent in support of the cause would only be following a sort of passion or warm whim. And talking much in favour of it may even in this secure and more liberal reign hurt a man in his rising in life.[494]

The *abstract* point of *right* would involve us in a discussion of remote and perplexed questions; and after all, we should have no clear principle of decision. That establishment, which, from political necessity, took place in 1688, by a breach in the succession of our kings, and which, whatever benefits may have accrued from it, certainly gave a shock to our monarchy, the able and constitutional Blackstone wisely rests on the solid footing of authority: "Our ancestors having most indisputably a competent jurisdiction to decide this great and important question, and having, in fact decided it, it is now become our duty, at this distance of time, to acquiesce in their determination."[495]

Mr Paley, the present Archdeacon of Carlisle, in his *Principles of Moral and Political Philosophy*, having, with much clearness of argument, shewn the duty of submission to civil government to be founded neither on an indefeasible *jus divinum*, nor on *compact*, but on *expediency*, lays down this rational position:

> Irregularity in the first foundation of a state, or subsequent violence, fraud, or injustice, in getting possession of the supreme power, are not sufficient reasons for resistance, after the government is once peaceably settled. No subject of the British Empire conceives himself engaged to vindicate the justice of the Norman claim or conquest, or apprehends that his duty in any manner depends upon that controversy. So likewise, if the house of Lancaster, or even the posterity of Cromwell, had been at this day seated upon the throne of England, we should have been as little concerned to enquire how the founder of the family came there.[496]

In conformity with this doctrine, I myself, though fully persuaded that the House of Stuart had originally no right to the crown of Scotland; for that Baliol, and not Bruce, was the lawful heir; should yet have thought it very culpable to have rebelled, on that account, against Charles the First, or even a prince of that house much nearer the time, in order to assert the claim of the posterity of Baliol.

However convinced I am of the justice of that principle, which holds allegiance and protection to be reciprocal, I do however acknowledge, that I am not satisfied with the cold sentiment which would confine the exertions of the subject within the strict line of duty. I would have every breast animated with the *fervour* of loyalty; with that generous attachment which delights in doing somewhat more than is required, and makes 'service perfect freedom'. And, therefore, as our most gracious Sovereign, on his accession to the throne, gloried in being born a Briton; so, in my more private sphere, *Ego me nunc denique natum gratulor.*[497] I am happy that a disputed succession no longer distracts our minds; and that a monarchy, established by law, is now so sanctioned by time, that we can fully indulge those feelings of loyalty which I am ambitious to excite. They are feelings which have ever actuated the inhabitants of the Highlands and the Hebrides. The plant of loyalty is there in full vigour, and the Brunswick graft now flourishes like a native shoot. To that spirited race of people I may with propriety apply the elegant lines of a modern poet, on the 'facile temper of the beauteous sex':

> *Like birds new-caught, who flutter for a time,*
> *And struggle with captivity in vain;*
> *But by-and-by they rest, they smooth their plumes,*
> *And to* new masters *sing their former notes.*[498]

Surely such notes are much better than the querulous growlings of suspicious Whigs and discontented Republicans.

Kingsburgh conducted us in his boat across one of the lochs, as they call them, or arms of the sea, which flow in upon all the coasts of Skye, to a mile beyond a place called Greshornish. Our horses had been sent round it in the morning to meet us. By this sail we saved eight miles of bad riding. Mr Johnson said, "When we take into the computation what we have saved and what we have gained by this agreeable sail, it is a great deal." He said, "It is very disagreeable riding in Skye. The way is so narrow, one only at a time can travel, so it is quite unsocial; and you cannot indulge in meditation by yourself, because you must be always attending to the steps which your horse takes." This was a just and clear description of its inconveniences.

He said Sir Alexander would make a wilderness of his estate. While I sailed in Kingsburgh's boat and thought of the emigration, it did not hurt me. I fancied him sailing in America just as he did about Skye.[499]

Mr Donald Macqueen told us, that the oppression, which then made so much noise, was owing to landlords listening to bad advice in the letting of their lands; that interested and designed people flattered them with golden dreams of much higher rents than could reasonably be paid; and that some of the gentlemen tacksmen, or upper tenants, were themselves in part the occasion of the mischief, by over-rating the farms of others. That many of the tacksmen, rather than comply with exorbitant demands, had gone off to America, and impoverished the country, by draining it of its wealth; and that their places were filled by a number of poor people, who had lived under them, properly speaking, as servants, paid by a certain proportion of the produce of the lands, though called sub-tenants. I observed, that if the men of substance were once banished from a Highland estate, it might probably be greatly reduced in its value; for one bad year might ruin a set of poor tenants, and men of any property would not settle in such a country, unless from the temptation of getting land extremely cheap; for an inhabitant of any good county in Britain, had better go to America than to the Highlands or the Hebrides. Here, therefore, was a consideration that ought to induce a chief to act a more liberal part, from a mere motive of interest, independent of the lofty and honourable principle of keeping a clan together, to be in readiness to serve his king. I added, that I could not help thinking a little arbitrary power in the sovereign, to control the bad policy and greediness of the chiefs, might sometimes be of service. In France a chief would not be permitted to force a number of the king's subjects out of the country. Dr Johnson concurred with me, observing, that 'were an oppressive chieftain a subject of the French king, he would probably be admonished by a *letter*'.

During our sail, Dr Johnson asked about the use of the dirk, with which he imagined the Highlanders cut their meat. He was told, they had a knife and fork besides, to eat with. He asked, how did the women do? And was answered, some of them had a knife and fork too; but in general the men, when they had cut their meat, handed their knives and forks to the women, and they themselves eat with their fingers. The old Tutor of Macdonald always eat fish with his fingers, alleging that a knife and fork gave it a bad taste.[500] I took the liberty to observe to Mr Johnson that he did so. "Yes," said he; "but it is because I am short-sighted, and afraid of bones; for which reason I'm not fond of eating many kinds of fish, because I must take my fingers."

Perhaps I put down too many things in this Journal. I have no fanners in my head, at least no good ones, to separate wheat from chaff. Yet for as much as I put down, what is written falls greatly short of the quantity of thought. A page of my Journal is like a cake of portable soup. A little may be diffused into a considerable portion.[501]

Mr Johnson observed of Macpherson's *Dissertations on Scottish Antiquities*, which he had looked at when at Coirechatachan, that you might read half an hour and ask yourself what you had been reading. There were so many words to so little matter, there was no getting through the book. (I had begun by saying they were very unsatisfactory, in which he agreed.)[502]

Kingsburgh had brought provisions for us, but we were not hungry, and after taking leave of him, rode on.[503] We passed through a wild moor, in many places so wet that we were obliged to walk, which was hard on Mr Johnson. Once he had advanced on horseback to a very bad step. There was a steep declivity on his left, to which he was so near that there was not room for him to dismount in the usual way. He alighted on the other side, as if he had been a *young buck* indeed. He fell at his length upon the ground, but got up immediately, and was not hurt. We were relieved by seeing several branches of the sea, that universal connexion. Our journey or ride was computed only seven miles, but was in fact a very long and tedious expedition. A guide, who had been sent with us from Kingsburgh, explored the way (much in the same manner as, I suppose, is pursued in the wilds of America) by observing certain marks known only to the inhabitants.[504]

We arrived at Dunvegan late in the afternoon. The great size of the castle, partly old and partly new, upon a rock on the sea, and nothing to be perceived at land but wild moorish hilly and rocky appearances, struck us – at least me. We went up a stair of twenty-two steps made by the late MacLeod as a land-access, the original one having been from the sea side, so that visitors who came by the land were under the necessity of getting into a boat, and sailed round to the only place where it could be approached.[505] I said, "This is feudal indeed."

But I shall by and by describe at once all about Dunvegan as well as I can. We were received by Mr Norman MacLeod, a young preacher, who as one of the clan did the honours of the house, MacLeod and Talisker not being yet come up.[506] We were introduced into a large dining-room with three windows, marble tables, a screen covered with many good prints; Brodie, Lady MacLeod's father's, portrait in the dress belonging to him as Lord Lyon of Scotland, and his lady; the young Laird of MacLeod, father to this Laird; ———, all family pictures, gave a kind of comfortable appearance, though the late Laird most gracelessly took from Dunvegan and left to his widow the family pictures, plate, etc.[507]

In a little appeared Lady MacLeod, mother of the laird, a sensible clever woman with whom Mr Johnson had been acquainted at Captain Brodie's in London; and before something was ready for us to eat, the Laird and Talisker arrived, having been detained on the road. We had venison collops from Cuillin, and something else. We then went to tea, where we saw Miss MacLeod (Maria, the Laird's eldest sister), and Miss Nannie, another of his sisters.[508] Two others were ill. We had admirable tea: ladies bred in England; everything agreeable.

The drawing-room was not large. It was formerly the bedchamber of Sir Roderick MacLeod, great-great-grandfather of the late Laird; and he chose it because behind it, at least on the rising ground to which its window looks, is a considerable cascade, the sound of which disposed him to sleep.[509] Above his bed was this inscription: "Sir Rorie McLeod of Dunvegan, Knight. GOD send good rest!" Perhaps some foolish painter put it on of his own accord. Perhaps Sir Rorie, who was called Rorie More ('Big Rorie'), from his size, chose it himself.[510] There were in this room prints of the months, published by Bowles, both in fruits and flowers, two sets coloured, and prints of Duncan Forbes, Lord Stair,[511] and the famous Ruins of Rome, very well copied by Lady MacLeod, a rich carpet, a good table, the tea in civilized order. Mr Johnson became quite joyous. He laughed and said, "Boswell, we came in at the wrong end of this island."

"Sir," said I, "it was best to keep this for the last."

He answered, "I'd have it both first and last."

In the evening there was a little repast of bread and cheese and porter and wine and punch only, as we had dined so late. I had a large old bedchamber, a large old-fashioned crimson bed, a light closet with a chest of drawers. I was quite at home.

TUESDAY 14 SEPTEMBER. Mr Johnson said in the morning, "Is not this a fine lady?" There was not a word now of his 'impatience to be in civilized life' – though indeed I should beg pardon: he found it here.

We had slept well and lain long. After breakfast we surveyed the castle, walked round the rock, walked in the garden. Mr Bethune the parish minister, Magnus MacLeod of Claggan, and Bay, another substantial man of the clan, dined. Magnus is brother to Talisker, and has children who would be next in succession to the Chief, as Talisker, the next heir, has none. We had admirable venison from Harris, good soup – in a word, all that a good table has. This was really the hall of a chief. Lady MacLeod had been much obliged to my father, who had settled by arbitration a variety of perplexed claims between her and Brodie, which made a good connexion between her and me.

MacLeod started the subject of making women do penance in the church for fornication. Mr Johnson said it was right. "Infamy," said he, "is attached to the crime by universal opinion so soon as it is known. I would not be the man who, knowing it alone, would discover it, as a woman may reform; nor would I commend a parson who discovers the first offence. But if mankind know it, it ought to be infamous. Consider of what importance the chastity of women is. Upon that, all the property in the world depends. We hang a thief for stealing a sheep. But the unchastity of a woman transfers sheep and farm and all from the right owner. I have much more reverence for a common prostitute than for a woman who conceals her guilt. The prostitute is known. She cannot deceive. She cannot bring a strumpet into the arms of an honest man, without his knowledge."[512]

I said there was a great difference between the licentiousness of a single woman and that of a married woman. JOHNSON. "Yes, sir; there is a great difference between stealing a shilling and a thousand pounds; between simply taking a man's purse, and murdering him first and then taking it. But when one begins to be vicious, it is easy to go on. Where single women are licentious, you rarely find faithful married women." BOSWELL. "And yet we are told that in some nations in India, the distinction is strictly observed." JOHNSON. "Nay, don't give us India. That puts me in mind of Montesquieu, who is really a fellow of genius, too, in many particulars; whenever he wants to support a strange opinion, he quotes you the practice of Japan or of ———, of which he knows nothing.[513] To support polygamy, he tells you of the island of Formosa, where there are ten women born for one man. He had but to suppose another island, where there are ten men born for one woman, and so make marriage between 'em."[514]

At supper, Lady MacLeod mentioned Dr Cadogan's book on the gout. Mr Johnson said, "'Tis a good book in general, but a foolish one as to particulars. 'Tis good in general, as recommending temperance and exercise and cheerfulness. 'Tis only Dr Cheyne's book told in a new way.

And there should come out such a book every thirty years, dressed in the mode of the times. 'Tis foolish, as it says the gout is not hereditary, and one fit of the gout when gone is like a fever when gone."

"But," said Lady MacLeod, "he does not practise what he teaches."[515] JOHNSON. "I cannot help that, madam. That does not make his book the worse. People are influenced more by what a man says, if his practice is suitable to it, because they are blockheads. The more intellectual people are, the readier will they attend to what a man tells them. If it is just, they will follow it, be his practice what it will. No man practises so well as he writes. I have, all my life long, been lying till noon. Yet I tell all young men, and tell them with great sincerity, that nobody who does not rise early will ever do any good. Only consider! You read a book; you are convinced by it; you do not know the author. Suppose you afterwards know him, and find that he does not practise what he teaches; are you to give up your former conviction? At this rate you would be kept in a state of *equilibrio* when reading every book, till you knew how the author practised."

"But," said Lady MacLeod, "you would think better of Dr Cadogan if he acted according to his principles." JOHNSON. "Why, madam, to be sure, a man who acts in the face of light is worse than a man who does not know so much. But I think there is something noble in publishing truth, though it condemns one's self."

I spoke of Cadogan's recommending good-humour.[516] Mr Johnson said, "A man grows better-humoured as he grows older, by experience. He learns to think himself of no consequence and little things of little importance; and so he becomes more patient, and better pleased. All good-humour and complaisance is acquired. Naturally a child seizes directly what it sees, and thinks of pleasing itself only. By degrees, it is taught to please others, and to prefer others; and that this will ultimately produce the greatest happiness. If a man is not convinced of that, he never will practise it. (Common language speaks the truth as to this. We say, a person is well-*bred*; as it is said that all material motion is in a right line, and is never *per circuitum*, in another form, unless by some particular cause; so it may be said intellectual motion is.)" Lady MacLeod asked if no man was naturally good. JOHNSON. "No, madam, no more than a wolf." BOSWELL. "Nor no woman, sir?" JOHNSON. "No, sir." Lady MacLeod started, saying low, "This is worse than Swift." What is within the parenthesis was said at an after time, but I bring it in here for connexion.

MacLeod of Ullinish had come in the afternoon. We were a jolly company at supper. It was fine to see the Laird surrounded by so many of his clan. They listened with wonder and pleasure while Mr Johnson harangued. I am vexed that I cannot take down his full strain of eloquence.

WEDNESDAY 15 SEPTEMBER. The gentlemen of the clan went away early in the morning to the harbour of Loch Bracadale to take leave of some of their friends who were going to America. It was a very wet day. We looked at Rorie More's horn, which is a large cow's horn with the mouth of it ornamented with silver. It holds rather more than a bottle and a half. Every Laird of MacLeod, it is said, must as a proof of his manhood drink it off full of claret without taking it from his right arm. He holds the small end of it backwards, and so keeps it at his mouth. The silver mouth to it is above an inch deep – a thin plate with such plaited carving upon it as is commonly found on the Highland dirks or forks and knives, with some other kind of figuring. And under the mouth, round the horn on the outside, are silver knobs which serve as nails to keep the piece of silver on. From Rorie More many of the branches of the family are descended – in particular the Talisker branch – so that his name is much talked of. We also saw his bow, which hardly any man now can bend, and his *claymore* which was wielded with both hands, and is of a prodigious size.[517] We saw some old pieces of iron armour, immensely heavy. The broadsword which is now called the *claymore* is much smaller than the sword used in Rorie More's time, and is of modern invention. There is hardly a target now to be found in the Highlands. After the disarming act they made them serve as covers to their buttermilk barrels, a kind of change like beating spears into pruning-hooks.

Sir George Mackenzie's works (the folio edition) were lying in a window in the dining room.[518] I made Mr Johnson read some of the *Characteres Advocatorum*. He allowed power of mind, and that Sir George understood very well what he tells, but there was too much declamation; and that the Latin was not correct. He found fault with *appropinquabant* in the character of Gilmour. I tried him with the opposition between *gloria* and *palma* in the comparison between Gilmour and Nisbet, which Lord Hailes in his Catalogue of the Lords of Session thinks difficult to be understood. I in my little Account of the Kirk of Scotland attempted to explain it thus: "The popular party has most eloquence; Dr Robertson's most influence"; *penes illam gloria, penes hanc palma.*[519] I was very desirous to hear Mr Johnson. He said: "I see no difficulty. Gilmour was admired for his parts. Nisbet carried his cause by his skill in law. *Palma* is victory."

I said the character of Nicholson in this book resembled that of Burke: for it is said, in one place, *In omnes lusos et jocos se saepe resolvebat*; and, in another, *accipitris more e conspectu aliquando astantium sublimi se protrahens volatu, in praedam miro impetu descendebat.*[520]

"No, sir," said Mr Johnson. "I never heard Burke make a good joke in my life."

"But he's a hawk, sir," said I.

Mr Johnson, thinking that I meant this of his joking, said, "No, sir, he's not the hawk there. He's the beetle in the mire."

I kept to the hawk, crying, "But he soars as the hawk." JOHNSON. "Yes, sir; but he catches nothing."

MacLeod asked, "What is the particular excellence of Burke's eloquence?" JOHNSON. "Copiousness and fertility of allusion; a power of diversifying his matter by placing it in various relations. Burke has great knowledge, and great command of language; though, in my opinion, it has not in every respect the highest elegance." BOSWELL. "Do you think, sir, that Burke has read Cicero much?" JOHNSON. "I don't believe it, sir. Burke has great knowledge, great fluency of words, and great promptness of ideas, so that he can speak with great illustration on any subject that comes before him. He is neither like Cicero, nor like Demosthenes, nor like any one else, but speaks as well as he can."[521]

Mr Donald MacLeod, late tenant in Canna but now dispossessed of it, was still with us. He was an obliging serviceable man. His father was one of MacLeod's ministers; and the late Laird educated him, and in particular had him several years at school near London. He was at present in that kind of wandering state that many a Highland younger brother is. I was sometimes angry at his appearing unanimated, speaking a few words slowly and with a weak voice, and then sitting with his mouth open. He was tall and a good sportsman. He gained me at last by saying of Mr Johnson, "Well, it is really a happiness to be in this man's company."[522]

Our money was now near an end. He went to Loch Bracadale today and took with him a bill of mine for £30 drawn on Sir W. Forbes & Co. to his order, for which he was to get money for me from the master of the vessel which carries away the emigrants.[523] There is hardly any specie in Skye. Mr Macqueen said he had the utmost difficulty to pay his servants' wages or to pay for any little thing which he has to buy. The rents are paid in bills which the drovers give; and these the Lairds get money for at Edinburgh, and never bring it here. The people consume a great deal of snuff and tobacco, for which they must pay ready money; and pedlars who come about selling goods, as there is not a shop in the island, carry away the cash. If there were encouragement given to fishing and manufactures, and the Lairds were to stay more at home, there might be a circulation of money introduced. I got one-and-twenty shillings in silver at Portree, which was a wonderful store.

On the 65 page of the first volume of Sir George Mackenzie's folio edition, Mr Johnson pointed out a paragraph beginning with *Aristotle*, and told me there was an error in the text which he bid me try to discover. I hit it at once. It stands that the devil answers *even* in *engines*. I corrected it to *ever* in *enigmas*. "Sir," said he, "you're a good critic. This would have been a great thing to do in the text of an ancient author."

We had a venison pasty today and most excellent roast beef. But I need say no more as to dinner or supper than that there is abundance of good things genteelly served up. Amidst the difficulties of the family, Lady MacLeod, who is a heroine for the clan, entertained us like princes. She has at the same time the greatest economy. She is butler herself, even of the porter. We had porter from the cask, as in London; claret, port, sherry, and punch. The claret we soon quitted. MacLeod and Talisker and I drank port. The rest of the men drank punch. Lady MacLeod and her daughters eat oat-bread. Mr Johnson and I had excellent cakes of flour. She is resolved to live just as the farmers do; I should think however that the ladies might eat wheat-bread. Mr Johnson said that it would not be above a shilling a week of odds among three.

THURSDAY 16 SEPTEMBER. Last night much care was taken of Mr Johnson. He had hitherto most strangely slept without a night-cap. Miss MacLeod made him a large flannel one, and he was prevailed with to drink a little brandy when he was going to bed – all to do his cold good. He has great virtue in not drinking wine or any fermented liquor, because he could not do it in moderation. He told us so on Tuesday night. Lady MacLeod would hardly believe him, and said, "I'm sure, sir, you would not carry it too far." JOHNSON. "Nay, madam, it carried me."

He took the opportunity of a long illness to leave it off. It was prescribed to him then not to drink wine; and having broke off the habit, he has never returned to it. He was in high spirits this morning.

In the argument on Tuesday night about natural goodness, he denied that any child was better than another, but by difference of instruction; though the greater attention given by one child than another, and a variety of imperceptible causes (such as instruction being counteracted by servants), made it be thought that of two children equally well educated, one should naturally be much worse than another.[524] He owned this morning that one might have a greater aptitude to learn than another, and that we inherit dispositions from our parents. Said he, "I inherited a vile melancholy from my father, which has made me mad all my life, at least not sober."

Lady MacLeod wondered he should tell this. "Madam," said I, "he knows that with that madness he is superior to other men."

I have often been astonished with what exactness and perspicuity he will explain the whole process of any art. He this morning gave us all the operation of coining, and at night he gave us all the operation of brewing spirits. Mr Macqueen said when he heard the first he thought he had been bred in the Mint. When he heard the second, that he had been bred a brewer.

It was curious to have him on this remote point of the world. Lady MacLeod was entertained with my simile, that it was like a dog who has got hold of a large piece of meat, and runs away with it to a corner, where he may devour it in peace, without any fear of others taking it from him. "In London, Reynolds, Beauclerk, and all of them are contending who shall have Mr Johnson. We are feasting upon him undisturbed at Dunvegan."

It was still a storm of wind and rain. Mr Johnson walked out with MacLeod, and saw Rorie More's cascade in grand fullness, by which MacLeod got such a toothache that he could not appear at supper. Every room in the house smoked but the drawing-room. We began tonight a comfortable custom of retreating to the drawing-room, where we took our glass warmly and snugly. This day we had Mr John Bethune, minister of Harris, a young man who said little and did not seem to have much to say to such a man as Mr Johnson. Colonel MacLeod, whom Mr Johnson called a very pleasing man, was at present very different from what he uses to be, and I have seen him. Instead of being all life and gaiety, he was grave and low-spirited and seldom spoke. He had formerly had something of the same kind. It had returned upon him by his taking a most anxious concern in MacLeod's affairs, striving to settle with the gentlemen on the estate, and finding many of the clan, who owed much to the family, by no means disposed to act a generous or affectionate part to their chief in his distress, but bargaining with him as with a stranger. However, he was always agreeable and polite, and would at times talk very well.

Thursday 16 September

Mr Johnson said he would go to Sweden with me. I said we should like to be with the King. Said Mr Johnson, "I doubt if he would speak to us."

Said the Colonel, "I'm sure Mr Boswell would speak to him." This was a good remark as to my forwardness. He added with a genteel civility, "And with great propriety."

Let me value my forwardness. It has procured me much happiness. I do not think it is impudence. It is an eagerness to share the best society, and a diligence to attain what I desire. If a man is praised for seeking knowledge though mountains and seas are in his way, is it not laudable in me to seek it at the risk of mortification from repulses? I have never yet exerted ambition in rising in the state. But sure I am, no man has made his way better to the best of company. Were my *places* to be ranged after my name, as 'Member of the Club at the Turk's Head', etc., I should make as great a figure as most peers. There is a meaning in this if it were well expressed.

After the ladies were gone, we talked of the Highlanders' not having sheets; and so on we went to the advantage of wearing linen. Mr Johnson said, "All animal substances are less cleanly than vegetable. Wool, of which flannel is made, is an animal substance; flannel therefore is not so cleanly as linen. I remember I used to think tar dirty. But when I knew it to be only a preparation of the juice of the pine, I thought so no longer. It is not disagreeable to have the gum that oozes from a plum-tree upon your fingers, because it is vegetable; but if you have any candle-grease, any tallow upon your fingers, you are uneasy till you rub it off." And then he came out with this saying: "I have often thought that if I kept a seraglio, the ladies should all wear linen gowns, or cotton; I mean stuffs made of vegetable substances. I would have no silk; you cannot tell when it is clean. It will be very nasty before it is perceived to be so. Linen detects its own dirtiness."

To hear Mr Johnson, while sitting solemn in arm-chair, talk of his keeping a seraglio and saying too, "I have *often* thought," was truly curious. Mr Macqueen asked him if he would admit me. "Yes," said he, "if he were properly prepared; and he'd make a very good eunuch. He'd be a fine fat animal.[525] He'd do his part well."

"I take it," said I, "better than you would do your part."

Though he treats his friends with uncommon freedom, he does not like a return. He seemed to me to be a little angry. He got off from my joke by saying, "I have not told you what was to be my part" – and then at once he returned to my office as eunuch and expatiated upon it with such fluency that it really hurt me. He made me quite contemptible for the moment. Luckily the company did not take it so clearly as I did. Perhaps, too, I imagined him to be more serious in this extraordinary raillery than he really was. But I am of a firmer metal than Langton and can stand a rub better.[526]

This morning he described Langton's house in Lincolnshire. He said the old house of the family was burnt. A temporary building was erected; and to this they have been always adding as the family increased. It was like a shirt made for a man when he was a child, and enlarged always as he grew older.

We talked tonight of Luther's allowing the Landgrave of Hesse two wives, and that it was with the consent of the wife to whom he was first married. Mr Johnson said there was no harm so far as she only was concerned, because *volenti non fit injuria.*[527] But it was an offence against the general order of society, and against the law of the Gospel, by which one man and one woman are united. "And," said he, "no man can have two wives but by preventing somebody else from having one."

FRIDAY 17 SEPTEMBER. After dinner yesterday, we had a conversation upon cunning. MacLeod said that he was not afraid of cunning people, but would let them play their tricks about him like monkeys. "But," said I, "they'll scratch."

"And," said Mr Macqueen, "they'll invent new tricks as soon as you find out what they do."

Mr Johnson said that cunning had effect from the credulity of others rather than the abilities of those who are cunning. He said it required no great talents to lie and deceive. This led us to consider whether it did not require great abilities to be very wicked. Mr Johnson instructed us nobly. Said he, "It requires great abilities to have the *power* of being very wicked; but not to *be* very wicked. A man who has the power which great abilities procure him, may use it well or ill; and it requires more abilities to use it well than to use it ill. Wickedness is always easier than virtue, for it takes the short cut to everything. It is much easier to steal a hundred pounds than to get it by labour or any other way. Consider only what piece of wickedness requires great abilities when once the person who is to be wicked has the power, for *there* is the distinction. It requires great abilities to conquer an army, but none to massacre it after it is conquered."

This day was rather better than any that we have had since we came to Dunvegan. Mr Macqueen had often talked to me of a curious piece of antiquity near this; what he called a temple of the Goddess Anaitis.[528]

He has sent Pennant a description of it. We were every day talking of going to see it; and it would have been a shame for me to have neglected it, though I should have been wet to the skin. He and I set out after breakfast, attended by his man, a fellow quite like a savage. And I must observe here that in Skye there seems to be much idleness; for men and boys follow you as colts will follow passengers upon a road. The usual figure of a Skye boy is a *lown* with bare legs and feet, a dirty kilt, ragged coat and waistcoat, a bare head, and a stick in his hand, which I suppose is partly to help the lazy rogue to walk, partly to serve as a kind of arms to him.[529]

We walked what is called two miles, but may be four, northeast from the castle, till we came to the sacred place. The country around is black dreary moor on all sides except to the sea-coast, towards which there is a view through a valley, and the farm of Bay shows some good ground. The place itself is green ground, being well drained by reason of a deep glen or valley on each side, in each of which there runs a rivulet or brook with a good quantity of water; for in each there are several cascades, which make a considerable appearance and sound; and at some places there are cascades formed by other brooks running into these. Upon the west there is one which has five separate falls formed by different projections of rock. The first thing we came to was an earthen mound or dike extending from the one precipice to the other. A little farther on was a strong stone wall, not high but very thick, extending in the same manner. On the outside of it were the ruins of two houses, one on each side of the entry or gate to it. The wall at the entry is four lengths and a half of my cane.[530] The wall is built all along of dry stone; but of stones of so large a size as to make a very firm and durable rampart. It has been built all about the consecrated ground except where the precipice is steep enough to form an enclosure of itself. The sacred spot will be more than two acres. There are within it the ruins of many houses (none of them large), a cairn, many graves marked by stones thus: ᎒᎒᎒; but what Mr Macqueen insists on is that the ruin of a small building standing east and west was actually the temple of the Goddess Anaitis, where her statue was kept, and from whence processions were made to wash it in one of the brooks. There is a hollow road really visible for a good way from the entrance. But Mr Macqueen walked with great attention along what he saw to be a continuation of it, for a good way, till there is an easy descent to the brook on the west. As I have often observed what looked like visible roads in moors, that is to say continued pieces of ground greener than the rest, and perhaps a little lower, I could not be sure that he was right here. All the houses, temple as well as the rest, have not more than a foot or a foot-and-a-half in height remaining of their walls. The temple is in length, within the walls, five lengths of my cane and six hands; in breadth, two lengths and a few hands, I think six too, so that it has been but a poor building. The waters on each side join at the north end of the sacred ground, which is like a theatre elevated above the neighbouring ground, and then the water or river formed by them runs away due north towards the sea.

Whatever this place has been it has been a most striking solemn scene. The sight lost in some places on a wild moor around; the hills in some other places bounding the prospect; and then, within, the space itself, so much concentrated and closely bound in by precipices, sometimes rocky, sometimes just green steep declivities – and waters beneath. I wish I could draw. Let me try to make an awkward sketch of it.[531] It is to be supposed that when this was a place of worship, the banks or steeps on each side of the brooks were covered with wood. When that circumstance is added, I can hardly conceive a more awful rude retreat. Mr Macqueen has collected a great deal of learning with regard to the temples of Anaitis, of which he supposes this to have been one. My sketch of it may convey some idea. But there is no exactness in it. I may truly be said to 'write about it, Goddess, and about it'.[532]

When we got home, and were enjoying ourselves over admirable roasted venison, we first talked of portraits. Mr Johnson agreed in thinking them valuable in families. I asked if he would rather have fine portraits or like ones. "Why," said he, "their chief excellence is in being like."

"But," said I, "are you of that opinion as to the portraits of ancestors whom one has never seen?"

Said he, "It then becomes of more consequence that they should be like – that you may see them. And I'd have them in the dress of the times, which makes a piece of history. One should like to see how Rorie More looked. *Truth*, sir, is of the greatest value in these things."

Mr Macqueen observed that if you hold that there is no matter though portraits are not like if well painted, you may be indifferent whether a piece of history is true or not, if well told.

Mr Johnson said at breakfast today that it was but of late that historians bestowed pains and attention in consulting records, to attain to accuracy. Bacon in writing his History of Henry VII does not seem to have consulted any, but just taken what he found in other histories, with what he learnt by tradition. He agreed with me that there should be a chronicle kept in every family, to preserve the characters and transactions of successive generations.

Friday 17 September

I started Anaitis after dinner. Mr Macqueen had laid stress on the name given to the place by the country people, *Aunnit*; and said he, "I knew not what to make of this piece of antiquity, till I met with the *Anaitidis delubrum*, in Asia Minor, mentioned by Pausanias and the elder Pliny."

Mr Johnson, who is wonderfully acute, examined Mr Macqueen as to the meaning of the word *Aunnit* in Erse; and it came out to be a water-place, or a place near a water. "Which," said Mr Macqueen, "agrees with all the descriptions of those temples, which were situated near rivers, that there might be water to wash the statue."[533]

"Nay," said Mr Johnson, "the argument from the name is gone. The name is exhausted by what we see. We have no occasion to go to a distance for what we can pick up under our feet. Had it been an accidental name, the similarity between it and Anaitis might have had something in it; but it turns out to be a mere physiological name."

MacLeod said Mr Macqueen's knowledge of etymology had destroyed his conjecture. "Yes," said Mr Johnson, "Mr Macqueen is like the eagle mentioned by Waller, who was shot with an arrow feathered from his own wing."[534]

Mr Macqueen would not yield his conjecture. "Sir," said Mr Johnson, "you have one possibility for you, and all possibilities against you. It is possible it may be the temple of Anaitis. But it is also possible that it may be a fortification. Or it may be a place of Christian worship, as the first Christians often chose remote and wild places to make an impression on the mind. Or if it was a heathen temple, it may have been built near a river, for the purpose of lustration; there is such a multitude of divinities to whom it may have been dedicated that the chance of its being a temple of Anaitis is hardly anything. 'Tis like throwing a grain of sand upon the sea-shore today and thinking you may find it tomorrow. No, this temple, like many an ill-built edifice, tumbles down before 'tis roofed in."

He had a kind of *conceit* in his discourse; for after Mr Macqueen spoke of an altar, he said, "Mr Macqueen is fighting *pro aris et focis*."

It was wonderful how well time passed in a remote castle and in dreary weather. After supper, we talked of Pennant. It was objected that he was superficial. Mr Johnson defended him warmly. He said, "Pennant has greater variety of inquiry than almost any man, and has told us more than perhaps one in ten thousand could have done in the time that he took. He has not said what he was to tell; so you cannot find fault with him for what he has not told. If a man comes to look for fishes, you cannot blame him if he does not attend to fowls."

Friday 17 September

"But," said Col. MacLeod, "he mentions the unreasonable rise of rents in the Highlands, and says: 'The gentlemen are for emptying the bag, without filling it.' For that is the phrase he uses. Why does he not tell how to fill it?" JOHNSON. "Sir, there is no end of negative criticism. He tells what he observes, and as much as he chooses. If he tells what is not true, you may find fault with him. But though he tells that the land is not well cultivated, he is not obliged to tell how it may be well cultivated. If I tell that many of the Highlanders go barefooted, I am not obliged to tell how they may get shoes. Pennant tells a fact. He need go no farther except he pleases. He exhausts nothing. And no subject whatever has yet been exhausted. But Pennant has surely told a great deal. Here is a man six foot high, and you're angry because he is not seven."

This was a capital *Oratio pro Pennantio*, which they who have read this gentleman's Tours, and recollect the Savage and the Shopkeeper at Monboddo, will probably impute to the spirit of contradiction.[535] But still I think he had better have given more attention to fewer things, than thrown together such a number of imperfect accounts. But I think with diffidence.

SATURDAY 18 SEPTEMBER. At breakfast Lady MacLeod complained of the difficulties under which the family now laboured. "Madam," said Mr Johnson, "consider what a son you have. He is as fine a young gentleman as I ever knew since I came into this world. I never knew any one who at his age had advanced his understanding so much."

Before breakfast Mr Johnson came up to my room to forbid me to mention that this was his birthday; but I told him I had done it already, at which he was displeased, I suppose from wishing to have nothing particular done on his account. MacLeod was not present when Mr Johnson gave his mother the high character of him. But I told him of it, as I knew it would confirm him in his laudable resolutions. The lady and I got into a warm dispute. She wanted to build a house upon a farm which she has taken, about five miles from the old castle, and to make gardens and everything fine there. All of which I approved of; but insisted that the seat of the family should always be upon the rock of Dunvegan. "Ay," said Mr Johnson, "in time we'll build all round this rock. You may make a very good house at the farm, but it must not be such as to tempt the Laird of MacLeod to go thither to reside. Most of the great families of England have a secondary house, which is called a jointure-house; let this be of that kind."

The lady insisted that the rock was very inconvenient. That there was no place near it where a good garden could be made; that it must always be a rude place; that it was Herculean labour to make a dinner here; that the climate was such that one might have half an hour fair now and then, though it rained in general; and therefore one should be close to where the farm is. Said Mr Johnson, "The Laird will not mind being wet. No, we'll keep the old rock, and we'll have an armoury, though Sir Alexander Macdonald said that arms would rust."

I was very keen. I was vexed to find the alloy of modern refinement in a lady who had so much old family spirit. "Madam," said I, "if once you quit this rock, this centre of gravity, there is no knowing where you may settle. You move five miles first; then to St Andrews, as the late Laird did; then to Edinburgh; and so on till you end at Hampstead, or in France. No, no; keep to the rock. It is the very jewel of the estate. It looks as if it had been let down from heaven by the four corners, to be the residence of a chief. Have all the comforts and conveniencies of life upon it; but never leave Rorie More's cascade."

"But," said she, "is it not enough if we keep it? Must we never be more convenient than Rorie More was? He had his beef brought to dinner in one basket and his bread in another. Why not as well be Rorie More all over as live upon his rock? And would not we tire of looking perpetually on this rock?"

"No, madam," said I, "your eye will never wear away the old rock."

Said she, "It is very well for you, who have a fine place and everything easy, to talk so, and think of chaining honest folks to a rock. You would not live upon it yourself."

"Yes, madam," said I, "I would live upon it were I Laird of MacLeod, and would be unhappy if I were not upon it."

Said Mr Johnson, with a strong voice and most determined manner: "Madam, rather than quit the old rock, Boswell would live in the pit. He'd make his bedchamber in the dungeon."

I felt a degree of elation at finding my resolute feudal enthusiasm thus confirmed by such a sanction. The lady was puzzled a little. She still returned to her pretty farm, rich ground, fine garden. "Madam," said Mr Johnson, "were it in Asia, I would not leave the rock."

The lady was rational in her notions to a certain degree. But the ancient family residence must be a primary object; and if the situation is in a place where there can be little done in farming or gardening, it has, besides the veneration acquired by the mere lapse of time during which the family has lived here, many circumstances of natural grandeur suited to the seat of a Highland chief. It has the sea – islands – rocks – hills – a noble cascade. And when the family is again in opulence, much may be done by art.

Mr Donald Macqueen went away today, in order to preach at Bracadale next day, as the minister there was to go and preach for him.[536] We were so comfortably placed at Dunvegan that Mr Johnson could hardly be moved from it. I proposed to him that we should leave it on Monday. "No, sir," said he. "I'll not go before Wednesday. I'll have some more of this good."

However, as the weather was at this season so bad and so very uncertain, and we had a good deal to do yet, Mr Macqueen and I prevailed with him to agree to set out on Monday if the day should be good. Mr Macqueen, though it was inconvenient for him to be away from his harvest, engaged to wait on Monday at Ullinish for us. When he was going away, Mr Johnson said, "I shall ever retain a great regard for you," then asked him if he had the *Rambler*. Mr Macqueen said no, but his brother had it. JOHNSON. "Have you the *Idler*?"

"No, sir." JOHNSON. "Then I'll order one for you at Edinburgh, which you will keep in remembrance of me."

Mr Macqueen was much pleased with this. He expressed himself in the strongest terms as to his admiration of Mr Johnson's wonderful knowledge, and every other quality for which he is distinguished. I asked Mr Macqueen if he was satisfied to be a minister in Skye. He said he was. But he owned that his forefathers having been so long there, and he himself being born there, made a chief ingredient in his contentment.

I should have mentioned that, on our left hand, between Portree and Dr MacLeod's, Mr Macqueen told me there had been a college of the Knights Templars; that tradition said so, and that there was a ruin remaining of their church, which had been burnt.[537] I must get him to explain this better. Mr Johnson has weakened my belief in remote tradition. In the dispute about Anaitis, Mr Macqueen said Asia Minor was peopled by Scythians, and as they were the ancestors of the Celts, the same religion might be in Asia Minor and Skye. Said Mr Johnson, "What can a nation that has not letters tell of its original? I have always difficulty to be patient when I hear authors gravely quoted as giving accounts of savage nations, which accounts they had from the savages themselves. What can the Macraes tell about themselves a thousand years ago? There is no tracing the connection of ancient nations but by language, and therefore I'm always sorry when language is lost, because languages are the pedigree of nations. If you find the same language in distant countries, you may be sure that the inhabitants of each have been the same people; that is to say, if you find the languages a good deal the same; for finding a word here and there will not do; as Butler, in his *Hudibras*, by way of ridicule, finds the word *penguin* in the Straits of Magellan, signifying a bird with a white head; and that word has the signification in Wales of a whiteheaded wench: *pen*, head, *guin*, white; therefore the people near the Straits of Magellan are Welsh."[538]

A young gentleman of the name of Maclean, nephew to the Laird of the Isle of Muck, came this morning; and just as we sat down to dinner, came the Laird of the Isle of Muck himself; his lady, sister to Talisker; a Miss Maclean, his niece; a Miss Macqueen, a relation (both of them young girls); and a Miss Mally MacLeod, daughter of the late Hammer, who wrote a treatise on the second sight, etc., under the designation of Theophilus Insulanus. She was, as I was told, past sixty; but affected youthfulness.

It was curious to hear the Laird called by his title. 'Muck' would not do well, but he was called 'Isle of Muck', which went off with great readiness. His lady was called Mrs Maclean. He was a hearty Highlander, and his lady a cheerful woman as could be. We were immediately quite easy with them; and Mr Johnson, hearing that their island lay between Skye and Mull, cried, "We'll go to the Isle of Muck."

They offered us a hearty welcome, but as we found out that it would be inconvenient for them to go home so soon as our time required, we laid aside the scheme. The name is ugly, though it is worse as now written; the Erse is *Mouack*, the sow's island, and Buchanan calls it *Insula Porcorum*. It is so called from its form. Some call it Isle of *Monk*. The Laird insists on this.[539] It was formerly church lands belonging to Icolmkill, and a hermit lived in it. It is two miles long, and about three-quarters of a mile broad. The Laird said he had sevenscore of souls upon it. Last year he had fourscore children inoculated; some of them indeed were eighteen years of age. He agreed with a surgeon to come and do it at half-a-crown a head. It is very fertile in corn. They export some; and its coasts abound in fish. A tailor comes there six times in a year. They get a good blacksmith from the isle of Eigg when they want him.

It was after supper before these particulars were told us. This addition to our society had just landed from the Long Island. In the evening we had an excellent dance, but Mr Johnson did not come to it. Neither did he come to supper for these two last nights, but only joined us after supper. Tonight he supped.

Saturday 18 September

SUNDAY 19 SEPTEMBER. It was rather worse weather than any that we have had yet. At breakfast Mr Johnson said that some cunning men chose fools for their wives, thinking to manage them; but they always failed. "There is a spaniel fool and a mule fool. The spaniel fool may be made to do by beating. The mule fool will neither do by words nor blows; and the spaniel fool often turns mule at last: and suppose a fool to be made do pretty well, you must have the continual trouble of making her do. Depend upon it, no woman is the worse for sense and knowledge."[540]

Whether he meant merely to say a polite thing, or to give his opinion, I could not be sure; but he said men knew that women were an overmatch for them; and therefore they chose the weakest or most ignorant. If they did not think so, they never could be afraid of women knowing as much as themselves. I must have this more amply discussed with him.[541]

He came to my room this morning before breakfast to read my Journal, which he has done all along. He often before said, "I take great delight in reading it." Today he said, "You improve. It grows better and better." I said there was a danger of my getting a habit of writing in a slovenly manner. "Sir," said he, "it is not written in a slovenly manner. It might be printed, were the subject fit for printing."[542]

He sat in his room with a volume of Lord Bacon's works, the *Decay of Christian Piety*, Monboddo's *Origin of Language*, and Sterne's sermons beside him, while Mr Bethune preached in the dining-room.[543] We had some of the neighbours assembled. There was just an ordinary Presbyterian forenoon's service, which was very decent, and which is always here when the family cannot go to church. He asked me today how we were so little together. I told him my Journal took up so much time. But at the same time, it is curious that although I will run from one end of London to another to have an hour with him, I should omit to seize any spare time to be in his company when I am in the house with him. But my Journal is really a task of much time and labour, and Mr Johnson forbids me to contract it.

I omitted to mention that Mr Johnson told Mr Macqueen that he had found the belief of the second sight universal in Skye, except among the clergy, who seemed determined against it. I took the liberty to say to Mr Macqueen that the clergy were actuated by a kind of vanity. Say they, "The world takes us to be credulous men in a remote corner. We'll show them that we are more enlightened than they think." The worthy man said that his disbelief of it was from his not finding sufficient evidence. But I could perceive that he was prejudiced against it.

After dinner today we talked of the extraordinary fact of Lady Grange's being sent to St Kilda.[544] Mr Johnson said, "If MacLeod would let it be known that he had such a place for naughty ladies, he might make it a very profitable island."

We had in the course of our tour heard of St Kilda poetry. Mr Johnson said, "It must be very poor, because they have very few images."

"But," said I, "there may be a poetical genius to combine these, and in short to make poetry of them."

"But, sir," said he, "a man cannot make fire but in proportion as he has wood. He cannot coin guineas but in proportion as he has gold."[545]

He came the length this day of contracting Monboddo and calling him 'Mony'. This was a piece of kindness, for he does so to all his friends. At tea he talked of his intending to go to Italy in 1775. MacLeod said he would like Paris better. Mr Johnson said there was none of the *literati* now alive to see whom he would cross a sea. He said he could find in Buffon's book all that he could say.[546]

After supper he said he was sorry that prize-fighting was gone out; that every art should be preserved, and the art of defence was important; that it was absurd that our soldiers should have swords and not be taught the use of them; that prize-fighting made people accustomed not to be alarmed at seeing their own blood, or feeling a little pain from a wound. He said the heavy claymore was an ill-contrived weapon. A man could only strike once with it. It employed both his hands, and he must of course be soon fatigued with wielding it; so that if his antagonist can only keep playing awhile, he is sure of him. He said, "I'd fight with a dirk against Rorie More's sword. I could ward off a blow with a dirk, and then run in upon my enemy. When within that heavy sword, I have him. He's quite helpless, and I could stab him at my leisure, like a calf."

He said it was thought by sensible military people that the English did not enough avail themselves of their superior strength of body against the French; for that must always have a great advantage in pushing with bayonets; that he had heard an officer say that if women could be made to stand, they'd do as well as men in a mere interchange of bullets from a distance; but if a body of men should come close up to 'em, then, to be sure, they must be overcome. "Now," said he, "in the same manner the weaker-bodied French must be overcome by our strong soldiers."

He said as to duelling that there is no case in England where one or other *must* die; that if you have overcome your adversary either by killing him or disarming him, your honour, or the honour of your family, is restored, as much as it can be by a duel. That it would be cowardly to make a man renew the combat when you know that you have the advantage of him. You might just as well go and cut his throat while he's asleep in his bed. That when a duel begins, it is supposed there may be an equality; because it is not always skill that prevails. "It depends much on presence of mind; nay, on accidents. The wind may be in a man's face – he may fall – many such things may decide the superiority. A man is punished by being called out and subjected to the risk that is in a duel." But as I suggested that the injured person is equally subjected to risk, Mr Johnson owned he could not explain the rationality of duelling.

I was under the greatest apprehensions for fear of the itch, which is really very common in these parts (especially among the young people), and very little minded. I this day perceived several pimples or rather blisters on the palm of my right hand, which were hot, painful, and itchy; but I was assured it never began so. I was, however, uneasy. The horror of having so vile a distemper and carrying it home made me shudder. I may appear to talk in too strong terms of a *minor* disease. But I feel what I write. As yet in the Highlands I was only bit with fleas at Anoch and Glenelg, and when changing my shirt at Armadale I found what I thought a *bug* sticking fast on my left arm. Perhaps it was some other sucking animal.

MONDAY 20 SEPTEMBER. When I awaked, the storm was higher still. I read some of Pennant's *Tour* in bed, and was very well pleased. I have read little here. Indeed I have been always writing. I found in my closet a large Prayer-Book and Bible and Apocrypha with prints, all in one volume. I read in it daily.

The storm abated about nine, and the sun shone; but it rained again soon, and it was not a day for travelling. At breakfast, Mr Johnson told us that there was once a pretty good tavern in Catherine Street, where very good company met in an evening, and each man called for his own half-pint of wine, or gill, if he pleased; they were frugal men, and nobody paid but for what he himself drank. The house furnished no supper, but a woman attended with mutton pies, which anybody might purchase.[547] Mr Johnson was introduced to this company by Cumming the Quaker, and used to go there sometimes when he drank wine.[548] He said that in the last age, when his mother lived in London, there were two sets of people, those who gave the wall and those who took it; the peaceable and the quarrelsome. When he returned to Lichfield after having been in London, his mother asked him whether he was one of those who gave the wall, or those who took it. Now it is fixed that every man keeps to the right; or, if one is taking the wall, another yields it, and it is never a dispute.

He was very severe on Lady Macdonald; he said he would have her sent to St Kilda. She was as bad as negative badness could be, and stood in the way of what was good. That insipid beauty would not go a great way, and that such a woman might be cut out of a cabbage, if there was a skilful artificer.

MacLeod was too late in coming to breakfast. Mr Johnson said laziness was worse than the toothache. "No," said I, "a basin of cold water or a horse-whip will cure laziness."

"No," said Mr Johnson, "it will only put off the fit; it will not cure the disease. I have been trying to cure laziness all my life, and could not do it."

"But," said I, "if a man does in a shorter time what might be the labour of a life, there is nothing to be said." JOHNSON. "Suppose that flattery to be true, the world has nothing to say to a man; but that will not justify him to himself."

After breakfast he said a Highland chief should now endeavour to do everything to raise his rents by means of the industry of his people; that formerly it was right to have his house full of idle people – they were his defenders, his servants, his dependants, his friends. "Now they may be better employed. The system of things is now so much altered that the family cannot have influence but by riches, because it has no longer the power. An individual of a family may have it; but it cannot now belong to the family unless you could have a perpetuity of men with the same views. One man like Sir Alexander destroys what twenty ancestors have gained. MacLeod has four times the land that the Duke of Bedford has. I think with his views he may in time make himself the greatest man in the King's dominions, for land may always be improved to a certain degree. And," said he, "don't sell land to throw money into the funds, as is done, or to try any other species of trade. Depend upon it, this rage of trade will destroy itself. You and I shall not see it, but the time will come when there will be an end on't. Trade is like gaming. If a whole company are gamesters, it must cease, for there is nothing to be won. When all nations are traders, there is nothing to be gained by trade. And it will stop the soonest where it is brought to the greatest perfection. Then, only the proprietors of land will be the great men."

I said it was hard for MacLeod to find ingratitude in so many of his people. "Sir," said he, "gratitude is a fruit of great cultivation. You do not find it among gross people."

I should doubt of this. Nature seems to have implanted it. The lion mentioned by Valerius Maximus had it.[549] I should think culture, which brings luxury and selfishness with it, may weaken the principle or passion of gratitude. This too must be discussed.

Mr Johnson said this morning, when talking of our setting out, that he was in the state that Lord Bacon represents kings. He desired the end but did not like the means. He wished much to get home, but was unwilling to travel in Skye. "And," said I, "you are like kings too in this, that you must act under the direction of others."

This day (half an hour past three) I have brought up my Journal to a minute, at least to this very forenoon. We had at dinner Ullinish and ————. I must observe that Mr Johnson read all my Journal to the foot of the preceding page, and said to me, "It is a very pretty Journal." It has therefore his sanction, and I am encouraged to go on. After dinner he let me copy his *Ode on Skye*.[550]

There was a dance at night; but I kept out of the way, and danced only one reel before supper. We were more jovial than ordinary tonight, and sat up till two in the morning. But there was no excess. The weather had changed, and it was to be our last night here.

TUESDAY 21 SEPTEMBER. Never was I so long of hearing from my dear wife as I have been now. Her last letter was dated the 1st of this month. She could write but once a week, and her letter of the 8th instant had not been sent on to Dunvegan. I could not help being uneasy. Mr Johnson has the advantage of me, in having no wife or child to occasion anxious apprehensions in his mind. It was a good morning, so we resolved to set out.

We have truly had a very comfortable residence at Dunvegan. The castle is upon a rock just upon the sea-shore. It was inaccessible every way but by a stair on the side near the sea, till the late Laird built a stair of two-and-twenty steps on the land side. On the right hand after you come up this stair is an old tower, to which is joined a large building four storeys high, which it is said was here when Leod, the first of this family, came from the Isle of Man and married the heiress of the MacCrails, the ancient possessors, and conquered as much as married. He surpassed the house of Austria; for he was *felix* both *bella gerere* et *nubere*.[551] He was like the heroes mentioned by John Home in his *Agis*: "They sack'd the cities," etc.[552]

John Breck, the grandfather of the late Laird, began to repair it or rather complete it. He, like some of those who had their epitaphs written before they died, had an inscription cut upon a large stone above one of the lower windows, of which I have a copy. It was composed by Mr Dugald Macpherson, the parish minister. It still remains to celebrate what was not done, and to serve as a memento of the uncertainty of life, and the presumption of man:

> *Joannes Macleod Beganoduni Dominus gentis suæ Philarchus, Durinesiæ Haraiæ Vaternesiæ, &c.: Baro D. Floræ Macdonald matrimoniali vinculo conjugatus turrem hanc Beganodunensem proavorum habitaculum longe vetustissimum diu penitus labefectatam Anno æræ vulgaris* MDCLXXXVI *instauravit.*

> *Quem stabilire juvat proavorum tecta vetusta,*
> *Omne scelus fugiat, justitiamque colat.*
> *Vertit in aerias turres magalia virtus,*
> *Inque casas humiles tecta superba nefas.*[553]

On the left hand after you come up this stair is a large building along the top of the rock with a parapet and a row of false cannon of stone.[554] This was one of the oldest parts of what was built upon the rock that was ever inhabited. Adjoining to it is a square tower in which is the drawing-room. There has been a wall here along the edge of the rock. Part of it remains and is covered with ivy. On the opposite corner is the remains of another tower, which was formed by the late Laird into a pigeon-house above and a little-house below. These towers are said to be the oldest buildings here. A square is formed along the rock by buildings of different kinds, by the late Laird: lodging rooms, kitchen, servants' apartments. But all of them are in sad disrepair. The court or close, clear of the buildings – that is to say, within them – is thirty canes long and thirteen broad. I shall have my cane measured, which will ascertain the number of feet.[555]

Rorie More's horn is ten inches in circumference at the root. In length, following the curves, two feet; black for about three inches next the top, and sharp there. Mr Johnson laid me half-a-crown I should not show him so large a horn in the Lothians. I was wrong in my description of the carving on the silver mouth of it. It has alternate circles filled up with plaited work and a beast which I took to be a griffin with a ribbon or ———— between.[556] The bow is five feet eight inches. The claymore, from the knob to the guard, thirteen inches and a half; from the guard to the point, full three feet. Rorie More was not denominated 'More' from his size, but from his great spirit. I had the true ancient spirit in this castle.[557]

There is, under the shade of the rock on the ————, two rows of sycamores planted by the late Laird, which grow pretty well; and from the drawing-room window you see a few ashes and other trees also planted by him. Before the castle on the land side, nothing is to be seen but wild hills interspersed with humps of whin-rock. The gradation of them begins directly. The cascade is grand; and on the ———— and ———— there are some good spots of ground which might be cultivated. The sea before the castle is curiously broken with islands and necks of land. The late Laird planted the Island of ————. But it was neglected in his absence, and cattle destroyed the trees. There is a well in the court of the castle. There is an inn at Dunvegan, as it is a convenient port for the Long Island. There is a blind man here who has been thirty years in the house. He was blind since he was three years of age, and he carries china and everything else quite safely.[558]

I cannot enough praise the genteel hospitality with which we were treated. The lady had sense and most meritorious resolution. She told me she believed she never would leave Dunvegan, so heroically resolved is she to retrieve the family. Miss Bell, the youngest daughter, appeared a few times. But Miss MacLeod and Miss Nanny were always with us.[559] They had lived much in Hampshire, and had the agreeable language and manners of English girls. As I left Dunvegan, I warmly wished for the prosperity of the family. In the state in which it now is, it is like Corsica in miniature; at least it resembles it in struggling to emerge from distress, and in having a chief of singular merit.

MacLeod and Talisker set out with us. We passed by the parish church, Duirinish. The churchyard is not enclosed, but a pretty murmuring brook runs along one quarter of it. In it is a pyramid erected to the memory of Thomas, Lord Lovat, by his son Lord Simon, who suffered on Tower Hill. It is of freestone, and I suppose about thirty feet high. There is upon it a square piece of marble with the arms of Lovat, and on the base a larger piece with an inscription on it, which I am persuaded was the composition of Lord Lovat himself, being quite his style – full of vainglory as to his own family and flattery of the MacLeods.[560]

This pyramid was erected by SIMON LORD FRASER of LOVAT, in honour of Lord THOMAS his Father, a Peer of Scotland, and Chief of the great and ancient clan of the FRASERS. Being attacked for his birthright by the family of ATHOLL, then in power and favour with KING WILLIAM, yet, by the valour and fidelity of his clan, and the assistance of the CAMPBELLS, the old friends and allies of his family, he defended his birthright with such greatness and fermety of soul, and such valour and activity, that he was an honour to his name, and a good pattern to all brave Chiefs of clans. He died in the month of May, 1699, in the 63d year of his age, in Dunvegan, the house of the LAIRD of MAC LEOD, whose sister he had married: by whom he had the above SIMON LORD FRASER, and several other children. And, for the great love he bore to the family of MAC LEOD, he desired to be buried near his wife's relations, in the place where two of her uncles lay. And his son LORD SIMON, to shew to posterity his great affection for his mother's kindred, the brave MAC LEODS, chooses rather to leave his father's bones with them, than carry them to his own burial-place, near Lovat.

I have preserved this inscription, though of no great value, thinking it characteristical of a man who has made some noise in the world. Mr Johnson said it was poor stuff, such as Lord Lovat's butler might have written; and he justly stigmatized Lovat's character, and repeated some good verses from one of the magazines on the several personages who suffered in 1745. (This he did at Ullinish. I shall look for the verses.)[561]

I saw a strange thing in this churchyard: a parcel of people assembled at a funeral before the grave was dug; and there was the coffin with the corpse in it lying on the grass, while the people alternately lent a hand in making a grave. One man at a little distance was busy cutting a turf for it with the crooked spade which is used in Skye, a very awkward instrument. The iron part of it is like a plough coulter. It has just a rude tree for a handle, and a good way up a pin is placed for the foot to press upon.[562] A traveller might, without further inquiry, have set this down as the mode of burying in Sky. I was told, however, that the usual way is to have a grave previously dug by the kirk officer. I could not help having a fallacious feeling for the corpse which was kept so long waiting.

I observed today that the usual way of carrying home their grain here is in loads on horseback. They have also a few sledges, or *cars* as they are called in Ayrshire, clumsily made and rarely used. They are made of two crooked trees. Two ends drag on the ground; two lean on a horse, one on each side, like the thills of a cart or chaise; and for a good way there are cross bars between them and a back of sticks.[563]

We went a mile off the road to Ullinish and viewed MacLeod's farm, which is a very large and beautiful one upon the sea-coast, a peninsula or great neck of land. Mr Johnson said it was quite an English farm. We got to Ullinish about six; found a very good farm-house of two storeys. Ullinish himself, a plain honest man in brown, much like an English justice of peace; not much given to talk, but sufficiently sagacious, and somewhat droll. His daughter, who was never out of Skye, a very well-bred

Tuesday 21 September

girl. Our reverend friend, Mr Donald Macqueen, kept his appointment, and met us here.

We talked of Phipps's voyage to the North Pole. Mr Johnson said it was conjectured that our former navigators have kept too near land, and so have found the sea frozen far north, because the land hinders the free motion of the tides; but, in the wide ocean, where the waves tumble at their full convenience, it is imagined that the frost does not take effect.[564]

Though we came so late, we had dinner, tea, and supper. I had a good room at night. Several books lay on the head of an escritoire. The *Scots Acts*, Bankton's *Institutions*, Milton's *Poems*, *Fingal*, some of the works of Dryden, etc. Mr Donald Macqueen slept in a closet by me.[565]

WEDNESDAY 22 SEPTEMBER. Donald MacLeod, who had gone to Bracadale to get us £30 for my bill, had not yet returned. This looked odd. An express was sent last night for him, but word came that he was gone to Portree. We were also informed that he had been mortally drunk, had been throwing away money, and had some stolen from him. This was offensive, as Mr Johnson said.

I was vexed at first, thinking myself to blame for having trusted such a man. But when I considered that I did not know of his failings, and saw him well received everywhere, I found that I might make myself easy in what concerned the imputation of folly. Talisker dispatched a baron-officer with a letter to him and another to James Macdonald at Portree, that if any money remained, it might be had for us. All however despaired of our recovering any; not because the man was dishonest, for he was never suspected of that, but because when he drank he became quite extravagant.

In the morning I walked out and saw the ship, the *Margaret of Clyde*, fairly pass by with a number of emigrants on board. It was a kind of melancholy sight. After breakfast we walked to see a subterraneous house about a short mile off. Mr Johnson and Ullinish rode to it. It was upon the side of a rising ground. It was discovered by a fox's having taken up his abode in it, and in chasing him they dug into it. It was ten sticks long, following a very gentle curve till we reached the upper end, where it was choked up by the digging. However, it seemed to have been not much longer, for we got a man with a crooked spade to dig a little beyond that, and he did not find the appearance of its continuance. Besides, just adjoining to where they had dug for the fox at that end (for they had dug at both ends), we found the foundations of little stone houses, which seemed to be four feet wide, and three feet high.[566]

Ullinish's servant went in with a candle, and we followed. Mr Johnson crept into it wonderfully. It has been fairly dug in the earth; the sides of it are faced with pebbles or whinstones of the ordinary size. The roof is formed of flagstones laid across, as in the subterraneous place at Raasay. Mr Macqueen, who is always for making everything as ancient as possible, boasted that it was the habitation of some of the first inhabitants of the island, and what a curiosity it was to find a specimen of the houses of the aborigines here, which he believed could be found nowhere else; and it was plain that they lived without fire. Mr Johnson well observed that they who made this were not in the rudest state, for that it was more difficult to make it than to make a house; therefore, to be sure, those who made it had houses, and had this only as a hiding-place. This seems clear. It appeared to me that the vestiges of houses just by it confirmed Mr Johnson's opinion.

We then proceeded a little way farther, to the top of a rising ground on which are the remains of what is said to have been the first residence of Leod, the ancestor of the MacLeods. We found a circular wall of ten feet in thickness, built without mortar, of very large whinstones, for raising which it seems certain that machinery had been employed. The wall is admirably built, and the stone is everlasting. Some of it seemed to be almost iron. One of the stones, which composed one side of the door or entry, had the very look almost of solid iron, and when I struck it, it sounded like a smith's anvil. I saw on each side of the entry an opening in which the bolt of this fortress had run. It was found some years ago sunk in the ground. It was of iron, very thick and long. A coulter for a plough and several spades were made of it. It was a pity to destroy it. The diameter of the circle within the walls is forty feet. (When I am precise in dimensions, it is from actual measurement.) Mr Johnson believed it to be only a temporary retreat. Indeed, we could not perceive a well, but that may be filled up. We saw, however, the vestiges of five different houses or apartments within it. Mr Macqueen conjectures that these were inhabited, and that the circular wall defended them.

From this old tower, or dun or whatever it shall be called, is a grand view of the mouth of Loch Bracadale, and at a distance, Barra and South Uist; and on the land side, the Cuillin, a prodigious range of mountains, capped with rocks like pinnacles in a strange variety of shapes.[567] They resemble the mountains near Corte, of which I have a print. They make part of a great forest for deer.[568] Martin erroneously writes the name *Quillin*.[569]

Many heavy showers fell when we were out. When we got home, dinner was on the table; so instead of setting out for Talisker, as we intended, without dining, we took a good meal, after which we were going to take boat to depart; but it was reconsidered, and found too late. Upon which we determined to employ the afternoon in seeing what we could here. Ullinish carried us in his boat down to the shore of an island possessed by him, but to which there is access by land when the sea is out.

The coast is an exceeding high rock. But there is first a stratum of rocky substance, not very high. We scrambled up that and went into an immense cave, an *antrum immane* indeed, much more so than that of the Sibyl to which that description is annexed by Virgil, which I likewise have visited.[570] It is one hundred and eighty feet long, thirty feet broad where it is broadest, and from twenty to thirty in other places. Mr Johnson thought it only twenty feet high, but most of us thought it thirty; some, forty. By throwing stones to the roof of it, I guessed it to be at least thirty. Near to it is another large cave, parallel with the sea and open at both ends; and nearer Ullinish, another in the same direction with the immense one, very near a circle, but not high in the roof. I forget its size, but it was considerable. The immense cave, we were told, had a remarkable echo, but we found none. They said it was owing to the great rains having made it damp. Such are the excuses by which the exaggeration of Highland narratives is palliated. There were several continued droppings, or rather runnings, from the roof.

We sailed a little farther down the shore, and saw a singular appearance: a piece of rock standing by itself like the front wall of an old castle, with an opening like a window quite through it, which has been made by the beating of wind and rain within these seven years; for Ullinish and his son both remember when it was not there.

Mr Johnson had never catched any fish in the sea. Two little girls were fishing from a rock. We borrowed their lines, and Mr Johnson drew one or two cuddies, but he let them go again. I saw as we walked from the shore a mineral spring, very strong of steel, or rather iron. There is a plentiful garden at Ullinish, and several trees; and just above the house is a hill, called ———, 'the hill of strife', where Mr Macqueen says justice was of old administered.[571] It is like the *mons placiti*, the Moots hill of Scone, or those *laws*, as we call them on the south of Tay, such as North Berwick Law and several others. It is curious that it should happen now to be just by the sheriff's residence.

While we were at dinner, snow had fallen on Cuillin, so that the earthy mountainous parts were white; and there was a good deal of hail while we were on the sea. I was glad to get safe home, for some of the

Wednesday 22 September

boatmen, whether in earnest or not I cannot tell, said, before we took boat, that they heard an English ghost cry; and my superstition and fear are both easily excited.[572]

The sheriff had excellent peats, and the evening went on admirably. Mr Johnson talked a good deal on the subject of literature. Speaking of the noble family of Boyle, he said that all the Lords Orrery, till this, have been writers. The first wrote several plays. The second was Bentley's antagonist; the third wrote the Life of Swift, and several other pieces. His son Hamilton, Earl of Orrery, wrote several papers in the *Adventurer* and *World*. He said he knew well Swift's Lord Orrery. He was a feeble-minded man. He was much hurt by the counter-Life written by Delany.[573] Mr Johnson comforted him by saying they were both right. Delany had seen most of the good side of Swift, my lord of the bad.[574] MacLeod asked if it was not wrong in Orrery to expose the defects of a man with whom he lived in intimacy. JOHNSON. "Why no, sir, after the man is dead, and it is done historically." He said if Lord Orrery had been rich, he would have been a very liberal patron. That his conversation was like his writing, neat and elegant, but without strength. That he grasped at more than his abilities could reach. Tried to pass for a better talker, and a better writer, and a better thinker than he was. He said there was a quarrel between him and his son Hamilton, in which my lord was criminal, because it arose from Hamilton's not allowing his wife to keep company with my lord's mistress. My lord showed his resentment in his will – leaving his library by his son, because he could not make use of it, or something to that purpose.[575]

I mentioned my lord's affectation of ending all his letters about Swift in different ways, and never 'I am, etc.' (an observation which I have heard Sheridan make); and that a foreign lady said to me that this was peculiar to, or at least most frequent among, the English. I took up a volume of Dryden, containing *The Conquest of Granada*, *Amboyna*, *The Assignation*, etc., and all of the dedications had such conclusions. Mr Johnson said it was more elegant than 'I am'. He said when addressing the Duke of York, the mode Dryden used was more respectful. I agreed that *there* it was better. It was making his escape from the royal presence with a genteel sudden timidity, in place of having the resolution to stand still and make a formal bow.[576]

Orrery's attack on his son in his will led us to talk of the dispositions a man should have when dying. I said I did not see why a man should alter his behaviour to those whom he thought ill of when well, merely because he was dying. Mr Johnson said, "I should not scruple to speak against a party when dying; but not against an individual." He said it was told of Sixtus Quintus that on his death-bed, in the intervals of his last pangs, he signed death-warrants.[577] Mr Macqueen said he should not do so. He would have more tenderness of heart. Said Mr Johnson, "I believe I should not either; but Mr Macqueen and I are cowards. It would not be from tenderness of heart, for the heart is as tender when a man is in health as when sick, though his resolution may be stronger. Sixtus Quintus was a sovereign as well as a priest, and if the criminals deserved death, he was doing his duty to the last. You would not think a judge died ill who should be carried off by an apoplectic fit while pronouncing sentence of death. Consider a class of men whose business it is to distribute death – soldiers, who die scattering bullets. Nobody thinks they die ill on that account."

Talking of biography, he said he did not know any literary man's life in England well-written. It should tell us his studies, his manner of life, the means by which he attained to excellence, his opinion of his own works, and such particulars. He said he had sent Derrick to Dryden's relations, and he believed Derrick had got all he should have got, but it was nothing. He said he had a kindness for Derrick, and was sorry he was dead.[578]

His notion as to the poems given by Macpherson as the works of Ossian, was confirmed here. Mr Macqueen always evaded the point, saying that Mr Macpherson's pieces fell far short of what he knew in Erse, and were said to be Ossian's. Said Mr Johnson, "I hope they do. I am not disputing that you may have poetry of great merit, but that Macpherson's is not a translation from ancient poetry. He got no manuscript of *Fingal*.[579] You do not believe it. I say before you, you do not believe it, though you are very willing that the world should believe it." Mr Macqueen could not answer to this.[580] Said Mr Johnson, "I look upon Macpherson's *Fingal* to be as gross an imposition as ever the world was troubled with. Had it been really an ancient work, a true specimen how men thought at that time, it would have been a curiosity of the first rate. As a modern production, it is nothing."[581]

Mr Johnson said he could never get the meaning of an Erse song. They told him the chorus was generally unmeaning. "I take it," said he, "they are like a song which I remember. It was composed in Queen Elizabeth's time on the Earl of Essex, and the burthen was: "Radaratwo, radarati, radaratadara tandore."

"But," said Mr Macqueen, "there would be words to it which had meaning."

Wednesday 22 September

Said Mr Johnson, "I recollect one stanza:

> *O then bespoke the prentices all,*
> *Living in London both proper and tall,*
> *For Essex's sake they would fight all.*
> *Radaratwo, radarati, etc.* "[582]

When Mr Macqueen began again upon the beauty of Ossian's poetry, Mr Johnson cried, "Ay, radaratwo, radarati."

Mr Rorie MacLeod, son to the sheriff, said he believed Macpherson's book to be a forgery; for that the Erse songs of Ossian which he had heard had no resemblance to Macpherson's English. Mr Macqueen is the most obstinate man I ever found. He has not firmness of mind sufficient to break. He is like a supple willow. No sooner is he pressed down than he rises again, just where he was. He always harped on this: "Macpherson's translations are far inferior to Ossian's originals."

"Yes," said I, "because they are not the same. They are inferior as a shilling is to a guinea, because they are not the same."

It was really disagreeable to see how Macqueen shuffled about the matter.

THURSDAY 23 SEPTEMBER. I took Ossian down to the parlour in the morning and tried a test proposed by Mr Rorie. Mr Macqueen had said he had some of him in the original. I made him read what he had, which was a passage on page 50, quarto edition, and Rorie looked on with me on the English, and said it was pretty like.[583] But when Mr Macqueen read a description of Cuchullin's sword, with a verse translation by Sir James Foulis, Rorie said that was much liker than Macpherson's translation of the former passage. Mr Macqueen repeated in Erse a description of one of the horses in Cuchullin's car. Rorie said Macpherson's English was nothing like it.[584]

When Mr Johnson came down, I told him that Mr Macqueen had repeated a passage pretty like; and that he himself had required Macpherson's Ossian to be no liker than Pope's Homer. "Well," said he, "this is just what I always said. He has found names, and stories, and phrases – nay passages in old songs – and with them has compounded his own compositions, and so made what he gives to the world as the translation of an ancient poem."[585]

"But," said I, "it was wrong in him to pretend that there was a poem in six books." JOHNSON. "Yes, sir. At a time too when the Highlanders knew nothing of *books* and nothing of *six* – or perhaps were got the length of counting six. We have been told, by Condamine, of a nation that could count no more than four. I'd tell Monboddo that. It would help him. There's as much charity in helping a man downhill as in helping him uphill." BOSWELL. "I don't think there's as much charity." JOHNSON. "Yes sir, if his *tendency* be downwards. Till he's at the bottom, he flounders. Get him to it, and he's quiet. Swift tells that Stella had a trick, which she learnt from Addison, to encourage a very absurd man in absurdity, rather than strive to pull him out of it."[586]

Mr Macqueen evaded our questions about Ossian in so strange a manner that I said if Macpherson was capitally tried for forgery, two such witnesses would hang him; because the truth that comes from an unwilling witness makes the strongest impression, gives the fullest conviction. Mr Johnson said, "I should like to see Mr Macqueen examined in one of our courts of justice about Ossian."

Said I, "Were he to evade as he has done now, in one of our courts, he would be committed." JOHNSON. "I hope he would. Sir, he has told Blair a little more than he believes, which is published; and he sticks to it. Sir, he is so much at the head of things here that he has never been accustomed to be closely examined; and so he goes on quite smoothly." BOSWELL. "He has never had anybody to work him." JOHNSON. "No, sir. And a man is seldom disposed to work himself; though he ought to work himself, to be sure." Mr Macqueen stood patiently by while all this passed.[587]

Mr Johnson told us that Garrick, though accustomed to face multitudes, was so disconcerted by a new mode of appearance – as a witness in Westminster Hall – that he could not understand what was asked. It was a cause where a man claimed a *free benefit*; that is to say, a benefit without paying the expense of the house; but the meaning of it was disputed. Garrick was asked, "Sir, have you a free benefit?"[588]

"Yes."

"Upon what terms have you it?"

"Upon – the – terms – of – a free benefit." He was dismissed for stupidity.

Mr Johnson is often too hard on Garrick. When I asked him, going from Forres to Nairn, why he did not mention him in the Preface to Shakespeare, he said, "I would not disgrace my page with a player. Garrick has been liberally paid for mouthing Shakespeare. If I should praise him, I should much more praise the nation who paid him. He has not made Shakespeare better known.[589] He cannot illustrate Shakespeare.

Thursday 23 September

He does not understand him. Besides, Garrick got me no subscriptions. He did not furnish me with his old plays. I asked to have them, and I think he sent me one. It was not worth while to ask again.[590] So I have reasons enough *against* mentioning him, were reasons necessary. There should be reasons *for* it."

I mentioned Mrs Montagu's high praises of Garrick. JOHNSON. "It is fit she should say so much, and I should say nothing." He said Reynolds was fond of her book, and he wondered at it; for neither he nor Mrs Thrale nor Beauclerk could get through it.[591]

Last night Mr Johnson gave us an account of the whole process of tanning, and of the nature of milk and the various operations upon it, as making whey, etc. His variety of knowledge is quite amazing, and it gives one much satisfaction to find such a genius bestowing his attention on the useful arts. Ullinish was much struck with his knowledge. "And," said he, "he is a great orator, sir. It is music to hear this man speak."

A strange thought struck me: to try if he knew anything of an art (or invention, or whatever it should be called), which is no doubt very useful in life, but which certainly lies far out of the way of a philosopher and poet – I mean the trade of a butcher. I began with observing that Banks tells us the art was not known in Otaheite; for instead of bleeding their dogs to death, they strangle them. This he told me himself; and I supposed that their hogs would certainly be slaughtered in the same way. Mr Johnson said, "This would be owing to their not having knives, though they have sharp stones with which they can cut a carcass in pieces tolerably."

By degrees, he showed that he knew something even of butchery. He said an ox was knocked down and a calf stunned, but a sheep had its throat cut without anything done to stupefy it. That the butchers had no view to the ease of the animals, but only to make them quiet, which they did not mind with sheep. He said Hales was of opinion that every animal should be blooded without having any blow given to it, because it bleeds better. I said it would be cruel. Mr Johnson said, "No, sir. There is not much pain if the jugular vein be properly cut." He said the kennels of Southwark run with blood two or three days in the week. That he was afraid there were slaughter-houses in more streets in London than one thinks – speaking with a kind of horror of butchering. And yet he said that any of us would kill a cow rather than not have beef. I said we *could* not. "Yes," said he, "any one may. The business of a butcher is a trade indeed; that is to say, there is an apprenticeship served to it. But it may be learnt in a month."

I mentioned a club in London at the Boar's Head in East-cheap, the very tavern where Falstaff and his joyous companions met; and the members of it all assume Shakespeare's characters. One is Falstaff, another Prince Henry, another Bardolph, and so on. Mr Johnson said, "Don't be of it. Now that you have a name, you must be careful to avoid many things not bad in themselves, but which will lessen your character.[592]

"This," said he, "every man who has a name must observe. A man who is not publicly known may live in London as he pleases without any notice being taken of him. But it is wonderful how a person of any consequence is watched. There was a Member of Parliament who wanted to prepare himself to speak on a question that was to come on in the House, and he and I were to talk it over together. He did not wish it should be known that he talked with me; so he would not let me come to his house, but came to me. Some time after he made his speech in the House, Mrs Cholmondeley, a very airy lady, told me, 'Well, you could make nothing of him' – naming the gentleman, which was a proof that he was watched.

"I had once some business to do for Government, and I went to Lord North's. It was dark before I went. Yet a few days after, I was told, 'Well, you have been with Lord North.' That the door of the Prime Minister should be watched is not so wonderful; but that a Member of Parliament should be watched, or my door should be watched, is wonderful."

We set out this morning in Ullinish's boat, having taken leave of him and his family. There was an ease in his house, an appearance as if everything went on daily just as we saw it, that was very agreeable. It made one quite free of the idea that our company was any burden. Mr Donald Macqueen still favoured us with his company, for which we were much obliged to him.[593] As we sailed along, Mr Johnson got into one of his fits of railing at the Scots. He owned that we were a very learned nation for about 100 years, from about 1550 to about 1650. But that we lost our learning during the Civil War and had never recovered it. He said we afforded the only instance of a people among whom the arts of civil life did not advance in proportion with learning; that we had hardly any trade, any money, or any elegance before the Union. That it was strange how with all the advantages that other nations have, we had not any of those arts which are the fruit of industry, till we came in contact with a civilized nation. "We have taught you," said he; "and we'll do the same in time to all barbarous nations – to the Cherokees – and at last to the orang-outangs" – laughing as if Monboddo had been present.

I said we had wine before the Union. "No sir," said he; "you had some weak stuff, the refuse of France, which would not make you drunk." BOSWELL. "I assure you, sir, there was a great deal of drunkenness." JOHNSON. "No, sir; there were people who died of dropsies which they contracted in trying to get drunk."

I must here glean some of his conversation at Ullinish, which I have omitted. He said for five years of his life he made him a bowl of punch every night. He repeated his remark that a man in a ship was worse than a man in a jail. "The man in a jail," said he, "has more room, better food, and commonly better company, and is in safety."

"Ay, but," said Mr Macqueen, "the man in the ship has the pleasing hope of getting to shore." JOHNSON. "Sir, I am not talking of a man's getting to shore, but of a man while he is in a ship; and then, I say, he is worse than a man while he is in a jail. A man in a jail *may* have the pleasing hope of getting out. A man confined for a certain time *has* it."

MacLeod mentioned his schemes for carrying on fisheries, with spirit, and how he would wish to understand well the construction of boats. I said he might go to a dockyard and work, as Peter the Great did. "Nay," said Mr Johnson, "he need not work. Peter the Great had not the sense to see that the mere mechanical work may be done by anybody, and that there is the same art in constructing a vessel whether the boards are well or ill wrought. Sir Christopher Wren might as well have served his time to a bricklayer, and first indeed to a brickmaker."

There is a beautiful little island in the Loch of Dunvegan, called Isay. MacLeod said he would give it to Mr Johnson, on condition of his residing on it three months in the year, nay, one month. Mr Johnson was highly pleased with the fancy. I have seen him please himself with little things, even with mere ideas, as this was. He talked a great deal of this island – how he would build a house, how he would fortify it, how he would have cannon, how he would plant, how he would sally out and *take* the Isle of Muck; and then he laughed with a glee that was astonishing, and could hardly leave off. I have seen him do so at a small matter that struck him, and was a sport to no one else. Langton told me that one night at the Club he did so while the company were all grave around him; only Garrick in his smart manner addressed him, "Mighty pleasant, sir; mighty pleasant, sir."

Poor Langton's Will was a sport of this kind; but there I own Mr Johnson carried me along with him, as he made it really most ludicrous; and perhaps the contrast of Chambers's gravity, who had helped Langton to make the Will, gave additional keenness to our risibility. MacLeod humoured Mr Johnson finely as to his island; told him that as it was the practice in this country to name every man by his lands, he begged leave to drink him in that manner: "*Island Isay*, your health!"

Ullinish, Talisker, and Mr Macqueen all joined in their different manners, while Mr Johnson bowed to each in excellent good humour.

We had a fine sail this day. There cannot be a finer harbour than the basin which we saw sheltered from every wind. MacLeod showed us an arm of the sea which runs up with very deep water for a mile, upon which he intends to build a town. We sailed up another arm. The shore was varied with hills and rocks and cornfields, and natural wood or bushes.[594]

We landed near to the house of Fernilea. He himself was waiting on the shore, with a horse for Mr Johnson. The rest of us walked up. We found at Fernilea a very comfortable house. His wife is daughter to Bernera. When I took off my *scalck* with hearty readiness, he said, "Fare fa' you!"[595]

His parlour was paved with flagstones, not in squares, but just in the shapes which they naturally had in the quarry. I liked this better. It had more variety. I preferred it by the same rule that Mr Johnson prefers the variety of the English conclusions of letters to the common style, 'I am, etc.' We had here an excellent dinner, in particular a remarkable leg of boiled mutton with turnips and carrots. MacLeod has really shown us a chief and his clan. We saw some of them with him at Dunvegan. We now saw him with some of them. On both sides there was the most agreeable kindness. I expressed to MacLeod the joy which I had in seeing this. Said he, "Government has deprived us of our ancient power, but it cannot deprive us of our domestic satisfactions. I would rather drink a bottle of punch in one of their houses" (meaning his people) "than a bottle of claret in my own."

Here he said at once what every chieftain should think. All that he can get by raising his rents is more luxury in his own house. Is it not far better to share the profits of his estate to a certain degree with his kinsmen, and so have both social intercourse and patriarchal influence? Fernilea seemed to be a worthy, sensible, kind man.

We had a very good ride for about three miles to Talisker, though we had showers from time to time. At Talisker, we found Mrs MacLeod, the Colonel's lady, a civil genteel woman. She had some resemblance of Tom Davies's 'mighty pretty wife'; at least she put me in mind of her.[596] We found here too Donald Maclean, the young Laird of Coll (nephew to Talisker). I had a letter to him from his uncle, Professor MacLeod at Aberdeen. Mr Johnson said he was a fine fellow. He was a little brisk young man, had been a good deal in England studying farming, and was resolved to improve his father's lands without hurting the people or losing the ancient Highland fashions. He had seen Donald MacLeod at Loch Bracadale, who had been paying some small debts which he owed to some of the emigrants, but had £21 of our money remaining, and was trying to muster up what he had given away of it. This was so far good news.

Talisker is really a fine place. It is situated in a rich bottom, containing ———— acres. Before it is a wide expanse of sea, on each hand of which are immense rocks. On the left there is a rock of considerable size, quite detached, standing in the sea.[597] A good way to the northwest are three columnal rocks rising to sharp points, also detached from the main rock, and advanced before each other into the sea, the outermost being the lowest; the middle one the next lowest; and the innermost of an immense height, and (what is remarkable) higher than the main rock.[598] They are called 'MacLeod's Maidens'. On the upper end of the valley or bottom is a large black rock ———— feet from the level of the bottom. Mr Johnson said it was like a haystack, which is indeed the appearance which it has from Talisker. The end of it there is quite round; but it goes backward a good way and has a considerable body to its head, as Arthur's Seat has. Mr Pennant took a drawing off it.[599]

The billows break with prodigious force and noise on the coast of Talisker. There are here a good many trees, mostly planted by the late Talisker, and some of them by this gentleman. They are very well grown. Talisker is an extensive farm. The possessor of it has for these ———— generations been the next heir to MacLeod, as there has been but one son always in the family; and no rent ever was paid for Talisker till the distress of the family obliged this gentleman to pay £100 a year.[600] The court before the house is most injudiciously paved with the round bluish-grey pebbles which are found upon the seashore, so that you walk as if upon cannon-bullets driven into the ground. The house is a very bad one. However we found a comfortable parlour, paved like the one at Fernilea; and the bedrooms, though small, were furnished with so much contrivance of convenience and neatness that we did very well. Mr Johnson had a room to himself, MacLeod and I one between us. I had a very clever bed raised some feet from the ground, that a large chest might be kept under it, and MacLeod had a cradle. Our tea was in good order, and we had a genteel supper. The Colonel had claret, port, sherry, and punch, with porter in abundance. Though he was depressed by lowness of spirits, he disturbed nobody with his complaints. He was attentive and polite. Only I missed that vivacity which I found about him at Edinburgh.

We talked of the assiduity of the Scotch clergy in visiting and privately instructing their people, and how in this they excelled the English clergy. Mr Johnson would not let this pass. He tried to turn it off by saying, "There are different ways of instructing. Our clergy pray and preach."

MacLeod and I pushed the subject, upon which he grew warm, and broke forth, "I do not believe your people are better instructed. If they are, it is the blind leading the blind, for your clergy are not instructed themselves. There is Macaulay – the most ignorant booby and the grossest bastard." (Coll says Mr Johnson said Macaulay was as obstinate as a mule and as ignorant as a bull, but I do not recollect this.) Mr Johnson took himself well, and said, "When I talk of the ignorance of your clergy, I speak of them as a body. I do not mean that there are not individuals who are learned." (Looking at Mr Macqueen.) "I suppose there are in Muscovy. The clergy of England have produced the most valuable books in support of religion, both in theory and practice. What have your clergy done since you sunk into Presbyterianism? Can you name one book of any value in religion written by them?"

We could not. Said he, "I'll help you. Forbes wrote very well, but I believe he wrote before Episcopacy was quite extinguished." And then, pausing a little, he said, "Yes, you have Wishart AGAINST repentance."[601]

"But, sir," said I, "we are not contending for the superior learning of our clergy, but for their superior assiduity."

He bore us down again with thundering against their ignorance, and said, "I see you have not been well taught, for you have not charity." He had been in a manner forced into this, for when he began, he said, "Since you *will* drive the nail." He again thought of good Mr Macqueen, and taking him by the hand, said, "Sir, I did not mean any disrespect to you."

Here I must observe that he conquered by leaving the argument, which was just where I put it.[602] The assiduity of the Scottish clergy is certainly greater than that of the English. His taking up the topic of their not having so much learning, was, though most ingenious, yet a fallacy in logic. It was as if there should be a dispute whether a man's hair is well dressed, and Mr Johnson should say, "Sir, his hair cannot be well dressed, for he has a dirty shirt. No man who has not clean linen has his hair well dressed."[603]

He used tonight an argument against the Scottish clergy being learned which I doubt was not just. Said he, "As we believe a man dead till we know that he is alive, so we believe men ignorant till we know that they are learned."

Now our maxim in law is to believe a man alive till we know he is dead. However, indeed, it may be answered that we must first know that he is alive, and that we have never known the learning of the Scottish clergy. Mr Macqueen, though he was of opinion that Dr Johnson had deserted the point really in dispute, was much pleased with what he said, and owned to me, he thought it very just; and Mrs MacLeod was so much captivated by his eloquence, that she told me 'I was a good advocate for a bad cause'.[604]

FRIDAY 24 SEPTEMBER. This was a good day. Dr Johnson told us, at breakfast, that he rode harder at a fox-chase than any body. "The English," said he, "are the only nation who ride hard a-hunting. A Frenchman goes out upon a managed horse, and capers in the field, and no more thinks of leaping a hedge than of mounting a breach. Lord Powiscourt laid a wager, in France, that he would ride a great many miles in a certain short time. The French academicians set to work, and calculated that, from the resistance of the air, it was impossible. His lordship however performed it."

Talisker, Mr Macqueen, and I, walked out, and looked at no less than fifteen different waterfalls near the house, in the space of about a quarter of a mile. We also saw Cuchullin's well, said to have been the favourite spring of that ancient hero. I drank of it. The water is admirable. On the shore are many stones full of crystallizations in the heart.

Though our obliging friend, Mr Maclean, was but the young laird, he had the title of Coll constantly given him. After dinner, he and I walked to the top of Prieshwell, a very high rocky hill, from whence there is a view of Barra, the Long Island, Bernera, the Loch of Dunvegan, part of Rum, part of Raasay, and a vast deal of the Isle of Skye.[605] Coll, though he had come into Skye with intention to be at Dunvegan, and pass a considerable time in the island, most politely resolved first to conduct us to Mull, and then to return to Skye. This was a very fortunate circumstance; for he planned an expedition for us of more variety than merely going to Mull. He proposed we should see the islands of Eigg, Muck, Coll, and Tyr-yi. In all of these islands he could shew us every thing worth seeing; and in Mull he said he should be as if at home, his father having lands there, and he a farm.[606]

SATURDAY 25 SEPTEMBER. It was resolved that we should set out, in order to return to Sleat, to be in readiness to take boat whenever there should be a fair wind. Talisker, having been bred to physic, had a tincture of scholarship in his conversation, which pleased Dr Johnson, and he had some very good books; and being a colonel in the Dutch service, he had introduced the ease and politeness of the continent into this rude region, in consequence of his and Mrs MacLeod's having been abroad and improved in the art of living.[607]

Mr Johnson wrote a letter today; and it was long before we could get him roused to depart. He did not come to breakfast, but had it sent to him. When he had finished, it was twelve o'clock, and we should have been away by ten. He said to me, "Do you remember a song which begins,

> Ev'ry island is a prison
> Strongly guarded by the sea.
> Kings and princes, for that reason,
> Pris'ners are as well as we?"

I suppose he had been thinking of our situation.[608] He would fain have had a boat from this, in place of riding back to Sleat. A scheme for it was proposed. He said, "We'll not be driven tamely from it." But it proved impracticable.

Last night we talked of Dr Birch. Mr Johnson said he knew more small particulars than anybody. I said Percy knew a great many; that he flowed with them, like one of the brooks here. But said he, "If Percy is like one of the brooks here, Birch was like the River Thames. Birch excelled Percy in that, as much as Percy excels Goldsmith." He was not pleased with Lord Hailes for publishing only such memorials and letters as were unfavourable for the Stuart family. He said, "If a man fairly warns you, 'I am to give all the ill, do you find the good,' he may. But if he publishes to give a view of a reign, let him tell all the truth. I would tell truth of the two Georges, or of that scoundrel King William." He said Granger's Biographical Dictionary might have been better done. He said, "The dog is a Whig. I do not like much to see a Whig in any dress. But I hate to see a Whig in a parson's gown."[609]

We took leave of MacLeod and the family of Talisker, and set forward. Young Coll was now our leader. Mr Macqueen was to go with us half a day more. We stopped at a little hut where we saw one old woman grinding with the quern, the ancient Highland mill, which it is said was used by the Romans. It consists of two circular whinstones like iron plates, roughened by having holes made in them by a pickaxe. These stones are placed one above another. In the centre of the upper one is an opening in which a frame of wood, which serves as the hopper, is fixed, and into which the grain is thrown. There are four holes in the upper stone by way of uniformity, but only one is necessary, *viz.*, that into which a stick is fixed by which the stone is turned about. The upper end of the stick is supported by being placed in a little semi-circular opening formed of straw-rope, fixed to the wattling of the roof. The woman turned about the stick, and the upper stone had a pin of wood near the middle fixed in the under one, on which pin it moved as on an axis. The upper stone is convex, and the under concave, by which the meal falls down on all sides of it from the centre. I cannot draw it. But young Coll has promised to send me one from Mull, as he has set up a mill on his estate there, and is abolishing the quern, which is a very poor and tedious implement.[610] I must try if Mr Johnson can describe it. Generally two women work at it. They can grind a boll in a day, as young Coll told me.

The cottages in Skye are frequently built by having two stone walls at several feet distance filled up with earth, by which a thick and very warm wall is formed. The roof is generally bad. The couples, such as they are, do not reach to the extremity of the wall, but only rise from the inner side of it; so that the circumference of the roof is a good deal less than that of the walls of the house, which has an odd appearance to strangers; and the storm finds a passage between the roof and the wall, as the roof does not advance so as to project over the wall. They are thatched sometimes with straw, sometimes with heath, sometimes with ferns. The thatch is fixed on by ropes of straw or of heath; and to fix the ropes there is a stone tied in the end of each. These stones hang round the bottom of the roof, and make it look like a lady's head in papers; but I should think that when there is wind they would come down and knock people on the head.

I observed a good many kind of enclosures in Skye, by earthen dikes or mounds of a great thickness, the making of which must have cost much labour. When a road passes through them, there is a little rude gate.[611] A tree is fixed in a hole in the ground, so as to turn about as on an axis, and it is loosely fixed both above and below to the dike by ropes of heath. From it issue horizontally several smaller trees with unequal ends just as they grow, and across them are some small bars or branches interwoven. They open very easily, by the slightest pull at one of the trees, and fall back again to their former situation. I find I can do nothing in

Saturday 25 September

the way of description of any visible object whatever. Whether it is owing to my not seeing with accuracy, or to my not having the use of words fitted to such sort of description, I cannot say.

We had some pretty good natural road for ——— miles, till we got to Sligachan, within a mile of Sconser, which was steep and rocky. We had a full view of Raasay, just opposite to us. It was pleasing to see it again. We dined at the inn at Sconser, where I received a letter from my dear wife, of date the 8th current.[612] I can hardly express the comfort which it gave me. But it made me impatient to be home, when I found that she was under continual apprehensions. I wrote to her from Sconser. Her letter told that Joseph's wife had got a son, which was joyful news to him, and as we all liked him, we were all glad. We had here an inn in a poor state, James Macdonald the landlord being about to emigrate. Our landlady was Mr Macqueen's daughter. We sent our horses round a point of land, that we might shun some very bad road, and go by boat.

We here took leave of Mr Macqueen. Mr Johnson said, "Dear sir, do not forget me." I promised to write to him from time to time letters full of questions concerning the Isle of Skye, which he promised to answer, and so by degrees he would write an account of it. Mr Johnson wished he would, and I thought this the best way to lead him on insensibly. Mr Johnson promised to look over the papers. He said Mr Macqueen should tell all that he could, distinguishing what he knows, what is traditional, and what is conjectural.

It was seven when we took our boat. We had many showers, and it soon grew pretty dark. Mr Johnson sat silent and patient. Once he said, as he looked on the black coast of Skye – black as being composed of rocks seen in the dusk – "This is very solemn." Our boatmen were bad singers. It was like hearing wild Indians when they sung. A very little imagination was necessary to give one the impression of being upon an American river.

We landed at Strollamus, from whence we got a guide to walk before us two miles to Coirechatachan. We could get no horse for our baggage. So I took one portmanteau before me, and Joseph another. We had just one star that seemed to afford us light. It was about eleven when we arrived. We were most hospitably received by the master and mistress, who were just going to bed, but with unaffected ready kindness got a good fire on, and at twelve o'clock at night had supper on the table.[613]

James Macdonald, of Knockow, Kingsburgh's brother, whom we had seen at Kingsburgh, was there. He shewed me a bond granted by the late Sir James Macdonald, to old Kingsburgh, the preamble of which does so

Saturday 25 September

much honour to the feelings of that much-lamented gentleman, that I thought it worth transcribing. It was as follows:

I, Sir James Macdonald, of Macdonald, Baronet, now, after arriving at my perfect age, from the friendship I bear to Alexander Macdonald of Kingsburgh, and in return for the long and faithful services done and performed by him to my deceased father, and to myself during my minority, when he was one of my Tutors and Curators; being resolved, now that the said Alexander Macdonald is advanced in years, to contribute my endeavours for making his old age placid and comfortable,

therefore he grants him an annuity of fifty pounds sterling.

Dr Johnson went to bed soon. When one bowl of punch was finished, I rose, and was near the door, in my way up stairs to bed; but Coirechatachan said, it was the first time Coll had been in his house, and he should have his bowl; and would not I join in drinking it? The heartiness of my honest landlord, and the desire of doing social honour to our very obliging conductor, induced me to sit down again. Coll's bowl was finished; and by that time we were well warmed. A third bowl was soon made, and that too was finished. We were cordial, and merry to a high degree; but of what passed I have no recollection, with any accuracy. I remember calling Coirechatachan by the familiar appellation of Corrie, which his friends do. A fourth bowl was made, by which time Coll, and young Mackinnon, Coirechatachan's son, slipped away to bed. I continued a little with Corrie and Knockow; but at last I left them. It was near five in the morning when I got to bed.

SUNDAY 26 SEPTEMBER. I awaked at noon, with a severe head-ach. I was much vexed that I should have been guilty of such a riot, and afraid of a reproof from Dr Johnson. I thought it very inconsistent with that conduct which I ought to maintain, while the companion of the *Rambler*. About one he came into my room, and accosted me, "What, drunk yet?"

His tone of voice was not that of severe upbraiding; so I was relieved a little. "Sir," said I, "they kept me up."

He answered, "No, you kept them up, you drunken dog."

This he said with good-humoured *English* pleasantry. Soon afterwards, Coirechatachan, Coll, and other friends assembled round my bed. Corrie had a brandy-bottle and glass with him, and insisted I should take a dram. "Ay," said Dr Johnson, "fill him drunk again. Do it in the morning, that we may laugh at him all day. It is a poor thing for a fellow to get drunk at night, and sculk to bed, and let his friends have no sport."

Finding him thus jocular, I became quite easy; and when I offered to get up, he very good-naturedly said, "You need be in no such hurry now."[614]

I took my host's advice, and drank some brandy, which I found an effectual cure for my head-ach. When I rose, I went into Dr Johnson's room, and taking up Mrs Mackinnon's prayer-book, I opened it at the twentieth Sunday after Trinity, in the epistle for which I read, "And be not drunk with wine, wherein there is excess." Some would have taken this as a divine interposition.

Mrs Mackinnon told us at dinner, that old Kingsburgh, her father, was examined at Mugstot, by General Campbell, as to the particulars of the dress of the person who had come to his house in woman's clothes, along with Miss Flora Macdonald; as the General had received intelligence of that disguise. The particulars were taken down in writing, that it might be seen how far they agreed with the dress of the 'Irish girl' who went with Miss Flora from the Long Island. Kingsburgh, she said, had but one song, which he always sung when he was merry over a glass. She dictated the words to me, which are foolish enough:

> *Green sleeves and pudding pies,*
> *Tell me where my mistress lies,*
> *And I'll be with her before she rise,*
> *Fiddle and aw' together.*
>
> *May our affairs abroad succeed,*
> *And may our king come home with speed,*
> *And all pretenders shake for dread,*
> *And let his health go round.*
>
> *To all our injured friends in need,*
> *This side and beyond the Tweed! —*
> *Let all pretenders shake for dread,*
> *And let his health go round.*
> *Green sleeves, etc.*[615]

While the examination was going on, the present Talisker, who was there as one of MacLeod's militia, could not resist the pleasantry of asking Kingsburgh, in allusion to his only song, "Had she *green sleeves?*" Kingsburgh gave him no answer. Lady Margaret Macdonald was very angry at Talisker for joking on such a serious occasion, as Kingsburgh was really in danger of his life. Mrs Mackinnon added that Lady Margaret was quite adored in Skye. That when she travelled through the island,

Sunday 26 September

the people ran in crowds before her, and took the stones off the road, lest her horse should stumble and she be hurt. Her husband, Sir Alexander, is also remembered with great regard. We were told that every week a hogshead of claret was drunk at his table.

This was another day of wind and rain; but good cheer and good society helped to beguile the time. I felt myself comfortable enough in the afternoon. I then thought that my last night's riot was no more than such a social excess as may happen without much moral blame; and recollected that some physicians maintained, that a fever produced by it was, upon the whole, good for health: so different are our reflections on the same subject, at different periods; and such the excuses with which we palliate what we know to be wrong.[616]

MONDAY 27 SEPTEMBER. Donald MacLeod arrived this morning. He looked miserably both from distress of mind and from the great fatigues of riding over the country in quest of money and us. He brought with him two-and-twenty pounds, which I was glad to get. He said he had given eight in payment of debt to a poor family of emigrants, and he expected to get some money which was owing to him. The difference between losing eight pounds and thirty was such as made me easy, though he should not get the eight which he said he would.

The plenty at Coirechatachan was wonderful, and the neatness with which things were set down. Yet I had still some squeamishness when I thought of the dirtiness of the lower Highlanders. My immediate fears of the itch were now off, for the pimples on the palm of my hand had almost disappeared. Besides, Mr Johnson treated the distemper lightly, as a thing that might pass off in a few days. The weather was still so bad that we could not travel. I saw a closet here, with a good many more books than what were lying about. Mr Johnson told me he found a library in his room at Talisker, and observed that it was one of the remarkable things of Skye that there were so many books in it.

One thing is strange. Coirechatachan, with all his abundance, has no garden at all, not even a turnip or carrot or cabbage – in short, literally no garden. At dinner they talked of the crooked spade, and maintained that it was better than the usual garden spade, and that there was an art in tossing it, by which those used to it could work very easily with it. "Nay," said Mr Johnson, "it may be useful in land where there are many stones to raise, but it certainly is not a good instrument for good land. A man may toss it, to be sure, but he will toss a light spade much better. Its weight makes it an encumbrance. A man *may* dig any land with it, but he has no occasion for such a weight in digging good land. You may take a field-piece to shoot sparrows. But all the sparrows you can bring home will not be worth the charge."

He was quite social and easy amongst them; and, though he drank no fermented liquor, toasted Highland beauties with great readiness. His conviviality engaged them so much, that they seemed eager to shew their attention to him, and vied with each other in crying out, with a strong Celtic pronunciation, "Toctor Shonson, Toctor Shonson, your health!"[617]

I had a good cup of coffee this afternoon. Dr Macdonald's wife, 'Mrs Dr Roy' (i.e., red Doctor), as Malcolm MacLeod toasted her, was a neat, pretty little girl. She sat down upon Mr Johnson's knee, and upon being bid by some of the company, put her hands round his neck and kissed him. "Do it again," said he, "and let us see who will tire first." He kept her on his knee some time, while he and she drank tea. He was now like a *buck* indeed. All the company laughed in great glee, and they were all pleased to see him have so much good humour. To me it was a very high scene. To see the grave philosopher – the Rambler – toying with a little Highland wench! There was a coincidence of opposed ideas. But what could he do? He must have been surly, and weak too, had he not behaved as he did. He would have been laughed at, and not more respected, though less loved.[618]

He read tonight, as he sat in the company, a great deal of this volume of my Journal, and said to me, "The more I read of this, I think the more highly of you."

"Are you in earnest?" said I.

Said he, "It is true, whether I am in earnest or no."

I went to bed at two in the morning, but the rest of the company sat still at their punch. The manner in which they were attended struck me as singular: the bell being broken, a smart lad lay on a table in the corner of the room, ready to spring up and bring the kettle, whenever it was wanted. They drank on and sung Erse songs till near five. I lay in great uneasiness. I was quite sombre in the dark, and could get no rest. I trembled to think how long I had been from home, and all the gloomy chances that imagination can figure disturbed me. I felt the utmost impatience to get home, and was tormented for some time. Near five those who lay in the same room with me came up. Unluckily Coll found a bottle of punch standing; upon which in tumbled all the company, and they drank it, and another which Coirechatachan brought. They made many apologies for disturbing me. I said I once thought of rising and going down to them. Honest Corrie said that to have had me do that, he would have given a cow. I thought I suffered so much tonight that the scene would make a figure in my Journal, but it makes but a wretched one.[619]

TUESDAY 28 SEPTEMBER. The weather was worse than yesterday. I felt as if imprisoned. Mr Johnson said it was irksome to be detained thus. Yet he seemed to have less uneasiness or more patience than I had. What made our situation worse here was that we had no rooms that we could command, for the good people here had no notion that a man could have any occasion but for a mere sleeping place; so, during the day, the bedrooms were common to all the house. Servants eat in Mr Johnson's, and mine was a kind of general rendezvous for all under the roof, children and dogs not excepted. The ladies indeed had no place during the day but Mr Johnson's room, except the parlour. I had always some good quiet time to write in it, before Mr Johnson was up; and by degrees I accustomed the ladies to let me sit at my Journal, and not mind me.

Mr Johnson was this morning for going to see as many islands as we could, never minding the uncertainty of the season, which might detain us in one place for many weeks. He said to me, "I have more the spirit of adventure than you." For my part I was anxious to get to Mull, from whence we might almost any day reach the mainland.

It was between eleven and twelve before we breakfasted today. This was certainly very disorderly living in a farmer's family; and I . . . t the table, which was kept . . . constantly full. Yet it . . .[620] She offered me even the Paris-plaster medallion of the Prince. She told me the print of Mrs Brooks was bought by her husband at the sale of one of the emigrants.[621]

Happily the weather cleared up between one and two, and we got ready to depart. But they would not let us go without a *snatch*, as they called it, which was in truth a very plentiful dinner.

I must not forget that in the morning Mr Johnson told us that the few ancient Irish gentlemen who remain have the highest pride of family. Mr Sandford, a friend of his, whose mother was Irish, told him that O'Hara, who was true Irish both by father and mother, and he, and Mr Ponsonby, son to the Earl of Bessborough, the greatest man of the three, but of an English family, went to see one of those ancient Irish; and that he distinguished them thus: "O'Hara, you are welcome. Mr Sandford, your mother's son is welcome. Mr Ponsonby, you may sit down."[622]

He talked both of threshing and thatching. He said it was very difficult to determine how to agree with a thresher. "If you pay him by day's wages, he'll thresh no more than he pleases, though to be sure the negligence of a thresher is more easily detected than that of most labourers, because he must always make a sound while he works. If you pay him by the piece, by the quantity of grain which he produces, he will thresh only while the grain comes freely, and though he leaves a good deal in the ear, it is not worth while to thresh the straw over again; nor can you fix him to do it sufficiently, because it is so difficult to prove how much less a man threshes than he ought to do. Here then is a dilemma. But for my part, I'd engage him by the day. I'd rather trust his idleness than his fraud." He said a roof thatched with Lincolnshire reeds would last seventy years, as he was informed when in that county. He told it to a great thatcher in London, who said he believed it might be true. This showed that Mr Johnson is at pains to get the best information on every subject.

He said it was difficult for a farmer in England to find day-labourers, because the lowest manufacturers can always get more than a day-labourer. "There is no matter," said he, "how high the wages of manufacturers are, but it would be of very bad consequence to raise the wages of those who procure the immediate necessaries of life, because that would raise the price of provisions. Here, then, is a problem for politicians. It is not reasonable that the most useful body of men should be the worst paid, yet it does not appear how it can be ordered otherwise. It were to be wished that a mode for its being otherwise were found out. In the mean time, it is better to give temporary assistance to poor labourers, at times when provisions are high, than to raise their wages; because if wages are once raised, they'll never get down again."

While we were at dinner, Mr Johnson kept a close whispering conference with Mrs Mackinnon about the particulars that she knew of the Prince's escape.[623] The company were entertained and pleased to observe it. Upon that subject there was a warm union between the soul of Mr Samuel Johnson and that of an Isle of Skye farmer's wife. It is curious to see people, though ever so much removed from each other in the general system of their lives, come close together on a particular point which is common to each. (I could illustrate this by a variety of instances from the ancient and modern world, but must be sparing of my paper, my own two books being now exhausted, and this small one which Mr Johnson gave me being all that remains.) We were merry with Coirechatachan on Mr Johnson's whispering with his wife. She cried, "I'm in love with him. What is it to live and not love?"

So she humoured our merriment. At the same time, she was really most heartily taken with his conversation. Upon her saying something,

Tuesday 28 September

which I did not hear or cannot recollect, he seized her hand keenly and kissed it. Here was loyalty strongly exemplified.

She told us a very extraordinary dream which she had during her first marriage. She saw the late Sir Alexander Macdonald; but recollecting that he was dead, she asked him if it was not so. "No," said he, "I am not dead. I am alive."

Said she, "You mean, sir, that you are alive in another state – in heaven" (or "happiness").

"Yes," said he; "and I'll tell you anything that you'll ask me."

"Why, then," said she, "sir, will you tell me if this unfortunate man will ever be restored to the throne of Britain?"

"Yes," said he. "He certainly will."

There was something so generous in her making this her first question – in her loyalty going before her concern for her family and everything else – that I was touched in a most sensible manner, and took hold of her hand across the table, shook it eagerly, and made her health go round. She had then nine children, and the smallpox of a very fatal kind was raging in Skye. She asked how her children would come off. He said she would lose but two; and those that survived would be a great comfort to her. This has exactly happened. She asked if Lady Margaret would marry again. He said, "No." She asked what kind of man Sir James would be. He said, "He'll be the best man you ever had, while you have him"; which meant that they would not have him long. She said that everything else which Sir Alexander told her in this dream has turned out so exactly that she had a firm faith in the restoration which was also told.

Mr Johnson said to me afterwards that he did not believe this dream. "For," said he, "she has dreamt something, and has always added to it, as she told it."

Last night I showed Coirechatachan in Baker's *Chronicle* two passages of King James VI's (or rather I's, as it is an English book) character that apply to Mr Johnson: his method of riding, and the accuracy of his extemporaneous discourse.[624]

As we were going, the Scottish phrase of 'honest man', which signifies kindness and regard, was often and often repeated by many of Mr Johnson. I myself was shown as much kindness and regard as I could desire; and I must take some merit from my assiduous attention to him, and the happy art which I have of contriving that he shall be easy wherever he goes, that he shall not be asked twice to eat or drink anything (which always disgusts him), that he shall be provided with water at his meals, and many such little things, which, if not attended to, would fret him.

Tuesday 28 September

I have also an admirable talent of leading the conversation; I do not mean leading as in an orchestra, by playing the first fiddle, but leading as one does in examining a witness: starting topics, and making the company pursue them. Mr Johnson appeared to me like a great mill, into which a subject is thrown to be ground. That is the test of a subject. But indeed it requires fertile minds to furnish materials for this mill. It vexes me when I see it unemployed, but sometimes I feel myself quite barren, and have nothing to throw in. I know not if this mill be a good figure; Pope makes his mind a mill for turning verses.[625] It is fine to see how the nonsense is thrown off from Mr Johnson's mill, or specious error crushed.

We set out about four. Young Coirechatachan went with us. We had as fine an evening as I ever saw, and arrived at Ostaig, the house of Mr Martin Macpherson, minister of Sleat. It is a pretty good house, built by his father upon a farm near the church . . . as I ever saw anywhere. Coll went to pay a visit at Camascross, and was not to come up till next day. We had here Mr and Mrs Macpherson and Miss Mackinnon, all of whom we had seen at Coirechatachan. Mr Johnson and I and young Mr Mackinnon and James Macdonald, the factor or bailie, made up the company. Miss Macpherson sung lively Erse songs to us.[626]

Mr Johnson had a good room to himself with a press stored with books, Greek, Latin, and French and English, most of which had belonged to the father of our host, the learned Dr Macpherson; who, though his *Dissertations* have been mentioned in a former page as unsatisfactory, was a man of distinguished talents. Dr Johnson looked at a Latin paraphrase of the song of Moses, written by him, and published in the *Scots Magazine* for 1747, and said, "It does him honour; he has a great deal of Latin, and good Latin."[627]

Dr Macpherson published also in the same magazine, June 1739, an original Latin ode, which he wrote from the Isle of Barra, where he was minister for some years. It is very poetical, and exhibits a striking proof how much all things depend upon comparison: for Barra, it seems, appeared to him so much worse than Skye, his *natale solum*, that he languished for its 'blessed mountains', and thought himself buried alive amongst barbarians where he was. My readers will probably not be displeased to have a specimen of this ode:

> *Hei mihi! quantos patior dolores,*
> *Dum procul specto juga ter beata;*
> *Dum feræ Barræ steriles arenas*
> *Solus oberro.*

Tuesday 28 September

Ingemo, indignor, crucior, quod inter
Barbaros Thulen lateam colentes;
Torpeo languens, morior sepultus,
Carcere cæco.

After wishing for wings to fly over to his dear country, which was in his view, from what he calls 'Thule', as being the most western isle of Scotland, except St Kilda; after describing the pleasures of society, and the miseries of solitude, he at last, with becoming propriety, has recourse to the only sure relief of thinking men – *Sursum corda*, the hope of a better world – and disposes his mind to resignation:

Interim fiat, tua, rex, voluntas:
Erigor sursum quoties subit spes
Certa migrandi Solymam supernam,
Numinis aulam.

He concludes in a noble strain of orthodox piety:

Vita tum demum vocitanda vita est.
Tum licet gratos socios habere,
Seraphim et sanctos Triadem verendam
Concelebrantes.[628]

The Bailie and young Mackinnon in one bed, and I in another, had the room opposite to Mr Johnson's.

WEDNESDAY 29 SEPTEMBER. After a very good sleep, I rose more refreshed than I had been for some nights. We were now nearer the shore, and saw the sea from the windows, which made our voyage seem nearer, and there was more convenience for us here than at Coirechatachan.

I altered my opinion of Mr Macpherson. I saw that what I have censured in him at Coirechatachan was only mistake or inaccuracy. He said there was an Erse Bible, confounding Erse with Irish. He said there were Erse manuscripts, thinking modern writings were understood.[629] At least I viewed him now with a most favourable eye, because I saw real goodness of character in him. He was a young man with his own hair cut short and round, with a pleasing countenance and most unaffected kindness. He said Mr Johnson was an honour to mankind, and if the expression might be used, was an honour to religion.

Coll and Donald MacLeod got up to us at breakfast, after which the Bailie went home.[630] The day was windy and rainy; so that we had just seized a happy interval for our journey last night. We had very good entertainment here, and time enough to ourselves. The day slipped along imperceptibly. We talked of Shenstone. Mr Johnson said he was a good layer out of land, but would not allow him excellence as a poet.[631] He said he had, he believed, tried to read all his Love Pastorals, but did not get through them. I repeated the stanza,

> She gazed as I slowly withdrew;
>   My path I could hardly discern;
> So sweetly she bade me adieu,
>   I thought that she bade me return.[632]

He said, "That seems to be pretty." I said he seemed to have had thought, from his short maxims in prose. Mr Johnson would not allow him that merit. Mr Macpherson said Garrick had written a very pretty epitaph for him.[633] Mr Johnson here was too severe, as usual, on Garrick, for he said, "Then if he could get up, he should pull it down. He was above having an epitaph upon him by Garrick." When I defended Garrick, Mr Johnson said, "The next subject you talk to him of, 'tis two to one he is wrong." He agreed however with Shenstone, that it was wrong in the brother of one of his correspondents to burn his letters.[634] "For," said he, "Shenstone was a man whose correspondence was an honour." He said Hammond's *Elegies* were poor things. He called Hanbury Williams a wretched scribbler, and said he had no fame but from boys who drank with him.

I mentioned to him a droll Scottish poem which I had just seen on occasion of his being entertained by the professors at St Andrews. He desired to hear it. I read it all but two lines about skait which were rather indecent, and explained it. He laughed, but said nothing. While he was in this mood, I was unfortunate enough, simply perhaps, but, I could not help thinking, undeservedly, to come within 'the whiff and wind of his fell sword'.[635] I asked him if he had never been accustomed to wear a night-cap. He said, "No."

I asked if it was best not to do it. He said he had that custom by chance: "And perhaps no man shall ever know whether 'tis best to sleep with or without a night-cap."

Something occurred where he was laughing at some deficiency, I fancy in the Highlands, and said, "One might as well go without ———" (I forget what), "or without shoes and stockings."

I, thinking to have a little hit at his own deficiency, ventured to say: "Or without a *night-cap*."

But I had as well have let it alone, for he was at me directly. "I do not see the connexion there" (laughing), and then, "Nobody before was ever foolish enough to ask whether it was best to wear a night-cap or not. This comes of being a little wrong-headed." And he carried the company along with him. And yet the truth is that if he had always worn a night-cap, as is the common practice in England, and found the Highlanders not doing it, he would have had a sally at their barbarity; so that I had him fair enough.

THURSDAY 30 SEPTEMBER. There was as great a storm of wind and rain as I have almost ever seen.[636] Mr Johnson said he did not grudge Burke's being the first man in the House of Commons, for he was the first man everywhere; but he grudged that a fellow who makes no figure in company, and has a mind as narrow as the neck of a vinegar cruet, should make a figure in the House of Commons merely by having the knowledge of a few forms, and being furnished with a little occasional information.[637]

He said the first time he saw Dr Young was at Mr Richardson's (*Clarissa*). He was sent for to come to him, that the Doctor might read to him his *Conjectures on Original Composition*, which he did, and Mr Johnson made his remarks; and he was surprised to find the Doctor receive as novelties what Mr Johnson thought very common thoughts. He said he believed Young was not a great scholar, nor had studied regularly the art of writing. He said there were very fine things in his *Night Thoughts*, though you could not find twenty lines together without some extravagance. He repeated two passages from his *Love of Fame* – the characters of Brunetta and Stella. He said Young pressed him much to come to Welwyn. He always intended it, but never went. He was sorry when he died. He said the cause of quarrel between Young and his son was that his son insisted that Young should turn away a clergyman's widow who lived with him, and who, having great influence over the father, was saucy to the son. Mr Johnson said she could not conceal her resentment at him for saying to Young that an old man should not resign himself to the management of anybody. I asked him if there was any improper connexion between them. "No sir, no more than between two statues. He was past fourscore, and she, a very coarse woman, read to him, and I suppose made his coffee and frothed his chocolate, and did such things as an old man wishes to have done for him."

This is another proof that Wilson, the barber at Stevenage, who pretended to know Dr Young well, and told me he kept a mistress, which I have mentioned in my Journal, spring 1772, was telling a lie.[638] I once spoke of it to Percy, who said there was no more foundation for such a suspicion than between Mr Johnson and Mrs Williams.

Mr Johnson said Dr Doddridge was author of one of the finest epigrams in the English language. It is in Orton's Life of him. He repeated it. The subject is his family motto, *Dum vivimus vivamus.* I shall copy it.[639]

I should have mentioned that we had MacLeod's horses all the way to this place. We sent them back yesterday. Each of us wrote him a letter. I have transcribed a paragraph of mine on the last leaf of the second volume of this Journal.[640]

I asked if it was not strange that Government should permit so many infidel writings to pass without censure. Mr Johnson said, "Sir, it is mighty foolish. It is for want of knowing their own power. The present family on the throne came to the crown against the will of nine-tenths of the people. Whether these nine-tenths were right or wrong is not our business now to inquire. But such being the situation of the Royal Family, they were glad to encourage all who would be their friends. Now you know every bad man is a Whig; every man who has loose notions. The Church was against this family. They were, as I say, glad to encourage any friends; and therefore, since the accession of this family, there is no instance of any man being kept back on account of his bad principles and hence this inundation of impiety."

There was something not quite serene in his humour tonight after supper, for he spoke of hastening away to London without stopping much at Edinburgh. I said he had General Oughton and many others to see. "Nay," said he; "I shall neither go in jest, nor stay in jest. I shall do what is fit."

"Ay, but," said I, "all I desire is that you will let me tell you when it is fit." JOHNSON. "Sir, I shall not consult you." BOSWELL. "If you are to run away from us, as soon as you get loose, we will keep you confined in an island."[641]

Yet he was very good company upon the whole. Donald MacLeod insisted to have an extraordinary bowl of punch tonight. I humoured him. He gave a very good gradation as to Mr Johnson. "First, when you see him," said he, "you are struck with awful reverence; then you admire him; and then you love him cordially."

Poor fellow, I thought this merited my sitting up a little longer with him than was quite agreeable to me, and made up for the £8 of our money which he had failed to bring us.

I looked a little at Voltaire's *War, 1741,* read Lord Kames against hereditary indefeasible right, and some of Congreve. If a man would keep an exact account of everything that he reads, it would much illustrate the history of his mind. I would have every minute circumstance marked: what a man reads, how much, at what times, and how often the same things. Mr Johnson told me that from twenty-one to fifty-six he had read no Greek; at least not above five chapters of the New Testament. He saw a Xenophon's *Cyropaedia* in Mr Thrale's library, and took it down; and he was not sensible that he had lost anything of it. He read all the New Testament that year, and has since read a good deal of Greek.[642]

Coll and Mr Mackinnon slept in my room, and Donald MacLeod on a bed on the floor.

FRIDAY 1 OCTOBER. There was pretty good weather. The Bailie came up, and asked us to go to Armadale, which we agreed to do.[643] I was very placid at Ostaig. The green hills and the brooks of Sleat had a kind of superior value when I recollected Sir James Macdonald.

I showed to Mr Johnson verses in a magazine on his Dictionary, composed of uncommon words taken from it: "Little of *Anthropopathy* has he", etc.[644] He read a few of them, and said, "I'm not answerable for all the words in my dictionary." I told him how Garrick kept a book of all who had either praised or abused him. Mr Johnson, on the subject of his own reputation, said, "Now that it has been so current a topic, I wish I had done so too." But he said it could not well be done now, as so many things are scattered in newspapers. I told him I would try to collect all.

He said he was angry at the boy of Oxford who wrote in his defence against Kenrick; because it was doing him hurt to answer Kenrick. He said he was told afterwards, the boy was to come to him to ask a favour.[645] He first thought to treat him rudely on that account. But then he considered, he had meant to do him all the service in his power; and he took another resolution, told him he would do what he could for him in the affair, and did so; and the boy was satisfied. He said he did not know how his pamphlet was done, as he had read very little of it. The boy made a good figure at Oxford, but died. He said attacks on authors did them much service. "A man who tells me my play is very bad, is less my enemy than he who lets it die in silence. A man whose business it is to be talked of, is much helped by being attacked." Garrick, I said, had been so helped. "Yes," said he; "though Garrick has more opportunities than almost any man to keep the public in mind of him, by exhibiting himself to such numbers, he would not have had more reputation than others, had he not been so much attacked. Every attack produces a defence; and so attention is engaged. There is no sport in mere praise when people are all of a mind."

"Then," said I, "Hume is not the worse for Beattie's attack."

"Yes," said he, "because Beattie has confuted him. I do not say but that there may be some attacks which will hurt an author. Hume was the better of other attacks." (He certainly could not include those of his old preceptor Dr Adams, and Tytler.) Talking of loose men being all Whigs, I mentioned Hume as a Tory. "Sir," said he, "Hume is a Tory by chance, as being a Scotsman, but not upon principle of duty; for he has no principle. If he is anything, he is a Hobbist."[646]

I said Goldsmith was the better of attacks. "Yes," said he; "but he does not think so yet." He said the *Critical* reviewers, on occasion of he and Goldsmith doing something together (i.e., publishing each a book at the same time, Mr Johnson the *Idler*), let them know that they might review each other. Goldsmith was for accepting. He said, "No. Set them at defiance." He told me it was said to old Bentley, upon the attacks against him, "Why, they'll write you down."

"No, sir," said he. "Depend upon it, no man was ever written down, but by himself."

Mr Johnson observed to me that the advantage of attacks to authors was in matters of taste, where you cannot confute, as so much may be said on either side. He told us he did not know who was the author of the *Adventures of a Guinea*; but that the bookseller had sent the first volume to him in manuscript to have his opinion if it should be printed, and he thought it should.[647]

Mr Johnson had a horse to carry him to Armadale, and Mr Macpherson and Donald MacLeod and I walked at his foot. Coll and the Bailie attended the ladies, who were all to be with us. When we got to it, we found Mr Archibald Macdonald, who had taken a lease of it, and a Mr Simson from Islay, who had a vessel along with him of twelve tons, and readily agreed to land us in Mull. This was a much better opportunity for us than going in Sir Alexander's open boat.

Miss Katie, the Bailie's sister, and Captain MacLeod, whom we formerly saw, were here. The house had quite a different air from what it had in Sir Alexander's time. We made a company of fourteen. We had a good dinner, excellent strong beer got on purpose for me, tea in good order, and a fiddler and a dance at night; then a good supper; and both at dinner and supper, excellent punch. At night both brandy punch and rum punch.

The Bailie had much of my friend Hallglenmuir's manner. He was most attentive and obliging. He had a chest of books carried up to Mr Johnson's room, who observed it would have been long before Sir Sawney would have thought of it. His factor's hospitality disgraced the knight.

We had many Erse songs. Mr Johnson had always been merry with Miss Macpherson; asked her to go to London, and said many little jocular complimentary things to her which afforded us amusement.[648] Her brother discovered veins of pleasantry. He imitated Mr Johnson's method of talking surprisingly well. He even said a thing a little in his way tonight. He had a dispute with Coll. Said Coll, "I'll bet a guinea."

Said Macpherson, "But, sir, till you win your bet, we shall not be convinced."

Macpherson danced freely. I saw in Skye that clergymen may without offence live much as other people do, who live innocently cheerful. At Dunvegan Mr Bethune danced very well on Saturday night, and next morning preached very well; and there did not seem to be any incongruity. Mr Johnson was now in good humour at Armadale, and I was very much so.

SATURDAY 2 OCTOBER. I was quite as I could wish here. I had my former room, with Joseph to sleep in a bed by me; so that I had a home, while all but Mr Johnson were crowded into common rooms. I had now got the habit of taking a *scalck* or dram every morning. It really pleased me to take it. They are a very sober people, the Highlanders, though they have this practice. I always loved strong liquors. I was glad to be in a country where fashion justified tasting them. But I resolved to guard against continuing it after leaving the isles. It would become an article of happiness to me. I thought with satisfaction when I got up that it waited me, as one thinks of his breakfast; so much is a man formed by habit.

I told Mr Johnson this morning that Sir Alexander said to me once that he left Skye with the blessings of his people. Said Mr Johnson, "You'll observe this was when he *left* it. It is only the back of him that they bless." He said Sir Alexander should have come and lived among them, and made his house the court of Skye, had he and his lady been fit for it.[649] They should have had so many of the gentlemen's daughters to receive their education in the family, to learn pastry and such things from the housekeeper, and manners from my lady. That was the way in the great families in Wales – at Lady Salusbury's, Mrs Thrale's grandmother's, and at Lady Philipps's.[650] He designed the families by the ladies, as he spoke of what was properly their province. There were always six young ladies at Sir John Philipps's. When one was married, her place was filled up. There was a large school room where they learned needlework, etc.

I observed that at the courts in Germany young people were educated. There is an academy for the pages. Mr Johnson said that manners were best learnt at these courts. "You are admitted with great facility to the Prince's company, and yet must treat him with great respect. At a great court, you are at such a distance that you get no good."

I said, "Very true. A man sees the court of Versailles, as if he saw it on a theatre."

He said the best book that ever was written upon good breeding grew up at the little court of Urbino – *Il Cortegiano* by Castiglione. He said I should read it, which I shall do.

I am glad always to have his opinion of books. At Macpherson's, he read some of Whitby's Commentary, which he commended; said he had heard him called rather lax, but he did not perceive it. He had looked at a novel called *The Man of the World* at Raasay, but thought there was nothing in it.[651] He said today while reading my Journal, "This will be a great treasure to us some years hence." He told me before that he was to copy part of it about Raasay, which he had not. I said I wished he would translate it. "How?" said he. BOSWELL. "Into good English." JOHNSON. "Sir, it is very good English."

He said today that Sir Alexander exceeded *L'Avare* in a farce. I said he was quite a character for a play. Foote would take him finely. The best way to make him do it would be to bring Foote to be entertained at his house for a week, and then it would be *facit indignatio*.[652] Said Mr Johnson, "I wish he had him. I, who have eat his bread, will not give him him; but I should be glad he came honestly by him. Nay," said he; "they are both characters." And then he took off my lady: "Thomson, some wine and water," with her mouth full; adding, "People are generally taught to empty their mouths of meat before they call for drink. She wants to be whipped in a nursery."

He said he was angry at Thrale for sitting at General Oglethorpe's without speaking. He censured a man for degrading himself to nonentity. I observed that Goldsmith was on the other extreme, for he spoke at all ventures. "Yes," said he; "Goldsmith, rather than not speak will talk of what he knows himself to be ignorant, which can only end in exposing him. I wonder if he feels that he exposes himself."[653]

"If," said I, "he was with two tailors – " and was going on.

Mr Johnson took it up – "Or with two founders, he'd fall a-talking on the method of making cannon, though both of them would soon see that he did not know what metal a cannon was made of."

We were very social and merry in his room this forenoon. We had again a good dinner, and in the evening a great dance. We made out five country squares without sitting down; and then we performed with

Saturday 2 October

much activity a dance which I suppose the emigration from Skye has occasioned. They call it 'America'. A brisk reel is played. The first couple begin, and each sets to one – then each to another – then as they set to the next couple, the second and third couples are setting; and so it goes on till all are set a-going, setting and wheeling round each other, while each is making the tour of all in the dance. It shows how emigration catches till all are set afloat.[654] Mrs Mackinnon told me that last year when the ship sailed from Portree for America, the people on shore were almost distracted when they saw their relations go off; they lay down on the ground and tumbled, and tore the grass with their teeth. This year there was not a tear shed. The people on shore seemed to think that they would soon follow. This is a mortal sign.

I recollect another anecdote, which Dr Donald Macqueen told me he had from the late Sir Alexander Macdonald. When Lord Lovat came in sight as a prisoner, Sir Everard Fawkener said to Sir Alexander, "*Raro antecedentem scelestum deseruit poena pede claudo.*"[655] This happened at Fort Augustus.

I had written letters all forenoon. It was a very bad day, and at night there was a great deal of lightning. I was really fatigued with violent dancing. I do not like dancing. But I force myself to it, when it promotes social happiness, as in the country, where it is as much one of the means towards that end as dinner; so I danced a reel tonight to the music of the bagpipe, which I never did before. It made us beat the ground with prodigious force. I thought it was better that I should engage the people of Skye by taking a cheerful glass and dancing with them rather than play the abstract scholar.

I looked on this tour to the Hebrides as a co-partnery between Mr Johnson and me. Each was to do all he could to promote its success; and I am certain that my gayer exertions were of much service to us. Mr Johnson's immense fund of knowledge and wit was a wonderful source of admiration and delight to them. But they had it only at times; and they required to have interstices agreeably filled up, and even little elucidations of his grand text. Besides, they observed that it was I who always 'set him a-going'. The fountain was locked up till I interfered. (I want a word here, as Macklin used to say when lecturing on oratory.) It was curious to hear them, when any dispute happened when Mr Johnson was out of the room, saying, "Stay till Mr Johnson comes. Say that to *him*."

Had they been barbarians, he was an Orpheus to them. But I cannot give them that character with any justice.

I should mention that on Sunday last, Raasay sent his boat to Sconser for us, begging to have us again in his island, and if it was not convenient, he would come over and spend the evening with us. So Mr Donald MacLeod informed me.

Yesterday Mr Johnson said, "I cannot but laugh to think of myself roving among the Hebrides at sixty. I wonder where I shall rove at fourscore." This evening he disputed the truth of what is said as to the people of St Kilda catching cold whenever strangers come. He said, "How can there be a physical effect without a physical cause?" He laughed and said that the arrival of a ship full of strangers would kill them. "For," said he, "if one stranger gives them one cold, two strangers must give them two colds; and so in proportion."

I wondered to hear him ridicule this, as he had praised Macaulay for putting it in his book. He said the evidence was not adequate to the improbability of the fact. That if a physician, rather disposed to be incredulous, should go to St Kilda and report the fact, he would begin to look about him. They said it was annually proved by MacLeod's steward, on whose arrival all the inhabitants caught cold.[656] He turned jocular then and said, "The steward always comes to seek something from them, and so they fall a-coughing. I suppose the people in Skye all take a cold when Sir Alexander comes."

They said Sir Alexander came only in summer. JOHNSON. "That is out of tenderness to you. Bad weather and he, at the same time, would be too much."

SUNDAY 3 OCTOBER. Mr Johnson told me there were two faults in my Journal: one was expatiating too much on the luxury of the little-house at Talisker. This fault, however, he mentioned as if he liked it – as if my expatiating had been congenial with his own feelings. The other fault was in my representation of the dispute about the Scottish clergy (*vid. supra*). "For," said he, "I did not say the man's hair could not be well dressed because he had not a clean shirt, but because he was bald."[657]

We did not get up till ten o'clock. Joseph said the wind was still against us. Mr Johnson said, "A wind, or not a wind? That is the question." For he can amuse himself at times with a little play of words, or rather of sentences. I remember when he turned his cup at Aberbrothock, where we drank tea, he muttered, "*Claudite jam rivos, pueri.*" I added, "*Sat prata biberunt.*"[658] I am most scrupulously exact in this Journal. Mr Johnson said it was a very exact picture of his life.[659]

While we were chatting in the indolent style of men who were to stay here all day at least, we were suddenly roused with being told that the wind was fair, that a little fleet of herring vessels was passing by for Mull, and that Mr Simson's vessel was lying off the shore for us. Hugh Macdonald, the skipper, came to us, and we were hurried to get ready, which we soon did. I just wrote a few lines to my wife. I felt my heart light at the thoughts of getting away. Breakfast was got ready for us. Mr Johnson with composure and solemnity repeated the observation of Epictetus, that, "As man has the voyage of death before him, whatever he does, he should always be ready at the Master's call; and an old man should never be far from the shore, lest he should not be able to be in readiness."[660]

He had a horse, and I and the other gentlemen walked about an English mile to the shore, where the vessel was. Donald MacLeod, poor man, gave me a good bill upon Mr MacLeod of Ose for the deficient £8. Mr Johnson said he should never forget Skye, and returned thanks for all civilities.

CHAPTER SIX

Coll

———

SAMUEL JOHNSON

Having waited some days at *Armidel*, we were flattered at last with a wind that promised to convey us to *Mull*. We went on board a boat that was taking in kelp, and left the Isle of *Sky* behind us. We were doomed to experience, like others, the danger of trusting to the wind, which blew against us, in a short time, with such violence, that we, being no seasoned sailors, were willing to call it a tempest.[661] I was seasick and lay down. Mr *Boswell* kept the deck. The master knew not well whither to go; and our difficulties might perhaps have filled a very pathetick page, had not Mr *Maclean* of *Col*, who, with every other qualification which insular life requires, is a very active and skilful mariner, piloted us safe into his own harbour.

In the morning we found ourselves under the Isle of *Col*, where we landed; and passed the first day and night with Captain *Maclean*, a gentleman who has lived some time in the East Indies; but having dethroned no Nabob, is not too rich to settle in his own country.[662]

Next day the wind was fair, and we might have had an easy passage to *Mull*; but having, contrarily to our own intention, landed upon a new Island, we would not leave it wholly unexamined. We therefore suffered the vessel to depart without us, and trusted the skies for another wind.

Mr *Maclean* of *Col*, having a very numerous family, has, for some time past, resided at *Aberdeen*, that he may superintend their education, and leaves the young gentleman, our friend, to govern his dominions, with the full power of a Highland Chief. By the absence of the Laird's family, our entertainment was made more difficult, because the house was in a great degree disfurnished; but young Col's kindness and activity supplied all defects, and procured us more than sufficient accommodation.

Here I first mounted a little Highland steed; and if there had been many spectators, should have been somewhat ashamed of my figure in the march. The horses of the Islands, as of other barren countries, are very low: they are indeed musculous and strong, beyond what their size gives reason for expecting; but a bulky man upon one of their backs makes a very disproportionate appearance.

From the habitation of Captain *Maclean*, we went to *Grissipol*, but called by the way on Mr *Hector Maclean*, the Minister of *Col*, whom we found in a hut, that is, a house of only one floor, but with windows and chimney, and not inelegantly furnished. Mr *Maclean* has the reputation of great learning: he is seventy-seven years old, but not infirm, with a look of venerable dignity, excelling what I remember in any other man.

His conversation was not unsuitable to his appearance. I lost some of his good-will, by treating a heretical writer with more regard than, in his opinion, a heretick could deserve. I honoured his orthodoxy, and did not much censure his asperity. A man who has settled his opinions, does not love to have the tranquillity of his conviction disturbed; and at seventy-seven it is time to be in earnest.[663]

Mention was made of the *Earse* translation of the New Testament, which has been lately published, and of which the learned Mr Macqueen of Sky spoke with commendation; but Mr Maclean said he did not use it, because he could make the text more intelligible to his auditors by an extemporary version. From this I inferred, that the language of the translation was not the language of the Isle of *Col*.[664]

He has no publick edifice for the exercise of his ministry; and can officiate to no greater number, than a room can contain; and the room of a hut is not very large. This is all the opportunity of worship that is now granted to the inhabitants of the Island, some of whom must travel thither perhaps ten miles. Two chapels were erected by their ancestors, of which I saw the skeletons, which now stand faithful witnesses of the triumph of Reformation.[665]

The want of churches is not the only impediment to piety: there is likewise a want of Ministers. A parish often contains more Islands than one; and each Island can have the Minister only in its own turn. At *Raasa* they had, I think, a right to service only every third Sunday. All the provision made by the present ecclesiastical constitution, for the inhabitants of about a hundred square miles, is a prayer and sermon in a

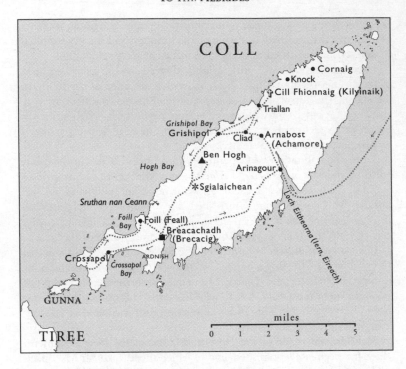

little room, once in three weeks: and even this parsimonious distribution is at the mercy of the weather; and in those Islands where the Minister does not reside, it is impossible to tell how many weeks or months may pass without any publick exercise of religion.

After a short conversation with Mr *Maclean*, we went on to *Grissipol*, a house and farm tenanted by Mr *Macsweyn*, where I saw more of the ancient life of a Highlander, than I had yet found.[666] Mrs *Macsweyn* could speak no *English*, and had never seen any other places than the Islands of *Sky*, *Mull*, and *Col*: but she was hospitable and good-humoured, and spread her table with sufficient liberality. We found tea here, as in every other place, but our spoons were of horn.

The house of Grissipol stands by a brook very clear and quick; which is, I suppose, one of the most copious streams in the Island. This place was the scene of an action, much celebrated in the traditional history of *Col*, but which probably no two relaters will tell alike.

Some time, in the obscure ages, *Macneil* of *Barra* married the Lady

Maclean, who had the Isle of *Col* for her jointure. Whether *Macneil* detained *Col*, when the widow was dead, or whether she lived so long as to make her heirs impatient, is perhaps not now known. The younger son, called *John Garve*, or *John the Giant*, a man of great strength, who was then in *Ireland*, either for safety, or for education, dreamed of recovering his inheritance; and getting some adventurers together, which, in those unsettled times, was not hard to do, invaded *Col*. He was driven away, but was not discouraged, and collecting new followers, in three years came again with fifty men. In his way he stopped at *Artorinish* in *Morvern*, where his uncle was prisoner to *Macleod*, and was then with his enemies in a tent. *Maclean* took with him only one servant, whom he ordered to stay at the outside; and where he should see the tent pressed outwards, to strike with his dirk; it being the intention of *Maclean*, as any man provoked him, to lay hands upon him, and push him back. He entered the tent alone, with his *Lochaber-axe* in his hand, and struck such terror into the whole assembly, that they dismissed his uncle.[667]

When he landed at *Col*, he saw the sentinel, who kept watch towards the sea, running off to *Grissipol*, to give *Macneil*, who was there with a hundred and twenty men, an account of the invasion. He told *Macgill*, one of his followers, that if he intercepted that dangerous intelligence, by catching the courier, he would give him certain lands in *Mull*. Upon this promise, *Macgill* pursued the messenger, and either killed, or stopped him; and his posterity, till very lately, held the lands in *Mull*.[668]

The alarm being thus prevented, he came unexpectedly upon *Macneil*. Chiefs were in those days never wholly unprovided for an enemy. A fight ensued, in which one of their followers is said to have given an extraordinary proof of activity, by bounding backwards over the brook of *Grissipol*. *Macneil* being killed, and many of his clan destroyed, *Maclean* took possession of the Island, which the *Macneils* attempted to conquer by another invasion, but were defeated and repulsed.

Maclean, in his turn, invaded the estate of the *Macneils*, took the castle of Brecacig, and conquered the Isle of *Barra*, which he held for seven years, and then restored it to the heirs.[669]

From *Grissipol*, Mr *Maclean* conducted us to his father's seat; a neat new house, erected near the old castle, I think, by the last proprietor.[670] Here we were allowed to take our station, and lived very commodiously, while we waited for moderate weather and a fair wind, which we did not so soon obtain, but we had time to get some information of the present state of *Col*, partly by inquiry, and partly by occasional excursions.

Col is computed to be thirteen miles in length, and three in breadth. Both the ends are the property of the Duke of *Argyle*, but the middle belongs to *Maclean*, who is called *Col*, as the only Laird.

Col is not properly rocky; it is rather one continued rock, of a surface much diversified with protuberances, and covered with a thin layer of earth, which is often broken, and discovers the stone. Such a soil is not for plants that strike deep roots; and perhaps in the whole Island nothing has ever yet grown to the height of a table. The uncultivated parts are clothed with heath, among which industry has interspersed spots of grass and corn; but no attempt has yet been made to raise a tree. Young *Col*, who has a very laudable desire of improving his patrimony, purposes some time to plant an orchard; which, if it be sheltered by a wall, may perhaps succeed. He has introduced the culture of turnips, of which he has a field, where the whole work was performed by his own hand. His intention is to provide food for his cattle in the winter. This innovation was considered by Mr *Macsweyn* as the idle project of a young head, heated with *English* fancies; but he has now found that turnips will really grow, and that hungry sheep and cows will really eat them.

By such acquisitions as these, the *Hebrides* may in time rise above their annual distress. Wherever heath will grow, there is reason to think something better may draw nourishment; and by trying the production of other places, plants will be found suitable to every soil.

Col has many lochs, some of which have trouts and eels, and others have never yet been stocked; another proof of the negligence of the Islanders, who might take fish in the inland waters, when they cannot go to sea.

Their quadrupeds are horses, cows, sheep, and goats. They have neither deer, hares, nor rabbits. They have no vermin, except rats, which have been lately brought thither by sea, as to other places; and are free from serpents, frogs, and toads.

The harvest in *Col*, and in *Lewis*, is ripe sooner than in *Sky*; and the winter in *Col* is never cold, but very tempestuous. I know not that I ever heard the wind so loud in any other place; and Mr *Boswell* observed, that its noise was all its own, for there were no trees to increase it.

Noise is not the worst effect of the tempests; for they have thrown the sand from the shore over a considerable part of the land; and it is said still to encroach and destroy more and more pasture; but I am not of opinion, that by any surveys or landmarks, its limits have been ever fixed, or its progression ascertained. If one man has confidence enough to say, that it advances, nobody can bring any proof to support him in denying it. The reason why it is not spread to a greater extent, seems to be, that the wind and rain come almost together, and that it is made close and heavy by the wet before the storms can put it in motion. So thick is the bed, and so small the particles, that if a traveller should be caught by a sudden gust in dry weather, he would find it very difficult to escape with life.

For natural curiosities, I was shown only two great masses of stone, which lie loose upon the ground; one on the top of a hill, and the other at a small distance from the bottom.[671] They certainly were never put into their present places by human strength or skill; and though an earthquake might have broken off the lower stone, and rolled it into the valley, no account can be given of the other, which lies on the hill, unless, which I forgot to examine, there be still near it some higher rock, from which it might be torn. All nations have a tradition, that their earliest ancestors were giants, and these stones are said to have been thrown up and down by a giant and his mistress. There are so many more important things, of which human knowledge can give no account, that it may be forgiven us, if we speculate no longer on two stones in *Col*.

This Island is very populous. About nine-and-twenty years ago, the fencible men of *Col* were reckoned one hundred and forty, which is the sixth of eight hundred and forty; and probably some contrived to be left out of the list. The Minister told us, that a few years ago the inhabitants were eight hundred, between the ages of seven and of seventy. Round numbers are seldom exact. But in this case the authority is good, and the errour likely to be little. If to the eight hundred be added what the laws of computation require, they will be increased to at least a thousand; and if the dimensions of the country have been accurately related, every mile maintains more than twenty-five.

This proportion of habitation is greater than the appearance of the country seems to admit; for wherever the eye wanders, it sees much waste and little cultivation. I am more inclined to extend the land, of which no measure has ever been taken, than to diminish the people, who have been really numbered. Let it be supposed, that a computed mile contains a mile and a half, as was commonly found true in the mensuration of *English* roads, and we shall then allot nearly twelve to a mile, which agrees much better with ocular observation.

Here, as in *Sky* and other Islands, are the Laird, the Tacksmen, and the under tenants.

Mr *Maclean*, the Laird, has very extensive possessions, being proprietor, not only of far the greater part of *Col*, but of the extensive Island of *Rum*, and a very considerable territory in *Mull*.

Rum is one of the larger Islands, almost square, and therefore of great capacity in proportion to its sides. By the usual method of estimating computed extent, it may contain more than a hundred and twenty square miles.

It originally belonged to *Clanronald*, and was purchased by *Col*; who, in some dispute about the bargain, made *Clanronald* prisoner, and kept him nine months in confinement.[672] Its owner represents it as mountainous, rugged, and barren. In the hills there are red deer. The horses are very small, but of a breed eminent for beauty. *Col*, not long ago, bought one of them from a tenant; who told him, that as he was of a shape uncommonly elegant, he could not sell him but at a high price; and that whoever had him should pay a guinea and a half.

There are said to be in *Barra* a race of horses yet smaller, of which the highest is not above thirty-six inches.

The rent of *Rum* is not great. Mr *Maclean* declared, that he should be very rich, if he could set his land at two-pence halfpenny an acre. The inhabitants are fifty-eight families, who continued Papists for some time after the Laird became a Protestant. Their adherence to their old religion was strengthened by the countenance of the Laird's sister, a zealous Romanist, till one Sunday, as they were going to mass under the conduct of their patroness, *Maclean* met them on the way, gave one of them a blow on the head with a *yellow stick*, I suppose a cane, for which the *Earse* had no name, and drove them to the kirk, from which they have never since departed. Since the use of this method of conversion, the inhabitants of *Egg* and *Canna*, who continue Papists, call the Protestantism of *Rum*, the religion of the *Yellow Stick*.[673]

The only Popish Islands are *Egg* and *Canna*. *Egg* is the principal Island of a parish, in which, though he has no congregation, the Protestant Minister resides. I have heard of nothing curious in it, but the cave in which a former generation of the Islanders were smothered by *Macleod*.[674]

If we had travelled with more leisure, it had not been fit to have neglected the Popish Islands. Popery is favourable to ceremony; and among ignorant nations, ceremony is the only preservative of tradition. Since protestantism was extended to the savage parts of Scotland, it has perhaps been one of the chief labours of the Ministers to abolish stated observances, because they continued the remembrance of the former religion. We therefore who came to hear old traditions, and see antiquated manners, should probably have found them amongst the Papists.

Canna, the other Popish Island, belongs to *Clanronald*. It is said not to comprise more than twelve miles of land, and yet maintains as many inhabitants as *Rum*.

We were at *Col* under the protection of the young Laird, without any of the distresses, which Mr *Pennant*, in a fit of simple credulity, seems to think almost worthy of an elegy by Ossian.[675] Wherever we roved, we were pleased to see the reverence with which his subjects regarded him. He did not endeavour to dazzle them by any magnificence of dress: his only distinction was a feather in his bonnet; but as soon as he appeared, they forsook their work and clustered about him: he took them by the hand, and they seemed mutually delighted. He has the proper disposition of a Chieftain, and seems desirous to continue the customs of his house. The bagpiper played regularly, when dinner was served, whose person and dress made a good appearance; and he brought no disgrace upon the family of *Rankin*, which has long supplied the Lairds of *Col* with hereditary musick.

The Tacksmen of *Col* seem to live with less dignity and convenience than those of *Sky*; where they had good houses, and tables not only plentiful, but delicate. In *Col* only two houses pay the window tax; for only two have six windows, which, I suppose, are the Laird's and Mr *Macsweyn's*.

The rents have, till within seven years, been paid in kind, but the tenants finding that cattle and corn varied in their price, desired for the future to give their landlord money; which, not having yet arrived at the philosophy of commerce, they consider as being every year of the same value.

We were told of a particular mode of undertenure. The Tacksman admits some of his inferiour neighbours to the cultivation of his grounds, on condition that performing all the work, and giving a third part of the seed, they shall keep a certain number of cows, sheep, and goats, and reap a third part of the harvest. Thus by less than the tillage of two acres they pay the rent of one.

There are tenants below the rank of Tacksmen, that have yet smaller tenants under them; for in every place, where money is not the general equivalent, there must be some whose labour is immediately paid by daily food.

A country that has no money, is by no means convenient for beggars, both because such countries are commonly poor, and because charity requires some trouble and some thought. A penny is easily given upon the first impulse of compassion, or impatience of importunity; but few will deliberately search their cupboards or their granaries to find out something to give. A penny is likewise easily spent; but victuals, if they are unprepared, require houseroom, and fire, and utensils, which the beggar knows not where to find.

Yet beggars there sometimes are, who wander from Island to Island. We had, in our passage to *Mull*, the company of a woman and her child, who had exhausted the charity of *Col*. The arrival of a beggar on an Island is accounted a sinistrous event. Every body considers that he shall have the less for what he gives away. Their alms, I believe, is generally oatmeal.

Near to *Col* is another island called *Tireye*, eminent for its fertility. Though it has but half the extent of *Rum*, it is so well peopled, that there have appeared, not long ago, nine hundred and fourteen at a funeral. The plenty of this Island enticed beggars to it, who seemed so burdensome to the inhabitants, that a formal compact was drawn up, by which they obliged themselves to grant no more relief to casual wanderers, because they had among them an indigent woman of high birth, whom they considered as entitled to all that they could spare. I have read the stipulation, which was indited with juridical formality, but was never made valid by regular subscription.[676]

If the inhabitants of *Col* have nothing to give, it is not that they are oppressed by their landlord: their leases seem to be very profitable. One farmer, who pays only seven pounds a year, has maintained seven daughters and three sons, of whom the eldest is educated at *Aberdeen* for the ministry; and now, at every vacation, opens a school in *Col*.[677]

Life is here, in some respects, improved beyond the condition of some other Islands. In *Sky* what is wanted can only be bought, as the arrival of some wandering pedlar may afford an opportunity; but in *Col* there is a standing shop, and in *Mull* there are two. A shop in the Islands, as in other places of little frequentation, is a repository of every thing requisite for common use. Mr *Boswell's* journal was filled, and he bought some paper in *Col*. To a man that ranges the streets of *London*, where he is tempted to contrive wants for the pleasure of supplying them, a shop affords no image worthy of attention; but in an Island, it turns the balance of existence between good and evil. To live in perpetual want of little things, is a state not indeed of torture, but of constant vexation. I have in *Sky* had some difficulty to find ink for a letter; and if a woman breaks her needle, the work is at a stop.

As it is, the Islanders are obliged to content themselves with succedaneous means for many common purposes. I have seen the chief man of a very wide district riding with a halter for a bridle, and governing his hobby with a wooden curb.[678]

The people of *Col*, however, do not want dexterity to supply some of their necessities. Several arts which make trades, and demand apprenticeships in great cities, are here the practices of daily economy. In every house candles are made, both moulded and dipped. Their wicks are small shreds of linen cloth. They all know how to extract from the Cuddy, oil for their lamps. They all tan skins, and make brogues.

As we travelled through *Sky*, we saw many cottages, but they very frequently stood single on the naked ground. In *Col*, where the hills opened a place convenient for habitation, we found a petty village, of which every hut had a little garden adjoining; thus they made an appearance of social commerce and mutual offices, and of some attention to convenience and future supply. There is not in the *Western Islands* any collection of buildings that can make pretensions to be called a town, except in the Isle of *Lewis*, which I have not seen.

If *Lewis* is distinguished by a town, *Col* has also something peculiar. The young Laird has attempted what no Islander perhaps ever thought on. He has begun a road capable of a wheel-carriage. He has carried it about a mile, and will continue it by annual elongation from his house to the harbour.

Of taxes here is no reason for complaining; they are paid by a very easy composition. The *malt-tax* for *Col* is twenty shillings. Whisky is very plentiful: there are several stills in the Island, and more is made than the inhabitants consume.

The great business of insular policy is now to keep the people in their own country. As the world has been let in upon them, they have heard of happier climates, and less arbitrary government; and if they are disgusted, have emissaries among them ready to offer them land and houses, as a reward for deserting their Chief and clan. Many have departed both from the main of *Scotland*, and from the Islands; and all that go may be considered as subjects lost to the *British* crown; for a nation scattered in the boundless regions of *America* resembles rays diverging from a focus. All the rays remain, but the heat is gone. Their power consisted in their concentration: when they are dispersed, they have no effect.

It may be thought that they are happier by the change; but they are not happy as a nation, for they are a nation no longer. As they contribute not to the prosperity of any community, they must want that security, that dignity, that happiness, whatever it be, which a prosperous community throws back upon individuals.

The inhabitants of *Col* have not yet learned to be weary of their heath and rocks, but attend their agriculture and their dairies, without listening to American seducements.

There are some however who think that this emigration has raised terrour disproportionate to its real evil; and that it is only a new mode of doing what was always done. The Highlands, they say, never maintained their natural inhabitants; but the people, when they found themselves too numerous, instead of extending cultivation, provided for themselves by a more compendious method, and sought better fortune in other countries. They did not indeed go away in collective bodies, but withdrew invisibly, a few at a time; but the whole number of fugitives was not less, and the difference between other times and this, is only the same as between evaporation and effusion.

This is plausible, but I am afraid it is not true. Those who went before, if they were not sensibly missed, as the argument supposes, must have gone either in less number, or in a manner less detrimental than at present; because formerly there was no complaint. Those who then left the country were generally the idle dependants on overburdened families, or men who had no property; and therefore carried away only themselves. In the present eagerness of emigration, families, and almost communities, go away together. Those who were considered as prosperous and wealthy sell their stock and carry away the money. Once none went away but the useless and poor; in some parts there is now reason to fear, that none will stay but those who are too poor to remove themselves, and too useless to be removed at the cost of others.

Of antiquity there is not more knowledge in *Col* than in other places; but every where something may be gleaned.

How ladies were portioned, when there was no money, it would be difficult for an *Englishman* to guess. In 1649, *Maclean* of *Dowart* in *Mull* married his sister *Fingala* to *Maclean* of *Coll*, with a hundred and eighty kine; and stipulated, that if she became a widow, her jointure should be three hundred and sixty. I suppose some proportionate tract of land was appropriated to their pasturage.

The disposition to pompous and expensive funerals, which has at one time or other prevailed in most parts of the civilized world, is not yet suppressed in the Islands, though some of the ancient solemnities are worn away, and singers are no longer hired to attend the procession.

Nineteen years ago, at the burial of the Laird of *Col*, were killed thirty cows, and about fifty sheep. The number of cows is positively told, and we must suppose other victuals in like proportion.

Mr *Maclean* informed us of an odd game, of which he did not tell the original, but which may perhaps be used in other places, where the reason of it is not yet forgot. At New-year's eve, in the hall or castle of the Laird, where, at festal seasons, there may be supposed a very numerous company, one man dresses himself in a cow's hide, upon which other men beat with sticks. He runs with all this noise round the house, which all the company quits in a counterfeited fright: the door is then shut. At New-Year's eve there is no great pleasure to be had out of doors in the *Hebrides*. They are sure soon to recover from their terrour enough to solicit for re-admission; which, for the honour of poetry, is not to be obtained but by repeating a verse, with which those that are knowing and provident take care to be furnished.[679]

Very near the house of *Maclean* stands the castle of *Col*, which was the mansion of the Laird, till the house was built. It is built upon a rock, as Mr *Boswell* remarked, that it might not be mined. It is very strong, and having been not long uninhabited, is yet in repair. On the wall was, not long ago, a stone with an inscription, importing, that *if any man of the clan of Maclonich shall appear before this castle, though he come at midnight, with a man's head in his hand, he shall there find safety and protection against all but the King.*

This is an old Highland treaty made upon a very memorable occasion. *Maclean*, the son of *John Garve*, who recovered *Col*, and conquered *Barra*, had obtained, it is said, from *James* the Second, a grant of the lands of *Lochiel*, forfeited, I suppose, by some offence against the state.

Forfeited estates were not in those days quietly resigned; *Maclean*, therefore, went with an armed force to seize his new possessions, and, I know not for what reason, took his wife with him. The *Camerons* rose in defence of their Chief, and a battle was fought at the head of *Loch Ness*, near the place where *Fort Augustus* now stands, in which *Lochiel* obtained the victory, and *Maclean*, with his followers, was defeated and destroyed.[680]

The lady fell into the hands of the conquerours, and being found pregnant was placed in the custody of *Maclonich*, one of a tribe or family branched from *Cameron*, with orders, if she brought a boy, to destroy him, if a girl, to spare her.

Maclonich's wife, who was with child likewise, had a girl about the same time at which Lady *Maclean* brought a boy, and *Maclonich* with more generosity to his captive, than fidelity to his trust, contrived that the children should be changed.

Maclean being thus preserved from death, in time recovered his original patrimony; and in gratitude to his friend, made his castle a place of refuge to any of the clan that should think himself in danger; and, as a proof of reciprocal confidence, *Maclean* took upon himself and his posterity the care of educating the heir of *Maclonich*.[681]

This story, like all other traditions of the Highlands, is variously related, but though some circumstances are uncertain, the principal fact is true. *Maclean* undoubtedly owed his preservation to *Maclonich*; for the treaty between the two families has been strictly observed: it did not sink into disuse and oblivion, but continued in its full force while the chieftains retained their power. I have read a demand of protection, made not more than thirty-seven years ago, for one of the *Maclonichs*, named *Ewen Cameron*, who had been accessary to the death of *Macmartin*, and had been banished by *Lochiel*, his lord, for a certain term; at the expiration of which he returned married from *France*, but the *Macmartins*, not satisfied with the punishment, when he attempted to settle, still threatened him with vengeance. He therefore asked, and obtained shelter in the Isle of *Col*.

The power of protection subsists no longer, but what the law permits is yet continued, and *Maclean* of *Col* now educates the heir of *Maclonich*.[682]

There still remains in the Islands, though it is passing fast away, the custom of fosterage. A Laird, a man of wealth and eminence, sends his child, either male or female, to a tacksman, or tenant, to be fostered. It is not always his own tenant, but some distant friend that obtains this honour; for an honour such a trust is very reasonably thought. The terms of fosterage seem to vary in different islands. In *Mull* the father sends with his child a certain number of cows, to which the same number is added by the fosterer. The father appropriates a proportionable extent of ground, without rent, for their pasturage. If every cow brings a calf, half belongs to the fosterer, and half to the child; but if there be only one calf between two cows, it is the child's, and when the child returns to the parents, it is accompanied by all the cows given, both by the father and by the fosterer, with half of the increase of the stock by propagation. These beasts are considered as a portion, and called *Macalive* cattle, of which the father has the produce, but is supposed not to have the full property, but to owe the same number to the child, as a portion to the daughter, or a stock for the son.

Children continue with the fosterer perhaps six years, and cannot, where this is the practice, be considered as burdensome. The fosterer, if he gives four cows, receives likewise four, and has, while the child continues with him, grass for eight without rent, with half the calves, and all the milk, for which he pays only four cows when he dismisses his *Dalt*, for that is the name for a foster child.[683]

Fosterage is, I believe, sometimes performed upon more liberal terms. Our friend, the young Laird of *Col*, was fostered by *Macsweyn* of *Grissipol*. *Macsweyn* then lived a tenant to Sir *James Macdonald* in the Isle of *Sky*; and therefore *Col*, whether he sent him cattle or not, could grant him no land. The *Dalt*, however, at his return, brought back a considerable number of *Macalive cattle*, and of the friendship so formed there have been good effects. When *Macdonald* raised his rents, *Macsweyn* was, like other tenants, discontented, and, resigning his farm, removed from *Sky* to *Col*, and was established at *Grissipol*.[684]

These observations we made by favour of the contrary wind that drove us to *Col*, an Island not often visited; for there is not much to amuse curiosity, or to attract avarice.

The ground has been hitherto, I believe, used chiefly for pasturage. In a district such as the eye can command, there is a general herdsman, who knows all the cattle of the neighbourhood, and whose station is upon a hill, from which he surveys the lower grounds; and if one man's cattle invade another's grass, drives them back to their own borders. But other means of profit begin to be found; kelp is gathered and burnt, and sloops are loaded with the concreted ashes. Cultivation is likely to be improved by the skill and encouragement of the present heir, and the inhabitants of those obscure vallies will partake of the general progress of life.

The rents of the parts which belong to the Duke of Argyle, have been raised from fifty-five to one hundred and five pounds, whether from the land or the sea I cannot tell. The bounties of the sea have lately been so great, that a farm in Southuist has risen in ten years from a rent of thirty pounds to one hundred and eighty.[685]

He who lives in *Col*, and finds himself condemned to solitary meals, and incommunicable reflection, will find the usefulness of that middle order of Tacksmen, which some who applaud their own wisdom are wishing to destroy. Without intelligence man is not social, he is only gregarious; and little intelligence will there be, where all are constrained to daily labour, and every mind must wait upon the hand.

After having listened for some days to the tempest, and wandered about the Island till our curiosity was satisfied, we began to think about our departure. To leave *Col* in October was not very easy. We however found a sloop which lay on the coast to carry kelp; and for a price which we thought levied upon our necessities, the master agreed to carry us to *Mull*, whence we might readily pass back to *Scotland*.

James Boswell

We were carried to the vessel in a small boat which she had, and we set sail very briskly about one o'clock. I was much pleased with the motion for many hours. Mr Johnson grew sick, and retired under cover, as it rained a good deal. I kept above, that I might have fresh air. I eat bread and cheese, and drank whisky and rum and brandy. The worthy Bailie had sent with us half a sheep and biscuits and apples and beer and brandy.

There was a little room or den at the forecastle, with two beds, and a fire in it. Dinner was dressed, and I was persuaded to go down. I eat boiled mutton and boiled salt herring, and drank beer and punch. I exulted in being a stout seaman, while Mr Johnson was quite in a state of annihilation. But I soon had a change; for after imagining that I could go with ease to America or the East Indies, I turned woefully sick, and was obliged to get above board, though it rained hard.

I regretted that we passed the island of Eigg, where there is a very large cave in which all the inhabitants were smoked to death by the MacLeods. They had murdered some MacLeods who were sailing near their coast. MacLeod and a number of the clan came to revenge the murder. The people of Eigg saw them coming, and all retired into this cave, which has a low and narrow entry, so that but one man can get in it at a time, but afterwards becomes spacious and lofty like a church. MacLeod and his people landed, and could not find a soul. They might perhaps have gone away. But one of the Eigg people, after waiting a long time in the cave, grew impatient, and went out to see what was become of the enemy. Perceiving them not gone, he returned. There was a deep snow upon the ground, by which means he was tracked by the print of his feet.

The MacLeods came to the mouth of the cave. Nothing could be done in the way of fighting, because but one man at a time could either go out or in, and would be killed directly. MacLeod called in to them that if they would give up the murderers, he would be satisfied. This they refused to do. Upon which he ordered a quantity of peats to be laid in the mouth of the cave and to be set on fire, and thus the people of Eigg,

Sunday 3 October

man, woman and child, were smoked to death. Young Coll told us he has been in the cave, and seen great quantities of bones in it; and he said one can still observe where families have died, as big bones and small, those of a man and wife and children, are found lying together. This happened in ——————————— time.[686]

I was also sorry that we passed by the Isle of Muck. But Mr Simson wanted to get forward; and besides, we knew that the Laird could not be yet at home, on account of contrary winds. I saw on the southeast as we sailed along, Morar, the present Laird of which had Prince Charles delivered to his care by Mackinnon. I wished much to have seen him, because it is said he owns that he has the second sight, which is hereditary in his family.[687]

On the same quarter I saw Loch Moidart, into which the Prince entered on his first arrival, and within which is a lesser loch called Lochninua, where the Prince actually landed. The hills around, or rather mountains, are black and wild in an uncommon degree. I gazed upon them with much feeling. There was a rude grandeur that seemed like a consciousness of the royal enterprise, and a solemn dreariness as if a melancholy remembrance of its events had remained. Its being Sunday gave a religious cast to the scene.[688]

Mr Simson was brisk in his hopes for a while, for the wind was for a while for us. He said if it continued so, he would land us at 'I' (i.e., Icolmkill) that night. But when the wind failed, it was resolved we should make for the Sound of Mull, and land in the harbour of Tobermory. We got up with the five herring vessels for a while. But four of them got before us, and one little wherry fell behind us. When we got in full view of the point of Ardnamurchan, the wind changed, and was full against our getting to the Sound. We were then obliged to tack, and get forward in that tedious manner.

As we advanced, the storm grew greater, and the sea very rough. Coll then began to talk of making for Eigg or Canna or Coll. Macdonald, our skipper, said he would get us into the Sound. We struggled a good while for this. Then he said he would push forward till we were near the land of Mull, where we might cast anchor till the morning; for although before this there had been a good moon, and I had pretty distinctly seen not only the land of Mull, but up the Sound, and the country of Morvern as at one end of it, the night was now grown very dark.

Our crew consisted of old Macdonald our skipper, a man with one eye, and another sailor. Mr Simson himself, Coll, and Hugh Macdonald his servant, all helped. Simson said he would willingly go for Coll if young Coll or his servant would undertake to pilot us to a harbour, but as the island is low land, it was dangerous to run upon it in the dark. Coll and his servant seemed a little dubious. The scheme of running for Canna seemed then to be embraced, but Canna was ten leagues off, all out of our way; and they were afraid to attempt the harbour of Eigg.

All these different plans being in agitation, I was much frightened. The old skipper still tried to make for the land of Mull; but then it was considered that there was no place there where we could anchor in safety. Much time was lost in striving against the storm. At last it became so rough, and threatened to be so much worse, that Coll and his servant took more courage, and said they would undertake to hit one of the harbours in Coll. "Then," said the skipper, "let us run for it, in GOD's name." And instantly we turned towards it.

The little wherry which had fallen behind us had hard work. The master begged that, if we made for Coll, we should put out a light to him. Accordingly one of the sailors waved a glowing peat for some time. I had a short relief when I found we were to run for a harbour before the wind. But it was very short, for I soon heard that our sails were very bad, and were in danger of being torn in pieces, in which case we would be driven upon the rocky shore of Coll. It was very dark indeed, and there was a very heavy rain almost incessantly. The sparks of the peat-fire in the boat flew terribly about. I dreaded that the vessel might take fire. Then, as Coll was a sportsman, and had powder on board, I figured that we might be blown up. Simson and he both appeared a little frightened, which made me more so; and the perpetual talking, or rather shouting, which was carried on in Erse, alarmed me. A man is always suspicious of what is saying in an unknown tongue; and if fear be his passion at the time, he grows more afraid.

The boat often lay so much to a side that I trembled lest she should be overset; and indeed they told me afterwards that they had run her sometimes to within an inch of the water, so anxious were they to make what haste they could before the night should be worse. I saw tonight what I never saw before, a prodigious sea with immense billows coming upon a vessel, so as that it seemed hardly possible to escape. There was something grandly horrible in the sight. I am glad I have seen it once. Amidst all these terrifying circumstances, I endeavoured to compose my mind. It was not easy to do it, for all the stories that I had heard of the dangerous sailing among the Hebrides, which is proverbial, or at least often mentioned, came full upon my recollection. It distressed me to think how much my dearest wife would suffer should I now be lost, and in what a destitute, or at least wretchedly dependent, state she would be left. I upbraided myself as not having a sufficient cause for putting myself in such danger.

Piety afforded me a good deal of comfort. I prayed fervently to GOD, but I was confused, for I remember I used a strange expression: that if it should please him to preserve me, *I would behave myself ten times better*. Be the expression what it may, I shall never forget – at least I hope so – the good resolutions which I then formed. While I prayed, I was disturbed by the objections against a particular providence and against hoping that the petitions of an individual would have any influence with the Divinity; objections which have been often made, and which Dr Hawkesworth has lately revived in his preface to the *Voyages to the South Seas*; but Dr Ogden's excellent doctrine on the efficacy of intercession prevailed. I was really in very great fear this night.

It was half an hour after eleven before we set ourselves in the course for Coll. As I saw them all busy doing something, I asked Coll with much earnestness what I could do. He with a lucky readiness put into my hand a rope which was fixed to the top of one of the masts, and bid me hold it fast till he bid me pull. This could not be of the least service; but by employing me, he kept me out of their way, who were busy working the ship; and at the same time diverted my fear to a certain degree, by making me think I was occupied. There did I stand firm to my post while the wind and rain beat upon me, always expecting a call to pull my rope.

The man with one eye steered. Old Macdonald and Coll and his servant lay upon the forecastle looking sharp out for the harbour. It was necessary to carry much *cloth*, as they termed it, that is to say, much sail, in order to keep the vessel off the shore of Coll. This made terrible plunging in a rough sea. At last they spied the harbour of Lochiern, and Coll cried, "Thank GOD, we're safe!" We run up till we were opposite to it, and then were wafted, I may say, though not gently, into it, where we cast anchor. The comfort which I felt may easily be imagined.

Mr Johnson had all this time been quiet and unconcerned. He had lain down on one of the beds, and having got free of sickness, was quite satisfied. The truth is, he knew nothing of the danger we were in: but, fearless and unconcerned, might have said, in the words which he has chosen for the motto to his *Rambler*, *Quo me cunque rapit tempestas, deferor hospes*.[689] Once during the doubtful consultations he asked whither we were going; and upon being told that it was not certain whether to Mull or Coll, he cried, "Coll for my money."

I now went down, with Coll and Simson, beside him. He was lying in philosophic tranquillity, with a greyhound of Coll's at his back keeping him warm. Coll is quite the *juvenis qui gaudet canibus*.[690] He had when we left Talisker two greyhounds, two terriers, a pointer and a large Newfoundland water-dog. He lost one of his terriers by the road, but had five dogs still with him.

I was miserably sick and very desirous to get to shore. When I was told that I could not get ashore that night, as the storm had now increased, I looked woefully, as Coll informed me. Shakespeare's phrase, which he puts into the Frenchman's mouth, of the English soldiers when starved, "Piteous they will look, like drowned mice," might have been applied to me.[691]

There was in the harbour before us a Campbeltown vessel, the *Betty*, Kenneth Morison master. She was taking in kelp at Coll, and was bound for Ireland. This was a lucky opportunity for us to get across to Mull in a strong ship after seeing Coll, which we could do while she took in the rest of her loading, part of which she was to get just at Coll's house. She was about twenty yards from us. Coll and Simson sent our boat to beg beds in her for two gentlemen, and that she would send her boat, which was larger. They were to go and leave me with Mr Johnson in our vessel. I was so very uneasy that I imagined I should be better in the other vessel; so went with them, and flattered myself with finding a spacious cabin. But behold, there was only a little confined place. I wished to return to the former vessel, but was ashamed to give more trouble. I began to think it was wrong for me to leave Mr Johnson. But I considered that he was quite well; that I had left Joseph to take care of him; that the crew would have more room to warm themselves by my being away; and that my extreme sickness was a sufficient excuse for my trying everything I could for relief.

Morison very genteelly yielded his bed to Simson. Coll and I had the other, for the cabin held just two. It was a very small one, and we were squeezed into it in a very uneasy manner. I was soaked to the skin all this time, for I had only a greatcoat which defended me little. I threw off tonight only my boots and greatcoat. I lay in considerable pain, for though the ship was at anchor, there was a great rolling, which made my sickness continue; and as the storm grew much worse and beat furiously upon the ship, I could not help being frightened that she might be set to sea again. I recollected reading in the newspapers of ships being driven from their moorings. I got some broken slumbers. My head was very cold, as having only my wig for a night-cap. In the morning I fell upon

WALKING UP THE HIGH STREET p. 23 'assailed by the evening effluvia of Edinburgh'

TEA p. 24 'The mistress of the house was so attentive to his singular habit.'

VERONICA: A BREAKFAST CONVERSATION p. 25 'Her fondness for him endeared her still more to me.'

SETTING OUT FROM EDINBURGH p. 39 'my man Joseph Ritter, a fine stately fellow above six feet high'

THE JOURNALIST p. 41 'Auchinleck is the Field of Stones: there would be bad going barefooted there.'

SCOTTIFYING THE PALATE p. 41 'I prevailed with him to let a bit of one of them lie in his mouth.'

THE PROCESSION p. 43 'the landlord walking before us with a candle and the waiter with a lantern'

THE VISION p. 70 'I began to think that Lord Errol's father (beheaded on Tower Hill) might appear.'

LODGING AT MACQUEEN'S p. 111 'I fancied that a spider was travelling towards my mouth.'

THE RECONCILIATION p. 116 'You deserved about as much as to believe it from night to morning.'

THE DANCE ON DUNCAAN p. 155 'We sat down and drank brandy and punch, then we danced a reel.'

THE RECOVERY p. 273 'Sir, they kept me up.' He answered, 'No, *you* kept *them* up, you drunken dog.'

SAILING AMONG THE HEBRIDES p. 309 'always expecting a call to pull my rope'

THE CONTEST AT AUCHINLECK p. 440 'Cromwell's coin unfortunately introduced . . . Toryism.'

IMITATIONS AT DRURY LANE THEATRE p. 587 'My dear sir, I would *confine* myself to the *cow!*'

REVISING FOR THE SECOND EDITION p. 598 'A few observations had escaped me.'

the expedient of wrapping my coat around it, which made me warm enough.

MONDAY 4 OCTOBER. Between eight and nine I got up and went above deck. By this time, Mr ———— Macdonald from Campbeltown, another of the owners of the ship (she belonged to Morison and him jointly) was come on board from the shore, where he had been all night. We soon got ready, and were carried in the ship's boat alongside of Simson's vessel. We saw nothing of the poor wherry and were afraid.

We took in Mr Johnson and Joseph, and Simson's boat carried Coll's servant, the dogs, and the baggage. Mr Johnson was quite well, though he had not tasted victuals, except a dish of tea without bread, since Saturday night. I was happy that he was not angry at my leaving him. I may here mention that when he lived in the Temple, and had no regular system of living, he has fasted for two days, that is to say from Sunday night till Wednesday morning. He went about and visited, though not at meal-times. He drank tea during that time, but ate no bread. This was not intentional fasting, but happened just in the course of a studious life or a literary life.[692]

There was a little poor public house close upon the shore, to which we would have gone had we landed last night. But this morning Coll resolved to take us directly to the house of Captain Lauchlan Maclean, a descendant of his family, who had made money in the East Indies, and come home and taken a farm in Coll.[693] We had about an English mile to go to it. Coll and Joseph and some other men, I forget whether part of the crew or people of the island, ran to some little horses that were going on a field, and catched one of them. We had a saddle with us which was clapped upon it, and a straw halter was put on his head. Mr Johnson was then mounted, and Joseph very slowly and gravely led the horse. I said to Mr Johnson I wished the Club saw him in this attitude.[694]

It was a prodigious rain, and I was wet to the skin, both at the neck and legs. Captain Maclean had but a poor temporary house, or rather hut, just a little larger than the common country house. However, it was a very good haven to us. He gave me a dry shirt and dry stockings directly. There was a blazing peat-fire, and Mrs Maclean, daughter of the minister of the parish, got us tea. I felt still the motion of the sea. Mr Johnson said it was not imagination, but a continuation of motion in the fluids, like that of the sea itself after the storm is over.

There were some books on the board which served as a chimney-piece.

Mr Johnson took up Burnet's *History of His Own Times*. He said the first part of it was quite dramatic: while he went about everywhere, saw everywhere, and heard everywhere.[695] He said by the first part he meant so far as it appeared that Burnet himself was actually engaged in what he narrated; and this he said one might easily distinguish. The Captain censured him for his high praise of Lauderdale in a dedication, when he shows him in his history to have been so bad a man. Mr Johnson said, "I do not think myself that a man should say in a dedication what he could not say in a history. But there is a great difference; for the known style of a dedication is flattery. It professes to flatter. There is the same difference between what a man says in a dedication and a history, as between a lawyer pleading a cause and reporting it."

Mr Macdonald from the ship was now with us. He had been here last night. The day slipped along easily enough. We had a very good dinner: the best shortbread just baked by Mrs Maclean, and pleasant rum punch soured with lemon shrub. I had not tasted lemon for more than a month. The wind turned fair for Mull in the evening, and Mr Simson resolved to sail next morning. It was so fair that I began to waver whether we should not go with him; and Mr Johnson said to me, "I'll do what you please." However, I considered that it would be weak just to land on Coll, and run away from it without seeing the old castle or anything else; and as we had the Campbeltown vessel to take us to Mull in a day or two, I determined to stay.

At night I was a little disconcerted. There were but three rooms or divisions in the house. The Captain and Mrs Maclean had one. Mr Johnson had another, with Joseph on a straw-bed beside him. And in the room where we sat all day were two beds. Simson and Macdonald had the one. The other was for young Coll and me. I have a mortal aversion at sleeping in the same bed with a man; and a young Highlander was always somewhat suspicious as to scorbutic symptoms. I once thought of sleeping on chairs; but this would have been uncivil and disobliging to a young gentleman who was very civil and obliging to us. Upon inspection, as much as could be without his observing it, he seemed to be quite clean, and the bed was very broad. So I lay down peaceably, kept myself separated from him, and reposed tolerably.

TUESDAY 5 OCTOBER. Simson went off about seven. I rose and wrote my Journal till about nine, and then went to Mr Johnson, who sat up in bed and talked and laughed. I said it was curious to look back ten years to the time when we first talked of visiting the Hebrides. How distant and improbable the scheme then appeared! Yet here we were actually among them. "Sir," said he, "people may do anything almost by talking of it. I really believe I could talk myself into building a house upon island Isay, though I'd probably never come back again to see it. I could easily persuade Reynolds to do it. There would be no great sin in persuading him to do it. Sir, he'd reason thus: 'What will it cost me to be there once in two or three summers? Why, perhaps £500, that is, £150 a year; and what is that in comparison of having a fine retreat to which a man can go, or to which he may send a friend?' – and he'd never find out that he may have this within twenty miles of London. Then I'd tell him that he may marry one of the Miss MacLeods, a lady of great family. Sir, it is surprising how people will go to a distance for what they may have at home. Mrs Langton came up to Knightsbridge with one of her daughters, and gave five guineas a week for a lodging and having a warm bath, that is, mere warm water. *That*, you know, could not be had in Lincolnshire. They said it was made either too hot or too cold there."

The house here was built of stone without mortar, and had no plaster or finishing at all. It was as cold as a stable. The Captain is going to build. Before the house where he now lives, there is like a rampart of whinstone upon the ridge of a rising ground running to the sea. We were here about four miles from the east end of the island.

After breakfast Mr Johnson and I and Joseph mounted horses, and Coll and the Captain walked with us about a short mile across the island. We called for Mr Hector Maclean, the minister.[696] His parish consists of Coll and Tyree. He was about seventy-seven, a decent old man in a full suit of black and a black wig. He was like a Dutch minister or one of the assembly of divines at Westminster. Mr Johnson said he was a fine old man – was as well dressed and had as much dignity in his appearance as the dean of a cathedral. We saw his wife and another daughter. A glass of whisky and cheese and barley-bread were served about by Miss, who was dressed in a clean printed linen gown. The old gentleman, we were told, has a valuable library, though he has but poor accommodation for it. He has no manse, only a small farm-house; and his books are kept in large chests. Coll says he is determined to purchase the library when the old man dies. It was curious to see him and Mr Johnson. Neither of them heard very quickly; so each of them talked in his own way, and at the same time. Mr Hector said he had a confutation of Bayle by Leibnitz. Said Mr Johnson, "What part of Bayle do you mean? The greatest part of his writing is not confutable. It is historical and critical."

Tuesday 5 October

Mr Hector said, "The irreligious part." And proceeded to talk of Leibnitz's controversy with Clarke, calling him a great man.

Mr Johnson said that Leibnitz persisted in affirming that Newton called space the *sensorium numinis*, notwithstanding he was corrected and desired to observe that Newton said *quasi sensorium numinis*. "No," said he, "Leibnitz was as paltry a fellow as I know. As he was patronized by Queen Caroline, Clarke treated him too well."

During the time that Mr Johnson was thus going on, old Mr Hector was standing with his back to the fire, cresting up erect, pulling down the front of his periwig, and talking what a great man Leibnitz was. To give an idea of the scene would require a page with two columns; but it could not be quite well represented but by two players. The old gentleman said Clarke was very wicked for going so much into the Arian system. "I will not say he was wicked," said Mr Johnson. "He might be mistaken."

Said Mr Hector, "He was wicked to shut his eyes against the Scriptures." Adding, "Worthy men since, in England, have confuted him to all intents and purposes."

"I know not," said Mr Johnson, "*who* has confuted him *to all intents and purposes*." Here again there was a double talking.

I regretted that Mr Johnson did not practise the art of accommodating himself to different sorts of people. Had he been softer with this venerable old man, we might have had more conversation. But Mr Johnson's forcible spirit and impetuosity of manner may be said to spare neither sex nor age. I have seen even Mrs Thrale stunned. But I have often maintained that it is better so. Pliability of address I take to be inconsistent with that majestic power which he has, and which produces such noble effects. A bar of iron nor a lofty oak will not bend like a supple willow, or like many plants between those. What though he presses down feeble beings in his course? They get up again like stalks of rye-grass. He told me afterwards he liked firmness in an old man, and was pleased to see Mr Hector so orthodox. "At his age," said he, "it is too late for a man to be asking himself questions as to his belief."

Mr Hector said he had taken up a list of his parishioners between seven and seventy by order of the General Assembly, and found nine hundred. According to this there must be about 1,200 souls in Coll. There must be two hundred under seven, and I should think fifty may be reckoned above seventy.[697]

The island is computed to be twelve English miles long, and three broad at an average. It is very populous. The inhabitants live mostly in little rural villages, for so I may call a number of houses close to each other, almost; at least with but small interstices. I saw at one place near the west end of the island, a village where I counted above thirty houses, and saw they would exceed forty. Fifty-eight families lived in it. Their stacks of corn were not much unlike their thatched houses. The village looked at a little distance like a very full barn-yard.[698] The people in Coll live more comfortably than those in Skye; for each has a little garden – a kale-yard, which few have in Skye; and the people here appeared to be better dressed.

It was very agreeable, as we went along, to see all the people come from their work and shake hands with the young laird. Mr Johnson wished that he had more conversation than that of a mere farmer; and indeed he seemed to be just a young country lad who had been a while in England. He had worked there with his own hands, while he lived at farmers' houses in Hertfordshire, in order to learn to improve his paternal acres, or rather *miles*. Mr Johnson said that was like the Czar of Muscovy. By this, however, his manners were not those of a chieftain in point of dignity. But if he had not reverence from his people, he had their affection.

I could find no traces of learning about him; though he had been educated under the care of his uncle, the professor at Aberdeen. But he had a constant good humour, and readiness of conversation upon common things. Then he had a clear sharp voice, and was not afraid to talk to Mr Johnson; informed him as to many particulars, and stuck to his point when Mr Johnson opposed what he said, until very handsomely driven off. With all this he had as much civility as could be wished, and very great attention to have everything right about Mr Johnson.

We rode near to the shore opposite to the Captain's on the north of the island. There we saw the ruins of a church or chapel. The place is called Kilyinaik or the Kirktown. It has not been large; the wall remains for about the highth of four feet all along, without any gap. The inside was covered with water. Beside it was a place of graves. There were two stones over lairds of Coll, and not many other stones. The family has never had any built burial place; and this place here has never been so much as enclosed. I could see no vestige that it has.[699] We returned to near the minister's. The Captain walked a little farther with us, and then turned back.

We went on about two miles till we came to Grishipoll, or the rough pool.[700] It is just on the seaside, and the waves beat very high. It is about the middle of the island on the north side. On the beach here there is a singular variety of globular stones. I picked up one, which I called a

Siberian turkey's egg, and another which was very like a small cucumber. By the by, Mr Johnson told me that Gay's phrase, 'as men should serve a cucumber', in the *Beggar's Opera*,[701] has no waggish meaning with reference to men flinging away cucumbers as too *cooling*, which some have thought; for it has been a common saying in England of every great physician, that he prescribed that a cucumber should be well sliced and dressed with vinegar, and then thrown out, as good for nothing. So the phrase is just 'adorning beauty' as people should always serve a cucumber – in conformity with the ordinary prejudice.[702] This is my commentary.

I saw here growing in the sand on the sea-shore and among small pebbles, a large green plant very like to kale or cole-worts. It has a salt taste. It is purgative. The cattle will not eat it. Indeed it has rather a harshness on the palate.

We found at Grishipoll an excellent slated house of two storeys. It was built by the present Coll while his eldest brother was alive; and just as it was finished he succeeded to the estate. The tenant, with whom we dined, was Mr Macsweyn. His predecessors had been in Skye from a very remote period, upon the estate belonging to MacLeod; but probably before the MacLeods had it, as the name is certainly Norwegian, from Sueno, King of Norway. This Mr Macsweyn left Skye upon MacLeod's raising his rents. He then got this farm from Coll, whom he had *fostered*.

I must explain what is meant by fostering. It has been a custom in the Highlands and isles for substantial farmers or tacksmen to take the children of the lairds into their houses, a little after they are weaned, and keep them till they are fit for education; and then they gave them by way of portion a number of cattle, which were called *mackalive* cattle. The custom I fancy may still prevail; at least it did lately. This same young Coll was fostered by a Campbell in the island of Tyree, and got forty mackalive cattle. It seems it has not been required that the fosterers should be of the same clan with the children. Young Coll should be a hero, for he may be said to have been fostered by a wolf, as Romulus and Remus were nursed. The Macleans have suffered so much from the ravages of the Campbells that his being fostered by a Campbell may be compared to the Roman emblem. Girls were given to be fostered as well as boys. The present Lady Coll, sister to Talisker, was also fostered by Mr Macsweyn. It is a strange custom.[703]

Macsweyn was now about seventy-seven, but looked as fresh and was as stout as a man of fifty. His son Hugh really looked older, and as Mr Johnson observed, had more the manners of an old man than he. I had often heard of such instances, but never saw one before. Mrs Macsweyn was a decent old gentlewoman, not much failed, though she had been above fifty years married. She was dressed in tartan, and could speak nothing but Erse. She said she had taught Sir James Macdonald Erse, and would teach me soon. I could now sing a verse of the words to *Hatyin foam eri*,[704] upon Allan, the famous captain of Clanranald, who fell at Sheriffmuir, and of whom his servant who lay on the field watching his dead body, being asked next day who that was, answered, "He was a man yesterday." And I had picked up I suppose thirty words.

We had here the best goose that I ever eat. Mr Johnson was much pleased with it; and we had whisky in a clam-shell, according to the ancient Highland custom. Mr Johnson drank a little water out of it.[705] In the forenoon Mr Johnson said that it would require great resignation to live in one of these islands. "I don't know," said I; "I have felt myself at times in a state of almost physical existence, satisfied to eat, drink and sleep, and walk about and enjoy my own thoughts; and I can figure a continuation of this."

"Ay, sir," said he; "but if you were shut up here, your own thoughts would torment you; you would think of Edinburgh or London, and that you could not be there."

We were entertained at Macsweyn's with a primitive heartiness. He and Coll got a horse; and Macsweyn, Junior, walked before us to Breacacha, the family seat, where his wife was waiting to be landlady to us.[706] It is called Breacacha, or the spotted field, because in summer it is enamelled with clover and daisies, as young Coll told me.[707] I should have mentioned that at Grishipoll the hearths were formed of the round sea-pebbles, such as those with which the court at Talisker was paved, but as it was most inconvenient at the latter, it was very rational at Grishipoll; because, as Mr Johnson observed, it kept the fire, which is always made in these islands upon the hearth, from moving, and so served both as hearth and fender. As we rode along in the forenoon, we saw a wonderful plenty of whinstone upon the surface of the earth. Mr Johnson said, "I see a plain of stone." There are however innumerable spots of earth between them, on which corn grows; and when it is cut, they set it up on the stony places to dry. I observed that the corn in Coll is very short, so that there is less straw produced than I ever saw anywhere else.

We rode from Grishipoll aslant the island to the southwest. We passed by a place where there is a large lump of whinstone, I may call it a rock – 'a vast weight for Ajax'. The tradition is that a giant threw such a lump at his mistress up to a hill or little mountain at a small distance to the southwest, and that she in return threw this lump down to him. It was all in sport: *Malo me petit lasciva puella*.[708] The hill is called Ben Hogh, the hill of Hogh, a neighbouring farm. Coll said that each of these stones is supported by a number of small ones. I got off my horse and inspected the one below. I did perceive stones under it, but I could not be sure but they were pieces of itself. I could however put my cane a great way under it. Mr Johnson said there was no matter whether there were stones under it or not. It could hardly fall anywhere here that it would not rest upon stones. The question was, had it a root in the earth? I really thought not. Coll said the one on the hill was much more plainly detached. How this has happened it is difficult to say. There is no large rock near of which it could have been a part. Perhaps some violence of nature has burst or pounded a large rock originally here, and so scattered its fragments around. At present the appearance is like the pieces of a broken loaf of sugar. No loaf is to be seen, only bits of sugar of different sizes.

A little farther on, we came to two triangular flagstones Δ Δ placed I imagine about ten yards from each other. (I afterwards measured: fourteen of my paces.) They have probably been a Druidical temple. Of latter times they are used for putting a trick on any stranger who is passing that way. He is desired to lie down behind the easternmost one (or westernmost, according to the route he is on) and told that he will hear everything that is said by the company, who stand at the other stone; and while he is lying in patient attention, the company get off and leave him; and when he at last gets up, he finds himself all alone. The stones are called Sgeulachdan, that is to say, 'Long tales'. Coll said if it had not been too late, he would have made me go through the ceremony.[709]

There is a curious custom at Coll. On the last night of the old year, a man puts upon him a cow's skin and runs round the house, while a number of people make a noise chasing him and beating upon the skin, which sounds like a drum. This brings out the strangers who are in the house to see what is the matter; and most of the family go out to decoy strangers, or for their diversion. Then the door is shut, and nobody gets in without repeating a verse of their own composition. It need not be extemporary. Some will be preparing for it all the year. When they are all got in, the evening is spent in great merriment, and the verses of each are criticized with emulation. Mr Johnson, who is for all old customs, said he would keep up this.[710]

About ten days at Christmas time the people in Coll make merry. All the men in the island are divided into two parties. Each party is headed by a gentleman. The Laird perhaps heads one, and Captain Maclean another; or other two gentlemen of the family are leaders. There is a ball thrown down in the middle of a space above the house, or on a strand near it; and each party strives to beat it first to one end of the ground with clubs or crooked sticks. The club is called the *shinny*. It is used in the low-country of Scotland. The name is from the danger that the shins run. We corrupt it to *shinty*. The leader of the party which prevails receives the bet which the opposite leader has lost to him, and gives it to the people to drink.[711]

As we advanced, we came to a large extent of plain ground. I had not seen such a place for a long time. Coll and I took a gallop upon it by way of race. It was very refreshing to me, after having been so long taking short steps in hilly countries. It was like stretching a man's legs after being cramped in a short bed. We also passed close by a large extent of sand hills, I dare say near two miles square. Mr Johnson was like to be angry with me for being pleased with them. I said I saw only dryness and cleanliness. He said he never had had the image before. It was horrible, if barrenness and danger could be so. I heard him, after we were in the house of Breacacha, repeating to himself as he walked about the room, "And smother'd in the dusty whirlwind, dies."[712]

I suppose he had been repeating the whole of the simile in *Cato*, as the sandy desert had struck him strongly. The sand has blown of late over a good deal of meadow. But it is not so thick but that grass grows in summer. It is very alarming. People in the island tell that their fathers told them they saw ploughed land over most of the space which is now covered with sand.

Coll's house is situated on a bay called Breacacha Bay, from the place where the family residence has always been. We found here a neat gentleman's house with four rooms on a floor, three storeys and garrets. The dining-room and the other three rooms on that floor were well wainscoted with good fir, and were very snug in dry weather. The storm, which beats on the front of the house and on one end, from the southwest, has hurt the timber of the windows much, so that they let in rain. There are two neat wings or pavilions to the house.

On our arrival here, we felt ourselves very comfortable. There was in the dining-room a map of the world and many tables, one large, one covered with wax-cloth. We had not been in so good a house since we were in Lord Erroll's. Mr Johnson relished it much at first, but soon remarked that there was nothing becoming a chief about it. It was quite a tradesman's box. It was at present a kind of waste house. However, young Coll did very well. Macsweyn, Junior, and his wife were busy to get things right; and a very clever girl, a Maclean, a native of the island, who had been five years a servant-maid at Glasgow and was come home on a visit to her relations, was got to officiate.

Mr Johnson seemed quite at home. He told me he could easily enough say 'Lady Raasay', but could not bring his tongue to pronounce readily the address to a laird by his title alone, as 'MacLeod', 'Raasay'. By this time he had improved, for he called, "Now, Coll, if you could get us a dish of tea."

We had it directly, and we had a very good supper served on china. We had a bold tune from the piper, a decent comely fellow with a green cloth waistcoat with silver lace; and then he helped to serve at table. His name was Neill Rankin. These Rankins have been pipers to the family of Maclean for many generations. They used to have a college in Mull for teaching the bagpipe, but it has not been in practice now for sixteen years. I forgot to mention that there was a college for the bagpipe in Skye kept by the MacCrimmons, the hereditary pipers of the Laird of MacLeod. It subsisted in a certain degree till last year, that an admirable piper went to America. MacLeod's present piper, whom we heard every day, is yet no professor, though he has a good ear, and plays very well.[713]

Mr Johnson and I had each an excellent bedroom on the dining-room floor. We had a dispute which of us had the best curtains. He rather had, as his were linen. But I insisted that I had the best posts, which was undeniable. Said he, "If you have the best posts, we'll have you tied to 'em and whipped."[714]

And so he got the better of me. As he did in this mere trifle, he will do at times in disputes of serious import. I can never forget Goldsmith's lively saying, the fruit of many a severe defeat which he has suffered.[715] Said he one day when we dined at Colman's, "There's no arguing with Johnson, for if his pistol misses fire, he knocks you down with the butt-end of it."

WEDNESDAY 6 OCTOBER. After a sufficiency of sleep, we assembled at breakfast. We were just as if in barracks. Everybody was master.[716]

We went and viewed the old castle of Coll, which is about two gun-shots from the present house, very near to the shore, and founded on a rocky bottom. The late Coll, brother to the present laird, lived in it till within ——— years of his death. He died in 1754. There were thirty cows killed for his funeral, and about fifty sheep. There were gentlemen at it from the mainland as well as the neighbouring islands.

We surveyed the old castle very minutely. It was more entire than any that I ever saw. It has never been a large feudal residence, Coll being but a second son of the Maclean family. There was a wall had gone all round; and one square tower was plainly very ancient, as was also a round tower which had an arched roof, and a parapet wall around the top. It served as a spying place towards the sea. There were battlements towards the east. There were two doors or gates to the castle on the ground. Above each was a place for throwing stones down in case of an attack. On the second storey we saw a vault which was, and still is, the family prison. There was a woman put into it by the Laird for stealing peats, within these ten years; and any offender would be put in yet, for from the necessity of the thing, as the island is remote from any power established by law, the Laird must exercise his jurisdiction to a certain degree. There were several other pieces of building within the walls, I know not of what age. All the roofs of all the different buildings here were covered with slates of an uncommon size. One of them was as long as my cane, and they were also uncommonly broad and thick. The walls, as in all old castles, were of an immense thickness. There was a bedroom, as it was called, and indeed it was used as such, in the thickness of the wall. It had two slits by way of windows.

Mr Johnson examined all this remaining specimen of ancient life with wonderful eagerness. It was very inconveniently arranged. There was one narrow passage which he tried to get through, but found it would not do. He persisted however; opened his waistcoat and pressed through. There was in the thickness of the walls on the southwest what Coll called a closet. It was a narrow passage or stripe to the southwest corner, and then it run at a right angle to the north for a little way. Mr Johnson had first looked at it from the entry into it. I went in and reported that it was a circular closet. I was mistaken, to be sure, in every sense; for the line which it formed had nothing of the circle. Coll agreed with me. This incited Mr Johnson's curiosity to a keener pitch, as he was almost positive we were wrong, from the cursory view he had taken. "How the plague is it circular?" said he. And back he went, and proceeded into it, and confuted us.

This old castle exemplified Gray's verses on one: "Huge windows that exclude the light / And passages that lead to nothing."[717] Besides the two doors on the ground, there was one to the square tower from the battlements. In the prison, which is a good large vault, we were shown in a corner a hole into which Coll said greater criminals used to be put. It was now filled up with rubbish of different kinds, particularly broken bottles. Coll said it was of a great depth. "Ay," said Mr Johnson. "All such places *that are filled up* were of a great depth."

Wednesday 6 October

He is very quick in showing why he does not give credit to what he is told, when that is the case. Since we came into Coll, somebody told him of 10,000 somethings, I do not recollect what. He said to me, "Why, sir, you know 10,000 is an even number." He made a similar observation on the number of people in the parish of Sleat being given him without any small fractions, as I may say (such as 1555), but in round hundreds. I think this was one of his instances of shrewd correction, and to be sure it is hardly to be believed that exact regular numbers will happen; so, when a man mentions such, it is probable he has not been exact. Mr Macpherson at Sleat told us there had not been above 1000 Highlanders engaged abroad in the last war.[718] He must be mistaken, I should imagine.

After seeing the castle, we looked at a small house, just a hut, built to the north of it, touching the wall. It is called *Teigh Franchich*, i.e., the Frenchman's house. Coll could not tell what was the history of it.[719] A poor man with a wife and —— children now lived in it. Mr Johnson walked into it and we followed. He gave some charity. There was one bed for all the family. It was very smoky. When he came out, he said to me, "*Et hoc secundum sententiam philosophorum est esse beatus.*"

I said the philosophers, when they placed happiness in a cottage, supposed cleanliness and no smoke. He said they did not think about either.

We walked a little in the garden, a piece of ground enclosed with a stone dike, and well stored with garden stuff.[720] But not a tree is to be found in Coll. They have tried many in the garden, but as soon as they got higher than the dike, they died. We saw a few very young fruit-trees on the southwest wall, and a nursery of firs. Mr Johnson prescribed sowing the seeds of hardy trees, such as birch. Coll showed us four very good rooms on the ground floor. One of them was a charter-room. The papers were confusedly kept. He without scruple opened both a little trunk and a cabinet where they lay, and let me look. I shall afterwards mention some of them.

He and I went and took a ride, I upon a black stoned-horse, he on a bay mare followed by a foal which sucked her when there was any halt. We saw a very pretty turnip-field near the house, which young Coll hoed all with his own hand. He had one last year. These have been the first in the Western Isles. We rode along a fine strand on the south, or rather southwest, side of the island, for it lies southeast and northwest.[721] The strand may be a mile and a half, admirable airing ground. Young Coll has tried to make roads in the island. We saw two pieces very well executed. The day was clear and only a little windy. We saw Mull, Icolmkill, Fladda,

Wednesday 6 October

the Dutchman's Cap (the two last small islands between Coll and Mull), as also Cairnbulg, a rock in the sea on which was a fortification of old.

We came to a farm called Crossapoll, i.e., the pool of the Cross.[722] The tenant, Maclean, is a most industrious man. He has ten children. He gives a college education at Aberdeen to his eldest son, who in the vacation keeps a school here, having so much paid him by the gentlemen of the island.

We were now within about a mile and a half of the west end of the island. We crossed over to the north side and looked at an appearance of lead, which seemed very promising. It has been long known, for I found in Coll's cabinet letters to the late laird from Sir John Erskine and Sir Alexander Murray, respecting lead – Sir John's directly so, and Sir Alexander's so as mentioning it in such a way as I understood it – and I fancy Coll never had any other view of lead but this. We passed along through a great extent of ground blown over with sand, till we came to another very good airing strand on the north side of the island; then turned to the right by the village of Foill, where I counted so many houses, and so got home.[723]

After dinner came Mr Maclean of Cornaig, brother to Isle of Muck, who is a cadet of the family of Coll. He possesses the two ends of Coll, which belong to the Duke of Argyll, as part of the estate of Maclean, which the Duke has, but which is now contested at law by Sir Allan Maclean.[724] The two ends of Coll were church lands belonging to Icolmkill. At the Reformation Maclean got them back. Coll used to have a lease of the two ends. The last rent was £45. Upon the Duke's demanding a high rent, Coll would no longer be tenant; so this gentleman, Cornaig (which is the name of the principal place on the lands), took them in 1771 for nineteen years at £105. His brother, Isle of Muck, has a share with him. Cornaig told me they were resolved to *go the length of their tether* rather than let a Campbell into Coll; and the Campbells had offered near as much. Mr Johnson well observed that landlords err much when they calculate merely what their land *may* yield. "The rent must be in a proportionate ratio of what the land may yield, and of the power of the tenant to make it yield. A tenant cannot make by his land but according to the corn and cattle which he has. Suppose you should give him twice as much land as he has, it does him no good unless he gets also more stock. It is clear then," said he, "that the Highland landlords who let their substantial tenants go, are infatuated; for the poor small tenants cannot give them good rents, from the very nature of things. They have not the means of raising more from their farms."

Wednesday 6 October

Cornaig was a tall stout man with grey hair, tied, but he was but middle-aged. Mr Johnson found him the most distinct man that he had met with in these isles. He said he did not shut his eyes or put his fingers in his ears, which he seemed to think, with justice too, was a good deal the mode with most of the people whom we have seen of late.

At night came Crossapoll and his eldest son, really an ingenious lad. He had taken a pretty good view of Staffa. We were jovial tonight. Cornaig sung Erse songs. We had no liquor but whisky punch without souring. The cellars of Coll were quite empty. I came to like it well enough. I sat till after three in the morning with them, and then left them to finish a new bowl. This day was fair but windy.

THURSDAY 7 OCTOBER. Captain Maclean came to breakfast. Crossapoll and his son had set out early. There came on a dreadful storm of wind and rain, which continued all day, and rather increased at night. The windows of the dining-room let in a deal of rain; and as the wind was from the southwest, it was directly against our getting to Mull.

We were in a strange state of abstraction from the world. We could neither hear from our friends, nor write to them. It gave me much uneasiness to think of the anxiety which my dear wife must suffer. Coll had brought Lucas *On Happiness*, Daillé *On the Fathers*, and More's *Dialogues*, from the minister's, and Burnet's *Own Times* with Salmon's *Remarks*, from the Captain's; and he had of his own some books of farming and Gregory's Geometry. Mr Johnson read a good deal of Burnet and of the latter, and he even made notes in the end of his journal about geometry.[725] I read a little of Young's *Six Weeks' Tour through the Southern Counties*. I wrote a deal of journal today.

We got up late, and the day moved on without my being at all splenetic. I am grown a hard-minded fellow. Mr Johnson when we were at Captain Maclean's, on my talking of Garrick's having rye-bread on his table at breakfast, said he had probably seen it at some great man's; and he observed how strangely people are swayed by what others tell them, and how few have the resolution to say plainly that they like wheat-bread best. "I could undertake," said he, "to make Langton eat all the kinds of grain in bread, and think each best."[726]

We were to have gone with Mr Johnson this morning to the mine. He said, when the storm was raging, "We may be glad we are not *damnati ad metalla*." This book which he gave me will soon be done. But he bid me not contract my Journal, and rather beg some paper.[727]

FRIDAY 8 OCTOBER. The Campbeltown ship was to come down to the harbour here to take in nine tuns of kelp, but could not get forward. Coll was of opinion that Mr Johnson and I had better freight her to set us down in Mull, which might be done with a wind that would not bring her hither. And supposing her here, she must wait a day for her ladening, and then the wind might come contrary again; so that by taking her directly from Lochiern, we had several more chances to get away. Morison and Macdonald, the two Masters, came here today. Mr Johnson was clear for freighting them. He felt today the weight of this barren way of passing time. He said, "I want to be on the mainland, and go on with existence. This is a waste of life." He has talked little here.

I shall here insert, without regard to chronology, some of his sayings. He told us that a man had been well received for two years among the gentlemen of Northamptonshire by calling himself his brother. At last he grew so impudent as by his influence to get tenants turned out of their farms. Allen the printer, who is of that county, came to Mr Johnson, asking him with much appearance of doubtfulness if he had a brother; and upon being assured he had none alive, he told Mr Johnson of the imposition, and immediately wrote to the country and the fellow was dismissed. Mr Johnson said it pleased him that so much was got by using his name. Said he, "It is not every name that can carry double; do both for a man's self and his brother" (laughing). "I should be glad to see the fellow."

He said a man could have no redress for his name being used, or ridiculous stories told of him in the newspapers, except he could show he had suffered damage. Some years ago some foolish piece was published 'by S. Johnson'. Some of Mr Johnson's friends wanted him to be very angry about this. He said it would be in vain, for the answer would be, "'S. Johnson' may be Simon Johnson, or Simeon Johnson, or Solomon Johnson; and even if it had been full Samuel Johnson, it might be said, 'It is not you. It is a much cleverer fellow.'"[728]

He and Beauclerk and Langton, and Lady Sydney Beauclerk, mother to our friend, were one day driving in a coach by Cuper's Gardens, which were then let to nobody. Mr Johnson for a joke proposed he and Beauclerk and Langton should take them; and they amused themselves scheming how they would all do. Lady Sydney grew angry, and said an old man should not put such things in young people's heads. Mr Johnson said she had no notion of a joke; had come late into life, and had a mighty unpliable understanding.

He said Carte's *Life of the Duke of Ormonde* was considered as a book of authority, but it was ill-written; the matter diffused in too many words; no animation, no compression, no vigour; that two good volumes in duodecimo might be made out of the two in folio.

Joseph informed us that he found several lice upon our shirts when we threw them off. This was very disagreeable. Mr Johnson made himself merry with the Scots. "I remember," said he, "a song against them, I think in James Ist's time: 'Your waistcoats and doublets were but thin, Where many a louse was shelter'd in.'" But he owned that this poet did not know the meaning of a doublet, which is the same with waistcoat.

I observed of our confinement here that this was just what Seneca complains so grievously of while in Corsica. "Yes," said Mr Johnson, "and he was not farther from home than we are. The truth is, he was much nearer."[729]

Captain Maclean went home today. It rained at times, and the wind was still contrary. Cornaig attended me while I rummaged through the cabinet and looked at all the papers. I shall now put down some anecdotes of the family and introduce some curious things which I found in the cabinet. The first laird of Coll was a younger son of the family of Maclean. His father gave him the middle part of Coll for his patrimony, but made it the jointure lands of Lady Maclean. MacNeil of Barra married her, and came and lived in Coll. Young Coll was so impatient to get possession that he got some of the clan to assist him against MacNeil. They killed him at Grishipoll, and then Coll took the estate. Some generations after, Maclean wanted to resume Coll, and there was a bloody battle, or skirmish rather, in which Coll prevailed; and since that time his chief never disturbed him.[730]

Coll had the £20 land of Lochiel. He was living there. The Camerons came upon him and killed him. His lady was with child. She was put under the care of Cameron, called Maclonich, with orders that if she bore a son, he should be put to death; if a daughter, she might be allowed to live. Maclonich's wife and Lady Maclean were brought to bed at the same time, the former of a daughter, the latter of a son. Maclonich generously made the children be exchanged; so that young Coll was saved. Thus the young laird of Coll had the same good fortune with Cyrus. Perhaps both the stories are fables. There is, however, for Coll's story all that tradition can go. When young Coll grew up, he came home to this island and was joyfully received by his people.[731]

Ever since that time there has been the greatest kindness shown by Coll's family to all the Maclonichs. Poor boys of that tribe from Lochaber would beg their way to Coll and be brought up about the kitchen till able to work for themselves. The chief of the tribe has always been educated by Coll. The present chief was with Coll at Aberdeen getting education. He would be a soldier. Coll could not get him a commission, so he is a sergeant in the train of artillery. I saw above the door upon the battlements of the old castle a vacant place where was a square stone, with an inscription in Erse bearing that if a Maclonich should come there at midnight with a man's head in his hand, he should be protected.[732] The meaning was, if he should even be a murderer. So late as the year 1737 this privilege was demanded. I found the following letter:

To The Laird of Coll / DR SIR, The long standing tract of firm affectionate friendship 'twixt your worthy predecessors and ours affords us such assurance as that we may have full relyance on your favour and undoubted friendship in recommending the bearer, Ewen Cameron, our Cousin, son to the deceast Dugall McConnill of Innermaillie, sometime in Glenpean, to your favour and conduct; who is a man of undoubted honesty and discretion, only that he has the misfortune of being alledged to have been accessory to the killing of one of Macmartin's family about fourteen years ago, upon which alledgeance the Macmartins are now so sanguine on revenging that they are fully resolved for the deprivation of his life, to the preventing of which you are relyed on by us, as the only fit instrument and a most capable person. Therefore your favour and protection is expected and intreated during his good behaviour, and failing of which behaviour you'll please use him as a most insignificant person deserves. Sir, he had upon the alledgeance foresaid been transported at Lochiel's desire to France to gratify the Macmartins; and, upon his return home about five years ago, married. But now he is so much threatened by the Macmartins that he is not secure enough to stay where he is, being Ardmurchan, which occasions this trouble to you. Wishing prosperity and happiness to attend still yourself, worthy Lady, and good family, we are in the most affectionate manner, Dr Sir, your most obliged, affectionate, and most humble servants, / DUIGALL CAMERON of Strone. / DUGALL CAMERON of Barr. / DWGALL CAMERON of Inviriskvoulline. / DUGALL CAMERON of Invinvalie. / Strone, 11 March 1737.[733]

Ewen Cameron was protected, and his son has now a farm from the Laird of Coll, in Mull.

I take the oldest charter of Coll which the family has, to be one granted by James V at Edinburgh, 1 December 1528:

Jacobus, DEI gratia Rex Scotorum, omnibus probis hominibus totius terre sue, clericis et laicis, salutem. Sciatis quia quondam Johannes Makclane, avus predilecti nostri Johannis Makclane de Coill, terras subscriptas sibi [hereditave] pertinentes habuit ipsi per quondam nobilissimum progenitorem nostrum Jacobum secundum Scotorum Regem bone memorie, cuius anime propitietur DEUS, concessas; et quod sue litere et evidentie —— terrarum per suos inimicos destruuntur et earundem registrum combustum . . .[734]

The family of Coll was very loyal in the time of the great Montrose, from whom I found two letters in his own hand-writing. The first is as follows.

For my very loving friend the Laird of Coall. / Strethearne 20 Jañ 1646 / SIR, I must heartily thank you for all your willingness and good affection to his Majesty's service, and particularly the sending alongs of your son, to who I will heave ane particular respect, hopeing also that you will still continue ane goode instrument for the advanceing ther of the King's service, for which, and all your former loyal carriages, be confident you shall fynd the effects of his Mãs favour, as they can be witnessed you by your very faithfull freinde, / MONTROSE.

The other is

For the Laird off Coall / Petty, 17 April 1646 / SIR, Having occasion to write to your fields, I cannot be forgetful of your willingness and good affection to his Majesty's service. I acknowledge to you, and thank you heartily for it; assuring, that in what lies in my power, you shall find the good. Meanwhile I shall expect that you will continue your loyal endeavours, in wishing those slack people that are about you to appear more obedient than they do, and loyal in their Prince's service, whereby I assure you you shall find me ever your faithful friend, / MONTROSE.

These are honourable documents, and should be carefully preserved. I have written the first just after the original.[735] From the second letter it would seem that Coll's zeal had rather failed a little, for the style is not so warm as that of the first. It gently hints complaints.

I found a contract of marriage in 1649 between Sir Lachlan MacLain of Dowart, as taking burden for his sister Finvoll (it should be Finvola, which they say is the same with Flora) and John MacLain, Laird of Coll.[736] The knight gives with her nine score head of *keye* (cows); and she is to have as her jointure eighteen score, and (as I read it) the half of the house – thus,[737] – and the half of all future conquests, i.e., what should be gained.

I found a curious piece on the death of the present laird's father:

Friday 8 October

'Nature's Elegy upon the death of Donald Maclean of Coll.'[738] Mr Johnson read the whole of this curious piece, and he wondered who wrote it. I suppose it has been some country schoolmaster. He said the epitaph was not so very bad. I asked what 'art's corrective' meant. "Why," said Mr Johnson, "that he was so exquisite that he set art right when she was wrong."

I found among the Coll papers a copy of a letter from the late MacLeod to the late Kingsburgh, in which he tells him that the Young Pretender will probably pay him a visit in expectation of his protection; that he knows the danger of assisting him, and the reward offered by Government, by which he may aggrandize his family beyond many in Scotland; and hopes he will do his duty to himself, family, and country. What a shocking exhortation! He also uses the name of Sir Alexander Macdonald, and says he can assure Kingsburgh his sentiments are the same with his (MacLeod's). I cannot justly convict him of writing this infamous letter, as I have not seen the original; but I take it to be genuine, since I do not see that a forgery would have been laid up by the late laird of Coll, to whom I found many original letters from MacLeod.[739] I also found a copy of a letter from Lochiel and Keppoch to Invernochiel, dated Glenivash, 20 March 1746,[740] desiring to communicate their sentiments to the leading men among the Campbells; upbraiding them for their cruelty in burning houses, and attacking women, children, and cattle. But I shall transcribe it.

> Yesternight we had a letter from Clunie, Younger, giving an account of the success of the party sent by his R. H. under the command of Lord George Murray.[741] A copy of which letter we thought proper to send you enclosed, as you happen for the present to be stationed contiguous to the Campbells. It is our general desire that you instantly communicate to Airds, the Sheriff, and other leading men amongst them, our sentiments (which, GOD willing, we are determined to execute) by transmitting this our letter and the copy enclosed, to any most convenient to you.[742]
>
> It is our opinion that, of all men in Scotland, the Campbells had the least reason of any to engage in the present war against his R. H.'s interest, considering that they had always appeared in opposition to his royal family since the reign of King James the 6th, and have been guilty of so many acts of rebellion and barbarity during that time that no injured prince but would endeavour to resent it when GOD was pleased to put the power in his hand. Yet his present Majesty and his R. H. the Prince R. are graciously pleased by their respective declarations to forgive all past miscarriages to the most virulent and inveterate enemy, and even bury

them in oblivion, provided they returned to their allegiance. And though they should not appear personally in arms in support of the royal cause, yet their standing neuter would entitle them to the good graces of their injured sovereign. But in spite of all the lenity and clemency that a prince could show or promise, the Campbells have openly appeared with their wonted zeal for rebellion and usurpation, in a most officious manner.

Nor could we ever form a thought to ourselves that any men endowed with reason and common sense could use their fellow creatures with such inhumanity and barbarity as they do; and of which we have daily proof by their burning of houses and stripping of women and children and exposing to the open field and severity of the weather, burning of corns (i.e., corn or grain), houghing of cattle, and killing of horses. To enumerate the which would be too tedious at this time. They must naturally reflect that we cannot but look on such cruelty with horror and detestation and hearts full of revenge. Will certainly endeavour to make reprisals, and are determined to apply to his R. H. for leave and orders to enter their country with full power that we are to act at discretion; and if we are so lucky as to obtain it, we shall show them that we are not to make war against brute creatures, but against men. But as GOD was pleased to put so many of their people in our custody, we hope to prevail with his R. H. to hang a Campbell for every house that shall hereafter be burnt by them.

Notwithstanding the scandalous and malicious aspersions contrived by our enemy against us, they could never, since the commencement of the war, impeach us with any act of hostility that had the least tendency to [such] cruelty as they exercised against us, though we had it in our power. It's barbarous enough to exert it, when courage fails, against men. It betrays cowardice to a degree to vent their spleen against brutes, houses, women, and children, who cannot resist. We are not ignorant of this villainous intention, by the intercepted letter from Airds to the Sheriff, which plainly discovers that it was by application that their General Cumberland granted orders for burning, which he could not be answerable for to the British Parliament; it being most certain that such barbarity could never be countenanced by any Christian senate. We are, sir, your most humble servants, / DONALD CAMERON of Lochiel. / ALEX. MACDONALD of Keppoch.

P. S. I cannot omit taking notice that my people have been the first that have felt the cowardly barbarity of my pretended Campbell friends. I shall only desire to have an opportunity of thanking them for it in the open field. / DONALD CAMERON.

I read this letter to Mr Johnson and called it a good one. Said he, "It is a very good one, upon their principles."743

Friday 8 October

Since I mentioned MacLeod's letter to Kingsburgh, Hugh Macsweyn (i.e., the younger Macsweyn) told me that he was present when MacLeod wrote a letter to Kingsburgh, but whether it was the same with the copy, he could not tell. He said the Duke of Cumberland was by while MacLeod wrote, so that the letter was quite under his direction. This MacLeod alleged as his excuse.

In the year 1745 the Laird of Coll assisted Government by sending sixty militia to Inveraray, which he raised at his own expense. They were sent home, as the Argyllshire battalion was made up before they arrived. Coll never had the least acknowledgment from Government for his service and expense. I found a copy of a letter from him to General Campbell, explaining how arms from the Prince's party had been brought into Coll. He tells the General that a brother of his, Lauchlan, whom he describes as of a very idle, odd character, and whom indeed he disinherited, had got these arms from an Irish officer. "This *blade*," says he, "got them from the *Teague.*" Young Coll told me that Lauchlan was a pretty fellow, and a poet, though very wild.[744] All the boats in Coll were destroyed, except one for the laird's use, lest the Prince should escape in one.

I found many excellent letters to Coll from Mr John MacLeod of Muiravonside, who had a pension of £40 Scots as lawyer for the family. I found the bond of pension discharged. There was one very religious letter on the death of Coll's lady. He talks in his letters with great affection of his son, whom he calls 'my dear absent friend', and says he must be supplied at any rate; and he mentions his hope as to *the good cause* – he plainly means so, with much faith. It would seem from these letters that though the laird sent sixty men, he was in his heart of the principles which warmed the breast of his ancestor, Montrose's correspondent. I found some letters from the present Lord Justice-Clerk when at the bar, exceedingly full and accurate with respect to some of Coll's family settlements.[745]

I found a copy or scroll of an agreement among the inhabitants of Tyree, mentioning that they were oppressed by strangers coming among them, from a belief that their island was more fertile than others, and begging grain from them; by giving away quantities of which, they were impoverished, and were also burdened with the maintenance of the strangers, as they were often stopped by storms; and therefore they resolved to give nothing to strangers, under a penalty which I forget. This agreement, I was told, never took place. Mr Johnson said he was glad of it. Young Coll, whom I called 'Rum', as Raasay's eldest son is called 'Rona', said that he intended to make the inhabitants of Rum enter into such an agreement; for strangers impoverish them by coming and getting wool in gifts, and live long upon them at times.[746] I found a letter from President Duncan Forbes – nothing in it but something about the two ends of Coll, which the laird and he understood. It is a pity that the Duke of Argyll has them. He would exchange them for some of Coll's lands in Mull; but Coll will not do that, because the lands in Mull are some of the best and . . .[747]

There are several districts of sandy desert in Coll. There are forty-eight lochs of fresh water, but many of them are very small, mere pools. About one-half of them, however, have trout and eel. There is a great number of horses in the island, mostly of a small size. Being overstocked, they sell some in Tyree, and on the mainland. Their black cattle, which are chiefly rough-haired, are reckoned remarkably good. The climate being very mild in winter, they never put their beasts in any house. The lakes are never frozen so as to bear a man, and snow never lies above a few hours. They have a good many sheep, which they eat mostly themselves, and sell but a few. They have goats in several places. There are no foxes; no serpents, toads, or frogs, nor any venomous creature. They have otters and mice here, but had no rats till lately that an American vessel brought them. There is a rabbit-warren on the northeast of the island, belonging to the Duke of Argyll. Young Coll intends to get some hares, of which there are none at present. There are no black cock, moor-fowl, nor partridges; but there are snipe, wild duck, wild geese, and swans, in winter; wild pigeons, plover, and great numbers of starlings, of which I shot some, and found them pretty good eating. Woodcocks come hither, though there is not a tree upon the island. There are no rivers in Coll, but only some brooks, in which there is a great variety of fish. In the whole isle there are but three hills, and none of them considerable for a Highland country.

The people are very industrious. Every man can tan. They get oak and birch bark and lime from the mainland. Some have pits, but they commonly use tubs. I saw brogues very well tanned, and every man can make them. They all make candles of the tallow of their beasts, both moulded and dipped; and they all make oil of fish. The little fish called cuddies produce a great deal. They boil their livers to make it. They sell some oil out of the island, and they use it much for light in their houses, in little iron (or unpainted black metal) lamps, most of which they have from England; but of late their own blacksmith makes them. He is a good workman; but he has no employment in shoeing horses, for they all go barefooted here, except some better ones of young Coll's, which were now in Mull. There are two carpenters in Coll; but most of the inhabitants can do something as boat-carpenters. They can all dye. They use heath for yellow; and for red, a moss which grows on stones. They make broadcloth, and tartan and linen, of their own wool and flax, enough for themselves, as also stockings.

Their bonnets come from the mainland. There is a man goes every year with a boat to Greenock and brings home a quantity of hardware, ribbons, and other small things; and keeps a little shop at the small village, where is the house in which public worship is held, as there is no church. It is a wretched hut, pretty long, with four little windows one way and two another, glass in none of 'em; only a bunch of straw is used to stop them in case of rain. There are also two people in the island who occasionally act as pedlars. In these particulars they are more improved than the Skye people; for there the pedlars are strangers, and I could hear of no shop except that of a glover at Portree, who, as Ullinish told me, makes very good gloves remarkably cheap. I did not think the luxury of gloves had been in Skye till he informed me. They have much need of them when they are to shake hands with strangers.

In Coll it is a practice to have cottars who are obliged to furnish two horses each for work, as also a third of the seed-corn; and for this and their work through the year, they have a third of the crop and three milk-cows grazed. This is a good method to make servants have a common interest with their masters.[748] The plough is a good deal used here, but they have also a spade for digging corn land upon steep places and among rocks. It is different from the Skye crooked spade, being much straighter: I have drawn it the wrong way, and too straight. The Skye one is: I have seen many as crooked. The ——— is made of one piece of wood, both in Skye and Coll.[749]

The inhabitants of Coll have increased considerably within these thirty years, as appears from the parish registers; for I find that when application was made to the Lords for disuniting it and Tyree, which were then one parish, Coll was said to contain between seven and eight hundred examinable persons; and the highest number would be given upon that occasion.[750] Now, the minister told us, there are nine hundred examinable persons. There are but three considerable tacksmen on Coll's property here: Macsweyn, Captain Maclean, and Mr Maclean of Knock; and they only have cottars, as above. The rest is let to small tenants, who pay four, three, or even two guineas.[751]

Crossapoll has the highest rented farm of any of them. His rent is £7. Upon this he has always lived creditably for one of his station. He has seven daughters and three sons, and his wife is with child. His eldest son

(Donald) he has educated for the Church of Scotland. He was taught by the tutor of Coll's sons. (Coll has eight sons and a daughter.) He then went to Aberdeen, where he gained a burse in King's College, upon a competition. Coll has now procured him a burse for four years as a student of divinity. He goes to Aberdeen from the opposite mainland, and returns on foot; and when at home, teaches his sisters and brothers to read and write. Mr Johnson said there was something noble in a young man's walking two hundred miles and back again, every year, for the sake of learning. He said he would send him his small Dictionary.[752] He did not know his merit when he was with us, or he would have talked to him. I talked a little to him. He teaches a few other children besides his father's. He told me he taught them first to read English, and then Erse was easily learnt. He can read the Irish character too. His father is like a judge among his neighbours.

Cornaig left us after dinner. I saw in the morning a good number of people who had come to Coll with complaints of each other's trespasses. Cornaig told them, "If you do not agree, we have the lawyer here from Edinburgh, who will take you to task" (or some such phrase). They said they were never used to take that way. They hoped Coll would settle matters himself.

SATURDAY 9 OCTOBER. We had agreed with the Campbeltown ship to put us in Mull for three guineas. The wind was still unfavourable, but it was a fine morning. As, in our present confinement, any thing that had even the name of curious was an object of attention, I proposed that Col should show me the great stone, mentioned in a former page, as having been thrown by a giant to the top of a mountain. Dr Johnson, who did not like to be left alone, said he would accompany us as far as riding was practicable. Coll and I rode out first as far as our horses could go up the hill where the stone thrown up by the giant lies. A servant held our horses. Mr Johnson sat down on the ground with a whin-rock at his back, and his hat tied down with his handkerchief, and read old Gataker on Lots and on the Christian Watch, a very learned book of the age of —— which Coll found in the garret.[753] Mr Johnson said it was a treasure here. He had a most eremitical appearance. He sat there while Coll and I walked up to the stone.

It is really a curious sight. It is of a triangular form, or rather like a huge coffin. I measured it with my handkerchief, and marked with a pencil how many lengths of that, and to a knot which I made on it. I put down the measurement with a lead pencil, and when we got home reduced it to feet by a foot-rule. It lies east and west. It is on the south side above nine feet long. Breadth, west end, about five feet; breadth, east end, four hands and a half. In circumference, tracing all its turns, about twenty-two feet. Highth, about four feet. It is clearly detached from the earth or any rock. The top of the hill is rocky, but it is supported upon three stones of no great size. I saw two others lying loosely under it. Perhaps they have also been supports, but it does very well without them. There is all the appearance that it has been set up artificially; yet it is difficult to conceive how it has been done. It is a very hard granite, and has over much of it a crust of crystallized substance, as many of the stones in Coll; and it has a great deal of the two kinds of moss with which Coll abounds growing upon it. I pulled a little of the moss and picked off a little of the crust, and put them up.

The other stone lying below, which I have mentioned already, is much larger. I have now measured it with my cane, which gives me a rough computation. It is three canes and more than one in highth (for I could not reach the top) – four broad – six long. It really seems to be as much detached as the one on the hill, and to have stones for supporters; but as it rests upon earth, it has sunk; while the other has kept up, as it rests on rock. Coll says tradition is not clear which of them was thrown by the giant, which by his mistress. When a compound ratio is taken of the smaller one being thrown up, and the larger thrown down, the difficulty of performing either will be pretty equal.

Mr Johnson was so much engaged with Gataker that he said he did not miss us. His avidity for variety of books, while we were in Col, was frequently expressed; and he often complained that so few were within his reach. Upon which I observed to him, that it was strange he should complain of want of books, when he could at any time make such good ones.[754]

We returned by the house, where I refreshed myself with a glass of whisky and a bit of bread. Mr Johnson two days ago very justly reproved me for taking the *scalck* or dram every morning. He said, "For shame!" And that it was now really become serious. It was lucky that he corrected me. I refrained from it since, as a regular morning mode; but this forenoon I was fatigued with walking up the hill, and it was a reasonable indulgence.

We resolved at last to go and see the lead mine in company. It was curious to see Mr Johnson mounted on the large bay mare, without shoes and followed by a foal. He and I had a good gallop on the south strand. When we came to Crossapoll, I alighted and viewed the burying place. Coll had told me that there never was a church or chapel there. I was expatiating on a very singular thing which I had found in Coll – a burying ground not at all connected with the sanctity of a religious edifice, which seemed to be a token of uncommon coldness of mind, of a deficiency in a principle or prejudice which all nations have had. But before I had time to write down this piece of curiosity, young Maclean of Crossapoll told me that there were vestiges of what was said to have been an old chapel. He showed me today the roots of the walls of the chapel, and also of a wall which had enclosed the consecrated ground. I fancy the place has its name from a cross having been there: Crossapoll, the Pool of the Cross. There has been a very ancient burying place here; I saw some very ancient tombstones, one with a broadsword engraven upon it with a kind of foliage. It was of a blue slate. I saw also many very recent ones, and graves without stones. It serves for a burying place equally with the one beside the ruins of the chapel near the minister's.[755]

I forgot to mention that at the minister's, Mr Johnson asked if the people here had any superstitions. The minister said, "No."

Their not choosing to cut peats at the increase of the moon was mentioned by somebody. "There," said Mr Johnson, "is a superstition."

Said the minister, "It's not a superstition. It's a whim." The correction I thought not amiss. However, Mr Johnson maintained that there are superstitions not connected with religion.[756]

We went to the mine. The sea rose very high in foaming waves on the shore. Mr Johnson contemplated it intensely. He looked at the mine, and young Maclean and I dug some pieces of ore with a pickaxe, which were very heavy. We rode with Mr Johnson through a long tract of sand-hills.[757] Coll and Maclean said there were vestiges of houses which had been blown over with sand. Mr Johnson would not believe it. I desired we might be shown them. This led us a strange zigzag journey among the sand-hills. There was a good deal of wind, and good deal of sand was blown in our faces. I cried, "This is quite Arabian." It was easy riding; for our horses could trot down apparent precipices without danger, the sand always sliding away from their feet. Mr Johnson observed that if the sand had been dry, it would have been impossible to ride here. We came at last to what they said was a house blown over. Mr Johnson said it was a house abandoned and the stones taken away for other purposes. He bid me observe the large stones, which form the foundations of the houses here, were still standing higher than the sand; and that if they were not blown over, it was clear nothing higher than they could be blown over.

Saturday 9 October

This was quite convincing to me. But it made not the least impression on Coll, young Maclean, and another man, who were not to be argued out of a Highland tradition.[758]

The sky overcast and threatened a storm. We hastened home by the north strand, turning at Foill.

We did not sit down to dinner till between six and seven. We really lived plentifully here, and had true welcome; as Mr Johnson said, we were in nobody's way. We had a *spring* from the piper at breakfast, at dinner, and at supper. The peats were good and made a cheerful fire. Those at Dunvegan, which were damp, Mr Johnson called 'a sullen fuel'. I slept admirably here; and my room came to be like a home, from being accustomed to pass time comfortably in it. We had wheat bread, both loaf and biscuit, from Captain Maclean's. There was abundance of cream both at dinner and supper. I said young Coll's want of dignity made him seem rather a favourite servant of the laird's than the young laird himself. He was quite companionable with all the people. But I observed they all kept themselves uncovered when they spoke with him. Perhaps he is right to be thus easy. He is of a very diminutive figure, and better adapted for being liked than reverenced. We had to serve us at table, the piper, Allan Maclean the gardener, a very decent-looking man, and Hugh Macdonald, his own servant. Joseph also attended. Everybody seemed happy.

Mr Johnson told me he had never seen Blenheim. He had not gone formerly; and he would not go now just as a common spectator for his money. He would not put it in the power of some man about the Duke of Marlborough to say, "Johnson was here. I knew him, but I took no notice of him." This is a very proper pride in one who has arrived at his consequence. He said he would be very glad to see Blenheim if properly invited, which in all probability would never be the case, as it was not worth his while to seek for it. He had a prudent and delicate resolution against asking Beauclerk to carry him there, which I should not have thought of, but have asked him slapdash.[759] "I doubt," said he, "if Beauclerk be on that footing with the Duke as to carry anybody there; and I would not give him the uneasiness to see that I knew it, or even to put himself in mind of it."

I must study to have more of this kind of delicacy. It is the same to many men with regard to the mind as to the body. I would not strip myself naked before every one, and would be shocked to occasion another being so exposed. Mental nakedness should be avoided with equal scrupulousness.

Saturday 9 October

The sky predicted well. There came on a very extraordinary storm. I went to bed snug, as being in a good warm place; was quite well as to immediate existence, and had no uneasiness but the recollection that my wife would be in impatience and fear. I had Ovid's Epistles with me, which I bought at Inverness, and sometimes looked at, particularly those of Penelope and Ulysses.[760]

SUNDAY 10 OCTOBER. We had one of the most terrible storms of wind and rain that I ever remember. It made such an awful impression on us all, as to produce, for some time, a kind of dismal quietness in the house.[761]

When Mr Johnson wondered who had written the 'Elegy on Coll', he said it was the Ghost of Ossian.[762] I said Ossian would have had grander images; for that it could not be denied that there were some in *Fingal*. But I said there was a certain sameness in *Fingal*, though every one is not sensible of it. That it was like the paper with which a room is finished, where you have a number of birds and a number of figures and a number of trees and a number of flowers; and as there is a variety of objects, one does not at once perceive that the finishing is composed of pieces all exactly the same. By the time your eye has made the round of the pattern, you forget what you first looked at. So is it with Ossian's poetry to a considerable degree. I said this from a very imperfect recollection of them. But I take it to be just. I shall try at some idle time ———[763]

The day was passed without much conversation; only, upon my observing that there must be something bad in a man's mind who does not like to give leases to his tenants, but to keep them in a perpetual wretched dependence on his will, Mr Johnson said I was right. "It is a man's duty," said he, "to extend comfort and security among as many people as he can. He should not wish to have his tenants mere ephemerae – mere beings of an hour."[764]

I objected that they might grow insolent, which was very disagreeable; and I put him in mind that he had said that an English tenant was so independent, that, if provoked, he would *throw* his rent at his landlord. "Depend upon it," said he, "it is the landlord's own fault if it is thrown at him. A man may always keep his tenants under dependence enough, though they have leases. He must be a good tenant, indeed, who will not fall behind in his rent, if his landlord will let him; and if he does fall behind, his landlord has him at his mercy. Indeed," said he, "the poor man is always much at the mercy of the rich, no matter whether master or tenant. If the tenant lets his landlord have a little rent beforehand, or has lent him money, then the landlord is in his power. There cannot be a greater man than a tenant who has lent money to his landlord; for he has under subjection the very man to whom he should be subjected."

I had lain awake a good while last night, and had thought much of my long absence from home. Imagination suggested a variety of gloomy ideas. It was really heavy, it was distressing, to consider that I might be shut up here for another week or even a fortnight; and that after I got to Mull and Icolmkill I might be detained by storms in either of those places, I knew not how long. I grew quite impatient, and resolved to make for the mainland directly. All this day I ruminated on my nocturnal uneasiness. I found the enamel of philosophy which I had upon my mind, broke, worn off, or worn very thin, and fretfulness corroding it.

I talked with Coll, and found by his calculation that going to Icolmkill would probably consume ten days. I considered that in that case we should not reach Auchinleck before the sitting down of the Session; so that I should lose having Mr Johnson at the romantic seat of our family, and with my father, and upon my own land of Dalblair, all which was of much more value than our being at Icolmkill. But I was against mentioning my objections to Mr Johnson, for fear he should fix me down; for I still had a great desire to be at Icolmkill. It had been in my mind from the first time that Mr Johnson and I talked of visiting the Hebrides. I had mentioned too to many people that we were to see 'that ancient seat of religion and learning'. I read Martin's account of it over again, and was in doubt how to determine. Then I had heard Coll talk of our visiting Sir Allan Maclean, his chief, in a pretty island in our way to Icolmkill; and Lochbuie, a curious laird who has a large old castle, in our way from it. At last the arguments against going preponderated, and I fairly tabled my intention for the mainland to Mr Johnson. He said, "But don't say that I would not go with you to Icolmkill."

This piqued my spirit, and set me up again. "Poor Iona!" said I. "It is lucky that though sometimes the one is against going thither, sometimes the other, we are never both at a time against it." I now thought I would keep my mind in a sort of indecision whether to go or not, just as I found it agreeable after we were loose from Coll.

I had with me on this jaunt a Bible which I had in a present from Lord Mountstuart when we were in Italy together.[765] I value it highly, and always have it with me. I read in it frequently. I also read this day Dr Ogden's fourth sermon.

Sunday 10 October

MONDAY 11 OCTOBER. The morning was fine and the wind fair and moderate. My mind was sound as ever, and the enamel of philosophy entire. It had not been broke, I take it, for it is not easily repaired. Coll was in a hurry to get us down to the harbour where the ship lay. But he was too late of beginning. We did not get away till about eleven.

It seems young Macsweyn and his wife live in the house here to take care of it. She was one of the hardest-favoured women that I ever saw, swarthy and marked with the smallpox, and of very ungainly manners. She had never been upon the mainland. Mr Johnson said of her and before her, "That is rather being behindhand with life. I'd go and see Glenelg," and he laughed.

"Why," said I, "you have never seen, till now, anything but your native island."

"But," said he, "by seeing London I have seen as much of life as the world can show."

"You have not seen Pekin," said I.

"Sir," said he in a sort of anger, "what is Pekin? Ten thousand Londoners would *drive* all the people of Pekin. They'd drive them like deer."

I should have mentioned that in the old castle here is a little-house. I rebuked Coll, as I did Raasay, by observing that his ancestors were more civilized than the family now is in that very essential particular; for there is not one at the new house. Coll promised to me that he would erect one soon. Mr Johnson and I talked of it. I called it now *Domus Taliskeriana*.[766] Mr Johnson said I had that much at heart. He said if ever a man thinks at all, it is there. He generally thinks then with great intenseness. He sets himself down as quite alone, in the first place. I said a man was always happy there, too. Mr Johnson said he did not know that. I told him of an elegant one at the Dutch ambassador's, when I was at Paris – quilted seats, etc. "Sir," said he, "that is Dutch; quilted seats retain a bad smell. No, sir, there is nothing so good as the plain board."

I was for having books and prints. He did not insist for that. He told me he knew a gentleman who had a set of the *Spectator* in that place.

I find myself insensibly acquiring some of Mr Johnson's expressions, such as beginning a sentence with "Why, sir." Lord Hailes and I had once a serious dispute whether I should introduce that expression in quoting Mr Johnson in my *Tour to Corsica*. I have the letters by me upon it. I have even learnt a more curious expression, which is to resume a subject with "No, sir," though there is no negation in the case. As thus he will say, after having talked of Langton and praised him, "No, sir, I know no better man than Langton."[767]

It should be mentioned that I found here several letters to the late Coll from my father's old companion at Paris, Sir Hector Maclean, also in the style of Jacobite faith like those of honest old Mr John MacLeod. Not least I recollect one from the time of settling the colony in Georgia.[768] It dissuades Coll from letting people go there, and assures him there will soon be an opportunity of employing them better at home. I saw from this letter that emigration from the Highlands, though not in such numbers at once as now, has always been practised. As Mr Johnson observed, instead of improving their country, they diminished their people.[769]

We had a tedious ride today. Coll and I had no bridles but halters with wooden curbs, so that our beasts were not easily directed along. As we went along, the wind turned against us and checked my brisk spirits.

We stopped at Captain Maclean's, and entered. His house was very cold, the earthen floor was damp. His wife had the midwife in the house, as she expected every moment to lie in, and he himself did not seem fond of having us as his guests. I said the Oriental heat had burnt up his Highland hospitality. Mr Johnson said he believed he made us welcome enough in his own way, but he was a coarse man. We dined and passed the day and evening tolerably. The minister dined with us, and went home in the afternoon.

The Captain had been above twenty years in the East Indies, in the service both of Government and of the Company. He was lame from a wound which he had from a cannon-ball. This made Mr Johnson and me disposed to think well of him and of his entertainment; and I shall agree with Mr Johnson that he made us welcome in his own way.

Coll and I were laid in one bed again and Mr Johnson in another beside us. I pretended great anxiety about the weather and that we should be up in time if the wind was fair. So a little after lying down, which I did not do till late and Coll was asleep, I got up and put on my breeches and greatcoat, and so in interrupted slumbering I lay till six in the morning.[770]

TUESDAY 12 OCTOBER. I wrote a good deal of journal early in the morning. Coll rose between seven and eight. He thought the wind would do. So we hurried breakfast and set out for the harbour. Before we reached it, there was such a storm that we could not stir. The ship's boat durst not come on shore. They turned back most expertly. We were compelled to turn.

Coll and I had walked down before. We met Mr Johnson and the baggage and Joseph, and turned them. Coll had said to me that if we were stopped, we should go up to Macsweyn's and wait. I insisted on doing it directly. When we returned to the Captain's, of whom we had taken leave, it was not a very cordial meeting on either side.[771] I was wet to the skin, and resolved to have one drying for all. So Coll and I walked, and Mr Johnson followed us on horseback. By the road, I fell into a brook and wet myself to the middle very much. My boots were almost filled with water. I stood in two lochs, as they would say here, where a loch is used to denote pieces of water of any size. Mr Johnson said in England they have several gradations: pits, pools, meres, lakes.

When we reached Grishipoll, I got myself all shifted – got on waistcoat and breeches of Joseph's, and a good Highland coat of old Macsweyn's, of black cloth with hollow silver buttons, which had lasted him fifty years, and which pass from generation to generation in the Highlands. It was a short coat. Mr Johnson said I looked much better in it, and if I were to go a-courting, should wear such a coat.

I had taken hardly any breakfast, for fear of being sick at sea; so was keenly hungry. I had some barley bread and cheese, on which I feasted. A strange resolution was taken in the family that we should have no dinner till late in the evening, and tea in the mean time. Mr Johnson opposed the tea *till after dinner*; but they persisted, and he took it very readily. He said to me afterwards, "You must consider, sir, a dinner here is a matter of great consequence. It is a thing to be first planned and then executed. I suppose the mutton was brought some miles off, from some place where they knew there was a sheep killed." His minute observation strikes me with wonder. He said life had not got at all forward by a generation in Macsweyn's family. "For," said he, "the son is exactly formed upon the father. What the father says, the son says; and what the father looks, the son looks."

He was disgusted with the coarse manners here. He said to me, "I know not how it is, but I cannot bear low life. And I find others, who have as good a right as I to be disgusted, bear it better, by having mixed more with different sorts of men. You would think that I have mixed pretty well, too."

He read a good deal of my Journal in the little book which I had from him, and was pleased; for he said, "I wish thy books were twice as big." He helped me to supply blanks which I had left in first writing it, when I was not quite sure of what he had said; and he corrected any mistakes that I had made. He said, "They call me a scholar. And yet how very little literature is there in my conversation."

"Sir," said I, "that must be according to your company. You would not give literature to Coll and Macsweyn. Stay till we meet Lord Elibank."

We had a tolerable little chat by ourselves this evening. Old Mrs Macsweyn did not appear till supper. Mr Johnson said when he thought that she could not read, it was strange. There was something shocking in it. We had a very decent supper, after which a glass of whisky punch, while Mr Johnson and old Mrs Macsweyn drank tea. I have not seen him drink tea at night since he left Edinburgh. By Coll's advice, Mary Macdonald, a comely black girl who had been three years at Glasgow, washed my feet with warm water, which was Asiatic enough; and then I lay down in clean sheets upon a bed of straw, which I preferred to one of their feather-beds.[772]

Coll had a bed in the room with me. I soon fell asleep.

WEDNESDAY 13 OCTOBER. Coll called me up, with intelligence that it was a good day for a passage to Mull; and just as we rose, a sailor from the vessel arrived for us. We got all ready with dispatch. Mr Johnson was displeased at my bustling and walking quickly up and down. He said it did not hasten us a bit. It was getting on horseback in the ship. "All boys do it," said he; "and you are longer a boy than others."

He himself has no alertness, or whatever it may be called; so he may dislike it, as *Oderunt hilarem tristes.*[773]

Let me here mark a few detached things. There are what may be called rivers which run into Loch Eirach. One upon the left, as you enter it, comes in quite fresh. The one upon the right, which runs by Captain Maclean's house, is met by a loch, or arm of the sea, so that salmon go up it a little way. Neither are rivers of any size, comparatively speaking. I saw at Grishipoll a fir tree which had been thrown ashore. There adhered to it a number of shells in clusters, with kind of stalks or branches of sea-warc connecting them to the timber. They say a bird is hatched in each of these shells. I put up two or three of them.[774]

There are many wrecks or things thrown ashore in Coll. There was lately some excellent mahogany, and some years ago there were some casks of Malaga. The country people, finding it sweet and mild, drank of it without fear of intoxication, till they were mortally drunk. There is here the bird called a curlew. It is a sucking bird, like a woodcock, but as large as a wild duck.[775] We had two to dinner one day. They eat pretty well, and had no fishy taste. There is in the sand on the seashore a plant which they call sea holly. Young Maclean said it was eringo. It has prickly leaves, and they are at different places formed into roses.

Solan geese fly about Coll, but do not breed here. The seamaws or gulls are very numerous. So are the cormorants or scarts. The island has a good many small birds, but I cannot be exact as to them. I saw larks enough. There is a deal of the aromatic plant called gaul.[776] There is no tree whatever but dwarf juniper and short willows. There is a kind of plant grows on the hills and rocks, somewhat like ivy till you come near it, when it is rather like willow.

Before we reached the harbour, the wind grew high again. However, the small boat was waiting, and took us on board. We waited for some time in a kind of uncertainty what to do. At last it was determined that, as a good part of the day was over, and it was dangerous to be at sea at night, we should not sail till the morning, when the wind would probably be gentler with the first of the tide. We resolved not to go ashore again, but lie here in readiness.

Mr Johnson and I had each a bed in the cabin. Coll sat at the fire in the forecastle, with the two captains and Joseph and his servant and the two sailors. They eat mutton and potatoes and drank whisky. I licked some oatmeal, of which I found a barrel in the cabin. I had not done this since I was a boy. Mr Johnson told me he used to be fond of it when a boy. I note this because I can tell him that *he* too had somewhat of an oatmeal education.[777]

He and I eat some roasted potatoes at night. He indeed eat only one. Captain Macdonald pressed him much to eat mutton or butter or cheese – in short, pressed him to all that was on board. He made Mr Johnson grow surly. Mr Johnson said to me, "I know not whether a man should blame himself for not making a proper return to awkward civility. Here now is this man who thinks he is doing the best he can to me, and I can hardly use him well."

I got some of Ovid's Epistle from Penelope to Ulysses by heart, which served well to divert the tedious hours; and there was a Belfast newspaper in the ship, of no very old date, which was to my hungry mind as Irish meal is to a town when meal is scarce.[778]

Wednesday 13 October

CHAPTER SEVEN

Mull

SAMUEL JOHNSON

As we were to catch the first favourable breath, we spent the night not very elegantly, nor pleasantly in the vessel, and were landed next day at *Tobor Morar*, a port in *Mull*, which appears to an unexperienced eye formed for the security of ships; for its mouth is closed by a small island, which admits them through narrow channels into a bason sufficiently capacious. They are indeed safe from the sea, but there is a hollow between the mountains, through which the wind issues from the land with very mischievous violence.[779]

There was no danger while we were there and we found several other vessels at anchor; so that the port had a very commercial appearance.

The young Laird of *Col*, who had determined not to let us lose his company, while there was any difficulty remaining, came over with us. His influence soon appeared; for he procured us horses, and conducted us to the house of Doctor *Maclean*, where we found very kind entertainment, and very pleasing conversation. Miss *Maclean*, who was born, and had been bred at *Glasgow*, having removed with her father to *Mull*, added to other qualifications, a great knowledge of the *Earse* language, which she had not learned in her childhood, but gained by study, and was the only interpreter of *Earse* poetry that I could ever find.[780]

The Isle of *Mull* is perhaps in extent the third of the *Hebrides*. It is not broken by waters, nor shot into promontories, but is a solid and compact mass, of breadth nearly equal to its length.[781] Of the dimensions of the larger Islands, there is no knowledge approaching to exactness. I am

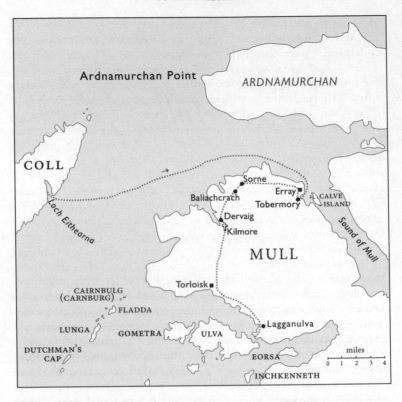

willing to estimate it as containing about three hundred square miles.

Mull had suffered like *Sky* by the black winter of seventy-one, in which, contrary to all experience, a continued frost detained the snow eight weeks upon the ground.[782] Against a calamity never known, no provision had been made, and the people could only pine in helpless misery. One tenant was mentioned, whose cattle perished to the value of three hundred pounds; a loss which probably more than the life of man is necessary to repair. In countries like these, the descriptions of famine become intelligible. Where by vigorous and artful cultivation of a soil naturally fertile, there is commonly a superfluous growth both of grain and grass; where the fields are crowded with cattle; and where every hand is able to attract wealth from a distance, by making something that promotes ease, or gratifies vanity, a dear year produces only a comparative want, which is rather seen than felt, and which terminates commonly

14–16 October

in no worse effect, than that of condemning the lower orders of the community to sacrifice a little luxury to convenience, or at most a little convenience to necessity.

But where the climate is unkind, and the ground penurious, so that the most fruitful years produce only enough to maintain themselves; where life unimproved, and unadorned, fades into something little more than naked existence, and every one is busy for himself, without any arts by which the pleasure of others may be increased; if to the daily burden of distress any additional weight be added, nothing remains but to despair and die. In *Mull* the disappointment of a harvest, or a murrain among the cattle, cuts off the regular provision; and they who have no manufactures can purchase no part of the superfluities of other countries. The consequence of a bad season is here not scarcity, but emptiness; and they whose plenty was barely a supply of natural and present need, when that slender stock fails, must perish with hunger.

All travel has its advantages. If the passenger visits better countries, he may learn to improve his own, and if fortune carries him to worse, he may learn to enjoy it.

Mr *Boswell's* curiosity strongly impelled him to survey *Iona*, or *Icolmkil*, which was to the early ages the great school of Theology, and is supposed to have been the place of sepulture for the ancient kings. I, though less eager, did not oppose him.

That we might perform this expedition, it was necessary to traverse a great part of *Mull*. We passed a day at Dr *Maclean's*, and could have been well contented to stay longer. But *Col* provided us horses, and we pursued our journey. This was a day of inconvenience, for the country is very rough, and my horse was but little. We travelled many hours through a tract, black and barren, in which, however, there were the reliques of humanity; for we found a ruined chapel in our way.[783]

It is natural, in traversing this gloom of desolation, to inquire, whether something may not be done to give nature a more cheerful face, and whether those hills and moors that afford heath cannot with a little care and labour bear something better? The first thought that occurs is to cover them with trees, for that in many of these naked regions trees will grow, is evident, because stumps and roots are yet remaining; and the speculatist hastily proceeds to censure that negligence and laziness that has omitted for so long a time so easy an improvement.

To drop seeds into the ground, and attend their growth, requires little labour and no skill. He who remembers that all the woods, by which the wants of man have been supplied from the Deluge till now, were self-sown, will not easily be persuaded to think all the art and preparation necessary, which the Georgick writers prescribe to planters. Trees certainly have covered the earth with very little culture. They wave their tops among the rocks of *Norway*, and might thrive as well in the Highlands and *Hebrides*.

But there is a frightful interval between the seed and timber. He that calculates the growth of trees, has the unwelcome remembrance of the shortness of life driven hard upon him. He knows that he is doing what will never benefit himself; and when he rejoices to see the stem rise, is disposed to repine that another shall cut it down.

Plantation is naturally the employment of a mind unburdened with care, and vacant to futurity, saturated with present good, and at leisure to derive gratification from the prospect of posterity. He that pines with hunger, is in little care how others shall be fed. The poor man is seldom studious to make his grandson rich. It may be soon discovered, why in a place, which hardly supplies the cravings of necessity, there has been little attention to the delights of fancy, and why distant convenience is unregarded, where the thoughts are turned with incessant solicitude upon every possibility of immediate advantage.

Neither is it quite so easy to raise large woods, as may be conceived. Trees intended to produce timber must be sown where they are to grow; and ground sown with trees must be kept useless for a long time, inclosed at an expence from which many will be discouraged by the remoteness of the profit, and watched with that attention, which, in places where it is most needed, will neither be given nor bought. That it cannot be plowed is evident; and if cattle be suffered to graze upon it, they will devour the plants as fast as they rise. Even in coarser countries, where herds and flocks are not fed, not only the deer and the wild goats will browse upon them, but the hare and rabbit will nibble them. It is therefore reasonable to believe, what I do not remember any naturalist to have remarked, that there was a time when the world was very thinly inhabited by beasts, as well as men, and that the woods had leisure to rise high before animals had bred numbers sufficient to intercept them.

Sir *James Macdonald*, in part of the wastes of his territory, set or sowed trees, to the number, as I have been told, of several millions, expecting, doubtless, that they would grow up into future navies and cities; but for want of inclosure, and of that care which is always necessary, and will hardly ever be taken, all his cost and labour have been lost, and the ground is likely to continue an useless heath.

Having not any experience of a journey in *Mull*, we had no doubt of reaching the sea by daylight, and therefore had not left Dr *Maclean's* very early. We travelled diligently enough, but found the country, for road there was none, very difficult to pass. We were always struggling with some obstruction or other, and our vexation was not balanced by any gratification of the eye or mind. We were now long enough acquainted with hills and heath to have lost the emotion that they once raised, whether pleasing or painful, and had our mind employed only on our own fatigue. We were however sure, under *Col's* protection, of escaping all real evils. There was no house in *Mull* to which he could not introduce us. He had intended to lodge us, for that night, with a gentleman that lived upon the coast, but discovered on the way, that he then lay in bed without hope of life.[784]

We resolved not to embarrass a family, in a time of so much sorrow, if any other expedient could be found; and as the Island of *Ulva* was over against us, it was determined that we should pass the strait and have recourse to the Laird, who, like the other gentlemen of the Islands, was known to *Col*. We expected to find a ferry-boat, but when at last we came to the water, the boat was gone.

We were now again at a stop. It was the sixteenth of October, a time when it is not convenient to sleep in the *Hebrides* without a cover, and there was no house within our reach, but that which we had already declined.

JAMES BOSWELL

THURSDAY 14 OCTOBER. I had slept pretty well. Mr Johnson had been up twice. Between six and seven the day was just as we could wish. We hauled in our anchors, which was a tedious operation, and at last set sail from Coll. We had a fine breeze. Mr Johnson was very uneasy for a while. He got up, and looked out of the cabin hatchway, and was pale as death. He then went to bed again, and was quiet all the time.

We descried off Rum a vessel making fine sail towards us. She came up quickly. It was cheerful to see her approach. At first our captains took her to be one of the desperate armed Irish smuggling vessels, which they called *buckers*. But she proved to be a king's cutter commanded by Mr Craufurd. She came close up to us, after having first hailed us with a speaking trumpet. She asked, "From whence?"

"From Coll."

"Where are you bound for?"

"Larne."

"With what are you loaded?"

"Kelp."

"What news in Coll?"

"None."

Her strength and the excellence of her rigging gave one a feeling of security; and seeing about twenty men above deck was a more lively scene than I had seen for some time. She soon left us, and run before us for . . .[785]

When Mr Johnson awaked this morning, he called, "*Lanky!*" having, I suppose, been thinking of Langton, but corrected himself instantly and cried, "*Bozzy!*" He has a way of contracting the names of his friends. Goldsmith feels himself so important now as to be displeased at it. Tom Davies was telling how Mr Johnson said, "We're all in labour for a name to *Goldy's* play."

Goldsmith cried, "I have often desired him not to call me *Goldy*."[786]

On Monday we had a dispute at the Captain's whether sand-hills could be fixed. Mr Johnson said, "How the devil can you do it?" but instantly took himself: "How can you do it?" I never before heard him use such a phrase.

I must endeavour to recollect what I may have omitted on former occasions. When I boasted at Raasay of my independency of spirit, and that I could not be bribed, he said, "Yes, you may be bribed by flattery." He has particularities which it is impossible to explain. He never wears a nightcap, as I have already mentioned, but puts his handkerchief on his head in the night. Coll told me he saw him washing his handkerchief, and that Joseph informed him that he never would give his handkerchiefs to wash, but always washed and dried them himself. The day that we left Talisker, he bid us ride on. He then turned the head of his horse back towards Talisker, then wheeled round to the same direction with ours, and then came briskly on. He sets open a window in the coldest day or night that is ablow and stands before it. This may do for his constitution, but most people, amongst whom I am one, must say, with the frogs in the fable, "This may be sport to you, but it is death to us."[787]

It is curious to hear the Highlanders always calling him *honest man*. By honest, they, as the Scotch in general, mean good or worthy in general. Old Macsweyn used it in another sense; for when his son told that he saw Mr Johnson with his handkerchief tied on his head, bringing peats to himself in a stormy night, the old man said that was *main honest.*

It is in vain to try to find a meaning in every one of Mr Johnson's particularities, which I suppose are mere habits contracted by chance; of which every man has some which are more or less remarkable. His speaking to himself, or rather repeating, is a common habit with studious men accustomed to deep thinking; and of course they will laugh by themselves if the subject which they are musing on is a merry one. Smith the moral theorist has this habit much. Mr Johnson is often uttering pious ejaculations when he appears to be talking to himself; for sometimes his voice grows stronger, and parts of the Lord's Prayer are heard. I have sat beside him with more than ordinary reverence on such occasions. Last night, when I told him I was going to sleep, he said, "GOD bless you, for Christ's sake."[788]

We got safely and agreeably into the harbour of Tobermory, before the wind rose, which it always has done for some days, as noon came onward. Tobermory is really a noble harbour. An island lies before it; and it is surrounded by a hilly theatre. The island is too low; otherwise this would be quite a secure port. But as the island is not high enough, some storms blow very hard here. Not long ago, fifteen sail of vessels were blown from their moorings. There will sometimes be sixty or seventy sail here. There was today twelve or fourteen vessels. To see such a fleet was the next thing to seeing a town. The vessels were from different places: Clyde, Campbeltown, Newcastle, etc. One was returning to Lancaster from Hamburg. After having been shut up in Coll, the sight of such an assemblage of moving habitations, containing such a variety of people engaged in different pursuits, gave me much gaiety of spirit. Mr Johnson said, "Boswell is now all alive. He is like Antaeus; he gets new vigour whenever he touches land."[789]

I went to the top of a hill fronting the harbour, and took a good view of it. We had here a tolerable inn, kept by a Mr Macarthur.

Mr Johnson had owned to me this morning that he was out of humour. Indeed, he showed it a good deal in the ship; for when I was expressing joy on being landed in Mull, he said he had no joy when he thought it would be five days before he should get to the mainland. I was afraid he would now take a sudden resolution to give up seeing Icolmkill. A dish of tea, some good wheaten cakes (scones) and fresh butter did him service, and his bad humour went off. I told him that I was diverted to hear all the people with whom we were as we travelled, say, "Honest man! He's pleased with everything. He's always content!"

Thursday 14 October

"Little do they know," said I.

He laughed and said, "You rogue."

We sent to find horses to carry us forward for Sir Allan Maclean's. Dr Maclean, who is married to Coll's aunt, was not at home, or we were to have gone to his house at Erray, which is but a mile off. Coll went and drank punch with the two captains and Joseph and one Nisbet, master of a Newcastle ship.[790]

Mr Johnson and I sat and talked a good deal. I told him how I had seen in Leandro Alberti's *Tour of Italy* a good deal of what Addison says in his *Remarks*. Mr Johnson said that the collection of passages from the classics had been made by another man than he.[791] "But," said he, "it is impossible to detect a man as a plagiary in such a case, because all who set about making such a collection must find the same. But," said he, "if you find the remarks in another, then Addison's learning in that book tumbles down." He said it was a tedious book, and if it were not attached to Addison's previous reputation, one would not think much of it. Had he written nothing else, his name would not have lived. He said, "Addison does not seem to have gone deep in Italian literature. He shows nothing of it in his subsequent writings. He shows a great deal of French learning."

Mr Johnson said, "There is perhaps more knowledge circulated in the French language than in any other. There is more original knowledge in English."

"But the French," said I, "have the art of accommodating literature."

"Sir," said he, "we have no such book as Moréri's Dictionary."

"Their *Ana*," said I, "are good."

He said few of them were; and we have one book of that kind better than any of them: Selden's *Table Talk*. "As to original literature," said he, "the French have a couple of tragic poets who go round the world, Racine and Corneille; one comic poet, Molière."

I mentioned Fénelon. "Why," said he, "*Telemachus* is pretty well."

I mentioned Voltaire. Said he, "He has not stood his trial yet. And what makes Voltaire chiefly circulate is collection – as his *Universal History*."

I mentioned the Bishop of Meaux. He said, "Nobody reads him."[792]

He would not allow Massillon and Bourdaloue to go round the world. He praised the French industry. He asked me if he had mentioned in the *Rambler* the description in Virgil of the entrance into hell, and applied it to the press. "For," said he, "I do not much remember them" (i.e., the papers in the *Rambler*).

I told him no. Upon which he repeated it.[793] "Now," said he, "almost all these apply exactly to an author. All these are about a printing-house."

I would have had him to dictate an essay on it, and I would write. He would not then, but said perhaps he would write a paper on it.

The Sunday evening that we sat by ourselves at Aberdeen, I asked him several particulars of his life from his early years, which he readily told me, and I marked down before him. This day I proceeded in my inquiries, also marking before him. I have them on separate leaves of paper. I shall lay up authentic materials for THE LIFE OF SAMUEL JOHNSON, LL.D., and if I survive him, I shall be one who shall most faithfully do honour to his memory. I have now a vast treasure of his conversation at different times since the year 1762 when I first obtained his acquaintance; and by assiduous inquiry I can make up for not knowing him sooner.[794]

Nisbet, the Newcastle man, would be in to sit a while with us. He was much in liquor, and spoke nonsense about his being a man for 'Wilkes and Liberty', and against the ministry. Mr Johnson was angry that a fellow should come into *our* company who was fit for *no* company. He left us soon.

Coll had gone up to see his aunt, and she insisted that we should come to her house that night, and horses were sent. Mr Campbell, the Duke of Argyll's factor in Tyree, came. He was a genteel agreeable man. He was going to Inveraray, and promised to put letters in the post office for us. Mr Johnson now showed that anxiety to have an opportunity to write made him so impatient to get to the mainland. We had tongue and fowls and greens to dinner about seven o'clock, and a little brandy punch, and then we set out for Dr Hector Maclean's.

Mr Johnson was mounted on a little strong Mull sheltie, and another sheltie carried the baggage. Coll and I and the servants walked. A Highlander led Mr Johnson's horse, and Coll's servant walked, holding a candle which burned till we saw the light of a candle at Dr Maclean's. It was a curious procession for about a mile.

We arrived at a strange confused house built by Mackinnon the proprietor about sixty years ago. We had been refreshed by the sight of two or three trees near the inn. We perceived several here. We were conducted through a large unfinished cold kitchen to a narrow timber stair, and then along a passage to a large bedroom with a coach roof, ornamented with some bad portraits, prints of several eminent physicians and others, and a piece of shell-work made by Miss Maclean, the Doctor's daughter. We were received by Mrs Maclean, a little brisk old woman in a bedgown with a brown wig, and Miss Maclean, a little plump elderly young lady

Thursday 14 October

in some dress which I do not recollect farther than that she had a smart beaver hat with a white feather.[795]

Dr Maclean had been above thirty years at Glasgow, so that his wife and daughter were not mere Highland ladies. We had here too Mr Angus Maclean, a third cousin of the Doctor's, a fine old gentleman of seventy-nine with little or no failure. He had been at the battle of Sheriffmuir. He was a tall comely man, a widower; had been unlucky in the world and now lived among his relations, chiefly with Dr Maclean. Mr Johnson observed when he heard his history that he had not now long to struggle with difficulties. Though dressed in a shabby kilt with shabby tartan hose, a coat and waistcoat of coarse dark brown cloth grown old, a wig too little for his head, with no curls, also aged, and a coloured handkerchief about his neck, he had the air of a gentleman. One could not but have a respect for him. Mr Johnson was taken with the appearance of the room. He cried to me, "You're not observing. This is the prettiest room we have seen since we came to the Highlands."

We had beef collops, potatoes, sowans and cream for supper. Mr Johnson took sowans and cream heartily. We had a bowl of rum punch. After supper when we were by ourselves, Mr Johnson asked me to give him paper to write letters. I begged he would write short ones and not *expatiate*, as we should set off early. He turned in bad humour; said, "What must be done, must be done; the thing is past a joke."

"Nay, sir," said I, "write as much as you please; but do not blame me if we are kept six days before we get to the mainland. You was very impatient in the morning, but no sooner do you find a good room with a few prints than you do not think of moving."

I got him paper enough, and we parted quietly.[796]

Let me bring up all with me. In the morning I said to him before we landed, "At Tobermory we shall see Dr Maclean, who has written the history of the Macleans." JOHNSON. "I have no great patience to stay to hear the history of the Macleans. I'd rather hear the history of the Thrales."

When on Mull I said, "Well, sir, this is the fourth of the Hebrides that we have been upon." JOHNSON. "Nay, we cannot boast of the number we have seen. We thought we should see many more. We thought of sailing about easily from island to island; and so we should, had we come at a better season; but we, being wise men, thought it should be summer all the year where we were. However, sir, we have seen enough to give us a pretty good notion of the system of insular life."

Coll and I had each a bed in a room at the other end of the passage.

Thursday 14 October

There was a parrot in it which Mrs Maclean had had for sixteen years. She said it could speak very well in Glasgow, but it had rusted in Mull, where the family had now been for seven years. Mr Johnson had his favourite coach-roofed room. Let me not forget that at Capt. Maclean's he read a good deal in *The Charmer*, a collection of songs.[797] I read some in it too.

When I was going to bed, Joseph perceived that the sheets were not clean. I looked at them, and was shocked at their dirtiness. I threw off only my boots and coat and waistcoat, and put on my greatcoat as a nightgown, and so lay down. The mixture of brandy punch at the inn and rum punch here, joined with the comfortless bed, made me rest very poorly.

FRIDAY 15 OCTOBER. After I had tossed long in weariness, Joseph came and called me and let in light. I would have risen, but was afraid to put my hand anywhere in the dark, for fear of spiders, or some uncleanly circumstance of sloth. I was not well at all, but I got up, sat down to my Journal, and soon was better.

Another damp to my gay prospect of advancing with celerity occurred. There was a violent storm of wind and rain. We should have been wet to the skin immediately had we set out; but it was absolutely impossible for us to get forward, because the rivers were swelled. There was no help for it. We were doomed to stay here all this day. I could hardly keep from repining indecently. Mr Johnson said, "Now that I have had an opportunity to write to the mainland, I'm in no such haste." I was amused with his being so easily satisfied; for the truth was, that the gentleman who was to convey our letters, as I was now informed, was not to set out for Inveraray for some time; so that it was probable we should be there as soon as he: however, I did not undeceive my friend, but suffered him to enjoy his fancy.

I wrote to my dear wife. It was a relief to me to think that she would hear of me, though I could not hear of her till I got to Inveraray. I also wrote to my father. I told him that, having been now for some time in countries where great attention is paid to dreams, I had been gloomy from having dreamt that I had lost him. I hoped in GOD he was well, and longed much to see him. It gives me pain to consider that there is much doubt if he has now that warm affection for me which he once had, and which I really have for him. I have now made up to him for all the uneasiness which my follies gave him. The satisfaction which I feel on his living till that was the case, is very great. I shall do my part now as well as I can; and shall never check my sincere affection for him (an affection which has much of the tenderness of a child) though he should appear cold.

At breakfast we had currant jelly, which led Coll to talk of Sir Alexander Macdonald's having treacle to breakfast as a sweetmeat, which I told him, as I was witness to it. Mr Johnson said, "We had it not at Armadale. We had nothing there but the *animated* looks of his lady. The difference between that woman when alive, and when she shall be dead, is only this. When alive she calls for beer. When dead she'll call for beer no longer."

I wrote journal a good part of the forenoon, and looked at a manuscript history of the Macleans by the Doctor, Tytler's *Queen Mary*, and the Account of Montrose's Funeral. Mr Johnson looked into the manuscript. We had a roasted turkey and some other things for dinner, by candlelight. When I spoke of having great resolution in going forward, Mr . . .[798]

Dr Johnson asked in the evening to see Dr Maclean's books. He took down Willis *De Anima Brutorum* and pored over it a good deal.

Miss Maclean produced some Erse poems by John Maclean, who was a famous bard in Mull, and had died only a few years ago. He could neither read nor write. She read and translated two of them: one, a kind of elegy on Sir John Maclean's being obliged to fly his country in 1715; another, a dialogue between two Roman Catholic young ladies, sisters, whether it was better to be a nun or to marry. I could not perceive much poetical imagery in the translation. Yet all of our company who understood Erse seemed charmed with the original. There may perhaps be some choice of expression and some excellence of arrangement that cannot be shown in translation.[799]

After we had exhausted the Erse poems, of which Dr Johnson said nothing, Miss Maclean gave us several tunes on a spinet, which, though made so long ago as in 1667, was still very well toned. She sung along with it. Dr Johnson seemed pleased with the music, though he owns he neither likes it nor has hardly any perception of it. At Mr Macpherson's, in Sleat, he told us that he knew a drum from a trumpet, and a bagpipe from a guitar, which was about the extent of his knowledge of music. Tonight he said that if he had learnt music he should have been afraid he would have done nothing else than play. It was a method of employing the mind, without the labour of thinking at all, and with some applause from a man's self.

We had the music of the bagpipe every day at Armadale, Dunvegan, and Coll. Dr Johnson appeared fond of it, and used often to stand for some time with his ear close to the great drone.[800]

The penurious gentleman of our acquaintance, formerly alluded to, afforded us a topic of conversation tonight. Dr Johnson said I ought to write down a collection of the instances of his narrowness, as they almost exceeded belief. Coll told us that O'Kane, the famous Irish harper, was once at that gentleman's house. He could not find in his heart to give him any money, but gave him a key for a harp, which was finely ornamented with gold and silver and with a precious stone, and was worth eighty or a hundred guineas. He did not know the value of it; and when he came to know it, he would fain have had it back, but O'Kane took care that he should not. JOHNSON. "They exaggerate the value; everybody is so desirous that he should be fleeced. I am very willing it should be worth eighty or a hundred guineas, but I do not believe it." BOSWELL. "I do not think O'Kane was obliged to give it back." JOHNSON. "No, sir. If a man with his eyes open, and without any means used to deceive him, gives me a thing, I am not to let him have it again when he grows wiser. I like to see how avarice defeats itself; how, when avoiding to part with money, the miser gives something more valuable."

Coll said the gentleman's relations were angry at his giving away the harp-key, for it had been long in the family. JOHNSON. "Sir, he values a new guinea more than an old friend."[801]

Coll also told us that the same person having come up with a sergeant and twenty men working on the high road, he entered into discourse with the sergeant, and then gave him sixpence for the men to drink. The sergeant asked, "Who is this fellow?" Upon being informed, he said, "If I had known who he was, I should have thrown it in his face." JOHNSON. "There is much want of sense in all this. He had no business to speak with the sergeant. He might have been in haste and trotted on. He has not learnt to be a miser; I believe we must take him apprentice." BOSWELL. "He would grudge giving half a guinea to be taught." JOHNSON. "Nay, sir, you must teach him gratis. You must give him an opportunity to practise your precepts."

Let me now go back and glean Johnsoniana. The Saturday before we sailed from Sleat, I sat awhile in the afternoon with Dr Johnson in his room, in a quiet serious frame. I observed that hardly any man was accurately prepared for dying, but almost every one left something undone, something in confusion; that my father, indeed, told me he knew one man (Carlisle of Limekilns), after whose death all his papers were found in exact order, and nothing was omitted in his will. JOHNSON. "Sir, I had an uncle who died so, but such attention requires great leisure and great firmness of mind. If one was to think constantly of death, the business of life would stand still. I am no friend to making religion appear too hard. Many good people have done harm by giving severe notions of it. In the same way as to learning: I never frighten young people with difficulties; on the contrary, I tell them that they may very easily get as much as will do very well. I do not indeed tell them that they will be Bentleys."

The night we rode to Coll's house, I said, "Lord Elibank is probably wondering what is become of us." JOHNSON. "No, no; he is not thinking of us." BOSWELL. "But recollect the warmth with which he wrote. Are we not to believe a man when he says that he has a great desire to see another? Don't you believe that I was very impatient for your coming to Scotland?" JOHNSON. "Yes, sir, I believe you was; and I was impatient to come to you. A young man feels so, but seldom an old man."

I however convinced him that Lord Elibank, who has much of the spirit of a young man, might feel so. He asked me if our jaunt had answered expectation. I said it had much exceeded it. I expected much difficulty with him, and had not found it. "And," he added, "wherever we have come, we have been received like princes in their progress."

He said he would not wish not to be disgusted in the Highlands, for that would be to lose the power of distinguishing, and a man might then lie down in the middle of them. He wished only to conceal his disgust.

At Captain Maclean's, I mentioned Pope's friend Spence. JOHNSON. "He was a weak conceited man."[802] BOSWELL. "A good scholar, sir?" JOHNSON. "Why, no, sir." BOSWELL. "He was a pretty scholar." JOHNSON. "You have about reached him."

Last night at the inn, when the factor in Tyree spoke of his having heard that a roof was put on some part of the buildings at Icolmkill, I unluckily said, "It will be fortunate if we find a cathedral with a roof on it." I said this from a foolish anxiety to engage Dr Johnson's curiosity more.

He took me short at once. "What, sir? How can you talk so? If we shall *find* a cathedral roofed! As if we were going to a *terra incognita*: when everything that is at Icolmkill is so well known. You are like some New England men who came to the mouth of the Thames. 'Come,' said they, 'let us go up and see what sort of inhabitants there are here.' They talked, sir, as if they had been to go up the Susquehanna, or any other American river."

SATURDAY 16 OCTOBER. This day there was a new moon, and the weather changed for the better. Dr Johnson said of Miss Maclean, "She is the most accomplished lady that I have found in the Highlands. She knows French, music, and drawing, sews neatly, makes shell-work, and can milk cows; in short, she can do everything. She talks sensibly, and is the first person whom I have found that can translate Erse poetry literally."

We set out, mounted on little Mull horses. Mull corresponded exactly with the idea which I had always had of it: a hilly country, diversified with heath and grass, and many rivulets. Dr Johnson was not in very good humour. He said it was a dreary country, much worse than Skye. I differed from him. "Oh, sir," said he, "a most dolorous country!"

We had a very hard journey today. I had no bridle for my sheltie, but only a halter; and Joseph rode without a saddle. At one place, a loch having swelled over the road, we were obliged to plunge through pretty deep water. Dr Johnson observed, how helpless a man would be were he travelling here alone and should meet with any accident, and said he longed to get to 'a country of saddles and bridles'. He was more out of humour today than he has been in the course of our tour, being fretted to find that his little horse could scarcely support his weight; and having suffered a loss, which, though small in itself, was of some consequence to him while travelling the rugged steeps of Mull, where he was at times obliged to walk.

The loss that I allude to was that of the large oak-stick, which, as I formerly mentioned, he had brought with him from London. It was of great use to him in our wild peregrination; for, ever since his last illness in 1766, he has had a weakness in his knees, and has not been able to walk easily. It had too the properties of a measure, for one nail was driven into it at the length of a foot, another at that of a yard. In return for the services it had done him, he said this morning he would make a present of it to some museum, but he little thought he was so soon to lose it. As he preferred riding with a switch, it was entrusted to a fellow to be delivered to our baggage-man, who followed us at some distance; but we never saw it more. I could not persuade him out of a suspicion that it had been stolen. "No, no, my friend," said he, "it is not to be expected that any man in Mull who has got it will part with it. Consider, sir, the value of such a *piece of timber* here!"

As we travelled this forenoon, we met Dr Maclean, who expressed much regret at his having been so unfortunate as to be absent while we were at his house.

We were in hopes to get to Sir Allan Maclean's at Inchkenneth tonight; but the eight miles of which our road was said to consist were so very long that we did not reach the opposite coast of Mull till seven at night,

Saturday 16 October

though we had set out about eleven in the forenoon; and when we did arrive there, we found the wind strong against us. Coll determined that we should pass the night at MacGuarie's, in the island of Ulva, which lies between Mull and Inchkenneth, and a servant was sent forward to the ferry to secure the boat for us; but the boat was gone to the Ulva side, and the wind was so high that the people could not hear him call, and the night so dark that they could not see a signal. We should have been in a very bad situation had there not fortunately been lying in the little sound of Ulva an Irish vessel, the *Bonetta*, of Londonderry, Captain McClure, master. He himself was at MacGuarie's, but his men obligingly came with their long-boat and ferried us over.

CHAPTER EIGHT

Ulva

Samuel Johnson

While we stood deliberating, we were happily espied from an *Irish* ship, that lay at anchor in the strait. The master saw that we wanted a passage, and with great civility sent us his boat, which quickly conveyed us to *Ulva*, where we were very liberally entertained by Mr *Macquarry*.

To *Ulva* we came in the dark, and left it before noon the next day. A very exact description therefore will not be expected. We were told, that it is an Island of no great extent, rough and barren, inhabited by the *Macquarrys*; a clan not powerful nor numerous, but of antiquity, which most other families are content to reverence. The name is supposed to be a depravation of some other; for the *Earse* language does not afford it any etymology.[803] *Macquarry* is proprietor both of *Ulva* and some adjacent Islands, among which is *Staffa*, so lately raised to renown by Mr *Banks*.

When the Islanders were reproached with their ignorance, or insensibility of the wonders of *Staffa*, they had not much to reply.[804] They had indeed considered it little, because they had always seen it; and none but philosophers, nor they always, are struck with wonder, otherwise than by novelty. How would it surprise an unenlightened ploughman, to hear a company of sober men, inquiring by what power the hand tosses a stone, or why the stone, when it is tossed, falls to the ground!

Of the ancestors of *Macquarry*, who thus lies hid in his unfrequented Island, I have found memorials in all places where they could be expected.[805]

Inquiring after the reliques of former manners, I found that in *Ulva*,

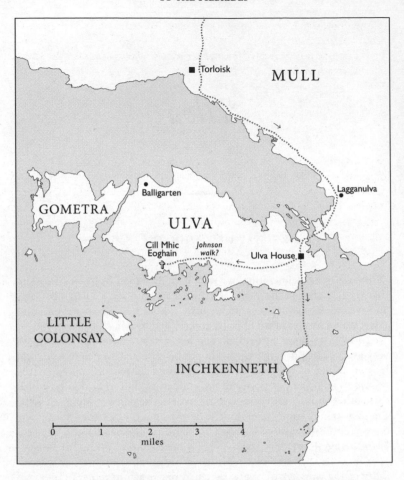

and, I think, no where else, is continued the payment of the *Mercheta Mulierum*; a fine in old times due to the Laird at the marriage of a virgin. The original of this claim, as of our tenure of *Borough English*, is variously delivered. It is pleasant to find ancient customs in old families. This payment, like others, was, for want of money, made anciently in the produce of the land. *Macquarry* was used to demand a sheep, for which he now takes a crown, by that inattention to the uncertain proportion between the value and the denomination of money, which has brought much disorder into *Europe*. A sheep has always the same power of supplying human wants, but a crown will bring at one time more, at another less.[806]

Ulva was not neglected by the piety of ancient times: it has still to show what was once a church.

JAMES BOSWELL

MacGuarie's house was mean, but we were agreeably surprised with the appearance of the master, whom we found to be intelligent, polite, and much a man of the world. Though his clan is not numerous, he is a very ancient chief, and has a burial place at Icolmkill. He told us his family had possessed Ulva for nine hundred years; but I was distressed to hear that it was soon to be sold for payment of his debts.[807]

Captain McClure, whom we found here, was of Scotch extraction, and properly a MacLeod, being descended of some of the MacLeods who went with Sir Norman of Bernera to the battle of Worcester, and after the defeat of the royalists, fled to Ireland, and, to conceal themselves, took a different name.[808] He told me there was a great number of them about Londonderry, some of good property. I said they should now resume their real name. The Laird of MacLeod should go over and assemble them, and make them all drink the large horn full, and from that time they should be MacLeods. The Captain informed us he had named his ship the *Bonetta* out of gratitude to Providence; for once, when he was sailing to America with a good number of passengers, the ship in which he then sailed was becalmed for five weeks, and during all that time, numbers of the fish bonetta swam close to her and were catched for food; he resolved therefore that the ship he should next get should be called the *Bonetta*.

MacGuarie told us a strong instance of the second sight. He had gone to Edinburgh and taken a man-servant along with him. An old woman who was in the house said one day, "MacGuarie will be at home tomorrow and will bring two gentlemen with him"; and she said she saw his servant return in red and green. He did come home next day. He had two gentlemen with him; and his servant had a new red and green livery, which MacGuarie had bought for him at Edinburgh upon a sudden thought, not having the least intention when he left home to put his servant in livery; so that the old woman could not have heard any previous mention of it. This, he assured us, was a true story.

MacGuarie insisted that the *Mercheta Mulierum*, mentioned in our old charters, did really mean the privilege which a lord of a manor or a baron had to have the first night of all his vassals' wives. Dr Johnson said the belief of such a custom having existed was also held in England, where there is a tenure called *Borough-English*, by which the eldest child does not inherit, from a doubt of his being the son of the tenant.[809] MacGuarie told us that still, on the marriage of each of his tenants, a sheep is due to him, for which the composition is fixed at five shillings. I suppose Ulva is the only place where this custom remains.

Talking of the sale of an estate of an ancient family, which was said to have been purchased much under its value by the confidential lawyer of that family, and it being mentioned that the sale would probably be set aside by a suit in equity, Dr Johnson said, "I am very willing that this sale should be set aside, but I doubt much whether the suit will be successful, for the argument for avoiding the sale is founded on vague and indeterminate principles: as that the price was too low, and that there was a great degree of confidence placed by the seller in the person who became the purchaser. Now, how low should a price be? Or what degree of confidence should there be to make a bargain be set aside? A bargain, which is a wager of skill between man and man. If, indeed, any fraud can be proved, that will do."

When Dr Johnson and I were by ourselves at night, I observed of our host, "*Aspectum generosum habet.*"

"*Et generosum animum,*" he added. For fear of being overheard in the small Highland houses, I often talked to him in such Latin as I could speak, and with as much of the English accent as I could assume, so as not to be understood in case our conversation should be too loud for the space.

We had each an elegant bed in the same room; and here it was that a circumstance occurred, as to which he has been strangely misunderstood. From his description of his chamber, it has erroneously been supposed that his bed being too short for him, his feet, during the night, were in the mire; whereas he has only said that when he undressed he felt his feet in the mire: that is, the clay floor of the room, on which he stood before he went into bed, was wet, in consequence of the windows being broken, which let in the rain.[810]

Saturday 16 October

CHAPTER NINE

Inchkenneth

SAMUEL JOHNSON

In the morning we went again into the boat, and were landed on *Inch Kenneth*, an Island about a mile long, and perhaps half a mile broad, remarkable for pleasantness and fertility. It is verdant and grassy, and fit both for pasture and tillage; but it has no trees. Its only inhabitants were Sir *Allan Maclean*, and two young ladies, his daughters, with their servants.[811]

Romance does not often exhibit a scene that strikes the imagination more than this little desert in these depths of Western obscurity, occupied not by a gross herdsman, or amphibious fisherman, but by a gentleman and two ladies, of high birth, polished manners, and elegant conversation, who, in a habitation raised not very far above the ground, but furnished with unexpected neatness and convenience, practised all the kindness of hospitality, and refinement of courtesy.

Sir *Allan* is the Chieftain of the great clan of *Maclean*, which is said to claim the second place among the Highland families, yielding only to *Macdonald*. Though by the misconduct of his ancestors, most of the extensive territory, which would have descended to him, has been alienated, he still retains much of the dignity and authority of his birth. When soldiers were lately wanting for the *American* war, application was made to Sir *Allan*, and he nominated a hundred men for the service, who obeyed the summons, and bore arms under his command.[812]

He had then, for some time, resided with the young ladies in *Inch Kenneth*, where he lives not only with plenty, but with elegance, having

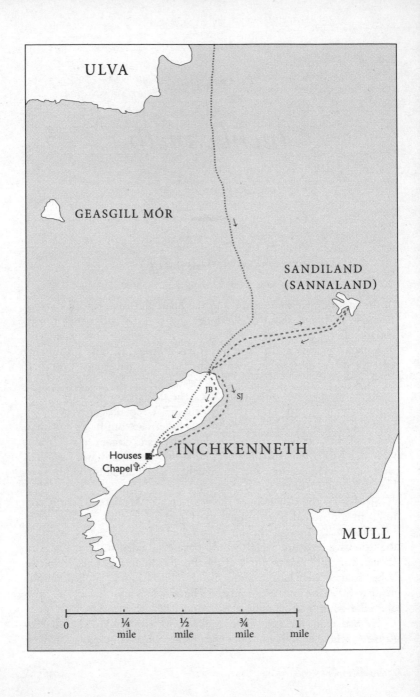

ULVA

GEASGILL MÓR

SANDILAND
(SANNALAND)

JB

SJ

INCHKENNETH

Houses
Chapel

MULL

0   ¼   ½   ¾   1
     mile   mile   mile   mile

conveyed to his cottage a collection of books, and what else is necessary to make his hours pleasant.

When we landed, we were met by Sir *Allan* and the Ladies, accompanied by Miss *Macquarry*, who had passed some time with them, and now returned to *Ulva* with her father.[813]

We all walked together to the mansion, where we found one cottage for Sir *Allan*, and I think two more for the domesticks and the offices. We entered, and wanted little that palaces afford. Our room was neatly floored, and well lighted; and our dinner, which was dressed in one of the other huts, was plentiful and delicate.

In the afternoon Sir *Allan* reminded us, that the day was Sunday, which he never suffered to pass without some religious distinction, and invited us to partake in his acts of domestick worship; which I hope neither Mr *Boswell* nor myself will be suspected of a disposition to refuse. The elder of the Ladies read the *English* service.

Inch Kenneth was once a seminary of ecclesiasticks, subordinate, I suppose, to *Icolmkill*. Sir *Allan* had a mind to trace the foundations of the college, but neither I nor Mr *Boswell*, who *bends* a keener *eye on vacancy*, were able to perceive them.[814]

Our attention, however, was sufficiently engaged by a venerable chapel, which stands yet entire, except that the roof is gone. It is about sixty feet in length, and thirty in breadth. On one side of the altar is a bas relief of the blessed Virgin, and by it lies a little bell; which, though cracked, and without a clapper, has remained there for ages, guarded only by the venerableness of the place. The ground round the chapel is covered with grave-stones of Chiefs and ladies; and still continues to be a place of sepulture.

Inch Kenneth is a proper prelude to *Icolmkill*. It was not without some mournful emotion that we contemplated the ruins of religious structures, and the monuments of the dead.

On the next day we took a more distinct view of the place, and went with the boat to see oysters in the bed, out of which the boatmen forced up as many as were wanted. Even *Inch Kenneth* has a subordinate Island, named *Sandiland*, I suppose, in contempt, where we landed, and found a rock, with a surface of perhaps four acres, of which one is naked stone, another spread with sand and shells, some of which I picked up for their glossy beauty, and two covered with a little earth and grass, on which Sir *Allan* has a few sheep. I doubt not but when there was a college at *Inch Kenneth*, there was a hermitage upon *Sandiland*.[815]

Having wandered over those extensive plains, we committed ourselves again to the winds and waters; and after a voyage of about ten minutes, in which we met with nothing very observable, were again safe upon dry ground.

We told Sir *Allan* our desire of visiting *Icolmkill*, and entreated him to give us his protection, and his company. He thought proper to hesitate a little, but the Ladies hinted, that as they knew he would not finally refuse, he would do better if he preserved the grace of ready compliance. He took their advice, and promised to carry us on the morrow in his boat.

We passed the remaining part of the day in such amusements as were in our power. Sir *Allan* related the *American* campaign, and at evening one of the Ladies played on her harpsichord, while *Col* and Mr *Boswell* danced a *Scottish* reel with the other.

We could have been easily persuaded to a longer stay upon *Inch Kenneth*, but life will not be all passed in delight. The session at *Edinburgh* was approaching, from which Mr *Boswell* could not be absent.

James Boswell

SUNDAY 17 OCTOBER. Being informed that there was nothing worthy of observation in Ulva, we took boat and proceeded to Inchkenneth, where we were introduced by our friend Coll to Sir Allan Maclean, the chief of his clan, and to two young ladies, his daughters.

Inchkenneth is a pretty little island, a mile long and about half a mile broad, all good land. As we walked up from the shore, Dr Johnson's heart was cheered by the sight of a road marked with cart-wheels, as on the mainland; a thing we had not seen for a long time. It gave us a pleasure similar to that which a traveller feels when, whilst wandering on what he fears is a desert island, he perceives the print of human feet.

Military men acquire excellent habits of having all conveniencies about them. Sir Allan Maclean, who had been long in the Army, and had now a lease of this island, had formed a commodious habitation, though it consisted but of a few small buildings, only one storey high. He had, in his little apartments, more things than I could enumerate in a page or two. Among other agreeable circumstances it was not the least to find here a parcel of the *Caledonian Mercury*, published since we left

Edinburgh, which I read with that pleasure which every man feels who has been for some time secluded from the animated scenes of the busy world.

Dr Johnson found books here. He bade me buy Bishop Gastrell's *Christian Institutes*, which was lying in the room. He said, "I do not like to read anything on a Sunday but what is theological; not that I would scrupulously refuse to look at anything which a friend should show me in a newspaper, but in general, I would read only what is theological. I read just now some of Drummond's *Travels*, before I perceived what books were here. I then took up Derham's *Physico-Theology*."

Every particular concerning this island having been so well described by Dr Johnson, it would be superfluous in me to present the public with the observations that I made upon it in my Journal. Dr Johnson here showed so much of the spirit of a Highlander that he won Sir Allan's heart; indeed, he has shown it during the whole of our tour. One night in Coll he strutted about the room with a broadsword and target, and made a formidable appearance; and another night I took the liberty to put a large blue bonnet on his head. His age, his size, and his bushy grey wig with this covering on it, presented the image of a venerable *sennachie*; and, however unfavourable to the Lowland Scots, he seemed much pleased to assume the appearance of an ancient Caledonian.

We only regretted that he could not be prevailed with to partake of the social glass. One of his arguments against drinking appears to me not convincing. He urged that in proportion as drinking makes a man different from what he is before he has drunk, it is bad, because it has so far affected his reason. But may it not be answered that a man may be altered by it *for the better*; that his spirits may be exhilarated without his reason being affected? On the general subject of drinking, however, I do not mean positively to take the other side. I am *dubius, non improbus*.

Some days earlier I had been in great indecision as to the trip to Icolmkill. Mr Johnson, however, appeared to be placidly indifferent. I had attempted to rouse him to a decision by stating the case for both sides. "Sir," said I, "if we include Icolmkill in our tour, it will take us a week to go to it, and we may perhaps not be able to get to Auchinleck before the Session, which would be losing something more valuable to me – seeing you upon our old castle. But, on the other hand, I have always had Icolmkill as a capital object in my mind, since we first talked of visiting the Hebrides. We should think our tour imperfect, and have a regret, if we did not see it. I may go at another time, but then I should not see it with you. Come, what do you say?" JOHNSON. "Sir, you have put it very well on both sides. I can only say, '*Non nostrum est tantas componere lites.*'"[816]

"But," said I, "give your opinion. Be my council. I shall be king, and determine after I have heard you."

He said, "Do as you will."

This day what had appeared so difficult and dubious seemed easy and clear. Sir Allan said if the weather was good he would conduct us by sea, if bad, by land; that was to say, he would either take us all the way by sea, or cross over to Mull, ride along to the Point of Ross, and from thence cross over to Iona. MacGuarie made a kind of promise of coming with his boat and going with us, but Sir Allan was the man on whom we depended.

I was quite easy with Sir Allan almost instantaneously. He knew the great intimacy that had been between my father and his predecessor, Sir Hector, and I suppose knew my character. He was himself of a very frank disposition. He talked with a strange unaccountable sort of hesitation whether he was to go with us or not; though he observed at the same time that we should be very ill off without him. Said I, "Is it not curious to hear him express uncertainty, when he knows it is certain he is to go with us? You had better do it with a good grace."[817]

I love little peculiar circumstances about any place. When I mentioned the track of cart-wheels, I should have marked that one of the young ladies had been overturned on the road a day or two before. It seems they rode in a cart, as the only carriage that they could get to take an airing in. Mr Johnson marked in his journal that in the islands they call a gentleman's boat his *carriage*. He did this because Mr Donald Macqueen, in his card to me, called Raasay's boat so; but upon inquiry I found that it was not a common mode of speech, and set Mr Johnson right. It was just a *conceit* of Mr Macqueen's, and Mr Johnson took it to be a general phrase. Thus it is that travellers generalize both as to phrases and customs.

Sir Allan said he had got Dr Campbell about a hundred subscribers to his *Britannia Elucidata*, of whom he believed twenty were dead.[818] Mr Johnson said he believed the delay of publication was owing to this: that after publication there would be no more subscribers, and few would send the additional guinea to get their books; in which they would be wrong, for there would be a great deal of instruction in the book. He said he thought highly of Campbell. "In the first place, he has very good parts. In the second place, he has very extensive reading; not, perhaps, what is properly called learning, but history, politics, and in short that popular knowledge which makes a man very useful. In the third place, he has learnt much by what is called the *vox viva*. He talks with a great many people."

Mr Johnson told us at Raasay a good story of Dr Campbell and him. He called on Dr Campbell, and they talked of Tull's *Husbandry*. Dr Campbell said something. Mr Johnson began to dispute it. "Come," said Dr Campbell, "we do not want to get the better of one another. We want to increase each other's ideas." Mr Johnson took it in good part, and the conversation then went on coolly and instructively. His candour in relating this anecdote does him much credit, and his conduct on that occasion proves how easily he could be persuaded to talk from a better motive than 'for victory'.

I was agreeably disappointed in Sir Allan. I had heard of him only as an officer in Lord Eglinton's Highland regiment, and as a great companion of the Earl's, so I apprehended that I should find a riotous bottle companion and be pressed to drink; in place of which, the Knight was as sober after dinner as I could wish, and let me do as I pleased. And what surprised me still more agreeably, though he swore, as Dr Campbell does, he was a man of religion like Dr Campbell. He said he always made his daughters read prayers every Sunday evening, as he thought it of great consequence that they should keep in mind their duty to GOD. He spoke warmly in favour of the Episcopal Church – said that his father had a chaplain of the Church of England, and that the people chose to attend worship with him rather than go to the Presbyterian kirk. Mr Johnson said they would all do so in the isles if they had an opportunity. Sir Allan agreed they would; and he said if he prevailed in his cause, he would build several chapels.

We had our tea comfortably; and at night prayer-books were brought. Miss Maclean read the evening service with a beautiful decency. We read the responses and other parts that congregations read. When she came to the prayer for the royal family, she stopped. I bid her go to the prayer for the clergy. She did so. Mr Johnson pointed out to her some prayers, which she read. After all, she and her sister sung the Hymn on the Nativity of our Saviour.

It was the 19th Sunday after Trinity. I shall ever remember it. Mr Johnson said it was the most agreeable Sunday evening that he had ever passed in his life; and it made such an impression on his mind, that he afterwards wrote the following Latin verses upon Inchkenneth:

Sunday 17 October

Insula Sancti Kennethi

Parva quidem regio, sed relligione priorum
  Nota, Caledonias panditur inter aquas;
Voce ubi Cennethus populos domuisse foroces
  Dicitur, et vanos dedocuisse deos.
Huc ego delatus placido per cærula cursu
  Scire locum volui quid daret ille novi.
Illic Leniades humili regnabat in aula,
  Leniades magnis nobilitatus avis:
Una duas habuit casa cum genitore puellas,
  Quas Amor undarum fingeret esse deas:
Non tamen inculti gelidis latuere sub antris,
  Accola Danubii qualia sævus habet;
Mollia non deerant vacuæ solatia vitæ,
  Sive libros poscant otia, sive lyram.
Luxerat illa dies, legis gens docta supernæ
  Spes hominum ac curas cum procul esse jubet,
Ponti inter strepitus sacri non munera cultus
  Cessarunt; pietas hic quoque cura fuit:
Quid quod sacrifici versavit femina libros,
  Legitimas faciunt pectora pura preces.
Quo vagor ulterius? quod ubique requiritur hic est;
  Hic secura quies, hic et honestus amor.[819]

We were all in a good frame. I was truly pious. I walked out in the dark to the cross, knelt before it, and holding it with both my hands, I prayed with strong devotion, while I had before me the image of that on which my Saviour died for the sins of the world. The sanctity of venerable Columbus filled my imagination. I considered that to ask the intercession of a departed saint was at least innocent, and might be of service. I indulged my inclination to what is called superstitious prayer. I said, "*Sancte Columbe, ora pro me.* O Columbus, thou venerable Saint, as we have all the reason that can be to believe that thou art in heaven, I beseech thee to pray GOD that I may attain to everlasting felicity."

I cannot be sure of the exact words (I am now writing at Glasgow, October 28). But what I said was to the above purpose. I felt a kind of pleasing awful confusion. I was for going into the chapel; but a tremor seized me for ghosts, and I hastened back to the house. It was exceedingly dark, and in my timorous hurry I stepped suddenly into a hollow place, and strained a sinew on my right foot. It was painful a while; but rubbing it with rum and vinegar cured it by next day at breakfast.[820]

I should have mentioned that after prayers I read to the company Dr Ogden's 2d and 9th Sermons on prayer, which, with their other distinguished excellence, have the merit of being short. I promised to send a copy of them to Miss Maclean.

Sir Allan had made an apology at dinner that he had neither red wine nor biscuits, but that he expected both. Luckily the boat arrived with them this very afternoon. We had a couple of bottles of port and hard biscuits at night, after some roasted potatoes, which is Sir Allan's simple fare by way of supper.

Sir Allan and Coll had each a bed in the room where I dressed. Mr Johnson and I had each one in the room where we passed the day. Mine was the camp-bed of the Hon. Roger Townshend, who was killed in America, and whose monument is in Westminster Abbey. Sir Allan's camp equipage was destroyed by a bomb. General Amherst desired him to take Colonel Townshend's, as he had been intimate with him, and settle as to the value of it with Lord Townshend, when he went to England. Sir Allan, when in London, begged my lord to accept of a £100 bank bill, but my lord would by no means have anything. There was something curious in sleeping in a camp-bed which had actually been in service in America. My old soldierly inclinations revived.

MONDAY 18 OCTOBER. We had agreed to pass this day with Sir Allan; and he engaged to have everything in order for our journey tomorrow. Before breakfast, I repaired to the chapel, knelt at the ruined altar, and prayed in a pleasing holy frame, 'with sense of gratitude and joy', as Parnell says. I thought I had so steady, so certain a prospect of celestial felicity that I should never again be vicious and could die with perfect peace. LORD, grant that when the period of my dissolution arrives, I may be in the same state! "Thou wilt keep him in perfect peace, whose mind is stayed on thee," etc.[821]

The night we were at Ulva, I told how Coll prescribed to me to have my feet washed and take a warm drink immediately, by which the cold which I contracted by being wet lasted only a quarter of an hour. Said Mr Johnson, "Coll does everything for us. We'll erect a statue to Coll."

"Yes," said I, "and we'll have him with his various attributes and characters, like Mercury or any other of the heathen gods. We'll have him as a pilot. We'll have him as a physician – and so on."

I this morning got a spade and dug a little grave in the floor of the chapel, in which I carefully buried what loose bones were there. I said, "Rest in peace, so far as I can contribute to it." I said I hoped somebody would do as much for me. JOHNSON. "Well said." He praised me for what I had done, though he said he would not do it. He showed, in the chapel at Raasay, his horror at dead men's bones. He showed it again at Coll's house. In the charter-room there was a remarkably large shin-bone of a man, which was said to have been a bone of John Garve, one of the lairds. The present Coll, with a strange unnaturality, took it home from the family burial-place, and now it is just a show, which is using an ancestor oddly.[822] I desired young Coll to have it put back to its place. Mr Johnson would not look at it, but started away from us. I lifted the bones today with my bare hands quite easily, conscious that I was doing a kind of pious office.

At breakfast I asked, "What is the reason that we are angry at a trader's having opulence?"

"Why, sir," said Mr Johnson, "the reason is (though I don't undertake to prove that there is a reason), we see no qualities in trade that should entitle a man to superiority. We are not angry at a soldier's getting riches, because we see that he possesses qualities which we have not. If a man returns from a battle, having lost one hand and with the other full of gold, we feel that he deserves the gold; but we cannot think that a fellow, by sitting all day at a desk, is entitled to get above us."

"But," said I, "may we not suppose a merchant to be a man of an enlarged mind, as Addison in the *Spectator* makes Sir Andrew Freeport?" JOHNSON. "Why, sir, we may suppose any fictitious character. We may suppose a philosophical day-labourer, who is happy in reflecting that by his labour he contributed to the fertility of the earth and to the support of his fellow-creatures; but we find no such philosophical day-labourer. A merchant may, perhaps, be a man of an enlarged mind; but there is nothing in trade connected with an enlarged mind."

I was very much taken with Inchkenneth. I said I was resolved to have it for an elegant retreat for our family during a month or two in summer. Sir Allan said, if he recovered it from the Duke of Argyll, I should have it on my own terms. I really indulged serious thoughts of buying it. My brother David always talked of purchasing an island. "Sir," said Mr Johnson, "so does almost every man, till he knows what it is."

Sir Allan and he and I walked awhile on the shore under the houses. We looked at a cave or cleft or recess of a rock, in which Sir Allan keeps his peats dry. We looked at a bed of oysters, which I had never seen anywhere before. I took up one, broke it between two stones, and eat it, by way of having a proof how I could live if I were thrown upon a coast where I could get only raw shell-fish; and I thought I could do. Mr

Johnson and I were also occupied in gathering little yellow shells like a more elegant species of whelks. Mr Johnson gathered for little Miss Thrale, I for my father.

I mentioned that I had heard Solander say he was a Swedish Laplander. JOHNSON. "Sir, I don't believe he's a Laplander. The Laplanders are not much above five feet high. He is as tall as you; and he has not the copper colour of a Laplander." BOSWELL. "But what motive could he have to make himself a Laplander?" JOHNSON. "Why, sir, he must either mean the word Laplander in a very extensive sense; or may mean a voluntary degradation of himself: 'For all my being the great man that you see me now, I was originally a barbarian'; as if Burke should say, 'I came over a wild Irishman,' which he might say in his present state of exaltation."

Coll and his dogs and Joseph were busy seeking for otters, of which this island has many. Sir Allan, Mr Johnson and I sailed in a little boat with two oars to a small island called Sannaland or Sandyland, very near Inchkenneth, in order to be on another isle, and to look for more shells. We found a great many of the small yellow whelks, and a good many small silver buckies, of which there are some on the coast of Inchkenneth. Mr Johnson lay down and gathered, as he is short-sighted. Sannaland is a small spot. It has, as Mr Johnson said, three parts: sand, rock, and rock covered with a little earth and grass upon it. It feeds a riding horse in summer. It is an appendage to Inchkenneth, so I am to have it; and I am also to have a right of game over all Sir Allan's lands in Mull. In summer I can have goats for milk, as there is a variety of fine herbage upon it. It is a kind of objection to Inchkenneth that sometimes the sea between it and Mull is at one place so shallow that people may wade over. This breaks the natural security of being surrounded by the sea. But it is a very rare thing to have so shallow a sea; and even then there are none can pass but people particularly well-acquainted with the place, as there are quicksands. I can have a battery of cannon on that quarter.

Mr Johnson said I should build me a fortification, if I came to live on Inchkenneth. "For," said he, "if you have it not, what should hinder a parcel of ruffians to land in the night and carry off what things you have in the house, which in a remote country would be more valuable than some of your cows and sheep; and this besides the danger of having your throat cut." I said I would have a large dog. "So you may," said he. "But a large dog is of no use but to alarm."

He however, I apprehend, thinks too lightly of the power of that animal. I have heard him say he would be afraid of no dog. He would take him up by the hinder legs, which would render him quite helpless, and then knock his head against a stone and beat out his brains. Beauclerk told me that at his house in the country two large dogs were fighting. Mr Johnson looked steadily at them for a little, and then, as one would separate two little boys who are foolishly hurting each other, he ran up to them and cuffed their heads till he had them asunder from one another. But few men have his intrepidity, Herculean strength, or contrivance. Most thieves or robbers would be afraid to encounter a mastiff.

Mr Johnson takes a kind of pleasure in laughing at his friends in trifles. There was a mere black barren rock in our view today as we sailed. He called to me, "This shall be your island, and it shall be called Inch Boswell." And then he laughed, with a strange appearance of triumph.

Coll was busy digging for rabbits after he could not find otters, being desirous to have rabbits in his lands of Quinish in Mull. I say *his* lands; for he always says 'my', and not 'my father's' lands; and indeed the old gentleman gives him full scope. There has been a custom in this family that the laird resigns the estate to his eldest son when he comes of age, reserving to himself only a certain life-rent. So young Coll told me. He said it was a voluntary custom. But I think I found an instance in the charter-room that there was such a resignation in consequence of a contract of marriage.[823] I must get a copy of the clause, as I neglected to attend to it exactly. If the custom was voluntary, it was only curious; but if by any obligation, it was dangerous; for Banks told me that in Otaheite, whenever a child is born (a son, I think) the father loses his right to the estate and honours, and this unnatural, or rather absurd, custom – as property is not natural either in one way or another – occasions the murder of many children.

Young Coll told us he could run down a greyhound. "For," said he, "the dog runs himself out of breath by going too quick, and then I get up with him and beat him at speed."

Mr Johnson observed that *I* explained the cause of this, by remarking that Coll had reason, and knew to moderate his pace, which the dog had not sense to know. Indeed, Coll is not a philosopher. Mr Johnson said, "He is a noble animal. He is as complete an islander as mortality can figure. He is a farmer, a sailor, a hunter, a fisher; he will run you down a dog. If any man has a tail, it is Coll. He is hospitable; and he has an intrepidity of talk, whether he understands the subject or not. I regret that he is not more intellectual."[824]

Mr Johnson observed that there was nothing of which he would not undertake to persuade a Frenchman in a foreign country. Said he, "I'll carry a Frenchman to St Paul's Churchyard, and I'll tell him, 'Sir, by our law you may walk half round the church, but if you walk round the whole, you will be punished capitally.' And he'll believe me at once. Now, no Englishman would readily swallow such a thing. He'd go and inquire at somebody else."

I said the Frenchman's credulity must be owing to his being accustomed to implicit submission; whereas every Englishman reasons upon the laws of his country, and instructs his representatives who compose the legislature.

Mr Johnson sailed near to the house to avoid walking. Sir Allan and I took a walk. I went to the beach where we landed yesterday, and looked for transparent white stones, but found hardly any pure ones. The gloss of being wet makes them all look transparent. Gathering pebbles is a gentle, pleasing amusement. I thought a pretty poem might be made upon it. We dined cheerfully and drank tea, after which Miss Maclean played several tunes on the harpsichord very well. I proposed a reel; so Miss Sibby and Coll and I danced, while Miss Maclean played, which was making the most of it.

As I have formerly observed, my exertions as a dancer are all forced by a reflex desire to promote lively good humour.

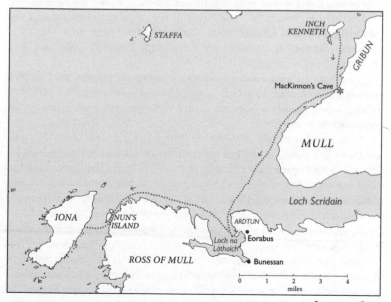

Journey to Iona

Iona

———————

SAMUEL JOHNSON

In the morning our boat was ready: it was high and strong. Sir *Allan* victualled it for the day, and provided able rowers. We now parted from the young Laird of *Col*, who had treated us with so much kindness, and concluded his favours by consigning us to Sir *Allan*. Here we had the last embrace of this amiable man, who, while these pages were preparing to attest his virtues, perished in the passage between *Ulva* and *Inch Kenneth*.[825]

Sir *Allan*, to whom the whole region was well known, told us of a very remarkable cave, to which he would show us the way. We had been disappointed already by one cave, and were not much elevated by the expectation of another.[826]

It was yet better to see it, and we stopped at some rocks on the coast of *Mull*. The mouth is fortified by vast fragments of stone, over which we made our way, neither very nimbly, nor very securely. The place, however, well repaid our trouble. The bottom, as far as the flood rushes in, was encumbered with large pebbles, but as we advanced was spread over with smooth sand. The breadth is about forty-five feet: the roof rises in an arch, almost regular, to a height which we could not measure; but I think it about thirty feet.

This part of our curiosity was nearly frustrated; for though we went to see a cave, and knew that caves are dark, we forgot to carry tapers, and did not discover our omission till we were wakened by our wants. Sir *Allan* then sent one of the boatmen into the country, who soon returned with one little candle. We were thus enabled to go forward, but could not venture far. Having passed inward from the sea to a great depth, we found on the right hand a narrow passage, perhaps not more than six feet wide, obstructed by great stones, over which we climbed and came into a second cave, in breadth twenty-five feet. The air in this apartment was very warm, but not oppressive, nor loaded with vapours. Our light showed no tokens of a feculent or corrupted atmosphere. Here was a square stone, called, as we are told, *Fingal's Table*.

If we had been provided with torches, we should have proceeded in our search, though we had already gone as far as any former adventurer, except some who are reported never to have returned; and, measuring our way back, we found it more than a hundred and sixty yards, the eleventh part of a mile.[827]

Our measures were not critically exact, having been made with a walking pole, such as it is convenient to carry in these rocky countries, of which I guessed the length by standing against it. In this there could be no great errour, nor do I much doubt but the Highlander, whom we employed, reported the number right. More nicety however is better, and no man should travel unprovided with instruments for taking heights and distances.

There is yet another cause of errour not always easily surmounted, though more dangerous to the veracity of itinerary narratives, than imperfect mensuration. An observer deeply impressed by any remarkable spectacle, does not suppose, that the traces will soon vanish from his mind, and having commonly no great convenience for writing, defers the description to a time of more leisure, and better accommodation.

He who has not made the experiment, or who is not accustomed to require rigorous accuracy from himself, will scarcely believe how much a few hours take from certainty of knowledge, and distinctness of imagery; how the succession of objects will be broken, how separate parts will be confused, and how many particular features and discriminations will be compressed and conglobated into one gross and general idea.

To this dilatory notation must be imputed the false relations of travellers, where there is no imaginable motive to deceive. They trusted to memory, what cannot be trusted safely but to the eye, and told by guess what a few hours before they had known with certainty. Thus it was that *Wheeler* and *Spon* described with irreconcilable contrariety things which they surveyed together, and which both undoubtedly designed to show as they saw them.[828]

When we had satisfied our curiosity in the cave, so far as our penury of light permitted us, we clambered again to our boat, and proceeded along the coast of *Mull* to a headland, called *Atun*, remarkable for the columnar form of the rocks, which rise in a series of pilasters, with a degree of regularity, which Sir *Allan* thinks not less worthy of curiosity than the shore of *Staffa*.

Not long after we came to another range of black rocks, which had the appearance of broken pilasters, set one behind another to a great depth. This place was chosen by Sir *Allan* for our dinner. We were easily accommodated with seats, for the stones were of all heights, and refreshed ourselves and our boatmen, who could have no other rest till we were at *Icolmkill*.[829]

The evening was now approaching, and we were yet at a considerable distance from the end of our expedition. We could therefore stop no more to make remarks in the way, but set forward with some degree of eagerness. The day soon failed us, and the moon presented a very solemn and pleasing scene. The sky was clear, so that the eye commanded a wide circle: the sea was neither still nor turbulent: the wind neither silent nor loud. We were never far from one coast or another, on which, if the weather had become violent, we could have found shelter, and therefore contemplated at ease the region through which we glided in the tranquillity of the night, and saw now a rock and now an island grow gradually conspicuous and gradually obscure. I committed the fault which I have just been censuring, in neglecting, as we passed, to note the series of this placid navigation.

We were very near an Island, called *Nun's Island*, perhaps from an ancient convent. Here is said to have been dug the stone that was used in the buildings of *Icolmkill*. Whether it is now inhabited we could not stay to inquire.

At last we came to *Icolmkill*, but found no convenience for landing. Our boat could not be forced very near the dry ground, and our Highlanders carried us over the water.[830]

We were now treading that illustrious Island, which was once the luminary of the *Caledonian* regions, whence savage clans and roving barbarians derived the benefits of knowledge, and the blessings of religion. To abstract the mind from all local emotion would be impossible, if it were endeavoured, and would be foolish, if it were possible. Whatever withdraws us from the power of our senses; whatever makes the past, the distant, or the future predominate over the present, advances us in the dignity of thinking beings. Far from me and from my friends, be such frigid philosophy as may conduct us indifferent and unmoved over any ground which has been dignified by wisdom, bravery, or virtue. That man is little to be envied, whose patriotism would not gain force upon the plain of *Marathon*, or whose piety would not grow warmer among the ruins of *Iona*!

We came too late to visit monuments: some care was necessary for ourselves. Whatever was in the Island, Sir *Allan* could command, for the inhabitants were *Macleans*; but having little they could not give us much. He went to the headman of the Island, whom Fame, but Fame delights in amplifying, represents as worth no less than fifty pounds.[831] He was perhaps proud enough of his guests, but ill prepared for our entertainment; however, he soon produced more provision than men not luxurious require. Our lodging was next to be provided. We found a barn well stocked with hay, and made our beds as soft as we could.

In the morning we rose and surveyed the place. The churches of the two convents are both standing, though unroofed. They were built of unhewn stone, but solid, and not inelegant. I brought away rude measures of the buildings, such as I cannot much trust myself, inaccurately taken, and obscurely noted. Mr *Pennant's* delineations, which are doubtless exact, have made my unskilful description less necessary.

The episcopal church consists of two parts, separated by the belfry, and built at different times. The original church had, like others, the altar at one end, and tower at the other; but as it grew too small, another building of equal dimension was added, and the tower then was necessarily in the middle.

That these edifices are of different ages seems evident. The arch of the first church is *Roman*, being part of a circle; that of the additional building is pointed, and therefore *Gothick*, or *Saracenical*; the tower is firm, and wants only to be floored and covered.

Of the chambers or cells belonging to the monks, there are some walls remaining, but nothing approaching to a complete apartment.[832]

The bottom of the church is so incumbered with mud and rubbish, that we could make no discoveries of curious inscriptions, and what there are have been already published. The place is said to be known where the black stones lie concealed, on which the old Highland Chiefs, when they made contracts and alliances, used to take the oath, which was considered as more sacred than any other obligation, and which could not be violated without the blackest infamy. In those days of violence and rapine, it was of great importance to impress upon savage minds the sanctity of an oath, by some particular and extraordinary circumstances. They would not have recourse to the black stones, upon small or common occasions,

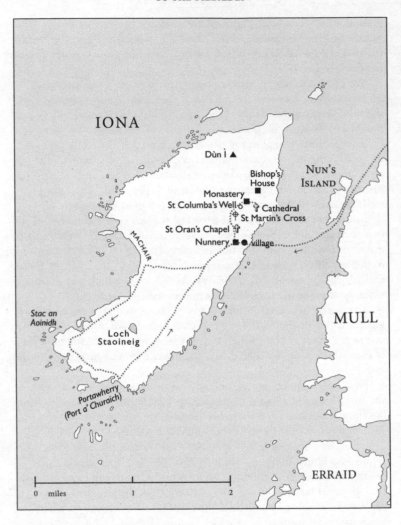

and when they had established their faith by this tremendous sanction, inconstancy and treachery were no longer feared.[833]

The chapel of the nunnery is now used by the inhabitants as a kind of general cow-house, and the bottom is consequently too miry for examination. Some of the stones which covered the later abbesses have inscriptions, which might yet be read, if the chapel were cleansed. The roof of this, as of all the other buildings, is totally destroyed, not only because timber quickly decays when it is neglected, but because in an island utterly destitute of wood, it was wanted for use, and was consequently the first plunder of needy rapacity.

The chancel of the nuns' chapel is covered with an arch of stone, to which time has done no injury; and a small apartment communicating with the choir, on the north side, like the chapterhouse in cathedrals, roofed with stone in the same manner, is likewise entire.

In one of the churches was a marble altar, which the superstition of the inhabitants has destroyed. Their opinion was, that a fragment of this stone was a defence against shipwrecks, fire, and miscarriages. In one corner of the church the bason for holy water is yet unbroken.[834]

The cemetery of the nunnery was, till very lately, regarded with such reverence, that only women were buried in it. These reliques of veneration always produce some mournful pleasure. I could have forgiven a great injury more easily than the violation of this imaginary sanctity.

South of the chapel stand the walls of a large room, which was probably the hall, or refectory of the nunnery. This apartment is capable of repair. Of the rest of the convent there are only fragments.

Besides the two principal churches, there are, I think, five chapels yet standing, and three more remembered. There are also crosses, of which two bear the names of St *John* and St *Matthew*.[835]

A large space of ground about these consecrated edifices is covered with grave-stones, few of which have any inscription. He that surveys it, attended by an insular antiquary, may be told where the Kings of many nations are buried, and if he loves to sooth his imagination with the thoughts that naturally rise in places where the great and powerful lie mingled with the dust, let him listen in submissive silence; for if he asks any questions, his delight is at an end.

Iona has long enjoyed, without any very credible attestation, the honour of being reputed the cemetery of the *Scottish* Kings. It is not unlikely, that, when the opinion of local sanctity was prevalent, the Chieftains of the Isles, and perhaps some of the *Norwegian* or *Irish* princes were reposited in this venerable enclosure. But by whom the subterraneous vaults are peopled is now utterly unknown. The graves are very numerous, and some of them undoubtedly contain the remains of men, who did not expect to be so soon forgotten.

Not far from this awful ground, may be traced the garden of the monastery: the fishponds are yet discernible, and the aqueduct, which supplied them, is still in use.[836]

There remains a broken building, which is called the Bishop's house, I know not by what authority. It was once the residence of some man above the common rank, for it has two stories and a chimney. We were shewn a chimney at the other end, which was only a nich, without perforation, but so much does antiquarian credulity, or patriotick vanity prevail, that it was not much more safe to trust the eye of our instructor than the memory.[837]

There is in the Island one house more, and only one, that has a chimney: we entered it, and found it neither wanting repair nor inhabitants; but to the farmers, who now possess it, the chimney is of no great value; for their fire was made on the floor, in the middle of the room, and notwithstanding the dignity of their mansion, they rejoiced, like their neighbours, in the comforts of smoke.

It is observed, that ecclesiastical colleges are always in the most pleasant and fruitful places. While the world allowed the monks their choice, it is surely no dishonour that they chose well. This Island is remarkably fruitful. The village near the churches is said to contain seventy families, which, at five in a family, is more than a hundred inhabitants to a mile. There are perhaps other villages; yet both corn and cattle are annually exported.

But the fruitfulness of *Iona* is now its whole prosperity. The inhabitants are remarkably gross, and remarkably neglected: I know not if they are visited by any Minister. The Island, which was once the metropolis of learning and piety, has now no school for education, nor temple for worship, only two inhabitants that can speak *English*, and not one that can write or read.[838]

The people are of the clan of *Maclean*; and though Sir *Allan* had not been in the place for many years, he was received with all the reverence due to their Chieftain. One of them being sharply reprehended by him, for not sending him some rum, declared after his departure, in Mr *Boswell's* presence, that he had no design of disappointing him, *for*, said he, *I would cut my bones for him; and if he had sent his dog for it, he should have had it.*[839]

When we were to depart, our boat was left by the ebb at a great distance from the water, but no sooner did we wish it afloat, than the islanders gathered round it, and, by the union of many hands, pushed it down the beach; every man who could contribute his help seemed to think himself happy in the opportunity of being, for a moment, useful to his Chief.

We now left those illustrious ruins, by which Mr *Boswell* was much affected, nor would I willingly be thought to have looked upon them without some emotion. Perhaps, in the revolutions of the world, *Iona* may be sometime again the instructress of the Western Regions.

JAMES BOSWELL

TUESDAY 19 OCTOBER. It was this day, and not yesterday, that I buried the bones. The day was charming for a voyage to Icolmkill. When I went out, I met Miss Maclean, who said, "I have been employed for you this morning. I have been scrambling among the rocks to get petrifications for you."

She gave me a few, but none of them were curious. I once more paid my devotions to GOD in the old chapel.

After breakfast we took leave of the young ladies, and of our excellent companion Coll, to whom we had been so much obliged. He had now put us under the care of his chief, and was to hasten back to Skye. There was a kindly regret at parting with him which was both proper and pleasing. He had been a kind of banker to me, in supplying me with silver. There remained six-and-sixpence due by me to him on settling our accounts today. He desired that I should purchase with it a cap to Joseph's young son. A small circumstance shows benevolence. He and Joseph had been often companions.[840]

Sir Allan had a good boat with four stout rowers. One of them, Lauchlan Dow ———, was a remarkably strong and clever fellow, either at sea or at land.[841] All of them, and he in particular, took a great liking for me before we parted, as Sir Allan told me by interpretation. We coasted along Mull till we reached Gribon, where is what is called Mackinnon's Cave, an *antrum immane* indeed, to which the one at Ullinish is nothing. It is in a rock of a great highth just upon the sea. Upon the left of its entrance there is a cascade, almost perpendicular from top to bottom of the rock, of no great size, but very pretty. There is a tradition that it was conducted thither artificially, to supply the inhabitants of the cave with water. Mr Johnson gave no credit to this tradition. As his faith in the Christian religion is firm upon good grounds, he is incredulous when there is no sufficient reason for belief, being in this just the reverse of modern infidels, who, however nice and scrupulous in weighing the evidences of religion, are yet often so ready to believe the most absurd and

Tuesday 19 October

improbable tales of another nature, that Lord Hailes said that somebody should write an "*Essai sur la crédulité des incrédules.*"[842]

The highth of this cave I cannot tell with any tolerable exactness, but it seemed to be very lofty, and to be a pretty regular arch. After advancing a little, we found it to be forty-five feet broad. Afterwards we found a passage or gallery about four or five feet broad – for we did not measure it. Then we came to a place fifteen feet broad. There we found a large stone table lying on the floor. Sir Allan said it had stood on supporters or pillars, and we saw some broken stones near it, but Mr Johnson was of opinion that machinery sufficient to raise it could not be erected in the cave; so that there was a mistake as to the pillars. Sir Allan said there were stone benches, too, around the table. I think I saw some stones which may be called such. Where the table is, the floor of the cave is a good deal elevated above the floor of the entrance, by gradual progression. The floor is sometimes of loose pebbles; sometimes of a fine dry sand; sometimes embarrassed with large stones, I suppose fragments of the rock. As we advanced, the arch of the roof became less regular, the rock filling up a considerable part of the space on the left, but so as a man could clamber up it. A yard or two beyond the table, we found another heap of fragments, beyond which I could perceive that I might go; but as we had but one candle with us, to be a proof when the air should grow bad, and to give us light, we did not choose to risk its going out. Tradition says that a piper and twelve men advanced into the cave, nobody knows how far, but never returned. At the heap to which we went, which was 485 feet from the entrance of the cave, the air was quite good, for the candle burnt freely without the least appearance of the flame's growing globular; and there was as much light from the large mouth, though distant, as that a man would not find himself quite in a dismal state, and would find his way out tolerably well. Mr Johnson said this was the greatest natural curiosity he had ever seen.

We saw the Island of Staffa, at no very great distance, but could not land upon it, the surge was so high on its rocky coast. We sailed close to a point called Ardtun, on the Mull coast, where we saw a miniature specimen of the Giant's Causeway, and some of the same kind of natural pilasters on rock as are described to be at Staffa. Sir Allan said people who had seen both were of opinion that the appearances at Ardtun were better than those at Staffa; prettier or finer, he said. If so, there must have been wondrous puffing about Staffa. He said if we had seen it, we should have had a controversy.

Sir Allan, anxious for the honour of Mull, was always talking of *woods* that he said were upon the hills of that island, which appeared at a distance as we sailed along. Said Mr Johnson, "I saw at Tobermory what they called a wood, which I unluckily took for *heath*. If you show me what I shall take for *furze*, it will be something."

Our rowers sung Erse songs, or rather howls. Sir Allan said the Indians in America sung in the same manner when rowing. We passed by the mouth of a large basin, arm of the sea, or loch, called Loch Scridain, upon the shore of which Mr Neil MacLeod, minister of Kilfinichen, lives. I had a letter to him from Kenneth Macaulay; and he was the best man we could get to show us Icolmkill with knowledge. But we were not sure of finding him at home, and thought it at any rate imprudent to go out of our way much, as we might lose a good day, which was very valuable. I however insisted that we should land upon the shore of Loch ———, which we came to a little after, but which, not being very far back into the country, cost us but a little deviation. My reason for insisting to land was to get some whisky or rum for our boatmen. The fellows were rather for pushing straight for Iona. But I could not be easy unless they had a *scalck*. Besides, the nearest public house was kept by Lauchlan Maclean, lately servant to Sir Allan; and we proposed to take him with us both as an additional rower and as quartermaster at Icolmkill, for which he was well fitted, having been with Sir Allan not only in the best parts of Scotland, but in many parts of England.[843]

Sir Allan, like all other officers, who, though by their profession obliged to endure fatigues and inconveniencies, are peculiarly luxurious, expatiated in prospect on the expertness with which Lauchlan would get on a good fire in a snug barn, and get us clean straw for beds, and dress us, along with Joseph, an Austrian campaigner, a tolerable supper. I take it the suffering, or at least the contemplating of hardships, to which officers are accustomed (for from Sir Allan's account even of the American expeditions, it appeared that though the poor common soldiers are often wretchedly off, the officers suffer little, having their commodious camp equipage, and their chocolate, and other comforts carried along in little room, and prepared by their men, who are most subservient beings), makes them fonder of all indulgences.

We went ashore upon a little rising ground, which is an island at high water. We sat down upon a seat of rock, and took a repast of cold mutton, bread and cheese and apples, and punch. Lauchlan Dow in the mean time ran to Lauchlan Maclean's house. When he returned with Lauchlan Maclean, we had the disappointment of finding that no spirits of any kind were to be found. A burial some days before had exhausted them.

Tuesday 19 October

Mr Campbell of ———,[844] a tacksman of the Duke of Argyll's, lived not far off. Sir Allan sent the two Lauchlans thither, begging the loan of two bottles of rum. We got them, with a message that Mr Campbell had expected us to dinner, having heard that we were to pass; that he was sorry he had not then seen us, and hoped we would be with him next day. We refreshed our crew.

The weather grew coldish. I proposed an expedient to keep our feet warm, which was to strew the boat plentifully with heath, the chief production of the island where we dined. Accordingly I fell to work and pulled, as did some of our men, and Mr Johnson pulled very assiduously. Sir Allan, who had been used to command men, and had no doubt superintended soldiers making roads or throwing up ramparts or doing some other kind of work, never stopped, but stood by *grieving* us (the Scottish expressive term for overseeing as a taskmaster, an overseer being called a *grieve*; as my lord Loudoun tells, a countryman said to him, Mr Dun our minister was *grieving* my father, who was busy gathering stones to mend a road).

We made ourselves very comfortable with the heath. The wind was now against us, but we had very little of it. We coasted along Mull, which was on our left. On our right was the Atlantic, with Staffa and other islands in it for some part of the way. Then we came to a large black rock in the sea; then to Nun's Island, which it is said belonged to the nuns of Icolmkill, and that from it the stone for the buildings of Icolmkill was taken; as the rocks still there are of the same kind of stone, and there is none such in Icolmkill.

It became very dusky, or rather dark, about seven; for our voyage, by going along the turnings of the coast, would be, Sir Allan said, forty miles from Inchkenneth to Iona; so that we were benighted. Mr Johnson said, as we were going up the narrow sound between Mull and Nun's Island, with solemn-like rocks on each side of us, and the waves rising and falling,[845] and our boat proceeding with a dancing motion, "This is roving among the Hebrides, or nothing is."

A man has a pleasure in applying things to words, and comparing the reality with the picture of fancy. We had long talked of 'roving among the Hebrides'. It was curious to repeat the words previously used, and which had impressed our imaginations by frequent use; and then to feel how the immediate impression from actually roving differed from the one in fancy, or agreed with it. It will be curious too, to perceive how the impression made by reading this my Journal some years after our roving will affect the mind, when compared with the recollection of what was felt at the time. Mr Johnson said I should read my Journal about every three years. Joseph made a very good observation. "Your journey," said he, "will always be more agreeable to you."

I often do not observe chronology, for fear of losing a thing by waiting till I can put it in its exact place. Joseph said this one night as I was going to bed, and was resuming to him with much complacency some of our past scenes on this expedition. He meant what I have often experienced: that scenes through which a man has gone improve by lying in the memory. They grow mellow. It is said, "*Acti labores sunt jucundi.*"[846] This may be owing to comparing them with present ease. But I also think that even harsh scenes acquire a softness by length of time;[847] and many scenes are like very loud sounds, which do not please till you are at a distance from them, or at least do not please so much; or like strong coarse pictures, which must be viewed at a distance. And I don't know how it is, but even pleasing scenes improve by time, and seem more exquisite in recollection than when they were present, if they have not faded to dimness in the memory. Perhaps there is so much evil in every human enjoyment when present, so much dross mixed with it, that it requires to be refined by time; and yet I do not see why time should not melt away the good and the evil in equal proportions, why the shade should decay and the light remain in preservation. I must hear Mr Johnson upon this subject.

The boat had so much motion tonight that I had a renewal of the uneasiness of fear at sea; and I wondered how I could so soon totally forget what I had endured when driven to Coll. People accustomed to sail give every little direction with so loud a tone that a fresh-water man is alarmed. Sir William Temple's observation on the boisterous manners of seamen, from their being used to contend with a boisterous element, will apply in some degree to all 'who go down into the sea' – at least while they are upon it. Coll talks loud at sea, and Sir Allan talks loud at sea. I asked if we should not be quieter when we were in the Sound between Mull and Icolmkill. Sir Allan said no. We should have a rougher sea, as we should then have a stronger current against us, and have the Atlantic quite open from each end of the Sound. I yielded so much to fear as to ask if it would not be better that we should go ashore for that night on Mull, and cross the Sound in the morning with daylight. Sir Allan was for going on. Mr Johnson said, "I suppose Sir Allan, who knows, thinks there is no danger."

"No, sir," said Sir Allan.

Mr Johnson was satisfied. I therefore had nothing to say, but kept myself calm. I am so much a disciple of Dr Ogden's that I venture to pray even upon small occasions if I feel myself much concerned. Perhaps when a man is much concerned, the occasions ought not to be called small. I put up a petition to God to make the waves more still. I know not if I ought to draw a conclusion from what happened; but so it was, that after we had turned the point of Nun's Island and got into the Sound of Icolmkill, the tide was for us, and we went along with perfect smoothness, which made me feel a most pleasing tranquillity.

In a little, I saw a light shining in the village at Icolmkill. All the inhabitants of the island, except perhaps a few shepherds or rather cowherds, live close to where the ancient buildings stood. I then saw the tower of the cathedral just discernible in the air. As we were landing, I said to Mr Johnson, "Well, I am glad we are now at last at this venerable place, which I have so long thought that you and I should visit. I could have gone and seen it by myself. But you would not have been with me; and the great thing is to bring objects together."

"It is so," said he, with a more than ordinary kind complacency. Indeed, the seeing of Mr Samuel Johnson at Icolmkill was what I had often imaged as a very venerable scene. A landscape or view of any kind is defective, in my opinion, without some human figures to give it animation. What an addition was it to Icolmkill to have the Rambler upon the spot! After we landed, I shook hands with him cordially.[848]

Upon hearing that Sir Allan Maclean was arrived, which was announced by his late servant Lauchlan whom we dispatched into the village, which is very near to the shore, the inhabitants – who still consider themselves as the people of Maclean, though the Duke of Argyll has at present possession of the ancient estate – ran eagerly to him. We went first to the house of ——— Macdonald, the most substantial man among them. Sir Allan called him the Provost. He had a tolerable hut with higher walls than common, and pretty well built with dry stone. The fire was in the middle of the room. A number of people assembled. What remained of our snuff was distributed among them. Sir Allan had a little tobacco, of which he gave several of them a little bit each. We regretted that there was not a drop of spirits upon the island, for we wished to have given them a hearty cup on occasion of a visit from Sir Allan, who had not been there for fourteen years, and in the interval had served four years in America. The people seemed to be more decently dressed than one usually finds those of their station in the isles.

Icolmkill pays £150 of rent. They sell about forty cattle and more than 150 bolls of barley; and what is remarkable, they brew a good deal of beer, which I could not find was done in any of the other isles. I was told that they imported nothing but salt and iron. Salt they might soon make. It is a very fertile island, and the people are industrious. They make their own woollen and linen webs, and indeed I suppose everything else, except any hardware for which they may have occasion. They have no shoes for their horses.

After warming ourselves in Mr Macdonald's, we were informed that our barn was ready, and we repaired to it. There was a fire in the middle of the floor, but the smoke was ceased before we went into the barn. We had cuddies and some oysters boiled in butter, that we might say we had fish and oyster sauce. Mr Johnson eat none of that dish. We had roasted potatoes, of which I think he eat one; and he drank a mug of sweet milk.[849] The fire was then carefully removed, and good hay was strewed at one end of the barn. Mr Johnson lay down with all his clothes and his greatcoat on. Sir Allan and I took off our coats and had them laid upon our feet. But we had also a pair of clean sheets which Miss Maclean had put up, and some very good blankets from the village; so that we had a tolerably comfortable bed. Each had a portmanteau for a pillow. Mr Johnson lay next the one wall, I next the other, Sir Allan in the middle. I could not help thinking in the night how curious it was to see the chief of the Macleans, Mr Samuel Johnson, and James Boswell, Esq. lying thus. Our boatmen were lodged somewhere in the village. Joseph, Lauchlan Maclean, and Donald MacDougal, a fine smart little boy-servant to Sir Allan, lay across the barn, at a little distance from our feet. It was just an encampment. There was a good deal of wind blew through the barn, so that it was rather too cool.

WEDNESDAY 20 OCTOBER. Between seven and eight we rose and went to see the ruins. We had for our cicerone ———, who calls himself the descendant of St Columbus's cousin. It is said their family has from time immemorial had ten acres of land in Icolmkill rent free, till it was lately taken from them by the Duke of Argyll. Sir Allan said if he recovered the island, they should be restored to their old possession. We had also a number of men following us. Our cicerone was a stupid fellow.[850]

We first viewed the monastery of the nuns. The church has been a pretty building. Mr Johnson took a very accurate inspection of all the ruins, and will give a very enlarged account of them in the *Tour*, or whatever he shall call it, which the world will gain by this expedition, to which I have had the merit of persuading him. I shall therefore only mention such circumstances as struck me on a cursory view.

It shocked one to observe that the nuns' chapel was made a fold for cattle, and was covered a foot deep with cow-dung. They cleared it off for us at one place and showed us the gravestone of a lady abbess. It was of that bluish stone or slate which is frequent in Highland churchyards. At one end was carved the abbess with her crosier at her side, and hands folded on her breast. At another, with the heads in an opposite direction, a Virgin and babe. I think the figures at each end were entire, whole lengths. Round the stone was an inscription telling who the lady was. But I am, I find, growing minute when I write, though for the reason which I have mentioned it is unnecessary; and besides, I did not give exact attention to the nuns, as I considered that so many people had examined them: Dr Pococke, Dr Walker, Mr Banks, Mr Pennant; and when I saw Mr Johnson setting himself heartily to examine them, my mind was quiescent, and I resolved to stroll among them at my ease, take no trouble to investigate, and only receive the general impression of solemn antiquity and the particular ideas of such objects as should of themselves strike my attention.[851]

We walked from the monastery of nuns to the great church or cathedral, as they call it, along an old pavement or causeway. They say that this was a street, and that there were good houses built on each side. Mr Johnson doubted if it was anything more than a paved road for the nuns. Some small houses now stand at various distances on each side of it. Mr Johnson said if there were houses there formerly, he did not imagine they were better. Indeed, when we saw how small a house the bishop had, it was not probable that inferior houses were better than what we now think poor cottages. Indeed, the houses here are all built of stone, as the inhabitants have without scruple made quarries of the walls of the religious buildings. The convent of monks, the great church, Oran's Chapel, and four more, are still to be discerned. Of some, more remains; of some, less. I restrain myself from saying anything in particular of them.

I was struck with a noble long cross called St Martin's Cross. But I must own that Icolmkill did not come up to my expectations, as they were high, from what I had read of it, and still more from what I had heard of it and thought of it, from my earliest years. Mr Johnson said it came up to his, because he had taken his impression from an account of it subjoined to Sacheverell's *History of the Isle of Man*, where it is said there is not much to be seen. Both he and I were disappointed when we were shown what are called the monuments of the kings of Scotland, Ireland, and Denmark, and of a king of France. There are only some gravestones

Wednesday 20 October

flat on the earth; and we could see no inscriptions. How far short was this of marble monuments, like those in Westminster Abbey, and which I had imaged here! The gravestones of Sir Allan Maclean's family, and of that of MacGuarie, had as good an appearance as the royal ones; if they were royal, which Mr Johnson doubted.

We were shown St Columbus's well. I drank out of it. Mr Johnson had his drink from it last night. We were told that here, as at Inchkenneth, the water was conveyed in leaden pipes. All that I could observe was that at the well the water came out of a flat freestone with a springing motion, as if conducted to the orifice by a pipe. But whether there was a lead pipe or not is a moot point. We also looked at the ———— house, which has been inconsiderable.[852]

We walked down again to our barn, where breakfast was prepared – milk, cheese, eggs, bread and butter. I slipped away and returned to the cathedral and its environs to perform some pleasing serious exercises of piety. I knelt before St Martin's Cross and said a short prayer. I went to the black stone on which the islanders of old used to swear. I had been shown a greyish piece of freestone, which they said was it; and I adopted their inaccurate information. I put my knees to this greyish freestone and said, "I here swear with all the solemnity that any honest, honourable, and brave man ever swore upon this stone, that I will stand by Sir Allan Maclean and his family." I had told Sir Allan that I would swear a covenant with him upon the black stone. I could not easily get him with me privately; so I went alone, and told him what I had done, which pleased him mightily; and I hope I shall have it in my power to convince him of my sincerity and steadiness.[853]

My easiness to receive information in the isles was too great. Had not Mr Johnson been with me, I might have brought home loads of fiction or of gross mistakes. No wonder that he is in a passion at the people, as they tell him with such readiness and confidence what he finds, upon questioning them a little more, is not true. Sir Allan told me plainly that the greyish freestone which stood like a stone at the end of a grave, near the wall of the monastery, was the famous black stone. I, either not attending to the striking objection that it was not black, or thinking that the epithet 'black' might have been given to it from its solemn purposes and not from its colour (for I do not clearly remember how I believed implicitly), very gravely thought myself kneeling on that stone where so many chiefs and warriors had knelt. Sir Allan told me afterwards, of his own accord, that the black stone was quite sunk into the earth. However,

I found (if Sir Allan could be credited as an antiquary a second time) that the black stone was sunk quite close to where the greyish stands; so that I really was upon the black stone while I swore to stand by Maclean.[854]

I then went into the cathedral, which is really grand enough when one thinks of its antiquity and of the remoteness of the place; and at the end, I offered up my adorations to God. I again addressed a few words to Saint Columbus; and I warmed my soul with religious resolutions. I felt a kind of exultation in thinking that the solemn scenes of piety ever remain the same, though the cares and follies of life may prevent us from visiting them, or may even make us fancy that their effects were only 'as yesterday when it is past',[855] and never again to be perceived. I hoped that ever after having been in this holy place, I should maintain an exemplary conduct. One has a strange propensity to fix upon some point from whence a better course of life may be said to begin. I read with an audible voice the fifth chapter of St James, and Dr Ogden's tenth sermon. I suppose there has not been a sermon preached in this church since the Reformation. I had a serious joy in hearing my voice, while it was filled with Ogden's admirable eloquence, resounding in the ancient cathedral of Icolmkill.

I had promised to write to my worthy old friend Grange from Icolmkill.[856] I therefore wrote a short solemn letter to him here. While I was writing it, Mr Johnson entered, that he might attentively view and even measure the ruins. I left him there, as I was to take a ride to the shore where Columbus landed, as it is said, and where the green pebbles called Icolmkill stones are found.

I eat some eggs for breakfast, while Sir Allan sat by me. ———— MacGinnis, whose horse I was to ride, came in. Sir Allan had been told that he had refused to send him some rum which he had; at which Sir Allan was in great indignation. "You rascal," said he, "don't you know that I can hang you if I please?"

I, not adverting to the chieftain's veneration from his clan, was supposing that Sir Allan had known of some capital crime that the fellow had committed, which he could discover and so get him condemned; and I said, "How so?"

"Why," said Sir Allan, "are they not all my people?"

Sensible of my inadvertency, and most willing to contribute what I could towards the continuation of feudal authority, "Very true," said I.

Sir Allan went on: "Refuse to send rum to me, you rascal! Don't you know that if I ordered you to go and cut a man's throat, you are to do it?"

"Yes, an't please your honour," said MacGinnis; "and my own too, and hang myself too."

The poor fellow denied that he had refused to send the rum. His making these professions was not merely a pretence in presence of Sir Allan. After he and I were out of Sir Allan's reach, he told me, "Had he sent his dog for the rum, I would have given it. I would cut my bones for him."

It was something very remarkable to find such an attachment to a chief, though he had then no connexion with the island, and had not been there for fourteen years. I was highly pleased with it, and so was Mr Johnson when I told him of it. Sir Allan, by way of upbraiding the fellow, said, "I believe you are a *Campbell*." MacGinnis is the name of a tribe of the Macleans.[857]

I had a pleasant ride over some fertile land, while MacGinnis run before me. I saw on the right three rocks on the shore, which looked like haystacks, as the mountain at Talisker does; till upon getting to the —— of them, they were seen not to be of a round form on all quarters.[858] The shore is about two miles from the village. They call it *Portawherry*, from the wherry in which Columbus came, as I suppose; though when you are shown the length of a vessel as marked on the beach by a heap of stones at each end of the space, they say, "Here is the length of the *curach*," using the Erse word.[859]

I had from my earliest years been shown by my father an Icolmkill stone, and then been told of the venerable antiquities of that place. So I was curious to gather some of the stones myself. I did so, and was in a fine placid humour. I knelt on the beach and offered up a short prayer, supposing it to be actually the place where the holy man landed.

It was far in the forenoon when I got back to the village. But Sir Allan and Mr Johnson did not scold much. I put up a stone of the wall of the cathedral, to be preserved as a memento for devotion, and a stone of the convent of monks, as a talisman for chastity. The former was red; the latter, black.

It seems there is no peculiar words in English to signify the distinction between a sacred society of females and one of males. I thought a convent had been appropriated to monks, a monastery to nuns. Mr Johnson said no; for a monastery signified a segregation from the world of a society of either sex.

We had a goodly number of the people to launch our boat; and when we sailed, or rather rowed, off, they took off their bonnets and huzza'd. I should have observed a striking circumstance: that in this island which once enlightened us all there is not now one man that can read, and but two that can speak English. There is not a school in it.

Wednesday 20 October

There is, near the village, a hill upon which St Columbus took his seat and meditated and surveyed the sea. Icolmkill struck me as not so remote as I had imagined, there being so small a sound between it and the large island of Mull. But on the quarter where Columbus landed, it seems far enough in the western ocean; and besides, being near Mull in old times was being near a very rude country, and is so to a certain degree to this day.

CHAPTER ELEVEN

Mull Again

SAMUEL JOHNSON

It was no long voyage to *Mull*, where, under Sir *Allan's* protection, we landed in the evening, and were entertained for the night by Mr *Maclean*, a Minister that lives upon the coast, whose elegance of conversation, and strength of judgement, would make him conspicuous in places of greater celebrity. Next day we dined with Dr *Maclean*, another physician, and then travelled on to the house of a very powerful Laird, *Maclean* of *Lochbuy*; for in this country every man's name is *Maclean*.[860]

Where races are thus numerous, and thus combined, none but the Chief of a clan is addressed by his name. The Laird of *Dunvegan* is called *Macleod*, but other gentlemen of the same family are denominated by the places where they reside, as *Raasa*, or *Talisker*. The distinction of the meaner people is made by their Christian names. In consequence of this practice, the late Laird of *Macfarlane*, an eminent genealogist, considered himself as disrespectfully treated, if the common addition was applied to him. Mr *Macfarlane*, said he, may with equal propriety be said to many; but I, and I only, am *Macfarlane*.

Our afternoon journey was through a country of such gloomy desolation, that Mr *Boswell* thought no part of the Highlands equally terrifick, yet we came without any difficulty, at evening, to *Lochbuy*, where we found a true Highland Laird, rough and haughty, and tenacious of his dignity; who, hearing my name, inquired whether I was of the *Johnstons* of *Glencoe*, or of *Ardnamurchan*.[861]

Lochbuy has, like the other insular Chieftains, quitted the castle that

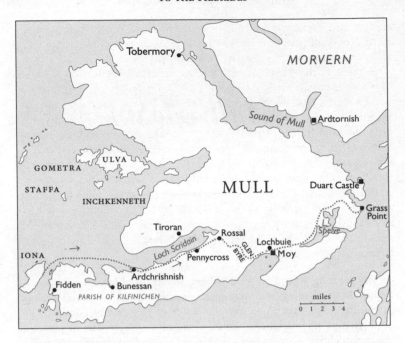

sheltered his ancestors, and lives near it, in a mansion not very spacious or splendid. I have seen no houses in the Islands much to be envied for convenience or magnificence, yet they bear testimony to the progress of arts and civility, as they shew that rapine and surprise are no longer dreaded, and are much more commodious than the ancient fortresses.

The castles of the *Hebrides*, many of which are standing, and many ruined, were always built upon points of land, on the margin of the sea. For the choice of this situation there must have been some general reason, which the change of manners has left in obscurity. They were of no use in the days of piracy, as defences of the coast; for it was equally accessible in other places. Had they been seamarks or light-houses, they would have been of more use to the invader than the natives, who could want no such directions on their own waters: for a watchtower, a cottage on a hill would have been better, as it would have commanded a wider view.

If they be considered merely as places of retreat, the situation seems not well chosen; for the Laird of an Island is safest from foreign enemies in the center: on the coast he might be more suddenly surprised than in the inland parts; and the invaders, if their enterprise miscarried, might more easily retreat. Some convenience, however, whatever it was, their position on the shore afforded; for uniformity of practice seldom continues long without good reason.

A castle in the Islands is only a single tower of three or four stories, of which the walls are sometimes eight or nine feet thick, with narrow windows, and close winding stairs of stone. The top rises in a cone, or pyramid of stone, encompassed by battlements. The intermediate floors are sometimes frames of timber, as in common houses, and sometimes arches of stone, or alternately stone and timber; so that there was very little danger from fire. In the center of every floor, from top to bottom, is the chief room, of no great extent, round which there are narrow cavities, or recesses, formed by small vacuities, or by a double wall. I know not whether there be ever more than one fire-place. They had not capacity to contain many people, or much provision; but their enemies could seldom stay to blockade them; for if they failed in the first attack, their next care was to escape.

The walls were always too strong to be shaken by such desultory hostilities; the windows were too narrow to be entered, and the battlements too high to be scaled. The only danger was at the gates, over which the wall was built with a square cavity, not unlike a chimney, continued to the top. Through this hollow the defendants let fall stones upon those who attempted to break the gate, and poured down water, perhaps scalding water, if the attack was made with fire. The castle of *Lochbuy* was secured by double doors, of which the outer was an iron grate.

In every castle is a well and a dungeon. The use of the well is evident. The dungeon is a deep subterraneous cavity, walled on the sides, and arched on the top, into which the descent is through a narrow door, by a ladder or a rope, so that it seems impossible to escape, when the rope or ladder is drawn up. The dungeon was, I suppose, in war, a prison for such captives as were treated with severity, and, in peace, for such delinquents as had committed crimes within the Laird's jurisdiction; for the mansions of many Lairds were, till the late privation of their privileges, the halls of justice to their own tenants.[862]

As these fortifications were the productions of mere necessity, they are built only for safety, with little regard to convenience, and with none to elegance or pleasure. It was sufficient for a Laird of the *Hebrides*, if he had a strong house, in which he could hide his wife and children from the next clan. That they are not large nor splendid is no wonder. It is not easy to find how they were raised, such as they are, by men who had no money, in countries where the labourers and artificers could scarcely be fed. The buildings in different parts of the Islands shew their degrees of wealth and power. I believe that for all the castles which I have seen beyond the *Tweed*, the ruins yet remaining of some one of those which the *English* built in *Wales*, would supply materials.

These castles afford another evidence that the fictions of romantick chivalry had for their basis the real manners of the feudal times, when every Lord of a seignory lived in his hold lawless and unaccountable, with all the licentiousness and insolence of uncontested superiority and unprincipled power. The traveller, whoever he might be, coming to the fortified habitation of a Chieftain, would, probably, have been interrogated from the battlements, admitted with caution at the gate, introduced to a petty Monarch, fierce with habitual hostility, and vigilant with ignorant suspicion; who, according to his general temper, or accidental humour, would have seated a stranger as his guest at the table, or as a spy confined him in the dungeon.

Lochbuy means the *Yellow Lake*, which is the name given to an inlet of the sea, upon which the castle of Mr *Maclean* stands. The reason of the appellation we did not learn.[863]

We were now to leave the *Hebrides*, where we had spent some weeks with sufficient amusement, and where we had amplified our thoughts with new scenes of nature, and new modes of life. More time would have given us a more distinct view, but it was necessary that Mr *Boswell* should return before the courts of justice were opened; and it was not proper to live too long upon hospitality, however liberally imparted.

Of these Islands it must be confessed, that they have not many allurements, but to the mere lover of naked nature. The inhabitants are thin, provisions are scarce, and desolation and penury give little pleasure.[864]

The people collectively considered are not few, though their numbers are small in proportion to the space which they occupy. *Mull* is said to contain six thousand, and *Sky* fifteen thousand. Of the computation respecting *Mull*, I can give no account; but when I doubted the truth of the numbers attributed to *Sky*, one of the Ministers exhibited such facts as conquered my incredulity.[865]

Of the proportion, which the product of any region bears to the people, an estimate is commonly made according to the pecuniary price of the necessaries of life; a principle of judgment which is never certain, because it supposes what is far from truth, that the value of money is always the same, and so measures an unknown quantity by an uncertain standard. It is competent enough when the markets of the same country, at different times, and those times not too distant, are to be compared; but of very little use for the purpose of making one nation acquainted with the state of another. Provisions, though plentiful, are sold in places of great pecuniary opulence for nominal prices, to which, however scarce, where gold and silver are yet scarcer, they can never be raised.

In the *Western Islands* there is so little internal commerce, that hardly any thing has a known or settled rate. The price of things brought in, or carried out, is to be considered as that of a foreign market; and even this there is some difficulty in discovering, because their denominations of quantity are different from ours; and when there is ignorance on both sides, no appeal can be made to a common measure.

This, however, is not the only impediment. The *Scots*, with a vigilance of jealousy which never goes to sleep, always suspect that an *Englishman* despises them for their poverty, and to convince him that they are not less rich than their neighbours, are sure to tell him a price higher than the true. When *Lesley*, two hundred years ago, related so punctiliously, that a hundred hen eggs, new laid, were sold in the Islands for a peny, he supposed that no inference could possibly follow, but that eggs were in great abundance. Posterity has since grown wiser; and having learned, that nominal and real value may differ, they now tell no such stories, lest the foreigner should happen to collect, not that eggs are many, but that pence are few.[866]

Money and wealth have by the use of commercial language been so long confounded, that they are commonly supposed to be the same; and this prejudice has spread so widely in *Scotland*, that I know not whether I found man or woman, whom I interrogated concerning payments of money, that could surmount the illiberal desire of deceiving me, by representing every thing as dearer than it is.

JAMES BOSWELL

We had a fine passage upon the sea today.[867] We set Lauchlan Maclean ashore at Ardtun. It has its name from two holes, which are called tuns. They are from the top of a rock of moderate highth, down to the sea. If a stone is thrown into one of them, it makes its way downwards till it bursts or plunges out upon the sea with a great noise; or I should rather say a considerable noise, for the account of it appeared exaggerated, after Lauchlan made the experiment.[868]

Wednesday 20 October

We wished to have called on Mr Campbell, who was so polite to us yesterday,[869] but found it would make us too late; so we pulled away along Loch Scridain till we landed near to Mr Neil MacLeod's, to whose house we walked. He met us, having heard of our landing from Donald, whom we sent forward.[870] He came to meet us. His first appearance was taking. He had a black wig and a smart air, like an English parson; and he had his hat covered with wax-cloth, which showed an attention to convenience. With him was a Lieutenant Hugh Maclean. His house was a good farm-house of one storey, dry and well furnished. His wife a very well-behaved woman. She was the daughter of the former minister; so, as Mr Johnson said, she knew how to live in the minister's house. We had tea first, and then an excellent supper. Mr MacLeod talked sensibly and distinctly. Mr Johnson said he was the cleanest-headed man he had met in the islands.[871] He said to Mr Johnson, "Sir, I have been often obliged to you, though I never had the pleasure of seeing you." Our evening went on well. Sir Allan, Mr Johnson, and I had each a good clean bed in the room where we supped. There were some good books here, and good pens and ink, which was no small rarity.

Mr MacLeod told us he had lived for some time in St Kilda, under the tuition of the minister or catechist there, and had there first read Horace and Virgil. Their scenes would be strongly contrasted with what was around him.[872]

THURSDAY 21 OCTOBER. Mr Johnson said the saying *Nitimur in vetitum* was not true; for that forbidding a thing did not make us have a greater liking for it.[873]

He said, "Pulteney was as paltry a fellow as could be. He was a Whig who pretended to be honest; and you know it is ridiculous for a Whig to pretend to be honest. He cannot hold it out." He called Pitt a meteor; Sir Robert Walpole, a fixed star. He said, "It required all the force of Government to prevent Wilkes from being chosen the Chief Magistrate of London, though the liverymen know he'd rob their shops, know he'd debauch their daughters."[874]

I said the history of England was so strange that if we had it not so well vouched as it is, it would hardly be credible. "Sir," said Mr Johnson, "if it were told as shortly, and with as little preparation for introducing the different events, as the history of the Jewish kings, it would be equally liable to objections of improbability." Mr MacLeod was pleased with the justice and novelty of the thought. Mr Johnson illustrated what he had said by mentioning Charles the First's concessions to his Parliament, which were greater and greater, in proportion as they grew more insolent and less deserving of trust. Had these concessions been related nakedly, without any detail of the circumstances which generally led to them, they would not have been believed.[875]

Sir Allan began to brag that Scotland had the advantage of England, by its having more water. "Sir," said Mr Johnson, "we would not have your water, to take the vile bogs which produce it. You have too much. A man who is drowned has more water than either of us." And then he laughed. (But this was surely robust sophistry; for the people of taste in England who have seen Scotland, own that its variety of rivers and brooks makes it naturally prettier than England in that respect.) "Sir," said Mr Johnson, pursuing his victory over Sir Allan, "your country consists of two things: stone and water. There is indeed a little earth above the stone in some places, but a very little; and the stone is always appearing. It is like a man in rags; the naked skin is always peeping out."

He took leave of Mr MacLeod, saying, "Sir, I thank you for your entertainment and your conversation."

Mr Campbell, who had been so polite yesterday, came up this morning on purpose to breakfast with us. He was a civil, jolly-looking man. Mr MacLeod thought as Mr Johnson did of Icolmkill. Mr Campbell had with him a manuscript account of it, by Mr Campbell, the schoolmaster of the parish. Mr MacLeod promised that a copy of it should be sent to me for Mr Johnson. Mr Johnson said, "If I shall find that I can make any use of it in case I publish anything about Icolmkill, may I do it? Or," said he, "I shall try to get Mr Campbell something for it from a bookseller, and let it be published as it is; and then I may make what use I please of it in the way of extract, as all the world may do." This was approved of by Mr MacLeod. Mr Johnson said, "I dare say I may get him five guineas for it; perhaps ten."[876]

This was the first indication that Mr Johnson gave of a design to give the world an account of his tour with me. I rejoiced at the thought.

We were furnished with horses here by Mr MacLeod and Mr Campbell; and I had a very pretty bay galloway belonging to Dr Alexander Maclean, another physician in Mull. We advanced well, till we came to this other physician's. He was one of the stoutest and most hearty men that I have seen, more of the farmer than of the doctor. He had a dinner prepared for us, so we could not refuse to stay and eat it. His wife did very well. We had a very good dinner.[877]

Mr Johnson said of the *Turkish Spy*, which lay in the room, that it told nothing but what everybody might have known at the time; and that what was good in it did not pay you for the trouble of reading to find it. He said it was written in London by Sir Robert Manley and Richard Sault.[878] Dr Maclean said, "This man is just a hogshead of sense." He and I took much to one another.

We had travelled on tolerably plain road in the forenoon, along the northern shore, at least in view of it. After dinner, we struck away to the southeast, and ascended a high mountain, from whence, had the weather been clear, Sir Allan said I might have seen Islay and Jura, besides many more smaller islands. We proceeded till we descended a sloping pathless moor or marshy meadow, and then came to a glen wilder in my mind than either Glenmoriston or Glen Shiel. It must be an excellent place for deer. It is part of Lochbuie's territory. We had sent on Donald to Moy, his seat, which is in a good plain on a branch of the sea called Loch Buy. As *buy* signifies yellow, I conjectured ingeniously that 'the Yellow Loch' might be said as well as 'the Red Sea', for it seemed not easy to explain how a loch came to be called yellow. But Sir Allan told me that a hill above the plain in which the house stands is called Ben Buy from its being of a yellowish hue, and from it the loch has been named.

We arrived between seven and eight. We had heard a great deal of Lochbuie's being a great roaring braggadocio, a kind of Sir John Falstaff both in size and manners. But it appeared that they had swelled him up to a fictitious size and clothed him with imaginary qualities. Coll said he was quite a Don Quixote, and that he would give a great deal to see him and Mr Johnson together. But the truth was that Lochbuie proved to be only a bluff, hearty, rosy old gentleman, of a strong voice and no great depth of understanding.[879] He was not taller than the common size. He was a good deal like Craigengillan, but had a longer face. His wife, Sir Allan's sister but much older than him, was a strange being to be a lady at the head of a family which I was told has £1000 a year. She had on a mean bed-gown, and behaved like the landlady of an ale-house. Sir Allan said they were just antediluvians. Their daughter was as wild as any filly in Mull, at least had as little notion of good-breeding. Mr Johnson tried to talk with her. But it would not do. The poor thing knew nothing. Though about seventeen, she had never read a play. Mr Johnson said my comparing of her to a filly was not just, for she had not the friskiness of a wild animal.

Lochbuie has spent a great deal of money in lawsuits. It was strange to see a man of his fortune, and one whose guineas have been liberally distributed to counsel, have a poor house, though of two storeys indeed. The dining-room, where we sat, had a bed in it; and neither the ceiling

Thursday 21 October

nor the walls were plastered, though they were prepared for it. We had tea, which was an immediate comfort. Lochbuie bawled out to Mr Johnson, "Are you of the Johnstons of Glen Croe, or of Ardnamurchan?"[880]

Mr Johnson gave a curious look. Sir Allan and I told Lochbuie that Mr Johnson was not Johns*ton*, but John*son*, and that he was an Englishman.[881]

Lochbuie tried not long ago to prove himself a fool, or what we call a facile man, in order to set aside a lease which he had granted to Gillean Maclean, his natural son; but it did not do, though I suppose there were foolish things enough proved. Mr Johnson told me that in England they will not allow a man to stultify himself, as they term it.[882] Lochbuie some years ago was fined in 500 merks, or paid that sum by way of damages to some gentlemen whom he imprisoned in the dungeon of his old castle. Sir Allan said he still imagines that he has an heritable jurisdiction.[883]

I must do Lochbuie the justice to mention that he was very hospitable. Our supper was indeed but a poor one. I think a sort of stewed mutton was the principal dish. I was afterwards told that he has no spit, and but one pot, in which everything is stewed. It is probable enough. He had admirable port. Sir Allan and he and I drank each a bottle of it. Then we drank a bowl of punch. I was seized with an avidity for drinking, and Lochbuie and I became mighty social. Another bowl was made. Mr Johnson had gone to bed as the first was finished, and had admonished me, "Don't drink any more *poonch*."

I must own that I was resolved to drink more, for I was by this time a good deal intoxicated; and I gave no answer, but slunk away from him, with a consciousness of my being brutish and yet a determination to go somewhat deeper. What I might have done I know not. But luckily before I had tasted the second bowl, I grew very sick, and was forced to perform the operation that Antony did in the Senate house, if Cicero is to be credited;[884] so that Mr Johnson's admonition to drink no more punch had its effect, though not from any merit of mine. I went to bed in the dining-room, which was my chamber; and my stomach being clear, I fell asleep immediately, while Sir Allan and Lochbuie finished the bowl beside me.

FRIDAY 22 OCTOBER. It humbled me to find that my holy resolutions at Icolmkill had been so ineffectual that the very day after having been there I had drank too much. I went to Mr Johnson before he was up. He first said none of our Club would get drunk, but then, taking himself, he said Burke would get drunk and be ashamed of it; Goldsmith would get drunk and boast of it, if it had been with a little whore or so, who had allowed him to go in a coach with her.[885]

Before Mr Johnson came to breakfast, Lady Lochbuie said he was a 'dungeon of wit', a very common phrase in Scotland, though Mr Johnson told me he had never heard it. She proposed that he should have some cold sheep-head for breakfast. Sir Allan was very angry at her vulgarity, and wondered how such a thought should come into her head. From a mischievous love of sport, I took the lady's part. "I think," said I, "it is but fair to give him an offer of it. If he does not choose it, he may let it alone."

"I think so," said the lady, looking at her brother with an air of victory. Sir Allan, finding the matter desperate, strutted about the room, and took snuff. When Mr Johnson came in, she called to him, "Do you choose any cold sheep-head, sir?"

"No, madam," said he, with a tone of surprise and anger.

"It's here, sir," said she, as if he had refused it to save the trouble of bringing it. He confirmed his refusal sufficiently; and I was entertained to see the ludicrous cross-purposes.

We walked in the garden after breakfast. Sir Allan anxiously called the attention of Mr Johnson to some trees growing in it. Ashes, I think. We walked down to the old castle, which is very near the present house, and surveyed it attentively. Lochbuie roared out, what excellent cellars he had in the vaults! Mr Johnson was offended at being disturbed in his antiquarian researches, or rather meditations, and said, "I don't care about cellars."

We viewed the *pit* for which Lochbuie had been fined by the Court of Justiciary. He said to me, "Your father has heard of this" (or "knows this"), alluding to my father's having sat as one of the judges on his trial. Sir Allan whispered me, that the laird could not be persuaded, that he had lost his heritable jurisdiction.[886]

We then set out for the ferry, by which we were to cross to the mainland of Argyllshire. Lochbuie and Sir Allan accompanied us. We were told much of a war-saddle on which Lochbuie used to be mounted. But we did not see it, for the young laird had it at one of the fairs for black cattle, Falkirk, I think.[887]

(I am glad to find that I remember so many particulars after the lapse of almost seven years. My Journal cannot have the same freshness and fullness when written now as when written recently after the scenes recorded. But I hope I shall preserve some valuable remains or fragments.)

CHAPTER TWELVE

Highlands Again

SAMUEL JOHNSON

From *Lochbuy* we rode a very few miles to the side of *Mull*, which faces *Scotland*, where, having taken leave of our kind protector, Sir *Allan*, we embarked in a boat, in which the seat provided for our accommodation was a heap of rough brushwood; and on the twenty-second of *October* reposed at a tolerable inn on the main land.[888]

On the next day we began our journey southwards. The weather was tempestuous. For half the day the ground was rough, and our horses were still small. Had they required much restraint, we might have been reduced to difficulties; for I think we had amongst us but one bridle. We fed the poor animals liberally, and they performed their journey well. In the latter part of the day, we came to a firm and smooth road, made by the soldiers, on which we travelled with great security, busied with contemplating the scene about us. The night came on while we had yet a great part of the way to go, though not so dark, but that we could discern the cataracts which poured down the hills, on one side, and fell into one general channel that ran with great violence on the other. The wind was loud, the rain was heavy, and the whistling of the blast, the fall of the shower, the rush of the cataracts, and the roar of the torrent, made a nobler chorus of the rough musick of nature than it had ever been my chance to hear before. The streams, which ran cross the way from the hills to the main current, were so frequent, that after a while I began to count them; and, in ten miles, reckoned fifty-five, probably missing some, and having let some pass before they forced themselves upon my notice. At

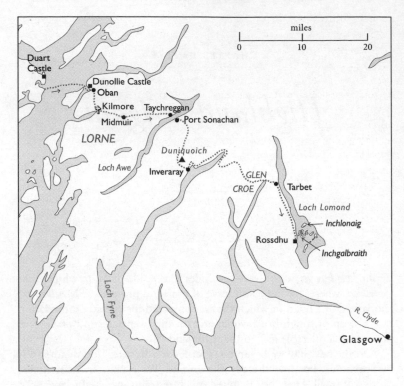

last we came to *Inverary*, where we found an inn, not only commodious, but magnificent.

The difficulties of peregrination were now at an end. Mr *Boswell* had the honour of being known to the Duke of *Argyle*, by whom we were very kindly entertained at his splendid seat, and supplied with conveniences for surveying his spacious park and rising forests.

After two days stay at *Inverary* we proceeded *Southward* over *Glencroe*, a black and dreary region, now made easily passable by a military road, which rises from either end of the glen by an acclivity not dangerously steep, but sufficiently laborious. In the middle, at the top of the hill, is a seat with this inscription, *Rest, and be thankful*. Stones were placed to mark the distances, which the inhabitants have taken away, resolved, they said, *to have no new miles*.[889]

In this rainy season the hills streamed with waterfalls, which, crossing the way, formed currents on the other side, that ran in contrary directions

22–27 October

as they fell to the north or south of the summit. Being, by the favour of the Duke, well mounted, I went up and down the hill with great convenience.[890]

From *Glencroe* we passed through a pleasant country to the banks of *Loch Lomond*, and were received at the house of Sir *James Colquhoun*, who is owner of almost all the thirty islands of the Loch, which we went in a boat next morning to survey. The heaviness of the rain shortened our voyage, but we landed on one island planted with yew, and stocked with deer, and on another containing perhaps not more than half an acre, remarkable for the ruins of an old castle, on which the osprey builds her annual nest.[891] Had *Loch Lomond* been in a happier climate, it would have been the boast of wealth and vanity to own one of the little spots which it incloses, and to have employed upon it all the arts of embellishment. But as it is, the islets, which court the gazer at a distance, disgust him at his approach, when he finds, instead of soft lawns and shady thickets, nothing more than uncultivated ruggedness.

JAMES BOSWELL

We bid adieu to Lochbuie and to our kind conductor Sir Allan Maclean on the shore of Mull, and then got into the ferry-boat, the bottom of which was strewed with branches of trees or bushes, upon which we sat. We saw the old Castle of Duart at a distance, while we sailed. I do not recollect distinctly any other objects.

We landed at Oban, having had a good day and a fine passage. Sir Allan had given us a card to introduce us to the Laird of MacDougall. But as we understood from his way of speaking, whether rightly or not, that the Laird would not be very willing to entertain us, we did not go to his castle, though very near. Sir Allan had recommended us to an inn at Oban, where we would get the best entertainment. But I think it was full, for we could not be accommodated. It was a thatched house of one storey. We went to another inn in this small village, if a very few houses should be so called. It was a slated house of two storeys, and we were well enough entertained; at least we were satisfied, though we had nothing like what is to be found in good inns upon a frequented road.

Here we found a newspaper, in which I read an account of the death of Alexander, Earl of Galloway, which affected me in a pretty sensible manner, as I had from my early years viewed him as a Great Man who had seen much of the world; and when I came to be well acquainted with him, had found him to be remarkably knowing in the affairs of life, lively, and like a man of fashion. There is a pleasure in being to a certain degree agitated by events. This I experienced on the present occasion.

It was comfortable to Mr Johnson and me, after so many states of uncertain confinement in islands, to be now on the mainland, and *sure*, if in health, to get to any place in Scotland or England in so many days. Here we discovered from the conjectures which were formed, that the people on the main land were entirely ignorant of our motions; for in a Glasgow newspaper we found a paragraph, which, as it contains a just and well-turned compliment to my illustrious friend, I shall here insert:

> We are well assured that Dr Johnson is confined by tempestuous weather to the isle of Sky; it being unsafe to venture, in a small boat upon such a stormy surge as is very common there at this time of the year. Such a philosopher, detained on an almost barren island, resembles a whale left upon the strand. The latter will be welcome to every body, on account of his oil, his bone, &c. and the other will charm his companions, and the rude inhabitants, with his superior knowledge and wisdom, calm resignation, and unbounded benevolence.[892]

I remember none of the conversation this night.

SATURDAY 23 OCTOBER. (Writing on 23 August 1782.) After a good night's rest, we breakfasted at our leisure. We talked of Goldsmith's *Traveller*, of which Mr Johnson said, I think, he had not written more than twenty lines. He spoke highly in praise of it; and while I was helping him on with his greatcoat, he began to repeat from it the character of the English, which he did with great energy.[893]

> *Stern o'er each bosom reason holds her state.*
> *With daring aims irregularly great,*
> *Pride in their port, defiance in their eye,*
> *I see the lords of humankind pass by,*
> *Intent on high designs, a thoughtful band,*
> *By forms unfashion'd; fresh from nature's hand;*
> *Fierce in their native hardiness of soul,*
> *True to imagin'd right, above control,*
> *While ev'n the peasant boasts these rights to scan,*
> *And learns to venerate himself as man.*

We could get but one bridle here, which, according to the maxim *detur digniori*, was, to be sure, appropriated to Mr Johnson's sheltie. My servant and I rode with halters. I ought to have put myself before my servant in this narrative. But I am not sure but he rode before me in the march. We had a fourth sheltie for the baggage. There came on a heavy rain. I recollect nothing of the country through which we passed. We crossed, I think, Loch Awe, a pretty wide lake, in a ferry-boat; and on this side of it, just on the shore, found a hut for our inn. We were much wet. I changed my clothes in part, and was at pains to get myself well dried. Mr Johnson resolutely kept on all his clothes, wet as they were, letting them steam before the smoky turf fire. I thought him in the wrong. But his firmness was a species of heroism.[894]

I remember but little of our conversation. I mentioned Shenstone's saying of Pope that he had the art of condensing sense more than anybody. Mr Johnson said, "It is not true, sir. There is more sense in a line of Cowley, than in a page" (or a sentence, or ten lines – I cannot be quite certain of the very phrase) "of Pope." He maintained that Archibald, Duke of Argyll, was a narrow man. I wondered at this; and observed that his building so great a house at Inveraray was not like a narrow man. "Sir," said he, "when a narrow man has resolved to build a house, he builds it like another man. But Archibald, Duke of Argyll, was narrow in his ordinary expenses, in his quotidian expenses."

The distinction is very just. It is in the ordinary expenses of life that a man's liberality or narrowness is to be discovered. I never before had heard the word 'quotidian' for 'daily', and I imagined it to be a word of Mr Johnson's own fabrication. But I have since found it in Dr Young's *Night Thoughts*, Night Fifth, 'Death's a destroyer of quotidian prey', and in my friend's *Dictionary*, supported by the authorities of Charles I and Dr Donne.[895]

It rained very hard as we journeyed on after dinner. I recollect the wind and rain and roar of brooks, which have since been so nobly described in the *Journey to the Western Islands*. We got at night to Inveraray, to a most excellent inn.[896] Even here Mr Johnson would not change his clothes. I put on a suit of our landlord's. The sight of good accommodation cheered us much. We supped well; and after supper, Mr Johnson, whom I had not seen taste any fermented liquor during all our expedition, had a gill of whisky brought to him.[897] "Come," said he, "let me know what it is that makes a Scotsman happy."

He drank it all but a drop, which I begged leave to pour into my glass, that I might say we had drank whisky together. I proposed Mrs Thrale should be our toast. He would not have *her* drank in whisky, but rather some insular lady; so we drank, I think, Miss Macpherson.[898] He owned tonight that he got as good a room and bed as at an English inn.

I had here the comfort of a letter from my dear wife, of whom I had not heard for many weeks; and I had the regale of a letter from Mr Garrick, in answer to mine to him from Inverness.[899]

Inverness, Sunday, 29 August, 1773 / My dear Sir, / Here I am, and Mr Samuel Johnson actually with me. We were a night at Fores, in coming to which, in the dusk of the evening, we passed over a bleak and blasted heath where Macbeth met the witches. Your old preceptor repeated, with much solemnity, the speech

> *How far is't called to Fores? What are these,*
> *So wither'd and so wild in their attire, &c.*

This day we visited the ruins of Macbeth's castle at Inverness. I have had great romantick satisfaction in seeing Johnson upon the classical scenes of Shakspeare in Scotland; which I really looked upon as almost as improbable as that 'Birnam wood should come to Dunsinane'. Indeed, as I have always been accustomed to view him as a permanent London object, it would not be much more wonderful to me to see St Paul's church moving along where we now are. As yet we have travelled in post-chaises; but to-morrow we are to mount on horseback, and ascend into the mountains by Fort Augustus, and so on to the ferry, where we are to cross to Sky. We shall see that island fully, and then visit some more of the Hebrides; after which we are to land in Argyleshire, proceed by Glasgow to Auchinleck, repose there a competent time, and then return to Edinburgh, from whence the Rambler will depart for old England again, as soon as he finds it convenient.

Hitherto we have had a very prosperous expedition. I flatter myself *servetur ad imum, qualis ab incepto processerit.*[900] He is in excellent spirits, and I have a rich journal of his conversation. Look back, Davy,[901] to Litchfield; run up through the time that has elapsed since you first knew Mr Johnson, and enjoy with me his present extraordinary tour.

I could not resist the impulse of writing to you from this place. The situation of the old castle corresponds exactly to Shakspeare's description. While we were there to-day, it happened oddly, that a raven perched upon one of the chimney-tops, and croaked. Then I in my turn repeated

> *The raven himself is hoarse,*
> *That croaks the fatal entrance of Duncan,*
> *Under my battlements.*

Saturday 23 October

I wish you had been with us. Think what enthusiastick happiness I shall have to see Mr Samuel Johnson walking among the romantick rocks and woods of my ancestors at Auchinleck! Write to me at Edinburgh. You owe me his verses on great George and tuneful Cibber, and the bad verses which led him to make his fine ones on Philips the musician. Keep your promise, and let me have them. I offer my very best compliments to Mrs Garrick, and ever am / Your warm admirer and friend, JAMES BOSWELL. / *To David Garrick, Esq; / London.*

His answer was as follows,

Hampton, September 14, 1773, / Dear Sir, / You stole away from London, and left us all in the lurch; for we expected you one night at the club, and knew nothing of your departure. Had I payed you what I owed you, for the book you bought for me, I should only have grieved for the loss of your company, and slept with a quiet conscience; but, wounded as it is, it must remain so till I see you again, though I am sure our good friend Mr Johnson will discharge the debt for me, if you will let him. Your account of your journey to *Fores*, the *raven, old castle*, &c. &c. made me half mad. Are you not rather too late in the year for fine weather, which is the life and soul of seeing places? I hope your pleasure will continue *qualis ab incepto*, &c.[902]

Your friend ———— threatens me much.[903] I only wish that he would put his threats in execution, and, if he prints his play, I will forgive him. I remember he complained to you, that his bookseller called for the money for some copies of his ————, which I subscribed for, and that I desired him to call again. The truth is, that my wife was not at home, and that for weeks together I have not ten shillings in my pocket. However, had it been otherwise, it was not so great a crime to draw his poetical vengeance upon me. I despise all that he can do, and am glad that I can so easily get rid of him and his ingratitude. I am hardened both to abuse and ingratitude.

You, I am sure, will no more recommend your poetasters to my civility and good offices.

Shall I recommend to you a play of Eschylus (the Prometheus), published and translated by poor old Morell, who is a good scholar, and an acquaintance of mine? It will be but half a guinea, and your name shall be put in the list I am making for him. You will be in very good company.

Now for the Epitaphs! [*These, together with the verses on George the Second, and Colley Cibber, as his Poet Laureat, of which imperfect copies are gone about, will appear in my* Life of Dr Johnson.][904]

I have no more paper, or I should have said more to you. My love and respects to Mr Johnson. / Yours ever, / D. GARRICK. / I can't write. I have the gout in my hand. / *To James Boswell, Esq., Edinburgh.*

My feelings this night were as agreeable as can be imagined.

SUNDAY 24 OCTOBER. (Writing on 24 August 1782.) We passed the forenoon calmly and placidly. I prevailed on Mr Johnson to read aloud Ogden's Sixth Sermon on Prayer, which he did with a distinct and agreeable solemnity. He praised my favourite preacher: his language, his acuteness, and said he fought infidels with their own weapons.

As a specimen of Ogden's manner, I insert the following passage from the sermon which Dr Johnson now read. The preacher, after arguing against that vain philosophy which maintains, in conformity with the hard principle of eternal necessity, or unchangeable predetermination, that the only effect of prayer for others, although we are exhorted to pray for them, is to produce good dispositions in ourselves towards them, thus expresses himself:[905]

A plain man may be apt to ask, But if this then, though enjoined in the holy Scriptures, is to be my real aim and intention, when I am taught to pray for other persons, why is it that I do not plainly so express it? Why is not the form of the petition brought nearer to the meaning? Give them, say I to our heavenly father, what is good. But this, I am to understand, will be as it will be, and is not for me to alter. What is it then that I am doing? I am desiring to become charitable myself; and why may I not plainly say so? Is there shame in it, or impiety? The wish is laudable: why should I form designs to hide it?

Or is it, perhaps, better to be brought about by indirect means, and in this artful manner? Alas! who is it that I would impose on? From whom can it be, in this commerce, that I desire to hide any thing? When, as my Saviour commands me, I have 'entered into my closet, and shut my door', there are but two parties privy to my devotions, God and my own heart, which of the two am I deceiving?

He wished to have more books; and upon inquiring if there were any in the house, he was told the waiter had some. They were brought to him. But I recollect none of them but Hervey's *Meditations*.[906] Mr Johnson thought slightingly of this admired book. He treated it with ridicule, and would not even allow the scene of the dying husband and father to be pathetic. I am not an impartial judge. For Hervey's *Meditations* were the delight of my dear, pious mother, and engaged my affections in my early years. He read a passage concerning the moon ludicrously, and showed how easily he could, in the same style, make reflections on that planet, the very reverse of Hervey's, representing her as treacherous to mankind. He did this very well. But I have forgotten the particulars. He then played himself in making a Meditation on a Pudding, of which I, a little after he had done, wrote down an imperfect note, the original of which I have preserved, and place as a loose leaf between this page and the opposite one.[907]

A Pudding

Flour that once waved in the golden grain and drank the dews of the morning. Milk pressed from the swelling udder by the gentle hand of the beauteous milkmaid, whose beauty and innocence might have recommended a worse draught; who, while she stroked the udder, indulged no ambitious thoughts of wandering in palaces, formed no plans for the destruction of her fellow-creatures. Let us consider: can there be more wanting to complete the Meditation on a Pudding? If more is wanting, more may be found. Salt which keeps the sea from putrefaction, that salt which is made the image of intellectual excellence, contributes to a pudding; and milk is drawn from the cow, that useful animal which eats the grass of the field, and supplies us with that which made the greatest part of the food of mankind in that age which the poets have agreed to call golden. It is made with an egg, that miracle of nature which the theoretical Burnet has compared to creation. An egg contains water within its beautiful smooth surface. An unformed mass, by the incubation of the parent, becomes a regular animal with bones and sinews and covered with feathers.

In a magazine, I think the Edinburgh weekly one, I found a saying of Mr Johnson's, something to this purpose: that the happiest part of a man's life is what he passes lying in bed in the morning. I read it out to him. He said, "I may perhaps have said this, for nobody talks more laxly than I do." I think I ventured to suggest to him that this was dangerous from one of his authority.

I spoke of living in the country, and upon what footing one should be with neighbours. For my own part, I said I would not wish to be too easy, for then a man's time is never his own. He said it depended much on what kind of neighbours a country gentleman has, whether he should be on an easy footing or not; and to be sure it is plain there can be no general rule as to this. I told him a strange characteristic sally of Sir John Dalrymple upon this subject. He said to me, he never was happy in the country till he was not on speaking terms with any of his neighbours, which he contrived in different ways to bring about. "Lord

Adam Gordon stuck long," said he. "At last the fellow poinded my pigs, and then I got rid of him."

"Nay, sir," said Mr Johnson, "Lord Adam got rid of Sir John, and showed how little he valued him, by putting his pigs in the pound."[908]

I told Mr Johnson I was in some difficulty how to act at Inveraray. The Duchess of Argyll, I knew, hated me, on account of my zeal in the Douglas Cause.[909] But the Duke of Argyll had always been very civil to me, and had paid me a visit in London. They were now at the castle. Should I go and pay my respects there? Mr Johnson was clear that I ought. But in his usual way, he was very shy of desiring to be there himself. His pride of character has ever made him keep aloof from any appearance of courting the great. Besides, he was impatient to get to Glasgow, where he expected letters. At the same time, he was secretly not unwilling to have attention paid him by so great a chieftain and so exalted a nobleman. He insisted I should not go to the castle this day before dinner, as it would look like asking an invitation. "But," said I, "if the Duke asks us to dine with him tomorrow, shall we accept?"

"Yes, sir," said he. I think he added, "To be sure." But he said, "He won't ask us." I mentioned how disagreeable my company would be to the Duchess. Mr Johnson treated this objection with a manly disdain. "That, sir," said he, "he must settle with his wife."

We dined well. I went to the castle just about the time when I supposed the ladies would be gone from dinner. I sent in my name, and was introduced. Found the amiable Duke sitting at the head of his table, with Campbell of Airds and several more gentlemen. I was very graciously received, drank some claret, and gave some particulars of the curious journey which I had been making with Dr Johnson. When we rose from table, the Duke came close to me, and said, "I hope you and Dr Johnson will dine with us tomorrow."

I thanked his grace, but told him Mr Johnson was in a great hurry to get back to London. The Duke, with an obliging complacency, said, "He will stay one day; and I will take care he shall see this place to advantage."

I said I should be sure to let him know his grace's invitation. This was as well as could be wished. As I was going away, the Duke said, "Mr Boswell, won't you have some tea?"

I thought it as well to put over the meeting with the Duchess this night; so respectfully agreed. I was conducted to the drawing-room by the Duke, who announced my name. But the Duchess took not the least notice of me. I did not mind this, as the Duke was exceedingly civil.[910]

Lady Betty Hamilton made tea, and I had some.[911] Miss Sempill, with whom I was pretty well acquainted, hardly acknowledged me, I suppose for fear of offending the Duchess. Miss Campbell of Carrick talked a little with me.

I was accompanied to the inn by Mr David Campbell, Writer to the Signet, one of the clan, whom I found at his chief's board. He sat a good while with Mr Johnson and me, and seemed to relish much Mr Johnson's forcible conversation. The Ayrshire election was mentioned. I told Mr Johnson there were some gentlemen in the county who, from a notion of independency, resolved to oppose every candidate who was supported by the peers. "Foolish fellows," said he. "Don't they see that they are as much dependent upon the peers one way as t'other? The peers have only to *oppose* a candidate to get him success. It is said the only way to make a pig go forward is to pull him back by the tail. These people must be treated like pigs."

He was much pleased with the Duke's invitation, and most readily accepted it.

MONDAY 25 OCTOBER. (Writing on 27 August 1782.)[912] My acquaintance, the Rev. Mr John Macaulay, one of the ministers of Inveraray and brother to Mr Kenneth at Cawdor, came to us this morning, and I think breakfasted with us. We then, accompanied by him, walked to the castle, where I presented Mr Johnson to the Duke. We were shown through the house; and I never shall forget the enchanting impression made upon my fancy by some of the ladies' maids tripping about in neat morning dresses. After seeing nothing for a long time but rusticity, their elegance delighted me; and I could have been a knight-errant for them.[913] Such is my amorous constitution.

We then had a little low one-horse chair, ordered for us by the Duke, in which I drove us about the place, Mr Macaulay riding before us on a good large horse. Mr Johnson was much pleased with the remarkable grandeur and improvements about Inveraray. He said, "What I admire here is the total defiance of expense."

He thought the castle too low, and wished it had been a storey higher. I need not have said 'he wished'. It was only his opinion. We did not ascend Duniquoich. I had a particular pride in shewing him a great number of fine old trees, to compensate for the nakedness which had made such an impression on him on the eastern coast of Scotland.

When we came in before dinner, we found the Duke and some gentlemen in the hall. Mr Johnson was much pleased with the large collection of arms, which are excellently disposed there.[914] I told what he had said to Sir Alexander Macdonald of his ancestors' not suffering their arms to rust. "Well," said the Doctor, "but let us be glad we live in times when arms *may* rust. We can sit today at his grace's table without any risk of being attacked, and perhaps sitting down again wounded." (He expressed being wounded or maimed, by words which I do not precisely remember.)

The Duke placed him by himself at table. I happened to sit in the middle, so that it was my duty to give about the soup, which I did with all imaginable ease, though conscious of the Duchess's peevish resentment. I was in fine spirits, and offered her grace some. I was in the right to be quite unconcerned, if I could. I was the Duke of Argyll's guest, and he had nothing to do with the Duchess of Hamilton's foolish anger.

I knew it was not the rule here to drink to anybody. But that I might have the satisfaction for once to look the Duchess in the face, with a glass in my hand, I rose a little and with a respectful air addressed her: "My lady Duchess, I have the honour to drink your grace's good health." I think I repeated all these words audibly and with a steady countenance. This was rather too much. But she had set me at defiance.[915]

She was very attentive to Mr Johnson. I know not how a middle state came to be mentioned. She asked Mr Johnson something about it. "Madam," said he, "your own relation Mr Archibald Campbell can tell you better about it. He was a bishop of the Nonjurant Communion, and wrote a book upon that subject."[916] He engaged to get it for her grace. He gave a full history of Mr Archibald Campbell, which I am sorry I do not recollect particularly.[917] He said he had been bred a violent Whig, but afterwards kept better company, and became a Tory. He said this with a fine smile, in pleasant allusion, as I thought, to the opposition between the political principles of the Duke's clan and his own. He added that Mr Campbell, after the Revolution, was thrown in gaol on account of his tenets; but, on application by letter to the old Lord Townshend, was released: that he always spoke of his Lordship with great gratitude, saying, 'though a *Whig*, he had humanity'.[918]

Luxury was introduced. He defended it. "We have now," said he, "a splendid dinner before us" (or words to that effect). "Which of all these dishes is unwholesome?" The Duke asserted that he had observed the grandees of Spain diminished in their size by luxury. Mr Johnson politely acquiesced in any observation which the Duke himself had made, but said that man must be very different from all other animals if he is diminished by good living, for the size of all other animals is increased by it.

I said something of my belief in the second sight. The Duchess said, "I fancy (or "I suppose") you will be a Methodist." This was the only sentence she ever deigned to utter to me; and I take it for granted she thought it a good hit on my credulity in the Douglas Cause.

A Colonel Livingstone, the Member for the County, was there. He talked a bit vaguely; and the result was that Mr Johnson afterwards remarked of him, "A mighty misty man, the Colonel." I told Mr Johnson a remark which I made. The Duke wanted to show a specimen of marble. He sent the Colonel for it, who brought a wrong piece; upon which he had to go back again to the other room, where it lay. He was conscious of an appearance of servility, but could not rebel. As he walked away, he whistled, to show his independency. Mr Johnson thought this a nice trait of character.

He talked a great deal, and was so entertaining that Lady Betty Hamilton went and placed her chair next his, leaned upon it, and listened eagerly. It would have made a fine picture to have drawn the sage and her at this time in their several attitudes. He did not know all the while that it was a princess of the blood who thus listened to him. I told him afterwards. I never saw him so gentle and complaisant as this day.

We went to tea. The Duke and I walked up and down the drawing-room, conversing. The Duchess persevered in her aversion to me, for which I really made allowance, considering how deeply she was interested for her son's cause, which I had opposed most heartily in every respect.[919]

She made Mr Johnson come and sit by her, while she served him with tea. I heard her say something of people being bad, and not what he thought them. He did not understand her, but I well knew it referred to me. I told him afterwards, and he thought it poor. She asked him why he made his journey so late in the year. "Why, madam," said he, "you know Mr Boswell must attend the Court of Session, and it does not rise till the twelfth of August."

She said, with spite, "I know *nothing* of Mr Boswell."

I heard this, and despised it. It was weak as well as impertinent. Poor Lady Lucy Douglas, to whom I mentioned it, observed, "She knew *too much* of Mr Boswell." I shall make no remark on her grace's speech. I indeed felt it as rather too severe; but when I recollected that my punishment was inflicted by so dignified a beauty, I had that kind of consolation which a man would feel who is strangled by a silken cord.[920]

Dr Johnson was all attention to her grace. I never saw him so courtly. He had afterwards a droll expression upon her dignity of three titles:

Hamilton, Brandon, Argyll. Borrowing an image from the Turkish empire, he called her a Duchess with three tails.

He was well pleased with our visit to the Duke, who was exceedingly polite to him; and upon his complaining of the shelties, which he had hitherto rode, being too small for him, his grace told him he should have a good horse to carry him next day.

Mr John Macaulay passed the evening with us at our inn . . . at this, and challenged him hotly – "Mr Macaulay, Mr Macaulay! Don't you know it is very rude to cry *eh! eh!* when one is talking?" Poor Macaulay had nothing to say for himself. But the truth is, it was a sin of ignorance, or mere rusticity. Afterwards, when Mr Johnson spoke of people whose principles were good but whose practice was faulty, Mr Macaulay said he had no notion of people being in earnest in their good professions, whose practice was not suitable. The Doctor grew angry, and said, "Are you so ignorant of human nature, sir, as not to know that a man may be very sincere in good principles, without having good practice?"[921]

Dr Johnson was unquestionably in the right; and whoever examines himself candidly will be satisfied of it, though the inconsistency between principles and practice is greater in some men than in others.

I recollect very little of this night's conversation. I am sorry that indolence came upon me towards the conclusion of our journey, so that I did not write down what passed with the same assiduity as during the greatest part of it.

TUESDAY 26 OCTOBER. Mr Macaulay breakfasted with us, nothing hurt or dismayed by his last night's correction. Being a man of good sense, he had a just admiration of Dr Johnson.

Either yesterday morning or this, I communicated to Dr Johnson, from Mr Macaulay's information, the news that Dr Beattie had got a pension of two hundred pounds a year. He sat up in his bed, clapped his hands, and cried, "O brave we!" – a peculiar exclamation of his when he rejoices.

As we sat over our tea, Mr Home's tragedy of *Douglas* was mentioned. I put Dr Johnson in mind that once, in a coffee-house at Oxford, he called to old Mr Sheridan, "How came you, sir, to give Home a gold medal for writing that foolish play?"[922] And defied Mr Sheridan to show ten good lines in it. He did not insist they should be together, but that there were not ten good lines in the whole play. He now persisted in this. I endeavoured to defend that pathetic and beautiful tragedy, and repeated the following passage:

——————— *Sincerity,*
Thou first of virtues! let no mortal leave
Thy onward path, although the earth should gape,
And from the gulf of hell destruction cry,
To take dissimulation's winding way.

JOHNSON. "That will not do, sir. Nothing is good but what is consistent with truth or probability, which this is not. Juvenal, indeed, gives us a noble picture of inflexible virtue:

> *Esto bonus miles, tutor bonus, arbiter idem*
> *Integer: ambiguae si quando citabere testis,*
> *Incertaeque rei, Phalaris licet imperet, ut sis*
> *Falsus, et admoto dictet perjuria tauro,*
> *Summum crede nefas animam praeferre pudori,*
> *Et propter vitam vivendi perdere causas.*"[923]

He repeated the lines with great force and dignity; then added, "And after this, comes Johnny Home with his *earth gaping*, and his *destruction crying* – pooh!"[924]

While we were lamenting the number of ruined religious buildings which we had lately seen, I spoke with peculiar feeling of the miserable neglect of the chapel belonging to the Palace of Holyrood House, in which are deposited the remains of many of the kings of Scotland, and of many of our nobility. I said it was a disgrace to the country that it was not repaired, and particularly complained that my friend Douglas, the representative of a great house and proprietor of a vast estate, should suffer the sacred spot where his mother lies interred to be unroofed, and exposed to all the inclemencies of the weather.[925] Dr Johnson, who, I know not how, had formed an opinion on the Hamilton side in the Douglas Cause, slyly answered, "Sir, sir, don't be too severe upon the gentleman; don't accuse him of want of filial piety! Lady Jane Douglas was not *his* mother."[926]

He roused my zeal so much that I took the liberty to tell him he knew nothing of the cause, which I do most seriously believe was the case. Had the Duchess of Argyll known that he was a *Hamiltonian*, her Grace would probably have honoured him with still more of her attention than he received, a part of which I cannot help presuming to impute to a desire of contrast with the neglect and scorn which a *Douglasian* should experience, but of which I hope there would now be no more, it being a principle with me that all offences whatever will in time be forgiven.[927]

Tuesday 26 October

We were now 'in a country of bridles and saddles', and set out fully equipped. The Duke of Argyll was obliging enough to mount Dr Johnson on a stately steed from his grace's stable. My friend was highly pleased, and Joseph said, "He now looks like a bishop."

We dined at the inn at Tarbet, and at night came to Rossdhu, the beautiful seat of Sir James Colquhoun, on the banks of Loch Lomond, where I, and any friends whom I have introduced, have ever been received with kind and elegant hospitality.[928]

WEDNESDAY 27 OCTOBER. When I went into Dr Johnson's room this morning, I observed to him how wonderfully courteous he had been at Inveraray, and said, "You were quite a fine gentleman, when with the Duchess."

He answered, in good humour, "Sir, I look upon myself as a very polite man." And he was right, in a proper manly sense of the word. As an immediate proof of it, let me observe, that he would not send back the Duke of Argyll's horse without a letter of thanks, which I copied.

> *To his Grace the Duke of Argyll* / Rossdhu, Oct. 27, 1773. / MY LORD, That kindness which disposed your grace to supply me with the horse, which I have now returned, will make you pleased to hear that he has carried me well. By my diligence in the little commission with which I was honoured by the Duchess, I will endeavour to show how highly I value the favours which I have received, and how much I desire to be thought, my lord, your grace's most obedient, and most humble servant, / SAM. JOHNSON.[929]

The Duke was so attentive to his respectable guest that on the same day he wrote him an answer, which was received at Auchinleck:[930]

> *To Dr Johnson, Auchinleck, Ayrshire* / Inveraray, Oct. 29, 1773. / SIR, I am glad to hear your journey from this place was not unpleasant, in regard to your horse. I wish I could have supplied you with good weather, which I am afraid you felt the want of. The Duchess of Argyll desires her compliments to you, and is much obliged to you for remembering her commission. I am, sir, your most obedient humble servant, / ARGYLL.

I am happy to insert every memorial of the honour done to my great friend. Indeed, I was at all times desirous to preserve the letters which he received from eminent persons, of which, as of all other papers, he was very negligent; and I once proposed to him that they should be committed to my care, as his *custos rotulorum*. I wish he had complied with my request, as by that means many valuable writings might have been preserved that are now lost.[931]

After breakfast, Dr Johnson and I were furnished with a boat, and sailed about upon Loch Lomond and landed on some of the islands which are interspersed. He was much pleased with the scene, which is so well known by the accounts of various travellers that it is unnecessary for me to attempt any description of it.

I recollect none of his conversation, except that, when talking of dress, he said, "Sir, were I to have anything fine, it should be very fine. Were I to wear a ring, it should not be a bauble, but a stone of great value. Were I to wear a laced or embroidered waistcoat, it should be very rich. I had once a very rich laced waistcoat, which I wore the first night of my tragedy."[932]

Lady Helen Colquhoun being a very pious woman, the conversation after dinner took a religious turn. Her ladyship defended the Presbyterian mode of public worship; upon which Dr Johnson delivered those excellent arguments for a form of prayer which he has introduced into his *Journey*.[933] I am myself fully convinced that a form of prayer for public worship is in general most decent and edifying. *Solemnia verba* have a kind of prescriptive sanctity, and make a deeper impression on the mind than extemporaneous effusions, in which, as we know not what they are to be, we cannot readily acquiesce. Yet I would allow also of a certain portion of extempore address, as occasion may require. This is the practice of the French Protestant churches. And although the office of forming supplications to the throne of heaven is, in my mind, too great a trust to be indiscriminately committed to the discretion of every minister, I do not mean to deny that sincere devotion may be experienced when joining in prayer with those who use no liturgy.

CHAPTER THIRTEEN

Lowlands Again

SAMUEL JOHNSON

Where the Loch discharges itself into a river, called the *Leven*, we passed a night with Mr *Smollet*, a relation of Doctor *Smollet*, to whose memory he has raised an obelisk on the bank near the house in which he was born.[934] The civility and respect which we found at every place, it is ungrateful to omit, and tedious to repeat. Here we were met by a post-chaise, that conveyed us to *Glasgow*.

To describe a city so much frequented as *Glasgow*, is unnecessary. The prosperity of its commerce appears by the greatness of many private houses, and a general appearance of wealth. It is the only episcopal city whose cathedral was left standing in the rage of Reformation. It is now divided into many separate places of worship, which, taken all together, compose a great pile, that had been some centuries in building, but was never finished; for the change of religion intercepted its progress, before the cross isle was added, which seems essential to a *Gothick* cathedral.

The college has not had a sufficient share of the increasing magnificence of the place. The session was begun; for it commences on the tenth of *October*, and continues to the tenth *of June*, but the students appeared not numerous, being, I suppose, not yet returned from their several homes. The division of the academical year into one session, and one recess, seems to me better accommodated to the present state of life, than that variegation of time by terms and vacations derived from distant centuries, in which it was probably convenient, and still continued in the *English* universities. So many solid months as the *Scotch* scheme of education joins together, allow and encourage a plan for each part of the year; but with us, he that has settled himself to study in the college is soon tempted into the country, and he that has adjusted his life in the country, is summoned back to his college.

Yet when I have allowed to the universities of *Scotland* a more rational distribution of time, I have given them, so far as my inquiries have informed me, all that they can claim. The students, for the most part, go thither boys, and depart before they are men; they carry with them little fundamental knowledge, and therefore the superstructure cannot be lofty. The grammar schools are not generally well supplied; for the character of a schoolmaster being there less honourable than in *England*, is seldom accepted by men who are capable to adorn it, and where the school has been deficient, the college can effect little.[935]

Men bred in the universities of *Scotland* cannot be expected to be often decorated with the splendours of ornamental erudition, but they obtain a mediocrity of knowledge, between learning and ignorance, not inadequate to the purposes of common life, which is, I believe, very widely diffused among them, and which countenanced in general by a national combination so invidious, that their friends cannot defend it, and actuated in particulars by a spirit of enterprise, so vigorous, that their enemies are constrained to praise it, enables them to find, or to make their way to employment, riches, and distinction.[936]

From *Glasgow* we directed our course to *Auchinleck*, an estate devolved, through a long series of ancestors, to Mr *Boswell's* father, the present possessor. In our way we found several places remarkable enough in themselves, but already described by those who viewed them at more leisure, or with much more skill; and stopped two days at Mr *Campbell's*, a gentleman married to Mrs *Boswell's* sister.[937]

Auchinleck, which signifies a *stony field*, seems not now to have any particular claim to its denomination.[938] It is a district generally level, and sufficiently fertile, but like all the *Western* side of *Scotland*, incommoded by very frequent rain. It was, with the rest of the country, generally naked, till the present possessor finding, by the growth of some stately trees near his old castle, that the ground was favourable enough to timber, adorned it very diligently with annual plantations.

Lord *Auchinleck*, who is one of the Judges of *Scotland*, and therefore not wholly at leisure for domestick business or pleasure, has yet found time to make improvements in his patrimony. He has built a house of hewn stone, very stately, and durable, and has advanced the value of his lands with great tenderness to his tenants.

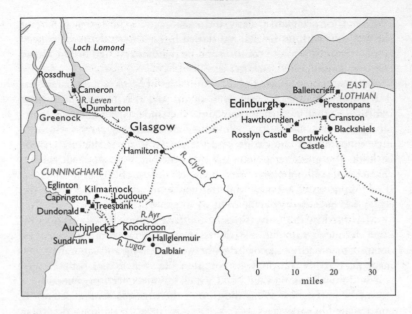

I was, however, less delighted with the elegance of the modern mansion, than with the sullen dignity of the old castle. I clambered with Mr *Boswell* among the ruins, which afford striking images of ancient life. It is, like other castles, built upon a point of rock, and was, I believe, anciently surrounded with a moat. There is another rock near it, to which the drawbridge, when it was let down, is said to have reached. Here, in the ages of tumult and rapine, the Laird was surprised and killed by the neighbouring Chief, who perhaps might have extinguished the family, had he not in a few days been seized and hanged, together with his sons, by *Douglas*, who came with his forces to the relief of *Auchinleck*.[939]

At no great distance from the house runs a pleasing brook, by a red rock, out of which has been hewn a very agreeable and commodious summerhouse, at less expence, as Lord *Auchinleck* told me, than would have been required to build a room of the same dimensions. The rock seems to have no more dampness than any other wall. Such opportunities of variety it is judicious not to neglect.

We now returned to *Edinburgh*, where I passed some days with men of learning, whose names want no advancement from my commemoration, or with women of elegance, which perhaps disclaims a pedant's praise.

The conversation of the *Scots* grows every day less unpleasing to the

27 October–22 November

English; their peculiarities wear fast away; their dialect is likely to become in half a century provincial and rustick, even to themselves. The great, the learned, the ambitious, and the vain, all cultivate the *English* phrase, and the *English* pronunciation, and in splendid companies *Scotch* is not much heard, except now and then from an old Lady.[940]

There is one subject of philosophical curiosity to be found in *Edinburgh*, which no other city has to shew; a college of the deaf and dumb, who are taught to speak, to read, to write, and to practice arithmetick, by a gentleman, whose name is *Braidwood*. The number which attends him is, I think, about twelve, which he brings together into a little school, and instructs according to their several degrees of proficiency.

I do not mean to mention the instruction of the deaf as new. Having been first practised upon the son of a constable of *Spain*, it was afterwards cultivated with much emulation in *England*, by *Wallis* and *Holder*, and was lately professed by Mr *Baker*, who once flattered me with hopes of seeing his method published. How far any former teachers have succeeded, it is not easy to know; the improvement of Mr *Braidwood's* pupils is wonderful. They not only speak, write, and understand what is written, but if he that speaks looks towards them, and modifies his organs by distinct and full utterance, they know so well what is spoken, that it is an expression scarcely figurative to say, they hear with the eye. That any have attained to the power mentioned by *Burnet*, of feeling sounds, by laying a hand on the speaker's mouth, I know not; but I have seen so much, that I can believe more; a single word, or a short sentence, I think, may possibly be so distinguished.

It will readily be supposed by those that consider this subject, that Mr *Braidwood's* scholars spell accurately. Orthography is vitiated among such as learn first to speak, and then to write, by imperfect notions of the relation between letters and vocal utterance; but to those students every character is of equal importance; for letters are to them not symbols of names, but of things; when they write they do not represent a sound, but delineate a form.

This school I visited, and found some of the scholars waiting for their master, whom they are said to receive at his entrance with smiling countenances and sparkling eyes, delighted with the hope of new ideas. One of the young Ladies had her slate before her, on which I wrote a question consisting of three figures, to be multiplied by two figures. She looked upon it, and quivering her fingers in a manner which I thought very pretty, but of which I know not whether it was art or play, multiplied the sum regularly in two lines, observing the decimal place; but did not add the two lines together, probably disdaining so easy an operation. I pointed at the place where the sum total should stand, and she noted it with such expedition as seemed to shew that she had it only to write.[941]

It was pleasing to see one of the most desperate of human calamities capable of so much help: whatever enlarges hope, will exalt courage; after having seen the deaf taught arithmetick, who would be afraid to cultivate the *Hebrides*?

Such are the things which this journey has given me an opportunity of seeing, and such are the reflections which that sight has raised. Having passed my time almost wholly in cities, I may have been surprised by modes of life and appearances of nature, that are familiar to men of wider survey and more varied conversation. Novelty and ignorance must always be reciprocal, and I cannot but be conscious that my thoughts on national manners, are the thoughts of one who has seen but little.

James Boswell

We were favoured with Sir James Colquhoun's coach to convey us in the evening to Cameron, the seat of Commissary Smollett.[942] Our satisfaction of finding ourselves again in a comfortable carriage was very great. We had a pleasing conviction of the commodiousness of civilization, and heartily laughed at the ravings of those absurd visionaries who have attempted to persuade us of the superior advantages of a *state of nature*.

Mr Smollett was a man of considerable learning, with abundance of animal spirits; so that he was a very good companion for Dr Johnson, who said to me, "We have had more solid talk here than at any place where we have been."

I remember Dr Johnson gave us this evening an able and eloquent discourse on the origin of evil, and on the consistency of moral evil with the power and goodness of GOD. He showed us how it arose from our free agency, an extinction of which would be a still greater evil than any we experience. I know not that he said anything absolutely new, but he said a great deal wonderfully well; and perceiving us to be delighted and satisfied, he concluded his harangue with an air of benevolent triumph over an objection which has distressed many worthy minds: "This then is the answer to the question, πόθεν τὸ κακόν?"[943] Mrs Smollett whispered me that it was the best sermon she had ever heard. Much do I upbraid myself for having neglected to preserve it.

Wednesday 27 October

THURSDAY 28 OCTOBER. Mr Smollett pleased Dr Johnson by producing a collection of newspapers in the time of the Usurpation, from which it appeared that all sorts of crimes were very frequent during that horrible anarchy.[944] By the side of the high road to Glasgow, at some distance from his house, he had erected a pillar to the memory of his ingenious kinsman, Dr Smollett; and he consulted Dr Johnson as to an inscription for it. Lord Kames, who, though he had a great store of knowledge, with much ingenuity and uncommon activity of mind, was no profound scholar, had, it seems, recommended an English inscription. Dr Johnson treated this with great contempt, saying, "An English inscription would be a disgrace to Dr Smollett." And in answer to what Lord Kames had urged as to the advantage of its being in English, because it would be generally understood, I observed that all to whom Dr Smollett's merit could be an object of respect and imitation would understand it as well in Latin; and that surely it was not meant for the Highland drovers, or other such people who pass and repass that way.

We were then shown a Latin inscription proposed for this monument. Dr Johnson sat down with an ardent and liberal earnestness to revise it, and greatly improved it by several additions and variations. I unfortunately did not take a copy of it as it originally stood, but I have happily preserved every fragment of what Dr Johnson wrote.

> *Quisquis ades, viator,*
> *Vel mente felix, vel studiis cultus,*
> *Immorare paululum memoriæ*
> *TOBIÆ SMOLLET, M.D.*
> *Viri iis virtutibus*
> *Quas in homine et cive*
> *Et laudes, et imiteris,*
> . . . . .
> *Postquam mira . . .*
> *Se . . . .*
> . . . .
> *Tali tantoque viro, suo patrueli,*
> . . . . . .
> *Hanc columnam,*
> *Amoris eheu! inane munumentum,*
> *In ipsis Leviniæ ripis,*
> *Quas primis infans vagitibus personuit,*
> *Versiculisque jam fere moriturus illustravit,*
> *Ponendam curavit*
> . . . .

The epitaph which has been inscribed on the pillar erected on the banks of the Leven, in honour of Dr Smollett, is as follows. The part which was written by Dr Johnson, it appears, has been altered; whether for the better, the reader will judge. The alterations are distinguished by italics.

Siste viator!
Si lepores ingeniique venam benignam,
Si morum callidissimum pictorem,
Unquam es miratus,
Immorare paululum memoriæ
TOBIÆ SMOLLET, M.D.
Viri virtutibus *hisce*
Quas in homine et cive
Et laudes et imiteris,
Haud mediocriter ornati:
Qui in literis variis versatus,
Postquam felicitate *sibi propria*
Sese posteris commendaverat,
Morte acerba raptus
Anno ætatis 51
Eheu! quam procul a patria!
Prope Liburni portum in Italia,
Jacet sepultus.
Tali tantoque viro, patrueli suo,
Cui in decursu lampada
Se potius tradidisse decuit,
Hanc Columnam,
Amoris, eheu! inane monumentum
In ipsis Leviniæ ripis,
Quas *versiculis sub exitu vitæ illustratas*
Primis infans vagitibus personuit,
Ponendam curavit
JACOBUS SMOLLET de Bonhill.
Abi et reminiscere,
Hoc quidem honore,
Non modo defuncti memoriæ,
Verum etiam exemplo, prospectum esse;
Aliis enim, si modo digni sint,
Idem erit virtutis præmium![945]

We had this morning a singular proof of Dr Johnson's quick and retentive memory. Hay's translation of Martial was lying in a window. I said I thought it was pretty well done, and showed him a particular epigram, I think of ten, but am certain of eight, lines. He read it, and tossed away the book, saying, "No, it is *not* pretty well." As I persisted in my opinion, he said, "Why, sir, the original is thus" (and he repeated it); "and this man's translation is thus"; and then he repeated that also, exactly, though he had never seen it before, and read it over only once, and that too without any intention of getting it by heart.

Here a post-chaise, which I had ordered from Glasgow, came for us, and we drove on in high spirits. We stopped at Dumbarton, and though the approach to the castle there is very steep, Dr Johnson ascended it with alacrity, and surveyed all that was to be seen. During the whole of our tour he showed uncommon spirit, could not bear to be treated like an old or infirm man, and was very unwilling to accept of any assistance; insomuch that, at our landing at Icolmkill, when Sir Allan Maclean and I submitted to be carried on men's shoulders from the boat to the shore, as it could not be brought quite close to land, he sprang into the sea and waded vigorously out.[946]

On our arrival at the Saracen's Head Inn at Glasgow, I was made happy by good accounts from home; and Dr Johnson, who had not received a single letter since we left Aberdeen, found here a great many, the perusal of which entertained him much. He enjoyed in imagination the comforts which we could now command, and seemed to be in high glee. I remember, he put a leg up on each side of the grate, and said, with a mock solemnity, by way of soliloquy but loud enough for me to hear it, "Here am I, an ENGLISH man, sitting by a *coal* fire."

FRIDAY 29 OCTOBER. The professors of the university being informed of our arrival, Dr Stevenson, Dr Reid, and Mr Anderson breakfasted with us. Mr Anderson accompanied us while Dr Johnson viewed this beautiful city. He had told me that one day in London, when Dr Adam Smith was boasting of it, he turned to him and said, "Pray, sir, have you ever seen Brentford?"

This was surely a strong instance of his impatience and spirit of contradiction. I put him in mind of it today, while he expressed his admiration of the elegant buildings, and whispered him, "Don't you feel some remorse?"

We were received in the college by a number of the professors, who showed all due respect to Dr Johnson; and then we paid a visit to the principal, Dr Leechman, at his own house, where Dr Johnson had the satisfaction of being told that his name had been gratefully celebrated in one of the parochial congregations in the Highlands, as the person to whose influence it was chiefly owing that the New Testament was allowed to be translated into the Erse language. It seems some political members of the Society in Scotland for Propagating Christian Knowledge, had opposed this pious undertaking, as tending to preserve the distinction between the Highlanders and Lowlanders. Dr Johnson wrote a long letter upon the subject to a friend, which being shown to them, made them ashamed, and afraid of being publicly exposed; so they were forced to a compliance. It is now in my possession, and is, perhaps, one of the best productions of his masterly pen.[947]

Professors Reid and Anderson, and the two Messieurs Foulis, the Elzevirs of Glasgow, dined and drank tea with us at our inn, after which the professors went away; and I, having a letter to write, left my fellow-traveller with Messieurs Foulis.[948] Though good and ingenious men, they had that unsettled speculative mode of conversation which is offensive to a man regularly taught at an English school and university. I found that, instead of listening to the dictates of the sage, they had teased him with questions and doubtful disputations. He came in a flutter to me and desired I might come back again, for he could not bear these men. "O ho! sir," said I, "you are flying to me for refuge!"

He never, in any situation, was at a loss for a ready repartee. He answered, with quick vivacity, "It is of two evils choosing the least." I was delighted with this flash bursting from the cloud which hung upon his mind, closed my letter directly, and joined the company.

We supped at Professor Anderson's. The general impression upon my memory is that we had not much conversation at Glasgow, where the professors, like their brethren at Aberdeen, did not venture to expose themselves much to the battery of cannon which they knew might play upon them. Dr Johnson, who was fully conscious of his own superior powers, afterwards praised Principal Robertson for his caution in this respect. He said to me, "Robertson, sir, was in the right. Robertson is a man of eminence, and the head of a college at Edinburgh. He had a character to maintain, and did well not to risk its being lessened."

SATURDAY 30 OCTOBER. We set out towards Ayrshire. I sent Joseph on to Loudoun, with a message that, if the Earl was at home, Dr Johnson and I would have the honour to dine with him. Joseph met us on the road, and reported that the Earl 'jumped for joy', and said, "I shall be very happy to see them."

We were received with a most pleasing courtesy by his lordship, and by the Countess his mother, who, in her ninety-fifth year, had all her faculties quite unimpaired. This was a very cheering sight to Dr Johnson, who had an extraordinary desire for long life. Her ladyship was sensible and well-informed, and had seen a great deal of the world. Her lord had held several high offices, and she was sister to the great Earl of Stair.

I cannot here refrain from paying a just tribute to the character of John, Earl of Loudoun, who did more service to the county of Ayr in general, as well as to individuals in it, than any man we have ever had. It is painful to think that he met with much ingratitude from persons both in high and low rank; but such was his temper, such his knowledge of 'base mankind',[949] that, as if he had expected no other return, his mind was never soured, and he retained his good humour and benevolence to the last. The tenderness of his heart was proved in 1745–6, when he had an important command in the Highlands, and behaved with a generous humanity to the unfortunate. I cannot figure a more honest politician; for, though his interest in our county was great, and generally successful, he not only did not deceive by fallacious promises, but was anxious that people should not deceive themselves by too sanguine expectations. His kind and dutiful attention to his mother was unremitted. At his house was true hospitality; a plain but a plentiful table; and every guest, being left at perfect freedom, felt himself quite easy and happy. While I live, I shall honour the memory of this amiable man.

At night, we advanced a few miles farther, to the house of Mr Campbell of Treesbank, who was married to one of my wife's sisters, and were entertained very agreeably by a worthy couple.

SUNDAY 31 OCTOBER. We reposed here in tranquillity. Dr Johnson was pleased to find a numerous and excellent collection of books, which had mostly belonged to the Reverend Mr John Campbell, brother of our host.[950] I was desirous to have procured for my fellow-traveller today the company of Sir John Cuninghame of Caprington, whose castle was but two miles from us.[951] He was a very distinguished scholar, was long abroad, and during part of the time lived much with the learned Cunningham, the opponent of Bentley as a critic upon Horace. He wrote Latin with great elegance, and, what is very remarkable, read Homer and Ariosto through every year. I wrote to him to request he would come to us, but unfortunately he was prevented by indisposition.

MONDAY I NOVEMBER. Though Dr Johnson was lazy and averse to move, I insisted that he should go with me and pay a visit to the Countess of Eglinton, mother of the late and present Earl. I assured him he would find himself amply recompensed for the trouble, and he yielded to my solicitations, though with some unwillingness. We were well mounted, and had not many miles to ride. He talked of the attention that is necessary in order to distribute our charity judiciously. "If thoughtlessly done, we may neglect the most deserving objects; and, as every man has but a certain proportion to give, if it is lavished upon those who first present themselves, there may be nothing left for such as have a better claim. A man should first relieve those who are nearly connected with him, by whatever tie; and then, if he has anything to spare, may extend his bounty to a wider circle."

As we passed very near the castle of Dundonald, which was one of the many residencies of the kings of Scotland, and in which Robert the Second lived and died, Dr Johnson wished to survey it particularly. It stands on a beautiful rising ground, which is seen at a great distance on several quarters, and from whence there is an extensive prospect of the rich district of Cunninghame, the western sea, the Isle of Arran, and a part of the northern coast of Ireland. It has long been unroofed; and, though of considerable size, we could not, by any power of imagination, figure it as having been a suitable habitation for majesty. Dr Johnson, to irritate my old Scottish enthusiasm, was very jocular on the homely accommodation of 'King Bob', and roared and laughed till the ruins echoed.

Lady Eglinton, though she was now in her eighty-fifth year, and had lived in the retirement of the country for almost half a century, was still a very agreeable woman. She was of the noble house of Kennedy, and had all the elevation which the consciousness of such birth inspires. Her figure was majestic, her manners high-bred, her reading extensive, and her conversation elegant. She had been the admiration of the gay circles of life, and the patroness of poets.

Dr Johnson was delighted with his reception here. Her principles in church and state were congenial with his. She knew all his merit and had heard much of him from her son, Alexander Earl of Eglinton. I had always been honoured with very obliging attention by her Ladyship. I was her ordinary counsel. She subscribed her letters to me 'your antediluvian friend'. Some time before her death she gave me *The Gentle Shepherd* in Allan Ramsay's own handwriting and all her letters from her deceased son, as she knew my intimacy with him. I cannot speak of him but with an emotion which agitates me more than I can express. All who knew his lordship will allow that his understanding and accomplishments were of no ordinary rate. From the gay habits which he had early acquired, he spent too much of his time with men, and in pursuits, far beneath such a mind as his. He afterwards became sensible of it, applied to business, and by a very able speech in the House of Lords upon the subject of banks and paper credit gave a proof of what he could do. He was cut off in the prime of his life, just when his country had the pleasing prospect of seeing him rise into consequence in the state. I cannot speak of him but with emotions of most affectionate regret. He was the patron of my early years. I lived under his roof in London and was first introduced by him into what alone deserves the name of life. His numerous relations and friends I hope will not suffer so distinguished a nobleman to sink into oblivion after the present age is past, but will have that elegant appearance which is preserved by the pencil of Sir Joshua Reynolds diffused by an engraving, and memoirs written of that life which every day communicated felicity to all around. The Countess his mother, knowing my intimacy with him, gave me all his letters to her, which, as well as those with which he honoured me, are unquestionable proofs of his brilliant vivacity.[952]

Often must I have occasion to upbraid myself that soon after our return to the mainland, I allowed indolence to prevail over me so much as to shrink from the labour of continuing my Journal with the same minuteness as before; sheltering myself in the thought that we had done with the Hebrides, and not considering that Dr Johnson's memorabilia were likely to be more valuable when we were restored to a more polished society. Much has thus been irrecoverably lost. When I talked of my being so fortunate in the friendship of Dr Johnson, Lady Eglinton said to me, "My friend, consider what a superior advantage you have, and make good use of it."[953]

In the course of our conversation this day, it came out that Lady Eglinton was married the year before Dr Johnson was born; upon which she graciously said to him that she might have been his mother, and that she now adopted him; and when we were going away, she embraced him, saying, "My dear son, farewell!"[954]

My friend was much pleased with this day's entertainment, and owned that I had done well to force him out.

TUESDAY 2 NOVEMBER. We were now in a country not only 'of saddles and bridles', but of post-chaises; and having ordered one from Kilmarnock, we got to Auchinleck before dinner.

My father was not quite a year and a half older than Dr Johnson,[955] but his conscientious discharge of his laborious duty as a judge in

Scotland (where the law proceedings are almost all in writing), a severe complaint which ended in his death, and the loss of my mother, a woman of almost unexampled piety and goodness, had before this time in some degree affected his spirits, and rendered him less disposed to exert his faculties; for he had originally a very strong mind and cheerful temper.[956] He assured me he never had felt one moment of what is called low spirits, or uneasiness without a real cause. He had a great many good stories, which he told uncommonly well, and he was remarkable for 'humour, *incolumi gravitate*', as Lord Monboddo used to characterize it. His age, his office, and his character had long given him an acknowledged claim to great attention, in whatever company he was; and he could ill brook any diminution of it. He was as sanguine a Whig and Presbyterian as Dr Johnson was a Tory and Church of England man; and as he had not much leisure to be informed of Dr Johnson's great merits by reading his works, he had a partial and unfavourable notion of him, founded on his supposed political tenets, which were so discordant to his own that, instead of speaking of him with that respect to which he was entitled, he used to call him 'a Jacobite fellow'.

Knowing all this, I should not have ventured to bring them together, had not my father, out of kindness to me, desired me to invite Dr Johnson to his house. I was very anxious that all should be well; and begged of my friend to avoid three topics, as to which they differed very widely: Whiggism, Presbyterianism, and – Sir John Pringle.[957] He said courteously, "I shall certainly not talk on subjects which I am told are disagreeable to a gentleman under whose roof I am; especially, I shall not do so to *your father*."

Our first day went off very smoothly. It rained, and we could not get out; but my father showed Dr Johnson his library, which, in curious editions of the Greek and Roman classics, is, I suppose, not excelled by any private collection in Great Britain. My father had studied at Leyden and been very intimate with the Gronovii and other learned men there. He was a sound scholar, and, in particular, had collated manuscripts and different editions of Anacreon, and others of the Greek lyric poets, with great care; so that my friend and he had much matter for conversation, without touching on the fatal topics of difference.

Dr Johnson found here Baxter's Anacreon, which he told me he had long inquired for in vain, and began to suspect there was no such book. Baxter was the keen antagonist of Barnes. His life is in the *Biographia Britannica*. My father has written many notes on this book, and Dr Johnson and I talked of having it reprinted.

Tuesday 2 November

WEDNESDAY 3 NOVEMBER. It rained all day, and gave Dr Johnson an impression of that incommodiousness of climate in the West, of which he has taken notice in his *Journey*; but, being well accommodated and furnished with variety of books, he was not dissatisfied.

Some gentlemen of the neighbourhood came to visit my father, but there was little conversation. One of them asked Dr Johnson how he liked the Highlands. The question seemed to irritate him, for he answered, "How, sir, can you ask me what obliges me to speak unfavourably of a country where I have been hospitably entertained? Who *can* like the Highlands? I like the inhabitants very well." The gentleman asked no more questions.

Let me now make up for the present neglect by again gleaning from the past. At Lord Monboddo's, after the conversation upon the decrease of learning in England, his lordship mentioned *Hermes* by Mr Harris of Salisbury, as the work of a living author for whom he had a great respect. Dr Johnson said nothing at the time, but when we were in our post-chaise, told me he thought Harris 'a coxcomb'. This he said of him not as a man but as an author; and I give his opinions of men and books, faithfully, whether they agree with my own or not. I do admit, that there always appeared to me something of affectation in Mr Harris's manner of writing; something of a habit of clothing plain thoughts in analytic and categorical formality. But all his writings are imbued with learning; and all breathe that philanthropy and amiable disposition, which distinguished him as a man.[958]

At another time during our tour, he drew the character of a rapacious Highland chief with the strength of Theophrastus or La Bruyère; concluding with these words: "Sir, he has no more the soul of a chief than an attorney who has twenty houses in a street, and considers how much he can make by them."[959]

He this day, when we were by ourselves, observed, how common it was for people to talk from books; to retail the sentiments of others, and not their own; in short, to converse without any originality of thinking. He was pleased to say, "You and I do not talk from books."

THURSDAY 4 NOVEMBER. I was glad to have at length a very fine day, on which I could show Dr Johnson the Place of my family, which he has honoured with so much attention in his *Journey*. He is, however, mistaken in thinking that the Celtic name, *Auchinleck*, has no relation to the natural appearance of it. I believe every Celtic name of a place will be found very descriptive. *Auchinleck* does not signify a *stony field*, as he has said, but a *field of flagstones*; and this place has a number of rocks which abound in strata of that kind.[960]

The 'sullen dignity of the old castle', as he has forcibly expressed it, delighted him exceedingly. On one side of the rock on which its ruins stand runs the river Lugar, which is here of considerable breadth, and is bordered by other high rocks, shaded with wood. On the other side runs a brook, skirted in the same manner, but on a smaller scale. I cannot figure a more romantic scene.

I felt myself elated here, and expatiated to my illustrious mentor on the antiquity and honourable alliances of my family, and on the merits of its founder, Thomas Boswell, who was highly favoured by his sovereign, James IV of Scotland, and fell with him at the battle of Flodden Field; and in the glow of what, I am sensible, will, in a commercial age, be considered as genealogical enthusiasm, did not omit to mention what I was sure my friend would not think lightly of, my relation to the Royal Personage, whose liberality, on his accession to the throne, had given him comfort and independence. I have, in a former page, acknowledged my pride of ancient blood, in which I was encouraged by Dr Johnson; my readers therefore will not be surprised at my having indulged it on this occasion.[961]

Not far from the old castle is a spot of consecrated earth, on which may be traced the foundations of an ancient chapel, dedicated to St Vincent, and where in old times was the 'place of graves' for the family. It grieves me to think that the remains of sanctity here, which were considerable, were dragged away and employed in building a part of the house of Auchinleck of the middle age, which was the family residence till my father erected that 'elegant modern mansion', of which Dr Johnson speaks so handsomely. Perhaps this chapel may one day be restored.

Dr Johnson was pleased when I showed him some venerable old trees under the shade of which my ancestors had walked. He exhorted me to plant assiduously, as my father had done to a great extent.

As we sauntered about, while I was every now and then turning round to my venerable friend, viewing him steadily, and wondering and exulting in having him in our shades, I told him that if I survived him, it was my intention to erect a monument to him here, among scenes which, in my mind, were all classical; for in my youth I had appropriated to them many of the descriptions of the Roman poets. He could not bear to have death presented to him in any shape, for his constitutional melancholy made the king of terrors more frightful. He turned off the subject, saying, "Sir, I hope to see your grandchildren!"

Thursday 4 November

This forenoon he observed some cattle without horns, of which he has taken notice in his *Journey*, and seems undecided whether they be of a particular race.[962] His doubts appear to have had no foundation, for my respectable neighbour, Mr Fairlie, who, with all his attention to agriculture, finds time both for the classics and his friends, assures me they are a distinct species, and that, when any of their calves have horns, a mixture of breed can be traced. In confirmation of his opinion, he pointed out to me the following passage in Tacitus: "*Ne armentis quidem suus honor, aut gloria frontis.*" (*De Mor. Germ.* §5), which he wondered had escaped Dr Johnson.[963]

On the front of the house of Auchinleck is this inscription: "*Quod petis, hic est; / Est Ulubris; animus si te non deficit aequus.*"[964] It is characteristic of the founder; but the *animus aequus* is, alas! not inheritable, nor the subject of devise. He always talked to me as if it were in a man's own power to attain it; but Dr Johnson told me that he owned to him, when they were alone, his persuasion that it was in a great measure constitutional, or the effect of causes which do not depend on ourselves, and that Horace boasts too much when he says, "*Æquum mi animum ipse parabo.*"[965]

But I must call myself off from my family and Place, upon which I could dwell the livelong day. Dr Johnson's approbation of family memoirs when we were at the Laird of MacLeod's encouraged me in preserving and continuing those which my grandfather and father wrote; and he last year promised to embody them in his lofty language, both in Latin and English, a most extraordinary favour which – I fear in part through my delay – has been irremediably lost to me and my family. For when shall we again have such a writer?

FRIDAY 5 NOVEMBER. The Reverend Mr Dun, our parish minister, who had dined with us yesterday with some other company, insisted that Dr Johnson and I should dine with him today. This gave me an opportunity to show my friend the road to the church, made by my father at a great expense for above three miles on his own estate, through a range of well-enclosed farms, with a row of trees on each side of it. He called it the *Via sacra*, and was very fond of it.

Dr Johnson, though he held notions far distant from those of the Presbyterian clergy, yet could associate on good terms with them. Mr Dun, though a man of sincere good principles, as a Presbyterian divine discovered a narrowness of information concerning the dignitaries of the Church of England, among whom may be found men of the greatest learning, virtue, and piety, and of a truly apostolic character. He talked before Dr Johnson of fat bishops and drowsy deans; and, in short, seemed to believe the illiberal and profane scoffings of professed satirists or vulgar railers. Dr Johnson was so highly offended that he said to him, "Sir, you know no more of our church than a Hottentot."

I was sorry that he brought this upon himself. But I hoped it would do him good.[966]

SATURDAY 6 NOVEMBER. I cannot be certain whether it was on this day or a former that Dr Johnson and my father came in collision. If I recollect right, the contest began while my father was showing him his collection of medals; and Oliver Cromwell's coin unfortunately introduced Charles the First, and Toryism. They became exceedingly warm and violent, and I was very much distressed by being present at such an altercation between two men, both of whom I reverenced; yet I durst not interfere. It would certainly be very unbecoming in me to exhibit my honoured father and my respected friend as intellectual gladiators, for the entertainment of the public; and therefore I suppress what would, I dare say, make an interesting scene in this dramatic sketch – this account of the transit of Johnson over the Caledonian Hemisphere.[967]

Yet I think I may, without impropriety, mention one circumstance, as an instance of my father's address. Dr Johnson challenged him, as he did us all at Talisker, to point out any theological works of merit written by Presbyterian ministers in Scotland. My father, whose studies did not lie much in that way, owned to me afterwards that he was somewhat at a loss how to answer, but that luckily he recollected having read in catalogues the title of *Durham on the Galatians*; upon which he boldly said, "Pray, sir, have you read Mr Durham's excellent commentary on the Galatians?"

"No, sir," said Dr Johnson.

My father then had him before the wind, and went on: "How came you, then, to speak with such contempt of the writings of our church? You may buy it at any time for half a crown or three shillings."

By this lucky thought my father kept him at bay, and for some time enjoyed his triumph; but his antagonist soon made a retort: "Sir, it must be better recommended before I give half the money for it."[968]

In the course of their altercation, Whiggism and Presbyterianism, Toryism and Episcopacy, were terribly buffeted. My worthy hereditary friend, Sir John Pringle, never having been mentioned, happily escaped without a bruise.

My father's opinion of Dr Johnson may be conjectured from the name he afterwards gave him, which was 'Ursa Major'. But it is not true, as has been reported, that it was in consequence of my saying that he was a *constellation* of genius and literature. It was a sly abrupt expression to one of his brethren on the bench of the Court of Session, in which Dr Johnson was then standing, but it was not said in his hearing.[969]

SUNDAY 7 NOVEMBER. My father and I went to public worship in our parish church, where in a comfortable pious union with the tenants of Auchinleck, to many of whom their farms have descended through many generations of the same family, I am much benefited, though there is no form of prayer or such solemnities as GOD prescribed to his own people the Jews and are to be found in some other Christian establishments. Dr Johnson stayed at home and I doubt not employed his time in private to very good purpose, yet, as God is worshipped in spirit and in truth, and the same doctrines preached as in the Church of England, my friend would certainly have shown more liberality had he attended. His uniform and fervent piety was manifested on many occasions during our tour which I have not mentioned. His reason for not joining in Presbyterian worship has been recorded in a former page.[970] Sunday is kept very strictly in the country parts of Scotland, which is certainly the best extreme.

The evening moved on well enough. I had a pleasing satisfaction in reading some of Dr Johnson's works in the library, looking up to him as at a great distance, as I formerly used to do, and then running into his room and chatting with him as friend and companion.

MONDAY 8 NOVEMBER. Notwithstanding the altercation that had passed, my father, who had the dignified courtesy of an old baron, was very civil to Dr Johnson, and politely attended him to the post-chaise which was to convey us to Edinburgh.

Thus they parted. They are now in another, and a higher, state of existence; and as they were both worthy Christian men, I trust they have met in happiness. But I must observe, in justice to my friend's political principles and my own, that they have met in a place where there is no room for Whiggism.

We came at night to a good inn at Hamilton. I recollect no more.[971]

TUESDAY 9 NOVEMBER. I wished to have shown Dr Johnson the Duke of Hamilton's house, commonly called the *Palace* of Hamilton, which is close by the town. It is an object which, having been pointed out to me as a splendid edifice from my earliest years, in travelling between

Auchinleck and Edinburgh, has still great grandeur in my imagination. My friend consented to stop and view the outside of it, but could not be persuaded to go into it.[972]

We arrived this night at Edinburgh, after an absence of eighty-three days. For five weeks together, of the tempestuous season, there had been no account received of us. I cannot express how happy I was on finding myself again at home.

WEDNESDAY 10 NOVEMBER. It was near ten before I got up. I had a certain degree of uneasiness from fearing that after my hardy and spirited tour I should sink into indolence. But I made myself easy by considering that it was allowable, natural, and happy that I should enjoy the comfort of repose when returned home.

Old Mr Drummond, the bookseller, came to breakfast. Dr Johnson and he had not met for ten years, and he was a good deal failed. There was respect on his side, and kindness on Dr Johnson's. Soon afterwards Lord Elibank came in, and was much pleased at seeing Dr Johnson in Scotland. His lordship said, hardly anything seemed to him more improbable than Mr Johnson's being in Scotland. Dr Johnson had a very high opinion of him. Speaking of him to me, he characterized him thus: "Lord Elibank has read a great deal. It is true, I can find in books all that he has read; but he has a great deal of what is in books, proved by the test of real life."

Indeed, there have been few men whose conversation discovered more knowledge enlivened by fancy. He published several small pieces of distinguished merit, and has left some in manuscript, in particular an account of the expedition against Cartagena, in which he served as an officer in the Army. His writings deserve to be collected. He was the early patron of Dr Robertson the historian, and Mr Home the tragic poet; who, when they were ministers of country parishes, lived near his seat. He told me, "I saw these lads had talents, and they were much with me." I hope they will pay a grateful tribute to his memory.

The morning was chiefly taken up by Dr Johnson's giving him an account of our tour. The subject of difference in political principles was introduced. JOHNSON. "It is much increased by opposition. There was a violent Whig, with whom I used to contend with great eagerness. After his death I felt my Toryism much abated." I suppose he meant Mr Walmesley of Lichfield, whose character he has drawn so well in his Life of Edmund Smith.

Captain Erskine came. So did Mr Nairne, and he and I accompanied

Dr Johnson to Edinburgh Castle, which he owned was 'a great place'. But I must mention, as a striking instance of that spirit of contradiction to which he had a strong propensity, when Lord Elibank was some days after talking of it with the natural elation of a Scotchman, or of any man who is proud of a stately fortress in his own country, Dr Johnson affected to despise it, observing that 'it would make a good *prison* in ENGLAND'.

Lest it should be supposed that I have suppressed one of his sallies against my country, it may not be improper here to correct a mistaken account that has been circulated as to his conversation this day. It has been said that, being desired to attend to the noble prospect from the Castle Hill, he replied, "Sir, the noblest prospect that a Scotchman ever sees is the high road that leads him to London." This lively sarcasm was thrown out at a tavern in London, in my presence, many years before.[973]

We had with us today at dinner at my house, the Lady Dowager Colville and Lady Anne Erskine, sisters of the Earl of Kellie; the Honourable Archibald Erskine, who has now succeeded to that title;[974] Lord Elibank; the Reverend Dr Blair; Mr Tytler, the acute vindicator of Mary Queen of Scots, and his son, the advocate.

Fingal being talked of, Dr Johnson, who used to boast that he had, from the first, resisted both Ossian and the Giants of Patagonia, averred his positive disbelief of its authenticity. Lord Elibank said, "I am sure it is not Macpherson's. Mr Johnson, I keep company a great deal with you; it is known I do. I may borrow from you better things than I can say myself, and give them as my own; but if I should, everybody will know whose they are."

The Doctor was not softened by this compliment. He denied merit to *Fingal*, supposing it to be the production of a man who has had the advantages that the present age affords, and said, "Nothing is more easy than to write enough in that style if once you begin."[975]

Young Mr Tytler stepped briskly forward, and said, "*Fingal* is certainly genuine; for I have heard a great part of it repeated in the original." Dr Johnson indignantly asked him, "Sir, do you understand the original?" TYTLER. "No, sir." JOHNSON. "Why, then, we see to what this testimony comes. Thus it is." He afterwards said to me; "Did you observe the wonderful confidence with which young Tytler advanced, with his front ready *brazed?*"[976]

I mention this as a remarkable proof how liable the mind of man is to credulity, when not guarded by such strict examination as that which Dr Johnson habitually practised. The talents and integrity of the gentleman who made the remark, are unquestionable; yet, had not Dr Johnson made him advert to the consideration that he who does not understand a language cannot know that something which is recited to him is in that language, he might have believed, and reported to this hour, that he had 'heard a great part of *Fingal* repeated in the original'.

For the satisfaction of those on the north of the Tweed, who may think Dr Johnson's account of Caledonian credulity and inaccuracy too strong, it is but fair to add that he admitted the same kind of ready belief might be found in his own country. He would undertake, he said, to write an epic poem on the story of Robin Hood, and half England, to whom the names and places he should mention in it are familiar, would believe and declare they had heard it from their earliest years.

One of his objections to the authenticity of *Fingal*, during the conversation at Ullinish, is omitted in my Journal, but I perfectly recollect it. "Why is not the original deposited in some public library, instead of exhibiting attestations of its existence? Suppose there were a question in a court of justice whether a man be dead or alive. You aver he is alive, and you bring fifty witnesses to swear it; I answer, 'Why do you not produce the man?'"

This is an argument founded on one of the first principles of the law of evidence, which Gilbert would have held to be irrefragable.

I do not think it incumbent on me to give any precise decided opinion upon this question, as to which I believe more than some, and less than others. The subject appears to have now become very uninteresting to the public. That *Fingal* is not from beginning to end a translation from the Gaelic, but that *some* passages have been supplied by the editor to connect the whole, I have heard admitted by very warm advocates for its authenticity. If this be the case, why are not these distinctly ascertained? Antiquaries and admirers of the work may complain that they are in a situation similar to that of the unhappy gentleman whose wife informed him, on her death-bed, that one of their reputed children was not his; and, when he eagerly begged her to declare which of them it was, she answered, "*That* you shall never know," and expired, leaving him in irremediable doubt as to them all.[977]

I beg leave now to say something upon second sight, of which I have related two instances, as they impressed my mind at the time. I own I returned from the Hebrides with a considerable degree of faith in the many stories of that kind which I heard with a too easy acquiescence, without any close examination of the evidence; but since that time my belief in those stories has been much weakened by reflecting on the careless inaccuracy of narrative in common matters, from which we may certainly conclude that there may be the same in what is more extraordinary. It is but just, however, to add that the belief in second sight is not peculiar to the Highlands and Isles.

Some years after our tour, a cause was tried in the Court of Session, where the principal fact to be ascertained was whether a ship-master, who used to frequent the Western Highlands and Isles, was drowned in one particular year or in the year after. A great number of witnesses from those parts were examined on each side, and swore directly contrary to each other upon this simple question. One of them, a very respectable chieftain, who told me a story of second sight which I have not mentioned but which I too implicitly believed, had in this case, previous to this public examination, not only said, but attested under his hand, that he had seen the ship-master in the year subsequent to that in which the court was finally satisfied he was drowned. When interrogated with the strictness of judicial inquiry, and under the awe of an oath, he recollected himself better, and retracted what he had formerly asserted, apologizing for his inaccuracy by telling the judges, "A man will *say* what he will not *swear*."[978]

By many he was much censured, and it was maintained that every gentleman would be as attentive to truth without the sanction of an oath, as with it. Dr Johnson, though he himself was distinguished at all times by a scrupulous adherence to truth, controverted this proposition; and, as a proof that this was not, though it ought to be, the case, urged the very different decisions of elections under Mr Grenville's Act from those formerly made.[979] "Gentlemen will not pronounce upon oath what they would have said, and voted in the House, without that sanction."

However difficult it may be for men who believe in preternatural communications, in modern times, to satisfy those who are of a different opinion, they may easily refute the doctrine of their opponents who impute a belief in second sight to superstition. To entertain a visionary notion that one sees a distant or future event, may be called superstition; but the correspondence of the fact or event with such an impression on the fancy, though certainly very wonderful, if proved, has no more connexion with superstition than magnetism or electricity.

After dinner various topics were discussed, but my record is miserably defective. I recollect only one particular. Lord Elibank praised Kaempfer's *History of Japan*. "What account," said Dr Johnson, "can a man give of a country who is allowed to travel through it only in a covered wagon, from which he can peep through a chink?"

The Doctor compared the different talents of Garrick and Foote as companions, and gave Garrick greatly the preference for elegance, though he allowed Foote extraordinary powers of entertainment. He said, "Garrick is restrained by some principle, but Foote has the advantage of an unlimited range. Garrick has some delicacy of feeling; it is possible to put him out; you may get the better of him; but Foote is the most incompressible fellow that I ever knew: when you have driven him into a corner, and think you are sure of him, he runs through between your legs, or jumps over your head, and makes his escape."

Dr Erskine and Mr Robert Walker, two very respectable ministers of Edinburgh, supped with us, as did the Reverend Dr Webster. The conversation turned on the Moravian missions, and on the Methodists. Dr Johnson observed in general that missionaries were too sanguine in their accounts of their success among savages, and that much of what they tell is not to be believed. He owned that the Methodists had done good, had spread religious impressions among the vulgar part of mankind; but he said they had great bitterness against other Christians, and that he never could get a Methodist to explain in what he excelled others; that it always ended in the indispensable necessity of hearing one of their preachers; that although the same prayers were admitted by the Methodist to be read at church, and the same doctrines to be preached, as in his meeting, still a man could not be right unless he heard a Methodist clergyman. Mr James Forrest, Clerk to the Society for Propagating Christian Knowledge, who had announced in a letter to me Dr Erskine's desire to see Mr Johnson, also supped with us.[980]

THURSDAY 11 NOVEMBER. Principal Robertson came to us as we sat at breakfast; he advanced to Dr Johnson, repeating a line of Virgil, which I forget. I suppose, either *Post varios casus, per tot discrimina rerum*, or *multum ille et terris jactatus, et alto*.[981] Everybody had accosted us with some studied compliment on our return. Dr Johnson said, "I am really ashamed of the congratulations which we receive. We are addressed as if we had made a voyage to Nova Zembla, and suffered five persecutions in Japan." And he afterwards remarked that to see a man come up with a formal air and a Latin line, when we had no fatigue and no danger, was provoking. I told him he was not sensible of the danger, having lain under cover in the boat during the storm; he was like the chicken that hides its head under its wing, and then thinks itself safe.[982]

Lord Elibank came to us. So did Sir William Forbes. Mr Johnson asked Lord Elibank why the Highlanders, after gaining the battle of Prestonpans, did not march directly for England. My Lord said Mr Hepburn of Keith had warmly advised that measure, and had remonstrated that then every man was increased to ten in the imagination of the English. But the majority were of a different opinion, and he was excluded from the next court martial. That the Highlanders run home with the booty which they had taken, to deposit it at their houses, and so there were few left; that they were at no pains to secure arms to themselves, though they might have taken those of the fugitive army, which however, were alleged to be picked up by the East Lothian peasants: "Of which," said he, "we still feel the bad effects, as they are poachers."

He said there was a contribution ordered from the City of Edinburgh of four thousand pair of shoes; that either intentionally or from the great hurry, they were made too little, pinched the feet, and were useless.

He said Craigie, who had a great antipathy at all the Duke of Argyll's party, sent an order to search Baron Maule's house for arms on purpose to affront him, as, to be sure, it was very indecent to suspect a man who held a judge's place under the Government. Baron Maule went in a great passion to Lord Milton, then Lord Justice-Clerk, one of the fastest-headed men and best politicians that this country ever had, and complained of what had been done. Milton wittily said to him, "Baron, you may be glad it is no worse. Had I been the person who sent to search your house for arms, I would have found them too."[983]

I was dull enough not to understand this at first. Lord Elibank's quickness made him grow in a passion because I did not. I took it to be an insinuation that Baron Maule *had* arms. But it was putting him in mind that Lord Milton was so much a more perfect politician than Craigie that if he had had a mind to do the Baron a mischief, he would not have been contented with merely raising a suspicion, but would have had art enough to have the arms which he wished to be found conveyed into the Baron's house.

I observed that the rash attempt in 1745 would make a fine piece of history. Dr Johnson said it would. Lord Elibank doubted whether any man of this age could give it impartially. JOHNSON. "A man, by talking with those of different sides who were actors in it, and putting down all that he hears, may in time collect the materials of a good narrative. You are to consider, all history was at first oral. I suppose Voltaire was fifty years in collecting his *Louis XIV*, which he did in the way that I am proposing." ROBERTSON. "He did so. He lived much with all the great people who were concerned in that reign, and heard them talk of everything; and then either took Mr Boswell's way, of writing down what he heard, or, which is as good, preserved it in his memory; for he has a wonderful memory." (With the leave, however, of this elegant historian, no man's memory can preserve facts or sayings with such fidelity as may be done by writing them down when they are recent.)

Dr Robertson said it was now full time to make such a collection as Dr Johnson suggested; for many of the people who were then in arms were dropping off; and both Whigs and Jacobites were now come to talk with moderation. Lord Elibank said to him, "Mr Robertson, the first thing that gave me a high opinion of you, was your saying in the Select Society,[984] while parties ran high, soon after the year 1745, that you did not think worse of a man's moral character for his having been in rebellion. This was venturing to utter a liberal sentiment while both sides had a detestation of each other."

"Ay," said I, "when Duke Archibald said upon James Stewart's trial that rebellion included every other crime."[985]

Dr Johnson observed that being in rebellion from a notion of another's right was not connected with depravity; and that we had this proof of it, that all mankind applauded the pardoning of rebels, which they would not do in the case of robbers and murderers. He said, with a smile, that he wondered that the phrase of *unnatural* rebellion should be so much used, for that all rebellion was natural to man. He said the value of a narrative of the 1745 (or by whatever epithet he called it) would be in preserving small incidents relative to characters which would interest, as coming home to individuals.

THURSDAY II – FRIDAY 19 NOVEMBER. As I kept no journal of anything that passed after this morning, I shall, from memory, group together this and the other days till that on which Dr Johnson departed for London. They were in all nine days: on which he dined at Lady Colville's, Lord Hailes's, Sir Adolphus Oughton's, Sir Alexander Dick's, Principal Robertson's, Mr Maclaurin's, and thrice at Lord Elibank's seat in the country, where we also passed two nights.[986] He supped at the Honourable Alexander Gordon's, now one of our judges by the title of Lord Rockville; at Mr Nairne's, now also one of our judges by the title of Lord Dunsinane;[987] at Dr Blair's, and Mr Tytler's; and at my house thrice: one evening with a numerous company, chiefly gentlemen of the law; another with Mr Menzies of Culdares, and Lord Monboddo, who disengaged himself on purpose to meet him; and the evening on which we returned from Lord Elibank's, he supped with my wife and me by ourselves. He breakfasted at Dr Webster's, at old Mr Drummond's, and at Dr Blacklock's; and spent one forenoon at my uncle Dr Boswell's, who showed him his curious museum, and made him a present of a Scotch pebble. He afterwards had it cut into a pair of sleeve-buttons, which he constantly wore; and, as he was an elegant scholar, and a physician bred in the school of Boerhaave, Dr Johnson was pleased with his company.

On the mornings when he breakfasted at my house, he had, from ten o'clock till one or two, a constant levee of various persons, of very different characters and descriptions. I could not attend him, being obliged to be in the Court of Session; but my wife was so good as to devote the greater part of the morning to the endless task of pouring out tea for my friend and his visitors.

Such was the disposition of his time at Edinburgh. He said one evening to me, in a fit of languor, "Sir, we have been harassed by invitations."

I acquiesced. "Ay, sir," he replied; "but how much worse would it have been if we had been neglected?"

From what has been recorded in this Journal, it may well be supposed that a variety of admirable conversation has been lost, by my neglect to preserve it. I shall endeavour to recollect some of it, as well as I can.

At Lady Colville's, to whom I am proud to introduce any stranger of eminence, that he may see what dignity and grace is to be found in Scotland, an officer observed, that he had heard Lord Mansfield was not a great English lawyer. JOHNSON. "Why, sir, supposing Lord Mansfield not to have the splendid talents which he possesses, he must be a great English lawyer from having been so long at the bar and having passed through so many of the great offices of the law. Sir, you may as well maintain that a carrier who has driven a pack-horse between Edinburgh and Berwick for thirty years does not know the road, as that Lord Mansfield does not know the law of England."

At Mr Nairne's he drew the character of Richardson, the author of *Clarissa*, with a strong yet delicate pencil. I lament much that I have not preserved it: I only remember that he expressed a high opinion of his talents and virtues; but observed, that his perpetual study was to ward off petty inconveniencies and procure petty pleasures; that his love of continual superiority was such that he took care to be always surrounded by women, who listened to him implicitly and did not venture to controvert his opinions; and that his desire of distinction was so great that he used to give large vails to the Speaker Onslow's servants that they might treat him with respect.

On the same evening, he would not allow that the private life of a judge in England was required to be so strictly decorous as I supposed.

"Why then, sir," said I, "according to your account, an English judge may just live like a gentleman." JOHNSON. "Yes, sir – if he *can*."

At Mr Tytler's, I happened to tell that one evening, a great many years ago, when Dr Hugh Blair and I were sitting together in the pit of Drury Lane playhouse, in a wild freak of youthful extravagance I entertained the audience prodigiously by imitating the lowing of a cow. A little while after I had told this story, I differed from Dr Johnson, I suppose too confidently, upon some point which I now forget. He did not spare me. "Nay, sir," said he, "if you cannot talk better as a man, I'd have you bellow like a cow."[988]

At Dr Webster's he said that he believed hardly any man died without affectation. This remark appears to me to be well founded, and will account for many of the celebrated death-bed sayings which are recorded.

One of the evenings at my house, Mr Ilay Campbell fought him very well against the system of *tacksmen* or upper tenants, and that same evening when he told that Lord Lovat boasted to an English nobleman that though he had not his wealth, he had two thousand men whom he could at any time call into the field, the Honourable Alexander Gordon observed that those two thousand men brought him to the block. "True, sir," said Dr Johnson, "but you may just as well argue, concerning a man who has fallen over a precipice to which he has walked too near, 'His two legs brought him to that.' Is he not the better for having two legs?"

At Dr Blair's I left him in order to attend a consultation, during which he and his amiable host were by themselves. I returned to supper, at which were Principal Robertson, Mr Nairne, and some other gentlemen.[989] Dr Robertson and Dr Blair, I remember, talked well upon subordination and government; and, as my friend and I were walking home, he said to me, "Sir, these two doctors are good men, and wise men." I begged of Dr Blair to recollect what he could of the long conversation that passed between Dr Johnson and him alone this evening, and he obligingly wrote to me as follows:

March 3, 1785. / DEAR SIR, As so many years have intervened since I chanced to have that conversation with Dr Johnson in my house, to which you refer, I have forgotten most of what then passed, but remember that I was both instructed and entertained by it. Among other subjects, the discourse happening to turn on modern Latin poets, the Doctor expressed a very favourable opinion of Buchanan, and instantly repeated, from beginning to end, an ode of his entitled *Calendae Maiae* (the eleventh in his *Miscellaneorum Liber*), beginning with these words, "*Salvete sacris deliciis sacrae*," with which I had formerly been unacquainted; but upon perusing it, the praise which he bestowed upon it as one of the happiest of Buchanan's poetical compositions, appeared to me very just.[990] He also repeated to me a Latin ode he had composed in one of the Western Islands, from which he had lately returned.[991] We had much discourse concerning his excursion to those islands, with which he expressed himself as having been highly pleased; talked in a favourable manner of the hospitality of the inhabitants, and particularly spoke much of his happiness in having you for his companion; and said that the longer he knew you, he loved and esteemed you the more. This conversation passed in the interval between tea and supper, when we were by ourselves. You, and the rest of the company who were with us at supper, have often taken notice that he was uncommonly bland and gay that evening, and gave much pleasure to all who were present. This is all that I can recollect distinctly of that long conversation. Yours sincerely, / HUGH BLAIR.

At Lord Hailes's, we spent a most agreeable day, but again I must lament that I was so indolent as to let almost all that passed evaporate into oblivion. Dr Johnson observed there that it is wonderful how ignorant many officers of the army are, considering how much leisure they have for study and the acquisition of knowledge. I hope he was mistaken, for he maintained that many of them were ignorant of things belonging immediately to their own profession: "For instance, many cannot tell how far a musket will carry a bullet." In proof of which, I suppose, he mentioned some particular person, for Lord Hailes, from whom I solicited what he could recollect of that day, writes to me as follows:

As to Dr Johnson's observation about the ignorance of officers in the length that a musket will carry, my brother, Colonel Dalrymple, was present, and he thought that the Doctor was either mistaken, by putting the question wrong, or that he had conversed on the subject with some person out of service.

Was it upon that occasion that he expressed no curiosity to see the room at Dunfermline, where Charles I was born? "I know that he was born," said he; "no matter where." Did he envy us the birth-place of the king?

Near the end of his *Journey*, Dr Johnson has given liberal praise to Mr Braidwood's academy for the deaf and dumb. When he visited it, a circumstance occurred which was truly characteristical of our great Lexicographer. "Pray," said he, "can they pronounce any *long* words?" Mr Braidwood informed him they could. Upon which Dr Johnson wrote one of his *sesquipedalia verba*, which was pronounced by the scholars, and he was satisfied. My readers may perhaps wish to know what the word was, but I cannot gratify their curiosity. Mr Braidwood told me it remained long in his school, but had been lost before I made my inquiry.[992]

Dr Johnson one day visited the Court of Session. He thought the mode of pleading there too vehement, and too much addressed to the passions of the judges. "This," said he, "is not the Areopagus."

At old Mr Drummond's, Sir John Dalrymple quaintly said the two noblest animals in the world were a Scotch Highlander and an English sailor. "Why, sir," said Dr Johnson, "I shall say nothing as to the Scotch Highlander, but as to the English sailor, I think he is as near the brute as a man can be."[993] Sir John said he was generous in giving away his money. JOHNSON. "Sir, he throws away his money, without thought and without merit. I do not call a tree generous that sheds its fruit at every breeze."

Sir John having affected to complain of the attacks made upon his *Memoirs*, Dr Johnson said, "Nay, sir, do not complain. It is advantageous to an author that his book should be attacked as well as praised. Fame is a shuttlecock. If it be struck only at one end of the room, it will soon fall to the ground. To keep it up, it must be struck at both ends." Often have I reflected on this since; and, instead of being angry at many of those who have written against me, have smiled to think that they were unintentionally subservient to my fame, by using a battledore to make me *virum volitare per ora*.[994]

At Sir Alexander Dick's, from that absence of mind to which every man is at times subject, I told, in a blundering manner, Lady Eglinton's complimentary adoption of Dr Johnson as her son; for I unfortunately stated that her ladyship adopted him as her son, in consequence of her having been married the year *after* he was born. Dr Johnson instantly corrected me. "Sir, don't you perceive that you are defaming the Countess? For, supposing me to be her son, and she was not married till the year after my birth, I must have been her *natural* son."

A young lady of quality, who was present, very handsomely said, "Might not the son have justified the fault?"[995]

My friend was much flattered by this compliment, which he never forgot. When in more than ordinary spirits, and talking of his journey in Scotland, he has called to me, "Boswell, what was it that the young lady of quality said of me at Sir Alexander Dick's?"

Nobody will doubt that I was happy in repeating it.

SATURDAY 20 – MONDAY 22 NOVEMBER. My illustrious friend, being now desirous to be again in the great theatre of life and animated exertion, took a place in the coach which was to set out for London on Monday the 22d of November. Sir John Dalrymple pressed him to come on the Saturday before to his house at Cranston, which being twelve miles from Edinburgh, upon the middle road to Newcastle (Dr Johnson had come to Edinburgh by Berwick, and along the naked coast), it would make his journey easier, as the coach would take him up at a more seasonable hour than that at which it sets out. Sir John, I perceived, was ambitious of having such a guest; but, as I was well assured that at this very time he had joined with some of his prejudiced countrymen in railing at Dr Johnson, and had said he wondered how any gentleman of Scotland could keep company with him, I thought he did not deserve the honour; yet, as it might be a convenience to Dr Johnson, I contrived that he should accept the invitation, and engaged to conduct him.

I resolved that, on our way to Sir John's, we should make a little circuit by Rosslyn Castle and Hawthornden, and wished to set out soon after breakfast; but young Mr Tytler came to show Dr Johnson some essays which he had written, and my great friend, who was exceedingly obliging when thus consulted, was detained so long that it was, I believe, one o'clock before we got into our post-chaise. I found that we should be too late for dinner at Sir John Dalrymple's, to which we were engaged; but I would by no means lose the pleasure of seeing my friend at Hawthornden – of seeing *Sam Johnson* at the very spot where *Ben Jonson* visited the learned and poetical Drummond. We surveyed Rosslyn Castle, the romantic scene around it, and the beautiful Gothic chapel, and dined and drank tea at the inn; after which we proceeded to Hawthornden and viewed the caves; and I all the while had *Rare Ben* in my mind, and was pleased to think that this place was now visited by another celebrated wit of England.[996]

By this time 'the waning night was growing old', and we were yet several miles from Sir John Dalrymple's. Dr Johnson did not seem much troubled at our having treated the baronet with so little attention to politeness; but when I talked of the grievous disappointment it must have been to him that we did not come to the *feast* that he had prepared for us (for he told us he had killed a seven-year-old sheep on purpose), my friend got into a merry mood, and jocularly said, "I dare say, sir, he has been very sadly distressed. Nay, we do not know but the consequence may have been fatal. Let me try to describe his situation in his own historical style. I have as good a right to make *him* think and talk as he has to tell us how people thought and talked a hundred years ago, of which he has no evidence. All history, so far as it is not supported by contemporary evidence, is romance. – Stay now. – Let us consider!" He then (heartily laughing all the while) proceeded in his imitation, I am sure to the following effect, though now, at the distance of almost twelve years, I cannot pretend to recollect all the precise words:

> Dinner being ready, he wondered that his guests were not yet come. His wonder was soon succeeded by impatience. He walked about the room in anxious agitation; sometimes he looked at his watch, sometimes he looked out at the window with an eager gaze of expectation, and revolved in his mind the various accidents of human life. His family beheld him with mute concern. "Surely," said he, with a sigh, "they will not fail me." The mind of man can bear a certain pressure; but there is a point when it can bear no more. A rope was in his view, and he died a Roman death.[997]

It was very late before we reached the seat of Sir John Dalrymple, who, certainly with some reason, was not in very good humour. Our conversation was not brilliant. We supped, and went to bed in ancient rooms which would have better suited the climate of Italy in summer than that of Scotland in the month of November.

Next morning at breakfast a scene truly ridiculous was exhibited. Sir John, who had boasted much of his seven-year old sheep which he had killed on purpose for Dr Johnson and which it was plain could not yet be all eat up, asked the Doctor whether he chose to have the *fore leg* or the *hind leg* to dinner, and having put the question, his lady voted *fore leg*. This contrivance failed, for it being explained to Dr Johnson that in the Scottish dialect *fore leg* meant *shoulder* in opposition to what alone is in England called *leg*, he honestly said, "I vote hind leg, to be sure."

He was certain of my vote, and Sir John, who could not in decency deny his guest what he liked best, was obliged to join. Poor Lady Dalrymple appeared much disconcerted, and was an innocent victim to the censure of Dr Johnson, who supposed she was unwilling to give us what was best. He said to me afterwards, "Sir, this is an odious woman. Were I Dalrymple, I'd go and entertain my friends at Edinburgh and leave her to herself. Did you observe her when we voted leg? Sir, she looked as if we had voted for roasting one of her children."

The truth, as I afterwards discovered, was that Sir John was not accurate in his information. There was no seven-year old sheep killed, and no leg in the house. Accordingly none appeared, for which some foolish excuse was made.

We went and saw the old castle of Borthwick. I recollect no conversation worth preserving, except one saying of Dr Johnson, which will be a valuable text for many decent old dowagers, and other good company in various circles to descant upon. He said, "I am sorry I have not learnt to play at cards. It is very useful in life; it generates kindness and consolidates society." He certainly could not mean deep play.

My friend and I thought we should be warmer and more comfortable at the inn at Blackshiels, two miles farther on. We therefore went thither in the evening, and he was very entertaining; but I have preserved nothing but the pleasing remembrance, and his verses on George the Second and Cibber, and his epitaph on Parnell, which he was then so good as to dictate to me.[998]

We breakfasted together next morning, and then the coach came and took him up. He had as one of his companions in it as far as Newcastle, the worthy and ingenious Dr Hope, botanical professor at Edinburgh. Both Dr Johnson and he used to speak of their good fortune in thus accidentally meeting; for they had much instructive conversation, which is always a most valuable enjoyment, and, when found where it is not expected, is peculiarly relished.[999]

NOTES

1 William Nairne, advocate, later Lord Dunsinane, see pp. 30, 442, 448, 449. Brief biographical details of individuals named in the text will be found in the Index.

2 He means the whole island of Britain, from 1603. Boswell gives the inscription as 'Maria Re. 1564' (p. 41), as does Johnson himself in writing to Mrs Thrale (Redford, *Letters*, vol. 2, p. 54). 'Re.' will be French *reine*, not Latin *regina*.

3 The 'invisible friend' was Robert Arbuthnot of Haddo, see p. 27. The house was that of Robert Watson, professor of logic, rhetoric and metaphysics.

4 After describing how Beaton was run through with the sword, Knox writes (*History of the Reformation*, p. 81): "While they were thus busied with the Cardinal, the Fray rose in the Town, the Provost assembles the Commonalty, and comes to the House-side, crying, *What have ye done with my Lord Cardinal? Where is my Lord Cardinal? Have ye slain my Lord Cardinal? . . .* And so was he brought to the *East-block-house* Head, and shewed dead over the Wall to the faithless Multitude, which would not believe before they saw; and so they departed without *requiem æternam, & requiescat in pace*, sung for his Soul. Now, because the Weather was hot, (for it was in *May*, as ye have heard) and his Funerals could not suddenly be prepared, it was thought best, to keep him from stinking, to give him great Salt enough, a Cope of Lead, and a Corner in the Bottom of the *Sea-Tower*, (a Place where many of God's Children had been imprisoned before) to await what Exequies his Brethren the Bishops would prepare for him. These Things we write merrily, but we would that the Reader should observe God's just Judgements . . . These are the Works of our God."

5 The lost street was called Swallow Street.

6 The three colleges were St Leonard's, St Salvator's and (for divinity only) St Mary's. St Leonard's was incorporated into St Salvator's in 1747. 'Hindred' is a characteristic Johnsonian spelling.

7 Johnson here uses 'society' where we would now prefer 'community', in the sense of 'a corporate body of persons having a definite place of residence' (*OED*): his 'literary societies' thus embraces schools of all kinds. For other examples see pp. 33, 99.

8 This was Dr James Murison, principal of St Mary's.

9 Thomas Hay, 9th earl of Kinnoul. A new rector was elected from among the professors each spring.

10 See p. 591. Boswell's notes (Pottle and Bennett, *Journal*, p. 40) show that the conversation turned on second sight: "Told me she never saw anything or heard, tho' she walked out in night-time. Only had dreams before her relations died."

11 Sir John Davies, *Discoverie of the True Causes why Ireland was Never Entirely Subdued until the Beginning of his Majesties Happy Reign* (1612), much quoted in Johnson's *Dictionary*.

12 It is celebrated for the signing in 1320 of the Declaration of Arbroath, an early expression of the importance of individual and national freedom and the acquiescence of rulers to the popular will.

13 See pp. 12, 51–52. By 'English' Johnson means that it was a licensed chapel of the Church of England, operating as an independent congregation. The Episcopal Church of Scotland was at this time suppressed by Act of Parliament, its clergy having sided with the Jacobites in the '45. Instrumental music had no place in Presbyterian worship, so there were probably no more than six organs in the whole of Scotland at this time, all in 'English chapels' – far fewer than in the previous century, when Sir Donald Macdonald of Sleat appears to have had one at Duntulm in Skye (Mackenzie, *Orain Iain Luim*, pp. 18–19, 237).

14 See p. 51. William Driver had bought the Ship Inn (at 107 High Street) in 1772. He named his son Johnson, and Johnson's son was also Johnson.

15 See pp. 52–57. James Burnett had been a judge of the Court of Session as Lord Monboddo since 1767. His book *Of the Origin and Progress of Language* shows him to have been an evolutionist before his time.

16 Boswell's father, Lord Auchinleck, for whom see pp. 435–41, was a circuit judge. They were at the New Inn (p. 57). It was where Union Street now turns north into King Street, and was demolished long ago to make way for a bank.

17 Boece's *Scotorum Historiae* (Paris, 1527) were translated into Scots by John Bellenden as the *History and Croniklis of Scotland* (1541). The critique of his work which follows is fair and well-balanced.

18 The magnificent Old Testament in Hebrew is still there: AUL MS 23, written, illuminated and bound in Naples 1492–94 (Roth, *Aberdeen Codex*, pp. 7–9). The Aretinus, however, has gone.

19 For the text see pp. 212–13.

20 The estate was that of Forvie, its owner a previous earl of Errol.

21 Perhaps the main interest of Dun Buy lies in its name. Strictly *dùn* means not a rock but a fortress.

22 See pp. 71–72. Boswell was using his legal connections to ensure hospitality along the route – 'Mr Frazer' was Alexander Fraser, son and heir of Alexander Fraser, Lord Strichen (1699–1775), one of the circuit judges of whom it was said (Ramsay, *Scotland and Scotsmen*, vol. 1, p. 93): "There were two of them, Justice-Clerk Erskine and Minto, who *ate*; two of them, Strichen and Drummore, who *drank*; and two that neither ate nor drank, Elchies and Killkerran." (The stones appear to have been a folly. Six fragments remained in 1962, but they have since disappeared.)

23 See p. 350.

24 The inn was the Red Lion in the High Street. For the other 'Scotish table' of which Johnson found reason to complain see p. 115.

25 By 'the family of Gordon' Johnson means the dukes of that name, see p. 75.

26 The chief was Alexander Stewart, 'the Wolf of Badenoch'.

27 The order to strip the lead off Elgin and Aberdeen cathedrals was dated 14 February 1568. For these two sentences Johnson originally wrote: "There is

now, as I have heard, a body of men, not less decent or virtuous than the Scotish council, longing to melt the lead of an English cathedral. What they shall melt, it were just that they should swallow." This reference to the dean and chapter of his native city of Lichfield was printed off, but Johnson changed his mind, explaining to the publisher (Lascelles, *Journey*, p. xxxiv): "The Dean did me a kindness about forty years ago. He is now very old, and I am not young. Reproach can do him no good, and in myself I know not whether it is zeal or wantonness."

28   For the inn see p. 76.

29   See pp. 146–47. In NLS H.32.a.31, a copy of the 1703 edition of Martin's book, is an inscription in Boswell's hand (he had borrowed it from the Advocates' Library): "This very Book accompanied Mr. Samuel Johnson and me, in our Tour to the Hebrides in Autumn 1773. Mr. Johnson told me that he had read Martin when he was very young. Martin was a native of the Isle of Sky where a number of his relations still remain. His Book is a very imperfect performance; & he is erroneous as to many particulars, even some concerning his own Island. Yet as it is the only Book upon the subject, it is very generally known. I have seen a second edition of it. I cannot but have a kindness for him, notwithstanding his defects. James Boswell. 16 April 1774."

30   *Macbeth*, act 1, scene 3.

31   Psalms 141: 5. Boswell's note (*Tour*): "Our friend Edmund Burke, who by this time had received some pretty severe strokes from Dr Johnson on account of the unhappy difference in their politics, upon my repeating this passage to him, exclaimed, 'Oil of vitriol!'"

32   Boswell's note (*Tour*): "This, I find, is a Scotticism. I should have said, 'It will not be long before we shall be at Marischal College.'"

33   "Do not reply to me." This and *ipse venit* ('he came himself') are adapted from the second line of the *Heroides* of Ovid: *Hanc tua Penelope lento tibi mittit, Ulixe – / Nil mihi rescribas tu tamen; ipse veni!* ("Your Penelope sends you this missive, Ulysses, slow of return that you are – but don't write anything back to me; come yourself!")

34   Boswell duly copied the letters from Elibank and Johnson into his journal, from which they were printed in the *Tour* (*To the Hebrides*, pp. 212, 213), but he forgot his own to Elibank (Pottle, *Journal*, p. 405): "London, 22 April 1773. MY DEAR LORD, This letter is intended as a *happy prologue to a swelling act*. It is to announce to your lordship that I do now seriously believe that our illustrious friend Mr Samuel Johnson will visit Scotland this year. I know your lordship's high respect for him, and your warm admiration of his wonderful genius; and therefore I need only hint to you that your throwing out to me a little of what you feel in abundance will, when read to him with my enthusiasm, fortify that resolution, which, I flatter myself, is already very strong. He talks of coming to Edinburgh about the beginning of August, that he may just see our courts of justice, and then he and I may set out directly on a tour through Scotland, particularly to see the Highlands and some of the Islands; after which we shall return to Edinburgh, where (and

at your lordship's country seat) we must try to keep him as long as we can. I shall not be many more weeks in London at this time, so I beg that your lordship may send me an epistle full of insensible attraction for Mr Johnson without delay. I have often told your lordship what influence you have with him; and my Johnsoniana contain compliments by him to your lordship more valuable than any titles which princes confer. I have the honour to be, my dear lord, Your obliged humble servant, James Boswell." For Elibank see pp. 442–43.

35   See note 172. William Scott, a native of Co. Durham, at that time a fellow of University College, was later to become an advocate and judge in the Admiralty and ecclesiastical courts, whose practice was based on civil or Roman law rather than English common law. He was a Member of Parliament from 1790 to 1821, when he was elevated to the Lords as Baron Stowell. Boswell's 'Commons' refers to Scott's receipt of a doctorate in civil law and his consequent admission to the Faculty of Advocates of England at Doctors' Commons in 1779.

36   Three types of closed vehicle were then generally available to travellers: the fly, a one-horse carriage for one or two passengers; the post-chaise, a fast coach for passengers and mail; and the stage-coach, a heavier vehicle for passengers and goods. Johnson fantasised (*Life*, 19 September 1777): "If I had no duties and no reference to futurity, I would spend my life in driving briskly in a post-chaise with a pretty woman; but," he added, "she should be one who could understand me, and would add something to the conversation."

37   Boswell's note (*Tour*, second and subsequent editions): "Such they appeared to me; but since the first edition, Sir Joshua Reynolds has observed to me, 'that Dr Johnson's extraordinary gestures were only habits, in which he indulged himself at certain times. When in company, where he was not free, or when engaged earnestly in conversation, he never gave way to such habits, which proves that they were not involuntary.' I still however think, that these gestures were involuntary; for surely had not that been the case, he would have restrained them in the public streets."

38   Boswell attended Glasgow University as a student of civil law in 1759–60. The stick produced two good jokes actually, see pp. 56, 359. The expression 'the *combination* and the *form*' in the following sentence derives from Aristotle's *Physics* via *Hamlet*, act 3, scene 4.

39   Johnson's prejudice against Scotland was real enough, but these lines are poor evidence for it. They simply point to the patriotism of the Irish and the Scots, the existence of poverty in London, and the higher age expectancy in London than in Scotland or Ireland.

40   Rev. 5: 9. 'Mr Crosbie' of the next sentence is Andrew Crosbie, advocate, the prototype of 'Counsellor Playdell' in Scott's *Guy Mannering*; when Boswell wrote these words in 1785 this extraordinary man was less than four months dead, the victim of poverty, disease and drink (Ramsay, *Scotland and Scotsmen*, vol. 1, p. 449–59).

41   For the principal reason, see p. 210.

42   For Chambers and Scott see p. 20.

43 Boyd's Inn, the White Horse, was demolished in 1868. It was near the corner of the Canongate and St Mary Wynd, now St Mary's Street (see pp. 32–33). On the wall of the tenement which replaced it is a carved inscription: "This is the first building / erected under the Improvement Act of 1867 / The Right Honourable / William Chambers / of Glenormiston / Lord Provost."

44 The word 'subsequently' is Pottle's (*Journal*, p. 407). Johnson's visit to Paris was in 1775.

45 This and two other little exchanges in Boswell's account of 14 August are taken from his notes. Otherwise his **Introduction** is from the *Tour*.

46 James's Court is still to be seen, behind the north side of the Lawnmarket (strictly 'Land Market', for the produce of the land, see pp. 32–33). According to Pottle and Bennett (*Journal*, p. 11) the 'late baronet' was perhaps Sir Gilbert Elliot (not to be confused with the judge of the same name, whose career is described by Ramsay in *Scotland and Scotsmen*, vol. 1, pp. 81–82).

47 In the *Literary Magazine* (1756) Johnson reviewed an essay in which Hanway had attacked tea-drinking. The magazine then published both Hanway's answer and Johnson's response to it. It was the only occasion on which Johnson took notice of any criticism of his work (*Life*).

48 The trial was of Calum MacGregor *alias* John Grant. He was indicted before the circuit court held at Aberdeen in May 1773 for the murder of John Stewart, tenant in Abergairn, on 25 December 1747. He pleaded prescription, and as this was an important and hitherto undecided point, the advocate-depute deserted the diet and MacGregor was recommitted on a new warrant so that the case might be argued before the Court of Session. His counsel argued that he was not guilty and had betrayed no symptoms of guilt, that twenty-five years had elapsed since the alleged crime, and that he had appeared in public, pursued his business, and maintained a fair character. "He indeed had changed his name; but that he was obliged to do by law." The indictment was dismissed (Maclaurin, *Arguments and Decisions*, pp. 595–615; Wimsatt and Pottle, *Boswell for the Defence*, p. 192).

49 The topic of conversation was Johnson's friend Bennet Langton, the making of whose will had afforded Johnson much amusement on 9 May that year (*Life*), see pp. 72, 265–66. The words 'our own' were altered to 'her own' in the third edition of the *Tour*, but Pottle states (*Journal*, p. 407): "Boswell and his wife never had separate rooms."

50 Boswell was as good as his word, but Veronica died aged 22 before his grant to her could be paid. He adds this note (*Tour*): "The saint's name of *Veronica* was introduced into our family through my great-grandmother Veronica, Countess of Kincardine, a Dutch lady of the noble house of Sommelsdyck, of which there is a full account in Bayle's Dictionary. The family had once a princely right in Surinam. The governor of that settlement was appointed by the States General, the town of Amsterdam, and Sommelsdyck. The States General have acquired Sommelsdyck's right; but the family has still great dignity and opulence, and by intermarriages is connected with many other noble families. When I was at The Hague I was received with all the affection of kindred. The present Sommelsdyck has an important charge in

the Republic, and is as worthy a man as lives. He has honoured me with his correspondence for these twenty years. My great-grandfather, the husband of Countess Veronica, was Alexander, Earl of Kincardine, that eminent Royalist whose character is given by Burnet in his *History of his own Times*. From him the blood of *Bruce* flows in my veins. Of such ancestry who would not be proud? And, as *Nihil est, nisi hoc sciat alter*, is peculiarly true of genealogy, who would not be glad to seize a fair opportunity to let it be known?" For Burnet's *History of my Own Times* see note 695.

51 The words in Boswell's manuscript note, from which this exchange is taken, were 'because Skye bad country'; J. D. Fleeman believed that this was a reference to infections or skin diseases (*Journey*, p. 176). Johnson wrote to Mrs Thrale from Skye (Redford, *Letters*, vol. 2, p. 77): "Mrs Boswel had warned us that we should *catch something*, and had given us Sheets for our security; for Sir Alexander and Lady Macdonald, she said, came back from Skie, so scratching themselves." No doubt Mrs Boswell is the 'lady at Edinburgh' referred to in a similar context at p. 95.

52 'Baron Smith's Chapel' in Black Friars Wynd (see pp. 32–33), now Blackfriars Street, was founded in 1722 by John Smith, Lord Chief Baron of the Exchequer.

53 Sir James Montgomery (1721–1803), a former Lord Advocate.

54 On the Douglas Cause see note 909.

55 Boswell brought this book with him on the tour, see pp. 43, 48, 339, 373, 394, 414.

56 See p. 3. This was probably the banker Robert Arbuthnot of Haddo, secretary to the Board of Trustees for Fisheries and Manufactures in Scotland, a friend of Beattie's. 'The celebrated Dr Arbuthnot' was John Arbuthnot, MD of St Andrews, physician to Queen Anne, writer, scholar, wit, campaigner for the Union and creator of 'John Bull'.

57 See note 86.

58 The reference is to Beattie's *Essay on Truth*, an attack on Hume's philosophy.

59 This exchange is taken from Boswell's notes of **15 August**, as are three other sentences and the 'shaving' anecdote with which the entry begins. Otherwise his account of this day is from the *Tour*.

60 See 'An Account of My last Interview with David Hume, Esq. Partly recorded in my Journal, partly enlarged from my memory, 3 March 1777', Scott and Pottle, *Private Papers*, vol. 12, pp. 227–32; Weis and Pottle, *Boswell in Extremes*, pp. 11–15; Milne, *Boswell's Edinburgh Journals*, pp. 256–59.

61 This letter has been published many times, see Hill and Powell, *Life*, vol. 5, p. 464.

62 Psalms 119: 99. The 'learned friend' was probably Malone.

63 The 'other gentleman' was Charles Hay, advocate, see note 86.

64 A surprising comment on the statesman Edmund Burke, footnoted by Boswell (*Tour*): "This was one of the points upon which Dr Johnson was strangely heterodox. For, surely, Mr Burke, with his other remarkable qualities, is also distinguished for his wit, and for wit of all kinds too; not merely that power of language which Pope chooses to denominate wit ('True

wit is Nature to advantage dressed; / What oft was thought, but ne'er so well expressed'), but surprising allusions, brilliant sallies of vivacity, and pleasant conceits. His speeches in Parliament are strewed with them. Take, for instance, the variety which he has given in his wide range, yet exact detail, when exhibiting his Reform Bill. And his conversation abounds in wit. Let me put down a specimen. I told him, I had seen, at a *blue stocking* assembly, a number of ladies sitting round a worthy and tall friend of ours, listening to his literature. 'Ay,' said he, 'like maids round a May-pole.' I told him, I had found out a perfect definition of human nature, as distinguished from the animal. An ancient philosopher said, man was a 'two-legged animal without feathers', upon which his rival sage had a cock plucked bare, and set him down in the school before all the disciples, as a 'Philosophic Man'. Dr Franklin said, man was 'a tool-making animal', which is very well; for no animal but man makes a thing, by means of which he can make another thing. But this applies to very few of the species. My definition of man is 'a Cooking Animal'. The beasts have memory, judgment, and all the faculties and passions of our mind, in a certain degree; but no beast is a cook. The trick of the monkey using the cat's paw to roast a chestnut, is only a piece of shrewd malice in that *turpissima bestia*, which humbles us so sadly by its similarity to us. Man alone can dress a good dish; and every man whatever is more or less a cook, in seasoning what he himself eats. 'Your definition is good,' said Mr Burke, 'and I now see the full force of the common proverb, "There is *reason* in roasting of eggs."' When Mr Wilkes, in his days of tumultuous opposition, was borne upon the shoulders of the mob, Mr Burke (as Mr Wilkes told me himself, with classical admiration), applied to him what Horace says of Pindar, '. . . numeris*que fertur* / Lege solutis'. Sir Joshua Reynolds, who agrees with me entirely as to Mr Burke's fertility of wit, said, that this was 'dignifying a pun'. He also observed, that he has often heard Burke say, in the course of an evening, ten good things, each of which would have served a noted wit (whom he named) to live upon for a twelvemonth."

In the second edition the following is added: "I find, since the former edition, that some persons have objected to the instances which I have given of Mr Burke's wit, as not doing justice to my very ingenious friend; the specimens produced having, it is alleged, more of conceit than real wit, and being merely sportive sallies of the moment, not justifying the encomium which they think with me, he undoubtedly merits. I was well aware, how hazardous it was to exhibit particular instances of wit, which is of so airy and spiritual a nature as often to elude the hand that attempts to grasp it. The excellence and efficacy of a *bon mot* depend frequently so much on the occasion on which it is spoken, on the peculiar manner of the speaker, on the person to whom it is applied, the previous introduction, and a thousand minute particulars which cannot be easily enumerated, that it is always dangerous to detach a witty saying from the group to which it belongs, and to set it before the eye of the spectator, divested of those concomitant circumstances, which gave it animation, mellowness, and relief. I ventured, however, at all hazards, to put down the first instances that occurred to me, as proofs of Mr Burke's lively and brilliant fancy; but am very sensible that his numerous friends could have suggested many of a superior quality. Indeed, the being in company with him, for a single day, is sufficient to shew that what I have asserted is well founded; and it was only necessary to have appealed to all who know him intimately, for a complete refutation of the heterodox opinion entertained by Dr Johnson on this subject. *He* allowed Mr Burke, as the reader will find hereafter, to be a man of consummate and unrivalled abilities in every light except that now under consideration; and the variety of his allusions, and splendour of his imagery, have made such an impression on *all the rest* of the world, that superficial observers are apt to overlook his other merits, and to suppose that *wit* is his chief and most prominent excellence; when in fact it is only one of the many talents that he possesses, which are so various and extraordinary, that it is very difficult to ascertain precisely the rank and value of each."

65 These are the words in Boswell's notes. In the *Tour* they were altered to 'if you met him for the first time in a street where you were stopped by a drove of oxen, and you and he stepped aside to take shelter'. Boswell's 'shower of cannon bullets' is hyperbolic, akin to 'raining cats and dogs'; 'up a stair' is Edinburgh dialect, and does not necessarily involve climbing, any more than does its Glasgow equivalent 'up a close'.

66 Boswell's note (*Tour*): "That cannot be said now, after the flagrant part which Mr John Wesley took against our American brethren, when, in his own name, he threw amongst his enthusiastic flock, the very individual combustibles of Dr Johnson's *Taxation no Tyranny*; and after the intolerant spirit which he manifested against our fellow-Christians of the Roman Catholic communion, for which that able champion, Father O'Leary, has given him so hearty a drubbing. But I should think myself very unworthy, if I did not at the same time acknowledge Mr John Wesley's merit, as a veteran 'Soldier of Jesus Christ', who has, I do believe, turned many from darkness into light, and from the power of Satan to the living GOD."

67 The friend was Burke, as Boswell's notes show.

68 Boswell's note (*Tour*): "If due attention were paid to this observation, there would be more virtue, even in politics. What Dr Johnson justly condemned, has, I am sorry to say, greatly increased in the present reign. At the distance of four years from this conversation, 21st February 1777, My Lord Archbishop of York, in his 'Sermon before the Society for the Propagation of the Gospel in Foreign Parts', thus indignantly describes the then state of parties: 'Parties once had a *principle* belonging to them, absurd perhaps, and indefensible, but still carrying a notion of *duty*, by which honest minds might easily be caught. But they are now *combinations of individuals*, who, instead of being the sons and servants of the community, make a league for advancing their *private interests*. It is their business to hold high the notion of *political honour*. I believe and trust, it is not injurious to say, that such a bond is no better than that by which the lowest and wickedest combinations are held together; and that it denotes the last stage of political depravity.' To find

a thought, which just showed itself to us from the mind of *Johnson*, thus appearing again at such a distance of time, and without any communication between them, enlarged to full growth in the mind of *Markham*, is a curious object of philosophical contemplation. That two such great and luminous minds should have been so dark in one corner – that *they* should have held it to be 'wicked rebellion in the British subjects established in America, to resist the abject condition of holding all their property at the mercy of British subjects remaining at home, while their allegiance to our common Lord the King was to be preserved inviolate' – is a striking proof to me, either that 'He who fitteth in Heaven', scorns the loftiness of human pride, or that the evil spirit, whose personal existence I strongly believe, and even in this age am confirmed in that belief by a Fell, nay, by a Hurd, has more power than some choose to allow."

69 In 1741 Capt. Samuel Goodere RN had his brother carried on board his vessel and strangled. The principal motive was jealousy.

70 Boswell's note (*Tour*): "It may be observed that I sometimes call my great friend *Mr* Johnson, sometimes *Dr* Johnson; though he had at this time a doctor's degree from Trinity College, Dublin. The University of Oxford afterwards conferred it upon him by a diploma, in very honourable terms. It was some time before I could bring myself to call him Doctor; but, as he has been long known by that title, I shall give it to him in the rest of this Journal." Boswell by no means always remembered to do this. The Dublin doctorate was conferred in 1765, the Oxford one in 1775.

71 The actor and dramatist David Garrick (1717–79) was a native of Lichfield and had been taught by Johnson as a boy.

72 *Remarks on the History of Scotland* by Sir David Dalrymple (Lord Hailes) had just appeared. It includes a chapter on Euphan McCullan, a 'poor woman, but rich in faith' in the parish of Kilconquhar in Fife. Hailes examines her alleged conversations with God and concludes (p. 263) that 'there was a time when all the suggestions of prejudice, or passion, or imbecility of mind, which presented themselves in the season of devotion, were held to be *answers from the Lord'*. He need not have used the past tense. The belief that random thoughts and impressions can be messages from God, depending on the sanctity of the individual in question (often demonstrated by the fulfilment of prophecy), remained a staple of demotic Presbyterianism in the island of Lewis until the twentieth century. One such saint, Norman MacDonald (*Tormod Sona*, 1853–1945), used the terminology of radio to describe the technique as 'listening-in' (Macleod, *Am Measg nan Lili*, pp. 23–33). Hailes points out that the murderers of Archbishop Sharp were motivated by prayer of this sort.

73 These two sentences were expanded by Pottle and Bennett (*Journal*, p. 23) from an obscure passage in Boswell's notes. Apart from this and two other short passages, Boswell's account of **16 August** is from the *Tour*.

74 In the Advocates' Library Johnson 'would look at little', according to Boswell's notes. Register House, still a prominent Edinburgh landmark today, was completed in 1789.

75 See p. 73. Boswell's note (*Tour*): "This word is commonly used to signify *sullenly, gloomily*; and in that sense alone it appears in Dr Johnson's Dictionary. I suppose he meant by it, 'with an *obstinate resolution*, similar to that of a sullen man'."

76 They were looking at the Treaty of Union at this point.

77 Boswell's note (*Tour*): "I have hitherto called him Dr William Robertson, to distinguish him from Dr James Robertson, who is soon to make his appearance. But *Principal*, from his being the head of our college, is his usual designation, and is shorter; so I shall use it hereafter."

78 The first part of this exchange is from Boswell's notes. They also offer an alternative version of the punchline: "It takes many kirks to make a church." In 1873–83 Sir William Chambers (for whom see note 43) had the stone walls partitioning St Giles' removed and the whole interior restored to something like its medieval integrity.

79 Blair had become minister of the New Church in 1768 and Edinburgh University's professor of rhetoric and belles lettres in 1772. He was renowned for his preaching (see p. 48).

80 "These are our miseries." Edinburgh University was on the site of the former Kirk o' Field, occupied today by 'Old College', whose foundation stone was laid in 1789. Neither South Bridge nor Chambers Street existed (the latter was named after Sir William Chambers in 1866). Access was from the Cowgate by a steep and narrow alleyway called College Wynd, roughly on the site of today's Guthrie Street, see pp. 32–33.

81 In Boswell's notes he is called 'Little Robertson'.

82 The infirmary was on the site of today's Infirmary Street. Drummond was six times Lord Provost between 1725 and 1764. He laid the foundation stone of North Bridge in 1763.

83 Boswell's note (*Tour*): "The stanza from which he took this line is, 'But then rose up all Edinburgh, / They rose up by thousands three; / A cowardly Scot came John behind, / And ran him through the fair body!'"

84 The words 'he had accused us of eating ox meat like dogs in Scotland' were cancelled in the printer's copy and do not appear in the *Tour*.

85 See notes 15 and 137.

86 Also present, as is clear from Boswell's notes, was Charles Hay, for whom see p. 27. In 1773 he was one of Boswell's closest friends, but after 1780 he is never mentioned in his journals. The reason is apparent from the entries for 25 January and 12 July 1777 (Milne, *Boswell's Edinburgh Journals*, pp. 287–88, 306): "I was disgusted with the vulgarity of Braxfield and with Hay's fulsome flattery of him . . . Charles Hay there. Disgusting meanness. Vexed to recollect intimacy with such."

87 This is the Rev. Dr Thomas Blacklock (1721–91), blind poet and scholar. A native of Annan, he was minister of Kirkcudbright from 1762 to 1765 and thereafter master of a boarding school in Edinburgh. On reading the first edition of the *Tour* he felt that he had been misrepresented, and wrote the following letter, which Boswell printed as an appendix to the second and third editions: "To JAMES BOSWELL, ESQ. DEAR SIR, Having lately had the

pleasure of reading your account of the journey which you took with Dr Samuel Johnson to the Western Isles, I take the liberty of transmitting my ideas of the conversation which happened between the doctor and myself concerning Lexicography and Poetry, which, as it is a little different from the delineation exhibited in the former edition of your Journal, cannot, I hope, be unacceptable; particularly since I have been informed that a second edition of that work is now in contemplation, if not in execution: and I am still more strongly tempted to encourage that hope, from considering that, if every one concerned in the conversations related, were to send you what they can recollect of these colloquial entertainments, many curious and interesting particulars might be recovered, which the most assiduous attention could not observe, nor the most tenacious memory retain. A little reflection, sir, will convince you, that there is not an axiom in Euclid more intuitive nor more evident than the doctor's assertion that poetry was of much easier execution than lexicography. Any mind therefore endowed with common sense, must have been extremely absent from itself, if it discovered the least astonishment from hearing that a poem might be written with much more facility than the same quantity of a dictionary. The real cause of my surprise was what appeared to me much more paradoxical, that he could write a sheet of dictionary *with as much pleasure* as a sheet of poetry. He acknowledged, indeed, that the latter was much easier than the former. For in the one case, books and a desk were requisite; in the other, you might compose when lying in bed, or walking in the fields, &c. He did not, however, descend to explain, nor to this moment can I comprehend, how the labours of a mere Philologist, in the most refined sense of that term, could give equal pleasure with the exercise of a mind replete with elevated conceptions and pathetic ideas, while taste, fancy, and intellect were deeply enamoured of nature, and in full exertion. You may likewise, perhaps, remember, that when I complained of the ground which Scepticism in religion and morals was continually gaining, it did not appear to be on my own account, as my private opinions upon these important subjects had long been inflexibly determined. What I then deplored, and still deplore, was the unhappy influence which that gloomy hesitation had, not only upon particular characters, but even upon life in general; as being equally the bane of action in our present state, and of such consolations as we might derive from the hopes of a future. I have the pleasure of remaining with sincere esteem and respect, Dear Sir, Your most obedient humble servant, Thomas Blacklock. Edinburgh, Nov. 12, 1785."

Boswell did not alter his text, but printed the following remarks after Blacklock's letter: "I am very happy to find that Dr Blacklock's apparent uneasiness on the subject of Scepticism was not on his own account (as I supposed), but from a benevolent concern for the happiness of mankind. With respect, however, to the question concerning poetry, and composing a dictionary, I am confident that my state of Dr Johnson's position is accurate. One may misconceive the motive by which a person is induced to discuss a particular topic (as in the case of Dr Blacklock's speaking of Scepticism);

but an assertion, like that made by Dr Johnson, cannot be easily mistaken. And indeed it seems not very probable, that he who so pathetically laments the *drudgery* to which the unhappy lexicographer is doomed, and is known to have written his splendid imitation of Juvenal with astonishing rapidity, should have had 'as much pleasure in writing a sheet of a dictionary as a sheet of poetry'. Nor can I concur with the ingenious writer of the foregoing letter, in thinking it an axiom as evident as any in Euclid, that 'poetry is of easier execution than lexicography'. I have no doubt that Bailey, and the 'mighty blunderbuss of law', Jacob, wrote ten pages of their respective Dictionaries with more ease than they could have written five pages of poetry. If this book should again be reprinted, I shall with the utmost readiness correct any errors I may have committed, in stating conversations, provided it can be clearly shown to me that I have been inaccurate. But I am slow to believe (as I have elsewhere observed), that any man's memory, at the distance of several years, can preserve facts or sayings with such fidelity as may be done by writing them down when they are recent: and I beg it may be remembered, that it is not upon *memory*, but upon what was *written at the time*, that the authenticity of my Journal rests."

88   Voltaire called this book by Baron d'Holbach 'a philippic against God'.

89   Dr John Gregory (1724–73) was professor of medicine at Edinburgh University. His son James (1753–1821), who was in his class when he died, completed the lectures as temporary professor, graduated in 1774, and was duly elected to the chair of medicine in his place in 1776. Boswell's uncle reappears at pp. 448–49.

90   Johnson's original 'Argument in Favour of the Scottish Law Doctrine of "Vicious Intromission"' may be found in Croker's *Life* (vol. 2 of 1831 edn, pp. 542–46). The document as printed, dated 14 January 1772, headed 'Unto the Right Honourable the Lords of Council and Session, the Petition of James Wilson late in Haghouse, now heritor in Kilmaurs' and subscribed 'JAMES BOSWELL' (34 pp.), is in the Advocates' Library (A105/1/72.07.01). A further petition under the same heading, dated 1 July 1772 and also subscribed by Boswell, is kept with it (A105/1/72.01.14). Both may be viewed on Harvard University Houghton Library's 'Eighteenth Century Collections Online'.

91   In the *Tour* Boswell footnotes Shore as 'Mistress of Edward IV' and Vallière as 'Mistress of Louis XIV'. The reference is to Johnson's best poem, 'The Vanity of Human Wishes', an imitation of the Tenth Satire of Juvenal, for which see also note 87.

92   Boswell's note (*Tour*): "Mr Maclaurin's epitaph, as engraved on a marble tombstone, in the Gray-Friars church-yard, Edinburgh: *Infra situs est / COLIN MACLAURIN / Mathes. olim in Acad. Edin. Prof. / Electus ipso Newtono suadente. / H. L. P. F. / Non ut nomini paterno consulat, / Nam tali auxilio nil eget; / Sed ut in hoc infelici campo, / Ubi luctus regnant et pavor, / Mortalibus prorsus non absit solatium: / Hujus enim scripta evolve, / Mentemque tantarum rerum capacem / Corpori caduco superstitem crede.*" The stone has been fixed to the outside of the southern wall of the church, along with Hugh Blair's, and is still (2007) in perfect condition. Blair's includes the words *Hunc Lapidem*

ponendum curabant ALUMNI ('whose students have arranged the placing of this stone'), which suggests that *H. L. P. F.* is for *hunc lapidem posuit filius.* The epitaph may thus be translated: "Buried here is / Colin Maclaurin, / formerly Professor of Mathematics in the University of Edinburgh, / elected with the backing of Newton himself. / His son has arranged the placing of this stone / not because he should look to his paternal name, / for he is in need of no such help; / but because in this unhappy place / where grief and fear hold sway, / comfort is certainly there for the living: / for read what is written about him / and believe that his intellect capable of such great powers / is still active in his extinguished body."

93 Webster, minister of the Tolbooth Church in St Giles', exemplified the best qualities of the Enlightenment: though 'not learned' in the classical sense, he was a popular evangelical preacher, a *bon viveur* and a statistician who compiled Scotland's first unofficial census.

94 Boswell had just been arguing the case; it was decided on 20 July 1773. His 'notes' were published in January 1774 as *The Decision of the Court of Session upon the Question of Literary Property.* The judge whose argument is mentioned was Lord Gardenstone, for whom see pp. 52–53.

95 A tax was levied on horses in 1784. Boswell's account of 17 **August** is taken from the *Tour.*

96 For William Scott see p. 20.

97 Boswell secretly perused the diary in Johnson's house on 5 May 1776 (*Life*, December 1784; Pottle, *Journal*, p. 410).

98 See p. 1.

99 Boswell's note (*Tour*): "Non illic urbes, non tu mirabere silvas: / Una est injusti caerula forma maris.—*Ovid. Amor.* L. II. El. xi. Nor groves nor towns the ruthless ocean shows; / Unvaried still its azure surface flows." This is Ovid's *Amores*, book 2, poem 11, lines 11–12, "There are no towns or woods there for you to gaze at – nothing but the deep blue form of the unjust sea."

100 See p. 79. The habit of wearing shoes spread gradually in Scotland – first to the aristocracy, last to the poor; first to the cities, last to the islands; first to adults, last to children; first in winter, last in summer; first on Sundays, last on weekdays (Gunn, 'Shoes May be Spared'). Johnson shows these processes half complete.

101 Boswell's note (*Tour*): "My friend General Campbell, Governor of Madras, tells me that they make *speldings* in the East Indies, particularly at Bombay, where they call them *Bambaloes.*" The *OED* has this word as 'bummalo'.

102 *Aeneid*, book 6, line 460: "Unwillingly, O queen, I left your shore."

103 Monro's was probably at Pettycur harbour, half a mile south-west of Kinghorn; the inn at Cupar where they had this conversation was Archibald's, whose precise location is unknown (Pottle, *Journal*, p. 455). Boswell's note (*Tour*): "The passage quoted by Dr Johnson is in the *Character of the Assembly-man*, Butler's *Remains*, p. 232, edit. 1754. 'He preaches, indeed, both in season and out of season; for he rails at Popery, when the land is almost lost in Presbytery; and would cry Fire! Fire! in Noah's flood.' There is reason to

believe that this piece was not written by Butler, but by Sir John Birkenhead; for Wood, in his *Athenæ Oxonienses*, Vol. II. p. 460, enumerates it among that gentleman's works, and gives the following account of it: '*The Assembly-man* (or *The Character of an Assembly-man*) written 1647, Lond. 1662–3, in three sheets in qu. The copy of it was taken from the author by those who said they could not rob, because all was theirs; so excised what they liked not; and so mangled and reformed it, that it was no character of an Assembly, but of themselves. At length, after it had slept several years, the author published it, to avoid false copies. It is also reprinted in a book entit. *Wit and Loyalty Revived*, in a collection of some smart satires in verse and prose on the late times. *Lond*. 1682, qu. said to be written by Abr. Cowley, Sir John Birkenhead, and Hudibras, alias Sam. Butler.' For this information I am indebted to Mr Reed, of Staple Inn." Pottle and Bennett remark (*Journal*, p. 37) that the most interesting thing about this note is that Boswell seems to have gone to press without it, and to have cancelled two leaves to get it in.

104   See p. 98. The passage from 'I *saw*' to 'help this' is from Boswell's notes, as are the paragraph beginning 'It looked as if' and the details of the travellers' meals at Kinghorn and St Andrews. Otherwise this account of **18 August** is from the *Tour*.

105   Glass's inn was the Black Bull at the corner of South Street and Heukster's Wynd, now called South Castle Street. The poem by Dr Archibald Pitcairne which was translated (or rather imitated) by Matthew Prior was 'Gualterus Danistonus ad Amicos' (Hill and Powell, *Life*, vol. 3, p. 119).

106   The purchase was made in 1772. Boswell says in his notes: "Mr W. bought whole College for £400." See note 3.

107   Boswell's note (*Tour*): "My Journal, from this day inclusive, was read by Dr Johnson." This takes the place of the following paragraph in the text, which was added after the journal was written, then deleted at proof stage: "My journal begins in an octavo paper book the day on which we left Edinburgh. It was read from that day by Dr Johnson. At first it is imperfectly kept, so that the matter is now in part supplied from memory and the expression filled up and corrected. It gradually grows more perfect, and by and by will be found to be verbatim as printed, with only small insertions of words and omissions of passages not fit for publication. I once thought of writing it anew, but Sir Joseph Banks, Sir Joshua Reynolds, and other friends thought it would be better to give the genuine transcript of what passed at the time and add notes to explain or enlarge. A great part of its value is its authenticity and its having passed the ordeal of Dr Johnson himself." See note 132.

108   Far from being pious, John Stewart, Lord Mountstuart, was self-indulgent and rakish. He was travelling with two companions in 1765 when Boswell met him in Rome. They visited Padua and Venice together before parting in Milan (Brady and Pottle, *Boswell on the Grand Tour*, pp. 54–114). Stewart later became 4th earl and 1st marquis of Bute.

109   Boswell's note (*Tour*): "Dr Johnson used to practise this himself very much."

110   Boswell may have been misinformed. It existed in manuscript, but is not mentioned in William Douglass, *Some Historical Remarks on the City of St.*

Andrews in North-Britain (London, 1728). For Douglass see Hill and Powell, *Life*, vol. 5, p. 479. Alternatively 'one Douglas' may have been the Aberdeen printer, publisher and bookseller Francis Douglas (*c.*1710–*c.*1790). He or his namesake – a relative, perhaps – was the author of a Pennantesque *General Description of the East Coast of Scotland, from Edinburgh to Cullen* (1st edn Paisley 1782, 2nd edn Aberdeen 1826). Again Martine's manuscript is not mentioned. It was finally published in 1797 by James Morison, printer to the university, as *Reliquiae Divi Andreae, or the State of the Venerable and Primitial See of St Andrews*. Perhaps the professors, aware of its value, were keeping it close to their chests.

111 Boswell's note (*Tour*): "Let youth in deeds, in counsel man engage; / Prayer is the proper duty of old age."

112 The 'Town Kirk' or Church of the Holy Trinity; James Sharp, archbishop of St Andrews since 1661, was murdered by Covenanters on Magus Muir, 3 May 1679. With the exception of the first paragraph, the dinner menu, and some words in the present paragraph, all of which are in Boswell's notes, this account of **19 August** is from the *Tour*.

113 St Salvator's College Mace, presented in 1461 by its founder, Bishop Kennedy, is of splendidly ornamented silverwork with an iron core, and is nearly four feet long; it is one of the university's three medieval maces. The arrow was competed for annually until 1754 by shooting at a mark: the winner recorded his victory by presenting a medal to be hung on the arrow. Three silver arrows and seventy silver medals survive (Cant, *University of St Andrews*, pp. 147–49, 153).

114 Presumably the Rev. David Lindsay, Episcopal priest at St Andrews from 1742 until his death in 1791.

115 This is a summary of Hope's words, whether Johnson's or Boswell's we cannot know. Sir William Hope's *The Compleat Fencing-Master: In which is fully Described the whole Guards, Parades & Lessons, Belonging to the Small-Sword* (London, 1691) was popularly called *The Scots Fencing-Master* because it contains a dedication 'To the Young Nobility and Gentry Of the Kingdom of Scotland' beginning 'My Lords and Gentlemen, I here present to You a SCOTS *Fencing-Master . . .*' Hope says: "If a Man should be forced to make use of *Sharps*, our *Scots-play* is in my Opinion, farr before any I ever saw abroad, as for security; and the Reason why I think it so, is, because all *French play* runneth upon *Falsifying* and *taking of time*, which appeareth to the Eyes of the Spectatours to be a farr neatter, & Gentiler way of playing than ours but no man that understands what secure *Fencing* is, will ever call that kind of play sure play, because when a Man maketh use of such kind of play, he can never so secure himself, but his Adversary (if he design it) may *Contre-temps* him every Thrust, now our *Scots* play is quit another thing, for it runneth all upon *Binding* or securing of your Adversaries Sword."

116 Johnson is referring to his friend Robert Chambers, with whom he had travelled from London to Newcastle on 6–10 August (p. 20).

117 J. P. de Crousaz, *A Commentary on Mr. Pope's Principles of Morality, or Essay on Man* (London, 1739). This caused Boswell much confusion (*Life*, November 1738), as he did not realise that there were two published translations of

Crousaz's *Examen*, one by Johnson and another by Elizabeth Carter.

118 James Thomson was the author of *The Seasons*. It was on James Craig's advice that the medieval roof of St Salvator's church was demolished in 1773.

119 The man who forgot his own name appears to have been Robert Irving of Bonshaw, WS, but Boswell's note on this is unclear. 'To Postumus' (Horace, *Odes*, book 2, poem 14) begins: *Eheu fugaces, Postume, Postume, / Labuntur anni nec pietas moram / Rugis* . . . "Ah Postumus, Postumus, the fleeting years glide away, and piety will never put a stop to wrinkles . . ."

120 John's vision in Patmos came to him through prayer (Rev. 1: 10).

121 Lt.-Col. John Nairne (d. 1782), presumably a relative of their companion William Nairne, lived at 4 South Street.

122 This is the reading of the third edition. The first has: "In the grotto, we saw a wonderful large lobster claw." The second: "In the grotto, we saw a lobster's claw uncommonly large."

123 This 'civil old man' was James Walker, minister of Leuchars from 1733 until his death on 27 December 1773. His successor, Thomas Kettle (1741–1808), describing the parish for Sir John Sinclair's *Statistical Account of Scotland*, mentions the tradition that its eastern part (the marsh called Sheuchy Dyke) was peopled by the crews of a Danish fleet wrecked on the coast, but finds no evidence to support the story. William Brown, one of the professors who entertained Johnson and Boswell, conducted an investigation on the ground, the results of which were later published in his 'Account of Sheuchy Dyke'. He found a firm tradition among the older inhabitants that following a battle, which he deduced to be Luncarty (*c.* 973), the defeated Danes encamped on the Tents Moors, and some of them settled there permanently. The tradition focused on a single family called Landsman. However, Sir Walter Scott commented (Croker, *Life*, 20 August): "The Danish colony at Leuchars is a vain imagination concerning a certain fleet of Danes wrecked on Sheughy Dikes."

124 The passage from 'Came to Dundee' to 'which I resumed' is from Boswell's notes, as are the details of the meal at Montrose. Otherwise this account of **20 August** is from the *Tour*. Peter Murray's inn at Dundee was in Couttie's Wynd, between the Nethergate and Whitehall Crescent, now occupied by university buildings. Arbroath and Aberbrothock are the same place: Shaw's inn was the White Hart on the corner of High Street and Kirk Wynd. The 'ruin' is Arbroath Abbey, which clearly revived Johnson's curiosity about Boswell's flirtation with Catholicism (in 1760, not 1759). By 'resumed' Boswell means 'recapitulated'.

125 Boswell's note (*Tour*): "*Then Jesus said unto them, verily, verily, I say unto you, except ye eat the flesh of the son of man, and drink his blood, ye have no life in you.* See St John's Gospel, chap. vi. 53 and following verses."

126 Boswell's note (*Tour*): "This description of Dr Johnson appears to have been borrowed from *Tom Jones*, Book XI, chap. ii. 'The other, who, like a ghost, only wanted to be spoke to, readily answered,' &c." For the inn at Montrose see p. 8; for the lemons, which were quickly used up, see pp. 110, 115, 312 and note 726.

127 The apothecary's shop was kept by a Patrick Stratton. The 'English chapel' was destroyed by fire in 1857; the town hall, on the east side of the High Street, was replaced by a modern building in 1963. See p. 8.

128 Boswell's note (*Tour*): "There were several points of similarity between them: learning, clearness of head, precision of speech, and a love of research on many subjects which people in general do not investigate. Foote paid Lord Monboddo the compliment of saying that he was 'an Elzevir edition of Johnson'. It has been shrewdly observed that Foote must have meant a diminutive or *pocket* edition." The Elzevir family were renowned for printing small, neat editions of the classics in the Netherlands during the seventeenth century; for 'the Elzevirs of Glasgow' see p. 432.

129 Heb. 13: 2. They were at the Boar's Head (1 High Street), still trading today as the Gardenstone Arms Inn. Some of the books mentioned in the following paragraph have been traced to Dundee University Library (Fleeman, *Journey*, p. 291).

130 Boswell's note (*Tour*, second and subsequent editions): "This, I find, is considered as obscure. I suppose Dr Johnson meant, that I assiduously and earnestly recommended myself to some of the members, as in a canvass for an election into Parliament."

131 From the first line of Virgil's *Georgics*: "The joy-giving corn."

132 Boswell's note (*Tour*): "My note of this is much too short. *Brevis esse laboro, obscurus fio.* Yet as I have resolved that *the very Journal which Dr Johnson read* shall be presented to the public, I will not expand the text in any considerable degree, though I may occasionally supply a word to complete the sense, as I fill up the blanks of abbreviation in the writing; neither of which can be said to change the genuine Journal. One of the best critics of our age conjectures that the imperfect passage above has probably been as follows: 'In his book we have an accurate display of a nation in war, and a nation in peace; the peasant is delineated as truly as the general; nay, even harvest sport, and the modes of ancient theft are described.'" Despite Boswell's resolve, the *Tour* is far from being 'the very Journal with Dr Johnson read', as countless alterations, deletions and additions were made. The critic was undoubtedly Malone, who helped Boswell prepare the *Tour* for publication.

133 "A certain regal quality."

134 Boswell's note (*Tour*): "Dr Johnson modestly said he had not read Homer so much as he wished he had done. But this conversation shows how well he was acquainted with the Moeonian bard; and he has shown it still more in his criticism upon Pope's Homer, in his Life of that poet. My excellent friend Mr Langton told me he was once present at a dispute between Dr Johnson and Mr Burke, on the comparative merits of Homer and Virgil, which was carried on with extraordinary abilities on both sides. Dr Johnson maintained the superiority of Homer."

135 This school, originally associated with Holyrood Abbey, was in Blackfriars' Wynd. In 1777–80 it was replaced by the building in Infirmary Street still known as High School Yards.

136 Arthur, Monboddo's only son, died next year, aged eleven. The 'Old Pretender',

known to Jacobites as James VIII and III, had died in 1766, and Boswell notes (*Tour*, second and subsequent editions): "I find, some doubt has been entertained concerning Dr Johnson's meaning here. It is to be supposed that he meant, 'when a king shall again be entertained in Scotland'."

137   With this we may compare Johnson's own account of his visit to Monboddo, in a letter to Mrs Thrale sent from Banff on 25 August (Redford, *Letters*, vol. 2, p. 57): "We travelled towards Aberdeen, another University, and in the way dined at Lord Monbodo's, the Scotch Judge who has lately written a strange book about the origin of Language, in which he traces Monkeys up to Men, and says that in some countries the human Species have tails like other beasts. He enquired for these longtailed Men of Banks, and was not well pleased, that they had not been found in all his peregrination. He talked nothing of this to me, and I hope, we parted friends, for we agreed pretty well, only we differed in adjusting the claims of merit between a Shopkeeper of London, and a Savage of the American wildernesses. Our opinions were, I think, maintained on both sides without full conviction; Monbodo declared boldly for the Savage, and I perhaps for that reason sided with the Citizen."

138   Down to here our source has been the *Tour*, with occasional additions from Boswell's notes. From this sentence onwards, however, Boswell's journal is fully written, and is therefore the source for the rest of his account of **21 August**, with some exceptions – the menu in this paragraph is taken from a previous point in the notes, while the *Cato* quotation and three sentences are from the *Tour*.

139   Since his appointment to the Court of Session in 1767, Monboddo had ridden to London most years in the spring 'to visit friends and to refresh his mind' (Cloyd, *James Burnett: Lord Monboddo*, p. 39). No doubt they met on one of these occasions.

140   The stick is Homeric, not the verse. In the *Tour* Boswell adds 'thus pleasantly alluding to his lordship's favourite writer', meaning Homer. The verse is from Addison's *Cato*, act 2, scene 5.

141   These two sentences are from the *Tour*. The journal merely states: "Gory, the black, was sent as our guide so far." See p. 39.

142   Pope, *An Essay on Man*, epistle 4, lines 219–24: "Heroes are much the same, the point's agreed, / From Macedonia's madman to the Swede; / The whole strange purpose of their lives, to find / Or make, an enemy of all mankind! / Not one looks backward, onward still he goes, / Yet ne'er looks forward farther than his nose." In the *Tour* Boswell cites the whole last line; 'Macedonia's madman' is Alexander, 'the Swede' is Charles XII.

143   See p. 437.

144   The church was Old St Paul's, whose ministers were the Revs James Riddoch and Thomas Gordon; Gordon was also Aberdeen University's professor of philosophy. The words 'the English' and 'well played by Mr Tait' do not appear in Boswell's journal. The account of **22 August** is from the journal, but over a dozen minor augmentations and clarifications of that kind have been added from the *Tour*.

145 The weaving of tartan cloth was indeed an ancient domestic art in the Highlands and Islands, as is well demonstrated by the blessings, chants and traditions collected by Alexander Carmichael in *Carmina Gadelica*, vol. 2, pp. 294–305.

146 'Waller the poet' is Edmund Waller (1606–87), squire of Beaconsfield in Buckinghamshire. The Aberdeen student was in fact his great-great-grandson, also Edmund (1757–1810). This young man's father, described later as 'a plain country gentleman', was Edmund Waller (*c.* 1726–88). He had been MP for Wycombe from 1747 to 1761.

147 The lines were first published under a portrait of Milton prefixed to Tonson's folio edition of *Paradise Lost* (1688): "Three poets, in three distant ages born, / Greece, Italy, and England, did adorn. / The first, in loftiness of thought surpassed; / The next, in majesty; in both, the last. / The force of nature could no further go; / To make a third, she joined the former two." Boswell's note (*Tour*): "London, 2d May, 1778. Dr Johnson acknowledged that he was himself the author of the translation above alluded to, and dictated it to me as follows: *Quos laudet vates Graius Romanus et Anglus / Tres tria temporibus secla dedere suis. / Sublime ingenium Graius; Romanus habebat / Carmen grande sonans; Anglus utrumque tulit. / Nil majus Natura capit: clarare priores / Quæ potuere duos tertius unus habet.*"

148 Boswell had fallen in love with Isabella Dallas when he was twenty-one. They met when he accompanied his father on the Northern Circuit. She married the Rev. James Riddoch (Pottle and Bennett, *Journal*, pp. 61–62, 415). She had a brother William (see note 152) and three younger sisters, Ann, Katherine and Margaret (Dallas, *History of the Family of Dallas*, p. 184). Margaret married the Rev. John Bowie, a native of Maryland who had come to study at King's College, Aberdeen. Their father was the Jacobite martyr James Dallas of Cantray, one of the first to attack and be killed at Culloden, 'a loyall, kind, brave young man, who rais'd his company at a great expence to serve his royall master', described by John Roy Stewart as *Triath eile mo rùin, / O Channtra an Tùir, / Air an àraich gun fhiach a léine* (Black, *An Lasair*, pp. 170–71): "Another leader I loved, from Cantray of the Tower, lay on the field without even his shirt." The Rev. James Hay told the Rev. Robert Forbes that Cantray's body was one of those merely covered with a little earth, 'for none durst do it in a proper time, or carry them away', but when taken up twenty days later it was uncorrupted and without smell (Paton, *Lyon in Mourning*, vol. 2, pp. 304–05, 354, and vol. 3, p. 55).

149 This is a difficult sentence, and some changes were made to it in the *Tour*. Boswell's note (*Tour*): "My worthy, intelligent, and candid friend, Dr Kippis, informs me, that several divines have thus explained the mediation of our Saviour. What Dr Johnson now delivered, was but a temporary opinion; for he afterwards was fully convinced of the propitiatory sacrifice, as I shall show at large in my future work, *The Life of Samuel Johnson, LL.D.*" Boswell was as good as his word (*Life*, 3 June 1781).

150 Bacon was not known as a poet, and the attribution to him of 'The Life of Man' caused a sensation in its day. The first of its four stanzas runs (Spedding,

Works, vol. 7, part 1, p. 272): "The world's a bubble, and the life of man / less than a span; / In his conception wretched, from the womb / so to the tomb: / Curst from the cradle, and brought up to years / with cares and fears. / Who then to frail mortality shall trust, / But limns the water, or but writes in dust." For more on this night's conversation see p. 353.

151 Boswell's note (*Tour*): "Dr Beattie was so kindly entertained in England, that he had not yet returned home." For the text of the diploma see pp. 212–13.

152 Mrs Margaret Dallas (*née* Hamilton), Mrs Riddoch's mother, was the widow of James Dallas of Cantray (see note 148) and the grandmother of the little girl called Stuart, or rather Stewart (p. 59), who was born in 1766. Stewart's parents – Mrs Riddoch's brother William and his wife Stewart, a daughter of Sir Alexander Mackenzie of Coul – had gone to the East Indies, leaving her in the care of her grandmother. William, the last Dallas of Cantray, died in China in 1773 or 1774. His daughter does not appear to have survived into adulthood (Dallas, *History of the Family of Dallas*, p. 190).

153 In the *Tour* this becomes 'my History of James IV of Scotland, the patron of my family'. Pottle and Bennett point out (*Journal*, p. 65) that this project, never heard of again, is one of over fifty works which Boswell planned to write at one time or another. They list a few, concluding: "Sir Alexander Macdonald, not being a fit subject for serious biography, was to be dealt with in a novel." By 'Old College' Boswell means King's College, founded in 1495.

154 The references are to *Observations on the Faerie Queene* (1754), by Johnson's friend the poet and historian Thomas Warton, and to Thomas Nugent's translation of *Réflexions Critiques sur la Poésie et la Peinture* (1719) by Abbé Jean-Baptiste Du Bos. Since Warton drew attention to his source, it is doubtful whether it should be described as plagiarism. For more of Gerard's talk see p. 105.

155 I take the poem and the preceding paragraph from Boswell's footnote (*Tour*). Apart from this and about half a dozen brief explanatory phrases from the *Tour* (mainly in the paragraph beginning 'Gerard said'), the account of **23 August** is from the journal. I am grateful to Mr Norman MacLeod for the following translation: "To the author, on his treatment of illnesses. The Healing Power, no match for such terrible illnesses, sheds tears over the raging fever and the body overcome by burning heat. And after a thousand treatments, and the efforts of medical skill, the fever still rages and will not allow itself to be controlled by treatment. We are prey to the flames. We only hope that the ash (destined for the cinerary urn) from this fire will hold out a little longer while the doctor looks for the cause and type of illness, the shadows of the flames, and firebrands without light. Growing hot with the fever, he treats and suffers these flames, but he himself fell down as the victim was ravaged by the fires of the fever. He, who was able to resist the lingering illness and the trembling limbs, sees himself being engulfed by the fire-producing fever. Thus the craftsman lights up with his instrument the walls already consumed, while slow destruction pulls down the ancient home. But if the devouring fire has burnt the unhappy building,

the one means of safety is now to bury the flames. Let there be flight. No one invites those with building skills at the point when the burnt-out house has nonetheless been destroyed by craftsmen.

"At length Sydenham, speaking against the school of thought surrounding the illness and the raging of the fever, looks for a cure for the disease. Not thoughtlessly does he find fault with the terrible fires of the body. The fluid which encourages the fever will not be false. It does not move the poison, here there is no moisture. What hope of safety is there if deceptive water burns within? He does not display his learned arguments with excessive pomposity. The heat which is within is greater than the fevers themselves. He calmly gives instructions for the harmless flames to burn the body, while checking the rapidly-burning flames with a sufficient amount of fire. He shows what destroys the fever, and the different treatments it demands, and demonstrates how the sick may be comforted. To this point Nature herself feared this heat, and often died in the uncertain fire by which it is heated.

"While he in a carefree manner renews the dormant fires of the blood, he also prepares it for burning, and that heat becomes a funeral pyre. Now with a heart free from care let them foment its flames. Medicine finds a way which Nature denies. Not only does Sydenham keep in check the lively tossing of the blood while recovery is as yet doubtful, hanging between hope and fear, but he tames the death-dealing malady – an evil which, we believe, the stars or angry Styx created. He has taken away the knives of Lachesis, he has taken away the poison of the disease, forbidding the existence of such fear. Who now disbelieves that the disease has been tamed to mildness by new skills, and that long-established illnesses can be eliminated?

"After so many thousands of deaths, and bodies being heaped up on a funeral pyre, cruel Plague, overcome by a small wound, lies dead. Although the flames from Heaven spread infections, whatever there is in those flames, there will be fire. Let the flames which have come down from Heaven burn more keenly. Do you think that they are only extinguished by an ice-cold watery death? You, victorious, prepare better cures, and you will be triumphant over a plague that conquers all. Live, a free man, now that the flames of fever have been conquered; there will be one fire for you and the world which remains."

156 See p. 136. It is unclear at first that these two paragraphs show how a zealous host can make guests feel like victims. In the *Tour*, 'the post-chaise' becomes 'being again in motion'; 'delicate' becomes 'fastidious'; 'doing too much' becomes 'doing too much to entertain him'.

157 Probably in the inn where the Buchan Arms now stands, at the north end of the bridge. With the exception of a sentence and two phrases brought in from the *Tour* for clarification, this account of 24 **August** is from Boswell's journal.

158 These men, respectively Lord Chief Justice and physician to the king, were both Scots. In the *Tour* Boswell also has Johnson say: "To have called me the greatest man in England, would have been an unmeaning compliment: but the exception marked that the praise was in earnest."

159 George Graham, author of *Telemachus, a Masque*, was a master at Eton; Goldsmith, the poet, had studied medicine at Edinburgh and Leyden. Boswell's note (*Tour*): "I am sure I have related this story exactly as Dr Johnson told it to me; but a friend who has often heard him tell it, informs me that he usually introduced a circumstance which ought not to be omitted. 'At last, sir, Graham, having now got to about the pitch of looking at one man, and talking to another, said *Doctor*, &c. What effect,' Dr Johnson used to add, 'this had on Goldsmith, who was as irascible as a hornet, may be easily conceived.'"

160 Writing to Mrs Thrale from Inverness on 28 August, Johnson explained how the invitation came about (Redford, *Letters*, vol. 2, pp. 60–61): "When I was at the English Church in Aberdeen, I happened to be espied by Lady Di. Middleton whom I had sometime seen in London. She told what she had seen to Mr Boyd, Lord Errols Brother, who wrote us an invitation to Lord Errols house called Slanes Castle."

161 'Northwest' was changed at proof stage to 'Northeast', but is perfectly correct, as the North Sea is in north-west Europe. Boswell always had great difficulty with the points of the compass.

162 This phrase becomes 'Mr Boyd's acquaintance with my father was enough' in the *Tour*. 'Mr Hall' may have been the Rev. Westley Hall, a dissenting minister. 'Miss Williams' was Dr Johnson's domestic companion Anna Williams, daughter of the Welsh physician Zachariah Williams (?1673–1755). Later in life she was known as Mrs (pronounced 'Mistress') Williams.

163 Horace, *Odes*, book 1, poem 2, *Iam satis terris nivis atque dirae* . . . "The Father has already sent enough dire snow and hail upon the earth; smiting the sacred hill-tops with his red right hand, he has filled the city and the people with fear . . ."

164 Mount Edgcumbe (in Cornwall) overlooks Plymouth Sound.

165 This sentence is from the *Tour*. The version of it in the journal makes little sense: "There is perhaps a weakness, that is to say, more fancy or warmth of feeling than is quite reasonable in me, but there is much pleasure arising from it."

166 Boswell's note (*Tour*): "Lord Chesterfield, in his letters to his son, complains of one who argued in an indiscriminate manner with men of all ranks. Probably the noble lord had felt with some uneasiness what it was to encounter stronger abilities than his own. If a peer will engage at foils with his inferior in station, he must expect that his inferior in station will avail himself of every advantage; otherwise it is not a fair trial of strength and skill. The same will hold in a contest of reason, or of wit. A certain king entered the lists of genius with Voltaire. The consequence was, that, though the king had great and brilliant talents, Voltaire had such a superiority that his majesty could not bear it; and the poet was dismissed, or escaped, from that court. In the reign of James I of England, Crichton, Lord Sanquhar, a peer of Scotland, from a vain ambition to excel a fencing-master in his own art, played at rapier and dagger with him. The fencing-master, whose fame and bread were at stake, put out one of his lordship's eyes. Exasperated at

this, Lord Sanquhar hired ruffians, and had the fencing-master assassinated; for which his lordship was capitally tried, condemned, and hanged. Not being a peer of England, he was tried by the name of Robert Crichton, Esq.; but he was admitted to be a baron of three hundred years standing. See the *State Trials*; and the *History of England* by Hume, who applauds the impartial justice executed upon a man of high rank."

167 See note 561.

168 The journal says 'ages' only. This is one of about half a dozen instances in the account of **25 August** where minor amplifications or corrections have been borrowed from the *Tour* (there is also one major amplification, see note 174). The passage in question is: "To hurl the dart, to ride the car, / To stem the deluges of war . . . / 'Twas this that rais'd th'illustrious line / To match the first in fame! / A thousand years have seen it shine / With unabated flame . . ."

169 Jean de Jullienne, a wealthy cloth manufacturer, lived in a house called *la grande Maison des Gobelins*.

170 Boswell's note (*Tour*): "He is the worthy son of a worthy father, the late Lord Strichen, one of our judges, to whose kind notice I was much obliged. Lord Strichen was a man not only honest, but highly generous; for after his succession to the family estate, he paid a large sum of debts contracted by his predecessor, which he was not under any obligation to pay. Let me here, for the credit of Ayrshire, my own county, record a noble instance of liberal honesty in William Hutchison, drover, in Lanehead, Kyle, who formerly obtained a full discharge from his creditors upon a composition of his debts; but upon being restored to good circumstances, invited his creditors last winter to a dinner, without telling the reason, and paid them their full sums, principal and interest. They presented him with a piece of plate, with an inscription to commemorate this extraordinary instance of true worth; which should make some people in Scotland blush, while, though mean themselves, they strut about under the protection of great alliance conscious of the wretchedness of numbers who have lost by them, to whom they never think of making reparation, but indulge themselves and their families in most unsuitable expence."

171 Boswell's note (*Tour*, second and subsequent editions): "Since the first edition, it has been suggested by one of the Club, who knew Mr Vesey better than Dr Johnson and I, that we did not assign him a proper place; for he was quite unskilled in Irish antiquities and Celtic learning, but might with propriety have been made professor of architecture, which he understood well, and has left a very good specimen of his knowledge and taste in that art, by an elegant house built on a plan of his own formation, at Lucan, a few miles from Dublin."

172 Boswell's note (*Tour*): "Our Club, originally at the Turk's Head, Gerrard Street, then at Prince's, Sackville Street, now at Baxter's, Dover Street, which at Mr Garrick's funeral acquired a *name* for the first time, and was called The Literary Club, was instituted in 1764, and now consists of thirty-five members. It has, since 1773, been greatly augmented; and though

Dr Johnson with justice observed, that, by losing Goldsmith, Garrick, Nugent, Chamier, Beauclerk, we had lost what would make an eminent club, yet when I mention, as an accession, Mr Fox, Dr George Fordyce, Sir Charles Bunbury, Lord Ossory, Mr Gibbon, Dr Adam Smith, Mr R. B. Sheridan, the Bishops of Kilaloe and St Asaph, Dean Marlay, Mr Steevens, Mr Dunning, Sir Joseph Banks, Dr Scott of the Commons, Earl Spencer, Mr Windham of Norfolk, Lord Elliot, Mr Malone, Dr Joseph Warton, the Rev. Thomas Warton, Lord Lucan, Mr Burke junior, Lord Palmerston, Dr Burney, Sir William Hamilton, and Dr Warren, it will be acknowledged that we might establish a second university of high reputation." On Langton's will see note 49.

173 The inn was either the Black Bull in Low Street (demolished in 1879) or the Ship near the market cross.

174 See pp. 15, 210. The last five sentences of this paragraph (which appear in the *Tour*) are in origin a footnote on the first three (which appear in both the journal and the *Tour*). The letter mentioned in the following paragraph is most recently edited by Redford, *Letters*, vol. 2, pp. 54–60; for Johnson's use of 'doggedly' see p. 31.

175 The inn at Cullen will have been the Horse's Head. 'Lawter' should read 'Lawtie': the minister of Cullen from 1717 to 1751 was the Rev. James Lawtie.

176 Condamine's *Histoire d'une jeune fille sauvage* was published in 1755. William Robertson had travelled three times to France in 1763–65 as secretary to James Burnett, advocate, to collect evidence in the Douglas Cause (see note 909). They met Memmie le Blanc, the 'savage girl', in Paris in 1765. Burnett became Lord Monboddo in 1767, and Robertson's English translation of Condamine's book appeared the following year, with Monboddo's preface, as *Account of a Savage Girl caught Wild in the Woods of Champagne*. Robertson subsequently became Lord Findlater's factor at Cullen, then, in 1777, deputy keeper of the Scottish Record Office.

177 See p. 54. Boswell's note (*Tour*): "It is the custom in Scotland for the judges of the Court of Session to have the title of *lords*, from their estates; thus Mr Burnett is Lord *Monboddo*, as Mr Home was Lord *Kames*. There is something a little awkward in this; for they are denominated in deeds by their *names*, with the addition of 'one of the Senators of the College of Justice'; and subscribe their Christian and surname, as *James Burnett, Henry Home*, even in judicial acts."

178 Boswell's note (*Tour*): "I do not know what was at this time the state of the parliamentary interest of the ancient family of Lowther, a family before the Conquest; but all the nation knows it to be very extensive at present. A due mixture of severity and kindness, economy and munificence, characterizes its present Representative." The reference in the text is to Sir James Lowther (*c.* 1673–1755), 4th baronet of Whitehaven in Cumberland; the reference in Boswell's note is to another Sir James Lowther (1736–1802), 3rd Viscount and (from 1784) 1st earl of Lonsdale, by whose patronage he hoped to enter Parliament.

179 Johnson had met Hailes on 17 August (pp. 37–38).

180 Boswell's note (*Tour*): "I am not sure whether the Duke was at home. But, not having the honour of being much known to his grace, I could not have presumed to enter his castle, though to introduce even so celebrated a stranger. We were at any rate in a hurry to get forward to the wildness which we came to see. Perhaps, if this noble family had still preserved that sequestered magnificence which they maintained when Catholics, corresponding with the Grand Duke of Tuscany, we might have been induced to have procured proper letters of introduction, and devoted some time to the contemplation of venerable superstitious state."

181 See p. 16. Robert Leslie's 'house' was the Red Lion, 44–46 High St.

182 The passage from 'In the afternoon' to here is from the *Tour*. All Boswell says in his journal is: "We drove over the very heath where Macbeth met the witches, according to tradition. Mr Johnson repeated solemnly again 'How far is't called to Forres?' etc., parodying it to me: 'All hail Dalblair!'" With the exception of this and four minor clarifications, Boswell's account of **26 August** is taken from his journal.

183 *Scots Magazine*, vol. 35, June 1773, p. 333, account of trials at Inverness: "Kenneth Leal, messenger in Elgin, indicted for robbing the Elgin mail in December last, was found guilty by the jury unanimously, and sentenced to be hanged, on the 7th of July, between Elgin and Fochabers, near Janet Innes's Cairn, the place where he robbed the mail, and his body to be hung in chains." Johnson had a horror of death, but Boswell never missed a hanging.

184 The Rev. Kenneth Macaulay had published his *History of St Kilda* in 1764, see pp. 96–97. Calder is an alternative spelling of Cawdor.

185 The two unnamed gentlemen in this paragraph were Valentine White and George Fern. Coote was not strictly governor, but commanding officer of the regiment which formed the garrison, the Enniskillen Fusiliers. See p. 100.

186 Johnson will be thinking of Lachlan MacQueen's daughter, see pp. 85–86, 110.

187 Neither structure survives today. Macbeth's real castle was destroyed in the eleventh century by Malcolm Canmore. Inverness Castle, fancifully called Macbeth's Castle, was on a different site, at the eastern edge of the town; it was blown up by Prince Charles's forces in 1746 and razed in 1834. Cromwell's Fort was on the right bank of the Ness to the north, and its site is now marked by a clock tower. The castellated structure which now dominates the city centre was built for administrative purposes in the 1830s.

188 Johnson refers here firstly to a work by the Scotsman Arthur Johnston, then to one by the Englishman Thomas May. For the custom of going barefoot see p. 41.

189 The Gaelic church was St Mary's in Church Street; for the 'English chapel' see p. 104. It was a room in a house in Baron Taylor's Lane, now Baron Taylor Street, still standing (Pottle, *Journal*, p. 461; Fleeman, *Journey*, p. 295).

190 Their names were John Hay and Lachlan Vass, see p. 106.

191 This military road, built *c.* 1730, ran along the eastern shore of the loch.

192 The reference is to a hill in Derbyshire well known to Johnson.

193 It is indeed as deep as this.

194 It is true that Loch Ness has never been known to freeze (MacilleDhuibh, 'The Loch that Never Freezes').

195 In Plutarch's *Life of Alexander*, when the hero invades India he encounters ten naked Hindu philosophers and asks each a single question. To the third he says: "Which is the craftiest of all animals?" The reply is: "That with which man is not yet acquainted."

196 This was *Taigh an Dìridh Mhóir*, 'the House of the Steep Climb', built in 1732 as a change-house on Wade's military road at Whitefield, halfway between Dores and Foyers, where the road turned sharply down from the hillside to the shore. The B852 now runs along the lochside the whole way, but a commemorative stone was placed by it in 1923 to mark the spot. See also pp. 107–08.

197 The site of Anoch is by today's A887 where it crosses *Allt an Eòin* ('the Stream of the Bird'). As the name implies (*aonach* 'market-stance'), it was a long-established drovers' inn on the route from Skye to the Lowlands. The landlord, Lachlan MacQueen, was a Gaelic poet, but none of his work appears to have survived. The 'Connection' was *The Old and New Testament Connected* by the orientalist Humphrey Prideaux, a very popular work first published in 1716–18.

198 Johnson met several ministers in the islands whom he would have been willing to describe as 'learned', but only one whom he would have called 'very learned': Donald MacQueen of Kilmuir in Skye.

199 Presumably this was Patrick Grant (1700–86), chief of the Grants of Glenmoriston since 1736.

200 See p. 110.

201 The exact location is known to tradition (it was shown to my friend Dr John MacInnes) and has been pinpointed to Ordnance Survey NH 144104, a little below the present road where it crosses a stream just over five miles east of the Cluanie Inn. Pottle's reservations about this identification (*Journal*, p. 466) are, I think, removed by note 254 below.

202 The mountains of Taurus in Turkey were the highest known to the ancient Greeks.

203 Loch Cluanie, now much larger following the construction of a dam in 1956.

204 The names of the glen and of the village are similar but unrelated. The glen is *Gleann Seile*, Glen Shiel, which takes its name from the river (*Seile* 'flowing one'). The village, 'Achanashela' in Blaeu's atlas of 1662, is *Achadh nan Seileach* 'the Field of the Willows'. There is no trace of it today.

205 Norman Macleod (1706–72), grandfather of the young chief whom we meet in chapters 4 and 5. As MP for Inverness-shire he travelled a great deal between Skye, Inverness and London.

206 Herodotus, *History*, book 4, §§2–4: "Because their husbands were absent from them for a long time, the Scythians' wives had associated with the

slaves . . . From their wives and their slaves a generation of young men had been born and bred." MacRae–MacLellan rivalry is a very old chestnut. The Rev. John MacRa mentions the 'vulgar error' that they fought each other at the thirteenth-century battle of Drimderfit, and shows them vying for status three centuries later ('Genealogy of the MacRas', pp. 204, 216). The Rev. Alexander Macrae addresses Johnson's story directly (*History of the Clan Macrae*, p. 336): "There is a well-known tradition that eighteen of the chief Maclennans of Kintail were killed in the Battle of Auldearn, in 1645, and that their widows were afterwards married by Macraes, who thus acquired possession of the Maclennan holdings, and so became the leading name in Kintail. But it is a tradition that has no trace of any foundation in fact."

207 This incident has not been identified, but it has the ring of truth.

208 Thucydides, *Peloponnesian War*, chapter 1, §6: "The Athenians were the first to lay aside their weapons, and to adopt an easier and more luxurious way of life."

209 A reference to the Act of 1747 which abolished heritable jurisdictions. On the legal vacuum thus created see pp. 188, 190–91.

210 The battle of Mulroy was fought in Brae Lochaber, over fifty miles south of Inverness, on 4 August 1688, in the reign of James VII and II.

211 See pp. 143, 303, 326–27.

212 This has not been done: the road to Glenelg still passes over Ratagan.

213 As the late Very Rev. Dr Tom Murchison pointed out ('Notes on the Murchisons', pp. 276–78), his name was in fact Murdoch Murchison (*Murchadh MacCalmain*), see pp. 112, 115. Perhaps Johnson misinterpreted *MacCalmain* as Gordon?

214 The twenty-foot high obelisk at Forres is firmly on record as 'King Sueno's Stone' since 1726. It dates from *c.* AD 850–950 and shows a teeming battle scene on one side and a cross on the other. Modern scholars disfavour the implied Danish or Norse connection and have proposed instead that it commemorates the defeat of the Picts by Kenneth mac Alpin in 843 or the death of another king of Scots, Dubh, in 966 (Sellar, 'Sueno's Stone', pp. 110, 112, 114). Though perhaps inspired by Shakespeare, Boswell's 'King Duncan's Monument' is in line with this.

215 *Leonidas* (1737) is a poem in nine books by Richard Glover (1712–85). Boswell calls *Manners* a 'brilliant and pointed' satire (*Life*, spring 1738); when it was published in 1739 the House of Lords decreed that it was scandalous and ordered the author into custody. He absconded.

216 This was in 1760; within two or three years Boswell's attitude to Derrick had changed. On Monday 28 March 1763 he informed his diary (Pottle, *Boswell's London Journal*, p. 228): "I wonder how I forgot to mention yesterday that just as I was going out to church a gentleman called upon me; and who was this but Derrick, who is now Master of the Ceremonies at Bath. I unluckily got acquainted with this creature when I was first in London, and after I found him out to be a little blackguard pimping dog, I did not know how to get rid of him. I now took care to let him see that I did not choose to renew my acquaintance with him." For Eglinton see pp. 434–35.

217 See p. 260. Derrick's correspondence was published in two volumes as *Letters Written from Leverpoole, Chester, Corke . . .* (1767), with his portrait as frontispiece.

218 The lines are by the Rev. Richard Gifford, vicar of Duffield near Derby, and are quoted in Johnson's *Dictionary* under 'wheel'. The poem was 'Contemplation' (1753).

219 Mrs Penelope Macaulay was a daughter of Alexander MacLeod of the Drynoch family, see pp. 99, 116. Boswell's note (*Tour*): "In Scotland, there is a great deal of preparation before administering the sacrament. The minister of the parish examines the people as to their fitness, and to those of whom he approves gives little pieces of tin, stamped with the name of the parish, as *tokens*, which they must produce before receiving it. This is a species of priestly power, and sometimes may be abused. I remember a law-suit brought by a person against his parish minister, for refusing him admission to that sacred ordinance."

220 "He is a coarse man." Johnson said even worse, see p. 268. It is believed today that what is most useful about the book, the descriptive and topographical parts, were indeed written by Macaulay, but that the antiquarian or speculative passages were by the Rev. Dr John MacPherson, for whom see pp. 136, 231, 280–81. Johnson's dislike of Macaulay sprang not from this but from his views on the Church of England.

221 *Macbeth*, act 1, scene 3: "The Thane of Cawdor lives, / A prosperous gentleman; and to be king / Stands not within the prospect of belief." Boswell's friend John Campbell of Cawdor (1695–1777), a former Lord of the Admiralty and of the Treasury, lived mostly in Wales, where he was brought up and where eventually he died, his father Sir Alexander having married a Pembrokeshire heiress.

222 This paragraph is from the *Tour*. Boswell's journal merely says: "I doubted if Mr Johnson would be present at a Presbyterian prayer. I told Macaulay so, and said that he might sit in the library. Macaulay said he'd let it alone rather than give Mr Johnson offence. I spoke of it to Mr Johnson, who said he had no objection." By 'tree' Johnson meant just that, indicating that he was willing to join an informal gathering of Presbyterians, but not a formal one before a pulpit. This may be the passage referred to at p. 441 where Boswell says that Johnson's 'reason for not joining in Presbyterian worship has been recorded in a former page', but it has not survived in manuscript. With the exception of this and five further sentences or phrases providing additional information, the account of **27 August** is taken either from the journal itself or (in the case of the words from 'where I eloped' to 'laborious occupation') from an additional passage written and cancelled in the course of preparing it for publication.

223 Born in Turin, Giuseppe Marc' Antonio Baretti came to live in London in 1751. He published an Italian and English dictionary in 1760, and was a friend of Johnson's and of the Thrales.

224 Boswell's note (*Tour*): "Dr Johnson did not neglect what he had undertaken. By his interest with the Rev. Dr Adams, master of Pembroke College,

Oxford, where he was educated for some time, he obtained a servitorship for young Macaulay. But it seems he had other views; and I believe went abroad." Aulay Macaulay spent a year, aged about seventeen, as a lieutenant of Marines, retired on half pay, lived to be eighty, and died in 1842.

225 This sentence is from the *Tour*; otherwise, with one tiny exception (see note 231), the account of **28 August** is from Boswell's journal. Valentine White is buried in Cawdor churchyard.

226 Boswell's *Account of Corsica*, including the 'Memoirs of Pascal Paoli', had been published in 1768 to considerable acclaim.

227 In the *Tour*, following Johnson's remark about a woman praying when she milks her cow, Boswell inserts '(which Mr Grant told us is done in the Highlands)'. Indeed it is, or was. In the late nineteenth century Alexander Carmichael collected numerous milking prayers (*Carmina Gadelica*, vols 1, pp. 258–71, and 4, pp. 62–81). Boswell footnotes the paragraph: "He could not bear to have it thought that, in any instance whatever, the Scots are more pious than the English. I think grace as proper at breakfast as at any other meal. It is the pleasantest meal we have. Dr Johnson has allowed the peculiar merit of breakfast in Scotland." See p. 123.

228 *Tour in Scotland*, a detailed account of travels on the mainland in 1769 by the Welsh naturalist Thomas Pennant, appeared in 1771. In 1772 he also visited the islands, and his description of this journey was published in 1774–76. Clearly one of Johnson's motivations for undertaking the trip was the feeling that Pennant, whose style he disliked, was upstaging him. Johnson's reference at p. 9 to a tendency to 'write of the cities of our own island with the solemnity of geographical description' is a veiled attack on the Welshman, but he was aware of his virtues as a scientist (p. 244). See also note 429.

229 See p. 55. In the *Tour*, instead of printing this paragraph, Boswell footnoted the previous: "Here Dr Johnson gave us part of a conversation held between a Great Personage and him, in the library at the Queen's Palace, in the course of which this contest was considered. I have been at great pains to get that conversation as perfectly preserved as possible. It will appear in Dr Johnson's Life." In the printer's copy the last sentence read 'It will appear to great advantage in Dr Johnson's Life', but Malone had the words 'to great advantage' removed. In the second and third editions the sentence was altered to: "It may perhaps at some future time be given to the public." Boswell gave a detailed account of the conversation in the *Life* at February 1767.

230 These words were maintained through the first and second editions of the *Tour*, but in the third Boswell deleted the reference to *Love in a Hollow Tree* (a comedy by Viscount Grimston, *Life*, 30 March 1781) and substituted '. . . good dinner and brilliant company, to borrow the expression of an absurd poet . . .'

231 The word 'to' is from the *Tour*. The point of Boswell's joke is that the MacGregors were a persecuted race whose very name had been proscribed by various acts of the Scots parliament.

232 Mrs MacKenzie's inn, 'the Horns', stood at the north-west end of Bridge Street, by the River Ness. No doubt it took its name from a stag's head, *Cabar Féidh* ('Deer's Antlers') being the MacKenzie war-cry. James Keith had succeeded Roderick MacKenzie of Redcastle, who lived in Inverness, as the town's collector of customs. They called on him next day.

233 Boswell's note (*Tour*): "It is remarkable that Dr Johnson read this gentle remonstrance, and took no notice of it to me."

234 For 'Oliver's fort' and 'Macbeth's Castle' see note 187. When in Rome, Boswell engaged James Alves to make a miniature of him for forwarding to Scotland (Brady and Pottle, *Boswell on the Grand Tour*, pp. 90–91, 285). The obituary of Alves in the *Inverness Journal*, 16 December 1808, states: "His life was singularly good, recluse, and inoffensive, and his death much regretted. He went abroad when young to improve himself in the fine arts, and studied eight years in Paris, and other eight years in Rome." Boswell's account of **29 August** is from his journal, with the addition of half-a-dozen phrases from the *Tour*, of which the reference to Reynolds is one.

235 This refers to Foote's comedy *The Orators*. In the *Tour* Boswell replaces the next paragraph with a footnote: "When upon the subject of this *peregrinity*, he told me some particulars concerning the compilation of his *Dictionary*, and concerning his throwing off Lord Chesterfield's patronage, of which very erroneous accounts have been circulated. These particulars, with others which he afterwards gave me – as also his celebrated letter to Lord Chesterfield, which he dictated to me – I reserve for his *Life*." Johnson's letter to Chesterfield, dated 7 February 1755, is justly famed for its fearlessness (*Life* at 1754): "Is not a patron, my Lord, one who looks with unconcern on a man struggling for life in the water, and, when he has reached ground, encumbers him with help?"

236 Carruthers's note (*Tour*, p. 96): "Mr Grant used to relate that on this occasion Johnson was in high spirits. In the course of conversation he mentioned that Mr Banks (afterwards Sir Joseph) had, in his travels in New South Wales, discovered an extraordinary animal called the kangaroo. The appearance, conformation, and habits of this quadruped were of the most singular kind; and in order to render his description more vivid and graphic, Johnson rose from his chair and volunteered an imitation of the animal. The company stared; and Mr Grant said nothing could be more ludicrous than the appearance of a tall, heavy, grave-looking man, like Dr Johnson, standing up to mimic the shape and motions of a kangaroo. He stood erect, put out his hands like feelers, and, gathering up the tails of his huge brown coat so as to resemble the pouch of the animal, made two or three vigorous bounds across the room! Mr Grant lived to the great age of eighty-five, and died at Calder Manse, June 28th, 1828. He had been minister of Calder, or Cawdor, for forty-eight years, and was highly esteemed as a divine, and as a fine specimen of an intelligent gentleman of the old school." The reason Boswell says nothing of this may be that he was upstairs writing the letter which appears at pp. 412–13.

237 In fact the *OED* has 'equitation' from 1562 onwards.

238 For Pembroke see p. 21. There is nothing about him here in Boswell's journal, and I take this paragraph from the *Tour*. Except for this and seven other phrases or sentences which provide additional information, the account of **30 August** is from the journal.

239 This 'temple' lies thirty-five yards east of the B862 Inverness–Dores road, directly opposite the Ballindarroch junction. It was described in 1831 as consisting of three concentric circles (Anderson, 'On Some of the Stone Circles', p. 213).

240 Lord Alemoor was a highly respected judge (Ramsay, *Scotland and Scotsmen*, vol. 1, p. 326): "If ever a Scotsman seemed born with talents to be Lord Chancellor of England, it was Lord Alemoor." Boswell appears to be referring to the incongruity that a man who exercised intellectual dominance over his fellow men should be unable to control a horse. See note 624.

241 Her fears were real. Here in *Taigh an Dìridh Mhóir* when still a change-house, twenty-seven years earlier, an officer of Cumberland's army had murdered the innkeeper and raped her granddaughter. Our travellers' hostess, who had taken over the house in 1747, was related to them; she was about the same age as the granddaughter and must have known her well (MacilleDhuibh, 'The House of the Steep Climb').

242 A play by George Farquhar, first produced in 1707. In act 4, scene 1, Archer says to Mrs Sullen: "I can't at this Distance, Madam, distinguish the Figures of the Embroidery." In Goldsmith's *She Stoops to Conquer*, act 3, Marlow spins the same yarn on Miss Hardcastle. "Odso! then you must shew me your embroidery. I embroider and draw patterns myself a little. If you want a judge of your work you must apply to me. (Seizing her hand.)"

243 The 'General's Hut' stood on the site of the present Foyers Hotel, near the parish church of Dores.

244 In the *Tour* this sentence reads: "Captains Urie and Darippe, of the 15th regiment of foot, breakfasted with us." The three officers were Capt. Lewis Ourry, Capt. Isaac Augustus D'Aripé and Lt. Henry Letch. Ourry had served with particular distinction, and their conversation was recalled by Johnson and Boswell on 7 April 1778 (*Life*): JOHNSON. "You may remember an officer at Fort Augustus, who had served in America, told us of a woman whom they were obliged to *bind*, in order to get her back from savage life." BOSWELL. "She must have been an animal, a beast." JOHNSON. "Sir, she was a speaking cat."

245 The road, then newly made, passed westwards over the hill from the southern end of Loch Ness by a series of hairpin bends. It was abandoned *c.* 1806. On Lachlan MacQueen see note 197; in the *Tour* 'one Macqueen' becomes 'a McQueen' and is footnoted: "*A* McQueen is a Highland mode of expression. An Englishman would say *one* McQueen. But where there are *clans* or *tribes* of men, distinguished by *patronymic* surnames, the individuals of each are considered as if they were of different species, at least as much as nations are distinguished; so that a *McQueen*, a *McDonald*, a *McLean*, is said, as we say a Frenchman, an Italian, a Spaniard."

246 For Prideaux' *Connexion* see note 197. *Cyrus's Travels* is the extremely popular

English translation of *Artamène, ou le Grand Cyrus* (ten volumes, 1649–53) by Madeleine de Scudery (1607–1701), a lively romance whose characters are portraits of notable persons of the author's day.

247 Lachlan MacQueen did not emigrate. He remained at Anoch for another fifteen years, then moved to another farm in the glen, and lived to be over ninety (Carruthers, *Tour*, p. 102).

248 On the remark about a sailor's life see p. 265. In the *Tour* (all editions) Boswell omits 'of arithmetic' and provides this footnote: "This book has given rise to much inquiry, which has ended in ludicrous surprise. Several ladies, wishing to learn the kind of reading which the great and good Dr Johnson esteemed most fit for a young woman, desired to know what book he had selected for this Highland nymph. 'They never adverted,' said he, 'that I had no *choice* in the matter. I have said that I presented her with a book which I *happened* to have about me.' And what was this book? My readers, prepare your features for merriment. It was *Cocker's Arithmetic*! Wherever this was mentioned, there was a loud laugh, at which Dr Johnson, when present, used sometimes to be a little angry. One day, when we were dining at General Oglethorpe's, where we had many a valuable day, I ventured to interrogate him, 'But, sir, is it not somewhat singular that you should *happen* to have *Cocker's Arithmetic* about you on your journey? What made you buy such a book at Inverness?' He gave me a very sufficient answer. 'Why, sir, if you are to have but one book with you upon a journey, let it be a book of science. When you have read through a book of entertainment, you know it, and it can do no more for you; but a book of science is inexhaustible.'"

249 I here augment the journal (in which the introduction is briefer, and only the last line of verse is quoted) from the *Tour*. This and the words 'called Anoch' (p. 109) are the only departures from the text of the journal in the account of **31 August**. In the *Tour* Boswell ascribes the verse to Swift, but it is from Pope's 'Mary Gulliver to Captain Lemuel Gulliver'.

250 I have suggested that the reason for their unease was that MacQueen had told them how in 1746, after Culloden, an English dragoon had gone to sleep one night in the stable – all that was ever found of him again was his boots (MacilleDhuibh, 'The Cow that Ate the Piper').

251 *Henry IV*, part 2, act 3, scene 1. In the *Tour* this sentence was emended to: "It reminded me of Henry the Fourth's fine soliloquy on sleep; for there was here as 'uneasy a pallet' as the poet's imagination could possibly conceive." This is the first of nine substantive improvements made to the account of **1 September** in the *Tour*, the rest of which are adopted into the text. They range from phrases altered to sentences added.

252 Much ink has been spilt over this sentence, metaphorically speaking. Suffice it to say that I believe it to be correctly punctuated and that 'an unfortunate' is a coded reference to Prince Charles. When in Glenmoriston from 23 July to 14 August 1746 he was in the depths of misery, which no doubt helps explain Boswell's tears.

253 The peak of *Faochag* ('Whelk') catches the eye as one enters Glen Shiel from the east. It is so called because it spirals up to a distinctive cone. Boswell

wrote '1715' in the journal and corrected it to '1719' in the *Tour*: the battle of Glenshiel (between Spanish and government troops, the earl of Seaforth aiding the Spanish) was fought on 10 June 1719.

254 In the *Tour* this becomes: "We came to a rich green valley, comparatively speaking, and stopped a while to let our horses rest and eat grass. We soon afterwards came to Auchnasheal . . ." At the word 'valley' Boswell then adds a footnote: "Dr Johnson, in his *Journey*, thus beautifully describes his situation here: 'I sat down on a bank, such as a writer of romance might have delighted to feign. I had, indeed, no trees to whisper over my head; but a clear rivulet streamed at my feet. The day was calm, the air soft, and all was rudeness, silence, and solitude. Before me, and on either side, were high hills, which, by hindering the eye from ranging, forced the mind to find entertainment for itself. Whether I spent the hour well, I know not; for here I first conceived the thought of this narration.' The *Critical Reviewers*, with a spirit and expression worthy of the subject, say, 'We congratulate the public on the event with which this quotation concludes, and are fully persuaded that the hour in which the entertaining traveller conceived this narrative will be considered, by every reader of taste, as a fortunate event in the annals of literature. Were it suitable to the talk in which we are at present engaged, to indulge ourselves in a poetical flight, we would invoke the winds of the Caledonian mountains to blow for ever, with their softest breezes, on the bank where our author reclined, and request of Flora, that it might be perpetually adorned with the gayest and most fragrant productions of the year.'" Evidently the 'rich green valley' of Boswell's journal was lower Glen Shiel, but after reading Johnson's *Journey* he doctored the sentence to make it refer instead to Johnson's 'narrow valley not very flowery, but sufficiently verdant' (p. 88), a good ten miles back along their route. It must have caused Boswell much agony that a location of such literary significance had escaped mention in his journal because Johnson had said nothing to him of what passed through his mind there. Boswell did not know of Johnson's decision to write the book until 21 October (see p. 403).

255 Milkshakes like this were called *omhan* or *umhan*, spelt by Martin 'oon'. They were made from boiled milk or whey, frothed up with a whisk called a *loinid* (Grant, *Highland Folk Ways*, pp. 196, 213, 298). Boswell's description of the *loinid* as 'a stick as is used for chocolate' echoes Martin's (*Description*, p. 126).

256 Hogg, *Jacobite Relics*, vol. 1, p. 152: "The laird of McIntosh is coming, / McCrabie and McDonald's coming, / McKenzie and McPherson's coming, / And the wild McCraw's coming. / Little wat ye wha's coming, / Donald Gun and a's coming." Boswell's note (*Tour*): "The McCraas, or Macraes, were since that time brought into the king's army, by the late Lord Seaforth. When they lay in Edinburgh Castle in 1778, and were ordered to embark for Jersey, they with a number of other men in the regiment, for different reasons, but especially an apprehension that they were to be sold to the East India Company, though enlisted not to be sent out of Great Britain without their own consent, made a determined mutiny, and encamped upon the lofty

mountain, Arthur's Seat, where they remained three days and three nights; bidding defiance to all the force in Scotland. At last they came down, and embarked peaceably, having obtained formal articles of capitulation, signed by Sir Adolphus Oughton, commander-in-chief, General Skene, deputy commander, the Duke of Buccleuch, and the Earl of Dunmore, which quieted them. Since the secession of the Commons of Rome to the *Mons Sacer*, a more spirited exertion has not been made. I gave great attention to it from first to last, and have drawn up a particular account of it. Those brave fellows have since served their country effectually at Jersey, and also in the East Indies, to which, after being better informed, they voluntarily agreed to go." Boswell's report of the mutiny was in the *Public Advertiser*, 29 September and 1 October 1778 (Reed and Pottle, *Boswell, Laird of Auchinleck*, pp. 22–23); there is a modern account in Prebble, *Mutiny*, pp. 91–141.

257 It was an Alexander MacLeod (son of Donald MacLeod of Balmeanach), then a lieutenant in the militia, who came close to arresting Prince Charles at Mugstot on 29 June 1746. By serving in the Dutch Army, Capt. John MacLeod was following a tradition which had been popular among the MacLeods and other kindreds since 1702, and which survived into the nineteenth century (see pp. 176, 270; note 812).

258 This 'King's house' was described in 1791–92 as 'a stage-house on the road from Fort Augustus to Bernera, called Sheil Inn' (Macrae, 'Parish of Glensheil', p. 411). It appears to have been on the site of the present Glenshiel Lodge.

259 *King Lear*, act 3, scene 4. Boswell's note (*Tour*): "It is amusing to observe the different images which this being presented to Dr Johnson and me. The Doctor, in his *Journey*, compares him to a Cyclops." See p. 95.

260 *Annual Register*, 1759, quoted by Pottle and Bennett, *Journal*, p. 112: "By the list of disabled officers . . . the army is much weakened. By the nature of the river, the most formidable part of this armament is deprived of the power of acting, yet we have almost the whole force of Canada to oppose. In this situation, there is such a choice of difficulties, that I own myself at a loss how to determine."

261 In the *Tour* the words 'and reminded him of his own remark at Aberdeen, upon old friendships being hastily broken off' are added (see p. 61). In fact, Boswell's whole account of 2 September was radically altered for publication, not so much because of his spat with Johnson as because it also contained a good deal of material which was potentially offensive to Sir Alexander Macdonald (see Chapter 3). For this day, therefore, while retaining the text of the journal, I add to it a paragraph from the *Tour* (see note 282) and draw attention to further variations (such as the above) in endnotes.

262 See p. 61. The point is clarified in the *Tour*: "That forming intimacies, would indeed be 'limning the water', were they liable to such sudden dissolution."

263 Sir Alexander was 9th baronet and chief of the MacDonalds of Sleat, having succeeded his brother Sir James in 1766; in 1776 he was made Baron Macdonald in the Irish peerage. His wife was Elizabeth Diana Bosville of Gunthwaite in Yorkshire. The couple were lodging at Armadale in a tenant's farmhouse, their Skye residence being at Mugstot in the north (see

p. 125). In a letter to Boswell of 26 November 1785, written in anger after reading the *Tour*, Macdonald described the circumstances (Scott and Pottle, *Private Papers*, vol. 16, p. 233): "Having withheld from me the notice of your intention to visit the Hebrides at a Season of the year when no man in his senses would have advised or undertaken such a Tour, you made an unexpected irruption at a corner of the Island where I have never resided, Sixty miles from my dwelling place, which I had quitted for the Season."

264   For John Campbell's *Britannia Elucidata* see p. 370. John Janes or Jeans was a dealer in mineral specimens and fossils: he scoured Scotland for them, polished them and brought them annually for sale to London. His son, 'a coarse and contemptible character', for whom see p. 126, succeeded him in the business, but was drowned on a dark night in 1809 by falling into the basin near London's New Pier (Anderson, 'Mr. Janes of Aberdeenshire', p. 156).

265   The piper will have been a MacArthur and the 'elderly Gentleman' will have been Roderick MacDonald, tacksman of Sandaig in Glenelg, see p. 126. Johnson misremembers the detail. The tune is 'Cille Chrìost' or 'Glengarry's March'. The church was that of Kilchrist at Tarradale in the Black Isle. The perpetrators were MacDonalds of Glengarry, the victims MacKenzies. The atrocity took place in 1603. There is a Culloden connection, however – Forbeses of Culloden had land in that area, at Ferintosh.

266   On 11 January 1728 the Irish House of Commons voted £200 to 'William *Maple* as an encouragement for discovering a new method of tanning Leather by a Vegetable of the Growth of this Kingdom' (Fleeman, *Journey*, p. 178). Seemingly Maple's achievement was to bring to the attention of the English-speaking world what had been known for centuries by Gaelic speakers about the use of tormentil (Scottish Gaelic *cairte-ciù, cairt-leamhna, leamhnach*) in tanning. This is mentioned by Isabel Grant (*Highland Folk Ways*, pp. 207, 243), but the best description of the process that I know is in Gaelic (MacRury, 'O Chionn Leith Cheud Bliadhna II', p. 390).

267   The Disarming Act (*An Act for the more effectual Disarming the Highlands in Scotland . . . and for restraining the Use of the Highland Dress*) was passed in 1746, then repeated and enlarged in a second Act of 1748. Both were promoted by Philip Yorke, 1st earl of Hardwicke, as Lord Chancellor; the legislation was repealed in 1782. Johnson appears to be saying that most of the men whom he and Boswell saw in the Highlands were wearing some kind of greatcoat and a blue bonnet; that some had stockings and shoes, others no footwear at all; and that whether they wore breeches or a 'fillibeg' (*féile beag* 'little kilt') under the coat did not make a great deal of difference to their appearance, since neither garment came below the knee. The gentleman whom they saw 'completely clothed in the ancient habit' was Malcolm MacLeod of Brae, see p. 140.

268   The journey was of fifteen miles. Coirechatachan lies west of Broadford at the foot of Beinn na Cailliche, for which see p. 135. Its name is *Coire a' Chatachain* 'the Corry of the Little Mackintosh', presumably reflecting the Mackintoshes' influence on the MacKinnons in the sixteenth century (MacilleDhuibh, 'The Cats of Skye'). The remains of the building are now

part of a sheep-fank; as 'Corry', the name has been transferred to a newer house further east.

269 Breacachadh in Coll, where a little collection of books was assembled from scratch for the travellers, see p. 324.

270 See note 382.

271 Apicius Caelius, a Roman epicure and glutton. In his treatise *In re Coquinaria* he refers to the toughness characteristic of newly killed meat.

272 See pp. 153–54.

273 Gaelic *sgailc* 'a thump', 'a box on the ears'. The semantics of 'punch' are comparable.

274 See pp. 411–12. Johnson is right about the derivation of the word (e.g. *uisge Arainn* 'Arran water' was whisky). Its application was only partly 'by way of eminence', however, and partly euphemistic.

275 See p. 154.

276 They had been in use since *c.* 1740.

277 This was earthenware as made by Josiah Wedgwood (1730–95) for Queen Charlotte (1744–1818), thoroughly up to date at this period. For the horn spoons mentioned in the following sentence see p. 294.

278 It was Johnson himself who popularised the spelling 'dirk' as opposed to 'durk'. The word was Gaelic *duirc* 'a tough little stump' (of a person or knife). When used in English slang of a person it becomes 'dork'. Johnson does not mention forks, which remained strangers to ordinary island tables for another century, as is shown by this anecdote, datable to 1862 when the lighthouse at the Butt of Lewis was built (Caimbeul, *Suathadh*, p. 98, translated): "When they had finished putting up the lighthouse and its associated buildings, four old men from Eoropie got the job of tidying up the site. On their first day they were brought in for a meal, soup and meat on a nice table with a tablecloth on it and, horror of horrors, knife, fork and spoon. Only one of them, Domhnall Gorm, had ever been away from home and seen food being eaten in this strange way. He warned the others not to make fools of themselves, but to keep an eye on him and do as he did. He started tucking in with the alien instruments, but after watching him for a while one of them declared, 'Let him get on with it, men, you'll soon see his blood blinding him.'" See note 849.

279 Johnson is referring to a body of opinion in 1766 within the Society in Scotland for the Propagation of Christian Knowledge, which ran most of the schools in the Highlands. In that year the Rev. James Stewart of Killin (1700–89) was translating the New Testament into vernacular Scottish Gaelic for publication by the Society. William Drummond (for whom see pp. 442, 448, 452) appears to have informed Johnson that there was some opposition to the project, and to him, on 13 August 1766, Johnson wrote one of his finest letters. Clearly Drummond showed it around in Edinburgh, for controversy ceased, and the work was duly published the following year. Boswell obtained the original from Drummond, and printed it in the *Life*.

280 In the *Tour* this sentence is omitted, and Lady Macdonald is described as 'formerly Miss Bosville of Yorkshire'.

281 Armadale Castle was burnt by Capt. Pottinger, RN, in 1690, during the chiefship of Sir Donald Macdonald (d. 1695), 3rd baronet of Sleat.

282 This paragraph does not appear in Boswell's journal, and is taken from the *Tour*. Conversely, all the offensive and gratuitous remarks in the preceding and following paragraphs were excised. It may thus be seen that this paragraph represents a carefully considered statement of Boswell's view of Sir Alexander. Nevertheless, after reading the *Tour*, on 26 November 1785 Lord Macdonald (as he had then become) sent Boswell an abusive but unsigned letter (Scott and Pottle, *Private Papers*, vol. 16, pp. 233–40). On 28 November Boswell wrote to his friend William Bosville, Lady Macdonald's brother, asking him to inform Macdonald that he had gone to a great deal of trouble to remove several remarks in case they caused offence, and that he then supposed that nothing hurtful remained. However, finding on revision that three more such passages had escaped him, he had expunged them from the second edition as it was going through the press. Sixteen sheets (256 pages) of the second edition were already printed off, he added, and might be seen at the printer's. In light of this explanation and apology, Boswell requested assurance from Lord Macdonald that no use of any kind would be made of the derogatory remarks in his letter. Receiving no satisfactory reply, he appointed John Courtenay his second and entrusted him with a written challenge which he was to present to Macdonald if no compromise could be found. Macdonald finally agreed to cancel or soften the harsher passages in his letter and to make no further use of them (Pottle and Bennett, *Journal*, pp. 114–15; Lustig and Pottle, *Boswell: The English Experiment*, pp. 8–16).

283 For Jeans and his son see note 264. There are Sandaigs in Glenelg and Knoydart; Rorie's was in Glenelg (see p. 129). Ronald Macdonald of Clanranald gave a lease of Keill and other lands of Canna to a certain Donald MacLeod for three nineteen-year terms, dating from Whitsuntide 1760, on 22 June 1761 (Campbell, *Canna*, pp. 115–16). Boswell deleted his compliment to MacLeod shortly after writing it; for the reason see p. 256.

284 'Captain Macdonald' is the former Lieutenant of Grenadiers referred to at p. 126. He is presumably the Donald Macdonald listed as one of the twenty-six original lieutenants of Montgomerie's Regiment (Stewart, *Sketches*, vol. 2, p. 15). It was raised in 1757, fought exclusively in America, and disbanded in 1775. It is to be distinguished from the Black Watch – the 42nd or 'old Highland regiment' mentioned at pp. 194–95, which was first raised in 1740, fought in America from 1756 to 1767, and remained in being until 2006. See notes 287 and 812.

285 Perhaps it was this comparison which emboldened Boswell (the elder of the two by five years) to speak his mind later that evening. Mrs MacDonald probably meant that both were young men of middle rank and modest fortunes who had inherited, or stood to inherit, country estates. There is also an insinuation they would both have been the better of a little less education and a little more maturity: in a word, they were schoolboys.

286 On the debts contracted by Macleod's predecessor (his grandfather) see p. 165. Mrs MacDonald and her husband Rorie were themselves victims of these difficulties, being about to lose their farm in Glenelg, see p. 129.

287 This paragraph was drastically altered in the *Tour*: "After dinner, when I alone was left at table with the few Highland gentlemen who were of the company, having talked with very high respect of Sir James Macdonald, they were all so much affected as to shed tears. One of them was Mr Donald Macdonald, who had been lieutenant of grenadiers in the Highland regiment, raised by Colonel Montgomery, now Earl of Eglintoune, in the war before last; one of those regiments which the late Lord Chatham prided himself in having brought from 'the mountains of the north': by doing which he contributed to extinguish in the Highlands the remains of disaffection to the present Royal Family. From this gentleman's conversation, I first learnt how very popular his Colonel was among the Highlanders; of which I had such continued proofs, during the whole course of my tour, that on my return I could not help telling the noble Earl himself, that I did not before know how great a man he was." See note 284; criticism of Sir Alexander is thus effected by praising the distinction and popularity of his late brother Sir James (for whom see pp. 130–32) and of his cousin the earl of Eglinton (brother of Boswell's beloved friend the previous earl, for whom see pp. 434–35).

288 The ode itself does not appear in Boswell's journal, but was printed in an appendix to the second and third editions of the *Tour* under the heading: "VERSES written by Sir Alexander (now Lord) Macdonald; addressed and presented to Dr Johnson, at Armadale in the Isle of Skye." I am grateful to Mr Norman MacLeod for the following translation: "O traveller who comes across our water to see the land of Skye, lo and behold, our people, tribe by tribe, are crowding the shores on all sides to welcome you. The MacDonalds, as many as the sea confines to these islands on our northern boundaries – for a long time now the sea has sustained these native people who are dependent on it, and it will continue to support them. Stop stirring up the seas, O Bearer of Storms, and I beg of you, do not harass our boats as part of your work, lest wives should have to lament the loss of their husbands and children grieve for their fathers. And you, in turn, do not be sorry that you have mourned a man – we know that in your heart reluctant grief boils up when they strike a body unexpectedly. Why not? More suffering is always displayed by those defending one who has been killed in a disaster than one who dies, while an open mind unlocks the deep recesses of grief. Farewell to mourning; hence keep tearful sights at a distance: we shall go, we shall go to the magnificent theatre where the works of Fingal are celebrated. Distinguished guest! Soon you will walk where one's mind, led on through the paths of ruins, will rejoice in exploring the rest, where the trumpeter sounded victories. Are you listening? The leader, rising again, breathes with his customary breathing, the powerful poet awakens the spirits of the dead, and renewed horror breaks out again with its usual force. Brandishing bronze weapons in his great hand thus would go the stern father of Ossian; may his ashes be at peace, and let loyal Macpherson stand guard over them." Sir Alexander refers to these verses in his letter of complaint to Boswell about the *Tour*, 26 November 1785 (Scott and Pottle, *Private Papers*, vol. 16, pp. 234–35): "As they evinced my belief in the Originality of Fingal's poems,

and contained a Compliment due to Mr. Macpherson, they have not been deemed worthy of any notice in your Memorabilia." In *To the Hebrides* they are promoted to the body of Boswell's text for the first time.

289 Sir James Foulis of Colinton (1714–91) was a private scholar whose particular interest was in what we would now call Celtic Studies. In 1780 he became a founding member of the Society of Antiquaries of Scotland. Their first *Transactions*, published the year after his death under the additional title *Archaeologia Scotica*, contained six of his papers, including 'An Inquiry into the Origin of the Name of the Scottish Nation'. See p. 261.

290 In the *Tour* this paragraph was altered: "Dr Johnson this day endeavoured to obtain some knowledge of the state of the country; but complained that he could get no distinct information about any thing, from those with whom he conversed." With the exception of Sir Alexander's ode, Boswell's account of **3 September** is taken from the journal.

291 The account of **4 September** is taken from the journal. In the *Tour*, the first two paragraphs were altered and the third omitted. The first begins: "My endeavours to rouse the English-bred chieftain, in whose house we were, to the feudal and patriarchal feelings, proving ineffectual, Dr Johnson this morning tried to bring him to our way of thinking. JOHNSON. 'Were I in your place, sir, in seven years I would make this an independent island . . .'" Sir Walter Scott commented (Croker, *Life*, 4 September 1773): "Dr Johnson seems to have forgotten that a Highlander going armed at this period incurred the penalty of serving as a common soldier for the first, and of transportation beyond sea for a second offence. And as for 'calling out his clan', twelve Highlanders and a bagpipe made a rebellion."

292 This paragraph was rewritten for publication: "We attempted in vain to communicate to him a portion of our enthusiasm. He bore with so polite a good-nature our warm, and what some might call Gothic, expostulations, on this subject, that I should not forgive myself, were I to record all that Dr Johnson's ardour led him to say. This day was little better than a blank." Boswell calls Lady Macdonald 'my beauty of a cousin' because he had convinced himself that Boswells and Bosvilles were branches of the same tree. He knew and liked her father, and addressed him once (when begging for a loan of £200) as 'my Chief' (Hill and Powell, *Life*, vol. 3, p. 540).

293 'Rorie' is Roderick MacDonald, tacksman of Sandaig (p. 126). His sons are James (Sir Alexander's factor for Sleat) and Donald (introduced at p. 126 as 'Lieutenant of Grenadiers').

294 In the *Tour* Boswell tells us instead that Sir James's monument 'was elegantly executed at Rome, and has the following inscription, written by his friend, George Lord Lyttelton'; they were in the church at Kilmore (*a' Chill Mhór*), which was presumably the 'house of prayer' singled out by Johnson at p. 147 as 'not in ruins'. It was built in 1687–96 and replaced in 1876, when the monument (a large wall-tablet) was moved into the new church beside it (Forbes, *Place-Names of Skye*, pp. 379–81; RCAHMCS, *Ninth Report*, pp. 185–86; Pottle, *Journal*, p. 467). In the account of **5 September**, this introductory paragraph is from Boswell's journal; the epitaph, the comments

on Sir James and the two letters that follow are from the *Tour* (part text, part footnote).

295 The first part of this paragraph is from the journal; in the *Tour* 'in this mean mansion' becomes 'at Armadale'. The second part (from 'BOSWELL') is not in the journal, and is taken from the *Tour*. Johnson is quoting *English Malady* by George Cheyne, MD.

296 In the *Tour* the second sentence is extended to embrace a quote from *Hamlet*, act I, scene 2: "The vigour of his mind was, however, sufficiently manifested, by his discovering no symptoms of feeble relaxation in the dull, 'weary, flat and unprofitable' state in which we now were placed."

297 On 9 September, see p. 155.

298 The ode and its introductory paragraph do not appear in the journal, and are taken from the *Tour*; conversely, the paragraph that follows appears in the journal only. Boswell footnotes the ode: "VARIOUS READINGS. Line 2. In the manuscript, Dr Johnson, instead of *rupibus obsita*, had written *imbribus uvida*, and *uvida nubibus*, but struck them both out. Lines 15 & 16. Instead of these two lines, he had written, but afterwards struck out, the following: *Parare posse, utcunque jactet / Grandiloquus nimis alta Zeno.*" Mr Norman MacLeod has kindly provided this translation: "Enclosed by the deep recesses of the sea, resounding with storms and shut in by rocks, how pleasing it is, O mist-covered Skye, to a weary traveller when you reveal a verdant bay. Care, I believe, is in exile from this locality; certainly charming peace dwells in these places: neither anger nor sorrow dares attack one's relaxation during this time. But it is of no advantage to a sick mind to hide oneself in a hollowed-out rock, nor to wander over the deserted mountains, nor from a cliff top to count the foaming waves. Human courage is not enough. It is not possible for anyone to prepare a relaxed frame of mind for himself, as the lofty, deceitful school of the Stoics snap their fingers too often. Almighty Father, you alone as judge control the force of a foaming breast and mind; when you feel expansive the waves surge forth, and when you are in a restraining mood, the waves recede."

299 Johnson later remarked that Browne, 'one of the first wits of this country, got into Parliament, and never opened his mouth' (*Life*, 5 April 1775). In the *Tour* the last sentence is removed and the following is put in its place: "I listened to this with the eagerness of one, who, conscious of being himself fond of wine, is glad to hear that a man of so much genius and good thinking as Browne had the same propensity."

300 The parenthesis is from the *Tour*. Except where indicated in endnotes, Boswell's account of **6 September** is taken from his journal.

301 Lachlan MacKinnon – Boswell left a blank in the journal for his first name, and failed to fill it in. He adds this footnote in the *Tour*: "That my readers may have my narrative in the style of the country through which I am travelling, it is proper to inform them, that the chief of a clan is denominated by his *surname* alone, as MacLeod, Mackinnon, Macintosh. To prefix *Mr* to it would be a degradation from *the* MacLeod, &c. My old friend, the Laird of Macfarlane, the great antiquary, took it highly amiss, when General Wade

called him Mr Macfarlane. Dr Johnson said, he could not bring himself to use this mode of address; it seemed to him to be too familiar, as it is the way in which, in all other places, intimates or inferiors are addressed. When the chiefs have *titles*, they are denominated by them, as *Sir James Grant, Sir Allan Maclean*. The other Highland gentlemen, of landed property, are denominated by their *estates*, as *Raasay, Boisdale*; and the wives of all of them have the title of *ladies*. The *tacksmen*, or principal tenants, are named by their farms, as *Kingsburgh, Coirechatachan*; and their wives are called the *mistress* of Kingsburgh, the *mistress* of Coirechatachan. Having given this explanation, I am at liberty to use that mode of speech which generally prevails in the Highlands and the Hebrides."

302 By *trea* Boswell means 'tray'. He will be indicating the disyllabic Gaelic pronunciation *treatha* as in *teatha* 'tea'.

303 In the *Tour* the paragraph to this point is reduced to a bland summary: "We here enjoyed the comfort of a table plentifully furnished, the satisfaction of which was heightened by a numerous and cheerful company." The section that follows, from 'and we for the first time' to 'any of the company', is not in the journal, but clearly deserves a place in our text. For Dr MacDonald, the physician, see p. 276.

304 In the *Tour* the last sentence is omitted and the following is put in its place: "On its being mentioned, that a present had here been made to him of a curious specimen of Highland antiquity, Dr Johnson said, 'Sir, it was more than he deserved: the dog is a Whig.'" As Johnson did not know Pennant but had read his books, this is to be understood as a literary rather than a political judgement, implying that Pennant was a machine and lacked a soul. His reply, in *Of London* (1790), p. 200, is a masterpiece. "I should have been a Whig at the Revolution. There have been periods since, in which I should have been, what I now am, a moderate Tory; a supporter, as far as my little influence extends, of a well-poised balance between the crown and people: but, should the scale preponderate against the *Salus populi*, that moment may it be said, *The dog's a Whig!*"

305 Johnson showed Boswell this ode, along with the previous one, on 9 September (see p. 155). Boswell subsequently obtained it from Mrs Thrale, and published it in the *Tour* at 6 September. I am grateful to Mr Norman MacLeod for the following translation: "I pass through a land where the bare rock mingles with the stony ruins in the mists and where the harsh landscape smiles at the fruitless toils of the husbandman. I wander amongst clans where the life of a wild people, embellished by no form of culture, is filthy and shapeless, and lies hidden in a foul state under the smoke of their peasant dwellings. Amongst the joltings of a tedious wandering, amongst the din of a strange language and with so many different customs, I ask you, dear Mrs Thrale, what is happening – whether a dutiful wife is soothing the cares of her husband, whether a dutiful mother is comforting her child, or whether she may diligently feed her mind with new knowledge by means of books: let this be our memory, and the reward of loyalty, let this loyalty be unshakeable, and may the shores of Skye learn to resound (and deservedly so) the pleasant name of Mrs Thrale. Written in Skye, 6 Sept. 1773."

306 Boswell's account of 7 **September** is taken entirely from his journal. In the *Tour*, 'several more books' becomes 'Craufurd's *Officers of State*, and several more'. After this, Malone's editing of the journal cuts ever deeper into non-controversial matters, so that Johnson's impersonation of Lady Macdonald is by no means the only material to be omitted. For Boethius see pp. 10–11. *Ecclesiastici, or, The History of the Lives, Acts, Deaths, and Writings of the Most Eminent Fathers of the Church* by Dr William Cave (1637–1713) went through various editions from 1683 onwards. For Baker's *Chronicle* see p. 279. The *Ecclesiastical History of Great Britain* by the Rev. Jeremy Collier appeared in 1708–14, and *The Lives and Characters, of the Officers of the Crown, and of the State in Scotland, from the Beginning of the Reign of King David I. to the Union of the Two Kingdoms* by George Crawfurd in 1726. With regard to Mrs Brooks (Brooke), Boswell added 'the actress' and 'my fair friend', then struck out the latter at proof stage. She had married James Brooke (?1728–1807) of Rathbone Place, London, an engraver and literary jack-of-all-trades. Unable to put up with his temper, she left him and her children and began a career on the stage at Edinburgh in 1761–62 when aged between thirty and thirty-five. Boswell appears to have had an affair with her from May 1761 to March 1762. According to the writer John Taylor she was a very beautiful woman; she died in 1782 (Pottle, *The Earlier Years*, p. 78; Pottle, *Journal*, pp. 420–21). See also p. 277.

307 For 'Clanranald' read 'Belfinlay'. Belfinlay, aged eighteen and a relative of the Coirechatachan family, was shot through both legs and clubbed on the head at Culloden, but survived until 1749. The picture is described and the inscription cited in Paton, *Lyon in Mourning*, vol. 2, pp. 326–27. Many other references to him can be found through the index in that work.

308 Martin MacPherson, 'the minister of Sleat', for whom see pp. 130, 138, note 398, etc., was the son of John MacPherson, author of *Dissertations on the Ancient Caledonians*, who was himself minister of Sleat from 1742 to 1765. One reads *Dissertations* with a sense of absolute despair that men like MacPherson and MacQueen, who could have told us so much about the cultural history of the Gael in their own time – ideally on the lines of Johnson's *Lives of the Poets* – preferred, as Boswell puts it so well, 'unsatisfactory conjectures as to antiquity before the days of record'. See notes 441, 502.

309 Boswell's final 'k' is indistinguishable from his 'h' (see also note 740). The printer read *taisck* (Gaelic *tamhasg*), but Boswell may have originally meant *taisch* (Gaelic *taibhs*). A *taibhs* may be any ghost, a *tamhasg* is more specifically a *doppelgänger*, the double of a living person (Black, *Gaelic Otherworld*, p. 241). This may be the first recorded instance of an English-speaking *taibhs* or *tamhasg*; Johnson and Boswell were told of another on 22 September (pp. 176, 259), and a much later one is noted in *Gaelic Otherworld*, p. 263.

310 James Moray, who in 1735 became the 13th laird of Abercairney in Perthshire, married Lady Christian Montgomerie (d. 1748), daughter of the 9th earl of Eglinton and sister of Lady Margaret Macdonald of Sleat. They had a large family. For Charles at Kingsburgh see p. 217; the 'sunshine of the breast' is

from Gray's 'Ode on a Distant Prospect of Eton College': "Gay hope is theirs by fancy fed, / Less pleasing when possest; / The tear forgot as soon as shed, / The sunshine of the breast."

311 Addison, *Cato*, act 5, scene 4, line 27. In the *Tour*, Boswell introduces this anecdote at the appropriate point in his description of the Prince's wanderings (*To the Hebrides*, pp. 216–25), as follows: "The mistress of Coirechatachan told me, that in the forenoon she went into her father's room, who was also in bed, and suggested to him her apprehensions that a party of the military might come up, and that his guest and he had better not remain here too long. Her father said, 'Let the poor man repose himself after his fatigues; and as for me, I care not, though they take off this old grey head ten or eleven years sooner than I should die in the course of nature.' He then wrapped himself in the bed-clothes, and again fell fast asleep."

312 To encourage fisheries, an Act of 1750 had placed a bounty of thirty shillings per ton on white herring.

313 In the *Tour* 'forenoon' is changed to 'afternoon' and Boswell footnotes 'Macgillicallum' as 'the Highland expression for Laird of Raasay'.

314 This is Malcolm MacLeod of Brae, who was with the Prince on his wanderings from 1 to 4 July 1746, see pp. 150–51 and note 267; 'camblet', 'bound' and 'a yellowish bushy wig' are brought in from the *Tour*, as is a passage at pp. 152–53 (see note 337). Otherwise Boswell's account of **8 September**, in both chapters 3 and 4, is from his journal.

315 See p. 158.

316 See pp. 154, 592–95.

317 The eating of eels was believed to cause madness; being biblical, the pork taboo probably dates from the Reformation (MacKenzie, *Scottish Folk-Lore*, pp. 41–55; Black, *Gaelic Otherworld*, pp. 120, 333). That pork and bacon were formerly eaten is attested by the prevalence of *muc* in place-names, e.g. the isle of Muck (pp. 173, 247).

318 See p. 164.

319 Johnson is thinking of Greek *proceleusma* 'incitement', and is clearly pleased to find the custom surviving in the Hebrides: note his remark about 'naval music', p. 151. There is a small collection of Gaelic rowing songs in Tolmie, *Songs of Occupation*, pp. 236–39.

320 This souterrain, *Uamha nan Ràmh*, is in a mound west of the road at Clachan. A natural fissure capped with massive stone slabs (see pp. 159, 257), it probably dates from the Iron Age. According to one tradition, Macleod of Raasay hid his silver in it when he came out for the Prince in 1745, but a servant was brutalised by Redcoats into revealing where it was (Nicolson, *Handbook*, p. 78); according to another, it was used for hiding oars the following year when Redcoats were searching the island for Prince Charles and destroying or confiscating boats. By 1990 it had become a rubbish-dump, but in spring that year it was cleared out and revealed to be 14 metres long and 1.5 metres high (MacLeod, *Raasay*, p. 9).

321 The botanist Joseph Banks, a friend of Johnson's, had circumnavigated the globe with Captain Cook in 1768–71. Elf-bolts or fairy arrows (*saighdean*

sìthe) are described in detail in Black, *Gaelic Otherworld*, pp. 14, 304–06; a modern archaeologist points out that, despite being 'very frequently picked up', none appear to exist now in the island (MacDonald, 'Raasay in Prehistory', p. 67). This is a puzzle.

322 See p. 159. The chapel, *Cill Mo Luaig*, is described in RCAHMCS, *Ninth Report*, p. 178, and in MacLeod, *Raasay*, pp. 232–35.

323 Martin Martin, *Description*, p. 106: "They preserve the memory of the deceased ladies of the place by erecting a little pyramid of stone for each of them, with the lady's name. These pyramids are by them called crosses; several of them are built of stone and lime, and have three steps of gradual ascent to them. There are eight such crosses about the village." See pp. 17–18, 160.

324 For a man who enjoyed a prodigious memory, Johnson's ignorance of the power of oral tradition is astonishing. This paragraph also demonstrates the lack of a vocabulary for folklore in the eighteenth century. Johnson's 'stated observances and practical representations' shows him feeling his way towards the concepts of calendar customs and material culture. The term 'folklore' was not invented until 1846; Johnson and Boswell had to make do with 'antiquities'.

325 In the *Odyssey*, Phæacia was a mythical land ruled by Alcinous, whose daughter Nausicaä welcomed Ulysses. In Raasay, the laird's eldest daughter Flora was a celebrated beauty. She married the future 5th earl of Loudoun in 1777 (see note 375).

326 See p. 317.

327 It is three miles broad. In the *Tour* Boswell simply called it 'a rugged island, about four miles in length'. Scalpay, Pabbay and the northern and eastern parts of Strath, including Coirechatachan, had been sold in 1751 by Iain Dubh, 17th of Mackinnon, to John Mackenzie of Delvine as trustee for Sir James Macdonald of Sleat (Sinclair, 'Clan Fingon', pp. 39–40).

328 Horace, *Odes*, book 2, poem 16. In the *Tour* Boswell cites a little more: *Otium Divos rogat in patenti / Prensus Ægæo . . .* "Storm-caught in the open Aegean, the mariner implores the gods for peace when dark clouds have hid the moon and the stars shine no longer sure for sailors . . ."

329 For the benefit of non-Scottish readers 'session' is glossed in the *Tour* as 'the parochial ecclesiastical court'. If MacQueen really said there was 'not now the least vestige' of belief in witchcraft in his parish, we may regard his claim as falling into a regular pattern of the exaggeration by parish clergy of their success in the struggle against superstition. In 1792 the minister of Tiree, the Rev. Archibald MacColl, declared his parishioners 'free of superstition'; a century later one of his Moderate successors, the Rev. John Gregorson Campbell, found enough material to fill two books on the subject (Black, *Gaelic Otherworld*, p. lxiii). Since MacQueen had actually discouraged his parishioners from bringing cases of witchcraft before his kirk session, he may have come to assume that belief in it no longer existed. For another example of the sensitivity of the clergy to this issue see p. 336; note also their refusal to believe in second sight (pp. 137, 248).

330 The bottle is mentioned again at p. 157. The Prince is also alleged to have given Malcolm a gun (Pottle, *Journal*, p. 421) and his silver spoon, knife and fork (Paton, *Lyon in Mourning*, vol. 2, p. 77). All that is known for sure about his pistols is that they were given to MacDonald of Milton (Flora's brother), who gave them to MacDonald of Armadale (*Lyon*, vol. 2, p. 32).

331 Boswell's note (*Tour*): "This old Scottish *member of Parliament*, I am informed, is still living (1785)."

332 This was John MacDonald (*c*. 1729–1809), 8th of Morar, for whom see p. 307. His father Allan (d. 1764), 7th of Morar, 'had the reputation of being an unmanly drunken creature all his life' (MacDonald, *Clan Donald*, vol. 3, p. 256).

333 See note 356. 'Ruins' is an odd word to use.

334 Boswell left a blank for the girls' names, and they are here supplied from Burke's *Landed Gentry*.

335 See note 273. In the *Tour*, for 'according to the Highland custom, filled round' Boswell substituted 'according to the custom of the Highlands, where a dram is generally taken every day'.

336 See p. 166. In the *Tour* at this point the words 'something between Proteus and Don Quixotte' are added. Had Boswell lived a little later he might have thrown in the Artful Dodger. 'The Adventures of MacCruslick' was the most popular 'trickster tale' in Gaelic, and in 1836 became the first traditional Gaelic story to be published as a monograph (Mackenzie, *Eachdraidh Mhic-Cruislig*). As a name for a comic character, 'MacCruslick' can be traced back to the seventh century AD (Black, *Gaelic Otherworld*, p. 446).

337 I do not know this song. John Macdonald, Aberdeen, suggested that 'Tullishole' might be for *tuilleadh sèoil* (better *tuilleadh siùil*) 'more sail' (Pottle and Bennett, *Journal*, pp. 134, 421–22). Depending on the position of the stress, it could equally represent *toll ìseal* ('lower hole'), a ship's hold. The passage from 'was so delighted' (p. 152, foot) to 'good humour and gaiety' is from the *Tour*, a leaf having been lost from Boswell's journal, and the words 'Many songs were sung' were supplied by Pottle and Bennett (*Journal*, p. 134). See note 314.

338 Both here and at p. 158 Boswell misunderstands Martin's reference to 'an artificial fort, three stories high' called 'Castle Vreokle': this is *Caisteal Bhròchail*, Brochel Castle. Martin describes Macleod of Raasay's seat 'in the village Clachan' as consisting of 'a little tower, and lesser houses, and an orchard with several sorts of berries, pot herbs, etc.' (*Description*, pp. 105–06). It was at Creagan Beaga in Oscaig (see note 348), and is on record as 'Castle Killmorocht' or 'the Castle of Kilmaluag' (RCAHMCS, *Ninth Report*, p. 185). A 'fire room' is a room with a fire-place (Pottle, *Journal*, p. 422); Raasay House is described and illustrated in Roberts, 'Raasay House', and MacLeod, *Raasay*, pp. 239–42. Today, much run down, it is in public ownership and serves mainly as an outdoor centre.

339 See note 403. The first half of this sentence was omitted from the *Tour*, as were some other passages in the account of 9 September; *gruitheam* (a compound of Gaelic *gruth* 'curd' and *ìm* 'butter') was suggested by Pottle

and Bennett (*Journal*, p. 134), Boswell having left a blank. Conversely, the words 'made of grain separated from the husks, and toasted by fire' are from the *Tour*, Boswell having merely written 'burnt with straw', which is unclear. Otherwise, the account of **9 September** is from the journal.

340 By 'feudal' Boswell means something like 'patrician'. Perhaps Malone disliked this pretentiousness, for in the *Tour* 'a very solid, easy, feudal chat' becomes 'some cordial conversation'. For Johnson's views on cheese at breakfast see p. 123.

341 In the *Tour*, Boswell deleted the words from 'and there is a question' to 'the Laird of MacLeod'. See pp. 143, 592–95.

342 Boswell probably means that he intends now to write up 12–15 September, leaving a gap for 9–11 September to be filled in later.

343 For Boswell's 'Danish fort' see notes 357, 362; his portrait of Charles Mackinnon (*c.* 1752–96) as a weedy intellectual appears to be borne out by the facts. Some of Mackinnon's correspondence with Adam Smith and the chemist Joseph Black, written from Kilmarie in Strathaird, has survived. Shortly after 1774 he sold Mishnish. His *Observations on the Wealth and Force of Nations* appeared in 1781, 1782 and 1784. In 1785 he published further essays on the authenticity of Ossian, musical accompaniment, fortifications and the existence of the body. He married Alexandra Macleod (for whom see note 508); they had three children, but separated in 1790. In 1789 he sold Strathaird, the last remaining part of his patrimony, a catastrophe which the poet William Ross, a native of the Mackinnon country, blamed on his 'tutor' (guardian) John Macleod of Raasay (Calder, *Gaelic Songs*, pp. 6–7). He died in poverty at Dalkeith (Sinclair, 'Clan Fingon', p. 40).

344 See pp. 133, 135, 252. On 30 August 1776 Boswell wrote to Mrs Thrale from Edinburgh (NLS MS 3278, f. 54r): "May I beg leave Madam to put you in mind of your promise to send me a copy of Dr. Johnson's Ode to you, which he read to me, in the Island of Rasay. I already engaged not to circulate it."

345 This brief paragraph is from the *Tour*, as are two other sentences and three short phrases; otherwise Boswell's account of **10 September** is from his journal.

346 The word 'east' is suggested by Pottle and Bennett (*Journal*, p. 137), as Boswell left a blank. The hill will have been Beinn a' Chapaill, the farm-house will have been at Screapadal. This was then a major centre of population, in which MacLeans had enjoyed a legal foothold ever since Farquhar Maclean of Dochgarroch was appointed bishop of the Isles in 1529 (MacLeod, *Raasay*, pp. 22–23, 41–42). It was cleared by George Rainy in 1852–54 (MacGill-Eain, *O Choille gu Bearradh*, pp. 306–07): *Dh' fhàg Rèanaidh Screapadal gun daoine, / Gun taighean, gun chrodh ach caoraich.* "Rainy left Screapadal without people, / With no houses or cattle, only sheep."

347 By 'keep-house' Boswell means 'store-room', but it is not clear whose usage he is reflecting. In Scots 'keep' is used to mean 'stores, provisions' and 'house' to mean 'room'. The same is true of *taigh* ('house') in Gaelic.

348 Gillies, *Life and Work of the Very Rev. Roderick Macleod*, p. 4: "Malcolm MacLeod of Raasay divorced his wife (decree recorded 5th December, 1735)

twenty-two years after he was married, a servant the name of Beaton being co-respondent . . . Malcolm . . . contracted an irregular marriage with a young clanswoman of his own, Janet MacLeod, in Oscaig." Boswell appears to be right about 'interested cunning' – tradition portrays young Janet as a flirtatious maidservant in Raasay House. Irregular or no, the marriage was legalised, and Janet became a 'lady' in Gaelic: *baintighearna dhubh Osgaig* 'the dark lady of Oscaig'. She bore Malcolm at least six sons and two daughters (MacInnes, 'Gleanings', pp. 5–8; MacAonghuis, 'Dioghlam', p. 135; MacLeod, *Raasay*, pp. 59–60, 71). The 'old castle' where she lived was Martin's 'little tower, and lesser houses' (note 338).

349 The castle was Brochel, on the north-eastern coast (RCAHMCS, *Ninth Report*, pp. 178–80; MacLeod, *Raasay*, pp. 235–39). The word 'northwestern' is suggested by Pottle and Bennett (*Journal*, p. 139), as Boswell left a blank. They were walking round the island anticlockwise. By 'Raasay' Boswell here means the person, not the place.

350 Boswell left blanks for the duration of Malcolm's imprisonment and the Captain's name. When in command of the *Furnace* in 1746, Ferguson, who was from the Mill of Inch in Aberdeenshire, scoured the Western Isles for Prince Charles, leaving rape and destruction in his wake. John MacCodrum, for whom see notes 441 and 808, pronounced a curse in the form of a thirteen-verse elegy when he heard of Ferguson's death in 1767 (Matheson, *Songs of John MacCodrum*, p. 173): "In many a country did he raise smoke, many a cheerful hall did he lay waste. Light would I deem a large mill-stone as an anchor to keep him down . . ."

351 Dick, a king's messenger, later became the guardian of other 'celebrity' prisoners – Old Clanranald, Capt. John MacKinnon of Elgol, Aeneas MacDonald the Paris banker, Alexander MacDonald of Boisdale, Dr John Burton of York. Flora was allowed to visit friends in the company of Dick's daughters. Lady Primrose, the widow of Hugh, 3rd Viscount Primrose, was a daughter of the Rev. Peter Drelincourt, Dean of Armagh.

352 This anecdote appears in the *Tour* at 13 September, following the description of Malcolm's imprisonment (*To the Hebrides*, p. 226). It ends: "'So,' said he, with a triumphant air, 'I went to London to be hanged, and returned in a post-chaise with Miss Flora Macdonald.'"

353 The Rev. Robert Forbes called this pipe a 'cuttie' (Paton, *Lyon in Mourning*, vol. 1, pp. 142–43): "Captain MacLeod took care to have one of the cutties the Prince had used and carried it to London with him, where meeting with one Dr Burton of York, a prisoner, and chancing to tell the story of the cuttie, the Doctor begged as a great favour to have the cuttie, which Malcolm gave him. The Doctor has made a fine shagreen case for it, and preserves it as a valuable rarity. This Dr Burton was made prisoner upon a suspicion of his having crossed England with an intention to kiss the Prince's hands. Malcolm in coming down from London made a stop at York for a day or two, and visited the Doctor and his cuttie." For the bottle see p. 150.

354 Richard Bentley, Master of Trinity College, Cambridge, ranged widely in his scholarship. Johnson later said (*Life*, 20 March 1776): "Take Bentley's and

Jason de Nores' Comments upon Horace, you will admire Bentley more when wrong, than Jason when right."

355 In the *Tour* (where the paragraph is placed last in the account of 10 September) this sentence was altered to: "That he imagined the duchess furnished the materials for her *Apology*, which Hooke wrote, and Hooke furnished the words and the order, and all that in which the art of writing consists." Nathaniel Hooke's principal work was *The Roman History* (4 vols, 1738–71, see p. 153 above), but as it made little money, his friends procured for him the position of amanuensis to the duchess, who gave him all the relevant anecdotes and documents. The work referred to as the *Apology* was her narrative of her time at court, written for her by Hooke and published in 1742 as *An Account of the Conduct of the Dowager Duchess of Marlborough, From her first coming to Court, To the Year 1710*. She had been the young Queen Anne's most trusted adviser, but their relationship was damaged beyond repair by her own brusque temper and sense of intellectual superiority. The purpose of the *Account* was to restore the tarnished reputations of the duchess and her late husband – not so much apology as apologia. David Mallet accepted money from the duchess to write the duke's Life, then did nothing because he expected her to furnish the materials in the same way. Mallet's real name was Malloch, and he was a son of the gardener at Abercairney House in Perthshire (Ramsay, *Scotland and Scotsmen*, vol. 1, p. 24); the Mallochs are MacGregors, Gaelic *mailgheach* 'beetle-browed' (Armstrong, *Dictionary*, p. 372).

356 This incised cross (3 ft 7 ins high) on a sloping rock at the old pier, nine feet above high-water mark, is described and illustrated in RCAHMCS, *Ninth Report*, pp. 184–85, and in *PSAS*, vols 41 (1906–07), pp. 435–36, and 67 (1932–33), p. 64. Boswell made two attempts to draw it, one blotted, the other scored out.

357 For the Oar Cave see pp. 145–46 and note 320. The 'Danish fortification' is in fact a Pictish broch, *Dùn Bhorghadail* or Dun Borrodale (RCAHMCS, *Ninth Report*, p. 181; MacDonald, 'Raasay in Prehistory', p. 69; MacLeod, *Raasay*, pp. 8, 231–32).

358 *Cill mo Luaig*, St Moluag's Chapel, is described in RCAHMCS, *Ninth Report*, p. 181, and MacLeod, *Raasay*, pp. 15–17, 232–35. The bones were those of the greatest hero in Raasay tradition, Faobairne MacCuidhein, himself a MacQueen, although many of his descendants called themselves MacKay (Maclean, 'Some Raasay Traditions', pp. 381–82; MacLeod, *Raasay*, p. 16).

359 Boswell wrote 'once in ——— Sundays' (Pottle, *Journal*, p. 422), and I have filled in the gap from Johnson's information (p. 293).

360 See p. 146. All that appears to remain of Martin's eight crosses (note 323) is two structures, one near the gate on the summit of the Battery and the other on a steep slope behind St Moluag's Chapel. Both have 'a large base of squared stone, with a second and possibly third step on top'. Their date and function are unknown (MacLeod, *Raasay*, p. 16). Boswell's circular buildings are equally puzzling: as Ann MacDonald points out ('Raasay in Prehistory', p. 71), they occupy an imposing site high above the sea at Doire

Domhain, looking directly into Portree Bay. "One may be a prehistoric cairn, others may be hut circles, or it has been speculated that the larger of the monuments may be an Iron Age wheelhouse of a kind normally found only on the Atlantic seaboard of the Outer Isles."

361 'Albin and the Daughter of Mey: an old tale, translated from the Irish' (*Scots Magazine*, vol. 18, January 1756, pp. 15–17) was the Scottish Gaelic Ossianic ballad 'Bàs Fhraoich' (which derives from the early Irish tale 'Táin Bó Fraích') rendered into twenty stanzas of English verse by Jerome Stone, schoolmaster at Dunkeld. Stone's poem is compared to 'Bàs Fhraoich' in Mackenzie's *Report*, Appendix, pp. 99–117. Its only resemblance to Malcolm's story (for which see Black, *Gaelic Otherworld*, pp. 112, 368–69) is that it involves a hero, a maiden, a monster and a lake. There is a biography of Stone in Ramsay, *Scotland and Scotsmen*, vol. 1, pp. 547–48.

362 Presumably *Eilean Taighe* 'House Island', which not only looks like a house but came to contain quite a number of them (during Raasay's century of forced population imbalance, 1850–1950). Boswell was probably wrong about Duncaan – recent scholarship suggests that it takes its name from a Pictish hero known to the Gael as Cano mac Gartnáin (Ó Baoill, 'Inis Moccu Chéin', p. 268). He will have lived in Boswell's 'Danish fort' (pp. 154, 159).

363 Johnson would have been commenting on Boswell's description, for he did not visit Brochel himself.

364 The entire passage from 'I perceived' in the previous paragraph to here (twenty-one sentences) was replaced in the *Tour* with: "In this remnant of antiquity I found nothing worthy of being noticed, except a certain accommodation rarely to be found at the modern houses of Scotland, and which Dr Johnson and I sought for in vain at the Laird of Raasay's new-built mansion, where nothing else was wanting."

365 Boswell left a blank for the figure, and it is supplied from Johnson's account (p. 143). 'Bow' in the Scots legal terms 'bowman' and 'steelbow' may be derived from Middle English *bu* 'homestead, livestock', as the dictionaries tell us, but the words Boswell would have heard around him were Gaelic *bó* 'cow' and *buachaille* 'cow-keeper, herdsman'.

366 Boswell left a line blank for recording more names of fishes. For Johnson's views on the Raasay fox see p. 145.

367 What Boswell appears to mean is that from the populated part of Raasay the eye is drawn west to the Cuillins, the high mountains on the west coast of Skye. The 'Heather Barn' burnt down in 1856 and was replaced with the present 'Top Barn' on the same site (MacLeod, *Raasay*, p. 110 and facing p. 56).

368 By *gaul* Boswell means the Scots – not Gaelic – word 'gall' ('gale, sweet-gale, bog-myrtle'), see p. 344. There was no coal in Raasay, but there was iron. It was mined intensively from 1911 to 1923 (Draper, 'Iron Ore Mine'; MacLeod, *Raasay*, pp. 160–62).

369 See p. 216. In the *Tour* the last three sentences are altered to: "Such are the observations which I made upon the island of Raasay, upon comparing it with the description given by Martin, whose book we had with us."

370 In the *Tour*, the five sentences from 'But Sir Alexander' to here were replaced with: "Old Raasay joined the Highland army in 1745, but prudently guarded against a forfeiture, by previously conveying his estate to the present gentleman, his eldest son."

371 I take this and one other sentence from the *Tour*. Otherwise the description of **11 September** is from Boswell's journal.

372 This was Macleod of Dunvegan, who had succeeded to his estate at the age of seventeen on 21 February 1772, see p. 127.

373 For the removal of heritable jurisdictions see pp. 188, 190–91; for Alexander MacLeod of Ullinish see pp. 173, 255.

374 Boswell's first blank might have been filled by 'a board ribbed lengthways', 'a long frame of wicker-work', 'three planks side by side', or even 'a door taken off its hinges'. Since he saw the women kneeling, the board, frame, planks or door must have been on the floor, as in Moses Griffith's illustration for Pennant of a waulking at Talisker in 1772 (see note 599). This would have been tiring, and when Boswell was no longer looking, no doubt the women sat down and used their feet instead of their hands, as Pennant describes them doing (*Tour 1772*, p. 284): "Six or seven pair of naked feet are in the most violent agitation, working one against the other." This practice survived in Lewis until the twentieth century (Macleod, *Living Past*, p. 196): "The men were put out, the skirts were tied just above the knee, the women sat on the floor and the thumping began." Boswell's second blank should be filled with 'urine', as he probably guessed from the smell, though it may have been mixed with soapy water, since the waulking was being done in a gentleman's kitchen (Campbell, *Hebridean Folksongs*, vols 1, pp. 3–16, and 3, pp. 2–5; Black, *Gaelic Otherworld*, p. 443).

375 In the *Tour* these two sentences are altered. "They dance here every night. The queen of our ball was the eldest Miss MacLeod, of Raasay, an elegant well-bred woman, and celebrated for her beauty over all those regions, by the name of Miss Flora Raasay." This is footnoted: "She had been some time at Edinburgh, to which she again went, and was married to my worthy neighbour, Colonel Mure Campbell, now Earl of Loudoun; but she died soon afterwards, leaving one daughter." This daughter (b. 1780) succeeded her father in 1786 as countess of Loudoun in her own right. See note 325.

376 From 'The Vanity of Human Wishes', see note 91. Johnson wrote 'grief', not 'pain'.

377 All ten daughters made good marriages.

378 By 'supply his place' Boswell means 'do his reflecting for him'. Instead of walking thirty miles Sir Alexander's horses walked eighty, and after reading the *Tour* he wrote indignantly to Boswell on 26 November 1785 (Scott and Pottle, *Private Papers*, vol. 16, p. 236): "Every consideration must yield to the accommodation of Dr Johnson (and yourself, of course); therefore, declining to accept the country horses, you set off with mine for Kingsburgh, about fifty miles, where (and at other places) you detained them several days, notwithstanding you might have been supplied at every gentleman's house upon the road; till moved, I presume, by retrospective compunction, you

returned the jaded animals, lame to the ground (without any apology), and consequently for a long time unfit for the journey which they were originally intended to perform. Thus the escape of the Pretender was the means of detaining me a prisoner 27 years after it happened . . ."

379 In his letter to Boswell of 26 November 1785, Lord Macdonald wrote (Scott and Pottle, *Private Papers*, vol. 16, p. 234): "At your own behaviour every one felt some degree of resentment when you told me your only errand into Sky was to visit the Pretender's conductress, and that you deemed every moment as lost which was not spent in her company."

380 See p. 212. Like many other important place-names (e.g. Brazil), Portree is a duonym, i.e. in origin it is *Port Ruighe* 'Slope Harbour', but since the king's visit in 1540 it has usually been spelt (and explained) as *Port Rìgh* 'King's Harbour'. The difference in pronunciation is minimal.

381 Martin, *Description*, pp. 98–99: "There is a large cave, in which many sea-cormorants do build. The natives carry a bundle of straw to the door of the cave in the night-time, and there setting it on fire, the fowls fly with all speed to the light, and so are caught in baskets laid for that purpose." The Scarf or Scart Caves (*Uamhan nan Sgarbh* 'Cormorant Caves') are on the south side of the entrance to Portree Harbour. See p. 211.

382 Johnson appears to contradict what he said about 'Sconsor' at p. 122. In fact there were inns at Sconser, Portree and Dunvegan, not to mention innumerable dram-shops throughout the island. Kingsburgh, Gaelic *Cinnseaborg*, probably means 'toll-town' – the first element looks like a Norse variant of Latin *census*, Gaelic *cìs* 'tax'.

383 Allan MacDonald was a son of Alexander MacDonald of Kingsburgh, Prince Charles's host, guide and protector on 29–30 June 1746. Allan's wife Flora, whom he married in 1750, was the Prince's most famous protector of all – on the dangerous crossing from Benbecula, 28–29 June 1746.

384 Lady Macleod was Emilia, daughter of Alexander Brodie of Brodie. Her husband John, younger of Macleod (*c.* 1726–66), had taken an active part in the '45. He died, much in debt, at Beverley in Yorkshire. For her daughters see p. 232.

385 See p. 127. He was a Member of Parliament from 1741 to 1754, which meant buying votes and living luxuriously in London. Coming out for the Government in 1745 involved large outlays for which he received no compensation. After 1754 he lived much at Edinburgh, St Andrews and Inverness. There is a description of Dunvegan Castle in RCAHMCS, *Ninth Report*, pp. 152–54.

386 Sir Donald Macdonald (*Domhnall Gorm Mór*, d. 1617), 7th of Sleat, appears to have repudiated his wife Flora, daughter of Ruairi Mór Macleod, in 1600; the MacDonalds prevailed at Coire na Creiche in 1601. The custom of handfast marriages is discussed by Martin, *Description*, p. 78.

387 This took place at *Uamh Fhraing*, St Francis's Cave in Eigg, in 1577; the victims were Clanranald MacDonalds. See pp. 306–07 and note 674.

388 For Ruairi Mór's horn see p. 235. Boethius (Boece) says that herring vanished from Inverness due to offence given to a saint, and that they always vanish

when blood is spilt by men fighting for them (Brown, *Scotland before 1700*, p. 74). No doubt the tradition about women has also to do with blood. According to Martin (*Description*, p. 16), it was believed that if a female were first to cross the Barvas River in Lewis on May-Day, no salmon would come up the river that year.

389 These were Hector MacLean and his wife Isabel, a MacLeod of the Talisker family. Muck is *Eilean nam Muc* 'the Isle of the Pigs', see note 317.

390 Alexander MacLeod of Ullinish, sheriff substitute, see pp. 166, 255.

391 This is the Pictish broch at Struanmore known as *an Dùn Beag* (*PSAS*, vol. 55, 1920–21, pp. 110–31; RCAHMCS, *Ninth Report*, pp. 142–43).

392 See pp. 256–57. This earth-house or souterrain is in *Cnoc Uilbhinnis* (Knock Ullinish), just north of the roadway from Ullinish Lodge to the main road (RCAHMCS, *Ninth Report*, p. 148).

393 Caisteal Ùistein at Kingsburgh, built *c.* 1580 by Hugh Macdonald, *Ùistean mac Ghilleasbaig Chlèirich* 'Hugh son of Archibald the Clerk' (RCAHMCS, *Ninth Report*, pp. 193–94; Nicolson, *Handbook*, pp. 27–30; Swire, *Skye*, p. 52).

394 For the caves and the '*English* ghost' see pp. 258–59. A 'cuddy' is the young of the saithe, coley or coalfish, Gaelic *cudaig* (perhaps from English 'haddock'). This fish was so useful that at each stage of its life it had a different name: *smalag, cudaig, saoidh, ucas.*

395 As tutor to young Macleod of Dunvegan, Col. John MacLeod of Talisker was responsible for managing the burden of debt under which the kindred was groaning. His first wife had been Mary MacLean of the Coll family. On the MacLeod tradition of entering the Dutch service see note 257. In better times 'the gay and the jovial' were by no means excluded from Talisker – the poet Alexander MacKenzie (d. 1642) called the place *ròd nan cliar* 'the anchorage of the poet-bands' (Watson, *Bàrdachd Ghàidhlig*, p. 231), and during the years 1675–1713 Col. MacLeod's grandfather John, 2nd of Talisker, presided over the extraordinarily talented 'Talisker circle' of poets and musicians, which included MacLeods, a MacKinnon, a MacKay from Gairloch and even Iain mac Ailein from Mull, for whom see pp. 208, 356 (Matheson, *Blind Harper*, pp. lxi–lxvii).

396 Peter the Great travelled through Europe incognito, learning industrial techniques as an ordinary craftsman, see p. 265; Donald Maclean ('Col', 'Coll', 'young Col', 'young Coll') remains with us throughout chapters 5–9. Curiously, the fonder of him Johnson and Boswell become, the shorter he seems to grow: at p. 144 he is 'a man of middle stature', at p. 267 he is 'a little brisk young man', by p. 337 he is 'a very diminutive figure'.

397 James MacDonald, the factor for Sleat, see pp. 129, 280, 281, 286.

398 This was Martin MacPherson, minister of Sleat from 1765 to his death (see note 308). He farmed at Ostaig. Johnson liked his sister Isabel (Isabella), who was in her twenties, see p. 287. He subsequently corresponded with her (Hill and Powell, *Life*, vol. 5, p. 547).

399 See p. 346. 'The Year of the Black Spring' (*Bliadhna an Earraich Dhuibh*) became proverbial in Gaelic for its severity. The Kintail poet Iain mac

Mhurchaidh (John MacRae) tells us that despite losing his milch cows, the sorest loss of all was his mares, without which he could not plough or harrow; he emigrated to North Carolina shortly after (MacilleDhuibh, 'Down to the Year of the Black Spring'). Johnson's gooseberry-gathering may have been at Armadale (p. 125), at Ullinish (p. 258), or both.

400 This is the *cas chrom* ('crooked leg'), see also pp. 255, 256, 275–76, 333. It is described and illustrated by Grant, *Highland Folk Ways*, pp. 103–05.

401 Johnson may have picked up some such terms as *mór-earrann* ('big division', arable land whose rigs were ploughed in rotation by different sub-tenants) and *geàrraidh* 'grazing land', which is from Old Norse *gerði* 'enclosure', not Gaelic *gearr* 'short'.

402 The 'frame of timber', a slipe or *carn*, is illustrated in Simmons, *Burt's Letters*, p. 42; see also note 410.

403 See pp. 153–54. The custom of burning off the husks is known as *gradanadh* 'graddaning' (from *grad* 'swift') or *eararadh*, *fuirireadh* 'parching'. It was described by Bishop John Leslie in 1578 (Brown, *Scotland before 1700*, p. 165) and by Domhnall mac Fhionnlaigh nan Dàn *c.* 1590–1600 (note 409; Black, *Gaelic Otherworld*, pp. 326–27). Archibald Constable, the translator of John Major's *Historia Majoris Britanniæ* of 1521, confused the practice with kiln-drying, but found a useful reference to it in Ireland in 1624 (Major, *History of Greater Britain*, p. 8). In both parching and kiln-drying the grain falls out of the husk without need for threshing.

404 For Raasay's barn see p. 164.

405 Probably manganese, which was mined in Raasay along with iron ore in 1911–23, see note 368. 'Black mass' does not adequately describe the diatomite mined in Skye *c.* 1890–1961 (Deveria, *A'Chailc*). For the lead mine in Coll see pp. 323, 324, 335–36.

406 These rocks were in the Sound of Harris, between Berneray and North Uist (Morrison, 'The Grianam Case', pp. 40–47). The case was brought to court in 1770 and settled in 1781. The kelp boom was at its height from 1790 to 1814 and caused unnatural displacement of population to rocky coastal areas, see for example note 698.

407 See p. 439. The Scots term *hummel* 'hornless' is unconnected to 'humble-' or 'bumble-bee', which denotes humming. In Gaelic 'hornless' is *maol*.

408 Down to this period there were more goats than sheep in the Highlands and islands. Goats were the mainstay of the poor: in 1798 there were estimated to be 1,500 in Arisaig and South Morar, and 800 in Moidart (Megaw, 'Goat-Keeping', p. 204). Sheep, on the other hand, were little more than pets. The only district traversed by Johnson and Boswell where large-scale sheep-farming had been introduced by 1773 was between Inveraray and Rossdhu.

409 This practice died out in the Highlands *c.* 1600. The long poem 'Òran na Comhachaig' ('The Owl's Song'), composed in that period by Domhnall mac Fhionnlaigh nan Dàn, laments its disappearance in Lochaber.

410 By 'crate' Johnson means a slipe, the unwheeled 'frame of timber' described earlier (p. 180); see also p. 255. Rope was regularly made from heather roots ('ropes of twisted heath', p. 82, 'ropes of heath', p. 271), but these were not

always obtainable, and straw was a common substitute ('ropes of straw or of heath', p. 271).

411 Turtles were a feature of civic banquets in Johnson's day. What he means is that diet is irrelevant to ageing.

412 Margaret Dalrymple (1684–1779), dowager countess of Loudoun, see pp. 432–33; Susanna Kennedy (1689–1780), countess of Eglinton, pp. 433–35. Johnson is trying to dispel a persistent belief that the secrets of good health and long life were to be found in the islands. It was to find data with which to assess this belief that Martin was encouraged to make his tour; his best example of longevity was from Jura, which Johnson and Boswell did not visit (Martin, *Description*, pp. 143–45).

413 See p. 363.

414 Johnson is notable for unequivocally describing as 'rape' Lovat's marriage *c.* 1696 to his cousin's widow, the dowager Lady Lovat. Pursued by his many enemies, he sought refuge at the court of the 'Old Pretender' in St Germains, but returned following his pardon in 1715.

415 Sir Ambrose Crowley, a native of Stourbridge in Worcestershire and a distant relative of Johnson's, had amassed a fortune through the development of the iron industry in Co. Durham.

416 Thus does Johnson describe the lowest two of the five castes of Gaelic society: the 'joint tenants' (Gaelic *tuath*) who emerged as 'crofters' in the nineteenth century, and the landless 'cottars' (*coitearan*, often referred to dismissively as *bodaich* 'peasants'), for whom no place at all was found in the nineteenth century. Above them, in ascending order, were the professionals, tacksmen and chiefs, already described. See note 751.

417 See pp. 119–20. The effects of the 'Disclothing Act' are discussed in Black, *An Lasair*, pp. 455–58.

418 For the Disarming Act of 1746 and 1748 see note 267. It forbade not only the carrying or possession of weapons or bagpipes but also the wearing of the Highland dress, the latter provision being known as the 'Disclothing Act'. Johnson's point about the 'loyal clans' is demonstrated by the poet Duncan Macintyre, who had served on the Government side in 1745–46 (MacLeod, *Songs of Duncan Ban Macintyre*, p. 15): "If Charles were to descend on us, / And we rose to take the field with him, / Red-tinted tartans could be got, / And the guns would be forthcoming."

419 *Scots Magazine*, vol. 35, June 1773, p. 333: "Edward Shaw Macintosh of Borlum, Alexander Mackintosh his natural brother, John Forbes miller at the mill of Reatts, William Davidson in Beldow of Reatts, Evan Dow Maclauchlan, and Donald Dow Robertson, both servants to Borlum, were indicted to stand trial for robbery, and entering into an association to murder and rob passengers on the highway. On the arrival of the members of court at Inverness on Thursday evening, May 13, the advocate-depute was informed, that two of the principal witnesses against this gang had been abstracted, and that Lady Borlum, and five gentlemen, were concerned in abstracting them: on which he obtained a warrant against them all; and a messenger was dispatched that same night, with a military party; by whom

they were carried in prisoners, the persons concerned in the abstraction on Saturday evening, and the two witnesses on Sunday evening. The gang had committed several robberies and thefts, and were a terror to the country. Borlum, and his two servants, and John Forbes, were fugitated for non-appearance. The remaining two were tried; and the jury, unanimously, found Alexander Macintosh guilty, art and part, of the haill crimes libelled, except that of stealing bear from Mr Blair, and, by a great plurality of voices, found William Davidson guilty, art and part, of robbing the house of James Macpherson weaver in Laggan of Killihuntly; and both were sentenced to be hanged, at Inverness, on the 2d of July, and the body of Mackintosh to be hung in chains."

420 This was not new. Those chiefs who had never possessed a barony or a regality had always 'usurped' this right in terms of feudal (though not of Celtic) law. As Boswell points out (p. 321), 'from the necessity of the thing . . . the Laird must exercise his jurisdiction to a certain degree'.

421 £164,232 16s was paid out in compensation, but most of it went to magnates like the duke of Argyll who had come out for the Government. Not all heritable jurisdictions were abolished. Baron courts (and thus those individuals who held the title of baron) were permitted to pursue for recovery of rent, to keep the peace at fairs and markets, and to hear civil cases concerning disputes up to £2 in value. These surviving rights may help explain the instances noted by Boswell (pp. 334, 394, 406) of chiefs continuing to assert judicial authority.

422 *Gentleman's Magazine*, vol. 19, October 1749, p. 472: "The good temperature of the air . . . puts me in mind of *Italy*, and I think there is a good prospect of it being altogether as fertile."

423 An evocation of the speech of Calgacus (Tacitus, *Agricola*, §30): *Ubi solitudinem faciunt, pacem appellant.* "Where they make a wilderness, they call it peace."

424 Caesar describes his war with the Helvetii in *De Bello Gallico*, book 1, §§1–29.

425 By 'the North' Johnson appears to mean all those lands whose peoples stopped the northern advance of Roman armies: Celts, Germans, Slavs. In *De Bello Gallico*, book 1, §29, Caesar totals the Helvetii, Tulingi, Latobrigi, Raurici and Boii at 368,000, of whom 92,000 could bear arms. In *Agricola*, §29, Tacitus says that at Mons Graupius 'more than 30,000 armed men were already on view, and still the stream flowed in'; in §37, after the battle, 'the enemy dead amounted to 10,000, while on our side there fell 360'.

426 See p. 364.

427 Johnson might have heard a different story had he visited Tiree, where the last peat-banks were exhausted in the 1840s.

428 Whether or not there was a causal connection between the Revolution of 1689 and the decline of the bagpipe, it is certainly true that the violin suddenly became popular in the Highlands after *c.* 1700, as is shown both by the Gaelic poetry of the time and by the chiefs' financial accounts. For MacCrimmons and Rankins see also p. 320.

NOTES

429 This is a criticism of Pennant, who had found Highlanders 'excessively inquisitive after your business, your name, and other particulars of little consequence to them' (*Tour 1769*, p. 194) and the natives of Rum 'expecting our landing, with that avidity for news common to the whole country' (*Tour 1772*, p. 276).

430 Donald MacLean, minister of the Small Isles from 1787 to his death (see pp. 300, 333–34), was a son of Neil MacLean of Crossapol (Maclean-Bristol, *From Clan to Regiment*, pp. 159–61, 174–77, 250–56, 708). In 1774 the Society in Scotland for the Propagation of Christian Knowledge established a school in Coll (Maclean-Bristol, *From Clan to Regiment*, pp. 280–81).

431 By 'grammar schools' Johnson means schools where Latin is taught, just as at p. 109 Boswell remarks that Lachlan MacQueen had learnt 'his grammar', i.e. Latin. These schools were at Kilmore (Sleat) and Bracadale.

432 Johnson's statement (p. 185) that each chief formerly told his people 'what religion they should profess' is nearer the mark. There were, and are, Catholics in many more places than Canna and Eigg. Their geographical distribution reveals the religious affiliation of the chiefs in the seventeenth century.

433 The reference is to Scalpay (Skye), not Scalpay (Harris), see note 327.

434 Johnson means *gruagach* 'long-haired one'. The minister was MacQueen, who in fact contributed a brief appendix on the *gruagach* ('Of the Gruagich') to Pennant's *Tour 1772*, part 2, published in 1776. There is a theory that the traditional connection between brownies and small islands like Trodda represents a 'Devil's island' form of incarceration for individuals with certain types of mental or physical handicap (Black, *Gaelic Otherworld*, pp. liii–lvi).

435 In the nineteenth century Alexander Carmichael made a massive collection of 'charms for the cure of different diseases' (*Carmina Gadelica*, vols 2 and 4) and of Gaelic traditions of this kind about the moon (*ibid.*, vols 1, pp. 122–23, and 3, pp. 274–305).

436 A *taibhs* is the thing seen. The power of seeing is *taibhsearachd*.

437 See p. 363.

438 The Rev. Martin MacPherson, see p. 137. He was born in Barra.

439 The natural philosopher Robert Boyle was perhaps the first scholar to conduct active research into second sight (Hunter, *Occult Laboratory*, pp. 2–12, 51–53). Before him, Francis Bacon had pondered the connections between superstitions, 'the force of the imagination' and what we would now call extra-sensory perception (Spedding, *Works of Francis Bacon*, vol. 2, part 2, pp. 666–67): "Being in Paris, and my father dying in London, two or three days before my father's death I had a dream, which I told to divers English gentlemen, that my father's house in the country was plastered all over with black mortar."

440 See pp. 137, 307.

441 Johnson's failure to elicit precise information reflects badly both upon him and upon MacQueen, the 'greatest master of *Hebridian* antiquities', who was 'always for making everything as ancient as possible' (p. 257),

and who appears to have been pathologically incapable of fixing his mind upon the cultural history of recent centuries. Gaelic was a written language and had been for a thousand years. Until earlier in the eighteenth century the Macleods were served by literate poets called Ó Muirgheasáin, the Macdonalds by literate poets called MacMhuirich. These held hereditary office. Thanks especially to James Macpherson, many of their manuscripts survive today. They include ancient genealogies. There were also countless non-literate poets, many of whom were attached to specific families. Among the most notable were Mary MacLeod (*Màiri nighean Alastair Ruaidh*, *c*.1615–*c*.1707) at Dunvegan and John MacCodrum (1693–1779) in North Uist, who had enjoyed the patronage of Sir Alexander Macdonald's late brother Sir James. Poets were necessarily also *seanchaidhean* (bearers of *seanchas*, i.e. traditional knowledge or, as Johnson says, 'talk'). Those who could write preserved their knowledge in writing, e.g. the so-called 'Book of Clanranald'. Ronald MacDonald in Eigg made a large collection of Gaelic poetry (*Comh-Chruinneachidh Orannaigh Gaidhealach*) which he published in 1776; whether he was motivated to do so by reports of Johnson's negative attitude is unclear, but he states in his preface that he had 'bestowed much labour and expence, during the course of two years, in collecting the poems now offered to the public', which suggests that he began collecting while Johnson and Boswell were on their tour.

442 The informal practice of genealogy persisted with great vigour, however, as Johnson had found when a boatman asked whether he could recite his own (p. 176).

443 The 'Bards or Senachies field', *Achadh nam Bard*, is in the parish of Snizort, and appears to have been held by the family of MacRury as hereditary poets and historians to the Macdonalds of Sleat (Forbes, *Place-Names of Skye*, p. 26). Johnson probably obtained his information about the perquisites of the smith, piper, etc. by quoting to his informant the following passage in Martin (*Description*, p. 76): "Before money became current, the chieftains in the isles bestowed the cow's head, feet, and all the entrails upon their dependants; such as the physician, orator, poet, bard, musicians, etc., and the same was divided thus: the smith had the head, the piper had the, etc."

444 This is likely to be correct. Coll MacDonald of Barrisdale is said to have brought out sixty well-armed men for the Prince, of whom 'every man had a target'; on the other hand, in a list of eighty recruits to the Clanranald regiment, only seven are noted as possessing one (Munro, *Taming the Rough Bounds*, p. 5; Macdonald, *Moidart*, pp. 171–73). Probably the target had gone out of use in the more southerly and easterly parts of the Highlands. See also p. 235.

445 The 'gentleman now living' appears to have been Donald MacLeod of Berneray ('the Old Trojan', 1692–1781), who supplied some men for the Government side as his chief required, then joined the MacLeods of Raasay to fight for Prince Charles in the Glengarry regiment. "According to local tradition, in the pursuit after Culloden," says Isobel Grant (*MacLeods*, p. 468), "the Old Trojan was attacked by a mounted man and, slipping, was

nearly run through. Another horseman came to his assistance, and the Old Trojan was able to kill his assailant and mount his horse. His rescuer merely told him to fly for his life, adding: 'You owe me a day's hard work at harvest time.'" This may be a separate incident (Morrison, 'The Grianam Case', p. 40), or merely a memory of what happened at Falkirk on 17 January 1746. Johnson's account is confirmed by the Old Trojan's epitaph in the churchyard of St Clement's, Rodel, Harris, probably composed by his son (Fleeman, *Journey*, p. 215): "When the standard of the house of Stuart, to which he was attached, was displayed, A.D: 1745, Tho past the prime of life, he took arms, had a share in the actions of that period, and in the battle of Falkirk, vanquished a dragoon hand to hand." The dragoons at Falkirk were on the left wing of the Government army, facing Keppoch's, Clanranald's and Glengarry's men on the Jacobite right.

446 Scottish Gaelic, which Johnson calls 'Earse', can be seen emerging in manuscripts such as the Book of Deer as a separate written language from the twelfth century onwards. There are two schools of orthography, one based on English and one on Irish. The greatest flowering of the 'English' school is the Book of the Dean of Lismore (1512–42). Hoping that their publications would be as serviceable in Ireland as in Scotland, the Reformers adopted the 'Irish' model. It was used for the Gaelic translation of Knox's Book of Common Order in 1567 and the metrical version of the Psalms from 1659 onwards, and is the system used today. The uncertainty of which Johnson speaks is caused by the gap between spelling (which represents an artificial norm and always lags behind) and the spoken language (which exists in various dialects and always forges ahead). This is as true of Irish and English as it is of Scottish Gaelic.

447 Spurious arguments of this type were used for centuries to justify imperialism.

448 See p. 356. It is far from certain that Iain mac Ailein was non-literate (Thomson, *Companion*, p. 5; Black, *An Lasair*, p. 402). His 'sacred history' is a hymn in seventeen eight-line stanzas beginning *A Thì chumhachdaich nan cumhdachdan* ('O powerful Lord of pronouncements'). It was written down by the young lady's father, Dr Hector MacLean (Ó Baoill, *MacLean Manuscripts*, p. 43), and has been published twice, without translation (Sinclair, *Gaelic Bards*, pp. 202–06; Sinclair, *Na Bàird Leathanach*, vol. 1, pp. 173–76).

449 It will be seen that Johnson had allowed personal animosity towards James Macpherson to cloud his judgement.

450 Irish, the parent language of Scottish Gaelic, provided precisely that 'written diction, which pervades all dialects' which Johnson claimed to be sadly lacking. The relationship of Scottish Gaelic to Irish resembled that of Schwyzerdütsch to High German today. Fifty years after the publication of the entire Bible in vernacular Scottish Gaelic (1801), the 'Irish' scriptures were still preferred by many for their dignity, and Irishisms survive in the Protestant theological discourse of Scottish Gaelic to this day.

451 Those writers of manuscripts who used the Irish orthographic model

were expected also to conform to Irish standards in grammar, syntax and vocabulary. Boswell's anxiety to purge his work of Scotticisms provides a perfect analogy.

452 Ossianic ballads existed, and Macpherson used them, which is why Gaelic-speaking readers of his 'translations' recognised names and images in them.

453 This is in the appendix (first published in 1765) to Hugh Blair's *Critical Dissertation on the Poems of Ossian* (Macpherson, *Poems of Ossian*, 1996 edn, p. 406): "From the reverend Mr John Macpherson minister of Slate in Sky, Mr Neil Macleod minister of Ross in Mull, Mr Angus Macneil minister of South Uist, Mr Donald Macqueen minister of Kilmuir in Sky, and Mr Donald Macleod minister of Glenelg, I have had . . . distinct and explicit testimonies to almost the whole epic poem of Fingal, from beginning to end, and to several also of the lesser poems, as rehearsed in the original, in their presence, by persons whose names and places of abode they mention, and compared by themselves with the printed translation. They affirm that in many places, what was rehearsed in their presence agreed literally and exactly with the translation."

454 See pp. 260–62.

455 This is an accurate description of the Book of the Dean of Lismore, which was in James Macpherson's possession and is now NLS MS Adv. 72.1.37.

456 Mariners since Magellan had reported sightings of very tall people in Patagonia. Commodore John Byron, RN, the poet's grandfather, reported an encounter in 1764 with an entire tribe who appeared to be between six and seven feet tall. Coming hard on the heels of Macpherson's editions of 'Ossian', which asserted the existence of a gigantic race in second-century Scotland as historical fact, this was met with scepticism. The controversy was renewed by the publication in 1773 of Hawkesworth's *Account of the Voyages*, in which Byron's log-book was enhanced for literary style (vol. 1, p. 28): "One of them, who afterwards appeared to be a Chief, came towards me: he was of a gigantic stature, and seemed to realise the tales of monsters in human shape: he had the skin of some wild beast thrown over his shoulders, as a Scotch Highlander wears his plaid . . ." Byron was hurt by being disbelieved, as his crew backed him up. Pennant assessed the evidence coolly, and suggested the existence of classes as well as tribes in Patagonian society (*Literary Life*, p. 65). They had a cult of height, so that the tallest men were chiefs. Byron may have encountered a rare gathering of this 'Brahman' caste (MacilleDhuibh, 'Patagonian Giants').

457 William Drummond of Hawthornden's *Cypresse Grove* is a gentle meditation on death (Kastner, *Poetical Works*, vol. 2, p. 72): "Who beeing admitted to see the exquisite Rarities of some Antiquaries Cabinet is grieued, all viewed, to haue the Courtaine drawen, and giue place to new Pilgrimes?"

458 Horace, *Epistles*, book 1, poem 2, lines 11–12: "Nestor hastens to allay the quarrel between the son of Peleus (Achilles) and the descendant of Atreus (Agamemnon)."

459 On the site of the present Royal Hotel, it was then almost the only building at Portree. Before being brought across to Raasay on the night of 30 June

1746, Prince Charles had got out of his wet clothes there, eaten, drunk, smoked, changed a guinea, bought a bottle of whisky and taken farewell of Flora MacDonald (see p. 219). The then landlord, Charles MacNab, was 'mighty inquisitive', but was warned to keep his thoughts to himself (Paton, *Lyon in Mourning*, vol. 2, pp. 21–27). On the name 'Portree' see note 380.

460 McGinnis and Williamson, *George Buchanan*, pp. 150–51: *Vix me in Britannis montibus natum, et solo / Inerudito et seculo, / Raræ audiebant . . .* "Scarcely and rarely did they pay me heed, born as I was in the British mountains, in an unlearned soil and time . . ." Buchanan (1506–82) was a Gaelic speaker from Killearn in Stirlingshire, and the same inferiority complex surfaces in a poem sent to one of the French reformers (*ibid.*, pp. 116–17): *Ad te carmina mitto, nec Latino / Nec Grajo sale tincta, sed Britannis / Nata in montibus horrida sub Arcto, / Nec cœlo neque seculo erudito.* "I send you poems, not steeped, I fear, in the virtuosity of Rome and Greece, but born in the British mountains, under shaggy Ursa Minor and the pole star, in an unlearned climate and time."

461 Lord Elibank was highly respected in his day for his erudition, his wit, and his support of literary causes, while writing almost nothing himself (see p. 442). In the *Tour* his letter to Boswell, which precedes the one to Johnson, is as follows: "August 21st, 1773. DEAR BOSWELL, I flew to Edinburgh the moment I heard of Mr Johnson's arrival; but so defective was my intelligence that I came too late. It is but justice to believe that I could never forgive myself, nor deserve to be forgiven by others, if I was to fail in any mark of respect to that very great genius. I hold him in the highest veneration; for that very reason I was resolved to take no share in the merit, perhaps guilt, of enticing him to honour this country with a visit. I could not persuade myself there was anything in Scotland worthy to have a summer of Samuel Johnson bestowed on it; but since he has done us that compliment, for heaven's sake inform me of your motions. I will attend them most religiously; and though I should regret to let Mr Johnson go a mile out of his way on my account, old as I am, I shall be glad to go five hundred miles to enjoy a day of his company. Have the charity to send a council-post with intelligence; the post does not suit us in the country. At any rate write to me. I will attend you in the North, when I shall know where to find you. I am, my dear Boswell, your sincerely obedient humble servant, ELIBANK." Boswell footnotes 'council-post': "A term in Scotland for a special messenger, such as was formerly sent with dispatches by the lords of the council."

462 "Aberdonian diploma for Samuel Johnson, LL.D. At Aberdeen, 23 August AD 1773, in the presence of the honourable gentlemen James Jopp, Esq., Provost; Adam Duff, William Young, George Marr, and William Forbes, Bailies; William Rainie, Dean of Guild; and John Nicoll, Treasurer of the said city. On this day Samuel Johnson, LL.D., a man of good birth and famous for his learning, was received and admitted into the number of burgesses and guild-brethren of the said city of Aberdeen. In token of the devoted love and affection and of the distinguished regard with which the said magistrates welcome him. Extracted by me, Alexander Carnegie."

Boswell made three errors of transcription, and these are here corrected in line with the text in the *Tour* (footnote to 23 August), which appears to have been set up from the original document rather than from the transcript.

463 Johnson's letter is from the *Tour*. Other than this and two short phrases, the only material in Boswell's account of 12 **September** (chapters 4 and 5) not taken from his journal is a clause referring to 'Highland Laddie' (note 467).

464 "... and that was all." By 'Sir James' Boswell means Sir Alexander Macdonald's much lamented elder brother (see pp. 130–32).

465 They met in Edinburgh on 10 November, see p. 442.

466 Altered in the *Tour* to 'a polite, agreeable woman'. The doctor's brother was Capt. Norman Macleod. The house was on the crest of the hill at Eyre, half a mile east of today's main road.

467 The remark about the song is taken from the *Tour*. The words are from 'Highland Laddie' as first published by Alan Ramsay in *The Tea-Table Miscellany* (1724, p. 169): "The Lawland Lads think they are fine, / But O they'r vain and idly gaudy! / How much unlike that gracefu' Mein, / And manly Looks of my Highland Laddie!" No trace survives of the eighteenth-century Kingsburgh House.

468 Kingsburgh and his family emigrated to North Carolina in August 1774. He and his five sons joined the British Army when the War of Independence broke out. Kingsburgh was taken prisoner. Flora returned to Scotland, and her husband followed her on his release in 1783. Flora died in 1790, aged 67, and Allan in 1792, aged 66.

469 This remark in the journal caused Boswell much agony, and he wrote to George III on 6 June 1785 seeking his permission to use the style 'Prince Charles'. Receiving no answer, on 15 June he accosted the king at his levee. After a show of displeasure the king, 'with a benignant smile equal to that of any of Correggio's angels', said, "I think and I feel as you do." Boswell then asked whether the style should be 'Prince Charles', and when the king hesitated, Boswell suggested, "Or shall it be 'the grandson of King James the Second'?" The king agreed, adding that he thought the matter of no consequence. Boswell volunteered the information that he was cousin in the seventh degree to Prince Charles (which also implied cousinship to George III), then withdrew in an ecstasy of delight (Lustig and Pottle, *The Applause of the Jury*, pp. 307–12). In the *Tour* the entry for 13 September therefore begins: "The room where we lay was a celebrated one. Dr Johnson's bed was the very bed in which the grandson of the unfortunate King James the Second lay, on one of the nights after the failure of his rash attempt in 1745–6, while he was eluding the pursuit of the emissaries of government, which had offered thirty thousand pounds as a reward for apprehending him." Boswell adds a footnote: "I do not call him *the Prince of Wales*, or *the Prince*, because I am quite satisfied that the right which the House of Stuart had to the throne is extinguished. I do not call him the *Pretender*, because it appears to me as an insult to one who is still alive, and, I suppose, thinks very differently. It may be a parliamentary expression; but it is not

a gentlemanly expression. I *know*, and I exult in having it in my power to tell, that *the only person* in the world who is intitled to be offended at this delicacy, thinks and feels as I do; and has liberality of mind and generosity of sentiment enough to approve of my tenderness for what even *has been* Blood Royal. That he is *a prince* by *courtesy*, cannot be denied; because his mother was the daughter of Sobiesky, king of Poland. I shall, therefore, *on that account alone*, distinguish him by the name of *Prince Charles Edward*."

470 Boswell's note (*Tour*): "This, perhaps, was said in allusion to some lines ascribed to Pope, on his lying, at John Duke of Argyll's, at Adderbury, in the same bed in which Wilmot, Earl of Rochester, had slept. 'With no poetic ardour fir'd, / I press the bed where Wilmot lay; / That here he lov'd, or here expir'd, / Begets no numbers, grave or gay.'" John Wilmot (1648–80), 2nd earl of Rochester, a favourite of Charles II, was a poet of genius and a notorious libertine.

471 The parliamentarian John Wilkes (1727–97), latterly Lord Mayor of London, was a champion of popular causes, democratic rights and personal freedoms. The king's architect, Sir William Chambers (1726–96), had just been brilliantly satirised by the poet and garden amateur William Mason (aided and abetted by Horace Walpole) in an anonymous *Heroick Epistle to Sir William Chambers* which went through ten editions in 1773 alone. On the surface the *Epistle* is a parody of Chambers's garden theories; underneath it is a political squib levelled at the Tory establishment.

472 Boswell's note (*Tour*): "With virtue weigh'd, what worthless trash is gold!"

473 Boswell's note (*Tour*, second and subsequent editions): "Since the first edition of this book, an ingenious friend has observed to me, that Dr Johnson had probably been thinking on the reward which was offered by government for the apprehension of the grandson of King James II, and that he meant by these words to express his admiration of the Highlanders, whose fidelity and attachment had resisted the golden temptation that had been held out to them."

474 'Lewis' is in error for 'Uist'. Both are parts of what was then commonly called 'the Long Island'.

475 The officer was Alexander son of Donald MacLeod of Balmeanach. Prince Charles was 'upon a hill near the house' (foot of p. 216), or, according to other accounts, down in the shore. 'Mugstot' (*Tour*) or 'Monkstadt' (journal) was the principal residence of the Macdonalds of Sleat. It is Norse *munkustaðr* 'monk's town'; the spellings *Mugstot*, *Mugasad*, *Mogstat*, *Mogastad* reflect Gaelic pronunciation.

476 Paton, *Lyon in Mourning*, vol. 1, pp. 296–306.

477 The following section ('From what she told us' to 'or at least very awful', p. 226) is from the *Tour*. This is the longest of several substantial passages in the account of 13 September which have been brought in from the *Tour*, mostly because they do not appear in the journal. All of these interpolations are indicated in endnotes.

478 This is Sir Alexander (1711–46), 7th baronet of Sleat, father of Sir Alexander (1744–95), 9th baronet, who is such a prominent figure in this book. The

7th baronet's wife, the much-loved Lady Margaret, was born Margaret Montgomerie, a daughter of the earl of Eglinton. She outlived her husband by fifty-three years, dying in 1799.

479 See p. 138.

480 The Rev. Robert Forbes. He and his friends used them as drinking vessels on special occasions; this was reported back to the Prince, who 'heartily enjoyed the idea' (Paton, *Lyon in Mourning*, vol. 1, p. xx). Stuck to the inside back cover of NLS Adv. MS 32.6.20 (vol. 5 of the 'Lyon') are two little lumps of leather. Underneath is the note: "The above are pieces of one of the Lugs of those identical Brogs, which the Prince wore, when disguised in the Female Dress under the Name of Bettie Burk, as Handmaid to Miss Flora MacDonald. See this Vol: pag: 1057. *Robert Forbes, A: M:*"

481 Capt. Donald Roy (*Domhnall Ruadh*), a brother of Hugh MacDonald of Baleshare in North Uist, was one of the few Sleat MacDonalds to join the Prince's army. He got a bullet through his foot at Culloden, and was acting at this time as Charles's principal agent among the Sleat MacDonalds. He was a Latin poet, taught by an uncle of the Rev. John MacPherson.

482 The 'fresh-water lake' was Loch Fada, one of the Storr Lochs north of Portree.

483 Boswell's note (*Tour*): "This old Scottish *member of parliament*, I am informed, is still living (1785)."

484 This refers to Lord George Murray (*c.* 1700–60), the Prince's lieutenant-general. The passage from 'He blamed' to 'ill founded' is from the proofs, where it was emended to: "He threw out some reflections on the conduct of the disastrous affair at Culloden, saying however that perhaps it was rash in him to do so. I am now convinced that his suspicions were groundless." In the margin Boswell wrote: "This paragraph I settled with General Murray, son of Lord George."

485 This is Andrew Lumisden (1720–1801), Jacobite politician and antiquary. The account (NLS MS 279) is published in Blaikie, *Origins of the 'Forty-Five*, pp. 403–19, with a biography of Lumisden at pp. lxxxiv–lxxxviii.

486 They landed not in Strath (the MacKinnon territory) but at the Rock of Scorrybreck in Portree Harbour. The Prince's command of Gaelic is also mentioned at p. 151. Linguistic competence is a relative concept, however: according to a later John Mackenzie (MacilleDhuibh, 'Cunnart', p. 81), *Cha robh aig a mhòrachd rìoghail ach droch Ghàelig.* "His royal highness had very poor Gaelic."

487 Angus of Scothouse (Scotus) and Coll of Barrisdale (both in Knoydart) were Glengarry MacDonalds. The latter was known as *Colla nan Cleas* ('Coll of the Tricks'), and his loyalty was notoriously suspect. Malcolm's brother-in-law was Capt. John MacKinnon (*c.* 1714–62) of Elgol.

488 Lewie Caw was the son of a surgeon in Crieff. He had come out for the Prince and was known to be skulking with his relations in Skye. The handkerchief tied around the head (p. 223) appears to have been regarded as a sign of sickness (MacilleDhuibh, 'Cunnart', p. 95).

489 Paton, *Lyon in Mourning*, vol. 1, p. 142: "Sir, I thank God I am in good

health, and have got off as design'd. Remember me to all friends, and thank them for the trouble they have been at. I am, Sir, Your humble servant, JAMES THOMSON. / Elliguil, July 4th, 1746."

490 "Let private citizens who believe themselves unfortunate consider this prince and his ancestors."

491 From Voltaire's *Siècle de Louis XIV*, chapter 15. A number of minor errors crept into Boswell's transcript, and these I have corrected. I would translate: "There is no example in history of a house so consistently unfortunate. The first of the kings of Scotland, his forefathers, who bore the name of *James*, after being eighteen years a prisoner in England, was assassinated, with his wife, at the hands of his subjects. *James* II, his son, was killed at the age of twenty-nine fighting the English. *James* III, imprisoned by his people, was then killed by rebels in a battle. *James* IV died in a combat which he lost. *Mary Stuart*, his granddaughter, driven from her throne, a fugitive in England, after languishing in prison for eighteen years, saw herself condemned to death by English judges, and was decapitated. *Charles* I, Mary's grandson, king of Scotland and England, sold by the Scots, and condemned to death by the English, died on a scaffold in the public square. *James*, his son, seventh of the name, and second in England, was driven from his three kingdoms; and to add insult to injury, his son was opposed even in the matter of his birth. This son's attempts to regain the throne of his fathers led only to the death of his friends at the hands of executioners; and we have seen Prince *Charles Edward*, reuniting in vain the virtues of his fathers and the courage of King John Sobieski, his maternal ancestor, performing exploits and suffering misfortunes of a most incredible nature. If anything gives support to those who believe in a fate which nothing can avoid, it is this unending series of misfortunes which has dogged the house of *Stuart* for more than three hundred years."

492 See note 352.

493 This paragraph is from the *Tour*, the next from the journal.

494 The following section ('The *abstract* point of *right*' to 'suspicious Whigs and discontented Republicans', p. 229) is taken from the *Tour*.

495 Boswell's note (*Tour*): "*Commentaries on the Laws of England*, Book I, chap. 3." This work by Sir William Blackstone (1723–80) was the first in which a comprehensive picture was painted of the law and constitution of England as a single organic structure.

496 Boswell's note (*Tour*, aimed at Hume): "Book VI, chap. 3. Since I have quoted Mr Archdeacon Paley upon one subject, I cannot but transcribe, from his excellent work, a distinguished passage in support of the Christian Revelation. After showing, in decent but strong terms, the unfairness of the *indirect* atttempts of modern infidels to unsettle and perplex religious principles, and particularly the irony, banter, and sneer, of one whom he politely calls 'an eloquent historian', the archdeacon thus expresses himself: 'Seriousness is not constraint of thought; nor levity, freedom. Every mind which wishes the advancement of truth and knowledge, in the most important of all human researches, must abhor this licentiousness, as

violating no less the laws of reasoning than the rights of decency. There is but one description of men to whose principles it ought to be tolerable. I mean that class of reasoners who can see *little* in christianity even supposing it to be true. To such adversaries we address this reflection. Had *Jesus Christ* delivered no other declaration than the following, "The hour is coming in the which all that are in the graves shall hear his voice, and shall come forth – they that have done well unto the resurrection of life, and they that have done evil unto the resurrection of damnation," he had pronounced a message of inestimable importance, and well worthy of that splendid apparatus of prophecy and miracles with which his mission was introduced and attested – a message in which the wisest of mankind would rejoice to find an answer to their doubts, and rest to their inquiries. It is idle to say that a future state had been discovered already. It had been discovered as the Copernican System was; it was one guess amongst many. He alone discovers who *proves*; and no man can prove this point but the teacher who testifies by miracles that his doctrine comes from GOD' (Book V, chap. 9). If infidelity be disingenuously dispersed in every shape that is likely to allure, surprise, or beguile the imagination – in a fable, a tale, a novel, a poem, in books of travels, of philosophy, of natural history, as Mr Paley has well observed – I hope it is fair in me thus to meet such poison with an unexpected antidote, which I cannot doubt will be found powerful." William Paley (1743–1805) was one of the principal exponents of theological utilitarianism.

497 Ovid, *Ars Amatoria*, book 3, lines 121–22: "I congratulate myself on not being born till now."

498 Boswell's note (*Tour*): "*Agis*, a tragedy, by John Home."

499 This paragraph is from the journal, the next from the *Tour*. In the *Tour* the present paragraph becomes: "The topic of emigration being again introduced, Dr Johnson said, that 'a rapacious chief would make a wilderness of his estate'."

500 See note 278. A Highland kindred was led by a tutor (Gaelic *taoitear*) during its chief's minority; this reference is to William MacDonald of Aird (d. 1730), who acted as tutor during the minority of Sir Alexander Macdonald of Sleat, 1720–30. The part of this paragraph as far as 'eat with their fingers' is taken from the *Tour*, as it is poorly expressed in the journal.

501 Pottle and Bennett (*Journal*, p. 165) helpfully quote an advertisement in the *London Chronicle*, 22 September 1761: "Portable soup, or solid broth, made from beef, veal, mutton, and chicken, is found exceedingly useful on various occasions; and has particularly recommended itself to gentlemen on journeys and at sea."

502 This book was referred to at p. 136 as '*Dissertations on the Ancient Caledonians*, etc.' Its full title is *Critical Dissertations on the Origin, Antiquities, Language, Government, Manners, and Religion, of the Ancient Caledonians, their Posterity the Picts, and the British and Irish Scots*.

503 Horses had been sent round by land to wait for them a mile beyond Greshornish (p. 229). In the *Tour* this sentence becomes: "As soon as we reached the shore, we took leave of Kingsburgh, and mounted our horses."

504 I have supplied the number of miles, as Boswell left it blank. The last sentence here is not in the journal and is taken from the *Tour*.

505 The second half of this sentence, from 'so that visitors', is taken from the *Tour*, as are two short phrases in the next paragraph but one.

506 The 'young preacher', Norman MacLeod (1745–1824), son of Donald MacLeod (1700–81), tacksman of Swordale on Loch Dunvegan, founded the best-known clerical dynasty in the Highlands. One of the young chief's former tutors, he was licensed to preach, but was then serving as parish schoolmaster of Duirinish. In 1775 he became minister of Morvern (Argyll). His younger son John (1801–82) succeeded him as minister of that parish. His elder son Norman (1783–1862), minister of Campsie, founded modern Gaelic prose literature. This younger Norman's great-grandson George (Lord MacLeod of Fuinary, 1895–1991) founded the 'Iona Community'.

507 The blank is for listing more portraits. Lady Macleod's brother, Alexander, had died aged eighteen in 1759, and was succeeded as laird of Brodie by his second cousin James (1744–1824), son of Joseph Brodie of Spynie. This led to the 'perplexed claims' mentioned at p. 233.

508 Lady Macleod bore five daughters, Maria (d. 1809), Ann ('Nannie', d. 1826), Alexandra (d. 1810), Isabella ('Bell', d. 1788), and Elizabeth (who died in infancy or childhood). For Alexandra see note 343.

509 Sir Roderick (*Ruairi Mór*, d. 1626), 15th of Dunvegan, much praised by poets, was considered the epitome of an old-style Highland chief.

510 Boswell changed his mind about Ruairi Mór in the *Tour*: "He was called Rorie *More*, that is, great Rorie, not from his size, but from his spirit."

511 This will be James Dalrymple (1619–95), 1st Viscount Stair, author of *Institutions of the Law of Scotland* (1681), an important contribution to the systematisation of Scots Law. His son Sir John, later 1st earl of Stair, signed the order for the massacre of Glencoe in 1692. The Bowleses were a dynasty of London printsellers, principally Thomas Bowles (?1689/90–1767).

512 The words 'without his knowledge' are from the *Tour*; apart from this and one other brief phrase, the account of **14 September** is from the journal. In the *Tour* 'if mankind know it' becomes 'being once divulged'.

513 The French political philosopher Charles Louis de Secondat de Montesquieu (1689–1755) argued, like Johnson, that beneficent liberal monarchy was the ideal form of government.

514 Boswell's note (*Tour*): "What my friend treated as so wild a supposition, has actually happened in the Western Islands of Scotland, if we may believe Martin, who tells it of the islands of Coll and Tyr-yi, and says that it is proved by the parish registers." Martin's words are these (*Description*, p. 165): "The isle of Coll produces more boys than girls; as if nature intended both these isles for mutual alliances, without being at the trouble of going to the adjacent isles or continent to be matched. The parish book, in which the number of the baptised is to be seen, confirms this observation."

515 Boswell's note (*Tour*): "This was a general reflection against Dr Cadogan, when his very popular book was published. It was said, that whatever precepts he might give to others, he himself indulged freely in the bottle.

But I have since had the pleasure of becoming acquainted with him, and, if his own testimony may be believed (and I have never heard it impeached), his course of life has been conformable to his doctrine."

516 In the *Tour* this becomes: "I expressed some surprize at Cadogan's recommending good humour, as if it were quite in our own power to attain it."

517 See p. 253. The relics on show at Dunvegan today are not quite as described here. The horn remains, the bow and part of the sword have disappeared, while Boswell somehow fails to mention Ruairi Mór's four-sided cup and the fairy flag (Pennant, *Tour 1772*, pp. 295–97; Pottle, *Journal*, p. 424; Black, *Gaelic Otherworld*, pp. 3, 293–95, 316).

518 Sir George Mackenzie of Rosehaugh (1636–91) was a writer on legal and historical topics. In 1682 he founded the Advocates' Library, the bulk of whose collections became the National Library of Scotland in 1925.

519 Corrected in the *Tour* to *penes illum gloria, penes hunc palma* ('one gets the glory, another the palm'). What Boswell calls his 'Account of the Kirk of Scotland' is his 'Sketch of the Constitution of the Church of Scotland', *The London Magazine*, April and May 1772 (Wimsatt and Pottle, *Boswell for the Defence*, p. 127).

520 Boswell footnotes these 'He often indulged himself in every species of pleasantry and wit' and 'Like the hawk, having soared with a lofty flight to a height which the eye could not reach, he was wont to swoop upon his quarry with wonderful rapidity'. On Burke's sense of humour (or lack of it) see pp. 28–29 and note 64.

521 The second half of this paragraph is from the *Tour*. Apart from this and five or six short phrases, Boswell's account of **15 September** is from his journal.

522 According to Harman (*An Isle called Hirte*, pp. 248–49), he was second son of Alexander MacLeod, a Skyeman educated at King's College, Aberdeen, who was minister or catechist in St Kilda from 1743 and was dead by 1758. Alexander MacLeod married Barbara, daughter of John MacPherson, tacksman of Orbost, and they had four children: Donald (d. 1813), tacksman of Achnagoyle, Colbost and St Kilda, our Donald, Mary, and Margaret. See also note 872.

523 It caused a great deal of trouble, see pp. 256, 267, 275, 284, 291. The paragraph eventually appears in the *Tour* at 24 September, with this sentence diplomatically altered to show that the matter was resolved: "We sent a bill for thirty pounds, drawn on Sir William Forbes and Co. to Lochbracadale, but our messenger found it very difficult to procure cash for it; at length, however, he got us value from the master of a vessel which was to carry away some emigrants."

524 For the sake of clarity, two or three words have been drafted into this sentence from the *Tour*. Apart from this and one short phrase towards the end, Boswell's account of **16 September** is from his journal.

525 Or 'gay animal' – the manuscript is unclear.

526 See p. 61. This unpleasant exchange went through two more drafts before

it reached print. First Boswell heavily inked over everything from 'Mr Macqueen' to 'stand a rub better', then he explained: "He . . . retaliated with such a keen sarcastic wit that I found myself, even at the distance of some years, so hurt by his raillery (of which I had preserved a minute in my journal) that though I can bear such attacks as well as most men, I could not be at ease till I had expunged every trace of this severe retort." Finally he rewrote this for the *Tour*: "To hear the grave Dr Samuel Johnson, 'that majestic teacher of moral and religious wisdom', while sitting solemn in an arm-chair in the Isle of Skye, talk, *ex cathedra*, of his keeping a seraglio, and acknowledge that the supposition had *often* been in his thoughts, struck me so forcibly with ludicrous contrast, that I could not but laugh immoderately. He was too proud to submit, even for a moment, to be the object of ridicule, and instantly retaliated with such keen sarcastic wit, and such a variety of degrading images, of every one of which I was the object, that, though I can bear such attacks as well as most men, I yet found myself so much the sport of all the company, that I would gladly expunge from my mind every trace of this severe retort."

527 "No harm is done to one who consents". Philip I, landgrave of Hesse (1504–67), took a second wife openly in marriage, and without being given the full facts of the case, Luther sanctioned it. As H. G. Haile has remarked (*Luther*, p. 276), 'a thousand times more apologies have been made by Lutheran writers for this slip than for all Luther's horrible attacks on Jewry'.

528 Anaitis, a Persian goddess, is mentioned by Strabo, Pausanias and the elder Pliny, among others (see p. 243). MacQueen appears to have developed his views gradually since 1764, when he wrote (Mackenzie, *Report*, Appendix, p. 35): "You will perhaps be surprised to hear, that the goddess of Victory, Andate (the Andraste of Dio), who had a temple at Camalodunum, had a particular veneration paid her in this part of the world. There are no less than the remains of four places of worship for her in this island: the most considerable of them lies within half a mile of the castle of Dunvegan (Anaid in Buy)." By 'Buy' he means Bay, and he cites the distance in Skye miles. Eight years later he discussed the site with Pennant, who reported (*Tour 1772*, pp. 298–99): "My learned friend supposes it to have been designed for the worship of the Earth, Bendis or Diana, which, according to Hesychius, was supposed to be the same. Plutarch gives the same goddess the title of *Anait*, the name of this place of worship; and Pliny speaks of a country in Armenia, called Anaitica, from Anaitis, a goddess in great repute there . . . "

529 In the *Tour* 'a kind of arms to him' becomes 'a kind of a defensive weapon'; *lown* or *loon* ('boy') is Scots, not Gaelic.

530 From the dimensions given by Boswell for the temple, Pottle and Bennett calculated (*Journal*, p. 179) that his cane was about thirty-nine inches long.

531 Reproduced in Pottle and Bennett, *Journal*, facing p. 180.

532 Pope, *Dunciad*, book 4, lines 249–52: "For thee we dim the eyes, and stuff the head / With all such reading as was never read: / For thee explain a thing till all men doubt it, / And write about it, Goddess, and about it."

In 1784 MacQueen read a paper to the Society of Antiquaries of Scotland entitled 'An Inquiry into the Nature of the Worship of Anaitis or Anait, whose Temples are numerous in the Isle of Skye, and vicinity' (*Archaeologia Scotica*, vol. 3, 1831, Appendix, p. 156); regrettably it was not printed, but no doubt it was on similar lines to the notes on the subject reproduced in MacLeod, 'Observations . . . by Rev. Donald MacQueen', pp. 385–86.

533   *Aunnit* becomes *Ainnit* in the *Tour*. The correct Gaelic spelling is *annaid*. MacQueen must have explained it from *abhainn* 'river' and *àite* 'place'. Vendryes, in his *Lexique*, defines its Old Irish etymon *andóit* as *église, plus anciennement 'partie d'église contenant des reliques'* ('church, more anciently part of a church containing relics') and traces it to a Brittonic variant of Low Latin *antitās* 'ancient foundation'. Other references to recent scholarship on the subject are given in Black, *Gaelic Otherworld*, p. 308. The *annaid* which Boswell visited is described in the *Ninth Report* of RCAHMCS, pp. 149–50. It is a high fortress-like enclosure, 200 feet long and 165 feet across the base, in the sharp angle formed by the confluence of Bay River and a tributary on its left bank about a mile from its mouth. It contains the ruins of what appear to be a rectangular building, an oblong one (perhaps a church), two smaller structures, four domed cells and two hut circles; outside the gateway are traces of another secondary building and three oval cells.

534   This is a reference to Edmund Waller's 'To a Lady Singing a Song of his Composing' – "That eagle's fate and mine are one, / Which, on the shaft that made him die, / Espied a feather of his own, / Wherewith he wont to soar so high."

535   The portion of this sentence from 'which they' to 'contradiction' is the longest of four items in the account of **17 September** taken from the *Tour*. The rest is from the journal. Judging from his own remarks on the Highland economy (pp. 191–94) Johnson had reached conclusions similar to Pennant's (*Tour 1769*, p. 208): "The rage of raising rents has reached this distant country: in *England* there may be reason for it, (in a certain degree) where the value of lands is increased by accession of commerce, and by the rise of provisions: but here (contrary to all policy) the great men begin at the wrong end, with squeezing the bag, before they have helped the poor tenant to fill it, by the introduction of manufactures."

536   The Rev. Roderick MacLeod, minister of Bracadale since 1768, was married to the Rev. Donald MacQueen's daughter Janet.

537   This can only be a reference to the two ruined medieval churches on Sgeabost Island (*Eilean Chaluim Chille*) in the River Snizort. Three or four grave-slabs have been found on the site, bearing the figures of knights carved in relief (RCAHMCS, *Ninth Report*, p. 192).

538   Two short phrases in this paragraph are from the *Tour*; otherwise Boswell's account of **18 September** is from his journal. It is generally accepted that 'penguin' is Welsh, Cornish or Breton. In the meaning 'white top' (*pen gwyn*), it was applied to small flat guano-covered islands in the Newfoundland seas which served as breeding-grounds for the flightless great auk. It then came to be applied to the great auk itself, and was duly transferred to the very

similar bird now known as the penguin. Neither of these birds has, or had, a white head (MacilleDhuibh, 'Why are Penguins so Called?').

539 In the *Tour* this becomes: "The laird insists that this is the proper name." He could only do so in defiance of basic facts. In Gaelic it is *Eilean nam Muc* ('the Isle of the Pigs'). It is not so called from its form but from some reputation attaching to it, if only in seamen's lore. George Buchanan called it *Insula Porcorum* in the geographical description of Scotland which is prefaced to his *Rerum Scoticarum Historia*.

540 The clause 'and the spaniel fool often turns mule at last' is from the *Tour*. Otherwise Boswell's account of 19 September is from his journal.

541 The *Tour* adds: "In justice to the sex, I think it but candid to acknowledge, that, in a subsequent conversation, he told me that he was serious in what he had said."

542 Boswell's note (*Tour*): "As I have faithfully recorded so many minute particulars, I hope I shall be pardoned for inserting so flattering an encomium on what is now offered to the public."

543 *The Causes of the Decay of Christian Piety* (1667) is believed to have been written by Dr Richard Allestree (1619–81).

544 Boswell's note (*Tour*): "The true story of this lady, which happened in this century, is as frightfully romantic as if it had been the fiction of a gloomy fancy. She was the wife of one of the Lords of Session in Scotland, a man of the very first blood of his country. For some mysterious reasons, which have never been discovered, she was seized and carried off in the dark, she knew not by whom, and by nightly journeys was conveyed to the Highland shores, from whence she was transported by sea to the remote rock of St Kilda, where she remained, amongst its few wild inhabitants, a forlorn prisoner, but had a constant supply of provisions, and a woman to wait on her. No inquiry was made after her, till she at last found means to convey a letter to a confidential friend, by the daughter of a Catechist, who concealed it in a clue of yarn. Information being thus obtained at Edinburgh, a ship was sent to bring her off; but intelligence of this being received, she was conveyed to MacLeod's island of Herries, where she died.

"In *Carstares's State Papers*, we find an authentic narrative of Connor, a catholic priest, who turned protestant, being seized by some of Lord Seaforth's people, and detained prisoner in the island of Herries several years; he was fed with bread and water, and lodged in a house where he was exposed to the rains and cold. Sir James Ogilvy writes (June 18, 1667 [1697]) that the Lord Chancellor, the Lord Advocate, and himself, were to meet next day, to take effectual methods to have this redressed. Connor was then still detained (p. 310). This shews what private oppression might in the last century be practised in the Hebrides.

"In the same collection, the Earl of Argyll gives a picturesque account of an embassy from *the great Macneil of Barra*, as that insular Chief used to be denominated. 'I received a letter yesterday from Macneil of Barra, who lives very far off, sent by a gentleman in all formality, offering his service, which had made you laugh to see his entry. His style of his letter runs as if he were of another kingdom' (p. 643)."

The extraordinary story of Lady Grange is told by Ramsay (*Scotland and Scotsmen*, vol. 1, p. 84), Grant (*MacLeods*, pp. 401–04), Swire (*Skye*, pp. 100–02), in the *ODNB*, and of course in books on St Kilda.

545 These thought-provoking comments offer a starting-point for a discussion of St Kildan verse. Harman lists thirty-six poems from there, of which twenty-one are elegies, seven are love-songs and three are religious (*An Isle called Hirte*, p. 238). Many anthologies of Gaelic verse include items from St Kilda, but it deserves to be asked whether they are chosen on merit or for curiosity value.

546 Boswell's note (*Tour*): "I doubt the justice of my fellow-traveller's remark concerning the French literati, many of whom, I am told, have considerable merit in conversation, as well as in their writings. That of Monsieur de Buffon, in particular, I am well assured is highly instructive and entertaining." Johnson did in fact go to Paris, with the Thrales, in 1775.

547 I take 'purchase' from the *Tour*. In the journal it is 'which anybody might have'. Otherwise the account of 20 September is taken entirely from the journal.

548 See pp. 237, 265. Born in 1709, Johnson was 'on the waggon' from about 1736 to 1757 and again from 1765 until his death in 1784 (Hill and Powell, *Life*, vol. 1, pp. 103–05).

549 Boswell altered 'Valerius Maximus' to 'Aulus Gellius' in the third edition of the *Tour*, footnoting it: "Aul. Gellius, Lib. v. c. xiv." It is the story of Androcles or Androclus, told by Aulus Gellius (*c.* AD 123–169) in the *Noctes Atticae* ('Attic Nights'), book 5, chapter 14.

550 See p. 133. Johnson had been thinking of Bacon's essay 'Of Empire' (Spedding, *Works*, vol. 6, part 2, p. 420): "The difficulties in princes' business are many and great; but the greatest difficulty is often in their own mind . . . For it is the solecism of power, to think to command the end, and yet not to endure the mean."

551 Leod (*Ljotr*), son of Olav the Black, king of Man, is believed to have lived in the thirteenth century and to have married a daughter of MacRaild, by whom he obtained Duirinish, Minginish, Bracadale, Lyndale and part of Trotternish. MacRaild, Gaelic *mac Ràilt*, is 'the son of Harold'. Harold may have been a son of Rollo (*Hrolf*), first duke of Normandy (Grant, *MacLeods*, pp. 24–27). '*Felix* both *bella gerere* et *nubere*' ('fortunate both in waging war and marriage') is adapted from a celebrated epigram on the policy of Austria: "Let others wage wars; do thou, O fortunate Austria, give thyself in marriage (*felix Austria nube*). For the kingdoms which Mars gives to others, Venus gives to thee." Albrecht Wittenberg, Boswell's German translator, drew attention to an error here (*Tagebuch*, p. 305): *Herr Boswell ist in der Anwendung des* felix Austria nube *nicht glücklich;* nubere *kann nur von Personen weiblichen Geschlechte gesagt werden, und also nicht vom Leod.* "Mr Boswell is unfortunate in his application of *felix Austria nube* – *nubere* may only be said of persons of the female sex, and therefore not of Leod." The words 'surpassed the house of Austria; for he' are the shortest of half-a-dozen passages from the *Tour* (two phrases, four separate sentences and two

memorial inscriptions) in the account of **21 September**. All the rest is from the journal.

552 *Agis*, act 4: "This facile temper of the beauteous sex / Great Agamemnon, brave Pelides, proved: / They sack'd the cities, and they slew the sires, / The brothers, and the lovers of the fair, / Who weep'd awhile, then wiped their wat'ry eyes, / And lost their sorrows in the hero's arms."

553 "John Macleod of Dunvegan, chief of his tribe, and ruler of Duirinish, Harris, Vaternish, etc.: married to Lady Florence Macdonald, in the year 1686 he repaired this tower of Dunvegan (by far the oldest dwelling of his ancestors), which for a long time had been in ruins deep within. 'Let him, whom it pleases to repair the old dwellings of our ancestors, / Avoid all crime and worship justice. / Courage changes little dwellings into lofty towers / And, wrongly, proud buildings into humble abodes.'" I take the inscription from the *Tour*.

554 The word 'parapet' was suggested by Pottle and Bennett (Boswell having left a blank), but Pottle later preferred 'balustrade' (*Journal*, pp. 195, 472). The false cannon serve as gargoyles.

555 See note 530.

556 See p. 235. I omit the word 'thus', Boswell's crude sketch, and the sentence: "This scratch will serve to help out the idea." The horn is described by MacLeod, 'Notes on the Relics'.

557 The bow has now disappeared, and so has part of the sword. The loss of the bow is particularly unfortunate, as Highland bows are described in great detail in seventeenth-century Gaelic verse, but none have survived. For Rorie More see p. 232.

558 The four blanks in this paragraph could perhaps be filled by 'south-east side', 'south', 'east', and 'Garbh-Eilean'.

559 See note 508.

560 Simon, Lord Lovat, was beheaded on Tower Hill on 9 April 1747 for the part he had played in the '45. Boswell says of the inscription at this point in the journal: "I took a copy of it, which is to be found on the last page of this volume." It is not in the surviving journal, but appears in the *Tour*, and I take it from there. The pyramid is still in the churchyard, but about 1850 the white marble tablet containing the inscription fell out and broke into fragments (Mackenzie, *History of the Macleods*, p. 120; Grant, *MacLeods*, p. 334).

561 Boswell gives them in the *Life* at 1747: "I have heard him repeat with great energy the following verses, which appeared in the Gentleman's Magazine for April this year; but I have no authority to say they were his own. Indeed one of the best critics of our age suggests to me, that 'the word *indifferently* being used in the sense of *without concern*, and being also very unpoetical, renders it improbable that they should have been his composition'. '*On Lord* LOVAT'*s Execution*. / Pity'd by *gentle minds* KILMARNOCK died; / The *brave*, BALMERINO, were on thy side; / RADCLIFFE, unhappy in his crimes of youth, / Steady in what he still mistook for truth, / Beheld his death so decently unmov'd, / The *soft* lamented, and the *brave* approv'd. / But LOVAT'S fate

indifferently we view, / True to no *King*, to no *religion* true: / No *fair* forgets the *ruin* he has done; / No *child* laments the *tyrant* of his *son*; / No *tory* pities, thinking what he was; / No *whig* compassions, *for he left the cause*; / The *brave* regret not, for he was not brave; / The *honest* mourn not, knowing him a knave!'"

562 I omit Boswell's sketch and the sentence which precedes it: "It is somewhat in this form."

563 See pp. 180, 183. The word 'thills' was suggested by Pottle and Bennett (*Journal*, p. 198), as Boswell left a blank. It could equally be 'trams'. I omit Boswell's sketch and the sentence which precedes it: "It is hardly worth while to draw it, but I shall scratch a little." With regard to Macleod's farm (next paragraph), it was 'about five miles from the old castle' (p. 244), so it must have been at Vatten or Feorlig on the Harlosh peninsula (Pottle, *Journal*, p. 472).

564 Capt. Constantine Phipps, RN, set out in April 1773 in search of a northern passage to India. There was much speculation in the newspapers about his progress. Finding the ice north of Spitzbergen impenetrable, he turned back; he passed Shetland on 7 September, but storms delayed his return to port until 24 September. This was of course the same weather that beset Johnson and Boswell.

565 By the *Scots Acts* Boswell means the volumes containing the last acts of the Scottish Parliament, principally *The Laws and Acts of Parliament, of our . . . Sovereign, Anne* (1702–07). Bankton's *Institutions* is *An Institute of the Laws of Scotland in Civil Rights* (1751–53), by Andrew Macdouall, Lord Bankton (1685–1760), of whom Ramsay paints a striking portrait in *Scotland and Scotsmen*, vol. 1, pp. 127–31.

566 For this souterrain see pp. 174–75, and for the 'crooked spade' see p. 179.

567 I omit Boswell's sketch and the words 'somewhat thus' which introduce it. The 'tower, or dun' is *an Dùn Beag*, see pp. 173–74.

568 Thus expanded in the *Tour*: "They make part of a great range for deer, which, though entirely devoid of trees, is in these countries called a forest."

569 It is odd to claim that a work which stands at the fountain-head of Highland ethnography is 'erroneous' simply because subsequent writers did not follow its lead. In Gaelic the name is *an Cuiltheann*.

570 *Aeneid*, book 6, lines 10–12: *At pius Aeneas arces quibus altus Apollo / Praesidet horrendaeque procul secreta Sibyllae, / Antrum immane, petit.* "But good Aeneas goes to the hill-top where throned Apollo sits aloft, and to a vast cavern, the far lone haunt of the dread Sybil."

571 MacQueen's 'hill of strife' may represent *Cnoc na h-Èirig*, more literally 'the Hill of Compensation', the name of a mound by the castle of Duntulm (Forbes, *Place-Names of Skye*, p. 119).

572 See p. 137. The geography of this excursion is still in doubt, and demands detailed investigation on the ground. According to the 'maximalist' theory, they took boat at the *Port Beag*, a few hundred yards south of Ullinish House; sailing west, they passed between Ullinish Point and Oronsay ('an island . . . to which there is access by land when the sea is out'), where they landed

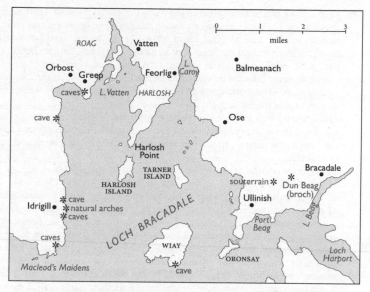

briefly. Then they sailed four miles north along the shore of Loch Bracadale to their *antrum immane*, the Piper's Cave or *Uamh an Òir* at Harlosh Point, of which Swire says (*Skye*, p. 167): "It connects with the Golden Cave at Dhubeag and Mac Coitir's Cave near Portree, with Fairyland, and, some say, with hell itself." This is a good summary of the 'cave of gold' legend, for which see note 827; the piper who never returned was a MacCrimmon. Disconcertingly, Nicolson claims that it was the great sea cave on Harlosh *Island* that Johnson and Boswell visited (*Handbook*, p. 40). A mile across Loch Vatten brought them to 'another large cave, parallel with the sea and open at both ends', the archway cave at Greep (Swire, *Skye*, p. 167). Here they were at Roag, the patrimony of Sweyn MacSweyn (pp. 294, 316–17). Continuing their anticlockwise circuit of Loch Bracadale, they viewed 'the great Archway Cave of Idrigall with its fine natural arches, where the tragic Lady Grange was once imprisoned' (Swire, *Skye*, p. 148). It is, in Boswell's words, 'nearer Ullinish'. A mile's sail southwards brought them within sight of Macleod's Maidens (see p. 267), one of which may have been the 'piece of rock standing by itself like the front wall of an old castle'; then, in the failing light, they headed eastwards for home, passing to the south of Wiay and Oronsay. This was a full thirteen-mile circuit of Loch Bracadale; unfortunately Johnson states that 'we never left the shore' (p. 176). There is therefore a 'minimalist' theory, according to which everything here described is to be found in Oronsay; there is also a 'compromise' one which has them landing on Wiay (Hill, *Footsteps*, p. 205; Pottle, *Journal*, p. 473; Fleeman, *Journey*, p. 303).

573 In the *Tour* this sentence becomes: "On the publication of Dr Delany's *Remarks* on his book, he was so much alarmed that he was afraid to read them." Strictly 'second' and 'third' should read 'fourth' and 'fifth'. The gentlemen in question are Roger Boyle, 1st earl (1621–79), Charles Boyle, 4th earl (1674–1731), John Boyle, 5th earl (1707–62), and Hamilton Boyle, 6th earl (1730–64). They are described in Budgell's *Memoirs ... of the Illustrious Family of the Boyles*, the 2003 edition of which includes a biography of its author, whose suicide is mentioned at p. 40 above.

574 This sentence begins 'He had seen' in the journal. 'Delany had seen' is from the *Tour*. This is one of half-a-dozen additions or clarifications adopted from the *Tour* in the account of 22 September, the others being complete clauses or sentences.

575 The relevant section of the will is in Pottle and Bennett, *Journal*, p. 203.

576 Orrery's *Life of Swift* was in the form of letters to his son Hamilton, one of which ends 'the conclusion ... turns my thoughts from Yahoos, to one of the dearest pledges I have upon earth, yourself: to whom I am a most / Affectionate Father / Orrery'. Dryden's dedication in the *Conquest of Granada* ends: "If at any time Almanzor fulfils the parts ... of the most unshaken friend, the greatest of Subjects, and the best of Masters, I shou'd then draw ... a true resemblance of your worth and vertues; at least as farr as they are capable of being copied, by the mean abilities of / Sir, / Your Royal Highnesse's / Most humble and most / obedient Servant / J. Dryden." Johnson took to doing this himself, as at p. 422, or when writing to Henry Thrale from Erray in Mull (Redford, *Letters*, vol. 2, p. 100): "I hope my mistress keeps all my very long letters ... I shall perhaps spin out one more before I have the happiness to tell you at home that I am Your obliged humble servant."

577 During his five-year papacy, Sixtus V (Felice Peretti, 1521–90) earned a reputation for stern justice. In his *History of the Popes* (vol. 1, p. 357), Ranke illustrates this with a tale not of his death-bed but of his coronation. "A prohibition had for some time existed against carrying short weapons, and more especially a particular kind of firearm. Four young men of Cora, nearly related to each other, were nevertheless taken with arms of this description about them. The day following was that of the coronation, and an occasion so auspicious was seized by their friends for entreating their pardon from the pontiff. 'While I live,' replied Sixtus, 'every criminal must die.' (*Se vivo, facinorosis moriendum esse.*) That very day the four young men were seen hanging on one gallows near the bridge of St Angelo."

578 See p. 96.

579 This short sentence is an interlinear addition. In the margin of the manuscript Boswell explains (Pottle, *Journal*, p. 425): "'He got no manuscript of Fingal' was added from uncertain recollection at the distance of some years. I am not sure it was said."

580 The journalist Edward Topham was told otherwise (*Letters from Edinburgh*, p. 143): "In a conversation with the Laird of Macleod, who was present at the time, and whose word, I am bold to say, I can depend upon, I asked

him whether this was the truth or not? His reply was this, 'Quite the contrary, I assure you: Doctor Johnson was very overbearing, and laughed at the Minister for giving credit to such an imposition. At last he asked him, whether he seriously did believe it? The gentleman's answer was, that he did.'" The fact that the following morning's 'test' was conducted in Johnson's absence (p. 261) appears to confirm that he could not be relied on to keep his temper over the matter.

581 Macpherson's work had been presented to the public (by Blair, especially) as the authentic voice of the third century AD. This made it as exciting to the public as the discovery of a new continent full of noble savages. Johnson's contention was that it was a mere invention, no Brazil but a Brobdingnag. The truth (that it was somewhere between the two) was tedious.

582 Boswell's note (*Tour*): "This droll quotation, I have since found, was from a song in honour of the Earl of Essex, called *Queen Elizabeth's Champion*, which is preserved in a collection of Old Ballads, in three volumes, published in London in different years between 1720 and 1730. The full verse is as follows: 'Oh! then bespoke the prentices all, / Living in London, both proper and tall, / In a kind letter sent straight to the Queen, / For Essex's sake they would fight all, / Raderer too, tandaro te, / Raderer, tandorer, tan do re.'" *A Collection of Old Ballads* appeared in three volumes, 1723–25.

583 The *Tour* names the book as *Fingal*, and expands the third sentence thus: "I desired him to mention any passage in the printed book, of which he could repeat the original. He pointed out one in page 50 of the quarto edition, and read the Erse, while Mr Roderick Macleod and I looked on the English; and Mr Macleod said, that it was pretty like what Mr Macqueen had recited." This page of *Fingal* (quarto edition, 1762) begins 'Everallin with the dark-brown hair' and ends 'on ocean's foamy waves' (Gaskill's edition, p. 83). Derick Thomson has shown (*Gaelic Sources*, pp. 32–37) that every sentence on this page, except one, derives from a passage in a genuine ballad.

584 In the first two parts of the test MacQueen appears to have been reading from a manuscript, and in the third to have been reciting from memory. The group's methodology was excellent. The comparison of manuscript text with Foulis produced the best result, the comparison of oral text with Macpherson the worst.

585 This is an accurate summary.

586 'Stella' was Swift's friend Esther Johnson; her trick, and Addison's, is described in Hill and Powell, *Life*, vol. 5, p. 243. Dr Johnson is clearly referring to a paper which was later published in translation by Pinkerton (*Voyages and Travels*, vol. 14, pp. 211–69) as 'Abridged Narrative of Travels through the Interior of South America, From the Shores of the Pacific Ocean to the Coasts of Brazil and Guyana, descending the River of Amazons; As read by Mr De la Condamine, member of the Academy of Sciences at Paris, at a Sitting of that Academy on the 28th April 1745'. At pp. 225–26 Condamine speaks of the language of the Tameos, whom he encountered by the Tiger River. "Poettarrarorincouroac signifies the number *three* in this tongue: happily for those who have transactions with them, their arithmetic goes

no farther. However incredible it may appear, this is not the only American nation with whom an equal poverty of numbers is common. The Brazilian tongue, a language spoken by people less savage and uncivilized, is equally barren; the people who speak it, where more than three is to be expressed, are obliged to use the Portuguese."

587 Boswell's note (*Tour*): "I think it but justice to say, that I believe Dr Johnson meant to ascribe Mr Macqueen's conduct to inaccuracy and enthusiasm, and did not mean any severe imputation against him."

588 Westminster Hall housed courts of law from the middle ages until 1834. For 'benefits' see also note 922.

589 Boswell's note (*Tour*, third and subsequent editions): "It has been triumphantly asked, 'Had not the plays of Shakespeare lain dormant for many years before the appearance of Mr Garrick? Did he not exhibit the most excellent of them frequently for thirty years together, and render them extremely popular by his own inimitable performance?' He undoubtedly did. But Dr Johnson's assertion has been misunderstood. Knowing as well as the objectors what has been just stated, he must necessarily have meant, that 'Mr Garrick did not as *a critic* make Shakespeare better known; he did not *illustrate* any one *passage* in any of his plays by acuteness of disquisition, or sagacity of conjecture': and what had been done with any degree of excellence in *that* way was the proper and immediate subject of his preface. I may add in support of this explanation the following anecdote, related to me by one of the ablest commentators on Shakespeare, who knew much of Dr Johnson: 'Now I have quitted the theatre,' cries Garrick, 'I will sit down and read Shakespeare.' ''Tis time you should,' exclaimed Johnson, 'for I much doubt if you ever examined one of his plays from the first scene to the last.'" The commentator in question will have been Malone.

590 This is dealt with in the *Life* at April 1772. Garrick told Johnson that he was welcome to use his library, but Johnson seemed to expect that Garrick should send books to him. Boswell concludes: "But, indeed, considering the slovenly and careless manner in which books were treated by Johnson, it could not be expected that scarce and valuable editions should have been lent to him."

591 Boswell's note (*Tour*, third and subsequent editions): "No man has less inclination to controversy than I have, particularly with a lady. But as I have claimed, and am conscious of being entitled to, credit, for the strictest fidelity, my respect for the public obliges me to take notice of an insinuation which tends to impeach it. Mrs Piozzi (late Mrs Thrale), to her *Anecdotes of Dr Johnson*, added the following postscript: '*Naples, Feb*. 10, 1786. Since the foregoing went to the press, having seen a passage from Mr Boswell's *Tour to the Hebrides*, in which it is said, that *I could not get through Mrs Montague's 'Essay on Shakspeare'*, I do not delay a moment to declare, that, on the contrary, I have always commended it myself, and heard it commended by every one else; and few things would give me more concern than to be thought incapable of tasting, or unwilling to testify my opinion of its excellence.'

"It is remarkable that this postscript is so expressed, as not to point out the person who said that Mrs Thrale could not get through Mrs Montague's book; and therefore I think it necessary to remind Mrs Piozzi, that the assertion concerning her was Dr Johnson's, and not mine. The second observation that I shall make on this postscript is, that it does not deny the fact asserted, though I must acknowledge from the praise it bestows on Mrs Montague's book, it may have been designed to convey that meaning.

"What Mrs Thrale's opinion is or was, or what she may or may not have said to Dr Johnson concerning Mrs Montague's book, it is not necessary for me to enquire. It is only incumbent on me to ascertain what Dr Johnson said to me. I shall therefore confine myself to a very short state of the fact.

"The unfavourable opinion of Mrs Montague's book, which Dr Johnson is here reported to have given, is known to have been that which he uniformly expressed, as many of his friends well remember. So much for the authenticity of the paragraph, as far as it relates to his own sentiments. The words containing the assertion, to which Mrs Piozzi objects, are printed from my manuscript Journal, and were taken down at the time. The Journal was read by Dr Johnson, who pointed out some inaccuracies, which I corrected, but did not mention any inaccuracy in the paragraph in question: and what is still more material, and very flattering to me, a considerable part of my Journal, containing this paragraph, *was read several years ago by Mrs Thrale herself*, who had it for some time in her possession, and returned it to me, without intimating that Dr Johnson had mistaken her sentiments.

"When the first edition of my Journal was passing through the press, it occurred to me, that a peculiar delicacy was necessary to be observed in reporting the opinion of one literary lady concerning the performance of another; and I had such scruples on that head, that in the proof sheet I struck out the name of Mrs Thrale from the above paragraph, and two or three hundred copies of my book were actually printed and published without it; of these Sir Joshua Reynolds's copy happened to be one. But while the sheet was working off, a friend, for whose opinion I have great respect, suggested that I had no right to deprive Mrs Thrale of the high honour which Dr Johnson had done her, by stating her opinion along with that of Mr Beauclerk, as coinciding with, and, as it were, sanctioning his own. The observation appeared to me so weighty and conclusive, that I hastened to the printing-house, and, as a piece of justice, restored Mrs Thrale to that place from which a too scrupulous delicacy had excluded her. On this simple state of facts I shall make no observation whatever."

The friend who advised Boswell to restore Mrs Thrale's name was probably Malone. No copy of the book has been found without it.

592 Boswell's note (*Tour*): "I do not see why I might not have been of this club without lessening my character. But Dr Johnson's caution against supposing one's self concealed in London, may be very useful to prevent some people from doing many things, not only foolish, but criminal."

593 Other than the words 'translation of the former passage' in the first paragraph and the second half of the last (see note 604), this sentence is the only part

of the account of **23 September** which is taken from the *Tour*. The rest is from the journal. Curiously, Boswell omits to mention that young Macleod of Dunvegan himself (to whom he quite properly refers throughout simply as 'MacLeod') was also still with them, as was his cousin Col. MacLeod of Talisker.

594 The basin is Loch Bracadale, the first arm of the sea is *Loch Beag Bhràcadail*, the second Loch Harport. Pennant agreed with Macleod that Bracadale was ripe for development (*Tour 1772*, p. 292): "This seems to me the fittest place in the island for the forming of a town. The harbour is deep and unspeakably secure. It is the Milford Haven of these parts; it opens at its mouth to the best part of the sea." When a town finally grew up in Skye, however, it was across the island at Portree, much as Sir James Macdonald had planned (p. 213).

595 Fernilea (*Fearann Eilghe* 'Ploughland') is halfway up Loch Harport on the south side. 'Fare fa' you' is a Scots expression: the line 'fair fa' your honest, sonsie face' is in Burns's 'To a Haggis', first published in 1786. Fernilea was bidding Boswell welcome in Boswell's language.

596 Thomas Davies was married to Susanna Yarrow (*c.* 1723–1801). The quote is from Charles Churchill's *Rosciad*: "With him came mighty Davies. On my life, / That Davies hath a very pretty wife! / Statesman all over! In plots famous grown! / He mouths a sentence, as curs mouth a bone." Talisker had been married to a sister of Hugh Maclean of Coll, but the lady here described is his second wife, Christine MacKay from Inverness.

597 This is *Stac an Fhùcadair* 'the Waulker's Stack', at least it is so named by Pennant (*Tour 1772*, p. 291); other sources make it merely *an Stac*. It must have suggested to him the idea of putting waulking-women into his Talisker print, in the background of which the stack is prominent (see note 599). Curiously, one of Macleod's Maidens, now collapsed into the sea, used to bear the same name (Nicolson, *Handbook*, p. 47): *Nic Cloisgeir mhór 's a triùir nighean, / A' Bheairt-Fhighe, 's am Fùcadair.* "Great Nic Cloisgeir with her three daughters, / The Loom, and the Waulker." The names seem suggestive of crashing, pounding and noise.

598 I omit Boswell's sketch and the word 'thus' which introduces it; I supply the word 'northwest' where he left a blank.

599 This is the hill called Preshal (or Prieshwell, as Boswell calls it later). He appears to have been told that Pennant had climbed it to get a view of Talisker from which to make a sketch. No doubt he had, but it was his servant, Moses Griffith, who did the sketching. A dozen women at work (foot-waulking and grinding with the quern) were added in the foreground. The result, published in 1774 (Pennant, *Tour 1772*, p. 286), is one of the most celebrated prints ever made of a Highland scene.

600 The number of generations was three; being unsure of the figure, Boswell printed 'for several generations' in the *Tour*.

601 Boswell's note (*Tour*): "This was a dexterous mode of description, for the purpose of his argument; for what he alluded to was a sermon published by the learned Dr William Wishart, formerly Principal of the college at

Edinburgh, to warn men *against* confiding in a death-bed *repentance*, of the inefficacy of which he entertained notions very different from those of Dr Johnson." Wishart's tract was published in 1748; he was clearly at one with Dugald Buchanan, who said in his hymn 'An Geamhradh' ('Winter') in the same period: *Cha dèan aithreachas crìche / Do dhìonadh on dórainn.* "Death-bed repentance / Will not defend you from anguish." Ramsay of Ochtertyre noted however that 'Dr Wishart seems to have had some peculiar notions on that head, for he would not attend criminals about to be executed' (*Scotland and Scotsmen*, vol. 1, p. 229).

602   Altered in the *Tour* to 'by deserting his ground, and not meeting the argument as I had put it'.

603   See p. 290. On assiduity, an example may be cited from the Fernilea/Talisker area itself. As a young man, the Rev. Angus John MacVicar (1878–1970) acted as assistant to the Rev. John Maclean of Bracadale (1841–1904) at the missionary chapel in Carbost. The advice given to him by the older man was, above all, *Bi cinnteach tadhal air na daoine a tha sean agus 'nan euslaintich.* "Be sure to visit the old and the sick." One old woman kept a tablecloth folded ready to put under the minister's knees when they prayed together on the cold clay floor of her house (Dòmhnallach, 'Ministearan').

604   Following the words 'though he was of opinion', four pages are missing from Boswell's journal, and the text is supplied from the first edition of the *Tour*. The lost portion may have consisted mainly of Boswell's expatiation on 'the luxury of the little-house at Talisker', see p. 290.

605   The parts of the 'Long Island' Boswell could see were Uist and Harris. By 'Bernera' he means neither the island of that name (*Bearnaraigh*) off Lewis, nor the barracks in Glenelg, but the fertile island in the Sound of Harris whose name (also *Bearnaraigh*) is now spelt Berneray in English. It was celebrated for its MacLeod tacksmen, Mrs MacLeod of Fernilea's family (p. 266). *Bearnaraigh* is Old Norse *Bjarnarøy* 'Bjorn's Island'; Bernera in Glenelg will be from Gaelic *bearn* 'gap' and *àirigh* 'shieling'. Cuchullin's well is described by Pottle, *Journal*, p. 475. The account of 24 September is from the *Tour*, the journal not having survived at this point; two paragraphs which appear in the *Tour* at 24 September appear elsewhere in the journal, and may be found here at pp. 236–37, 270.

606   Coll's lands were in Quinish in the north of the island. Nicholas Maclean-Bristol tells me that young Coll's farm was probably at Penmolloch. Spellings like 'Tyr-yi' and 'Tireye' (p. 300) reflect the trisyllabic pronunciation of Gaelic *Tiridhe*.

607   The surviving journal recommences at 'his and Mrs MacLeod's'. In the *Tour* the paragraph ends 'into this rude region.' The words 'in consequence of' were supplied by Pottle and Bennett (*Journal*, p. 218) as a link.

608   He had indeed. The letter was to Mrs Thrale, and is published in Redford, *Letters*, vol. 2, pp. 81–84. He begins by quoting the same piece of verse, and remarking: "We have at one time no boat, and at another may have too much wind, but of our reception here we have no reason to complain." The song is in *The Charmer*, pp. 223–24 (see note 797); it reappeared in

Ritson's *Select Collection of English Songs*, 1783, vol. 2, pp. 105–06, with the attribution 'by Mr Coffey' (?Charles Coffey, d. 1745). It begins 'Welcome, welcome, brother debtor'.

609   In the *Tour* this paragraph is switched to 24 September where it belongs. The biographer Dr Thomas Birch (1705–66) was celebrated for his anecdotes, but one from a different source is relevant here. Writing from Leith on 27 November 1773, the Rev. Robert Forbes reported (Paton, *Lyon in Mourning*, vol. 3, p. 292): "You know the famous Dr Johnson has been among us. Several anecdotes could I give you of him, but one is most singular. Dining one day at the table of one of the Lords of Session, the company stumbled upon characters, particularly it would appear of kings. 'Well, well,' said the bluff Doctor. 'George the 1st was a robber, George the 2nd a fool, and George the 3d is an idiot.' How the company stared I leave you to judge."

610   This statement is contradicted slightly by the *Tour*, which omits everything after 'the Romans', substituting 'but which, being very slow in its operation, is almost entirely gone into disuse'. Johnson describes the quern at pp. 197–98, remarking that 'these stones are found in *Lochaber*'. One wonders if this derives from Pennant, who saw one there four years earlier (*Tour 1769*, pp. 211–12). Particular places certainly enjoyed a reputation for the quarrying and manufacture of millstones: if Lochaber was one, Raasay was another (MacLeod, *Raasay*, p. 71).

611   A wattled gate of this kind is called in Gaelic *cachaileith*. I omit Boswell's sketch and the word 'thus' which introduces it.

612   I take the beginning of this sentence from the *Tour*. The journal merely has: "At Sconser I received a letter from my dear wife . . ." Apart from this, one other brief clarification, and sections at the start and finish where the manuscript is missing, Boswell's account of **25 September** is from his journal.

613   After the words 'had supper', six pages are missing from the journal, and the text is supplied from the *Tour*.

614   Boswell's note (*Tour*, third and subsequent editions): "My ingenuously relating this occasional instance of intemperance has I find been made the subject both of serious criticism and ludicrous banter. With the banterers I shall not trouble myself, but I wonder that those who pretend to the appellation of serious critics should not have had sagacity enough to perceive that here, as in every other part of the present work, my principal object was to delineate Dr Johnson's manners and character. In justice to him I would not omit an anecdote, which, though in some degree to my own disadvantage, exhibits in so strong a light the indulgence and good humour with which he could treat those excesses in his friends, of which he highly disapproved. In some other instances, the critics have been equally wrong as to the true motive of my recording particulars, the objections to which I saw as clearly as they. But it would be an endless task for an author to point out upon every occasion the precise object he has in view. Contenting himself with the approbation of readers of discernment and taste, he ought not to complain that some are found who cannot or will not understand him." Boswell is thinking mainly of Dr Wolcot ('Peter Pindar'), whose *Bozzy and*

Piozzi treats the episode with genuine wit. "'Twas *strange* that in *that* volume of divinity, / I op'd the Twentieth Sunday after Trinity, / And read these words – 'Pray be not drunk with wine, / Since drunkenness doth make a man a *swine*.' / 'Alas!' says I, 'the sinner that I am!' / And having made my speech, I took a *dram*."

615 'Green Sleeves' or 'Which Nobody can Deny' has been sung and danced in England and Scotland since the sixteenth century. The first appearance of a variant 'Green Sleeves and Pudding Pies' is in the seventh edition of Playford's *Dancing-Master* (1686). 'Green peas, mutton pies, / Tell me where my Bella lies' was still being chanted by Scottish children in 1897 (Nicholson, *Golspie*, p. 157). Closest of all is a version in Hecht's *Songs from David Herd's Manuscripts*, p. 177: "Green sleeves and pudden-pyes, / Come tell me where my true love lyes, / And I'll be wi' her ere she rise: / Fidle a' the gither! / Hey ho! and about she goes, / She's milk in her breasts, she's none in her toes, / She's a hole in her a——, you may put in your nose, / Sing: hey, boys, up go we! / Green sleeves and yellow lace, / Maids, maids, come, marry apace! / The batchelors are in a pitiful case / To fidle a' the gither."

616 Boswell's account of **26 September** is from the *Tour*, the relevant pages of his journal being missing. The journal resumes again with the words 'both from distress' in the second sentence of 27 September. Some of the eight words preceding 'both from distress' are conjectural (Pottle and Bennett, *Journal*, p. 225).

617 This paragraph, which reads like a trite summary of the following one, is taken from the *Tour*, as it does not appear in the journal. The following one *was* allowed into the published book, however, only the coffee and the lady's identity being suppressed. The rest of the account of **27 September** is from the journal, except for two full sentences and a phrase ('at their punch') taken from the *Tour*, and some words (especially in the first and last paragraphs) which were guessed by Pottle and Bennett (*Journal*, pp. 225–26, 426–27) where text was missing or difficult to read.

618 Margaret Macalister Williamson, Kingsburgh's great-great-grand-niece, told the story like this (Pierpoint, 'Dr. Johnson'): "Mrs Mackinnon's daughter, Margaret Macalister, then a young bride of sixteen, having just married Dr Macdonald of Gillen, took a bet with some sprightly young ladies that she would sit on Dr Johnson's knee in the drawing-room and kiss him. These young ladies had dared her to do it, saying he was too ugly for any woman to kiss." Judging from Malcolm's toast (which Boswell must have heard in Raasay) she was known in Gaelic as *Bean an Dotair Ruaidh*.

619 In the margin of his journal Boswell wrote: "Insert the ludicrous scene of Joseph and the . . ." As Pottle and Bennett point out (*Journal*, p. 227), the manuscript is defective and Boswell failed to insert the scene in the *Tour*, so we will never know what it was.

620 At this point in the journal both lower corners of a page are defective, and the following leaf is missing altogether. Nothing in the *Tour* corresponds to any of this, because after 'mainland' Boswell directed the printer to 'go to 379', i.e. the next surviving page. Pottle and Bennett point out (*Journal*,

pp. 227–28) that the first sentence on p. 379 shows Boswell talking to Mrs MacKinnon about Prince Charles, and suggest that the missing leaf contained material which helped him construct his account of the Prince's escape (pp. 216–25).

621 See p. 136.

622 The same story was published in 1780 by Arthur Young (*Tour in Ireland*, p. 70): "Another great family in Connacht is MacDermot, who calls himself Prince of Coolavin. He lives at Coolavin in Sligo, and, though he has not above £100 a year, will not admit his children to sit down in his presence. Lord Kingsborough, Mr Ponsonby, Mr O'Hara, Mr Sandford, etc. came to see him, and his address was curious: '*O'Hara! you are welcome; Sandford, I am glad to see your mother's son* (his mother was an O'Brien): *as to the rest of ye, come in as ye can.*'" It may be deduced that these men constituted a delegation from the Irish parliament during the years 1743–45. The 'Prince of Coolavin' was Charles MacDermott (1707–58), a descendant of the MacDermotts of Moylurg. Henry O'Hara (*c.* 1695–1745) was MP for Randalstown 1727–45. Sir Robert King, 1st Baron Kingsborough (1724–55), was MP for Boyle 1743–48. John Ponsonby (1713–87), third son of the earl of Bessborough, was MP for Newtownards and other places from 1739 to his death, and served as speaker of the Irish House of Commons from 1756 to 1771. There are three possible Sandfords: Henry Sandford (1719–96), MP for Co. Roscommon 1741–60; Robert Sandford (1692–1777), MP for Newcastle 1727–60; and William Sandford (1704–59), MP for Roscommon Borough 1733–59.

623 'While we were at dinner' becomes in the *Tour* 'While the punch went round'.

624 Boswell prefixed the second of these passages, not very accurately transcribed, to the *Tour* as a sort of motto: "He was of an admirable pregnancy of wit, and that pregnancy much improved by continual study from his childhood; by which he had gotten such a promptness in expressing his mind that his extemporal speeches were little inferior to his premeditated writings. Many, no doubt, had read as much, and perhaps more than he; but scarce ever any concocted his reading into judgement as he did." The description of James's riding (which immediately precedes it) is as follows: "It is said he had such a fashion in riding that it could not so properly be said he rode, as that his horse carried him; for he made but little use of his bridle; and would say, 'A horse never stumbled but when he was reined.'" For Johnson's riding see pp. 106–07.

625 'Second Epistle of the Second Book of Horace Imitated', lines 76–79: "This subtle Thief of Life, this paltry Time, / What will it leave me, if it snatch my Rhime? / If ev'ry Wheel of that unweary'd Mill / That turn'd ten thousand Verses, now stands still."

626 Two lines of text, about fourteen words, are lost after 'church'. Perhaps Boswell was praising the view, or the 'prospect' as he would have called it. In the *Tour*, all that follows 'church' is reorganised into a single sentence containing new information: "We were received here with much kindness

by Mr and Mrs Macpherson, and his sister, Miss Macpherson, who pleased Dr Johnson much, by singing Erse songs, and playing on the guittar."

627   It appears in *The Scots Magazine*, vol. 9, 1747, p. 590, under the heading '*Cantici Mosaici paraphrasis*', Exod. xv.', and contains twenty quatrains beginning *Rectorem celebro siderei poli*; see note 635. The words 'the father of our host' and everything from 'who, though his *Dissertations*' to the end of the Latin verses on p. 281 are taken from the *Tour*, as are the words 'when in that county' at p. 278. Otherwise Boswell's account of **28 September** is from his journal.

628   The poem appears in *The Scots Magazine*, vol. 1, 1739, pp. 273–74, headed: "*Bara, March* 1739. Ad amicum longe charissimum D. N____ M M____D, Ecclesiæ quæ dicitur *Sanctæ Mariæ* Pastorem vigilantissimum, Ode." This is the Rev. Norman MacLeod, a native of Ose in Bracadale, minister of St Mary's, Duirinish, from 1717. He had been drowned while crossing the Minch from Skye to Barra. Boswell omits to point out that in Barra, despite being parish minister, Mr MacPherson was little more than chaplain to the laird's family, the population having remained staunchly Roman Catholic. I am grateful to Mr Norman MacLeod, Walkerburn, for this translation of the four verses: "Woe is me! What great misery I endure, while I survey in the distance the mountain summits thrice blessed; while I, all by myself, wander across the barren sands of wild Barra. I mourn, I am angry, I am tortured because I am in the midst of barbarians who dwell in a far-off Thule; weak and inactive, I am dying, buried in a dark prison. Meanwhile, may it be your wish, O mighty one, that I be lifted up again as often as there springs to mind the certain hope of departing for celestial Jerusalem, to the court of divine will. Then at last life, life has to be summoned. Then we are allowed to have grateful friends celebrating the sacred seraphims and the awe-inspiring Trinity."

629   It was Boswell who was confused. Gaelic writings by Scots, exhibiting gradual divergence from the parent language (Irish), survive in manuscript from the twelfth century and in print from the sixteenth. By 1690 there was a complete Irish Bible 'carefully changed from Irish script into neat, easily-read Roman characters for the general good of Scottish Gaels' (*chum maitheas coitcheann na nGaóidheail Albanach, áthruighte go haireach as an litir Eireandha chum na mion-litre shoi-léighidh Romhanta*); it was much loved by many in Scotland until well into the nineteenth century. By 1767 both the Psalms and the New Testament had been published in the vernacular. Even in 1773, Irish orthography still exercised a strong pull on Scottish Gaelic writing, as is well demonstrated by the title of a work first published in Edinburgh in that year, *Eisempleir Shoilleir Ceasnnuighe*.

630   In the *Tour* this becomes: "Coll, who had gone yesterday to pay a visit at Camuscross, joined us this morning at breakfast. Some other gentlemen also came to enjoy the entertainment of Dr Johnson's conversation." Presumably the gentlemen in question were Donald MacLeod, the Rev. Martin MacPherson, James MacDonald (the *bàillidh* or factor), and John or Lachlan MacKinnon, younger of Coirechatachan.

TO THE HEBRIDES

631 As Johnson later explained in his Life of William Shenstone, his passion was the beautification of his Shropshire estate – he liked nothing better than 'to point his prospects, to diversify his surface, to entangle his walks, and to wind his waters'.

632 Boswell gives only the first line in his journal, but cites the full stanza in the *Tour*. Other than this, one short phrase and one sentence, the account of **29 September** is from the journal.

633 Pottle and Bennett point out (*Journal*, p. 233) that although the epitaph was attributed in the newspapers to Garrick, it was by Richard Graves, and was inscribed on an urn erected by Graves in Halesowen churchyard. It begins: "Whoe'er thou art, with rev'rence tread / The sacred mansions of the dead."

634 The correspondent was Anthony Whistler of Whitchurch, the burner his brother John.

635 *Hamlet*, act 2, scene 2. In the journal this paragraph begins: "He looked at a Latin paraphrase of the Song of Moses in the *Scots Magazine*, by Dr Macpherson, and said it did him honour; that he had a great deal of Latin, and good Latin." Boswell shifted this sentence to 28 September in the *Tour*, from which it now appears above, p. 280. Boswell had found the 'droll Scottish poem', Robert Fergusson's '*To the* PRINCIPAL *and* PROFESSORS *of the University of St* ANDREWS, *on their superb treat to Dr* SAMUEL JOHNSON', in the Edinburgh *Weekly Magazine* for 2 September 1773 (vol. 21, pp. 305–06). Fergusson speaks scornfully of the dainty dishes with which Johnson was probably regaled, recommends homelier fare such as haggis and sheep's head and trotters, and declares: "Then neist whan SAMY's heart was faintin, / He'd lang'd for scate to mak him wanton." Skate seems to have been regarded as an aphrodisiac.

636 The *Tour* adds 'which necessarily confined us to the house; but we were fully compensated by Dr Johnson's conversation'.

637 Boswell's note (*Tour*): "He did not mention the name of any particular person; but those who are conversant with the political world will probably recollect more persons than one to whom this observation may be applied."

638 I have added the word 'telling' to make sense of this sentence. The journal entry in question may be found in Wimsatt and Pottle, *Boswell for the Defence*, pp. 32–33.

639 Boswell gives it in the *Tour*. "The subject is his family-motto, *Dum vivimus, vivamus*; which, in its primary signification, is, to be sure, not very suitable to a Christian divine; but he paraphrased it thus: 'Live, while you live, the *epicure* would say, / And seize the pleasures of the present day. / Live, while you live, the sacred *preacher* cries, / And give to God each moment as it flies. / Lord, in my views let both united be; / I live in *pleasure*, when I live to *thee.*'"

640 Despite this, Boswell's has not survived (the volume having been taken apart at the time of revision for the printer), but Johnson's has. It is on display at Dunvegan, and is as follows (Redford, *Letters*, vol. 2, p. 85): "To MACLEOD OF MACLEOD. / DEAR SIR: / We are now on the margin of the sea, waiting for

a boat and a wind. Boswel grows impatient, but the kind treatment which I find wherever I go makes me leave with some heaviness of heart an Island which I am not very likely to see again. Having now gone as far as horses can carry us, we thankfully return them. My Steed will, I hope, be received with kindness; he has borne me, heavy as I am, over ground both rough and steep with great fidelity, and for the use of him, as for your other favours, I hope you will believe me thankful, and willing, at whatever distance we may be placed, to show my sense of your kindness by any offices of friendship that may fall within my power. Lady Macleod and the young Ladies have, by their hospitality and politeness made an impression on my mind which will not easily be effaced. Be pleased to tell them that I remember them with great tenderness and great respect. I am, Sir, Your most obliged and Most humble Servant, / SAM: JOHNSON. / We passed two days at Talisker very happily, both by the perfectness of the place, and elegance of our reception. / Ostig, Sept. 28, 1773."

641 This last remark of Boswell's is from the *Tour*, as are the words 'read to him, and' (p. 283, foot). Otherwise the account of 30 **September** is from the journal.

642 In Boswell's journal this paragraph begins: "I read a very pretty ode by Dr Macpherson, written from Barra, when he was minister there." See pp. 280–81, where the ode is quoted from the *Tour*.

643 This is explained in the *Tour*: "Mr James Macdonald, factor to Sir Alexander Macdonald in Sleat, insisted that all the company at Ostaig should go to the house at Armadale, which Sir Alexander had left, having gone with his lady to Edinburgh, and be his guests, till we had an opportunity of sailing to Mull."

644 Boswell found '*On* JOHNSON's DICTIONARY' in the Edinburgh *Weekly Magazine* for 14 January 1773 (vol. 19, pp. 81–82). Written by John Maclaurin, later Lord Dreghorn, it begins: "In love with a pedantic jargon, / Our poets now-a-days are far gone; / So that a man can't read their songs, / Unless he has the gift of tongues." Maclaurin warns young poets to use Johnson with care: "Always attentitively distinguish / The Greek and Latin words from English." They must use English ones only, or the result may resemble: "Little of *anthropopathy* has he, / Who in yon fulgid *curricle* reclines / Alone; while I, *depauperated* bard! / The streets *pedestrious* scour; why, with bland voice, / Bids he me not his *vectitation* share?"

645 In 1765 William Kenrick had published a violent review of Johnson's *Shakespeare*; James Barclay of Balliol College (*c*. 1747–70), who graduated BA in 1768, responded in Johnson's defence. The words 'he was told afterwards' are from the *Tour*. Apart from this and one other minor clarification, Boswell's account of 1 **October** is from his journal.

646 These remarks on Hume appear in the *Tour* at 30 September. Johnson means that Hume followed the paths trodden by Thomas Hobbes (1588–1679), a rationalist who insisted on the separation of philosophy from theology.

647 The author of *Chrysal, or the Adventures of a Guinea* (1760–65) was Charles Johnstone.

648 See note 398.

649 These references to Sir Alexander were expunged from the *Tour*, in which the account of 2 October begins: "Dr Johnson said, that 'a chief and his lady should make their house like a court. They should have a certain number of the gentlemen's daughters . . .'"

650 Hester Salusbury, Lady Cotton, was in fact Mrs Thrale's great-grandmother (Pottle, *Journal*, p. 427).

651 On reading Johnson's dismissive opinion of his novel in the *Tour*, Henry Mackenzie commented (*Anecdotes and Egotisms*, p. 189): "I am the less offended at that because I am confident he never read it."

652 Juvenal, *Satires*, book 1, line 79: *Si Natura negat, facit indignatio versum.* "When Nature refuses, sheer scorn produces verse."

653 In the *Tour* this last sentence is spoken by Boswell along with the next remark.

654 The dance did not survive, but thanks to these comments by Boswell, 'A Dance Called America' became the title of a song performed by the Gaelic rock band Runrig and of James Hunter's book *A Dance Called America: The Scottish Highlands, the United States and Canada* (Edinburgh, 1994).

655 Horace, *Odes*, book 3, poem 2, lines 31–32: "Though she seems to limp, Punishment seldom fails to catch up with a scoundrel." Boswell's award of a doctorate to MacQueen is both a mistake and a mark of esteem.

656 The second half of this sentence is from the *Tour*. Otherwise the account of 2 October is from the journal. The references to Sir Alexander in the last two paragraphs are expunged from the *Tour* by substituting respectively '(naming a certain person)' and 'he'.

657 On the 'little-house' see note 604; on the dispute see p. 268.

658 Virgil, *Eclogues*, poem 3, line 111: "Dam up the ditches, boys, the meadows have drunk enough." Virgil was referring to irrigation; according to custom, Johnson had turned his teacup upside down to show that he was finished.

659 In the *Tour*, the last three sentences are replaced by: "I must again and again apologize to fastidious readers, for recording such minute particulars. They prove the scrupulous fidelity of my *Journal*. Dr Johnson said it was a very exact picture of a portion of his life."

660 Epictetus, *Encheiridion*, chapter 7, 'The Voyage of Life'.

661 In his 'Remarks' on the *Journey* (Adam, *R. B. Adam Library*, vol. 2, foll. p. 45), Boswell told Johnson: "You treat the storm too lightly. Coll and all the islanders thought we were really in danger."

662 This is Capt. Lachlan MacLean (d. 1790), for whom see note 693. Johnson is referring to Robert Clive, whose enrichment after deposing the Nabob of Bengal was the subject of a parliamentary enquiry in May 1773, and who committed suicide in 1774.

663 See pp. 313–14.

664 Johnson is referring to *Tiomnadh Nuadh* (1767). Had he said 'dialect' his point might have had some force. The work was in the 'language' of Coll, but distanced from it in two or three minor respects: the survival of many Irish words and grammatical forms now more or less obsolete in the

vernacular, Irish having provided the traditional written standard of Scottish Gaelic; the survival of Irish forms of spelling, there being as yet no fixed Scottish Gaelic orthography; and the use of the Perthshire dialect as the new standard. MacLean can be forgiven for feeling that his own renderings were not inferior to those in the new book.

665 At Cill Fhionnaigh and Crossapol, see pp. 315, 336.

666 This was Sweyn MacSweyn (*Suain MacSuain*), a Skyeman from Roag, see pp. 305, 316. 'Sweyn' is an attempt to render the long diphthong in *Suain*. The preferred spelling in Skye and Raasay is MacSwan or MacSwain. The name must be distinguished from *MacSuibhne* – that of the MacSweens and MacSweeneys of Castle Sween (Argyll) and Fanad (Donegal).

667 Roderick Macneil of Barra (*fl.* 1409) married Anna, daughter of William Macleod, 5th of Dunvegan (d. 1402), widow of Lachlan Maclean, third son of Lachlann Lùbanach, 5th of Duart. Her younger son by her first marriage was *Iain Garbh* ('Thickset John', i.e. he was a big fellow but not tall). According to Maclean-Bristol, *Warriors and Priests*, p. 38, quoting from Allan MacLean of Crossapol's version of the 'Brief Genealogical & Historical Account of the Family and Surname of Maclean', Iain Garbh rescued his uncle, Macleod of Harris, from the custody of the Lord of the Isles at Ardtornish; this may have been Iain Borb (d. *c.* 1442), 6th of Dunvegan, though he is named in another version as Alexander Macleod (MacLean, *Breif Genealogical Account*, p. 79). Johnson had this part of the story back to front. The full story of Iain Garbh is in the *Breif Genealogical Account*, pp. 78–81, and was published by Hector MacDougall in both Gaelic and English (MacDhughaill, 'Seann Eachdraidh Chollach', pp. 178–201; *Clarsach na Coille*, pp. 263–77; *Handbook*, pp. 21–22, 45–47, 55–56).

668 This man was called *an Gille Riabhach* ('the Swarthy Lad'). Johnson has corrupted it to make it look like a surname, but it was quite a common forename – *Clann Mhic Ghille Riabhaich*, for example, were the Darrochs of Jura. Johnson is right about the lands in Mull, however: they were at Dervaig (MacDougall, *Clarsach na Coille*, p. 271; MacDhughaill, 'Seann Eachdraidh Chollach', p. 192).

669 This looks a little muddled. Perhaps what Johnson means is that Iain Garbh first invaded some outlying part of Macneil's territory (Boisdale, Mingulay or Vatersay), then took Breacachadh in Coll, and finally conquered the Macneil heartland of Barra. For another account of Iain Garbh's exploits see p. 326, and for his shin-bone see p. 374.

670 The new house at Breacachadh was built *c.* 1750 by Hector Maclean, 11th of Coll (MacDougall, *Handbook*, p. 34).

671 On Beinn Hogh – see pp. 334–35.

672 Other accounts state that it was Maclean of Duart who imprisoned Clanranald, *c.* 1608–09.

673 This story is so well known that *Creideamh a' Bhata Bhuidhe* 'the Religion of the Yellow Stick' is in effect the Gaelic for proselytism. It has been told not only of Rum but also of Coll and South Uist. In Coll the stick was wielded by Lachlan, 8th of Coll, or by a priest (Lachlan's wife and brother

were Catholics). In Rum it was Hector, 11th of Coll. In South Uist it was Colin Macdonald of Boisdale (Dwelly, *Dictionary*, p. 269; MacDougall, *Handbook*, p. 62; Campbell, *Canna*, p. 207; Maclean-Bristol, *From Clan to Regiment*, pp. 70, 112; MacilleDhuibh, 'The Religion of the Yellow Stick').

674 Johnson originally wrote (Lascelles, *Journey*, pp. xxxiv–xxxv): " . . . but a cave which contains memorials of an old transaction. / The inhabitants once laid hold on a boat manned by *Macleod*, and tying the crew hand and foot, pushed them off into the ocean. Which way they escaped is not told. *Macleod* was informed how his vassals had been treated, and demanded the offenders, whom the inhabitants refused to deliver. Nothing now remained but force. The people of *Egg* had a very capacious cavern, to which they all retreated, and where they imagined themselves safe; but *Macleod* used the usual method of forcing subterraneous fortresses, and kept a fire at the mouth till they were all destroyed." This was printed off before Johnson remembered that he had already told the story (p. 172); he was obliged to cancel and rewrite.

675 Accounts of Johnson's and Boswell's tour of 1773 were appearing in the newspapers while Pennant was writing up his tour of 1772. The *Edinburgh Evening Courant*, for example, reported on 13 November 1773 that 'they were confined by stormy weather for thirteen days to a barren island where they could get nothing to eat but oat meal'. This was a gleeful reflection of Johnson's celebrated definition of oats in his *Dictionary* (see also note 777). Pennant (himself a Welshman), assuming the reports to be true, described Coll as 'celebrated for being the place where Doctor *Samuel Johnson* had long and woeful experience of oats being the food of men in *Scotland*, as they are of horses in *England*'. The first part of his *Tour 1772* (the islands) was published in Chester on 19 May 1774; Johnson's *Journey* followed on 18 January 1775; the second part of *Tour 1772* (the mainland) came last, in 1776.

676 See p. 331.

677 This was Neil MacLean of Crossapol. His son was Donald, later minister of the Small Isles, see pp. 333–34.

678 This was young Coll, see p. 341.

679 By 'Mr *Maclean*' Johnson means young Coll. This 'game' is a curious (but entirely credible) aristocratic inversion of the well-known custom of expelling the old year, whose 'original' is the scapegoat of Leviticus 16 (Black, *Gaelic Otherworld*, pp. 530–31). In the demotic version the scapegoat runs around the outside of the house while his companions beat at the skin, then one by one they say their rhymes and are allowed in by the family to partake of bread, cheese and whisky. Here, in pantomime, the scapegoat runs around the inside of the house, drives everyone out, then, as 'king of the castle', readmits them on hearing them perform their verses. See also p. 318.

680 Johnson's geography is confused, as usual. The battle took place at Blarnicara by Corpach at the head of Loch Linnhe, near where Fort William now stood. John Stewart dates it to *c.* 1460 (*The Camerons*, p. 13), but if Iain Abrach was killed in the battle, as appears to be the case, it was fought in 1519, and Iain

Abrach's adversary was Ewen Cameron, 13th of Lochiel (Maclean-Bristol, *Warriors and Priests*, p. 91).

681 The Maclean in question will be John (Iain Cam, *fl.* 1528–58), 4th of Coll.

682 Boswell tells the same story, and quotes the 'demand of protection', at pp. 326–27. It was in Dr Hector MacLean's manuscript (*Breif Genealogical Account*, pp. 81–82).

683 The late Rev. William Matheson used to point out that fosterage of this kind survived into the twentieth century, see for example Sellar, 'O'Donnell Lecture 1985', p. 12. Though a Gaelic word (*mac-shealbh* 'filial property'), macalive (makhelve, macheliffe, mackhallow, makallow, meikalow, machtella etc.) is more to the fore in Scots and English legal documents and dictionaries. Currie cites examples (*Mull*, pp. 56–57, 171). A tutor of Macleod is on record as 'Machalvie', presumably *mac-shealbhach* 'custodian of the heir's filial property' (Grant, *MacLeods*, p. 46). *Dalta* is a fosterchild. See also p. 316.

684 According to Boswell (p. 316) young Coll was fostered by a Campbell in Tiree, and MacSweyn was a tenant on Macleod's estate, not Macdonald's. The name is strongly associated with Roag in Macleod's country, see notes 572, 666. Mrs MacSweyn was a MacDonald who claimed to have taught Gaelic to Sir James Macdonald (p. 317); perhaps that is what confused Johnson, who is much less reliable than Boswell on such matters.

685 This will be Kilbride on Boisdale's estate.

686 The massacre probably took place in the period 1510–17, during the reign of James IV or V (Grant, *MacLeods*, p. 136; Campbell, *A Very Civil People*, pp. 128–29). See also pp. 172, 298.

687 John Macdonald (1729–1809), 8th of Morar, see also pp. 151, 203.

688 By 'Loch Moidart' Boswell means the Sound of Arisaig (see map, p. 170). The four paragraphs ending here are summarised briefly in the *Tour*: "As we had been detained so long in Skye by bad weather, we gave up the scheme that Coll had planned for us of visiting several islands, and contented ourselves with the prospect of seeing Mull, and Icolmkill and Inchkenneth, which lie near to it."

689 Horace, *Epistles*, book 1, poem 1, line 15: "To wherever the storm drives me, I am borne as a willing guest." This sentence is from the *Tour*, and is footnoted: "For as the tempest drives, I shape my way. FRANCIS." Otherwise Boswell's account of 3 October (in both chapters 5 and 6) is taken from his journal, except for the words 'where we drank tea' at p. 290 and some conjectural readings at the foot of p. 310 ('into it', 'soaked', 'only a', 'little', 'boots and great—') where the corner of a page is missing (Pottle and Bennett, *Journal*, p. 252). 'Francis' is the translator Dr Philip Francis (?1708–73).

690 Horace, *Ars Poetica*, lines 161–62: *Imberbis iuvenis, tandem custode remoto, / Gaudet equis canibusque et aprici gramine Campi.* "The beardless youth, free at last from his tutor, finds joy in horses and dogs and the grass of the sunny Plain of Mars." For more on young Coll's dogs see pp. 177, 375–76.

691 *Henry VI*, part 1, act 1, scene 2.

692 Johnson lived at no. 1 Inner Temple Lane in London from 1760 to 1765 (Hill and Powell, *Life*, vol. 3, p. 535). This account of 4 October is from Boswell's journal.

693 See pp. 292, 341. Capt. Lachlan seems to have been of a family which had a wadset of Grishipol. He may well have been illegitimate. He was the first Coll man to join the Indian Army: he went out *c.* 1753, served in the Madras European battalion, and appears to have requested leave to come home in 1766 (Hill and Powell, *Life*, vol. 5, p. 284; Pottle, *Journal*, p. 428). He subsequently purchased the estate of Craigendmuir at Provan near Glasgow, became tacksman of Gallanach in Coll, and helped finance Sir Allan Maclean's bid to recover his patrimony, see note 724 (Maclean-Bristol, *From Clan to Regiment*, pp. 95, 143–47). The public house was at Arinagour; Capt. Lachlan's was at Arnabost, where its ruins may still be seen about 100 yards south of the modern farmhouse of Achamore.

694 Boswell's note (*Tour*): "This curious exhibition may perhaps remind some of my readers of the ludicrous lines, made, during Sir Robert Walpole's administration, on Mr George (afterwards Lord) Lyttelton, though the figures of the two personages must be allowed to be very different: 'But who is this astride the pony; / So long, so lean, so lank, so bony? / Dat be de great orator, Lytteltony.'"

695 In the *Tour* this is expanded to: "He said, 'The first part of it is one of the most entertaining books in the English language; it is quite dramatic: while he went about . . .'" Gilbert Burnet (1643–1715), a native of Edinburgh, was a popular preacher and historian who enjoyed a glittering career as chaplain to Charles II, chaplain to Queen Mary when princess of Orange, and bishop of Salisbury. His *History of my Own Times* was published posthumously in 1724–34 (see note 725).

696 See pp. 293–94. The manse appears to have been at Cliad, between Arnabost and Grishipol. This account of 5 October is taken from Boswell's journal.

697 1,200 is the population of Coll as given by Walker in 1764, 1765 and 1771 (*Report*, pp. 27, 28), but Nicholas Maclean-Bristol points out that it stood at only 938 in 1776 (*From Clan to Regiment*, p. 152). He believes that 'Mr Hector' exaggerated it both to Walker and to Boswell.

698 This was Foill (Feall), as Boswell points out later (p. 323). There are no houses there at all now, partly because of sand-blow, partly because after 1794 the people were cleared to the other side of Coll to work on kelp.

699 It was enclosed by 1889 (MacDougall, *Handbook*, p. 50). The name in Gaelic is *Cill Fhionnaich, Cill Fhionnaigh* or *Cill Fhionnáig* 'the church of St Findoca' – *Findsech, Findóc*, 'fair lady', 13 October, 'a virgin from Sliabh Guaire in Gailenga' (now part of Meath), also commemorated at Findogask in Perthshire, Innishail in Loch Awe, and Killinaig in Mull (Watson, *Celtic Place-Names*, pp. 286–87). The chapel and churchyard are described in RCAHMS, *Argyll*, vol. 3, pp. 148–49. Pottle and Bennett give the name as 'Kilymaik' (*Journal*, p. 258), but in light of the pronunciation, 'Kilyinaik' ('y' as in 'your') is a more logical reading of Boswell's manuscript. For this and other key readings I have used Yale University Library's Digital Collections website http://images.library.yale.edu/dlxc/ (a search for 'Hebrides' brings up images of the original manuscript of Boswell's journal).

700 Boswell's information was unreliable. The name is Norse: *gríss* 'boar' (perhaps a man's name), *bólstaðr* 'steading' (MacEchern, 'Place-Names of Coll', p. 321).

701 Polly Peachum marries Macheath in secret, and her mother remarks that after all the pains they have taken to dress her 'with care and cost, all tempting, fine, and gay, / As men should serve a cucumber, she flings herself away'. The 'Siberian turkey' is perhaps a figment of Boswell's imagination, on the lines of the Siberian crane, crow, falcon, finch, thrush, etc., mentioned in *OED*.

702 The word 'adorning' is guesswork. Pottle and Bennett (*Journal*, p. 259) could not read what precedes 'beauty', making it merely eight or nine letters beginning 'a'; neither can I.

703 See pp. 304–05. Boswell's claim that MacSweyn had fostered Hugh Maclean as well as his future wife must be incorrect, as MacSweyn and Maclean were about the same age. Probably they were foster-brothers, reared by MacSweyn's parents at Roag (Maclean-Bristol, *From Clan to Regiment*, pp. 128, 154, 158).

704 See p. 148. 'Hatyin foam eri' is 'Tha Tighinn Fodham Éirigh' ('I am Minded to Rise'), a well-known song of which various translations exist. The earliest, four quatrains and a chorus, is by Margaret Douglas Maclean Clephane (*c.* 1791–1830) of the Torloisk family, whose guardian was a young Edinburgh lawyer, Walter Scott. When Scott was writing *The Lady of the Lake* in 1808–10 he invited Margaret and her sisters to send him translations of Gaelic verse, and this one was among them. In 1815 Margaret married the future marquis of Northampton; following her death in Italy in 1830 Scott published it in a footnote to Croker's 1831 edition of the *Life* (at 5 October 1773), attributing it to 'a fair friend of mine'. The next (nine quatrains and chorus) is by Robert Carruthers, who says (*Tour*, 1852, p. 229): "Boswell boasts that he had learned a verse of the song; but we suspect it was only the chorous, which, though of the customary length of four lines, consists of but four words frequently repeated . . . The following crude version will give some idea of the original, though it may appear but what Andrew Fairservice calls 'nipperty-tipperty poetry nonsense.'" In his *MacDonald Bards* (1900, p. 32), Keith Norman MacDonald reproduced the same nine quatrains under the heading 'Translation of "Tha Tighinn Fodham Eiridh" by James Boswell', seemingly misled by Carruthers's disclaimer into thinking that Boswell had done the versifying himself. Finally there are, again, nine quatrains and a chorus in Black, *An Lasair* (2001, pp. 48–51). At p. 383 of that book I stated that 'Boswell made a translation of the song into English verse', to which I can only plead the saying: *Mas breug bhuam e, is breug thugam e.* "If it's a lie from me, it's a lie to me."

705 It was indeed an ancient custom (Pennant, *Tour 1772*, p. 301). The clam- or scallop-shell is metaphoric for whisky: *Si 'n t-slige chreachainn / An t-slige chreach sinn.* "The scallop-shell is / The shell that's robbed us."

706 This is explained in the *Tour*: "We set out after dinner for Breacacha, the family seat of the Laird of Coll, accompanied by the young laird, who had now got a horse, and by the younger Mr Macsweyn, whose wife had gone thither before us, to prepare every thing for our reception, the laird and his family being absent at Aberdeen."

707 *Breacachadh* suggests rather a 'variegated field' broken up by rocky outcrops,

much as described later in the paragraph; other etymologies have been suggested (MacEchern, 'Place-Names of Coll', pp. 327–28), but that is the safest.

708 Virgil, *Eclogues*, poem 3, lines 64–65: *Malo me Galatea petit, lasciva puella, / Et fugit ad salices, et se cupit ante videri.* "Galatea, saucy girl, throws an apple at me and runs into the willows to hide, first making sure I see her." The expression 'a vast weight for Ajax' reflects Pope's 'Essay on Criticism', lines 370–71, "When Ajax strives some rock's vast weight to throw, / The line too labours, and the words move slow."

709 They are in fact *sgialaichean* 'tale-tellers', as are standing stones elsewhere. They are 46 feet apart, 5–6 feet above ground, roughly 3 feet broad and a little over a foot thick. Hector MacDougall wrote of them (*Clarsach na Coille*, p. 271) *gu bheil an dara cuid dà fhamhaire no clann famhaire air an adhlac an sin is gur e clach chinn do gach aon a tha anns gach té* ('that either two ogres or ogre's children are buried there and that each is a headstone for one of them'), modifying this in his *Handbook*, p. 41, to 'a tradition that they mark the "grave of a giant" (or two giants)'. Perhaps we may connect them with the 'giants' responsible for the glacial deposits described in the previous paragraph (see also pp. 297, 334–35). *Famhair* suggests not so much a giant as an ogre – a coarse, unpredictable individual of mixed human/Fairy blood who lives in desert places and possesses some supernatural abilities.

710 To be understood, this must be read with Johnson's account at p. 303. What both men describe is an aristocratic inversion of demotic New Year customs as explained by young Coll, who appears to see little value in them other than as a seasonal joke to be played on 'strangers' (meaning, presumably, visiting friends and relations from the Lowlands or England).

711 For New Year's shinty matches see Black, *Gaelic Otherworld*, pp. 536–37. Boswell's explanation of the name is widely believed but unsatisfactory. A derivation from Gaelic *sìnteag* 'leap' is plausible but hard to prove.

712 Addison's *Cato*, act 2, scene 6, lines 55–57: "The helpless traveller, with wild surprize, / Sees the dry desart all around him rise, / And smother'd in the dusty whirlwind dies."

713 Neil Rankin (d. 1819) was a son of Hugh (*Eoghan*), son of Hector (*Eachann*), son of Conduiligh who founded the 'college in Mull'. It was at Kilbrennan by Ulva Sound and was discontinued in 1757. As it was customary for young Rankins and MacCrimmons to complete their education in each other's colleges, Neil finished his in Skye (Morrison, 'Clann Duiligh', pp. 70–71, 72, 74; MacLennan, 'Notices', June 1974; Maclean-Bristol, *From Clan to Regiment*, pp. 191, 293, 399). John (*Iain Dubh*, 1731–1822), eldest son of Malcolm MacCrimmon, served as piper to Macleod of Dunvegan from 1760 to 1769. He had a lease of Boreraig as piper from 1760 to 1775, but appears to have left in 1772 in a rage about being asked to pay rent. It is believed that the piper whom Boswell heard 'every day' was Angus MacKay (*Aonghas Mór*) and that he was succeeded on the same day-to-day basis by Kenneth (d. c. 1801), son of Donald MacCrimmon (*Domhnall Donn*) and cousin to Iain Dubh. The MacCrimmon who emigrated to America in 1772

was John's brother Donald (*Domhnall Ruadh*, 1743–1825). He became an officer in a loyalist corps in 1778 and had returned to Skye on half-pay by 1799, when he played for Macleod. Iain Dubh decided to emigrate in 1795, and got as far as Greenock, but changed his mind and returned to Skye (MacLennan, 'Notices', May–Aug. 1970, Dec. 1971).

714 A schools inspector who visited Coll in the decades around 1900 recalled the estate factor showing him 'two mahogany bedposts of long, spiral shape, carefully roped together and labelled' (Wilson, *Tales and Travels*, p. 183). "These, he said, were two of the posts belonging to the bed in which Johnson slept – all that was rescued when the furniture was being overhauled."

715 Having discovered that Goldsmith's witticism was derivative, Boswell altered this sentence in the *Tour*: "Goldsmith, I remember, to retaliate for many a severe defeat which he has suffered from him, applied to him a lively saying in one of Cibber's comedies, which puts this part of his character in a strong light."

716 Boswell means that all were equal. He used the image again in his journal for 9 March 1777, where he says of Treesbank, following the death in quick succession of James Campbell and his wife (Weis and Pottle, *Boswell in Extremes*, p. 92), "It was a picture of desolation to find both master and mistress gone; yet I know not how, there was a sort of feeling of ease, as in barracks." This account of **6 October** is from his journal.

717 Thomas Gray's 'A Long Story' begins: "In Britain's Isle, no matter where, / An ancient pile of building stands: / The Huntingdons and Hattons there / Employ'd the power of Fairy hands / To raise the cieling's fretted height, / Each pannel in achievements cloathing, / Rich windows that exclude the light, / And passages, that lead to nothing." In his edition of the *Tour* (1852, p. 232), Carruthers commented drily that 'Gray has "*Rich* windows," but the epithet would not have suited the windows of an old Highland castle'. The castle and house at Breacachadh are described and illustrated in RCAHMS, *Argyll*, vol. 3, pp. 177–84, 228–29.

718 The first digit of '1000' is doubtful. It may be '4000'. As at p. 32, the 'last war' is the Seven Years' War, 1656–63.

719 Nicholas Maclean-Bristol now keeps his peats in it. It is curious that young Coll did not mention that *Taigh an Fhrangaich* (or *an Fhraingich*) means equally 'the Frenchman's House' or 'Rankin's House', and that since the Rankins were hereditary pipers to the lairds of Coll (see p. 299), the latter is the obvious meaning. (This was first pointed out a century ago by the Rev. Dugald MacEchern, 'Place-Names of Coll', p. 319.) Pipers expected to be treated by chiefs as companions, not servants, frequently sleeping in the same room (Morrison, 'Clann Duiligh', p. 69). Young Coll seems to have been full of misinformation about his own island, perhaps because his mother was from Skye and he was fostered in Tiree: for another obvious example see p. 336.

720 Presumably this was on the site of the present (nineteenth-century) walled garden half a mile east of Breacachadh.

721 Boswell was confused. Coll stretches from north-east to south-west. Near

the south-western tip, Crossapol Strand faces due south. This passage was omitted in the published *Tour*.

722 More wrong information from young Coll, presumably. It is Norse *Crosabólstaðr* 'Cross Town'.

723 See p. 315.

724 Boswell was one of Sir Allan's counsel in his suit against the duke, see p. 393. It was partially successful, Sir Allan regaining Brolas (south Mull) in 1783. This was however the dregs of the Duart estate: *Diù Mhuile Bròlas*, 'the worst part of Mull is Brolas'. The two ends of Coll are separate properties to this day.

725 In the *Tour* 'journal' is corrected to 'pocket-book'. Johnson was clearly reading Thomas Salmon's *Impartial Examination of Bishop Burnet's History of His Own Times: Containing an Abridgment of that History, and Suitable Remarks on every Material Paragraph* (London, 1724). See note 695.

726 The journal contains more text at this point: ". . . ise to us; for he . . . t which he grate . . . and so made it more palatable." The gaps, each involving perhaps five or six words, are due to the lower corners of the leaf being defective. Pottle and Bennett guessed (*Journal*, p. 271) that Johnson was grating something over his food to make it more palatable. I would suggest that it relates to the lack of lemons for the punch, see pp. 51, 312, 324.

727 Boswell bought some in the shop at Cliad (pp. 300, 333), which was probably kept by Allan, brother of Neil MacLean, Crossapol (Maclean-Bristol, *From Clan to Regiment*, p. 159). This account of 7 **October** is from his journal.

728 There may be some confusion here. *Hurlothrumbo* is a 'foolish piece', but was published in 1729, when Dr Johnson was only twenty, by an older Samuel Johnson (1691–1773) from Cheshire. *A Compleat Introduction to the Art of Writing Letters* is not foolish, but was published in 1758 by an otherwise unknown 'S. Johnson' (Hill and Powell, *Life*, vol. 5, p. 553).

729 In the *Tour* the close-quotation marks are placed after 'we are', making the last sentence Boswell's, and the first sentence of the paragraph is expanded: "Talking of our confinement here, I observed, that our discontent and impatience could not be considered as very unreasonable; for that we were just in the state of which Seneca complains so grievously, while in exile in Corsica." Boswell knew that island well, having visited it in 1765 and published *An Account of Corsica* in 1768. Seneca was banished there by Emperor Claudius in AD 41, and in the *Account* (2006 edn, pp. 28–29) Boswell published two epigrams, translated for him by the young scholar Thomas Day, in which the poet complains of the island's barrenness, heat and plagues. The second ends *Hic solo haec duo sunt, exsul, et exsilium*: "Nought here, alas! surrounding seas enclose, / Nought but an exile, and an exile's woes."

730 See p. 295. The Maclean of Duart who tried to take Coll ('resume' is the wrong word) was Sir Lachlann Mór. As it happened during the minority of Lachlan, 6th of Coll, his opponent was Niall Mór of Quinish (Maclean-Bristol, *Murder under Trust*, pp. 1, 210). The skirmish in which they met was at *Sruthan nan Ceann* ('the Burn of the Heads') near Totronald in Coll. Some years later, in 1598, Sir Lachlann was killed in battle at Tràigh Ghruinneart in Islay.

731 This was *Iain Abrach* ('John of Lochaber', *fl.* 1499–1519), 2nd of Coll; his wife was Janet, daughter of Hugh MacLean of Urquhart, a progenitor of the Kingairloch family (Maclean-Bristol, *Warriors and Priests*, pp. 186, 191). Maclonich, also spelt in English Macgillonie or Macgillanaigh, is in Gaelic *Mac Gill' Onfhaidh* (or *Anfhaidh*), implying descent from a person called *Gill' Onfhaidh* 'Tempest Lad' (presumably from being born in a storm). The name Cameron (*Camshron* 'Bent Nose') is applied to a confederation of Lochaber tribes including MacLonichs, MacMartins, MacSorleys and MacQuilkins. For Cyrus see note 246.

732 See pp. 94, 303. MacDougall gives it from oral tradition (*Handbook*, p. 33): *Ma thig duine de Chloinn 'ic Ghille Onfhaidh a dh'ionnsuidh a' chaisteil so, ged a b'ann air a' mheadhoin-oidhche, agus ceann duine fo achlais, gheibh e an so dion agus fasgadh o gach neach, saor is an Righ.* "Should any MacLonich come to this castle, even if at midnight with a man's head in his oxter, he will find here defence and shelter from all persons, save only the King."

733 'Invinvalie' is Boswell's mistranscription of 'Inivirvalie' (*Inbhir Mhàillidh*, Innermaillie). 'Dugall McConnill of Innermaillie' is a patronymic: he is *Dùghall mac Dhomhnaill*, Dugald son of Donald, a MacLonich Cameron. The original letter is now back in Breacachadh Castle after being found in South Africa, see p. ix.

734 "James, by the grace of GOD King of Scots, to all good men of all his realm, clerks and laymen, greeting. Know ye, that because the late John Maclean, grandfather of our beloved John Maclean of Coll, held as his [heritable] property the lands below mentioned, which were granted to him by our late most noble ancestor, James the Second, King of Scots, of good memory (whose soul GOD rest), and because his papers and his proofs to the title of the lands are destroyed by his enemies and the register of the same burned . . ." This charter to lands in Lochaber (Lochiel) and Morvern (Drimnin, Achalennan) is now back in Breacachadh Castle (see p. ix) and will no doubt be published in full in due course. The text is incomplete here simply because a leaf is missing from Boswell's journal at this point and he chose to leave it out of the *Tour*. I have restored *hereditave* 'heritable' from the original, Boswell having accidentally omitted it; the other blank is a short word h— which neither Boswell nor I could make out. The next few lines, as far as the words 'still continue ane', are from the *Tour*.

735 This is explained by a footnote which Boswell subjoined to Montrose's second letter (*Tour*): "It is observable that men of the first rank spelt very ill in the last century. In the first of these letters I have preserved the original spelling." The originals are now back in Breacachadh Castle (see p. ix): for 'alongs' read 'alonge', for 'your fields' read 'those feilds', for 'acknowledge to you' read 'acknowledge it to you'.

736 Finvoll and Finvola represent variations (*Fionnghal, Fionnghala*) of the common name *Fionnghuala* 'Fair Shoulder', anglicised in modern times as 'Flora' in Scotland and 'Nuala' in Ireland. Flora MacDonald was widely known as *Fionnghal a' Phrionnsa* 'the Prince's Fionnghal'. See p. 302.

737 Pottle and Bennett, *Journal*, p. 276: "Boswell here traces the letters of the

doubtful word." The original document (dated Kilmaluag, Tiree, 7 July 1649) is now back in Breacachadh Castle (see p. ix). At this point the text reads: "I bind & obleis me & my foirsaids to giv to the said finnvoll the just & aequall halff of the houss & the aequall & just halff of all futuir conqueste."

738 There is no trace in Boswell's journal of the leaf or leaves containing the 'curious piece', nor is it among the papers found in South Africa. It is presented as follows in the *Tour*: "I found some uncouth lines on the death of the present laird's father, intituled 'Nature's Elegy upon the Death of Donald Maclean of Col'. They are not worth insertion. I shall only give what is called his Epitaph, which Dr Johnson said, 'was not so very bad' – 'Nature's minion, Virtue's wonder, / Art's corrective here lyes under.'" See p. 338.

739 See p. 331. This item is not among the papers found in South Africa. Unattested copies of the letter, such as this one in Coll, circulated widely in 1746. The original appears to have been destroyed. Kingsburgh told Forbes that the copies in circulation were inaccurate, the original being 'still worse'; he had never given a copy to anyone, and believed that some person who had seen the original had written it down from memory (Paton, *Lyon in Mourning*, vol. 3, p. 83). The unattested copy obtained by Forbes is as follows (*ibid.*, vol. 2, p. 1): "His royal highness, the Duke of Cumberland, has now certain information of the young Pretender's skulking in the Long Island. You know the danger of protecting or aiding him by any of our friends. I have warned my people of it, and ever[y]body knows the reward of putting the laws in execution. I am persuaded he will pay you a visit in expectation of your protection. It will then be in your power (I hope you will use it) to aggrandize your family beyond many in Scotland. I need not enlarge on this. I know Sir Alexander's writing to you would have greater weight with you than anything I can say, which he will probably do. But be assured that his sentiments and mine are the same on this head. You know your reward, and I hope you will do your duty to yourself, your family and country."

740 Again, this is not among the papers found in South Africa. 'Invernochiel' is Alexander Stewart of Invernahyle in Appin; Pottle and Bennett's 'Glenivask' (*Journal* p. 277) can only be a misreading of 'Glenivash', i.e. Glen Nevis, *Gleann Nibheis* (Lochiel and Keppoch were laying siege to Fort William). The original (National Archives of Scotland, Campbell of Stonefield papers, GD14/73) is addressed 'To Alexander Steuart Younger of Invernahyle Esq' and dated 'Glenevis 20th. March 1746'. The body of the letter is written by a clerk, but the postscript is in Lochiel's own hand. See note 309.

741 'Clunie, Younger' is Ewen Macpherson; 'R. H.' is his royal highness Prince Charles, the prince regent. On the morning of 17 March, Murray had simultaneously surprised thirty Government posts in Perthshire and taken them all.

742 'Airds' is Donald Campbell of Airds, deputy lieutenant of Argyll. His daughter Jean married Hector Maclean, 11th of Coll (d. 1754). There were no children of the marriage: Hugh, young Coll's father, who succeeded to

the chiefship in 1754, was Hector's half-brother. 'The Sheriff' is Archibald Campbell of Stonefield, sheriff-depute of Argyll.

743 There is another copy in the Stewart family papers, published in Stewart and Stewart's *Stewarts of Appin*, pp. 173–75. It is closer to the original than to Boswell's version, e.g. 'against Women & the Brute Creation' (GD14/73), 'against women and brute creation' (Stewart), 'against brute creatures' (Boswell). Invernahyle forwarded the original to Donald Campbell, governor of Castle Stalker in Appin, along with the following from himself (Stewart and Stewart, p. 175): "SIR,—As you have frequent opportunities of corresponding with the gentlemen of Argyleshire, I send you the enclosed for their perusal, which I request you will forward. I am heartfelt sorry that the burning of houses and destruction of cattle is once begun in our country, which must be hurtful to both parties, and a loss to the conqueror, and make friends and neighbours that (wish) well to one another's interests alter their sentiments. I own it is the only part of the war that gives me most trouble. If my friends and I should differ about the government of the nation, I always thought it was better we decided in the field than bring our sentiments upon innocent wives and children, who may possibly differ in sentiments from their parents. You may see by the enclosed it is believed that my friends in Argyleshire have been the cause of this violent procedure. I shall be very sorry it hold true, as I still continue to have a value and friendship in private life for them, they being mostly my good friends and relations; and I hope, if it is in their power, they will put a stop to it. I did not choose to be employed in forwarding such letters, but people, once engaged on either side of the question, must execute their orders.—I am, dear Sir, your humble servant, / (Signed) ALEXR. STEWART of Invernahyle." Invernahyle's native Gaelic idiom surfaces in the expressions 'the only (i.e. one) part of the war that gives me most trouble' (*an aon phàirt den chogadh as motha tha deanamh dragh dhomh*) and 'to have a value . . . for them' (*luach* 'value' and *luaidh* 'esteem' seemingly confused as in note 822). He was an officer in Prince Charles's army, and together these letters capture the strange and uneasy atmosphere in the Highlands in the early spring of 1746. There is a copy of both letters in NLS MS 2911, ff. 45v–46v, made at Airds by Sir William Burrell.

744 One song by this Lachlan (*c.* 1703–63) appears to have survived – sixty-four humorous lines in dispraise of the bagpipe – along with two which may be addressed to him, one mocking his verse, the other his coat. They are published but not translated (Ó Baoill, *Duanaire Colach*, pp. 29–31, 112–15). The 'Teague', previously misread as 'League' (Pottle, *Journal*, p. 431), was Capt. Ultan Kindelan or Lt. Maurice McMahon of the Ultonia Regiment of Spanish Infantry. These men had brought a cargo of Jacobite arms and money to Colonsay, Mull, Iona, Barra and South Uist in October–November 1745 (Campbell and Eastwick, 'MacNeils of Barra', pp. 85–88; Maclean-Bristol, *From Clan to Regiment*, pp. 124–26). Major-General John Campbell (who arrested McMahon after Culloden) led the Government militia, including the Argyllshire battalion, in 1745–46; he later became fourth duke of Argyll.

745 Muiravonside's son was Alexander MacLeod ('MacCruslick'), see p. 152. The Lord Justice-Clerk was Thomas Miller, who had defended James of the Glen and later became Lord President (Ramsay, *Scotland and Scotsmen*, vol. I, pp. 342–50). It appears from one of the documents now retrieved from South Africa that Boswell was not told the truth about the Macleans of Coll in the '45, for according to Hugh, young Coll's father, a hundred men were raised for the Government (Maclean-Bristol, *From Clan to Regiment*, p. 673): "These men joined his Majesty's Forces, & went to Culloden; & few of them ever returned."

746 This is an ancient custom variously called 'cadging', 'thigging' or 'genteel begging', Gaelic *faoighe*. Those who practised it took advantage of sacred traditions of hospitality, and it could indeed be burdensome (Black, *An Lasair*, pp. xxix–xxxii).

747 Here again a leaf or more is missing from the journal, and the text is taken from the *Tour* as far as the words 'they all make oil of' (p. 332, foot). The original of Forbes's letter, dated 1737, is now back in Breacachadh Castle; though acting for the duke, he agreed that Hector Maclean was paying a very high rent for the two ends of Coll, see pp. ix, 323.

748 See p. 338, where the topic is raised in conversation.

749 See pp. 179, 255. Boswell's two sketches are omitted. The term that escapes him is probably *cas chrom* 'crooked leg', although the Coll version was called the *cas dhìreach* 'straight leg'. A wooden spade is *caibe*.

750 See note 514. Tiree and Coll were legally one parish from 1618 to 1865 (Black, *Gaelic Otherworld*, p. 630), but from 1733, when Hector MacLean was appointed, funds were available for the minister, who resided in Tiree, to employ an assistant in Coll: hence the ambiguity. When on 25 August 1859 the assistant in Coll, James MacColl, was declared 'first minister of the parish' in view of the fragile state of his superior's health, the latter (Neil MacLean) died next day. His successor was the Rev. John Gregorson Campbell, the folklorist. I take the words 'as appears from the parish registers' from the *Tour*; with the exception of this and two passages drawn from the *Tour* where leaves are missing, Boswell's account of **8 October** is from his journal.

751 A 'tacksman' (from 'tack' or 'taking') was a large tenant; a 'cottar' had no land of his own, but usually enjoyed grazing rights on common land, at least for some goats; the 'small tenants' here referred to emerged as 'crofters' in the following century, once the tacksman class had been eliminated. See note 416.

752 Pottle draws attention (*Journal*, p. 431) to a copy of Johnson's two-volume octavo *Dictionary* (4th edn, 1770) inscribed: "To Mr Maclean, Teacher of Languages in the Island of Coll, from the Author." It was sold by Sotheby's in 1929 and was on offer again by Maggs in 1936. Nicholas Maclean-Bristol says that at one time it belonged to his grandmother (*From Clan to Regiment*, p. 164). In 1969 it was donated by Victor Rothschild, 3rd Baron Rothschild, to the library of Trinity College, Cambridge, where it is shelfmarked RW.48.5/6.

753 These were two books by Thomas Gataker, *Of the Nature and Use of Lots*

and *The Spirituall Watch*, published 1619 (in the age of James VI and I) and here evidently bound together. Gataker's 'lots' were of the decision-making kind.

754 In these first four paragraphs of the account of 9 October, the journal focuses on the rocks, but the *Tour* sweeps them aside with the dismissive remark that 'the stone . . . did not repay our trouble in getting to it', and focuses instead on Johnson. The present account is from the journal, with the addition of five sentences from the *Tour*: the third, fourth and sixth in paragraph 1, and the second and third in paragraph 4. For Boswell's cane see note 530.

755 See p. 315 and note 722. The Crossapol graveyard is described in full in Muir, *Characteristics*, p. 151, and RCAHMS, *Argyll*, vol. 3, p. 137. There are no traces of the chapel today. Also untraceable, presumably due to sand-blow or marine erosion, is a curative *clach thuill* ('holed stone') on Crossapol farm through which consumptives crept three times in the name of the Trinity (Black, *Gaelic Otherworld*, p. 228).

756 See note 329. St Thomas Aquinas defined superstition as 'a vice contrary to religion by excess, not that it offers more to the divine worship than true religion, but because it offers divine worship either to whom it ought not, or in a manner it ought not' (*Summa Theologica*, quoted in Opie and Tatem, *Dictionary of Superstitions*, p. vii).

757 In the *Tour* this becomes 'a very uncouth district, full of sand hills'. The location of the mine, Johnson's 'black vein . . . of lead' (p. 181), is now unknown. Probably it is under sand. MacDougall (*Handbook*, p. 35) says of Feall that 'this is where the vein of lead to which Dr Johnson refers is supposed to be'. The mineralogist Edward Clarke wrote in 1797 (Maclean-Bristol, *From Clan to Regiment*, p. 299): "Upon the seashore at the southern point of the island, is a remarkable vein of the purest lead ore, which runs into the rock. It is extraordinary no person has undertook to work it. I saw specimens of it . . . and was informed that blocks of the ore amounting to 20 or 30 pounds in weight, had frequently been taken from them."

758 The remark about Highland tradition is taken from the *Tour*. Apart from this and the stated changes to the first four paragraphs (note 754), Boswell's account of 9 October is from his journal.

759 Johnson's friend Topham Beauclerk was the duke's brother-in-law. Boswell means that had it been himself, he would have asked Beauclerk 'to carry him there'. For an outstanding example of his thoughtlessness in such matters see note 771.

760 In the *Tour*, instead of mentioning Ovid's *Epistles* here, Boswell adds them to the list of books in the account of 7 October (p. 324): "I read a little of Young's *Six Weeks Tour through the Southern Counties*; and Ovid's *Epistles*, which I had bought at Inverness, and which helped to solace many a weary hour."

761 This sentence is from the *Tour*. The journal merely states: "There was a kind of dismal quietness in the house." Apart from this and one other clarification from the *Tour* (in the paragraph beginning 'I objected'), Boswell's account of 10 October is from his journal.

762 See p. 329.

763 Boswell forgot to complete this sentence.

764 See p. 333.

765 See p. 43.

766 A 'Taliskerian House', see notes 604 and 657. Boswell had in fact mentioned it (p. 321), using Coll's word 'closet'. The term 'little-house' is a conjectural restoration, the manuscript being defective (Pottle and Bennett, *Journal*, p. 291), but this is what he had called it at Dunvegan and Talisker (pp. 253, 290). The Gaelic equivalent *taigh beag* is still very much in use today.

767 See for example Johnson's remark on the Union, p. 32. When in Corsica in October 1765, Boswell had quoted to General Paoli the following remark of Johnson's about James Macpherson (Brady and Pottle, *Boswell on the Grand Tour*, p. 192, cf. *Life*, 14 July 1763): "Why, Sir, if the fellow does not think as he speaks, he is lying; and I see not what honour he can propose to himself from having the character of a liar. But if he does really think that there is no distinction between virtue and vice, why, Sir, when he leaves our houses let us count our spoons." Lord Hailes gave Boswell seven folio pages of detailed remarks on the 'Account of Corsica', but the ensuing correspondence is mostly lost (Brady and Pottle, *Boswell in Search of a Wife*, pp. 14, 79, 97, 100; Cole, *General Correspondence*, vol. 2, p. 294). Both instances of 'why, Sir' survived into the published *Account*.

768 See p. 370. Sir Hector Maclean of Duart (1703–50) was born at Calais, fostered in Coll, and studied philosophy, mathematics and civil law at Edinburgh University, where he seems likely to have met the young Alexander Boswell (1707–82). In 1721 he went on to the Sorbonne, subsequently making his home in Paris (Currie, *Mull*, p. 28). Alexander passed advocate at Leyden University in Holland on 22 July 1727, then took a trip to Paris, where he dressed in the height of fashion. The city was full of Scots Jacobites in those days; one of them, James Drummond of Blair Drummond, later told the young James Boswell at Lord Kames's table that 'he had seen his father strutting abroad in red-heeled shoes and red stockings', whereupon 'the lad was so much diverted with it that he could hardly sit on his chair for laughing' (Ramsay, *Scotland and Scotsmen*, vol. 1, p. 161). For 'honest old Mr John MacLeod' see p. 331; the British colony in Georgia, including the city of Savannah, was founded in 1733 by General Oglethorpe, who returned to England ten years later.

769 In the *Tour* this paragraph was moved to its logical place at 8 October, following the conversation about 'art's corrective' (p. 329), and the final point was clarified: "The lairds, instead of improving their country, diminished their people." None of these letters were among those found in South Africa.

770 This was in Capt. MacLean's house at Arnabost. Boswell records his dislike of sleeping with men at p. 312. The account of 11 **October** is entirely from his journal; in the *Tour* it is reduced to less than 200 words.

771 What Boswell means is that on the way from the harbour to MacSweyn's at Grishipol, the party called in briefly at Capt. Lachlan MacLean's house at Arnabost, which they had left that same morning after spending the night

there. In the *Tour*, however, it is clarified that, despite Coll's good advice, Boswell (though perhaps not Johnson) had every intention of imposing on the Captain's hospitality yet again: "Captain Maclean's house being in some confusion, on account of Mrs Maclean being expected to lie-in, we resolved to go to Mr Macsweyn's, where we arrived very wet, fatigued, and hungry." Within three years the Captain's wife was dead; whether it happened at this confinement is unknown (Maclean-Bristol, *From Clan to Regiment*, p. 155).

772 By 'black' Boswell means 'black-haired'. The account of **12 October** is from his journal; it is expanded in the *Tour* by the addition of material from 14 October.

773 Horace, *Epistles*, book I, poem 18, line 89: *Oderunt hilarem tristes, tristemque iocosi*. "The grave dislike the gay, the gay the grave." This account of **13 October** is from Boswell's journal.

774 Boswell is referring to the belief that barnacle geese hatched in barnacles (Black, *Gaelic Otherworld*, p. 376). By 'put up' he means 'preserved as specimens': he uses the same expression at pp. 335 and 395. By 'Loch Eirach' he means Loch Eithearna, or Lochiern as he spelt it previously (p. 309), but he can hardly be blamed for being confused. Since its first appearance as 'Yurrn' in Blaeu's atlas of 1662 the second element has been variously spelt Yern, Irin, Grin, Ithiuirne, Iathairne, Eatharna and Eithearna. Its meaning is unknown. When Arinagour developed into a village in the nineteenth century it began to be called *Loch Àirigh nan Gobhar*, Loch Arinagour; Boswell's 'arm of the sea' is its narrow innermost reach where it penetrates *Bràighe 'n Loch* 'the Upland of the Loch', high tides bringing sea-water far up the *Mul Bhuidhe* 'Yellow Shingle' (MacDougall, *Handbook*, p. 48).

775 'Sucking bird' will be a reference to the curlew's extraordinary six-inch bill. The term is Boswell's own: at least, it is certainly not taken from the leading 'bird book' of the day, Pennant's *British Zoology* of 1768, nor is Boswell applying it to the woodcock, which has a three-inch bill.

776 Bog-myrtle, see p. 164.

777 Having fasted all day to avoid seasickness (see pp. 306, 342), Boswell drew the oats from the barrel with his fist and licked it off his palm. In the *Tour* he replaced 'licked' with 'eat', i.e. 'ate'. The reference to an 'oatmeal education' is a shy at Johnson's celebrated definition of oats, as the *Tour* makes clear: "Dr Johnson owned that he too was fond of it when a boy; a circumstance which I was highly pleased to hear from him, as it gave me an opportunity of observing that, notwithstanding his joke on the article of oats, he was himself a proof that this kind of food was not peculiar to the people of Scotland." See p. 590 and note 675.

778 Meal imported from Ireland was considered to be of poor quality.

779 Johnson means Tobermory (*Tobar Mhoire* 'the Well of the Virgin Mary'); having heard the name but not seen it in writing, perhaps, he confused it with Morar on the mainland. Boswell corrected him in his 'Remarks' (Adam, *The R. B. Adam Library*, vol. 2, foll. p. 45): "For Morar read Mori or Mory the Earse for Mary." The island is Calve (*Calbh*). The contention that the harbour is more vulnerable to winds off the land than off the sea,

for which see also p. 351, is a mystery to Tobermory folk. One native of the town, Alasdair H. Campbell, has speculated to me that since it consisted in 1773 of little more than an inn, there may have been some sort of gap in the hills which subsequent construction has closed. If so, it would have been in the neighbourhood of the distillery.

780 See p. 356. Hector MacLean, MD (1704–83), younger of Gruline, was a historian and collector of Gaelic verse. For his historical work see note 798. His verse collection, which is of great importance, is now in the Public Archives of Nova Scotia (Ó Baoill, *MacLean Manuscripts*, pp. 36–55). There are copies in Edinburgh and Aberdeen university libraries and in Glasgow University's department of Celtic. He wrote to Boswell on 4 July 1774 enclosing some poems (Maclean-Bristol, 'Re-Appraisal', p. 87). He was married to young Coll's aunt Catherine; for their daughter (Christina *or* Mary, *c.* 1741–1826) see note 799.

781 It is hard to imagine an island more 'broken by waters' and 'shot into promontories' than Mull – except, perhaps, for Skye.

782 See p. 179.

783 Their route took them by Sorne and Baliachcrach to Dervaig before crossing the hill to Torloisk (Currie, *Mull*, p. 106), so the 'ruined chapel' will have been Kilcolmkill (Kilmore), which occupies the highest ground in the churchyard at Dervaig. It appears to have been in use until 1754, when a new church, or rather 'house for worship', was erected nearby (MacArthur, 'Parish of Kilninian', p. 334; RCAHMS, *Argyll*, vol. 3, p. 144). The only loch on the route which could have 'swelled over the road' (p. 359) is Loch na Cuilce at Kilmore.

784 This is unique to Johnson's account, probably because Boswell's journal for 16 October is missing. In the *Tour* Boswell merely says that their plan was to get to Inchkenneth that night, failing which they determined on Ulva (pp. 359–60). First they will have reached the coast at Torloisk, home of Lachlan Maclean. He was certainly hale and hearty: he dined with Boswell, Sir Allan Maclean, young Coll (brother of the deceased), Macquarrie and others in Edinburgh on 18 February 1775 (*Life*), and lived to 1799. But travelling to Inchkenneth will have meant a stop at Lagganulva, home of his brother Archibald (*c.* 1727–82), who presumably commanded the distribution of ferry-boats. His name has come down to us variously as that of a successful merchant, a maker of Gaelic songs, and a lecher (notes 813, 978; Maclean-Bristol, *Hebridean Decade*, pp. 17–18, 25; Currie, *Mull*, pp. 80, 170–71). Clearly on that night, for whatever reason, he was unavailable, but some one advised them to ride the last mile to the ferry, as the boat was expected to leave shortly; for the rest see p. 360.

785 Boswell's account of **14 October** is taken from his journal, with two exceptions: (a) at this point a leaf of the manuscript is missing, and a portion of the text is supplied (with slight re-arrangement) from the *Tour*; (b) later in the account, two brief phrases have been brought in from the *Tour* for clarification. Some portions of the journal for 14 October were transferred in the *Tour* to 9 or 12 October.

786 The play was named *She Stoops to Conquer* just days before its first performance (Hill and Powell, *Life*, vol. 2, pp. 205–06). This anecdote reappears in the *Life* at 7 May 1773.

787 See p. 15. This presumably refers to a version of Aesop's fable about Zeus and the frogs (Gibbs, *Aesop's Fables*, p. 17). The frogs ask Zeus to send them a king. He responds by dropping a piece of wood into their pond. Frightened at first, the frogs take to jumping over it and making fun of it. Then they ask Zeus to send them another king. Irritated, he sends a water-snake which sets about killing them. Terrified, the frogs send Hermes with a message to Zeus, begging him to put an end to the slaughter, or as Boswell says, "This may be sport to you, but it is death to us." Zeus (a stern moralist, like Boswell's father) replies: "Since you rejected what was good, put up with it, or something even worse may happen!"

788 See p. 111. Boswell's note (*Tour*): "It is remarkable that Dr Johnson should have read this account of some of his own peculiar habits, without saying anything on the subject, which I hoped he would have done."

789 See p. 345. In Greek mythology, Antaeus was a gigantic wrestler whose strength was invincible as long as he was touching the earth. Hercules killed him by lifting him off the ground and squeezing him to death.

790 In the *Tour* this paragraph becomes: "We sent to hire horses to carry us across the island of Mull to the shore opposite to Inchkenneth, the residence of Sir Allan Maclean, uncle to young Coll, and chief of the Macleans, to whose house we intended to go the next day. Our friend Coll went to visit his aunt, the wife of Dr Alexander Maclean, a physician, who lives about a mile from Tobermorie."

791 Than Alberti, that is – the *Tour* has it as 'by another Italian'.

792 Boswell's note (*Tour*): "I take leave to enter my strongest protest against this judgment. Bossuet I hold to be one of the first luminaries of religion and literature. If there are who do not read him, it is full time they should begin."

793 The quotation (*Aeneid*, book 6, lines 273–77) is in the *Tour*, with Dryden's English rendering in a footnote: *Vestibulum ante ipsum, primisque in faucibus orci, / Luctus et ultrices posuere cubilia Curæ; / Pallentesque habitant Morbi, tristisque Senectus, / Et Metus, et malesuada Fames, et turpis Egestas, / Terribiles visu formæ; Lethumque, Laborque.* "Just in the gate, and in the jaws of hell, / Revengeful cares, and sullen sorrows dwell; / And pale diseases, and repining age; / Want, fear, and famine's unresisted rage; / Here toils and death, and death's half-brother, sleep, / Forms terrible to view, their sentry keep. DRYDEN." More literally: "Right in front of the doorway, and in the opening of the jaws of hell, grief and avenging pains have made their bed. Ghastly diseases dwell there, and joyless old age, and fear, and hunger that leads to crime, and squalid want, and shapes terrible to see, and death, and toil."

794 Boswell's note (*Tour*): "It is no small satisfaction to me to reflect that Dr Johnson read this, and, after being apprised of my intention, communicated to me, at subsequent periods, many particulars of his life, which probably could not otherwise have been preserved."

795 See note 780. By 'elderly' Boswell will mean 'like a church elder', i.e. officious, self-important.

796 Johnson wrote to Robert Chambers, to Henry Thrale, and then, 'having a little more time than was promised me', to Mrs Thrale as well (Redford, *Letters*, vol. 2, pp. 98–102). He saw fit to inform her: "I have not good health, I do not find that travelling much helps me. My nights are flatulent, though not in the utmost degree, and I have a weakness in my knees, which makes me very unable to walk."

797 In the *Tour* Boswell prefaces this by remarking that 'he sometimes amused himself with very slight reading; from which, however, his conversation showed that he contrived to extract some benefit'. The full title of the collection is *The Charmer: A Choice Collection of Songs, Scots and English*. It was first published in Edinburgh in 1749, with further editions in 1752, 1765 and 1782. Johnson quotes a verse from it at p. 270.

798 With the exception of the sentence beginning 'I was amused', which is from the *Tour*, Boswell's account of **15 October**, down to here, is from his journal. However, fifty-eight pages are missing from the manuscript, so the remainder is taken from the *Tour*. Two versions of the doctor's 'Breif Genealogical Account of the ffamily of McLean' were printed posthumously – one which he had given to Walter Macfarlane in 1734, and one which was later obtained by Alexander MacLean of Ardgour, see p. 603. Others remain unpublished, notably NLS Adv. MS 28.3.12, ff. 2r–19r, the writer of which is anonymous, and one at Breacachadh written by Allan MacLean of Crossapol, see note 667 (Maclean-Bristol, 'Re-Appraisal', p. 70). Also mentioned here are William Tytler's popular *Inquiry, Historical and Critical, into the Evidence against Mary Queen of Scots* (1760, 1767, 1772), and Thomas Saintserf's *Relation of the True Funerals of the Great Lord Marquesse of Montrose* (Edinburgh, 1661), a rare pamphlet.

799 See p. 208. The first of these, as John Mackenzie pointed out in 1841 (*Sar-Obair*, p. 394), is 'Òran do Shir Iain MacillEathain Dhubhairt' (mistitled 'do Shir Eachunn' by Mackenzie), ten eight-line stanzas, still never translated in print. The second is 'Trodan ris an Fheòil' ('Struggling with the Flesh'), an unusual and intriguing item, now rendered into English in Black, *An Lasair*, pp. 94–101. They appear on successive pages of Dr MacLean's collection (Ó Baoill, *MacLean Manuscripts*, p. 40). Miss MacLean's choice of 'Trodan ris an Fheòil' was piquant, as she had a relationship with Duncan MacKenzie, Aros, which in 1768 earned the couple a rebuke from the presbytery. They finally married in 1786 after her father's death (Carruthers, *Tour*, p. 252; Maclean-Bristol, *Hebridean Decade*, p. 19; Currie, *Mull*, pp. 105–06, 296–98).

800 Johnson seems to have suffered from *paracusis Willisii*, a form of deafness whose characteristic symptom is the ability to hear in noisy conditions. It has been suggested that listening to the big drone was 'an acoustic experiment' (Hill and Powell, *Life*, vol. 1, p. 500) which allowed him to 'detect certain aspects of harmonic structure' (Cheape, 'A Rare Instrument', p. 19).

801 There are other versions of this story (Ó Baoill, 'Some Irish Harpers', pp. 159–61). In his memoirs, written 1808–13 (O'Sullivan, *Carolan*, vol. 2, pp.

160–61), Arthur O'Neill (1734–1818) speaks of Ruairí Dall Ó Catháin ('Blind Roger O'Keane', *fl.* 1600–48): "Roger died in Scotland in a nobleman's house, where he left his harp and silver key to tune it. About forty years ago a blind harper named Echlin Keane, a scholar of [Cornelius] Lyons whom I often met and an excellent performer, went over to Scotland and called at the house where Roger's harp and key were, and the heir of the nobleman took a liking to Echlin and made him a present of the silver key, he being namesake to its first owner. But the dissipated rascal sold it in Edinburgh and drank the money." Dr James MacDonnell of Belfast had heard O'Neill tell the story before 1773 (Bunting, *Ancient Music*, introduction, p. 44). On 26 November 1785 Sir Alexander, now Lord Macdonald, who was described by John Gunn (*Historical Enquiry*, p. 47) as 'one of our best amateurs on the violin, and one of the best judges of musical talents of that period', wrote to Boswell (Scott and Pottle, *Private Papers*, vol. 16, p. 239): "O'Kane, the drunken blind Harper . . . after having slurred over some tunes for a week at my house under the inordinate influence of Bacchus, was dismissed with two Guineas in his pocket and a key which he valued more than one hundred Guineas, made of common Agate. His reason for putting so extraordinary a value upon it was because he said it belonged to Roderic O'Kane, a famous Harper in King Ch. 2d's time; being apprehensive of losing what he deemed a precious relict during his drunken vagaries, I am informed he deposited it afterwards in the hands of a relation of mine, who I am confident would restore it to me if I thought it of importance to claim it."

802 Boswell's note (*Tour*): "Mr Langton thinks this must have been the hasty expression of a splenetic moment, as he has heard Dr Johnson speak of Mr Spence's judgment in criticism with so high a degree of respect as to show that this was not his settled opinion of him. Let me add that, in the preface to the *Preceptor*, he recommends Spence's *Essay on Pope's Odyssey*, and that his admirable Lives of the English Poets are much enriched by Spence's anecdotes of Pope."

803 It is *MacGuaire*. Guaire ('noble', 'proud') was a relatively common name in medieval Ireland. Guaire Aidne, king of Connacht, was famed in literature for his generosity. Curiously, Johnson's best description of the evening's events is at p. 196.

804 Staffa was, and is, famed for its basaltic columns and *Uamh Fhinn* 'Fingal's Cave', argued by some to represent *an Uamh Bhinn* 'the Melodious Cave'. On Banks's return from Staffa with Dr Solander (for whom see p. 375) it was described as 'one of the greatest natural curiosities in the world' (*Gentleman's Magazine*, vol. 42, November 1772, p. 540); echoing this, Boswell remarked ('Some Anecdotes', p. 509) how amazing it was that it had 'never before been observed'. Banks's journal of the visit was published by Pennant, who had been unable to land there (*Tour 1772*, pp. 254–68): "Compared to this what are the cathedrals or the palaces built by men?"

805 It might be thought that by 'memorials' Johnson means books, but MacQuarries do not appear to be mentioned by Martin, Pennant or any historian of Scotland down to 1773. He can only mean stones: 'all places

where they could be expected' may therefore be safely defined as Ulva, Inchkenneth and Iona (see p. 393). As Johnson archly mentions 'what was once a church' in Ulva (p. 363) it may be deduced that, animated by piety on the morning of Sunday 17 October, he walked three miles to Cill Mhic Eoghain and back while Boswell slept, thus simultaneously confirming and contradicting its modern description in RCAHMS, *Argyll*, vol. 3, p. 276, according to which the entire structure visible today is evidently a private burial-enclosure of *c*. 1791: "Its walls appear to stand on more substantial footings, which may incorporate some fragments of the early church referred to, but apparently not visited, by Dr Johnson in 1773 . . . The earliest inscribed stone is a headstone erected to mark his burying-place in 1765 by John McGuarie of Balligarten." In answer to the argument that Boswell mentions no such walk, it may be pointed out that Johnson decided on 1 September to write the *Journey* (p. 89), but said nothing about it until 21 October (p. 403).

806 See p. 364. *Mercheta mulierum* appears to be of Celtic origin: Welsh *mercheta* 'debauching', Latin *mulierum* 'of married women'. Johnson was clearly pleased to find a little piece of evidence pertaining to this vexatious problem of legal history. In his *Dictionary*, citing John Cowell, *The Interpreter* (1607), he had defined 'Borough *English*' as 'a customary descent of lands or tenements, whereby, in all places where this custom holds, lands and tenements descend to the youngest son; or, if the owner have no issue, to his youngest brother'. Lord Hailes poured scorn on the idea that *mercheta mulierum* was ever sanctioned by Scots law, but could not avoid admitting that *jus primae noctis* prevailed at one time in many countries of Europe (Dalrymple, *Annals of Scotland*, vol. 1, pp. 324–29; Anderson, 'Enquiry', p. 64). A sheep rendered up in the way described was known as a *caora chàraidh* 'sheep of adjustment'; Fr Allan McDonald describes it as 'a sheep due as tribute to the proprietor' and says (*Gaelic Words*, p. 60): "All the tenants had to send a fat sheep to the tacksman at *Samhuinn* or Hallowtide. This exaction was strictly enforced." *Samhain*, the month of November, was the traditional time for weddings.

807 Ulva was sold to Capt. Dugald Campbell of Achnaba in 1777 for £9,080 (MacKenzie, *As it Was*, p. 13).

808 These Skye McClures or MacLures are *Mac-a-Leòir, MacillDheòir, Mac Ghill' Dheòir* 'Son of the Dewar's Servant', one of a group of names derived from ecclesiastical office, the best-known of which is *Gill' Easbaig, Gilleasbaig,* Gillespie, 'Bishop's Servant' (MacBain, 'Early Highland Personal Names', pp. 164–66). For dewars see note 850. The best-known Mac-a-Leòir was a poet from Skye who satirised John MacCodrum (1693–1779) on a visit to Uist; the motive may have been jealousy, as Sir James Macdonald made MacCodrum his bard, with a croft free of rent for life, in 1763 (Matheson, *Songs of John MacCodrum*, pp. xxi, xxiv–xxv, xxxiv, 272, 317).

809 This sentence may be read as an attempt to clarify Johnson's inscrutable statement (p. 362) that 'the original of this claim, as of our tenure of *Borough English*, is variously delivered'. In other words, Johnson explicitly endorsed

the connection between *mercheta mulierum* and Borough English that had been made long before (as he knew well) in Plot's *Natural History of Stafford-Shire* (p. 278): "I guess . . . that the places where now *Borow-English* obtains, were anciently lyable to the same ungodly *custom* granted to the *Lords* of *Manors* in *Scotland* by King *Evenus* or *Eugenius*, whereby they had the *privilege* of enjoying the first nights lodging with their *Tenants* brides." Plot was subsequently ridiculed by Dalrymple in *The Annals of Scotland*, vol. 1, pp. 315–16, the proofs of which Johnson corrected. Boswell's note (*Tour*): "Sir William Blackstone says in his Commentaries that he cannot find that ever this custom prevailed in *England*; and therefore he is of opinion that it could not have given rise to *Borough-English*."

810 See p. 196. In Scotland Latin was pronounced in the Continental way, in England like English. Boswell's account of **16 October** (in both chapters 7 and 8) is from the *Tour*, as his journal for this date is missing.

811 Sir Allan (*c.* 1710–83) was 6th baronet and 18th Maclean of Duart. His wife Una, of the Coll family, had died in 1760. He had three daughters, Maria, Sibella ('Miss Sibby', p. 377) and Ann, the youngest, who was away at school (Pottle, *Journal*, p. 434; Currie, *Mull*, pp. 107, 150). Due to the misfortunes of his ancestors, he owned no property at all, but had a tack of Brolas, which the Campbells had mortgaged to the Macleans (*ibid.*, pp. 107, 436). Inchkenneth was by far the best piece of land on the Brolas estate, and when Boswell 'indulged serious thoughts of buying it' (p. 374), it was on the assumption that he would help Sir Allan win back the whole of his patrimony (note 724), and that his victorious client would take up residence in Duart Castle.

812 He commanded a company in the Argyll militia on the Government side in 1745–46, then served as a captain in the Scots Brigade in the Netherlands. In 1756 he proposed raising a regiment of a thousand Highlanders, but this was sabotaged by the duke of Argyll, and he had to be content with a company in the 77th Foot, Lord Eglinton's Highlanders (Montgomerie's Regiment, see notes 284, 287), with whom he served in America in 1757–58 (Maclean-Bristol, *Hebridean Decade*, p. 8).

813 This was probably Macquarrie's second daughter Flora, who later married John, illegitimate son of Archibald Maclean of Lagganulva, for whom see notes 784, 825 and 978. Her elder sister Maria was married in 1771 to Gillean MacLean, WS, of Scallastle (Currie, *Mull*, p. 430).

814 *Hamlet*, act 3, scene 4: "Alas, how is't with you, / That you do bend your eye on vacancy, / And with the incorporal air do hold discourse?" The ruins on Inchkenneth are of a thirteenth-century parish church; there is no physical evidence for the early Christian college which was traditionally believed to exist on the site (RCAHMS, *Argyll*, vol. 3, pp. 138–40).

815 Perhaps by 'contempt' Johnson means 'irony', on the basis that Sandiland is not particularly sandy and scarcely a 'land'. Fleeman describes it as 'a low rocky reef with a little grass crown and not much sand' (*Journey*, p. 308). Boswell calls it 'Sannaland or Sandyland', and it is otherwise on record as Sandland, Samaland, Samalan, Samlan. The name is clearly Norse. Dr

Richard Cox tells me that he is inclined to agree with the assumed derivation from *sandr* 'sand' and *land* 'land', but wonders if it was originally a name for Inchkenneth itself, transferred to the smaller island when the larger one began to be called after the saint.

816 Johnson adapts Virgil, *Eclogues*, poem 3, line 108: *Non nostrum inter vos tantas componere lites.* "It's not for me to settle such a great dispute between you." The first part of this paragraph, from 'Some days' to 'take us a week', was written by Pottle and Bennett to create a link between the *Tour* and the surviving manuscript of the journal, which recommences with the words 'to go to it' (*Journal*, p. 314). The rest of the account of 17 **October** is from the journal, with the exception of four short sentences or passages of clarification and Johnson's ode to Inchkenneth, all of which are from the *Tour*.

817 See p. 341. Boswell speaks apostrophically to Sir Allan (no doubt with a change of tone) while addressing Johnson.

818 See p. 117. The historian Dr John Campbell (1708–75) was fourth son of Robert Campbell of Glenlyon. He was born in Edinburgh but brought up in England. In the *Tour* Boswell points out that *Britannia Elucidata* is 'since published under the title of *A Political Survey of Great Britain*'.

819 I am indebted to Mr Norman MacLeod for the following translation: "There is indeed a small kingdom, known by the religion of its forefathers, lying open amidst Scottish waters; here Kenneth, it is said, by his voice of authority, tamed a wild people and taught them to forget about false gods. Brought here over the dark blue sea by means of a pleasant voyage, I wished to get to know the place and what new knowledge it would provide. In that place Maclean, renowned in the eyes of our noble grandfathers, ruled from a humble abode. One lowly dwelling accommodated two girls along with their father. The god Love had appointed these girls to be goddesses of the deep. However, they did not lie hidden in an unrefined state in cold caves similar to the situation in which the cruel inhabitant of the Danube exists; they did not lack the pleasant comforts of an empty life, whether their periods of leisure demanded books or the lyre. That day had dawned when a race of people, learned in the laws pertaining to a northern country, gave instructions for the hopes and cares of mankind to be in the distant past. Amidst the roaring of the waves the services of a sacred culture did not cease; as well as piety here also was a feeling of care: at a time of sacrifice a woman studied the books and their pure hearts offered up prayers sanctioned by law. Where further should I wander? That which is looked for everywhere is here; this is a secure seat of quiet rest, here is honourable love."

820 Johnson wrote to Mrs Thrale of this visit to the chapel (Redford, *Letters*, vol. 2, p. 105): "Boswel, who is very pious, went into it at night to perform his devotions, but came back in haste for fear of Spectres."

821 Isaiah 26: 3. Boswell also thinks of 'A Hymn to Contentment' by Thomas Parnell: "Oh! by yonder mossy seat, / In my hours of sweet retreat, / Might I thus my soul employ / With sense of gratitude and joy."

822 MacDougall, *Clarsach na Coille*, pp. 276–77 (I translate): "One of Iain Garbh's bones, his humerus apparently, was kept by an old woman called

Màiri nighean Iain Bhàin in her own house at Triallan for some time after the Macleans lost the estate. When, at an advanced age, she realised that she was coming to the end of her days, she gathered together some of the old natives of the island and delivered up the bone to them. It was buried in its proper place, in the grave of the Macleans in Cill Fhionnaigh, along with the rest of Iain Garbh's earthly remains. Why she had it, apart from the value (*luaidh*) she placed on the memory of its owner when the warm marrow of humanity was in it, or what proof she had that it belonged to her beloved hero, is unclear. It was said that Cill Fhionnaigh had begun to be seriously threatened by blowing sand in the time of Alastair Ruadh, and that many of the bones had come to the surface – apparently that was why the new Mausoleum (*Tung*) was built at Ardnish. The bones of Iain Garbh appeared along with others, and according to one report, a son or brother of the laird of Coll brought this one home to Breacachadh, but others in the family, one of his brothers at least, was annoyed at him for so doing, or even for taking it out of the churchyard where it had a right to be. It was shortly after this, perhaps, that Màiri nighean Iain Bhàin acquired it. She was said to have looked after it so carefully that she always had it by her, even keeping it behind her bed when she was asleep at night." One of the 'old natives' (John Johnston, piper and hero of land reform) told MacDougall more than once that the precious relic was thirteen inches thick and proportionately long, more like a thigh-bone than a humerus (*cnaimh-mór a' ghàirdein*), but the others insisted that it was the latter. There is a shorter version of the same account in MacDhughaill, 'Seann Eachdraidh Chollach', p. 201.

823 Altered in the *Tour* to 'such an obligation in a contract of marriage'. The custom was widespread: young Lochbuie was regarded as chief in the same way, see note 825.

824 The last sentence here is from the *Tour*. Except for this and one short phrase, Boswell's account of **18 October** is from his journal.

825 This happened on 25 September 1774. Sir Walter Scott claimed that 'just opposite to Macquarrie's house the boat was swamped by the intoxication of the sailors, who had partaken too largely of Macquarrie's wonted hospitality' (Croker, *Life,* 19 October 1773), but despite Johnson's mention of Ulva, Macquarrie appears to have had nothing to do with it. The following is a traditional account, translated from a radio broadcast made by Neil Morison in 1936 or 1937 (Mac a Phi, *Am Measg nam Bodach*, pp. 56–58): "One event that took place in the lower half of Mull was as fresh in the traditions of the old people a century afterwards as it was the day it happened, and that was the drowning of *Domhnall Cholla* (Donald of Coll) in the Sound of Ulva . . . This Donald was the 'young Col' of whom Dr Johnson speaks so warmly. He was so highly regarded among his own compatriots that they would lower their voices almost to a whisper when speaking about him nearly a hundred years after his death. As it was told to me, this is how it happened. He, Maclaine of Lochbuie (*Mac'Illeathain Loch Buidhe*) and one or two other men left Erray House near Tobermory, making for Inchkenneth where Sir Allan Maclean lived. Unfortunately he never reached his destination. On the

way across the moor, at Achnasaul, he visited Hector Morrison, his ground-officer on the Quinish estate, and told him how annoyed he was at Lochbuie for shooting and killing birds on the journey. At any rate, they carried on to Lagganulva, where they called on Archibald of Laggan, brother of the laird of Torloisk. No sooner were they in the house than Lochbuie found an opportunity to ask the man of the house to have some of the moorhen that he had shot on the way prepared for a midday meal and placed on the table in front of Domhnall Cholla to carve them up. They sat in to their meal. The birds were served as requested, but when Domhnall Cholla realised what had happened he immediately threw them into the grate and would not take a bite. Then they resumed their journey to the ferry. Tragically, the boat was only a short way out from land when it overturned. Domhnall Cholla, his servant and six others were drowned. He was found, the only one marked – with a cut on his face. Hector Morrison took care of him, wrapped him in his cloak, and brought him to Coll. When I tell you that both Lochbuie and Domhnall Cholla were seeking the hand of Sir Allan's daughter, you will realise that there was no love lost between them. It's said that she preferred Domhnall. Before they took him away from Ulva Ferry she came from the Inch and asked for his watch; she opened it and took out a tiny piece of paper. People subsequently assumed that it was a marriage agreement between herself and the heir of Coll.

"It's very likely, as the old people used to tell me, that this was the origin of the verses that inspired the poet Thomas Campbell to write 'Lord Ullin's Daughter'. A sister of Campbell of Airds had the tack of Sunipol farm; her brother's family lived with her, along with the poet as tutor. Her chief tenant was Alexander MacLean from Coll, and the drowning made such an impression on the people's minds that I am sure he would often have spoken of it to the poet."

The man referred to as Lochbuie is Archibald (referred to briefly at p. 406), son and heir of John Maclaine of Lochbuie. He succeeded fully to the chiefship in 1778, joined the army, married a young heiress in New York in April 1784, and was murdered in a shipboard brawl four months later (Currie, *Mull*, pp. 119–36). The daughter of Sir Allan's who retrieved her 'tiny piece of paper' will have been Maria, then aged twenty-two, whose 'undoubted gifts and beauty' are referred to by Currie (*Mull*, p. 148); she and young Coll (with one of his dogs) are portrayed together in a painting reproduced on the cover of Maclean-Bristol's *Hebridean Decade*, and in his *From Clan to Regiment*, foll. p. 366. The report of the disaster in the *Scots Magazine*, vol. 36, September 1774, p. 503, gives the death toll as nine, not eight, and the number of survivors as three: "Archibald Murdoch, Esq; younger of Gartincaber, Mr Maclean of Coll, Mr Fisher from England, and Mr Malcolm Macdonald drover in Mull, with five attendants, unfortunately drowned in crossing a ferry in the isle of Mull. Mr Murdoch had gone to Mull on a visit to Mr Maclean of Lochbuy; and having dined in a friend's house, the melancholy accident happened in their return. The barge overset within a gunshot of the lands of Ulva and Mull. Mr Maclean of Lochbuy, and three young men in the barge, having got hold of the mast, continued dashing in the waves for three quarters of an hour, and were saved by the ferry-boat of Ulva, which reached them just as they were ready to sink."

826 For the disappointment see pp. 176, 258; now they were in *Uamh Chloinn Fhionghain*, the MacKinnons' Cave at Gribun (MacLean, *History of the Island of Mull*, vol. 1, p. 41). The MacKinnons held Gribun in the fourteenth and fifteenth centuries as long as their chiefs and abbots were influential in Iona and Inchkenneth. A MacKinnon from Gribun, *Gobha Dubh Ghrìobainn*, fought for Iain Garbh at Grishipol (MacDougall, *Clarsach na Coille*, p. 276). Subsequently, under pressure from the MacLeans, they were forced to exchange it for Mishnish, and the last of them were cleared out by 1600. Sir Walter Scott explained (Croker, *Life*, 19 October 1773): "A great number of the McKinnons, escaping from some powerful enemy, hid themselves in this cave till they could get over to the isle of Sky. It concealed themselves and their birlings, or boats, and they show McKinnon's harbour, McKinnon's dining-table, and other localities. McKinnon's candlestick was a fine piece of spar, destroyed by some traveller in the frantic rage for appropriation, with which tourists are sometimes animated."

827 Without knowing it, Johnson and Boswell had stumbled on the most enduring and widespread of British eschatological myths – the story of a warrior in the otherworld which found expression in English in the 'Romance of Thomas the Rhymer' and in Gaelic as traditions of *Uamh an Òir* 'the Cave of Gold' (Bruford, 'Legends', pp. 43–45, 54–55). Every Cave of Gold has a rear exit, usually at the other side of an island or peninsula; the MacKinnons' is said to be near Tiroran on the north shore of Loch Scridain (Maclean, *Isle of Mull*, p. 158). It is curious that Johnson, who did not believe in Fingal, should have reported the name 'Fingal's Table', while Boswell, who discusses the 'table' in detail (p. 386), fails to mention it. Some accounts claim that the cave takes its name from the piper, but the piper legend is migratory. 'Fingal's Table' is said to have been 'used by the disciples of the Columban Church who made the cave a kind of hermitage' (Macphail, *Handbook*, p. 58), so it is just possible that 'Fingal' is in error for 'Finguine', and that the table and cave take their name from the most notorious of these warrior clerics, Finguine the Green Abbot (*fl.* 1357–1405), brother of Niall, chief of the MacKinnons (Macquarrie, *Iona*, pp. 16–19). The Gaelic writer John MacCormick locates an unusually full telling of the *Uamh an Òir* story in this cave, while endorsing the Fingalian connection (*An t-Eilean Muileach*, p. 79): "It opens . . . into an arched chamber, 45 feet wide by 30 feet high, where is a square stone called Fingal's Table, on which tradition states that the Fingalian feasts were served. It appears to have been formed by a vein of trap rock which has afterwards been washed out by the sea."

828 This is a reference to Jacob Spon, *Voyage d'Italie, de Dalmatie, de Grece, et du Levant . . . par Jacob Spon . . . & George Wheler* (Lyon, 1678), and George Wheler, *Journey into Greece, by George Wheler Esq; in company of Dr. Spon of Lyons* (London, 1682), in which Wheler frequently contradicts his friend's account of what they had both seen and heard.

829 Having passed Ardtun (Johnson's 'Atun'), they appear to have been on the tidal rock that lies off the headland at Eorabus on the eastern shore of *Loch na Làthaich* ('the Loch of Mud', Bunessan Loch) in the Ross of Mull.

830 This is not the full story. As Boswell points out at p. 431, Johnson refused to be carried, jumped into the sea and waded ashore. His action was regarded as eccentric by the islanders and was long remembered. The following is my translation of a traditional account broadcast in 1936 or 1937 by the Rev. Dr Coll MacDonald (Mac a Phi, *Am Measg nam Bodach*, pp. 28–29): "Johnson was a massive, burly man, big-bellied and talkative. He was so short-sighted that he jumped out of Maclean of the Inch's galley before her stem had ploughed a furrow in the sands of Port Ronan. He was wet up to his thighs, and poor Boswell paid for the calamity. The huge old man exploded in rage and started berating and bullying him. 'I have been tormented like the Apostle Paul by the tumult of waves and placed in danger of my life amidst the dark vales and horrid peaks of this uncouth land. Should this wetting bring upon me a fatal disease, pray take care that my corpse rot in London's soil, and by no means amongst the savage chiefs and plunderers of the Highland clans.'"

831 This was Neil MacDonald, see pp. 390–91.

832 By 'episcopal church' Johnson means the diocesan church of the bishop of the Isles. The 'original church' or 'first church' is the abbey, whose arches are Romanesque. The 'building of equal dimension' or 'additional building' is the cathedral, and the 'chambers or cells belonging to the monks' are the adjoining cloisters. Pennant's description of the ruins appeared in 1774 (*Tour 1772*, pp. 237–50) while Johnson was working on the *Journey*.

833 Dr Hector MacLean writes, for example, of John, Lord of the Isles, vowing friendship to the Macleans in Iona 'upon certain Stones called black Stones where Men were used to make solemn Vows in those superstitious Times' (Macfarlane, *Genealogical Collections*, vol. 1, p. 122). According to Martin (*Description*, p. 158), the black stones, 'which are so called, not from their colour, for that is grey, but from the effects that tradition say ensued upon perjury', lay outside the church to the west of Torr an Aba. Pennant, who appears to have found them in a corner of the cloister, said they were black (*Tour 1772*, pp. 245, 248). Other early accounts speak of a single 'Black Stone' (see pp. 393–94), and in his remarks on the *Journey* (Adam, *R. B. Adam Library*, vol. 2, foll. p. 45) Boswell insisted on this – "p. 349 line 17 for *Stones* read *Stone*. p. 350 at the top might not a better word than *blackest* be found for the infamy of violating an oath on the *black* stone? p. 350 line 7 for *Stones* read *Stone*."

834 Pennant found the nunnery floor covered 'some feet thick with cow-dung', part of which he paid a man to remove (*Tour 1772*, p. 237), with the result that, as Boswell says (p. 392), it was now only one foot deep. Six visitors, from Sacheverell in 1688 to Johnson in 1773, charted the gradual reduction of the altar in the abbey church from 'one of the finest pieces of white marble I ever saw' to 'destroyed', some of them also, like Johnson, noting the powers that fragments of it were believed to possess (RCAHMS, *Iona*, pp. 140–41).

835 Mairi MacArthur points out to me that the 'five chapels yet standing' will be St Ronan's, St Oran's, St Mary's, St Michael's (as it has been called since restoration) and St Columba's (originally a separate oratory, see note 854). Boswell's 'Oran's Chapel, and four more' (p. 392) reflects the same calculation. The 'three more remembered' may be Cill Chainnich, Cill mo Ghobhannain and Cill mo Neachdainn. The four great free-standing crosses of St Oran, St John, St Martin and St Matthew are fully described in that order in RCAHMS, *Iona*, pp. 192–211; Johnson is the first writer to mention St John's. St Martin's is the best preserved, and is twice mentioned by Boswell (pp. 392, 393).

836 This garden ground lay between the abbey and *Torr an Aba* ('the Abbot's Mount') to the west, and on both sides of *Sruth a' Mhuilinn* ('the Mill Stream') to the north. Martin mentions 'an empty piece of ground between the church and the gardens, in which murderers and children that died before baptism were buried' (*Description*, p. 157); speaking of Torr an Aba, Pennant says (*Tour 1772*, p. 250): "Beneath seem to have been the gardens, once well cultivated, for we are told that the monks transplanted from other places, herbs both esculent and medicinal. Beyond the mount are the ruins of a kiln, and a granary: and near it, was the mill. The lake or pool that served it lay behind; is now drained, and is the turbary, the fuel of the natives." The lake was known as *an Lochan Mór* 'the Big Pool'; Sruth a' Mhuilinn was probably deepened *c.* 1750 to facilitate the draining of the loch, and is clearly the 'aqueduct' referred to by Johnson, but it is hard to know what to make of his 'fishponds'.

837 The Bishop's House (*Taigh an Easbaig*) lies just north of Sruth a' Mhuilinn, and enjoyed its own walled garden. Most of the fabric collapsed during the century after Johnson's visit (RCAHMS, *Iona*, pp. 252, 280).

838 At this period the minister of Kilfinichen and Kilviceon held services in Iona four times a year. In 1774 the Society in Scotland for the Propagation of Christian Knowledge established a school. In 1828 a 'parliamentary chapel' was built. A minister was appointed to it the following year, and in 1845 the island was made a *quoad sacra* parish of the Church of Scotland. Following the emergence of a Free Church congregation, a second new church was built in 1849.

839 See p. 395.

840 See note 825. In the *Tour* the passage from 'There was a kindly regret' to here is as follows: "We parted from him with very strong feelings of kindness and gratitude; and we hoped to have had some future opportunity of proving to him the sincerity of what we felt; but in the following year he was unfortunately lost in the Sound between Ulva and Mull; and this imperfect memorial, joined to the high honour of being tenderly and respectfully mentioned by Dr Johnson, is the only return which the uncertainty of human events has permitted us to make to this deserving young man." Among the papers now restored to Breacachadh from South Africa (see p. ix) is 'AN / ELEGY / TO THE MEMORY OF / Mr *MACLEAN*, younger of *Coll*, / Who was drowned with three Gentlemen, and five Attendants, on / the 25th

of September, 1774'. Printed in two columns on a single sheet, it consists of 122 lines beginning 'And is thy race, Maclean, already o'er? / And shall thy virtues rise to charm no more?' It is subscribed 'Musæus. *Spittle-hill, Dec. 22. 1774*'. Spittle-Hill is at Morpeth in Northumberland.

841 *Lachann Dubh* 'Black-Haired Lachlan'. Boswell had no reason to know his surname.

842 See note 827. The words from 'who, however nice' to 'another nature, that' are from the *Tour*; otherwise the account of **19 October** is taken from Boswell's journal.

843 The unnamed loch is Loch na Làthaich (see note 829); the public-house was at Bunessan.

844 Probably Fidden, which had Campbell tacksmen at this time. Fidden itself is on the Sound of Iona, but the farm may have expanded to take in Bunessan, which had been 'a good farm going to waste' in 1748. Ardfenaig, three miles west and strongly associated with Campbell tacksmen in the nineteenth century, was tenanted by MacLeans at this period (Currie, *Mull*, pp. 349–57, 435, 436, 438).

845 In the *Tour* at this point Boswell says that they 'sailed along by moonlight, in a sea somewhat rough, and often between black and gloomy rocks'.

846 Cicero, *De Finibus Bonorum et Malorum*, book 2, §32, *vulgo enim dicitur iucundi acti labores*, 'for there's a popular saying that toil is pleasant when it's over'.

847 Boswell's note (*Tour*): "I have lately observed that this thought has been elegantly expressed by Cowley: 'Things which offend when present, and affright, / In memory, well painted, move delight.'" This is Abraham Cowley's 'Ode upon His Majesty's Restoration and Return', verse 12, lines 8–9.

848 In the *Tour* Boswell says: "When we had landed upon the sacred place, which, as long as I can remember, I had thought on with veneration, Dr Johnson and I cordially embraced. We had long talked of visiting Icolmkill; and, from the lateness of the season, were at times very doubtful whether we should be able to effect our purpose." He speaks of the pleasure of being there with Johnson 'who was no less affected by it than I was', quotes the latter's words on 'the plain of Marathon' and 'the ruins of Iona' (p. 381), and adds a footnote: "Had our tour produced nothing else but this sublime passage, the world must have acknowledged that it was not made in vain. The present respectable President of the Royal Society was so much struck on reading it, that he clasped his hands together, and remained for some time in an attitude of silent admiration." This was Sir Joseph Banks, for whom see pp. 146, 263, 361, 376.

849 See p. 381. Neil MacDonald, later described as innkeeper as well as farmer, was the duke of Argyll's principal tenant in Iona (MacArthur, *Iona*, pp. 16, 24). The Rev. Dr Coll MacDonald's account, seemingly based on oral tradition, differs from Boswell's with regard to Johnson's appetite, as is normal in Gaelic stories about him (Mac a Phi, *Am Measg nam Bodach*, p. 29, translated): "He spent the night in Maclean's house facing Port Ronan, near the Nunnery (*an eaglais dhubh*, 'the black church'). He was given the

best food and drink in the house. Despite eating a chicken all by himself, like Donald Cumming, he was most displeased at not being provided with a utensil unknown in Iona in that era. He did not sleep well in a strange bed, and was astir early in the morning, most impatient to receive his breakfast." Donald Cumming was a character in a popular song (Mac-na-Ceàrdadh, *An t-Òranaiche*, pp. 71–73); for forks see note 278. Mairi MacArthur points out to me that Dr MacDonald referred to the house as Maclean's because that was how it was known in the 1930s. Formerly an inn, it is now Iona Cottage.

850   In the *Tour* Boswell adds that he was illiterate. He says just enough about the cicerone ('guide') to suggest that he was the hereditary coarb or keeper of the relics of the saint, a figure usually known elsewhere in Scotland as a *deòir* or 'dewar'. The Ó Muirgheasáins or Morisons, who served as poets to the Macleans in the sixteenth and seventeenth centuries, had performed precisely this office in Donegal (Thomson, *Companion*, pp. 219–20).

851   On the cow-dung in the nuns' chapel see p. 382. The gravestone described by Boswell is that of Anna Maclean (d. 1543), prioress of the Augustinian nunnery of Iona. It was fortunate that it had already been sketched by Lhuyd and Pennant, as a third of it was destroyed by the collapse of the vault in 1830 (RCAHMS, *Iona*, pp. 232–33). William Sacheverell, Martin Martin, the Rev. Dr Richard Pococke, the Rev. Dr John Walker and Thomas Pennant all wrote good descriptions which may be read today (see pp. 604–06), while J. F. Miller and other draughtsmen who accompanied Banks to Iona in 1772 left a valuable pictorial record (RCAHMS, *Iona*, pp. 150, 156, 157).

852   'St Columbus's Well' was probably constructed in the sixteenth century, and is still in use; no doubt by '——— house' Boswell means 'little house', but the abbey's reredorter or latrine-block measures 9.5 x 5.3 metres, which is hardly 'inconsiderable' (RCAHMS, *Iona*, pp. 130–31, 138).

853   See note 724.

854   Boswell had been the victim of a surpassingly ambivalent piece of tradition. Not only were the location and colour of the 'black stones' in doubt (note 833), their number varied as well. Several early accounts identify 'the Black Stone' as an ecclesiastical effigy of late medieval type, carved in relief as a grave-slab and preserved, until its destruction by a lunatic about 1820, in the oratory at the abbey church known as St Columba's Shrine (RCAHMS, *Iona*, p. 233).

855   Psalms 90: 4.

856   John Johnston of Grange, an Edinburgh advocate, was one of Boswell's closest friends, and the letter (Walker, *Correspondence*, pp. 284–85) is an eighteenth-century postcard: "Cathedral of Icolmkill, 20 October 1773 / MY WORTHY FRIEND: I promised to write to you from this venerable spot. You know I never fail either in my promises or good offices to you. But at present I would less fail than at any other time; for the sanctity of the place and the sight of the ruined monuments of religion and learning now around me have thrown me into so excellent a frame that our long friendship has the most lively impressions upon my soul. I am all superstition and warmth

of heart. I fervently pray GOD to bless us and make us eternally happy in heaven. It is grand to see the Rambler stalking about as I write. I am ever your most affectionate friend / JAMES BOSWELL."

857 See p. 384. 'MacGinnis' is *MacAonghais*, nowadays anglicised MacInnes, one of the most common surnames in Iona at that time. Clearly he could speak English. The abolition of heritable jurisdictions (pp. 188, 190–91) had in fact removed any vestigial right of Sir Allan's to 'hang him if he pleased' in 1747. The words 'and had not been there for fourteen years' are from the *Tour*; otherwise Boswell's account of **20 October** (in both chapters 10 and 11) is from his journal.

858 Boswell seems to have crossed to the machair on the western side of the island, then ridden south past Loch Staoineig, the three rocks being *Stac an Aoinidh* ('the Stack of the Steep Promontory') and its neighbours (Pottle, *Journal*, p. 481).

859 A *curach* is a boat constructed of skins on a timber frame. The word is masculine in Iona, feminine elsewhere. In *Port a' Churaich* ('Coracle Harbour') it is in the masculine form of the genitive case, and Boswell mistook it for 'wherry'.

860 These were the Rev. Neil MacLeod (*not* MacLean), minister of Kilfinichen and Kilviceon (1729–80), Dr Alexander MacLean of Pennycross (1725–86), and John Maclaine (*c.* 1700–78), 17th of Lochbuie. MacLeod had married his predecessor's daughter Margaret MacLean (d. 1789).

861 As the MacDonalds of Glencoe and Ardnamurchan traced their descent from different figures called John, the chiefs of both were patronymically *Mac Mhic Iain* 'the Son of the Son of John'. This gave each kindred the secondary surname *MacIain*, for which the Lowland surname Johnston provided a convenient English translation.

862 A reference to heritable jurisdictions, see pp. 93, 188, 190–91.

863 See p. 404.

864 By 'thin' Johnson means 'thin on the ground'.

865 What Johnson has in mind will be the Rev. John Walker's *Report*, which gives figures of 5,325 for Mull and 15,067 for Skye. Probably the minister with whom Johnson discussed the latter figure was MacQueen, whose parish of Kilmuir contained the largest single concentration of people which the two travellers had missed on their visit to Skye – East Side, now called Staffin.

866 This is John Leslie or Lesley (1527–96), bishop of Ross, author of a Latin history of Scotland (*De Origine Moribus*, etc.). Johnson wrote to George Steevens on 7 February 1774 asking him for a copy. In Fr James Dalrymple's translation, the matter of the eggs is as follows (Cody, *Historie of Scotland*, vol. 1, p. 63): "We remember in the tyme of King James the fyfte, leist athir strangers or quha cumis eftir vs beleiue vs nocht, that a hundir egs commonlie war cofte for a frenche sous of Turine." Turine is Tours.

867 Boswell says in the *Tour*: "We set sail again about mid-day."

868 Duncan M. MacQuarrie tells the same story differently – the place is *Àird Tunna*, 'Barrel Height', the 'barrel' being Boswell's sea-cavern, which 'at certain tidal conditions emits a loud "boom"' (*Placenames of Mull*, p. 47).

869 See p. 388.

870 Donald MacDougall, Sir Allan's boy-servant, see p. 391.

871 Johnson meant 'clean' in the sense 'not encumbered with anything useless', one of his own definitions of the word (Pottle, *Journal*, p. 435). In the *Tour* at this point Boswell says of MacLeod: "He seemed to be well acquainted with Dr Johnson's writings." The lieutenant who was with him will be Hugh MacLean of Ardchrishnish, later in Rossal and known to posterity as 'Hugh Rossal' (Currie, *Mull*, p. 359).

872 Until Neil MacLeod was fourteen, St Kilda had a minister, Roderick MacLennan, a 'serious and devout man' who spent as much time as he could visiting the unfortunate Lady Grange (see note 544). In Harman's opinion (*An Isle called Hirte*, p. 246) this may have been why MacLennan and his wife were removed to Tongue in 1743. He was succeeded by a catechist, Alexander MacLeod, a Skyeman educated at King's College, Aberdeen, who came to live in the island with his wife, two daughters and two sons and remained there until his death in or before 1758. One of his sons was that very Donald MacLeod who had the tack of Canna for a while and was only too well known to Boswell and Johnson, see notes 522 and 523. We may assume that Neil was Alexander MacLeod's foster-son.

873 Ovid, *Amores*, book 3, poem 4, line 17: *Nitimur in vetitum semper, cupimusque negata.* "We always strive for what's forbidden, and covet what's denied."

874 Wilkes was attacked at length even in Gaelic at this period (MacLeod, *Songs of Duncan Ban Macintyre*, pp. 396–405). Boswell's note (*Tour*): "I think it incumbent on me to make some observation on this strong satirical sally on my classical companion, Mr Wilkes. Reporting it lately from memory in his presence, I expressed it thus: 'They knew he would rob their shops, *if he durst*; they knew he would debauch their daughters, *if he could*'; which, according to the French phrase, may be said *renchérir* on Dr Johnson; but on looking into my Journal, I found it as above, and would by no means make any addition. Mr Wilkes received both readings with a good humour that I cannot enough admire. Indeed both he and I (as, with respect to myself, the reader has more than once had occasion to observe in the course of this Journal) are too fond of a *bon mot* not to relish it, though we should be ourselves the object of it. Let me add, in justice to the gentleman here mentioned, that at a subsequent period, he *was* elected Chief Magistrate of London, and discharged the duties of that high office with great honour to himself, and advantage to the city. Some years before Dr Johnson died, I was fortunate enough to bring him and Mr Wilkes together; the consequence of which was, that they were ever afterwards on easy and not unfriendly terms. The particulars I shall have great pleasure in relating at large in my LIFE OF DR JOHNSON." Which he did (*Life*, May 1776).

875 The words 'which were greater and greater' and the last sentence are from the *Tour*. Otherwise the account of **21 October** is from Boswell's journal.

876 None of this seems to have happened, but the manuscript survived, perhaps in more than one copy. In 1758 it was shown to Sir William Burrell at Airds in Appin. He made a partial transcript (NLS MS 2911, ff. 23r–25r), describing

it as 'the Observations of a very ingenious Man, (versed in the Antient Languages), which he made on the Spot; his Name is John Campbell, a Charity Schoolmaster at Airds, in Argyleshire' (Dunbar, *Sir William Burrell's Northern Tour*, pp. 90–93). In 1770 John Stewart of Ballachulish showed it to the Rev. Robert Forbes, from whose journal it is quoted at length in Craven, *Journals*, pp. 306–09, under the heading 'Observations taken at Icolmkill, by Mr John Campbell, March 5, 1749'. Mairi MacArthur tells me that she has seen a photocopy of the manuscript.

877 This was at Pennycross. When Boswell writes 'another physician' he is thinking of Dr Hector MacLean.

878 Boswell left blanks for these two names. I have supplied them from the *Life*, 10 April 1783, where, after giving Johnson's information, Boswell says in a footnote that 'the real authour was I. P. Marana, a Genoese'. *The Turkish Spy* is a collection of letters purporting to be written by a deist called Mahmoud who lived undetected in Paris for forty-five years. Mahmoud comments unrestrainedly on western life, ranging through matters as mischievous as the alleged discovery of America in 1170 by a Welshman called Madoc. The germ of the the enterprise was a little volume called *L'Espion Turc* which Giovanni Paolo Marana published in Paris in 1684. By 1686 he had prepared two more. The material was picked up in Amsterdam by the English publisher Henry Rhodes, and by 1693, when Marana died, the copyright was owned by Dr Robert Midgely, who appears to have written the rest of the eight-volume set (1687–93) with the help of a Grub Street hack called William Bradshaw. Between 1694 and 1770 it went through twenty-six editions, which is why spurious claims of authorship were made, notably by Sir Robert Manley's daughter (Hill and Powell, *Life*, vol. 4, pp. 199–200, 517–19; Williams, *Madoc*, pp. 73–74).

879 In the *Tour* this becomes 'a bluff, comely, noisy old gentleman, proud of his hereditary consequence, and a very hearty and hospitable landlord'.

880 Boswell misheard: Lochbuie certainly said Glencoe, as Johnson reported (p. 397). Lochbuie's various lawsuits are well described by Currie (*Mull*, pp. 56–69).

881 Lochbuie's failure to discern that Johnson was an Englishman suggests that English was not his first language. Explaining that the name was 'Johnson' and not 'Johnston' must have convinced him that he was right in the first place.

882 In the *Tour* this becomes: "On my mentioning this circumstance to Dr Johnson, he seemed much surprized that such a suit was admitted by the Scottish law, and observed, that 'in England no man is allowed to *stultify* himself'." Boswell puts in a footnote: "This maxim, however, has been controverted. See Blackstone's *Commentaries*, Vol. II, p. 292; and the authorities there quoted." We may now add: "See Currie, *Mull*, p. 66."

883 Lochbuie, who had built himself a new house in 1752, imprisoned Hector MacLean of Killean and Allan MacLean of Kilmory in his old castle of Moy 'for certain misdemeanors' on 13 October 1758. It appears that they were 'locked up at large within the building rather than being restricted to any

particular chamber' (RCAHMS, *Argyll*, vol. 3, pp. 227, 234–35). The trial took place in Edinburgh, Boswell's father being one of the judges. Lochbuie was ordered to pay £500 to the complainers and £300 in expenses (MacLean, *History of the Clan MacLean*, pp. 244–45; Pottle, *Journal*, pp. 435–36; Currie, *Mull*, pp. 58–60).

884 Whether Cicero alleged that Mark Antony 'performed an operation' is a moot point, but there is no doubt of the enduring attraction of the passage to schoolboys (*Philippics*, no. 2, §63): *In coetu vero populi Romani negotium publicum gerens magister equitum, cui ructare turpe esset, is vomens frustis esculentis vinum redolentibus gremium suum et totum tribunal inplevit.* "But at an assembly of the Roman people, during the conduct of public business, a certain cavalry officer, for whom it would be disgraceful even to belch, vomited and filled his own lap and the whole tribunal with fragments of food reeking of wine."

885 These were the last words of Boswell's journal to be written in 1773. The rest was written in 1779–80 (Pottle and Bennett, *Journal*, pp. 345, 436).

886 Boswell underlines 'pit' because of its use in the quasi-legal expression 'right of pit and gallows' (the power to impose sentences of imprisonment or death). For Sir Allan's own amnesia see note 857.

887 In the *Tour* this becomes: "We were told much of a war-saddle, on which this reputed Don Quixote used to be mounted; but we did not see it, for the young laird had applied it to a less noble purpose, having taken it to Falkirk fair *with a drove of black cattle.*" This was Archibald Maclaine, for whom see note 825.

888 Their most likely route was one of about twelve miles by the sides of Loch Uisg, Loch Spelve and Loch Don to the ferry at Grass Point. From there they were probably brought straight to Oban. Now a sizeable town, in 1773 it consisted of little more than a couple of inns. One, as Boswell tells us (p. 409), was full; another, *Taigh Clach a' Gheodha* ('Creek-Stone House'), on the site of what is now 14 Argyll Square, is famed in Gaelic literature for being tenanted by Mrs Campbell of Barr, who composed an anti-Jacobite song, now lost, which brought upon her the wrath of the poet Alexander MacDonald (Alastair mac Mhgr Alastair, *c.* 1698–1770). This, I think, is where Johnson and Boswell stayed.

889 What Johnson calls 'Glencroe' consists of Glen Kinglas to the west of the pass still referred to as the 'Rest and Be Thankful' (really *Bealach an Easain Duibh*, 'the Pass of the Little Black Ravine') and Glen Croe itself to the east.

890 See p. 422.

891 The isle of yew and deer was Inchlonaig, that of the castle and the osprey was Inchgalbraith. Johnson told Mrs Thrale (Redford, *Letters*, vol. 2, p. 111): "When I was upon the Deer Island, I gave the keeper who attended me a shilling, and he said it was too much. Boswel afterwards offered him another, and he excused himself from taking it, because he had been rewarded already."

892 This quotation is taken, with the sentence that introduces it, from the *Tour*,

as are various phrases and sentences in the 'sheep-head' and 'pit' anecdotes in Chapter II; otherwise Boswell's account of **22 October** is from his journal.

893 In the *Tour* Boswell adjusts this to 'the character of the British nation, which he did with such energy, that the tear started into his eye'. It was popularly believed that Johnson was the author of a substantial part of this poem of 438 verses. It had indeed been 'submitted to his friendly revision', but when Boswell asked him in 1783 to go through it marking the lines he had written, he could find only nine of which he could be sure (*Life*, February 1766).

894 Johnson and Boswell probably took the old drove road from Oban to Loch Awe by Kilmore, Glen Feochan, Midmuir and Taychreggan, then crossed the loch to the inn at Port Sonachan, near where the hotel now stands.

895 These words from 'and in my' to 'Donne' are from the *Tour*, as are the Goldsmith quotation at the beginning and the two letters at the end; otherwise the account of **23 October** is from Boswell's journal.

896 The present Argyll Arms Hotel. Johnson liked it too (p. 408).

897 Boswell had forgotten the brandy at Dunvegan (p. 237).

898 See pp. 178, 280, 287.

899 In the *Tour* this paragraph becomes: "I had here the pleasure of finding a letter from home, which relieved me from the anxiety I had suffered, in consequence of not having received any account of my family for many weeks. I also found a letter from Mr Garrick, which was a regale as agreeable as a pineapple would be in a desert. He had favoured me with his correspondence for many years; and when Dr Johnson and I were at Inverness, I had written to him as follows."

900 Horace, *Ars Poetica*, lines 125–27: *Si quid inexpertum scaenae committis, et audes / Personam formare novam, servetur ad imum / Qualis ab incepto processerit* . . . "If you trust an untried subject to the stage, and venture to create an original character, it must be kept to the end of the play as it was when brought on at the start . . ."

901 Boswell's note (*Tour*): "I took the liberty of giving this familiar appellation to my celebrated friend, to bring in a more lively manner to his remembrance the period when he was Dr Johnson's pupil."

902 See note 900.

903 This was William Julius Mickle (1735–88), translator of the *Lusiad*. Boswell explains in a footnote: "I have suppressed my friend's name from an apprehension of wounding his sensibility; but I would not withhold from my readers a passage which shows Mr Garrick's mode of writing as the Manager of a Theatre, and contains a pleasing trait of his domestic life. His judgment of dramatic pieces, so far as concerns their exhibition on the stage, must be allowed to have considerable weight. But from the effect which a perusal of the tragedy here condemned had upon myself, and from the opinions of some eminent critics, I venture to pronounce that it has much poetical merit; and its author has distinguished himself by several performances which show that the epithet *poetaster* was, in the present instance, much misapplied."

904 See note 998.

905 This paragraph (including the Ogden quotation) is from the *Tour*; otherwise Boswell's account of **24 October** is from his journal.

906 This book by James Hervey was one of the most popular religious works of its time. Boswell's attachment to it is demonstrated by 'A Contemplative Walk at Moffat, on a Summer Night. A Sketch in Imitation of Hervey's Style' (*Scots Magazine*, December 1758), of which, aged eighteen, he appears to have been the author.

907 In the *Tour* this sentence became: "He then indulged a playful fancy, in making a *Meditation on a Pudding*, of which I hastily wrote down, in his presence, the following note; which, though imperfect, may serve to give my readers some idea of it." The 'Meditation' itself was then polished, reorganised, and given a new beginning: "Let us seriously reflect of what a pudding is composed. It is composed of flour . . ."

908 For Sir John Dalrymple see pp. 453–54.

909 This concerned the succession to the dukedom of Douglas. Both claimants (Archibald Douglas and the duke of Hamilton) were minors, the real protagonists being the elderly dowager duchess of Douglas (Archibald's aunt, see note 940) and the nubile dowager duchess of Hamilton (the duke's mother). The case was finally settled on appeal to the House of Lords in 1769: Archibald was awarded the estates but not the dukedom (Steuart, *The Douglas Cause*). Boswell had been on his side since his admission to the bar in 1766, filling the newspapers with propaganda and even publishing a short 'novel', *Dorando*, an allegory of the Douglas Cause which contained uncomplimentary remarks about the duchess of Hamilton. Widowed in 1758, in 1759 she had married Col. John Campbell, who succeeded to the dukedom of Argyll in 1770. See pp. 27, 421.

910 In the *Tour* this sentence becomes: "I should have been mortified at being thus coldly received by a lady of whom I, with the rest of the world, have always entertained a very high admiration, had I not been consoled by the obliging attention of the Duke."

911 Lady Betty was the duchess's only daughter by her first husband.

912 Pottle and Bennett, *Journal*, p. 356. Boswell's account of **25 October** is taken mainly from his journal, but some material is brought in from the *Tour*, i.e. two sentences and two clauses (mostly unmarked) which enhance or clarify the narrative, and several passages (indicated in endnotes) which fill in gaps in the surviving manuscript.

913 Boswell's note (*Tour*): "On reflection, at the distance of several years, I wonder that my venerable fellow-traveller should have read this passage without censuring my levity."

914 It still presides threateningly, if a little inaccessibly, over the main staircase.

915 In the *Tour* this sentence became: "But some allowance must be made for human feelings."

916 Boswell's note (*Tour*): "As this book is now become very scarce, I shall subjoin the title, which is curious: 'The Doctrines of a Middle State between Death and the Resurrection: Of Prayers for the Dead: And the Necessity of Purification; plainly proved from the holy Scriptures, and the Writings of

the Fathers of the Primitive Church: And acknowledged by several learned Fathers and great Divines of the Church of England and others since the Reformation. To which is added, an Appendix concerning the Descent of the Soul of Christ into Hell, while his Body lay in the Grave. Together with the Judgment of the Reverend Dr Hickes concerning this Book, so far as relates to a Middle State, particular Judgment, and Prayers for the Dead as it appeared in the first Edition. And a Manuscript of the Right Reverend Bishop Overall upon the Subject of a Middle State, and never before printed. Also, a Preservative against several of the Errors of the Roman Church, in six small Treatises. By the Honourable Archibald Campbell.' Folio, 1721."

917 Boswell righted this omission in the *Tour*. "Dr Johnson and I passed some time together, in June 1784, at Pembroke College, Oxford, with the Reverend Dr Adams, the master; and I having expressed a regret that my note relative to Mr Archibald Campbell was imperfect, he was then so good as to write with his own hand, on the blank page of my *Journal*, opposite to that which contains what I have now mentioned, the following paragraph; which, however, is not quite so full as the narrative he gave at Inveraray." Johnson's paragraph is then quoted, but not accurately; here it is as it stands in the journal (Pottle and Bennett, *Journal*, facing p. 354): "The Honourable Archibald Campbel, was I believe the Nephew of the Marquis of Argile. He began life by engaging in Monmouth's rebellion, and to escape the Law, lived some time in Surinam. When he returned, he became zealous for Episcopacy and Monarchy, and at the revolution adhered not only to the Nonjurors, but to those who refused to communicate with the Church of England or to be present at any worship, where the usurper was mentioned as King. He was, I believe more than once apprehended in the reign of K. William, and once at the accession of George. He was the familiar friend of Hickes and Nelson, a man of letters, but injudicious, and very curious and inquisitive, but credulous. He died in 1743 or 44, about 75 years old." At the foot Boswell wrote: "The above was supplied by Dr Johnson at Oxford, 15 June, 1784. It is not quite so full as the narrative . . . at Inveraray." What seems to have happened is that Johnson 'talked with great regard' of Campbell at Oxford on 9 June 1784 (*Life*), Boswell mentioned that his note was imperfect, and on 15 June, the day before their return to London, Boswell produced his journal for Johnson to write in.

918 The last sentence here is from the *Tour*. In the journal, confusingly, it was placed after the one ending 'particularly' and read simply: "He mentioned his saying of Lord Townshend, 'For though a Whig, he had humanity.'" The *Tour* also amends 'the political principles of the Duke's clan and his own' to 'his own political principles and those of the Duke's clan'.

919 In the *Tour* this sentence becomes: "The Duchess still continued to show the same marked coldness for me; for which, though I suffered from it, I made every allowance, considering the very warm part that I had taken for Douglas, in the cause in which she thought her son deeply interested. Had not her grace discovered some displeasure towards me, I should have suspected her of insensibility or dissimulation."

920 The manuscript is defective, so the last two sentences here are taken from the *Tour*.

921 This paragraph utilises the last coherent fragment of manuscript as follows: 'Mr' to 'us', journal; 'at our inn', *Tour*; 'at this' to 'a man may', journal; 'be very sincere' onwards, *Tour* (Pottle, *Journal*, pp. 357, 436–37). No more can be made of it.

922 Sheridan arranged for *Douglas* to be staged in Dublin. The first two nights were a great success, and as was customary, the third was to be for the playwright's benefit. What happened next is carefully explained by the Dublin author and schoolmaster Samuel Whyte (*Miscellanea Nova*, pp. 45–47). The press reported that Home was a clergyman, and it was put about that he had profaned his office. This reduced the audience to the point where the play made a loss, and Whyte observed to Sheridan that a tactful gift was in order. Sheridan's first idea was a piece of plate, to which Whyte objected that as Home was not a family man, 'it might run him to expence in showing it'. Whyte suggested instead 'a piece of Gold in the way of a Medal' which Home could carry about with him, and a medal worth about twenty guineas was duly inscribed: "Thomas Sheridan, Manager of the Theatre Royal, Smock-alley, Dublin, presents this small token of his gratitude to the Author of Douglas, for his having enriched the Stage with a Perfect Tragedy." Whyte brought it to London for transmission to Home via the earl of Bute, though not without incident: "I was stopped by highwaymen, and preserved the well-meant offering, by the sacrifice of my purse, at the imminent peril of my life."

923 Juvenal, *Satires*, book 8, lines 79–84: "Be a good soldier, a good guardian, and an incorruptible judge. If you are ever summoned as a witness in a difficult and doubtful case, even if a Phalaris tells you to lie and brings up his bull beside you as he dictates his perjury, regard it as the height of infamy to value the breath of your body more than your honour, and to sacrifice the purpose of life for the sake of life." Boswell's note (*Tour*): "'An honest guardian, arbitrator just, / Be thou; thy station deem a sacred trust. / With thy good sword maintain thy country's cause; / In every action venerate its laws: / The lie suborn'd if falsely urg'd to swear, / Though torture wait thee, torture firmly bear; / To forfeit honour, think the highest shame, / And life too dearly bought by loss of fame; / Nor, to preserve it, with thy virtue give / That for which only man should wish to live.' For this and the other translations to which no signature is affixed, I am indebted to the friend whose observations are mentioned in notes." He means Malone. Pottle points out (*Journal*, p. 437) that, judging from the printer's copy, the following footnote by Malone, printed in the *Tour* at the words 'when he rejoices' (p. 420 above), was meant to be placed here: "Having mentioned, more than once, that my Journal was perused by Dr Johnson, I think it proper to inform my readers that this is the last paragraph which he read." From here on Boswell's text appears to have been written in summer 1785, when he was revising his manuscript for publication.

924 Boswell's note (*Tour*): "I am sorry that I was unlucky in my quotation. But

notwithstanding the acuteness of Dr Johnson's criticism, and the power of his ridicule, the tragedy of *Douglas* still continues to be generally and deservedly admired."

925 Boswell's first publication, a poem of fifty-one lines entitled 'An EVENING-WALK in the Abbey-church of Holyroodhouse', written in May 1758 at the age of seventeen, expresses similar sentiments (*Scots Magazine*, vol. 20, August 1758, p. 420). Baron Douglas resented this remark in the *Tour*, and treated Boswell coldly ever after.

926 The issue in the Douglas Cause had been whether or not Archibald Douglas was the legitimate son of Lady Jane Douglas, the late duke's sister. The House of Lords decided in 1769 that he was (see note 909). For one clue to the reason for Johnson's support for the Hamiltons see p. 53. For another, when Boswell was asked why all the people of extraordinary sense were Hamiltonians he replied (Ramsay, *Scotland and Scotsmen*, vol. 1, p. 340): "I cannot tell, but I am sure all persons of *common* sense are Douglassians."

927 This sentence is in the printer's copy, but was cancelled (Pottle, *Journal*, p. 437). Otherwise Boswell's account of **26 October** is from the *Tour*.

928 Boswell had once been in love with Sir James's daughter Kitty. She married in 1764 (Walker, *Correspondence*, p. 96).

929 For the 'commission' see p. 418.

930 It was not on the same day. Boswell copied the date on Johnson's letter as 'Oct. 27', but it looks a little like 'Oct. 29' – twelve years later it was so read by the printer of the *Tour*, and evidently also by Boswell himself. With the exception of '27' for '29', Boswell's account of **27 October** (in both chapters 12 and 13) is taken from the *Tour*.

931 Boswell's note (*Tour*): "As a remarkable instance of his negligence, I remember some years ago to have found lying loose in his study, and without the cover, which contained the address, a letter to him from Lord Thurlow, to whom he had made an application as Chancellor, in behalf of a poor literary friend. It was expressed in such terms of respect for Dr Johnson that, in my zeal for his reputation, I remonstrated warmly with him on his strange inattention, and obtained his permission to take a copy of it; by which probably it has been preserved, as the original I have reason to suppose is lost." The 'poor literary friend' was Alexander Macbean.

932 The tragedy was *Irene*, performed at Garrick's theatre in Drury Lane (*Life*, February 1749): "On occasion of his play being brought upon the stage, Johnson had a fancy that as a dramatic author his dress should be more gay than what he ordinarily wore; he therefore appeared behind the scenes, and even in one of the side boxes, in a scarlet waistcoat, with rich gold lace, and a gold-laced hat." The play was not a success.

933 See p. 200.

934 James Smollett, the novelist's cousin, lived at Cameron House, a mile north of Balloch. The obelisk is still to be seen today in the Vale of Leven town of Renton.

935 For university graduates, the teaching profession was generally regarded in Scotland as a step towards the ministry of the church. Those who remained in it were frequently ill-educated or frustrated – or both.

936 By 'national combination' Johnson appears to mean the view of Scotland's ruling elite. In his letter to Boswell (p. 591) George Dempster picks up the expression and uses it in the plural to mean political groupings.

937 James Campbell of Treesbank married Mary Montgomerie as his second wife.

938 See pp. 437–38.

939 In 1449 Richard Colville of Ochiltree slew Sir James Auchinleck. William, 8th earl of Douglas, then beheaded Colville and destroyed his castle – an act which led to Boswell's steadfast support for the Douglas family in its time of need (see note 909).

940 One of the direct consequences of Union was the gradual rejection of the Scots language by the elite, who began to mix in London with their new compatriots, and found that if they wished to be understood they must study English. Dr Johnson wrote to Mrs Thrale (Redford, *Letters*, vol. 2, p. 53) of 'an old Lady who talks broad Scotch with a paralytick voice, and is scarce understood by her own countrymen'. This was the illiterate duchess of Douglas, whom he had met on 16 August (p. 34), and whose blood was anything but blue. Johnson gave her the attention her rank demanded, and Boswell was forced to spend the evening translating bad Scots into good English: a comic scene, apparently (Hill and Powell, *Life*, vol. 5, p. 43).

941 This young lady, then aged about twelve, has been identified as Sarah, daughter of John Dashwood, subsequently Lord Despencer. She married the Rev. John Walcot of Bitterley, Shropshire (Fleeman, *Journey*, p. 247). Thomas Braidwood had established his pioneering 'Academy for the Deaf and Dumb' on a spectacular site east of St Leonard's Road about 1764. It achieved international renown, then closed in 1783 when Braidwood moved to London. The 'Dummie Hoose', as it was popularly called, was demolished about 1939, but the names of Braidwood and his school survive in the district – 'Dumbiedykes' is now a housing scheme, and its community centre is Braidwood House (Harris, *Place Names of Edinburgh*, p. 230).

942 See note 934. Smollett was a sheriff depute of Dunbartonshire and commissary of Edinburgh (a judge in a former bishop's court); when he died in 1775, Boswell sought the office of commissary for himself and was bitterly disappointed when he failed to secure it.

943 "Whence is evil?"

944 The 'Usurpation' is better known as Cromwell's 'Commonwealth' – 1649–60 in England, 1651–60 in Scotland.

945 I am grateful to Mr Norman MacLeod for the following translation: "Stop, O traveller! If you have ever marvelled at the charms and kindly grace of nature, if you have ever marvelled at a most skilled painter of life, tarry for a short time with the memory of Tobias Smollet, M.D., a man with those excellent qualities which as both man and citizen you should praise and attempt to imitate. He was a very distinguished man who engaged in many literary activities. In a state of happiness peculiar to himself, having committed his life to coming generations, he was snatched away by cruel death at the age of 51. Alas, how far away from his homeland he is! He lies

buried in the port of Livorno in Italy. To such a great man his kinsman would have preferred to have handed over his estate rather than this pillar: a monument of love but, alas, an empty monument, on the very banks of the Leven which as a child he filled with infant cries, and which became famous with his little verses now that he was on the point of death. James Smollet of Bonhill saw to the erection of this pillar. Continue on your way, and remember that this gift is indeed a mark not only to the memory of the deceased, but also to his way of life. For if these qualities are worthy in the eyes of others, this will be his reward for outstanding work!" Johnson's contribution was one of many: the first four lines were by John Ramsay of Ochtertyre at the request of Lord Kames, who was dissatisfied with the inscription as originally written by Professor George Stewart (Ramsay, *Scotland and Scotsmen*, vol. 1, p. 311). The manuscript annotated by Johnson is preserved at Cameron House. Boswell's account of **28 October** is taken from the *Tour*, with one minor alteration – in the *Tour* the words from 'The epitaph' to here take the form of a footnote.

946 See note 830. The Saracen's Head, mentioned next, was in the Gallowgate.

947 The friend was William Drummond, bookseller in Edinburgh. The letter was written on 13 August 1766 and appears in the *Life* following 6 November 1766. Boswell's account of **29 October** is taken from the *Tour*.

948 The brothers Robert and Andrew Foulis were printers, publishers, and founders of an Academy for Fine Arts in the city. On 'Elzevir' editions see note 128.

949 Boswell's note: "'The unwilling gratitude of base mankind.'—Pope." This quotation is from 'The First Epistle of the Second Book of Horace', line 14. The account of **30 October** is from the *Tour*.

950 Treesbank is three miles south of Kilmarnock on the Ayr road; the old house is long gone. Boswell had published an epitaph in twenty-eight lines on the Rev. John Campbell in the *Scots Magazine*, vol. 23, April 1761, p. 204: "In quiet peaceful silence here repose / The bones of one who never could have foes . . ."

951 Sir John appears to have had in his possession a Gaelic manuscript written at Inveraray *c.* 1640 (now NLS MS 1745), the least of many items which give the lie to Johnson's absurd claim (p. 207) that 'there is not in the world an Earse manuscript a hundred years old' (Black, 'A Scottish Grammatical Tract', p. 4). Boswell's account of **31 October** is taken from the *Tour*.

952 As described at p. 95, Eglinton befriended Boswell in 1760 and introduced him to London society. In 1769, aged 46, he was accidentally shot and killed by Mungo Campbell, an exciseman. Most of this paragraph (from 'She knew' to 'I can express' and from 'applied to business' to 'vivacity') was deleted by Boswell and Malone from the printer's copy (Pottle, *Journal*, pp. 438–39).

953 The last sentence was cancelled in the printer's copy (Pottle, *Journal*, p. 439). With the exception of this and the material mentioned in the previous note, Boswell's account of **1 November** is from the *Tour* as published. Lady Eglinton lived at Auchans Castle (Old Auchans), now a ruin, about three miles north-east of Troon.

954 In a letter to Mrs Thrale, 3 November 1773, Johnson preserved a little more of this exchange (Redford, *Letters*, vol. 2, p. 116): "She called Boswel the boy. 'Yes, Madam,' said I, 'we will send him to school.' 'He is already,' said she, 'in a good school'; and expressed her hope of his improvement."

955 He was more than two and a half years older than Johnson.

956 Boswell originally wrote (Pottle, *Journal*, p. 439): ". . . a most valuable wife, had before this time seriously impaired him. For he had originally a mind as strong as Dr. Johnson's, without the flaws which melancholy occasions." At no stage does he mention his stepmother, whom his father had married in 1769 after four years as a widower, and who must have welcomed Dr Johnson and presided at the dinner-table. His account of 2 **November** is taken from the *Tour*.

957 For Pringle see p. 65. He held liberal views on religion and was a friend of Benjamin Franklin.

958 Boswell's note: "This gentleman, though devoted to the study of grammar and dialectics, was not so absorbed in it as to be without a sense of pleasantry, or to be offended at his favourite topics being treated lightly. I one day met him in the street, as I was hastening to the House of Lords, and told him I was sorry I could not stop, being rather too late to attend an appeal of the Duke of Hamilton against Douglas. 'I thought,' said he, 'their contest had been over long ago.' I answered, 'The contest concerning Douglas's filiation was over long ago; but the contest now is, who shall have the estate.' Then, assuming the air of 'an ancient sage philosopher', I proceeded thus: 'Were I to *predicate* concerning him, I should say, the contest formerly was, What *is* he? The contest now is, What *has* he?'—'Right,' replied Mr Harris, smiling; 'you have done with *quality*, and have got into *quantity*.'" See p. 57 and note 909.

959 This paragraph and the previous one contain echoes of material which appears in the journal (but not the *Tour*) at 21 August and 4 September (pp. 57, 129). Presumably Boswell regretted these deletions and decided to restore them. It allowed him to assure Sir Alexander Macdonald that an offensive passage had been 'removed' (see note 282) when all he had done was pluck it out of its context and delete Sir Alexander's name. His account of 3 **November** is taken from the *Tour*.

960 See p. 425. Boswell is right. It will be Gaelic *Achadh nan Leac* 'the Field of the Flagstones'.

961 Boswell and George III were both descended from John Stuart, earl of Lennox, who died in 1526 (Pottle, *Journal*, pp. 439–40, 441).

962 See pp. 181–82.

963 Tacitus, *Germania*, §5: "Even the cattle lack natural beauty and majestic brows."

964 Horace, *Epistles*, book 1, poem 11, lines 29–30: "What you seek, here it is; it's even at Ulubrae, if you don't lack a well-balanced mind." Proverbial for its remoteness from Rome, Ulubrae was a decaying town in the Pontine marshes where frogs could be heard croaking. The point is that happiness depends on one's state of mind, not on where one lives.

965 Horace, *Epistles*, book 1, poem 18, lines 111–12 (the last words of the poem): *Sed satis est orare Iovem, quae ponit et aufert, / Det vitam, det opes; aequum mi animum ipse parabo.* "But it's enough to pray Jupiter, who gives and takes away, to grant me life and means; a well-balanced mind I will provide myself." Boswell's account of 4 **November** is from the *Tour* as published, with the exception of the words from 'As we sauntered about' to 'in our shades' and the final paragraph, which were cancelled in the printer's copy (Pottle, *Journal*, p. 440).

966 Boswell's account of 5 **November** caused him some trouble. He had a note which read: "Friday 5. Hallglenmuir and Usher. They went with us and dined at Mr. Dun's. 'Know no more of our church than a Hottentot.'" In the printer's copy he cancelled the last sentence, 'But I hoped it would do him good.' The words 'on his own estate' and the sentence 'Dr Johnson . . . good terms with them' appear for the first time in the second edition. On 9 March 1789, when the third edition had been in print for three years, Dun, his old friend and tutor, wrote to him stating that Johnson had not used the word 'Hottentot', and asking him to print a retraction in a subsequent edition of the *Tour* or in the *Life*. Boswell refused, but in the next reprint he turned 'Mr Dun, though a man of sincere good principles, as a Presbyterian divine . . .' into 'He indeed occasionally attacked them. One of them . . .' Our account of this day is therefore best described as from the second edition, with one sentence from the printer's copy. 'Hallglenmuir' was Alexander Mitchell, while 'Usher' was John Boswell, 'Old Knockroon', usher to the Lord High Commissioner to the General Assembly (Pottle, *Journal*, pp. 441–42).

967 The printer's copy for 6 November begins, tantalisingly, "The old story of *Bluebeard* . . ." This was cancelled. According to Sir Walter Scott, when Johnson challenged Auchinleck to say what good Cromwell had ever done he replied (Croker, *Life*, 6 November 1773): "God, Doctor! He gart kings ken that they had a *lith* in their neck." ("He taught kings that they had a joint in their necks.") This has the ring of truth, as the expression had the status of family folklore. Boswell recorded elsewhere (Pottle, *Journal*, pp. 442–43) that in the 1720s his father's cousin Thomas Cochrane, earl of Dundonald, a violent Whig, once entered a church in London on 30 January, the national fast on the anniversary of the execution of Charles I. He met Sir Watkin Williams Wynn, a prominent Tory, who said: "Cochrane, are you here? What! Do you feel like observing this day?" Cochrane replied: "Yes, Sir. I think that this day ought to be observed in England century after century to remind our king that he has a joint in his neck."

968 I have reconstructed this exchange from Boswell's cancelled copy and Malone's memorandum as cited in Pottle, *Journal*, p. 443. Otherwise the account of 6 **November** is from the printed *Tour*.

969 See p. 452. Boswell assured his father one day, says Ramsay of Ochtertyre, that Johnson was 'a constellation of virtues' (*Scotland and Scotsmen*, vol. 1, p. 176). "Yes, James," answered he; "the Doctor is Ursa Major, and you are Ursa Minor."

970 See p. 99. Boswell's account of 7 **November** is from cancelled printer's copy

as cited in Pottle, *Journal*, pp. 443–44, except for the passage from 'yet, as God is worshipped' to 'a former page', which is from the *Tour* as printed.

971 The inn was the Hamilton Arms in Muir Street. Built in 1696, it became a museum in 1967. Boswell's account of **8 November** is from the *Tour*.

972 Hamilton Palace was undermined by the very coal-workings which had brought such wealth to its owners, and was demolished in the 1920s. Boswell's account of **9 November** is from the *Tour*.

973 At the Mitre, 6 July 1763 (*Life*).

974 'Captain Erskine' of the previous paragraph but one. The original journal says of the visit to the Castle (Pottle, *Journal*, p. 445): "Captain Erskine had gone up before us." Presumably this was to make arrangements for the visit.

975 Boswell's note (*Tour*): "I desire not to be understood as agreeing *entirely* with the opinions of Dr Johnson, which I relate without any remark. The many imitations, however, of *Fingal*, that have been published, confirm this observation in a considerable degree." A well-known anecdote from the Edinburgh *Weekly Magazine* of 25 February 1773 may not go amiss here (vol. 19, p. 272): "*A* BON MOT. A Gentleman desiring to know Dr JOHNSON's opinion of Mr *Macpherson's* poem of *Fingal* at the same time asked him, whether there were *many* in these kingdoms that could produce such a composition? 'Yes, Sir,' replied the great POMPOSO, *'many men, many women, and many children.'*"

976 This was Alexander Fraser Tytler, later Lord Woodhouselee, the above-mentioned advocate. Tytler resented the aspersion, and appears to have written Boswell an insulting letter. On 18 November 1785 Boswell consulted Malone and Courtenay, who advised him to apologise. He did so, and on 30 November received a satisfactory reply. In the second edition he turned 'his son, the advocate' into 'some other friends' and revised this paragraph as follows: "One gentleman in company expressing his opinion that *Fingal* was certainly genuine, for that he had heard a great part of it repeated in the original, Dr Johnson indignantly asked him whether he understood the original; to which an answer being given in the negative, 'Why then,' said Dr Johnson, 'we see to what *this* testimony comes:—thus it is.'"

977 The ascertaining was done by Derick Thomson in his *Gaelic Sources* (1951); as more sources have come to light since then, it is time for a further appraisal. For the conversation at Ullinish see pp. 260–61.

978 John Wilson, ironmonger in Glasgow, had brought an action for payment of goods furnished to Archibald Maclean of Lagganulva (for whom see notes 784, 813, 825) in 1771. Maclean produced a receipt signed by Capt. John White, showing that the goods had been paid for. Wilson alleged that the receipt was a forgery, Capt. White having been drowned in 1770. Eighty witnesses, supported by fifteen pieces of writing, swore that White was alive until October 1771, others that he had died in 1770. The chieftain was Sir Allan Maclean; he wrote the letter on 6 February 1775 and was examined by the court on 14 June 1777 (Pottle, *Journal*, pp. 381, 448).

979 Under Grenville's Act (1770), instead of being a matter of debate for the

whole House of Commons, disputed elections were now tried by a select committee with all the solemnity of a court.

980 Boswell describes Dr Erskine as 'a distinguished member of the Society for Propagating Christian Knowledge'; also at supper were 'Miss Webster, and George'. The Moravian Brethren, a sect based in what is now the Czech Republic, were active as missionaries to the native and enslaved peoples of North America and the West Indies. Boswell's account of 10 **November** is from the *Tour*, augmented by some passages from a diary of 10 and 11 November which he wrote in Lord Elibank's house at Ballencrieff on 14 November 1773 (Pottle, *Journal*, pp. 444–46, 449). This diary is not as full as the *Tour*, however.

981 Boswell's notes (*Tour*): "Through various hazards and events we move." And: "Long labours both by sea and land he bore.—DRYDEN." The words are from the *Aeneid*, book 1, lines 204–05, *per varios casus, per tot discrimina rerum / tendimus in Latium* 'through various mishaps, through so many perilous chances, we journey towards Latium', and lines 3–4, *multum ille et terris iactatus et alto / vi superum* 'much buffeted on sea and land by violence from above'. Boswell's account of 11 **November** is based, in roughly equal proportions, on his diary of 10–11 November (Pottle, *Journal*, pp. 446–48) and the *Tour*. Some of the material is in the one, some in the other, some in both.

982 See pp. 292, 309.

983 Robert Craigie, Lord Glendoick, was successively Lord Advocate and (from 1752 to his death in 1760) President of the Court of Session, and owed nothing to Argyll; John Maule of Inverkeilor, advocate (1706–81), MP for the Aberdeen Burghs 1739–48, was of 'Argyll's party'. He was not appointed a Baron of the Exchequer until 1748, so the anecdote clearly dates from that year or later. Elibank and his brother Alexander Murray (1712–78) were Jacobite sympathisers, but avoided taking an active role in the '45. In 1752 Alexander, angered by a personal grievance, threw caution to the winds by becoming the leading conspirator in the abortive 'Elibank plot', whose object was the assassination of King George. He fled into exile and was created earl of Westminster in the Jacobite peerage.

984 Boswell's note (*Tour*): "A society for debate in Edinburgh, consisting of the most eminent men." He was a member of it himself. It still exists today.

985 James Stewart 'of the Glen' was accused of the murder of Colin Campbell of Glenure, factor on the forfeited estate of Charles Stewart of Ardsheal. The murder took place on 14 May 1752, and the trial was held at Inveraray in September that year. At one point Thomas Miller, senior counsel for the defence, rose to cross-examine Donald Campbell of Airds on the defendant's good character. The duke of Argyll, who sat on the bench as Lord Justice-General, forbade it on the grounds that it would allow the accused to rebut evidence. Miller insisted that his client was a God-fearing man who protected widows and orphans. Argyll asked what kind of character he had displayed in 1745. Miller admitted that Stewart had been a Jacobite officer, but pointed out that as he had received the royal pardon the defence had

the right, never before refused, to establish his good name. Argyll demanded to know how Miller could hope to prove the good character of a man who had been guilty of rebellion, 'a crime that embraced most other crimes, such as treason, murder, rapine, oppression and perjury', and refused to allow further questioning of Airds. It was the turning-point of the trial: Stewart, though innocent, was found guilty and hanged (Carney, *The Killing of the Red Fox*, pp. 108–09).

986 Boswell had to return to work by 12 November, as the Candlemas term of the Court of Session began on that day. However, he contributed a report of Johnson's visit to *The Caledonian Mercury*, 27 November 1773, from which we know that the visit to Lord Elibank's home (at Ballencrieff in East Lothian) was from Saturday 13th to Monday 15th, the dinner at Principal Robertson's on Tuesday 16th, and at Sir Adolphus Oughton's on Wednesday 17th (Pottle, *Journal*, pp. 385, 449).

987 See p. 40.

988 Boswell's note: "As I have been scrupulously exact in relating anecdotes concerning other persons, I shall not withhold any part of this story, however ludicrous.—I was so successful in this boyish frolic, that the universal cry of the galleries was, '*Encore* the cow! *Encore* the cow!' In the pride of my heart, I attempted imitations of some other animals, but with very inferior effect. My reverend friend, anxious for my *fame*, with an air of the utmost gravity and earnestness, addressed me thus: 'My dear sir, I would *confine* myself to the *cow!*'"

989 The printer's copy shows that one of the 'other gentlemen' was 'Mr Blair, a very able lawyer' – Robert Blair (1741–1811), later Lord President of the Court of Session. He was son of the Rev. Robert Blair, author of *The Grave* (Pottle, *Journal*, p. 449), and is not to be confused with 'Dr Blair', i.e. Hugh Blair.

990 Ford, *George Buchanan*, p. 153: "Hail, May Day, sacred to sacred delights, dedicated to joy and wine, games, jesting, and the delicate dances of the Graces . . . "

991 See pp. 133, 372.

992 See pp. 427–28. Boswell appends a footnote: "One of the best critics of our age 'does not wish to prevent the admirers of the incorrect and nerveless style which generally prevailed for a century before Dr Johnson's energetic writings were known, from enjoying the laugh that this story may produce, in which he is very ready to join them'. He, however, requests me to observe, that 'my friend very properly chose a *long* word on this occasion, not, it is believed, from any predilection for polysyllables (though he certainly had a due respect for them), but in order to put Mr Braidwood's skill to the strictest test, and to try the efficacy of his instruction by the most difficult exertion of the organs of his pupils'." The critic was probably Malone.

993 Thus the printer's copy; the *Tour* reads simply 'as to the English sailor, I cannot agree with you'. Apart from this and two similarly brief passages which were deleted prior to printing (Pottle, *Journal*, pp. 449–50), Boswell's account of 11–19 November is from the *Tour*.

994 Virgil, *Georgics*, book 3, lines 8–9: *Temptanda via est, qua me quoque possim / Tollere humo victorque virum volitare per ora.* "A path must be tried by which I, too, may lift myself off the ground and fly about triumphant on the lips of men." See pp. 285–86 and (on Dalrymple's *Memoirs*) note 997.

995 This was Lady Anne Lindsay, author of 'Auld Robin Gray' (Pottle, *Journal*, pp. 390, 450). For the 'adoption' see p. 435.

996 It appears from this that they drove to the village of Roslin and walked from the inn down to the castle (on the west bank of the North Esk), then up again to the chapel, which is doubly famous now thanks to Dan Brown's bestseller *The Da Vinci Code*. After dining at the inn they enjoyed a two-mile circular drive across by the bridge to the other side of the valley (which is spectacular here) and down to Hawthornden Castle, high above the right bank of the river. Ben Jonson had walked from London in 1618 to spend two or three weeks with Drummond at Hawthornden; the house is still privately owned and functions as a writers' retreat. Our two travellers must have walked down by some riverside path to view the man-made caves underneath the castle before returning to their chaise for the eight-mile drive by Dalkeith to Cranston. Dalrymple's house there is long since demolished (Pottle, *Journal*, p. 488).

997 Boswell's note: "'Essex was at that time confined to the same chamber of the Tower from which his father Lord Capell had been led to death, and in which his wife's grandfather had inflicted a voluntary death upon himself. When he saw his friend carried to what he reckoned certain fate, their common enemies enjoying the spectacle, and reflected that it was he who had forced Lord Howard upon the confidence of Russell, he retired, and by a *Roman death*, put an end to his misery.' Dalrymple's *Memoirs of Great Britain and Ireland*, Vol. I, p. 36."

998 See p. 413. The verse on George II and his poet laureate Colley Cibber goes (*Life*, 1740): "Augustus still survives in Maro's strain, / And Spenser's verse prolongs Eliza's reign; / Great George's acts let tuneful Cibber sing; / For Nature form'd the Poet for the King." The epitaph on Parnell, the subject of one of Johnson's *Lives of the Poets*, goes (*Life*, 1781): *Hic requiescit* Thomas Parnell, *S. T. P. / Qui sacerdos pariter et poeta, / Utrasque partes ita implevit, / Ut neque sacerdoti suavitas poetæ, / Nec poetæ sacerdotis sanctitas, deesset.* ("Here lies Thomas Parnell, Professor of Theology, who, at once priest and poet, so played both parts that the poet's sweetness was never false to the priest, nor the priest's piety false to the poet.")

999 Boswell's account of **20–22 November** is from the *Tour*, with the exception of the long passage from 'Next morning at breakfast' to 'the old castle of Borthwick' and the words 'warmer and' in the penultimate paragraph. These were removed from the printer's copy (Pottle, *Journal*, pp. 450–51). The reason that so much Dalrymple material was left in was that Boswell was unafraid of him. He and Johnson had sized him up and found him worthy of contempt. By 1785, when the *Tour* was published, Boswell's contempt had increased. After defaming Lord Barrington in a pamphlet Dalrymple had backed out of a duel, thus demonstrating that he could be attacked with impunity (Reed and Pottle, *Laird of Auchinleck*, pp. 419–20).

Boswell's Conclusion

———————

I have now completed my account of our tour to the Hebrides. I have brought Dr Johnson down to Scotland, and seen him into the coach which in a few hours carried him back into England. He said to me often that the time he spent in this tour was the pleasantest part of his life, and asked me if I would lose the recollection of it for five hundred pounds. I answered I would not; and he applauded my setting such a value on an accession of new images in my mind.

Had it not been for me, I am persuaded Dr Johnson never would have undertaken such a journey; and I must be allowed to assume some merit from having been the cause that our language has been enriched with such a book as that which he published on his return; a book which I never read but with the utmost admiration, as I had such opportunities of knowing from what very meagre materials it was composed.

But my praise may be supposed partial; and therefore I shall insert two testimonies not liable to that objection, both written by gentlemen of Scotland, to whose opinions I am confident the highest respect will be paid: Lord Hailes and Mr Dempster.

To James Boswell, Esq. / New Hailes, 6th Feb. 1775. / Sir, I have received much pleasure and much instruction from perusing the *Journey* to the Hebrides. I admire the elegance and variety of description, and the lively picture of men and manners. I always approve of the moral, often of the political, reflections. I love the benevolence of the author.

They who search for faults may possibly find them in this, as well as in every other work of literature. For example, the friends of the old family say that the era of planting is placed too late, at the Union of the two kingdoms. I am known to be no friend of the old family, yet I would place the era of planting at the Restoration, after the murder of Charles I had been expiated in the anarchy which succeeded it. Before the Restoration, few trees were planted, unless by the monastic drones; their successors (and worthy patriots they were), the barons, first cut down the trees, and then sold the estates. The gentleman at St Andrews, who said that there were but two trees in Fife, ought to have added that the elms of Balmerino were sold within these twenty years to make pumps for the fire-engines.[1]

In J. Major *De Gestis Scotorum*, L. i. C. 2., last edition, there is a singular passage: "Davidi Cranstoneo conterraneo, dum de prima Theologiae licentia foret, duo ei consocii et familiares, et mei cum eo in artibus auditores, scilicet Jacobus Almain Senonensis, et Petrus Bruxcellensis, Praedicatorii Ordinis, in Sorbonae curia die Sorbonico coram commilitonibus suis publice objecerunt, quod pane avenaceo plebeii Scoti, sicut a quodam religioso intellexerant, vescebantur, ut virum, quem cholericum noverant, honestis salibus tentarent, qui hoc inficiari tanquam patriae dedecus nisus est."[2] Pray introduce our countryman, Mr Licentiate David Cranston, to the acquaintance of Mr Johnson. The syllogism seems to have been this: "They who feed on oatmeal are barbarians; / But the Scots feed on oatmeal: / Ergo ———." The licentiate denied the *minor*. I am, sir, your most obedient servant, / Dav. Dalrymple.

To James Boswell, Esq., Edinburgh / Dunnichen, 16th February, 1775. / My dear Boswell, I cannot omit a moment to return you my best thanks for the entertainment you have furnished me, my family, and guests, by the perusal of Dr Johnson's *Journey to the Western Islands*; and now for my sentiments of it. imo. It is printed on a very imposing pick-pocket paper and print. Its solid contents might, and to a man in Johnson's circumstances they ought to, have been comprised in a two-shilling book. He does not want money, and an author who is not necessitous ought to watch the printers and publishers, being the only check upon their rapacity and extortion. Well said in me, who has got the book for nothing. 2d. I was well entertained. His descriptions are accurate and vivid. He carried me on the tour along with him. I am pleased with the justice he has done to your humour and vivacity. "The noise of the wind being all its own," is a *bon mot* that it would have been a pity to have omitted, and a robbery not to have ascribed to its author.[3]

There is nothing in the book, from beginning to end, that a Scotchman need to take amiss. What he says of the country is true, and his observations on the people are what must naturally occur to a sensible, observing, and reflecting inhabitant of a *convenient* metropolis, where a man on thirty pounds a year may be better accommodated with all the little wants of life than Coll or Sir Allan. He reasons candidly about the second sight, but I wish he had inquired more before he ventured to say he even doubted of the possibility of such an unusual and useless deviation from all the known laws of nature.[4] The notion of the second sight I consider as a remnant of superstitious ignorance and credulity, which a philosopher will set down as such till the contrary is clearly proved, and then it will be classed among the other certain, though unaccountable, parts of our nature, like dreams, and – I do not know what.

In regard to the language, it has the merit of being all his own. Many words of foreign extraction are used, where, I believe, common ones would do as well, especially on familiar occasions. Yet I believe he could not express himself so forcibly in any other style. I am charmed with his researches concerning the Erse language and the antiquity of their manuscripts. I am quite convinced; and I shall rank Ossian and his Fingals and Oscars amongst the nursery tales, not the true history of our country, in all time to come.[5]

Upon the whole, the book cannot displease, for it has no pretensions. The author neither says he is a geographer, nor an antiquarian, nor very learned in the history of Scotland, nor a naturalist, nor a fossilist. The manners of the people and the face of the country are all he attempts to describe or seems to have thought of. Much were it to be wished that they who have travelled into more remote, and of course more curious, regions, had all possessed his good sense. Of the state of learning, his observations on Glasgow University show he has formed a very sound judgment.[6] He understands our climate too, and he has accurately observed the changes, however slow and imperceptible to us, which Scotland has undergone in consequence of the blessings of liberty and internal peace. I could have drawn my pen through the story of the old woman at St Andrews, being the only silly thing in the book.[7] He has taken the opportunity of ingrafting into the work several good observations, which I dare say he had made upon men and things before he set foot on Scotch ground, by which it is considerably enriched.[8] A long journey, like a tall May-pole, though not very beautiful itself, yet is pretty enough when ornamented with flowers and garlands; it furnishes a sort of cloak-pins for hanging the furniture of your mind upon; and whoever sets out upon a journey without furnishing his mind previously with much study and useful knowledge erects a May-pole in December, and puts up very useless cloak-pins.

I hope the book will induce many of his countrymen to make the same jaunt, and help to intermix the more liberal part of them still more with us, and perhaps abate somewhat of that virulent antipathy which many of them entertain against the Scotch; who certainly would never have formed those *combinations* which he takes notice of, more than their ancestors, had they not been necessary for their mutual safety (at least for their success) in a country where they are treated as foreigners.[9] They would find us not deficient, at least in point of hospitality, and they would be ashamed ever after to abuse us in the mass.

So much for the tour. I have now, for the first time in my life, passed a winter in the country; and never did three months roll on with more swiftness and satisfaction. I used not only to wonder at, but pity, those whose lot condemned them to winter anywhere but in either of the capitals. But every place has its charms to a cheerful mind. I am busy planting and taking measures for opening the summer campaign in farming; and I find I have an excellent resource, when revolutions in politics perhaps, and revolutions of the sun for certain, will make it decent for me to retreat behind the ranks of the more forward in life.

I am glad to hear the last was a very busy week with you. I see you as counsel in some causes which must have opened a charming field for your humorous vein. As it is more uncommon, so I verily believe it is more useful than the more serious exercise of reason; and, to a man who is to appear in public, more éclat is to be gained, sometimes more money too, by a *bon mot* than a learned speech. It is the fund of natural humour which Lord North possesses that makes him so much the favourite of the House, and so able, because so amiable, a leader of a party.

I have now finished *my* Tour of Seven Pages. In what remains, I beg leave to offer my compliments, and those of *ma très chère femme*, to you and Mrs Boswell. Pray unbend the busy brow and frolic a little in a letter to, my dear Boswell, your affectionate friend, / George Dempster.[10]

I shall also present the public with a correspondence with the Laird of Raasay, concerning a passage in the *Journey to the Western Islands*, which shows Dr Johnson in a very amiable light.

To James Boswell, Esq. Raasay, April 10th, 1775. Dear Sir, I take this occasion of returning you my most hearty thanks for the civilities shown to my daughter by you and Mrs Boswell.[11] Yet, though she has informed me that I am under this obligation, I should very probably have deferred troubling you with making my acknowledgments at present if I had not seen Dr Johnson's *Journey to the Western Isles*, in which he has been pleased to make a very friendly mention of my family, for which I am surely obliged to him, as being more than an equivalent for the reception you and he met with. Yet there is one paragraph I should have been glad he had omitted, which I am sure was owing to misinformation; that is, that I had acknowledged MacLeod to be my chief, though my ancestors disputed the pre-eminence for a long tract of time.[12]

I never had occasion to enter seriously on this argument with the present laird or his grandfather, nor could I have any temptation to such a renunciation from either of them. I acknowledge, the benefit of being chief of a clan is in our days of very little significance, and to trace out the progress of this honour to the founder of a family of any standing, would perhaps be a matter of some difficulty.

The true state of the present case is this: the MacLeod family consists of two different branches: the MacLeods of Lewis, of which I am descended, and the MacLeods of Harris. And though the former have lost a very extensive estate by forfeiture in King James the Sixth's time, there are still several respectable families of it existing, who would justly blame me for such an unmeaning cession, when they all acknowledge me head of that family; which though in fact it be but an ideal point of honour, is not hitherto so far disregarded in our country but it would determine some of my friends to look on me as a much smaller man than either they or myself judge me at present to be. I will, therefore, ask it as a favour of you to acquaint the Doctor with the difficulty he has brought me to. In travelling among rival clans, such a silly tale as this might easily be whispered into the ear of a passing stranger; but as it has no foundation in fact, I hope the Doctor will be so good as to take his own way in undeceiving the public – I principally mean my friends and connexions, who will be first angry at me, and next sorry to find such an instance of my littleness recorded in a book which has a very fair chance of being much read. I expect you will let me know what he will write you in return, and we here beg to make offer to you and Mrs Boswell of our most respectful compliments. I am, dear sir, your most obedient humble servant, JOHN MACLEOD.

To the Laird of Raasay. London, May 8, 1775. DEAR SIR, The day before yesterday I had the honour to receive your letter, and I immediately communicated it to Dr Johnson. He said he loved your spirit, and was exceedingly sorry that he had been the cause of the smallest uneasiness to you. There is not a more candid man in the world than he is, when properly addressed, as you will see from his letter to you, which I now enclose. He has allowed me to take a copy of it, and he says you may read it to your clan, or publish it if you please. Be assured, sir, that I shall take care of what he has entrusted to me, which is to have an acknowledgment of his error inserted in the Edinburgh newspapers. You will, I dare say, be fully satisfied with Dr Johnson's behaviour. He is desirous to know that you are; and therefore when you have read his acknowledgment in the papers, I beg you may write to me; and if you choose it, I am persuaded a letter from you to the Doctor also will be taken kind. I shall be at Edinburgh the week after next.

Any civilities which my wife and I had in our power to show to your daughter, Miss MacLeod, were due to her own merit, and were well repaid by her agreeable company. But I am sure I should be a very unworthy man if I did not wish to show a grateful sense of the hospitable and genteel manner in which you were pleased to treat me. Be assured, my dear sir, that I shall never forget your goodness, and the happy hours which I spent in Raasay.

You and Dr MacLeod were both so obliging as to promise me an account in writing of all the particulars which each of you remember concerning the transactions of 1745–6. Pray do not forget this, and be as minute and full as you can; put down everything; I have a great curiosity to know as much as I can, authentically.[13]

I beg that you may present my best respects to Lady Raasay, my compliments to your young family, and to Dr MacLeod, and my hearty good wishes to Malcolm, with whom I hope again to shake hands cordially. I have the honour to be, dear sir, your obliged and faithful humble servant, JAMES BOSWELL.

ADVERTISEMENT, written by Dr Johnson, and inserted by his desire in the Edinburgh newspapers – referred to in the foregoing letter.

The author of the *Journey to the Western Islands*, having related that the MacLeods of Raasay acknowledge the chieftainship or superiority of the MacLeods of Skye, finds that he has been misinformed or mistaken. He means in a future edition to correct his error, and wishes to be told of more, if more have been discovered.[14]

Dr Johnson's letter was as follows:

To the Laird of Raasay. DEAR SIR, Mr Boswell has this day shown me a letter in which you complain of a passage in the *Journey* to the Hebrides. My meaning is mistaken. I did not intend to say that you had personally made any cession of the rights of your house, or any acknowledgment of the superiority of MacLeod of Dunvegan. I only designed to express what I thought generally admitted: that the house of Raasay allowed the superiority of the house of Dunvegan. Even this I now find to be erroneous, and will therefore omit or retract it in the next edition.

Though what I had said had been true, if it had been disagreeable to you, I should have wished it unsaid, for it is not my business to adjust precedence. As it is mistaken, I find myself disposed to correct, both by my respect for you and my reverence for truth.

As I know not when the book will be reprinted, I have desired Mr Boswell to anticipate the correction in the Edinburgh papers. This is all that can be done.

I hope I may now venture to desire that my compliments may be made, and my gratitude expressed, to Lady Raasay, Mr Malcolm MacLeod, Mr Donald Macqueen, and all the gentlemen and all the ladies whom I saw in the island of Raasay; a place which I remember with too much pleasure and too much kindness not to be sorry that my ignorance or hasty persuasion should, for a single moment, have violated its tranquillity.

I beg you all to forgive an undesigned and involuntary injury, and to consider me as, sir, your most obliged, and most humble servant, SAM. JOHNSON. London, May 6, 1775.[15]

It would be improper for me to boast of my own labours, but I cannot refrain from publishing such praise as I received from such a man as Sir William Forbes of Pitsligo, after the perusal of the original manuscript of my Journal.

To James Boswell, Esq. Edinburgh, March 7, 1777. MY DEAR SIR, I ought to have thanked you sooner for your very obliging letter, and for the singular confidence you are pleased to place in me, when you trust me with such a curious and valuable deposit as the papers you have sent me.[16] Be assured I have a due sense of this favour, and shall faithfully and carefully return them to you. You may rely that I shall neither copy any part, nor permit the papers to be seen. They contain a curious picture of society, and form a journal on the most instructive plan that can possibly be thought of; for I am not sure that an ordinary observer would become so well acquainted either with Dr Johnson, or with the manners of the Hebrides, by a personal intercourse, as by a perusal of your Journal. I am very truly, dear sir, your most obedient and affectionate humble servant, WILLIAM FORBES.

When I consider how many of the persons mentioned in this tour are now gone to 'that undiscovered country, from whose bourne no traveller returns',[17] I feel an impression at once awful and tender. REQUIESCANT IN PACE!

It may be objected by some persons, as it has been by one of my friends, that he who has the power of thus exhibiting an exact transcript of conversations is not a desirable member of society. I repeat the answer which I made to that friend: "Few, very few, need be afraid that their sayings will be recorded. Can it be imagined that I would take the trouble to gather what grows on every hedge, because I have collected such fruits as the *nonpareil* and the *bon chrétien*?"[18]

On the other hand, how useful is such a faculty if well exercised! To it we owe all those interesting apophthegms and memorabilia of the ancients, which Plutarch, Xenophon, and Valerius Maximus have transmitted to us. To it we owe all those instructive and entertaining collections which the French have made under the title of *Ana*, affixed to some celebrated name. To it we owe the *Table Talk* of Selden, the *Conversation* between Ben Jonson and Drummond of Hawthornden, Spence's *Anecdotes* of Pope, and other valuable remains in our own language. How delighted should we have been if thus introduced into the company of Shakespeare and of Dryden, of whom we know scarcely anything but their admirable writings! What pleasure would it have given us to have known their petty habits, their characteristic manners, their modes of composition, and their genuine opinion of preceding writers and of their contemporaries! All these are now irrecoverably lost. Considering how many of the strongest and most brilliant effusions of exalted intellect must have perished, how much is it to be regretted that all men of distinguished wisdom and wit have not been attended by friends, of taste enough to relish and abilities enough to register their conversation:

> *Vixere fortes ante Agamemnona*
> *Multi, sed omnes illacrymabiles*
> *Urgentur, ignotique longa*
> *Nocte, carent quia vate sacro.*[19]

They whose inferior exertions are recorded, as serving to explain or illustrate the sayings of such men, may be proud of being thus associated, and of their names being transmitted to posterity, by being appended to an illustrious character.

Before I conclude, I think it proper to say that I have suppressed everything which I thought could *really* hurt any one now living.[20] Vanity and self-conceit indeed may sometimes suffer. With respect to what *is* related, I considered it my duty to 'extenuate nothing, nor set down aught in malice';[21] and with those lighter strokes of Dr Johnson's satire, proceeding from a warmth and quickness of imagination, not from any malevolence of heart, and which, on account of their excellence, could not be omitted, I trust that they who are the subject of them have good sense and good temper enough not to be displeased.

I have only to add that I shall ever reflect with great pleasure on a tour which has been the means of preserving so much of the enlightened and instructive conversation of one whose virtues will, I hope, ever be an object of imitation, and whose powers of mind were so extraordinary that ages may revolve before such a man shall again appear.

NOTES

1   For both the era of planting and the gentleman at St Andrews see p. 7.
2   "When my compatriot David Cranston was taking his first course of theology, his fellow students and bosom friends were James Almain of Sens and Peter of Brussels, a Dominican, who attended my arts class with him. In the course of a discussion on Founder's Day in the courtyard of the

Sorbonne, they taunted him publicly before his fellows by maintaining that the common people of Scotland (as they had been assured by a certain religious) ate oaten bread. They did this knowing him to be quick-tempered and meaning to tease him with a fair joke, but he strove to repel the charge as if it had brought disgrace on his country."

3   For 'the noise of the wind being all its own' see p. 296. The passage from 'imo.' to '2d.' was deleted in the printer's copy (Pottle, *Journal*, p. 451); otherwise Boswell's **Conclusion** is taken from the *Tour* as published.

4   See p. 204.

5   This is a clear statement of the position that belief in Ossian's authenticity meant belief in his historicity.

6   See p. 425.

7   See p. 6.

8   Boswell's note (*Tour*): "Mr Orme, one of the ablest historians of this age, is of the same opinion. He said to me, 'There are in that book thoughts, which, by long revolution in the great mind of Johnson, have been formed and polished – like pebbles rolled in the ocean!'"

9   See p. 425. This was a *cri du coeur* from Dempster, whose nickname was 'Honest George': an improving landlord from Angus, he had been an MP in the Whig interest for Forfar Burghs since 1761, but was not a keen party man, and used his position as best he could to promote Scottish industries and agriculture.

10   Boswell's note (*Tour*): "Every reader will, I am sure, join with me in warm admiration of the truly patriotic writer of this letter. I know not which most to applaud – that good sense and liberality of mind, which could see and admit the defects of his native country, to which no man is a more zealous friend; or that candour, which induced him to give just praise to the minister whom he honestly and strenuously opposed."

11   Flora Macleod had visited Edinburgh during the winter and spring of 1775.

12   See p. 143.

13   See p. 164.

14   The document, in Johnson's hand, was among the papers found at Malahide in 1940. Johnson first wrote 'has misrepresented a question which in the Hebrides is of great importance', then deleted this and substituted 'has been misinformed or mistaken'. Malone wrote the heading and added a footnote: "The original MS is now in my possession." He then sent it to the printer as copy for the *Tour* (Pottle, *Journal*, p. 451).

15   Boswell's note (*Tour*): "Raasay was highly gratified, and afterwards visited and dined with Dr Johnson, at his house in London." The visit was in summer 1782 (*Life*, 7 September 1782).

16   Boswell's note (*Tour*, second and subsequent editions): "In justice both to Sir William Forbes and myself, it is proper to mention, that the papers which were submitted to his perusal contained only an account of our Tour from the time that Dr Johnson and I set out from Edinburgh (p. [39]), and consequently did not contain the elogium on Sir William Forbes (p. [25]),

which he never saw till this book appeared in print; nor did he even know, when he wrote the above letter, that this Journal was to be published." This was in response to a remark in Lord Macdonald's letter of complaint to Boswell of 26 November 1785, frequently referred to above (Scott and Pottle, *Private Papers*, vol. 16, p. 237): "Having read a Letter from a respectable person annexed to your publication who gives his sanction and approbation to the work in which he must have discovered his own just panegyric, I think it is time to justify myself."

17 *Hamlet*, act 3, scene 1.

18 Defined in Johnson's *Dictionary* as, respectively, a kind of apple and a kind of pear.

19 Horace, *Odes*, book 4, poem 9, lines 25–28: "Many brave men lived before Agamemnon, but all of them, unwept and unknown, lie buried in eternal night because they lack their sacred bard."

20 Boswell's note (*Tour*, second edition): "Having found, on a revision of this work, that, notwithstanding my best care, a few observations had escaped me, which arose from the instant impression, the publication of which might perhaps be considered as passing the bounds of a strict decorum, I immediately ordered that they should be omitted in the present edition. If any of the same kind are yet left, it is owing to inadvertence alone, no man being more unwilling to give pain to others than I am." In the third edition Boswell turned 'a revision of this work' into 'a revision of the first edition of this work' and 'present edition' into 'subsequent editions', after which he inserted: "I was pleased to find that they did not amount in the whole to a page." At the end he added: "A contemptible scribbler, of whom I have learned no more than that, after having disgraced and deserted the clerical character, he picks up in London a scanty livelihood by scurrilous lampoons under a feigned name, has impudently and falsely asserted that the passages omitted were *defamatory*, and that the omission was not voluntary, but compulsory. The last insinuation I took the trouble publicly to disprove; yet, like one of Pope's dunces, he persevered in 'the lie o'erthrown'. As to the charge of defamation, there is an obvious and certain mode of refuting it. Any person who thinks it worth while to compare one edition with the other, will find that the passages omitted were not in the least degree of that nature, but exactly such as I have represented them in the former part of this note, the hasty effusion of momentary feelings, which the delicacy of politeness should have suppressed." The 'contemptible scribbler' was John Wolcot, writing as 'Peter Pindar' in *Poetical and Congratulatory Epistle to James Boswell*. Boswell responded in the newspapers and in two letters in the *Gentleman's Magazine* (vol. 56, part 1, April 1786, pp. 285–86) which dealt with the issues raised by Lord Macdonald and Mrs Thrale (now Mrs Piozzi). Wolcot 'persevered in the lie o'erthrown' (a quote from Pope's 'Prologue to the Satires') in his extremely funny book *Bozzy and Piozzi*.

21 *Othello*, act 5, scene 2: "Speak of me as I am; nothing extenuate, / Nor set down aught in malice: / Then must you speak / Of one that lov'd not wisely, but too well."

Books & Articles Cited in the Notes

[Adam, R. B.], *The R. B. Adam Library relating to Dr. Samuel Johnson and his Era*, 3 vols, Buffalo, 1929

Anderson, George, 'On Some of the Stone Circles and Cairns in the Neighbourhood of Inverness', *Archaeologia Scotica: or Transactions of the Society of Antiquaries of Scotland*, vol. 3, 1831, pp. 211–22

Anderson, John, 'Enquiry into the Origin of the *Mercheta Mulierum*', *Archaeologia Scotica*, vol. 3, 1831, pp. 56–73

Anderson, P. J., 'Mr. Janes of Aberdeenshire', *Notes and Queries*, 10th series, vol. 2, July–Dec. 1904, pp. 155–56

Armstrong, Robert A., *A Gaelic Dictionary*, London, 1825

Black, Ronald, ed., 'A Scottish Grammatical Tract, c. 1640', *Celtica*, vol. 21, 1990, pp. 3–16

——, ed., *An Lasair: Anthology of 18th Century Scottish Gaelic Verse*, Edinburgh, 2001

——, ed., *The Gaelic Otherworld: John Gregorson Campbell's Superstitions of the Highlands & Islands of Scotland and Witchcraft & Second Sight in the Highlands & Islands*, Edinburgh, 2005

——, *see also* MacilleDhuibh, Raghnall

Blaikie, Walter Biggar, ed., *Origins of the 'Forty-Five*, Scottish History Society, Edinburgh, 1916

Boswell, James, *An Account of Corsica, the Journal of a Tour to that Island, and Memoirs of Pascal Paoli*, ed. by James T. Boulton and T. O. McLoughlin, Oxford, 2006 [1st edn London 1768]

——, 'Some Anecdotes of the Late Voyage of Mr. Banks and Dr. Solander in the Northern Seas', *London Magazine*, vol. 41, November 1772, pp. 508–09

Brady, Frank, and Pottle, Frederick A., eds, *Boswell on the Grand Tour: Italy, Corsica, and France 1765–1766*, London, 1955

——, eds, *Boswell in Search of a Wife*, London, 1957

Brown, P. Hume, *Scotland before 1700 from Contemporary Documents*, Edinburgh, 1893

Brown, William, 'An Account of Sheuchy Dyke', *Archaeologia Scotica: Transactions of the Society of the Antiquaries of Scotland*, vol. 2, part 1, 1818, pp. 192–98

Bruford, Alan, 'Legends Long since Localised or Tales Still Travelling?' *Scottish Studies*, vol. 24, 1980, pp. 43–62

Budgell, Eustace, *Memoirs of the Lives and Characters of the Illustrious Family of the Boyles; particularly, of the Late Eminently Learned, Charles Earl of Orrery*, ed. by Donald Brady, Waterford, 2003 [1st edn London 1732]

Bunting, Edward, *The Ancient Music of Ireland*, Dublin, 1840

Caimbeul, Aonghas, *Suathadh ri Iomadh Rubha*, Glasgow, 1973

Calder, George, ed., *Gaelic Songs by William Ross*, Edinburgh, 1937

Campbell, J. L., ed., *Hebridean Folksongs*, 3 vols, Oxford, 1969–81

——, *Canna: The Story of a Hebridean Island*, Oxford, 1984

——, *A Very Civil People; Hebridean Folk, History and Tradition*, ed. by Hugh Cheape, Edinburgh, 2000

——, and Eastwick, C., 'The MacNeils of Barra in the Forty-Five', *The Innes Review*, vol. 17, 1966, pp. 82–90

Cant, R. G., *The University of St Andrews: A Short History*, 2nd edn, Edinburgh, 1970 [1st edn Edinburgh 1946]

Carmichael, Alexander, *Carmina Gadelica*, 6 vols, Edinburgh, 1900–71

Carney, Seamus, *The Killing of the Red Fox: An Investigation into the Appin Murder*, Moffat, 1989

Carruthers, Robert, ed., *The Journal of a Tour to the Hebrides with Samuel Johnson, LL.D. by James Boswell*, London, 1852

Chambers, Robert, *Traditions of Edinburgh*, Edinburgh, 1996 [1st edn Edinburgh 1824]

Cheape, Hugh, 'A Rare Instrument by Donald MacDonald Bought for Nation', *The Piping Times*, vol. 57, no. 2, November 2004, pp. 9–21

Cloyd, E. L., *James Burnett: Lord Monboddo*, Oxford, 1972

Cody, Rev. Fr E. G., ed., *The Historie of Scotland Wrytten First in Latin by the Most Reuerend and Worthy Jhone Leslie Bishop of Rosse and Translated in Scottish by Father James Dalrymple . . . 1596*, 2 vols, Scottish History Society, Edinburgh, 1888–95

Cole, Richard C., ed., *The General Correspondence of James Boswell 1766–1769*, 2 vols, Edinburgh, 1993–97

Craven, Rev. J. B., ed., *Journals of the Episcopal Visitations of the Right Rev. Robert Forbes, M.A.*, London, 1886

Croker, John Wilson, ed., *The Life of Samuel Johnson, LL.D. including A Journal of a Tour to the Hebrides, by James Boswell, Esq.*, 1st edn, 5 vols, London, 1831 [and various other editions]

Crousaz, J. P. de, *A Commentary on Mr. Pope's Principles of Morality, or Essay on Man*, London, 1739

Currie, Jo, *Mull: The Island and its People*, Edinburgh, 2000

Dallas, James, *The History of the Family of Dallas*, Edinburgh, 1921

Dalrymple, Sir David, *Remarks on the History of Scotland*, Edinburgh, 1773

——, *Annals of Scotland*, 2 vols, Edinburgh, 1776–79

Deveria, Richard A. A., *A'Chailc: The Story of Skye Diatomite*, Dunoon, 2000

Dòmhnallach, Tormod E., 'Ministearan – an t-Urr. Aonghas Iain MacBhiocair (4)', *Am Pàipear*, March 2007, p. 11

Draper, Laurence, and Draper, Pamela, 'The Iron Ore Mine on Raasay', in MacKay, *Duanagan*, pp. 107–30

Dunbar, John G., ed., *Sir William Burrell's Northern Tour, 1758*, E. Linton, 1997

Dwelly, Edward, *The Illustrated Gaelic–English Dictionary*, 9th edn, Glasgow, 1977 [1st edn Herne Bay 1901–11]

Fleeman, J. D., ed., *Samuel Johnson: A Journey to the Western Islands of Scotland*, Oxford, 1985

Forbes, Alexander Robert, *Place-Names of Skye and Adjacent Islands*, Paisley, 1923

Ford, Philip J., *George Buchanan, Prince of Poets*, Aberdeen, 1982

Gibbs, Laura, ed., *Aesop's Fables*, Oxford, 2002

Gillies, Donald, *The Life and Work of the Very Rev. Roderick Macleod of Snizort, Skye*, n.p., [1969]

Grant, I. F., *The MacLeods*, London, 1959

——, *Highland Folk Ways*, London, 1961

Gunn, Douglas M., 'Shoes May be Spared', *Scots Magazine*, new ser., vol. 164, no. 1, January 2006, pp. 86–90

Gunn, John, *An Historical Enquiry respecting the Performance on the Harp in the Highlands of Scotland*, Edinburgh, 1807

Haile, H. G., *Luther: A Biography*, London, 1981

Harman, Mary, *An Isle called Hirte: History and Culture of the St Kildans to 1930*, Lusta (Skye), 1997

Harris, Stuart, *The Place Names of Edinburgh*, London, 2002 [1st edn Edinburgh 1996]

Hawkesworth, John, *An Account of the Voyages . . . for Making Discoveries in the Southern Hemisphere . . . Drawn Up from the Journals which were Kept by the Several Commanders*, 3 vols, London, 1773

Hecht, Hans, ed., *Songs from David Herd's Manuscripts*, Edinburgh, 1904

Hill, George Birkbeck, *Footsteps of Dr. Johnson (Scotland)*, London, 1890 [repr. Didsbury 1973]

——, and Powell, L. F., eds, *Boswell's Life of Johnson together with Boswell's Journal of a Tour to the Hebrides and Johnson's Diary of a Journey into North Wales*, 6 vols, Oxford, 1934–64

Hogg, James, ed., The *Jacobite Relics of Scotland*, 2 vols, Edinburgh, 2002–03 [1st edn Edinburgh 1819–21]

Hope, Sir William, *The Compleat Fencing-Master: In which is fully Described the whole Guards, Parades & Lessons, Belonging to the Small-Sword*, London, 1691

Hunter, Michael, *The Occult Laboratory: Magic, Science and Second Sight in Late Seventeenth-Century Scotland*, Woodbridge, 2001

Kastner, L. E., ed., *The Poetical Works of William Drummond of Hawthornden*, 2 vols, Manchester, 1913

Knox, John, *The History of the Reformation of the Church of Scotland*, Edinburgh, 1731 [1st edn London 1587]

Lascelles, Mary, ed., *A Journey to the Western Islands of Scotland* by Samuel Johnson, New Haven, 1971

Lustig, Irma S., and Pottle, Frederick A., eds, *Boswell: The Applause of the Jury 1782–1785*, London, 1982

——, eds, *Boswell: The English Experiment*, London, 1986

MacAonghuis, Iain, 'Dioghlam á Dùthchas Ratharsair', in MacKay, *Duanagan*, pp. 131–40

—— , *see also* MacInnes, John

Mac a Phi, Eoghan, ed., *Am Measg nam Bodach*, Glasgow, 1938

MacArthur, Rev. Archibald, 'Parish of Kilninian', in *The Statistical Account of Scotland*, ed. by Sir John Sinclair, new edn, vol. 20, Wakefield, 1983, pp. 323–40 [1st edn Edinburgh 1790s]

MacArthur, E. Mairi, *Iona*, 2nd edn, Edinburgh, 2002 [1st edn Edinburgh 1990]

MacBain, Alexander, 'Early Highland Personal Names', *TGSI*, vol. 22, 1897–98, pp. 152–68

MacCormick, John, *An t-Eilean Muileach, The Island of Mull: Its History, Scenes and Legends*, Glasgow, 1923

MacDhughaill, Eachann M., 'Seann Eachdraidh Chollach', *TGSI*, vol. 34, 1927–28, pp. 170–201

——, *see also* MacDougall, Hector

MacDonald, Revs A. and A., *The Clan Donald*, 3 vols, Inverness, 1896–1904

McDonald, Rev. Fr Allan, *Gaelic Words and Expressions from South Uist and Eriskay*, Dublin, 1958

MacDonald, Ann, 'Raasay in Prehistory', in MacKay, *Duanagan*, pp. 65–71

Macdonald, Rev. Charles, *Moidart; or Among the Clanranalds*, Edinburgh, 1989 [1st edn Oban 1889]

MacDonald, Keith Norman, MD, *MacDonald Bards from Mediæval Times*, Edinburgh, 1900

MacDougall, Hector, ed., *Clarsach na Coille* by the Rev. A. Maclean Sinclair, 2nd edn, Glasgow, 1928 [1st edn Glasgow 1881]

——, and Cameron, Rev. Hector, *Handbook to the Islands of Coll and Tiree*, Glasgow, [1937]

——, *see also* MacDhughaill, Eachann M.

MacEchern, Rev. Dugald, 'Place-Names of Coll', *TGSI*, vol. 29 (1914–19), pp. 314–35

Macfarlane, Walter, *Genealogical Collections concerning Families in Scotland*, ed. by James Toshach Clark, 2 vols, Scottish History Society, Edinburgh, 1900

MacGill-Eain, Somhairle, *O Choille gu Bearradh*, Manchester, 1989

——, *see also* Maclean, Dr Sam

McGinnis, Paul J., and Williamson, Arthur H., *George Buchanan: The Political Poetry*, Scottish History Society, Edinburgh, 1995

MacilleDhuibh, Raghnall, 'The Loch that Never Freezes', *WHFP*, 27 October 1995

——, 'Down to the Year of the Black Spring', *WHFP*, 28 March 1997

——, 'The Cats of Skye', *WHFP*, 16 September 2005

——, 'Cunnart, Eadar-Theangair ag Obair: *Eachdraidh a' Phrionnsa* le Iain MacCoinnich', in *Cànan & Cultar / Language & Culture: Rannsachadh na Gàidhlig 3*, ed. by Wilson McLeod, James E. Fraser and Anja Gunderloch, Edinburgh, 2006, pp. 73–110

——, 'Why are Penguins so Called?' *WHFP*, 24 Nov., 8 Dec., 22 Dec. 2006

——, 'The Cow that Ate the Piper', *WHFP*, 16 February 2007

——, 'The House of the Steep Climb', *WHFP*, 16 March 2007

——, 'The Patagonian Giants', *WHFP*, 29 March 2007

——, 'The Religion of the Yellow Stick', *WHFP*, 8 June 2007

——, *see also* Black, Ronald

MacInnes, John, 'Gleanings from Raasay Tradition', *TGSI*, vol. 56, 1988–90, pp. 1–20

[MacKay, Rebecca, *et al.*, eds], *Duanagan, Dain is Dualchas a Eilean Ratharsair, Fladaidh is Eilean Tighe: Songs, Poems, Stories and Prose emanating from the Rich Treasure of History and Traditions of Raasay, Fladda and Eilean Tighe*, Urras Dualchas Ratharsaidh, Raasay Heritage Trust, Raasay, 2001

Mackenzie, Alexander, *History of the Macleods*, Inverness, 1889

Mackenzie, Annie M., ed., *Orain Iain Luim: Songs of John MacDonald, Bard of Keppoch*, Scottish Gaelic Texts Society, Edinburgh, 1964

MacKenzie, Donald A., *Scottish Folk-Lore and Folk Life*, London, 1935

MacKenzie, Donald W., *As it Was, Sin mar a Bha: An Ulva Boyhood*, Edinburgh, 2000

Mackenzie, Henry, ed., *Report of the Committee of the Highland Society of Scotland, Appointed to Inquire into the Nature and Authenticity of the Poems of Ossian*, Edinburgh, 1805

——, *Contemporary Memoirs: The Anecdotes and Egotisms of Henry Mackenzie 1745–1831*, Bristol, 1996 [repr. of 1927 edn]

Mackenzie, John, *Eachdraidh Mhic-Cruislig, Sgialachd Ghàëlach*, Glasgow, 1836

——, ed., *Sar-Obair nam Bard Gaelach*, 1st edn, Glasgow, 1841

Maclaurin, John, *Arguments and Decisions, in Remarkable Cases, before the High Court of Justiciary, and other Supreme Courts, in Scotland*, Edinburgh, 1774

Maclean, Charles, *The Isle of Mull: Placenames, Meanings and Stories*, Dumfries, 1997

[MacLean, Dr Hector], 'A Brief Genealogical Account of the Family of Maclean from its First Settling in the Island of Mull and Parts Adjacent to the Year 1716', in Macfarlane, *Genealogical Collections*, vol. 1, pp. 118–43

——, *A Breif Genealogical Account of the ffamily of McLean from its First Settlement in the Island of Mull and Parts Adjacent*, Edinburgh, 1872

MacLean, J. P., *A History of the Clan MacLean*, Cincinnati, 1889

——, *History of the Island of Mull*, 2 vols, Greenville (Ohio) and San Mateo (California), 1923–25

Maclean, Dr Sam, 'Some Raasay Traditions', *TGSI*, vol. 49, pp. 377–97

——, *see also* MacGill-Eain, Somhairle

Maclean-Bristol, Nicholas, *Hebridean Decade: Mull, Coll and Tiree 1761–1771*, Society of West Highland and Island Historical Research, Coll, 1982

——, 'The Macleans from 1560–1707: A Re-Appraisal', in *The Seventeenth Century in the Highlands*, ed. by Loraine Maclean, Inverness, 1986, pp. 70–88

——, *Warriors and Priests: The History of the Clan Maclean, 1300–1570*, E. Linton, 1995

——, *Murder under Trust: The Crimes and Death of Sir Lachlan Mor Maclean of Duart, 1558–1598*, East Linton, 1999

——, *From Clan to Regiment*, Barnsley, 2007

MacLennan, Lt. John, 'Notices of Pipers', *The Piping Times*, vols 22–26, 1970–74

MacLeod, Angus, ed., *The Songs of Duncan Ban Macintyre*, Scottish Gaelic Texts Society, Edinburgh, 1952

Macleod, Donald, *The Living Past*, Stornoway, 2006

MacLeod, Fred T., 'Notes on the Relics preserved in Dunvegan Castle, Skye', *PSAS*, vol. 47, 1912–13, pp. 99–125

——, 'Observations on the Gaelic Translation of the Pentateuch, by Rev. Donald MacQueen, Skye, 1777–1783', *TGSI*, vol. 36, 1931–33, pp. 346–407

MacLeod, Norma, *Raasay: The Island and its People*, Edinburgh, 2002

Macleoid, an t-Urr. Iain, *Am Measg nan Lili: Tormod Sona a bha 'n Siadair Bharabhais*, Inverness, 1948

Mac-na-Ceàrdadh, Gilleasbuig, ed., *An t-Òranaiche*, new edn, St Andrew's (Nova Scotia), 2004 [1st edn Glasgow 1879]

Macphail, Rev. J. W., *Handbook to the Islands of Mull and Iona*, Glasgow, 1938

Macpherson, James, *Fingal, an Ancient Epic Poem*, London, 1762

——, *The Poems of Ossian*, ed. by Howard Gaskill, Edinburgh, 1996

Macquarrie, Alan, *Iona through the Ages*, Society of West Highland and Island Historical Research, Coll, 1983

MacQuarrie, Duncan M., *The Placenames of Mull*, Tobermory, 1982

MacRa, Rev. John, 'Genealogy of the MacRas', *Highland Papers*, vol. 1, ed. by J. R. N. Macphail, Scottish History Society, 1914, pp. 195–239

Macrae, Rev. Alexander, *History of the Clan Macrae*, Dingwall, 1899

Macrae, Rev. John, 'Parish of Glensheil', in *The Statistical Account of Scotland*, ed. by Sir John Sinclair, new edn, vol. 17, Wakefield, 1981, pp. 404–12 [1st edn Edinburgh 1790s]

MacRury, Rev. John, Snizort, 'O Chionn Leith Cheud Bliadhna II', *TGSI*, vol. 24, 1899–1901, pp. 383–94

Major, John, *A History of Greater Britain*, ed. by Archibald Constable, Scottish History Society, Edinburgh, 1892

Martin, Martin, *A Description of the Western Islands of Scotland*, Edinburgh, 1999 [1st edn London 1703]

Martine, George, *Reliquiae Divi Andreae, or the State of the Venerable and Primitial See of St Andrews*, St Andrews, 1797

Matheson, William, ed., *The Songs of John MacCodrum, Bard to Sir James Macdonald of Sleat*, Scottish Gaelic Texts Society, Edinburgh, 1938

——, ed., The *Blind Harper: The Songs of Roderick Morison and his Music*, Scottish Gaelic Texts Society, Edinburgh, 1970

Megaw, B. R. S., 'Goat-Keeping in the Old Highland Economy', *Scottish Studies*, vol. 7, 1963, pp. 201–09

Milne, Hugh M., *Boswell's Edinburgh Journals 1767–1786*, new edn, Edinburgh, 2003 [1st edn 2001]

Morrison, Alick, 'The Grianam Case, 1734–1781, the Kelp Industry, and the Clearances in Harris, 1811–1854', *TGSI*, vol. 52, 1980–82, pp. 20–89

Morrison, Neil Rankin, 'Clann Duiligh: Piobairean Chloinn Ghill-Eathain', *TGSI*, vol. 37, 1934–36, pp. 59–79

[Muir, Thomas Smyth], *Characteristics of Old Church Architecture*, Edinburgh, 1861

Munro, R. W., *Taming the Rough Bounds: Knoydart 1745–1784*, Society of West Highland & Island Historical Research, Coll, 1984

Murchison, Rev. T. M., 'Notes on the Murchisons', *TGSI*, vol. 39/40, 1942–50, pp. 262–93

Nicholson, Edward W. B., ed., *Golspie: Contributions to its Folklore*, London, 1897

Nicolson, Alexander, *Handbook to the Isle of Skye*, Glasgow, [1936]

Ó Baoill, Colm, 'Some Irish Harpers in Scotland', *TGSI*, vol. 47, 1971–72, pp. 143–71

——, 'Inis Moccu Chéin', *Scottish Gaelic Studies*, vol. 12, 1971–76, pp. 267–70

——, ed., *Duanaire Colach 1537–1757*, Aberdeen, 1997

——, *MacLean Manuscripts in Nova Scotia*, Aberdeen, 2001

Opie, Iona, and Tatem, Moira, eds, *A Dictionary of Superstitions*, Oxford, 1989

O'Sullivan, Donal, *Carolan*, 2 vols, London, 1958

Paton, Henry, ed., *The Lyon in Mourning, or a Collection of Speeches Letters Journals . . . by the Rev. Robert Forbes*, 3 vols, Scottish History Society, Edinburgh, 1895–96

Pennant, Thomas, *A Tour in Scotland; MDCCLXIX*, 3rd edn, Warrington, 1774 [repr. Perth 1979]

——, *A Tour in Scotland and Voyage to the Hebrides 1772*, Edinburgh, 1998 [1st edn Chester 1774–76]

——, *Of London*, London, 1790

——, *Literary Life*, London, 1793

Pierpoint, Robert, 'Dr. Johnson: Flora Macdonald', *Notes and Queries*, 10th series, vol. 10, July–Dec. 1908, p. 147

Pindar, Peter [John Wolcot], *Bozzy and Piozzi: or, the British Biographers*, 9th edn, London, 1788 [1st edn London 1786]

Pinkerton, John, *A General Collection of the Best and Most Interesting Voyages and Travels in all Parts of the World*, 17 vols, London, 1808–14

[Playford, M.], *The Dancing-Master: Or, Directions for Dancing Country Dances, with the Tunes to each Dance*, 14th edn, London, 1709 [1st edn 1651]

Plot, Robert, *The Natural History of Stafford-Shire*, Oxford, 1686 [repr. Manchester 1973]

Pococke, Richard, bishop of Meath, *Tours in Scotland 1747, 1750, 1760*, ed. by Daniel William Kemp, Scottish History Society, Edinburgh, 1887

Pottle, Frederick A., ed., *Boswell's London Journal 1762–1763*, London, 1950

——, ed., *James Boswell, The Earlier Years 1740–1769*, London, 1966

——, and Bennett, Charles H., eds, *Boswell's Journal of a Tour to the Hebrides with Samuel Johnson, LL.D. 1773*, 2nd edn, London, 1963 [1st edn 1936]

Prebble, John, *Mutiny: Highland Regiments in Revolt*, Harmondsworth, 1977

Ramsay, John, of Ochtertyre, *Scotland and Scotsmen in the Eighteenth Century*, ed. by Alexander Allardyce, 2 vols, Edinburgh, 1888

Ranke, Leopold von, *The History of the Popes*, 3 vols, 6th edn, London, 1913

RCAHMCS, *Ninth Report with Inventory of Monuments and Constructions in the Outer Hebrides, Skye and the Small Isles*, Edinburgh, 1928

RCAHMS, *Argyll: An Inventory of the Monuments*, vol. 3, *Mull, Tiree, Coll & Northern Argyll*, Edinburgh, 1980

——, *Argyll: An Inventory of the Monuments*, vol. 4, *Iona*, Edinburgh, 1982

Redford, Bruce, ed., *The Letters of Samuel Johnson*, 3 vols, Oxford, 1992

Reed, Joseph W., and Pottle, Frederick A., eds, *Boswell, Laird of Auchinleck 1778–1782*, New York, 1977

Ritson, Joseph, *Select Collection of English Songs*, 3 vols, London, 1783

Roberts, David, 'Raasay House', in MacKay, *Duanagan*, pp. 11–21

Roth, Cecil, *The Aberdeen Codex of the Hebrew Bible*, Edinburgh, 1958

Sacheverell, William, *An Account of the Isle of Man . . . with a Voyage to I-Columb-Kil*, The Manx Society, Douglas, 1859 [1st edn London 1702]

Scott, Geoffrey, and Pottle, Frederick A., eds, *Private Papers of James Boswell from Malahide Castle, 12: The Journal of James Boswell 1776–1777*, n.p., 1931

——, eds, *Private Papers of James Boswell from Malahide Castle, 16: The Journal of James Boswell 1783–1786*, n.p., 1932

Sellar, W. D. H., 'O'Donnell Lecture 1985, Celtic Law and Scots Law: Survival and Integration', *Scottish Studies*, vol. 29, 1989, pp. 1–27

——, 'Sueno's Stone and its Interpreters', in *Moray: Province and People*, ed. by W. D. H. Sellar, The Scottish Society for Northern Studies, Edinburgh, 1992, pp. 97–116

Simmons, Andrew, ed., *Burt's Letters from the North of Scotland*, new edn, Edinburgh, 1998 [1st edn London 1754]

Sinclair, Rev. A. Maclean, ed., *Gaelic Bards from 1411 to 1715*, Charlottetown, 1890

——, ed., *Na Bàird Leathanach: The Maclean Bards*, 2 vols, Charlottetown, 1898–1900

——, 'The Clan Fingon', *The Celtic Review*, vol. 4, 1907–08, pp. 31–41

Spedding, James, *et al.*, eds, *Works of Francis Bacon*, London, 1996 [repr. of 1879 edn]

Steuart, A. Francis, *The Douglas Cause*, Glasgow, 1909

Stewart, Col. David, *Sketches of the Character, Manners, and Present State of the Highlanders of Scotland*, 2 vols, 2nd edn, Edinburgh, 1822 [repr. Edinburgh 1977]

Stewart, John H. J., and Stewart, Lt.-Col. Duncan, *The Stewarts of Appin*, Edinburgh, 1880

Swire, Otta F., *Skye: The Island and its Legends*, 4th edn, Edinburgh, 2006 [1st edn Oxford 1952]

Thomson, Derick S., *The Gaelic Sources of Macpherson's 'Ossian'*, Edinburgh, 1951

——, *Companion to Gaelic Scotland*, 2nd edn, Glasgow, 1994 [1st edn Oxford 1993]

Tolmie, Frances, *One Hundred and Five Songs of Occupation from the Western Isles*, Llanerch, 1997 [repr. from *Journal of the Folk-Song Society*, no. 16, 1911]

Topham, Edward, *Letters from Edinburgh*, London, 1776

Vendryes, Joseph, *et al.*, eds, *Lexique Étymologique de l'Irlandais Ancien*, Paris, 1959–96

Walker, Rev. Dr John, *Report on the Hebrides of 1764 and 1771*, ed. by Margaret M. McKay, Edinburgh, 1980

Walker, Ralph S., ed., *The Correspondence of James Boswell and John Johnston of Grange*, London, 1966

Watson, William J., *History of the Celtic Place-Names of Scotland*, Edinburgh, 1926

——, ed., *Bàrdachd Ghàidhlig*, 3rd edn, Glasgow, 1959 [1st edn Inverness 1918]

Weis, Charles McC., and Pottle, Frederick A., eds, *Boswell in Extremes 1776–1778*, New York, 1970

Whyte, Samuel, *Miscellanea Nova*, Dublin, 1800 [repr. New York 1974]

Williams, Gwyn A., *Madoc: The Making of a Myth*, London, 1979

Wilson, John, *Tales and Travels of a School Inspector*, 3rd edn, Edinburgh, 2007 [1st edn Glasgow 1928, 2nd edn Stornoway 1998]

Wimsatt, William K., and Pottle, Frederick A., eds, *Boswell for the Defence 1769–1774*, New York, 1959

[Wittenberg, Albrecht], *Tagebuch einer Reise nach den Hebridischen Inseln mit Doctor Samuel Johnson*, Lübeck, 1787

Young, Arthur, *A Tour in Ireland*, Cambridge, 1925 [1st edn Dublin 1780]

Abbreviations

AUL	Aberdeen University Library
bt	baronet
JB	James Boswell
Journal	Pottle and Bennett, *Boswell's Journal of a Tour to the Hebrides*
Journey	Samuel Johnson, *A Journey to the Western Islands of Scotland*
Life	James Boswell, *The Life of Samuel Johnson, LL.D.*
NLS	National Library of Scotland
ODNB	*Oxford Dictionary of National Biography*
OED	*Oxford English Dictionary*
PSAS	*Proceedings of the Society of Antiquaries of Scotland*
RCAHMCS	Royal Commission on Ancient and Historical Monuments & Constructions of Scotland
RCAHMS	Royal Commission on the Ancient and Historical Monuments of Scotland
SJ	Samuel Johnson
TGSI	*Transactions of the Gaelic Society of Inverness*
Tour	James Boswell, *The Journal of a Tour to the Hebrides*
WHFP	*West Highland Free Press*
WS	Writer to the Signet
yr	younger

Glossary

abstract, to to remove quietly
adventitious additional
airing ground, airing strand beach or other place suitable for short walk or ride
ana (plural) collection of table-talk, gossip or literary anecdotes
Anaitidis delubrum (Latin) shrine of Anaitis
animus aequus (Latin) well-balanced mind
anthropopathy human sympathy
apophthegm pithy saying
a posteriori (Latin) from behind
archiepiscopal pertaining to archbishops
Areopagus supreme court of ancient Athens
Arian system the denial of Christ's divinity
Asiatic exotic
at length at last
augmented to puffed up to be
awful awe-inspiring
baron-officer estate official
bear barley
blade swashbuckling fellow
bland smooth, gentle, suave
bog marsh
bonetta bonito, a tropical fish
Boor Norwegian peasant farmer
brevis esse laboro, obscurus fio (Latin) I try to be brief, and I become obscure
brinded brindled, marked with streaks or spots
bubbled swindled
bucker, buccar (Scots) fast-sailing boat used in smuggling
buckies (Scots) whelks
bug bed-bug or house-bug (*Cimex lectularius*)
burden obligation
camblet camlet, cloth of wool and goat's hair

characteres advocatorum (Latin) the distinctive qualities of the advocates
charked burnt to charcoal
chevalier de Malthe (French) knight of Malta
cicerone (Italian) a guide
claymore (Gaelic *claidheamh mór* 'big sword') two-handed sword
climacteric point in human life at which great physical change takes place
cogitative of or pertaining to thought
complacency pleasure, enjoyment
conglobated concentrated
coot (Scots) guillemot
corry (Gaelic *coire* 'cauldron') mountain recess
court martial council of war
cradle portable or makeshift bed
crown paper paper cut in 15 x 20 in. sheets, originally watermarked with a crown
cuddy (Scots) young coalfish
curb type of horse's bit
curricle two-wheeled chaise drawn by two horses
custos rotulorum (Latin, 'guardian of the rolls') keeper of documents
Cyclops fabled one-eyed giant
damnati ad metalla (Latin) condemned to the mines
dear year a year of dearth
deny refute
depauperated impoverished
depeditation amputation of foot
depravation corruption
designed not impartial
detur digniori (Latin) give it to the worthier
diet loaf (Scots) sponge cake
discovered revealed
discriminated separate, discrete, distinct
dolus latet in universalibus (Latin) general terms are treacherous

doubted of suspected

dubius, non improbus (Latin) doubtful, not wicked

duffle thick coarse woollen cloth

dum vivimus vivamus (Latin) let us live while we live

effusion pouring or streaming out, shedding (as of blood)

elogium (Latin) panegyric

emersion emergence

empyreumatick burnt, acrid

enthusiasm excess of piety

eringo (Greek *eryngos*) sea-holly

esculent eatable

esse (Latin 'to be') existence

et hoc secundum sententiam philosophorum est esse beatus (Latin) and that, according to the opinion of philosophers, is happiness

ex aede Christi, Oxon. (Latin) formerly of Christ Church College, Oxford

fane temple

fare fa' you (Scots) good luck to you

feculent foul, toxic

fermety firmity, constancy

festal pertaining to a holiday

feudal patrician

fields territory

filiation paternity

fillibeg, filibeg (Gaelic *fèileadh beag*) kilt

fire rooms rooms with fire-places

flower flour

freight hire

fried chicken (Scots) friar's chicken, chicken broth with eggs dropped into it

frith firth

frontless shameless

fugitate, to (Scots law) to sentence to outlawry

fulgid flashing

gaul, gall (Scots) gale, sweet-gale, bog-myrtle

georgic agricultural, rural

glengore syphilis

Gothic of the Goths, an ancient Germanic nation

grammar Latin

gullet channel, creek, inlet

haill (Scots) whole

heath heather

hobby small, strong, active horse

impar sibi (Latin) unequal to himself

in little room tightly packed

incolumi gravitate (Latin, 'total seriousness') deadpan humour

Indian luxurious

indited composed, written

infatuated deprived of judgment

infidel atheist

infidelity atheism

insufficient unsuitable, incompetent

irrefragable unanswerable

jointure property settled on a woman at marriage to be enjoyed in widowhood

jus divinum (Latin) divine right

knotting knitting of threads into knots for fancywork, similar to 'tatting'

la vieille cour (French 'the old court') traditional courtesy

law (Scots, N. English) hill

licentiate student

liverymen freemen of the city of London

lown (Scots) rascal

macaroni dandy, fop

machair(e) (Gaelic) fertile seaside plain

mackalive (Gaelic *mac-shealbh* 'filial property') property given to a foster-son

manufacturers factory workers

minor friar

mons placiti (Latin) hill of pleading

mortmain transfer of property to a corporation

moss soft, spongy ground

mountain wine made from mountain grapes

nabob self-made millionaire

natale solum (Latin) native soil

nightgown dressing-gown

nihil est nisi hoc sciat alter (Latin) it's nothing if the other fellow doesn't know it

nil admirari (Latin) to wonder at nothing, regard nothing with admiration

numerisque fertur lege solutis (Horace, *Odes*, book 4, ode 2, lines 11–12) he is borne on in numbers, exempt from rule

occasionally on/for a particular occasion

operose labour-intensive, laborious

oratio pro Pennantio (Latin) speech in Pennant's defence

own claim or acknowledge as one's own

oxen cattle
oxter armpit
pandour Croatian foot-soldier
pathetic touching, full of pathos
pedestrious on foot
per circuitum (Latin) taking a circuitous route
peregrinity foreignness, wanderlust
perflation free passage of wind, ventilation
perpendicularly tubulated with a hole down the middle
petrification fossil
Phalaris Sicilian tyrant who roasted victims in a brazen bull
philosophical scientific
pick-pocket expensive
pilaster square column built into a wall but projecting from it
plumped fattened
policy plantation
posse (Latin 'to be able') potential
postern back door
pravity wickedness
precipitance impulse, impetuosity
pro aris et focis (Latin, 'for altars and fires') for hearth and home
pro bono publico (Latin) for public benefit
proceleusmatic inciting, encouraging
projector leader of an enterprise, speculator
propugnacula (Latin) bulwarks, outer defences
put up take away as specimen or souvenir
quasi sensorium numinis (Latin) like the seat of sensation of divine will
ratiocination reasoning
regale feast
renchérir (French) to take it further
reposited laid away, deposited
requiescant in pace (Latin) may they rest in peace
resuming summarising
rissered (Scots) sun-dried
salus populi (Latin) the people's welfare
sancte Columbe, ora pro me (Latin) holy Columba, pray for me
scalck (Gaelic *sgailc* 'thump, box on the ears') morning dram
scorbutic related to (or similar to) scurvy
season time of day

security evidence of ownership
seignory feudal lordship
sennachie (Gaelic *seanchaidh*) tradition-bearer.
sensorium numinis (Latin) seat of sensation of divine will
sesquipedalia verba (Latin) words of six syllables
shagreen a granular leather of horse's or ass's skin
sheltie Shetland pony
shieling summer pasture
shrub lemon-flavoured alcoholic drink
skait skate (the fish)
snatch snack
society community
solemnia verba (Latin) formal words
solicitude anxiety, uneasiness
sowans, sowens (Scots) a porridge-type dish made by steeping and straining oat-husks
sparagrass asparagus
specie coined money
speculatist speculative philosopher
spring lively dance-tune
state (Scots) statement, description
stated settled, established, fixed
stoned-horse stallion
subject of devise heritable property
succedaneous serving as a substitute
sursum corda (Latin) lift up your hearts
Sybil prophetess
taedium vitae (Latin) depression, weariness with life
target targe, small round shield
Teague Irishman
tender small craft that services a larger one
thills shafts
took himself checked himself
Triton a Greek sea-god
tubulated *see* **perpendicularly**
turbary peat-bank
turpissima bestia (Latin) that most disgraceful (or crafty) beast
vails tips, bribes
vectitation transport, conveyance
view picture, drawing, sketch (of a place)
vitiated spoiled, corrupted
vox viva (Latin) living voice
wands wattles
wanton whimsical, careless

Index

Macleod, Charles, half-bro. to John M. of
Raasay 156–57
Macleod, Christian, 10th dau. of John M.
of Raasay 152
MacLeod, Mrs (Christine MacKay, Inver-
ness), 2nd wife of John MacLeod of
Talisker 177, 266, 269, 270, 534
MacLeod, Donald, of Berneray ('the Old
Trojan', 1692–1781) 512–13
MacLeod, Donald (d. 1813), tacksman of
Achnagoyle 522
MacLeod, Donald (1700–81), tacksman of
Swordale 521
MacLeod, Donald, former tacksman of
Canna 126, 129, 134, 135, 138, 155, 213, 281,
286, 290, **522**, 539, 573; and JB's money
236, 256, 267, 275, 284, 291, 492, 522
MacLeod, Rev. Donald (c. 1729–81), min-
ister of Glenelg 514
Macleod, Lady (Emilia Brodie, 1730–1802),
mother of Norman, 20th of Dunvegan
171, 232, 237, 244, 254, 506, 541
Macleod, Flora (d. 1780), eldest dau. of
John M. of Raasay 152, 166–67, 499, 505,
593, 597
Macleod, Lady (Florence Macdonald), wife
of John M., 15th of Dunvegan 253, 527
MacLeod, Rev. George (Lord MacL. of
Fuinary, 1895–1991), founder of Iona
Community 521
Macleod, Isabella ('Bell', d. 1788), youngest
sister of Norman, 20th of Dunvegan 232,
237, 254, 521
MacLeod, Isabella, 5th dau. of John M. of
Raasay 152
Macleod, James (d. 1824), 12th of Raasay
152, 332
Macleod, Jane, 6th dau. of John M. of
Raasay 152
Macleod, Lady (Jane MacQueen, d. 1780),
wife of John M. of Raasay 143, 152, 155,
166, 168, 594
Macleod, Janet, 2nd dau. of John M. of
Raasay 152
Macleod, Mrs Janet, 2nd wife of Malcolm
Macleod, 10th of Raasay 156, 502
MacLeod, Mrs (Janet MacQueen), wife of
Rev. Roderick MacL. of Bracadale 524
MacLeod, John (d. 1713), 2nd of Talisker 507
MacLeod, John (1688–1773), of Muiravon-
side 331, 341

Macleod, John (c. 1714–86), 11th of Raasay
139–40, 141, **143**, **152**, 154, **161–68**, 169,
180, 211, 213, 216, 218, 221, 222, 225, 290,
332, 340, 370, 397, 501, 505, 592–95, 597
Macleod, John (*Iain Borb*, d. c. 1442), 6th of
Dunvegan 295, 543
MacLeod, John (*Iain Breac*, 1637–93), 15th of
Dunvegan 252–53, 255, 527
MacLeod, John (d. 1790/1), of Bay 233
MacLeod, John, 3rd son of John M. of
Raasay 152
MacLeod, Capt. John (1725/6–66), yr of M.,
father of Norman, 20th of Dunvegan
232, 506
MacLeod, Capt. John, of Balmeanach 114,
286, 489
MacLeod, Col. John (1714–98), 4th of
Talisker 65, 152, 168, **176–77**, 231–33,
237, **238**, 244, 254, 256, **266–70**, 274,
316, 397, 507, 534
MacLeod, Rev. John (1801–82), minister of
Morvern 521
MacLeod, Julia, 7th dau. of John M. of
Raasay 152
Macleod, Katherine, 3rd dau. of John M. of
Raasay 152
MacLeod, Magnus (b. c. 1719), of Claggan
233
MacLeod, Malcolm (b. 1711), of Brae **140**,
141, 148–62, 154, 155–57, 160, 168, 211, 213,
220, 276, 490, 594; and Prince Charles
150–51, 157, 218, 219, 220, 222–26
MacLeod, Malcolm (*fl.* 1745), 10th of Raasay
153, 156, 165, 217, 218, 225, 498, 505
MacLeod, Malcolm, 2nd son of John M. of
Raasay 152
MacLeod, Miss Mally (*Màili*, b. c. 1713),
dau. of William MacL. of Hamer 247
MacLeod, Margaret, 4th dau. of John M. of
Raasay 152
MacLeod, Mrs Margaret (4th dau. of
Donald MacLeod of Berneray), wife of
Alexander MacL. of Fernilea 266, 535
MacLeod, Mrs (Margaret MacLean, d.
1789), wife of Rev. Neil MacL. 402, 572
MacLeod, Maria (d. 1809), eldest sister of
Norman, 20th of Dunvegan 232, 237,
254, 521
MacLeod, Mary, 9th dau. of John M. of
Raasay 152
MacLeod, Mary (Màiri nighean Alastair
Ruaidh, c.1615–c.1707), poet 512

Watson, Dr Robert (*c.* 1730–81), professor of logic, rhetoric and metaphysics, St Andrews 43–44, 46–48, 49, 456

waulking 166, 534, 505

weapons 129, **206–07**, 245, 417–18, 523; bows 235, 522; cannons 265; dirks 124, 206, 224, 230, 235, 249, 295, 491; elf-bolts, fairy arrows 146, 498–99; guns, pistols 40, 500; Lochaber axes, bills 206, 295; shields, targets 206, 235, 369, 512; swords, claymores 235, 249, 369, 470, 522

weasels 144, 183

weather 120, 121, 136, 138, 407, 411, 413, 422, 545; storms 13, 172, 238, 250, 283, **292**, 296, **307–10**, 324, 338, 345, 355, 446, 499, 542

Webster, Miss —— (*fl.* 1773), Edinburgh 586

Webster, Rev. Dr Alexander (1707–84), preacher and statistician 38, 446, 448, 450, 468

Wedgwood, Josiah (1730–95), potter 491

wells, springs 3, 88, 393, 399

Welwyn (Hertfordshire) 283

Wesley, Rev. John (1703–91), preacher, Methodist leader 29, 62, 463

Westminster: abbey 373, 393, hall 262, 532

Wheler, Sir George (1650–1723), traveller 379, 567

Whigs 30, 229, 270, 284, 286, 402, 418, 436, 440, 441, 442, 448, 496, 528, 584

Whistler, Anthony (1714–1754), friend of Shenstone 540

Whistler, John, bro. of above 540

Whitby, Dr Daniel (1638–1726), divine 288

White, John (d. 1770/1), sea-captain 585

White, Valentine (*c.* 1717–1784), factor, Cawdor 100, 480, 484

Whitefield (Inverness-shire) 481

Whitefield, Rev. George (1714–70), preacher, Calvinistic Methodist leader 29–30

Whitehead, Paul (1710–74), satirist 95, 482

Whyte, Samuel (1733–1811), Dublin author and schoolmaster 579

Wiay (Skye) 529

Wilkes, John (1727–97), politician 215, 353, 402, 462, 573

Wilks, Robert (?1665–1732), actor 102

William III (1650–1702), king of England and Scotland 93, 270, 578

Williams, Anna ('Mrs Williams', 1706–83), poet, SJ's domestic companion 66, 103, 284, 477

Williams, Sir Charles Hanbury (1708–59), satirical writer and diplomatist 282

Williams, Zachariah (?1673–1775), physician 477

Williamson, Margaret Macalister (*fl.* 1897), descendant of Kingsburgh family 537

Willis, Dr Thomas (1621–75), physician 356

Wilmot, John (2nd earl of Rochester, 1648–80), poet 517

Wilson, ——, barber, Stevenage 283

Wilson, James, Kilmaurs (Ayrshire) 467

Wilson, John, ironmonger, Glasgow 585

Wilton House (Wiltshire), seat of earls of Pembroke 21

Windham, William (1750–1810), statesman 479

Wishart, Dr William (d. 1753), principal of Edinburgh University 268, 534–35

Wit and Loyalty Revived 469

witchcraft 35–36, 76, 149, 499

Wolcot, Dr John ('Peter Pindar', 1738–1819), satirist 536, 598

Wolf of Badenoch, *see* Stewart, Alexander

Wolfe, Maj.-Gen. James (1727–59), victor of Quebec 116

women 6, 79–80, 82–83, 85–86, 172, **183**, **199**, 230, 233, 234, 240, 248, 249, 330, 486, 507, 553; education of 78, 86, 287; work of 6, 10, 187, 271, 534

Wood, Anthony (1632–95), antiquary 469

Worcester, battle of (3 September 1651) 363

World, The 37, 259

Wren, Sir Christopher (1632–1723), architect 265

Wynn, Sir Watkin Williams (?1693–1749), Welsh politician 584

Xenophon (445–391 BC), historian 285, 595

Yale University ix, 546

York, duke of (later James VII and II) 259

Young Pretender, *see* Stuart, Prince Charles Edward

Young, Arthur (1741–1820), agriculturist 324, 555

Young, Dr Edward (1683–1765), poet 283, 411

Young, Frederick (b. *c.* 1732), son of Dr Edward Young 283

Young, William, bailie, Aberdeen 212, 515

Zeus, king of Greek gods 559